THE AFRICAN AMERICAN MALE SCHOOL ADAPTABILITY CRISIS (AMSAC)

ITS SOURCE AND SOLUTION PLANTED IN THE AFRICAN AMERICAN GARDEN OF EDEN

Joe L. Rempson

(Published for the Rempson Foundation)

authorHOUSE

AuthorHouse™
1663 Liberty Drive
Bloomington, IN 47403
www.authorhouse.com
Phone: 1 (800) 839-8640

© 2016 Joe L. Rempson. All rights reserved.

No part of this book may be reproduced, stored in a retrieval system, or transmitted by any means without the written permission of the author.

Published by AuthorHouse 03/11/2016

ISBN: 978-1-5049-7676-3 (sc)
ISBN: 978-1-5049-7677-0 (hc)
ISBN: 978-1-5049-7678-7 (e)

Library of Congress Control Number: 2016902062

Print information available on the last page.

Any people depicted in stock imagery provided by Thinkstock are models, and such images are being used for illustrative purposes only. Certain stock imagery © Thinkstock.

This book is printed on acid-free paper.

Because of the dynamic nature of the Internet, any web addresses or links contained in this book may have changed since publication and may no longer be valid. The views expressed in this work are solely those of the author and do not necessarily reflect the views of the publisher, and the publisher hereby disclaims any responsibility for them.

The Rempson Foundation is a private charitable
trust, a 501(c)(3) organization.
Its purpose is to promote the progress of African Americans
by strengthening the black family.
To strengthen the black family, inclusively, it will
undertake and sponsor activities to increase
the school and life success of black males.
The Foundation was created in 2002 and
made operational in 2006.
The author, Joe L. Rempson, is its President.

Dedication

To the memory of my mother and father,
especially to the memory of my out-of-wedlock father,
who did not live long enough even to see me finish high school,
and who, though an uneducated man, always said to me,
"boy, regardless of what nobody tells you, you go to school and get
yourself an education,"
and did his part by often buying the clothes and books that I needed,

and

To my son, Joseph, whose extraordinary
accomplishments seem almost unreal, and to his
wonderful family: my daughter-in-law, Denise,
and my two granddaughters, Caitlin and Jordan --
all being a source of great pride and inspiration, and all
giving me a certain peace of mind
and the comfort of knowing that, if I have
made no other contribution,
their existence alone suffices to have made my life worthwhile,

and

To my son's mother and my former wife, Elizabeth,
who did such a great job in rearing our son
and, in the process, provided me an education in child rearing
as valuable as my graduate training and
which helps to form the basis of my educational and life philosophy,
and finally,

Joe L. Rempson

To the memory of
all the supportive and encouraging teachers
that I have had along the way,
beginning with my first grade teacher, Ms. Laurie Mae Curry,
who, in my eyes, was like an angel;
my high school counselor, Mr. G. S. Hare,
who steered me into a tuition-free Buffalo State
Teachers College when, without resources, I had no
idea about what I would do after high school;
two of my undergraduate professors, Dr. Carl
Hines and Dr. Richard C. Brown,
especially Dr. Brown who showed such great interest and faith in me,
encouraging and helping me, for example, to apply for grants;
two of my graduate professors, Prof. E. Edmund Reutter, Jr., and
. Prof. A. Harry Passow, my dissertation sponsor; and
my dissertation editor and mentor, Dr. Robert A. Dentler,
who chopped up my dissertation and returned
it to me a more concise document
that more or less sailed through, and who, in addition,
gave me an opportunity to publish
and provided me entree into the world of research and scholarship.

Acknowledgements

I relied heavily upon the publications of Prof. Robert Norrell, Professor of History at the University of Tennessee, and Prof. John McWhorter, Associate Professor of English and Comparative Literature at Columbia University. Both were generous in giving me permission to do so, and I extend to them my deepest thanks. Lkewise, I extend my deepest thanks to Prof. Imani Michelle Scott (formerly K. Michelle Scott) of the Savannah College of Art and Design. My explanation of the root cause of dysfunctionality among segments of our African American community was borrowed from her, and she expressed delight in having me use it. In a similar manner, I relied on Paul Tough. Paul's research leading him to emphasize the role of the home in providing the security and love so essential to a child's school and life success was the cornerstone of my own emphasis. His emphasis, further, reinforced my belief in the value of the **practice of the art of loving**, and was a major factor which led me to advocate a **Child Family Rights Movement**. Though more than willing to grant his permission to cite his publications, Paul did not feel that I needed it, and sent a very encouraging response.

To be sure that I conformed to "fair use" guidelines, I also had to reach out to other authors – or to their publishers. It was a somewhat trying undertaking, it always being a relief, first, just to get a response, and, second, to get a favorable one. I am grateful for those acquired, have acknowledged them in the text, and here extend a collective thanks.

I extend thanks also to George Ryan and his internet design company, MyCustomLogo, now transformed into a new company, Hatchwise. George and his companies designed all of the logos so far created for my proposed experimental program, the African American Male Career Pathway Program (AMCAP), including the cover and back of this book.

Joe L. Rempson

The front and back cover logos, incidentally, are in the color in which all the logos are produced, only, due to cost considerations, the inside logos are in black and white. I provided the text, design specifications, and editing; George's companies did the rest.

Although I was not fortunate enough to benefit from the criticisms of scholars from the various disciplines upon which I have drawn, nor to reap the benefit of developmental editing, I am deeply indebted to my friend and colleague, Dr. Frank Donnangelo, for his copyediting. Frank spared me from some horrendous errors in accuracy of data, and, throughout, his punctuation and rewording have enhanced the readability and clarity of my discussion. After Frank's help, I continued, however, to make some changes and additions, my hope being that those changes and additions reflect what I learned from his copyediting. But from my periodic subsequent skimming of the manuscript, despite the fact that I had periodically thought that I had found all of my typograhical and construction errors (yes, I had to do my own typing, plus all else – it's a self-published book), I still found more. Occasionally, I even found, inexplicably, text that had been scrambled so as to render some portion unintelligible. Like myself, therefore, I am sure that you, too, will find errors of various sorts, only not of such a nature, I hope, that I fail to get across my message – just, instead, suffer a twinge of embarrassment.

While not fortunate enough to benefit from the criticisms of scholars from the various disciplines upon which I have drawn, I am deeply indebted to two scholars and to the personality who dominates the pages of this book: Prof. John McWhorter, Prof. Norrell, and, my hero, Booker T. Washington.

Prof. McWhorter is as courageous as he is scholarly and insightful, telling it like it is, the demands of fictive kinsip and political correctness notwithstanding. I think of him as the E. Franklin Frazier of our day. More than ever, he brought home to me, not only that something has to be done, but why: we are "Losing the Race." The fact that he is doing something about that "losing" reinforced my need to hang in and to pitch in.

Similarly, Prof. Norrell's revisionist biography of Washington is as instructive as it is inspirational. Norrell makes it evident that Washington's struggles were the struggles of us ex-slaves to survive and uplift ourselves, and he gives context to the labor, wisdom, and heroism exercised by Washingon in confronting those struggles. His depiction of those struggles puts Washington in a context at variance with the prevailing "story." It seems as if almost everything we blacks say about Washington distorts his place in our origin and history by, as black historian David H. Jackson Jr. (cited herein) states, labeling him an "accommodationist." This "accommodationist" label has made him unworthy of honor, instead, bringing condemnation, his name seldom receiving honorable mention, if any mention at all. Norrell has dealt a damaging blow to such treatment, and in doing so, he has encouraged me to do my part as well. Without that encouragement, I would not have probed as deeply, which Norrell's book made possible, and, therefore, left fallow, even in my own mind, a more true knowledge of our own African American background – knowledge which, as may be evident from this book, in addition to being inspiring and uplifting, has enabled me to address our most critical race problem, our black male school adaptability crisis, from a more realistic, in-depth, and instructive perspective.

As for my hero, Booker Taliaferro Washington, there is a lot, lot more that I want to read and know about him, but I have read enough to feel more than ever that my race, as the nation, is deeply indebted to him. At the nadir of our new life, starting out with more or less nothing, he constructed a pathway out and, through a lifetime of single-minded devotion and exhaustive labor, he put us on the road to adaptation. So, as I got further and further into my research, I said to myself: the least, therefore, that I can do to show our gratitude (the gratitude of his race) is to write a book of which he might be proud.

Contents

Dedication vii
Acknowledgements ix
Tables And Figures xv

1 Introduction 1

Part I
The Crisis

2 The African American School Adaptability Crisis
  (AMSAC): Present and Past 47

Part II
Causes and Context

3 To Blame or Not to Blame Ourselves: Cosby Versus
  Dyson / Loury versus Ferguson 69
4 The Crisis as an Outgrowth of Our Two Adaptation
  Traditions: Washington Versus Dubois In Our African
  American Garden of Eden 94
5 Why the Crisis? The Maladaptation of Our Students:
  Cool-Pose Culture versus School Culture 198
6 Why the Crisis? "Acting White" as a Cause 208
7 Why The Crisis: The Adaptation Of Our Community, A
  Window Into The Adaptation Of Our Students 269
8 Why the Crisis? The IQ Factor: Adaptation as a Function
  of Our Innate Ability 306
9 Why the Crisis? The Root Cause: Lack of a Positive Core
  Identity 358
10 The Role of Our Two Adaptation Traditions in Our
   Identity Formation 418
11 Of President Barak Obama and Others (Victimology:
   Our Second Bondage) 430

Part III
The Solution: The School "on the Hook"

12 Overcoming IQ as a Putative Obstacle to School (and Community) Adaptation 475
13 The African American Male Career Pathway Program (AMCAP) 523
14 AMCAP Goals, Hypotheses, Methodology 552
15 The Case For AMCAP Use of African American Male Counselors 582
16 Popular but Flawed Solutions to School Reform and Art of Loving (AOL) Schools as the Answer 599

Part IV
We African Americans "on the Hook"

17 The Case for Our Self-Responsibility Tradition as The Tradition of Choice: You be the Judge or Jury 633
18 A Child Family Rights Movement to Replace our Civil Rights Movement 699
19 Taking Us From Here: Unshackling Dr. King 713
20 Renewing Washington's Self-Responsibility Tradition: Proposals And Success Requirements 723

Appendix

A Washington's Compromise Address Of 1895* 785
B President Barak Obama: Trayvon Martin Case Remarks* 788

References 795
About the Author 899
Index 901

Tables And Figures

Tables

1. Black Male, Comparative, College Enrollment and Graduation Rate 56
2. Factors Found to Account for School Achievement 80
3. National Public High School Graduation Rates, Class of 2003 529
4. Two Traditions Compared on Seven Socioeconomic Variables 661

Figures

1. Racism as Security Blanket 12
2. Statue of Booker T. Washington "Lifting the Veil of Ignorance," by Charles Keck 75
3. Relative influences on learning 82
4. Booker T. Washington 100
5. W. E. B. DuBois 101
6. Tuskegee Normal and Industrial Institute 184
7. The Oaks, Washington's home at Tuskegee Institute built in 1899 with bricks made by faculty and students 185
8. Cotton States Exposition, 1896 185
9. Interior of Negro building, Atlanta Exposition 186
10. Tuskegee faculty, 1897 186
11. George Washington Carver, center front, with staff 187
12. Theodore Roosevelt visit to Tuskegee in 1905 187
13. Booker T. Washington Silver Anniversary lecture at Carnegie Hall 188

14. Handbill of Booker T. Washington 1909 Virginia tour 188
15. Booker T. Washington speaking in New Orleans 189
16. Interior view of library reading room at Tuskegee,
    Tuskegee students seated 189
17. History class at Tuskegee 190
18. Chemistry laboratory at Tuskegee 190
19. Studying botany – Tuskegee students 191
20. Upholstery (tailoring) class at Tuskegee 191
21. Roof construction by students at Tuskegee 192
22. Students working in print shop at Tuskegee 192
23. Field work by Tuskegee students 193
24. Outdoor work at Tuskegee 193
25. Tuskegee students cutting sugar cane 194
26. Hospital at Tuskegee, showing patients and staff 194
27. Commencement day parade at Tuskegee, 1914 195
28. Booker T. Washington's coffin being carried
    to his grave site at Tuskegee Institute 195
29. Langston Hughes, with Jessie Fauset and Zora Neale
    Hairston, at Tuskegee, 1927, in front of statue,
    "Lifting the Veil of Ignorance" 196
30. Booker T. Washington 1940 Issue 196
31. SS Booker T. Washington 197
32. Booker T. Washington National Monument,
    Hardy, Virginia 197
33. Black and white IQ distributions 328
34. Model of multiple dimensions of identity 367
35. Sample KIPP character growth card 505
36. AMCAP logo: practice of the art of loving logo 559
37. AMCAP logo: time perspective 560
38. AMCAP logo: AMCAP code 568
39. AMCAP logo: ant killer 577
40. System-Responsibility Tradition yin-yang 701

1

Introduction

Proverbs, 16:22 - "Understanding is a wellspring of life unto him that hath it: but the instruction of fools is folly."[1]
Galatians, 6:5 - "For every man shall bear his own burden."

I say to all African American males what I say in my <u>African American Career Pathway (AMCAP) Task Guide</u> to the students I hope to enroll in my proposed experimental program, AMCAP:

> We African-American males need to be able satisfactorily to do something that is essential to our manhood and to our role responsibility in family and community: to make a living.
>
> Having limited ability to make a living means limited ability to care for self or family or to be a solid citizen of the community. Instead, the care goes in the opposite direction. Rather than providing care, we must receive it. We become a drag and a burden.
>
> Yet the normal drives and desires of manhood remain. That we cannot satisfy them through making an honest living too often

---

[1] Source: King James Version of the Holy Bible, as are all other biblical references in this book.

leads us to try other ways, among them: parasitism (living off others), drugs, vice, crime (225).[2]

The situation reminds me of Franklin D. Roosevelt's, "I see one-third of a nation ill-housed, ill-clad, ill-nourished."[3] Primarily because of us African American males, similarly, I see one-fourth of our race disproportionately ill-educated, unemployed or underemployed, and ill-acculturated.

This book represents my lifelong desire to do something about this persistent situation and thereby contribute to the progress of my people. That desire ensues from no event or teaching; it simply emerged sometime during my adolescent years and I accepted and embraced it. The desire led me to seek jobs that would advance our students and, ultimately, upon retirement, to establish a private foundation, the Rempson Foundation, to express it. The hope had been that I would be able, on my own, to fund the foundation so that it could sponsor a program that would have some of the elements of the herein proposed **African American Male Career Pathway Program (AMCAP)**.

My idea for such a program had its origin when I was Dean of Students at Bronx Community College of the City University of New York. I had a proposal funded by the New York State Education Department to conduct a program to increase the retention and graduation rate of the College's minority males. It came to be called MCAP (Minority Male Career Pathway Program). Administrative and time constraints did not permit a valid test of its efficacy, but the research results showed that it held promise. Now that promise, built upon an enlargement of my original vision, was to be put to a more valid test by my foundation.

I could not do so, however, without funds. The current, July, 2015, amount in the Foundation's account, $25,479.84, hardly suffices. I therefore was reminded of what I call the **Washington $15 Gold**

---

[2] Throughout, numbers in parentheses designate references which are numbered in the References section at the end of the book, the page number(s) cited following the Reference number.

[3] Source: http://en.wikisource.org/wiki/Franklin_Roosevelt%27s_Second_Inaugural_Address. 24 November 2014.

Watch Pawning. I later tell the story of Booker T. Washington and his Tuskegee students and staff having made three unsuccessful attempts to build a kiln for brickmaking, his staff thereupon urging that the effort be abandoned. But Washington refused to give up. He pawned his gold watch [a present from a New England widow] for $15 and was able to make a fourth and successful try. Later, with the notoriety gained from his best-selling book, Up from Slavery, he turned that beginning success into fame.

Purpose

To start my Foundation's proposed program, AMCAP, I have no equivalent of a watch to pawn. Nor do I have the faintest hope that this book will be another Up from Slavery. But I thought that it might be successful enough to attract the funding and school needed for AMCAP, possibly even more. Evidence-based, AMCAP is designed to help solve our African American male school crisis. I call this crisis the **African American Male School Adaptability Crisis**, or **AMSAC**.

I have a second aim. It is to contribute to an understanding of our African American social problems, of which AMSAC is an inseparable part, and to offer as well some remedies. To stand our best chance to solve AMSAC, we must not limit our attempt to AMSAC itself, but must focus simultaneously on those community forces responsible for it. We deceive ourselves if we think that AMSAC is something for the school alone to solve; it is a crisis which can be solved *only* if we African American males and our community also make ourselves an active part of the solution.

One of the saddest things of my lifetime is to watch some of our people in the inner city too often more or less hand our problems over to white people to solve. A case in point is the crime and drug dealing in some of our inner-city neighborhoods. Among other things, we blame the police for not stopping it or for letting it happen, something we say they would not do in white neighborhoods (probably true because most white neighborhoods would not tolerate it). Yet, in response, when -- as in New York City for example -- they employ a stop-and-frisk policy, we cry racism and seek legal remedy. So be "dammed if you do, dammed if you don't." *Our own behavior* in this instance, as in other instances, serves both to cause the problem and to hinder its solution.

Regardless of the reasons for the behavior, it is *our behavior*, and rather than placing its remedy in the hands of white people -- and then standing back and criticizing them -- we must lead the way in its prevention and remedy. White people are no longer responsible for us. We are no longer in slavery. Nor otherwise under oppression. We are on our own, and must bear our own burdens. That requires us to do an eminently better job of *managing* our own life -- beginning with, and most fundamentally, our own *home* life. Whites have provided us a lot of help and support to enable us to do so. Those not satisfied with that help and support need to be reminded that we do not live in a perfect world, and they need to ponder what our life might be like if we lived elsewhere (indeed, look around!). As is, take full advantage of white help and support, rather than constantly complaining and protesting, and we can do quite well; it is a matter of *effective management*.

Instead of asking whites to control our inner-city behavior, let us be led by the example, as reported in the New York Times (January, 2013), of the black middle-class enclave of Chatham, on Chicago's South Side (315d). In response to a rising crime rate and other deviant behavior, to preserve the character of their neighborhood, block groups and volunteers swung into action to stem the tide and reverse the trend. Their reported considerable success so far is a lesson for all our poor neighborhoods as well. Of course, poor neighborhoods cannot be expected to have Chatham's structure, but therein lies our challenge. Others are not responsible for meeting that challenge; we are. We have to work to create such structures, fully understanding that the price of our failure to do so is the futile continuation of our too-often expectation of whites to do for us that which only we can do for ourselves.

Centrality of Family

As pertains to AMSAC and its inseparable social problems, I have come to believe that if they are to be solved, we must strengthen our families. As sociologist and professor emeritus of Harvard University, Lee Rainwater, puts it:

> It is in the family that the child learns the most primitive categories of existence and experience, and that he develops his most deeply held beliefs about the world and about himself. From the child's point of view, the household *is* [emphasis in original] the world; his experiences as he moves out of it into the larger world are always interpreted in terms of his particular experience in the home (215a:200).

And what is his "particular experience in the home?" This is Rainwater's thesis [bearing in mind that he is talking about the poor]:

> It is the central thesis of this paper that the caste-facilitated infliction of suffering by Negroes on other Negroes and on themselves appears most poignantly within the confines of the family, and that the victimization process as it operates in families prepares and toughens its members to function in the ghetto world, at the same time that it seriously interferes with their ability to operate in any other world (215a:176).

Rainwater's thesis is the belief herein, which is that due to home factors our students are hampered in their ability to function in the school world or, as Rainwater contends, in any other world. My belief, however, did not stem from Rainwater, nor for that matter from the infamous Moynihan Report (discussed in a later chapter), but evolved from life experience and exposure to the social sciences. We should not, in fact, have even needed the Moynihan Report to tell us what we should have already known, and it is ironic that so many of us made the report an occasion to deny what many of us have lived or have observed first hand. I do not think that I am unique when I say that I have seen the disproportionate dysfunctionality in my own large family of six brothers and three sisters, and its many grandchildren, nieces, nephews, and other kindred.

Even so, one cannot be sure that today many of us see it – or should I say, accept it. One does not discern it in the public discourse and the action is missing. Maybe something like an incident that has occurred while I am writing this introduction will shock us all into a more awake, active state. Republican candidates campaigning for their 2012 presidential nomination were asked by a conservative group to sign a marriage vow pledge that, at one point, contained the later deleted following statement:

> 'Slavery had a disastrous impact on African-American families, yet sadly a child born into slavery in 1860 was more likely to be raised by his mother and father in a two- parent household than was an African-American baby born after the election of the USA's first African-American President' (475a).

The statement caused such an uproar that it was deleted from the vow, but my research indicates that there is some history to support it. If one stops to think about conditions then and now, it is not unreasonable to believe that it is one of those inconvenient truths that we blacks find hard to face and do not want to accept -- maybe because (with good reason) we are ashamed to do so. My evidence-based view, however, is that if we face our demons, we will free ourselves to deal more effectively with them. Whether this deleted statement is true or not -- and there is ample reason to believe that it is true -- it starkly draws our attention to what I consider one of our **three major demons**, *fatherless families*, the other two being *IQ lag* and *crime*. I see all three as having their source from within: a negative core identity grounded in Victimology.

Practices and policies formulated without operationally taking these three major demons into account -- and the factors and forces which they reflect -- are doomed to failure, or at least to limited success. Think, for example, about the War on Poverty, school desegregation, or school reform. Their failure, or limited success, reflects a deficiency in addressing these parallel community factors and forces.

We continue to live in what E. Franklin Frazier called a "world of make-believe." As evident from the literature, we make-believe that (1) the expected gains from our civil rights victories have not materialized for so many of us because, to put it bluntly, we are still victims of a white racist society; and (2) the solution to our victimization is unceasing activism, however predictably futile, and the creation of a black identity and a competitive black world view. That is what we variously have seen, for example, in the Black Power Movement, nigrescence, Afrocentrism, critical race theory, Black Studies departments, black caucuses, the proliferation of black professional organizations and publications, and opportunistic protests and outrages. Not that there is a uniform black subscription to this make-believe world -- in some of its aspects, the majority of us are dissenters -- but thanks to our activists and ideologues, aided by many whites, it is this make-believe world which has come to dominate the black conversation and the black agenda. Our **three major demons** -- *IQ lag--fatherless families--crime* -- have no meaningful role in the conversation nor a discernible place on the agenda. Just the contrary; the three have been transmuted and politicized. Our IQ lag has become a school problem, fatherless families a child poverty problem,[4] and crime a police and race relations problem. The feeling which nurtures this mindset tends to run deep, producing a faith-like fervor. Seemingly casting themselves in an aura of grace, those who possess it – and they are omnipresent -- commonly convey the impression that they are staunch defenders of the race, others of us not sharing their fervor being, if *not really black*, at least suspect.

The Spirit of William Lloyd Garrison and Our Second Bondage

I stand accused. Nevertheless, in the spirit of abolitionist William Lloyd Garrison, "I will be as harsh as truth, and as uncompromising as justice." "I am in earnest—I will not equivocate—I will not excuse—I will not retreat a single inch—**AND I WILL BE HEARD**" [emphasis in original][5] Only with this byproduct book as my The Liberator, I can merely hope -- and pray -- that "**I WILL BE HEARD.**"

Garrison's call was for us to end our first bondage: slavery. My call is for us to end its replacement, **Victimology**, which has become our second bondage. The term and insight are borrowed from John McWhorter, who defines Vicimology as victimhood treated as an identity rather than as a problem to be solved. It is Victimology – mental and psychological slavery -- which now enslaves us. The results are ubiquitous and devastating, the inhibition and vitiation of our manhood being foremost.

---

[4] For an informative discussion of this demon, see Horowitz's article cited in bibliography, #389. Also see following link, which, in addition to the Horowitz's article, provides link to several other highly informative articles. http://www.discoverthenetworks.org/viewSubCategory.asp?id=1261 13 December 2014.

[5] http://en.wikipedia.org/wiki/William_Lloyd_Garrison. 24 November 2014.

Joe L. Rempson

As Elisabeth Lasch-Quinn argues in her book, <u>Race Experts: How Racial Etiquette, Sensitivity Training, and New Age Therapy Hijacked the Civil Rights Revolution</u> (discussed in Chapter 9), these consequences have left us "mired in a generational sense of complaint and outrage that never seems to subside." As evident from the almost daily dosage we get from the media, replacing the (by some counts) some 700 black riots of the 1960s have been persistent local and national black uproars or outrages over one perceived race wrong or another. No similar uproars or outrages, however, when it comes to such fundamental problems as out-of-wedlock births and young black male fratricide.

Paradoxically, this new self-imposed enslavement is primarily the outcome of our Civil Rights victories of the 1950s and 1960s. Those victories brought us tremendous success, but that success has been accompanied by disappointments, failures, and setbacks which have produced a disgruntled middle class, and which has left one-fourth of us behind (Abandoned is Eugene Robinson's description of those in this category). In explanation, we have declared ourselves victims -- victim of the white man's system that is stacked against us and which does not give us a fair shake and a fair chance. Its most common expression has come to be captured in that ubiquitous term, racism. Racism, we blacks generally believe, is everywhere; there is no escaping it and those of us blacks who think we can deceive ourselves. More than that, since Victimology has become part of black identity, it evokes the charge that -- if we think we have and can escape it -- we are not black because we *think white*.

The seeds of this victim mindset were planted in our African American Garden of Eden. The planter was the father of the tradition from which the seeds derive, the System-Responsibility Tradition of W. E. B. DuBois. DuBois preached and propagated victimhood, and the activists and ideologues of the 1960s gave widespread prominence to him and his gospel. The result, as John McWhorter declares, is that Victimology has come to permeate the entirety of black society. Not limited to the poor, we see it no less among our Talented Tenth (including our first black President, Barak Obama) and in federal laws designed to *protect* us. I discuss three main examples: the Trayvon Martin case, Affirmative Action, and a new federal study of school discipline.

To end the bondage, we must follow in the footsteps of the late black journalist Bob Teague. In one of the introductory pages to his book, <u>The Flip Side of Soul: Letters to My Son</u>, he has the following quotations (255a):

'If I were a black man, I'd be living in a state of constant fury.'
--Westbrook Pegler

'I'm trying to cut down on fury myself. Bad for digestion. Am thinking of switching to finesse.'
-- Bob Teague

Like Bob Teague, let's think of "switching to finesse." In fact, as he actually did, let's just do it.

I try to subscribe to Teague's formula. Born black – and proudly so -- I have always felt that, simultaneously, I am -- as my fellow blacks are -- an integral and equal part of the human race, subject to the same imperatives, what whites and others may say or think notwithstanding. In later life, it is more than abundantly clear to me that if we fail to embrace this affirmation, we automatically compound the ordinary problems of human existence. That is primarily because, as a result, we neither see nor accept the reality of our existence; rather, we deny that reality and create our own (*recomposition* is what Shelby Steele calls it).

That is a lesson that we can take, for example, from the Harper-Tuckman study (2006). Brian E. Harper is a black educational psychologists at Cleveland State University and Bruce W. Tuckman is an educational psychologist at Ohio State University. They "investigated racial centrality, public regard and private regard beliefs in relation to the grade point average of [289] African-American high-school students" (367b). To measure their beliefs they used a shortened 20-item version of the Multi-dimensional Model of Black Identity (MMBI). The model is premised on four distinct dimensions of racial identity: *racial salience*, the extent to which race is a relevant aspect of a respondent's self-concept at a particular moment in time; *racial centrality* a stable component of racial identity), the extent to which a respondent defines him or herself in terms of race; *private regard* (*racial regard*), or the extent to which a respondent has positive feelings towards her or his own race, and the *public regard*, or the extent to which respondent feels others have a positive view of blacks; and *racial ideology*, the way a respondent feels members of the race should behave.

The first three are the crucial dimensions and are conceived to function in concert rather than independently. The model measures other dimensions, which are not measured by the 20 items. The 20 items yield four racial identity clusters: *Idealized*, characterized by a high levels of racial centrality, private regard, and public regard; *Alienated*, characterized by low levels of racial centrality, private regard, and public regard; *Buffering/Defensive*, characterized by high level of racial centrality and private regard and a low level of public regard; and *Low connectedness/High affinity* (similar to the *Alienated*), characterized by a low level of racial centrality, a high level of private regard, and a low level of public regard.

Below and elsewhere more will be said about the study, the point to be made here is that, contrary to what some "think black" believers might predict, it revealed that the *Alienated* students had a significantly higher grade point average than the *Idealized* students. That is, the *less* central a role race played in their identity, the higher their academic achievement, and the *more* central a role it played the lower their academic achievement. My argument is that this is not an anomaly. When we make our *blackhood* central, we hinder our progress, whereas when, instead, we make our *personhood* central, we foster it.

I decided to take the inventory myself, just to see if my results validated my self-perception. So, I went online, found the test, and responded to and scored the 20 items.

Whereas I would have labeled myself *Low connectedness/High affinity*, the results showed that, instead, I belong in the *Alienated* identity cluster. The item that kept me out of the *Low connectedness/High affinity* dimension pertains to feeling good about black people, for I just do not feel good about us because we ourselves are not committed to addressing our own internal problems, something which eats at my existence.

In addition to the leadership factor, the commitment to address our own internal problems is undermined when -- as the late journalist

Westbrook Pegler (presaging black intellectual, author, and activist Cornell West, for example) says a black man should do, and as so many of the *Idealized*, in fact, do -- we choose to live in "a state of constant fury." Yet, as McWhorter in effect persuasively argues, we have come to make "a state of constant fury" a part of the bedrock of black identity. Pronounced among our lower class, and variously present among our middle class as well, the literature suggests this profile of our African American personality: a personality grounded in Victimology, the lack of a positive core identity being at its center, that lack associated with low self-responsibility, low self-acceptance, and aggression. What we get from this personality is a sense of madness. For too many of us this is what Victimology breeds: a syndrome which yields a sense of madness.

- The imagined is taken for the real.
- The symptoms are treated as the substance.
- The objective is viewed as the contrived.
- Racial sensitivity is transformed from a character trait into a disease.
- Individual responsibility is treated, not as an expectation, but as punishment.
- Justice is seen to lie, not in the process, but in the outcome.
- Personal acceptance is treated, not as a choice, but as a mandate.
- Race is used to account for every wrong and exonerate every evil.
- Remedies are held, not to lie in the exercise of any responsibility, but solely in the enforcement of rights.

Too often, our plight is explained as a product of racism. Racism is our security blanket. It gives us the ostensible feeling that *we* are OK; *racisum* is the problem. This "mark of oppression"(racism), as Kardiner and Ovesey might term it, is an evolution of what Frazier saw as intrinsic to black history, and what he observed in his analysis of the middle class of his time: an inferiority complex (discussed in Chapter 7). To alleviate its inferiority feeling, Frazier's thesis is that the black middle class created a world of make-believe in which it derived its status in American life, and in our race, primarily through its society life. Today, that feeling of inferiority intertwines with Victimology, and too many of us alleviate their combined trauma, not actively, through our society life, but, psychologically, through making a drumbeat of racism. Racism has come to provide a measure of comfort to us against

Figure 1. Racism as Security Blanket. Copyright ownership by Joe Louis Rempson.

the perceived ubiquitous evils perpetrated against us by white society. Failing to meet the requirements of adaptation, or whatever the demands of success might be, we use it as an excuse, and employ it to wrap ourselves in the security it affords us from our failure.

To be sure, the use of the term by some of us is not so self-serving. More or less, it is simply a meme (discussed elsewhere). Its use derives from our historically-rooted and transmitted racial sensitivity. That sensitivity, however, can prevent us from differentiating *racial bias* from *human nature*. Not necessarily an easy distinction, but a reasonably possible and necessary one. We tend to attribute to racial bias behavior which, given human nature, would be expected of any other similarly-situated human being. Although our first thought-response might be racism, we must dig further and question whether, in invoking it, we are the victim of our own tendency. Otherwise, we end up making racism that which too many of us make it: our security blanket.

To bring this madness to an end, we must undertake a cultural war. As our first bondage, slavery, was ended through a military war leading to an amendment to our constitution, I call for the ending of this second bondage through a cultural war which leads us to amend our culture. I see this war being waged by a **Child Family Rights Movement**, discussed below.

Centrality of Father to Family

On the alluded to role of the family, as I pondered how, out of our disorganized family life, a more viable family could be forged, I came to feel -- based then as much on observation and experience as on educational training -- that it cannot be done unless the father is made a viable part of it. So rather than focusing on the family per se, my evolved notion came to be that, instead, we must concentrate on the weak and too often missing link in the family structure, the father. To get our males to be responsible fathers is the key to strengthening our families, and if we strengthen our families, we will solve AMSAC and the social problems from which it is inseparable.

The achievement of this goal, responsible fatherhood, lies in our hands, the hands of us African American males. No one else can achieve it. Research and experience, discussed in Chapter 15, suggest that it requires males to bring up males. Few things encountered in my research have made this assertion stand out more than the preschool data which I discuss in Chapter 3. The data indicate that model preschool programs for our 3- and 4-year-olds have had long-term significant benefits for black females, *but not for black males*. Based on the literature, it can be inferred that one major reason may be that these programs, staffed as they are primarily by females, do not satisfy the "male hunger" which our 3- and 4-year-olds have (as do males of all ages) – that hunger traceable to absent fathers. Their female guides cannot satisfy that hunger and, therefore, spark in them the responsiveness that might contribute to their desired development. Nor can their male peer culture contribute significantly to their desired development. Others can help, foremost the school itself can, but without us African American males doing our part, the crisis will persist.

Therefore, my foundation's proposed program, AMCAP, focuses mainly on our African American male students. Other black male students are our racial brothers, however, it is neither they nor our daughters who have a crisis; it is we African American males who do. That is the conclusion which I can draw from the male-female differences in my large family, as well as from other large families in my life circle, a conclusion supported by the literature and the statistics. There are, however, program components which provide for the participation of all blacks males, whatever their definition of black.

Collective Fatherhood -- and Familyhood

Because it is we who have a crisis, I write this unintended book to you, my fellow African American males. I write to you as collective fathers. Black music and culture journalist, Steven Ivory, has it right: "Whether or not we are biological or step or universal dads [without an offspring or maybe even connection with someone with an offspring], all men shoulder some responsibility in how children turn out" (131: 247). Indeed, we are a family, a family of black men, and, as a family, we must look out for one another. I believe that we African American males, in unity, must step up and put our sons on the right pathway. They are us, and I, like so many others of us, dislike what they are doing to themselves and to us. John McWhorter rightly says they (and others among us) are engaged in self-sabotage, and the "self" is not just them personally but, to some degree, all of us. We must not stand by, let them run rampant, simply talk about it, and blame the white man and his system. We are obligated to do more.

I make an appeal to our black male athletes and entertainers to do something in particular. You can have a massive impact on our black male school crisis because so many of you are idolized by so many of us and our young black males. Though you may have disagreements with this book, please do not let your disagreements prevent you from supporting the proposed Student AMCAPs (described below) and helping to propagate the motto which guides my proposed evidence-based experimental program, the African American Male Career Pathway Program (AMCAP). The motto is: DISCOVER AND PURSUE YOUR CAREER PATHWAY (see Chapters 13, 14, and 15). Their home, school, library, and the

nternet (on which, for example, career inventories can be found) can assist them. And your voices, as any other support you may lend, can help to create Student AMCAPs and to popularize this motto. If the motto is made a part of our black male culture, the likely result will be major strides in their high school graduation rate and in their subsequent college and life success.

The "more" which all of us black males are obligated to do begins with our acceptance of responsibility for ourselves. We must say: yes, regardless of the cause, this is *our* crisis and *we* accept full and unqualified ownership of it. With that ownership goes the full and unqualified responsibility to do, on *our* part, all that we *ourselves* can do for *ourselves*. We must remind ourselves that, just as the system is composed of men, we, too, are men. And, as men, like other men, we must bear our own burden. That burden is borne, not through unceasing protest, as DuBois advocated, but, as Washington urged, through foundation-building. Foremost, that foundation-building requires us to look out for family and self. In <u>Manhood in the Making</u>, State University of New York, Stony Brook anthropologist, David Gilmore, explains that, throughout the world, men are protectors and providers (101). They look out for family and self. Nothing entitles us African American men to be exempted from that near universal male role.

But we are not alone. In this endeavor, as in others, we have our other, and some say better, half: our African American females. This is a crisis which we cannot separate from our overall social problems; we have to tackle both simultaneously. That requires all of us, African American males and African American females alike, to work together. So whereas I write especially to you, my fellow African American males, I write as well to our companions: our African American females.

White Support

I write also to our white compatriots. Throughout our history, you have led or supported us in all of the major thrusts in our upward climb -- from the ending of slavery, to the self-help program of Booker T. Washington, to the founding of the National Association for the Advancement of Colored People (NAACP), to the War on Poverty, to the Civil Rights Movement. Therapeutic sensibility makes it increasingly difficult, however, for you to support the kind of self-help focus proposed, but I say to you that your conscience must not be permitted to fall victim to condescension. It is far past time that many more of you get past any feeling of guilt or fear of repercussions if you support something (and it does not take much!) which puts you in the position of being accused of being insensitive, racist, or supremacists. We blacks must be upheld by you to the same standards by which you abide and which have enabled you to make such great progress.

Byproduct Book

To be sure, I did not start out to write a book, to say nothing of one this size (disregarding the fact that on several occasions my son has mused, "Dad, why don't you write a book!"). I started out to finish the task of formulating a solution to our crisis, the byproduct of which is this book. After completing the first draft of my <u>AMCAP Task Guide</u> for AMCAP, I began to write a handbook to guide the staff in its use. I wanted it to have data that would give it an understanding of the crisis. In the process of compiling that data – compiled into a paper, "Facts, Figures, and More," a portion of which has been excerpted and included in Chapter17 -- one thing led to another, and to another, and on it went. The process was somewhat like Joseph Campbell's "Follow your bliss" advice. Call it a kind of inner ethnographic journey, as the process more or less had the feeling of something within me working itself out somewhat in the fashion of a fetus maturing in the womb. What came out and where I ended up is before you in book form. Whether or not the book results in my getting the funding, the school, or the readership I seek, I feel rewarded. I have learned more than I ever knew and I understand better that which I might never have more fully understood. I have been left with enhanced insight, clarity, and certitude. If I can approximate a similar outcome for you and the rest of my readers, our race as well would have been rewarded; so, too, would our nation.

Focus on the Masses

No grand reward is sought. I am not so concerned about our being able to hold prestigious jobs, live in swank neighborhoods, or amass huge fortunes. Perhaps, in part, that is a product of having spent my early years in a family of sharecroppers on Southern farmlands in

Tennessee. Moreover, as black Pulitzer Prize-winning <u>Washington Post</u> journalist Eugene Robinson, for example, makes evident in his recent book, <u>Disintegration: The Splintering of Black America</u>, quite a few of us already fit those descriptions (227). My primary concern is the masses, or, to look at it another way, the less fortunate among us -- the abandoned one-fourth of our race. Indeed, "There, but by the grace of God go I." I just want most of us to do what so many of us do not do: live ordinary lives in that we work and love, attributes of the able, normal person, as Sigmund Freud saw it. I, as no doubt you, do not want so many of us to be living on the edge, depressed and deprived, with so many of our families and neighborhoods being in disarray. Many of us blacks may be able to identify with this revelation from Dr. George Jenkins (later referenced) regarding his growing up:

> I never felt confident when dealing with the constant confrontations that arise when you live in a neighborhood like mine. Somebody's always losing his temper; somebody's always getting shoved around. The root of these beefs is usually something so trivial or petty that I just couldn't get worked up about it (55a:15-16).

"Somebody's always losing his temper." That must end, or perhaps more realistically, meaningfully diminish. It is not a state of plenty which is my concern, but the end of so many of us "always losing our temper" -- engaged in "constant confrontations" over the "trivial or petty" -- and its more or less uniform replacement with work and love which produce a state of self-care and safety.

"average expectable environments"

As regards safety, I come to the second of our **three major demons**: *crime*. I am sure that none of us wants us to continue to carry this historical burden, especially to the extent to which it has evolved. Co-chair of the National Network for Safe Communities and Professor of Criminal Justice at John Jay College of Criminal Justice in New York, David M. Kennedy, in his recent book, <u>Don't Shoot: One Man, A Street Fellowship, and the End of Violence in Inner-City America</u>, expresses the reward that I seek on this count. He writes:

> We do not have to live with the death, and the hatred, and the gunshot survivors who walk the streets with their canes and colostomy bags, and the young men who say matter-of-factly that they expect to be dead before they see twenty-five, and the warrior-priest cops who go through door after door and it never changes, and whole communities of black men going to prison, and whole communities that are unable to get anywhere on anything of substance because people are afraid to go outside, and poisoned relations between those who need each other the most. We do not have to go on like this (144b:15).

I agree. Part of the reward that I seek lies in the hope that we will not continue to live like this. It is a hope for what the late world renown psychoanalyst, Erik Erikson, terms "**average expectable environments**," [emphasis added] from which all else will follow. In such environments, our children would be provided the security and love so indispensable to their growth and development and without which they are likely to falter and flounder – and thereby keep breeding the kind of home and community life described by Dr. Jenkins and David Kennedy.

This hope reminds me of the kind of spirit which Booker T. Washington expressed in his article, "Industrial Education for the Negro," referenced in a later chapter. In it, he had this to say:

> One farm bought, one house built, one home sweetly and intelligently kept, one man who is the largest tax payer or has the largest bank account, one school or church maintained, one factory running successfully, one truck garden profitably cultivated, one patient cured by a Negro doctor, one sermon well preached, one office well filled, one life cleanly lived--these will tell more in our favor than all the abstract eloquence that can be summoned to plead our cause (270:360).

Such results reflect the essence of the kind of ordinary, productive life that I have in mind and whose spirit is needed as much in our time as in Washington's time. With that spirit, we can create the "**average expectable environments**" which will enable us to forge a positive core identity.

We African American males are essential to the creation of such environments. From "**average expectable environments**," we are going to get responsible fathers, from responsible fathers we are going to get strengthened families, and from strengthened families we are going to get the solution to our crisis and problems. I write to make my case to you as to my basis for this assertion and offer a program and ideas that can make such environments possible.

I do so mindful of an observation made by black journalist and bestselling author, Ellis Cose, in his most recent book, <u>The End of Anger</u>. Writing about a couple of ex-offenders, he observes, "They remind me of dozens of young men I have met over the years who, given a different set of circumstances, could be thriving, well-respected members of society" (49:212). I suspect that our experience enables any of us to make a similar observation, that observation perhaps being applicable even to some members of our own family. "Given a different set of circumstances," we might have mused, "their life could have turned out differently." And this is what "**average expectable environments**" are about: giving our males (and really all our children and youth) a "different set of circumstances," namely, "**average expectable environments**" wherein they are provided security and love, or, as Erik Erikson puts it, a "hallowed presence."

A Diverse Audience

In writing to a diverse audience, I cover a somewhat broad territory and touch on matters which lie in the public, policy, practice, and academic domains. Those within these domains share an interest in our crisis and problems and have variously staked their claim, so to speak, or made their voices heard. So while writing especially to you, my fellow African American males -- and simultaneously to our African American females -- at the same time, I am speaking to all of you, and often in your language. I resume the public conversation that I initiated back in 1966 with my article in <u>The Urban Review</u> on the local control of schools in New York City, and that somewhat more recently, 1993, I continued in textbook form with a chapter on the human spirit in collaboration with my friend and colleague, Angela Anselmo of Baruch College of the City University of New York (220,226). The basic topic remains the same: the needs of our disadvantaged students.

Only today, the intensified problems of our males have evolved into a crisis that is manifested in ever-more alarming school data and in the kind of social problems and issues which are reflected in the prisonization of their values and to other outcomes suggested in Chapter 17 by "Facts, Figures, and More." The crisis contaminates our poor communities. To save ourselves -- to have life in most of our urban neighborhoods characterized by "**average expectable environments**" -- requires a distinct departure from that which has not worked.

Identifying the Problem

The key to any such departure is identifying the cause of the problem. We have a situation wherein the attributed causes are like a bundle of wires connected to a time bomb: which one do you cut to defuse it. Our time bomb is a crisis, and our quandary: an attack on which attributed cause will do the most to defuse it. At the outset, I had thought that I had answered this question fairly well. I had narrowed it down to males, further to the need of males for male nurturing, and even further their need for a route to manhood through career discovery and pursuit. In the process, I had to come to grips with the other causes that have been advanced. As pertains to our students in general, inclusive of our males, the major ones have been school segregation, teacher qualifications and expectations, color-biased instructional materials, class size, physical facilities, and cultural deprivation. The problem with these causes -- *and they are causes* -- is that they have been addressed without significant or enduring impact. Busing, multi-ethnic materials, modification of materials, special teacher training, compensatory education, and other attempts at solving them have not paid off. That does not mean, however, that these causes do not need addressing; all causes must be addressed. It simply means that addressing them alone, though perhaps helpful, has not solved our problems.

"acting white"

Then "acting white" was introduced as one major cause. In their classic ethnographic study (1986) reported in the Urban Review, "Black Students' School Success: Coping with the "Burden of 'Acting White,'" black anthropologist, Signithia Fordham, and the late black Nigerian American anthropologist, John Ogbu, drew this conclusion:

"*...one major reason* Black students do poorly in school is that they experience inordinate ambivalence and affective dissonance in regard to academic effort and success" [emphasis in original] (90:594)). A storm of controversy ensued that has not ended. Partly because of what it reveals about how we have tended broadly to treat the cause of the achievement gap between black and white students, I give extended attention to it. My conclusion is that the evidence *does not* support "acting white" as one *major* reason for black students' poor school performance. Rather, it is a symptom of *the main reason*, which is an underlying co-existent oppositional culture which does not value academic effort and success. "Acting white," however, may possibly have the effect of reducing the number and attainment of prospective Talented Tenth black students. By *value*, I refer, not to what our students *think* about the importance of education, but about the attitude and behavior which they display in its pursuit – which is what oppositional culture is about, their rejection of those attitudes and behaviors.

Intelligence Quotient (IQ)

An even more controversial cause, IQ, had been previously raised by late University of California at Berkley educational psychologist, Arthur Jensen, in his even more classic 1969 research review article in the Harvard Educational Review, "How Much Can We Boost IQ and Scholastic Achievement?" And in their 1994 book, The Bell Curve: Intelligence and Class Structure in American Life, late Harvard psychologist, Richard Herrnstein, and American Enterprise Institute political scientist, Charles Murray, again raised the IQ question, stirring a renewed storm. They accented the 15-point black-white IQ gap and their thesis that our IQ lag is a major reason for our educational and social problems outraged blacks and many whites. In Chapter 8, I give considerable attention to the controversy, taking the view that our response, though understandable, has been unfortunate. Demons are hard to face, and our 15-point IQ lag, when compared to whites, is one of our **three major demons**. We benefit by confronting and addressing it, as we should do in regard to our other major demons, *fatherless families* and *crime*. Rather than being, as accused, racists or bigots, Jensen-Herrnstein-Murray appear to have been led by where the data took them. That it took them to some perceived racial negatives does not necessarily make them wrong, racists, or bigots; scholarship requires that we let the chips fall where they may.

The weight of the evidence suggests that IQ is a major cause of black students' poor school performance, but, in general, a more decisive role is played by home-student-school factors. Nonetheless, IQ warrants attention because it is a cause which *can be and often is* decisive – which is what makes it a major cause. The problem is that it is a major cause about which we can *so far* do very little. At least that is the case when it come to their pure or *fluid* IQ -- their abstract thinking and problem-solving ability. In 1971, Robert Cattell identified another type of IQ about which a lot can be done. He called it *crystallized* intelligence -- knowledge and skills. Therefore, the thinking goes, interventions which address students' intelligence as a cause should focus, not on their pure or fluid IQ, but instead on their more malleable crystallized IQ, their knowledge and skills. In addition, whereas pure IQ is strongly correlated with school achievement, crystallized IQ is even more strongly correlated with it -- involving as it does both general and specific content knowledge and skills.

In sum, to address IQ as a major cause of our students' poor school performance, we should focus, not on their more or less permanent IQ (permanent after the ages 8-10), but instead, on their pliable achievement as represented by their general and specific content knowledge and skills, which is their other IQ -- their crystallized IQ. We should look, therefore, not at IQ scores, but at achievement measures (representing students' crystallized IQ), such as their grades and achievement tests.

That does not mean, however, that we should ignore IQ scores. Herrnstein and Murray point out that even a raise of three percentage points can make a big difference, and, moreover, research shows IQs indisputable association (not determination, but association) with an array of outcomes. Therefore, the extent to which pure or fluid IQ can be raised, we should try to raise it, only indirectly rather than directly. Evidence indicates that a rise has been brought about -- and may continue to be brought about -- through such indirect approaches as school achievement, improved prenatal care, nutrition, and an enriched home, school, and community environment.

Nor, it follows, should we -- as many schools have done -- eliminate IQ testing. We must remember that, like it or not, and notwithstanding the fact that we can do little about it, low IQ is a major cause of the poor school performance of many of our students. Teachers and educators need to know all they can about a given student so that they can better meet that student's needs. The research does not support the notion that what they know might result in low expectations. Further, if we cannot trust our educators with IQ test results, we should not entrust them with the care and education of our students. When and where warranted, teachers should be removed, not IQ tests.

Integral to our IQ concern -- and a factor in the success of our students -- is the need to focus on a related domain, our students' abilities. Bearing in mind that our goal is to enable our students to succeed in school and in life, more than we have done in the past, we must make our students' abilities something which we identify and cultivate. Success in school and life is not just about the cognitive domain, it is also about the range of domains which make school and life success possible, be it, for example, in athletics or the arts. In cooperation with various community agencies and entities, schools can and should play a greater role in making those domains available.

As for how we should otherwise treat our IQ lag as one of our **three major demons**, I make the case that we should acknowledge it and desist to engage in the discussion. Nothing is programmatically served by trying to address the many issues which are raised in the literature; let us leave that to the technical and scholarly experts -- and the issues can be quite technical and quite scholarly. We simply declare that although we would like to see a rise in our IQ, our IQ is not a preoccupation for us, for we can do quite well as it stands. To succeed, we just need much more drive, which will amplify our IQ -- make it more than measured or imagined -- and which we can get by working on such character traits as impulse control. We accept ourselves for who we are -- IQ and all, are proud of who we are, and strive to be the best of who we are capable of becoming. The fact is, we should add, that we live in a diverse world in which no people or persons are the same, and, in which, therefore, we must strive to accept and respect our differences -- *all* of them -- and, further, strive to transcend those differences in the interest of a common humanity and its implicit moral and civic egalitarianism. As the saying goes, case closed; in this instance, controversy closed.

The case should likewise be closed on a related issue: the black-white academic achievement gap. The goal of *closing* the gap has become a fetish, and it is time to end it, and, instead, focus on *reducing* the gap, perhaps based on some statistical estimate of the range of reduction which is possible. While the evidence suggests that the academic achievement of our black students can be substantially improved, it does not suggest that the magnitude of the improvement would be sufficient to close the gap. Rather, viewed in its totality, it suggests that our three major demons, *IQ lag-fatherless families-crime*, limit that magnitude and make the goal unrealistic. The shift would allow for a more productive use of energy and resources in meeting the individual needs of our students.

Main cause: character deficits

In the end, then, I ruled out IQ as a major cause which we can attack to defuse our crisis, opting instead for concentration on achievement and abilities. I also ruled out the school factors as a cause on which to focus since, beginning in the 1950s, they have been addressed without sufficient success. Left was the alluded to cause reflected in the "acting white" controversy: the culture of our students. Experience and the research evidence justify the conclusion that our students devalue academic striving and success as evident in their too commonly disruptive classroom and school behavior and in their delinquent school work, which, simply put, translates into their not behaving well enough nor working hard enough. And if you do not satisfactorily behave and work hard enough you are unlikely to achieve satisfactorily or to develop your abilities.

University of Pennsylvania psychologist (and MacArthur Fellowship winner), Angela Duckworth, drove this point home for me from a different perspective: character traits. Her teaching experience led her to come to a conclusion with which she did not start out: that the problem with our low-performing students lies, not just with the school, but also with the students themselves because, though "exhilarating and gratifying," "learning is hard" -- "often daunting, exhausting and sometimes discouraging." And, she points out, our low-performing students do not have the character traits required to work that hard. I, therefore.came to label our students' attitude, behavior, and work deficits as character deficits -- and the *main* cause.

Root cause: lack of a positive core identity

Still puzzling, however, is why, after all these years of freedom, and especially after The King Years (the Civil Rights Movement, 1954-68), we and our students are still haunted by the same maladaptive character issues.

I encountered what I believe to be the answer to that puzzle in an article by Prof. Imani Michelle Scott (formerly K. Michelle Scott) entitled, "A Perennial Mourning: Identify Conflict and the Transgenerational Transmission of Trauma Within the African American Community" (443). Scott wrote her article as a doctoral student at Nova Southeastern University. In the process of reading and pouring over it, I turned to Erik Erikson's Identity: Youth and Crisis (79). The two made it possible for me to connect the dots, so to speak -- to put together my cumulative experience and knowledge to get to the root of what is behind our character problem. What I had written (with Angela Anselmo) about the human spirit and learned about emotional intelligence and our *hidden* selves also came into play. What I ended up with is what I call the *root* cause, not only of AMSAC, but also its inseparable social problems: the *lack of a positive core identity*.

Scott's thesis is that the disconnectedness, instability, and aggression that we see in many of our African American neighborhoods reflect response to generations of transmitted unresolved inward struggle against oppression and our failure, as a result, to develop a positive core identity -- a unified, loved self. It became apparent to me that this thesis explains, not just our generalized neighborhood disorder, but, in addition, the disorder we see in the character deficits of our students. Our core identity, Erik Erikson explains, is the constant and enduring sense of self which gives us a **"subjective sense of an invigorating sameness and continuity"** [emphasis added]. Its "invigorating" force sustains us and we rely on it in our interactions, strivings, and challenges. When flawed – due to associated bad character traits -- we are more likely to falter; when firm and positive – due to associated good character traits -- we are more likely to succeed. Ours is flawed, Scott says, not only because of externally-caused trauma, but also because our own attitudes and behaviors have contributed. McWhorter goes further. In his bestselling Losing the Race: Self-Sabotage in Black America, he argues that the flaw is part of our identity, manifesting itself in cults of Victimology, Separatism, and Anti-intellectualism (160).

Attack our core identity issue, I said to myself, and we attack the twin factors (identity and character) which are at the root of our school crisis and social problems. My analysis is that our crisis and problems stem mainly from the lack of that which so many of us have never possessed: a positive core identity, a *"subjective sense of an invigorating sameness and continuity,"* and its associated sound character assets. According to Erikson (drawing upon his colleague Heinz Hartmann), the development of such an identity depends on coming up in **"average expectable environments."** Such environments foster a healthy character, a character which enables us *actively to master our environment, function in a unified, integrated fashion, and perceive the world and self correctly* (79: 92). It is our identity that is the foundation of such a character, an identity that we begin to forge at birth, Erikson explains, and continue over our life span, making appropriate adaptations at its various stages.

Many of us, in particular the disadvantaged one-fourth of us, have never acquired such a character because we have not been brought up in **"average expectable environments,"** the foundation of our identity and of a healthy character which is likely to stem from it. It is this Scott/Erikson-based revelation, persuasively supported by McWhorter in particular, which throughout informs my analysis and proposals.

The Role of Our Two Traditions

In addition to the Scott/Erikson-based revelation regarding identity and character, there is something else that has guided my analysis and proposals: the role of Booker T. Washington and W. E. B. DuBois in our history. In the process of my research, particularly as it pertained to "acting white," it became evident that blame and solutions tend to fall into one of two camps. My sensitivity to these camps was heightened with the controversy ignited by **Bill Cosby's Brown Anniversary**

(Pound Cake) Speech 2004. I came to interpret what I was seeing in my research as the **Self-Responsibility Tradition** of Booker Taliferro Washington and the **System-Responsibility Tradition** of William Edward Burghardt Dubois.

Although their thinking was not original, I came to see each as having fathered these traditions, and came to see these traditions as having dominated the span of black existence. University of Tennessee historian Robert Norrell's Up from History: The Life of Booker T. Washington, and late Kent State University historian August Meier's Negro Thought in America, 1880-1915: Racial Ideologies in the Age of Booker T. Washington, were particularly revealing (192;168). From them, and from my cumulative knowledge, I got a more vivid sense of what was at stake, which was nothing less than the adaptation of the race. It is a context quite different from a context in which the Washington-DuBois cleavage has been cast: as part of our civil rights struggle -- as a matter of fighting for or not fighting for our civil rights. Civil rights per se was not the dominant issue; after 1903, DuBois made it the issue, before that time, essentially agreeing with Washington. Adaptation was, and for many still is, the issue -- our way of life and our need to modify it to meet our **Adaptation Requirements**.

Washington understood and fully accepted adaptation to be the issue while DuBois, though understanding adaptation to be the issue, only conditionally accepted it as such. He conditioned his full acceptance on our acquisition of civil rights. Without civil rights, he did not feel that our adaptation was possible, which led him (among other reasons) to make these rights the central issue -- and as has turned out to be the case, mainly the only issue. To him, civil rights became the panacea. Thus, he rooted our uplifting and civic wellbeing in protest and confrontation in contrast to Washington's emphasis on compromise and accommodation. He placed victimhood over Washington's characterhood.

Our African American Garden of Eden

I imagine the two as having been in an African American Garden of Eden. Here we were now free and perilously positioned to embark upon a new life, replacing our slave existence with an autonomous one. To make this transition possible, planted about in the garden were trees of life, chief among them were the readiness trees of brain, property, and character, while planted in the center was a charming and enchanting civil rights tree. Washington directed us to eat freely of the *foundation fruits* of the brains, property, and character trees but forbade us from eating the *equality fruits* from the civil rights tree, fearing that their enchantment powers would so fix our attention on civil rights that we would come to see it as a cure-all and fail to see the need to eat freely from the others so that we could build a foundation for our success. While we heeded Washington's command during his lifetime, upon his death, we fell sway to DuBois's command, a la the biblical serpent, to eat freely the forbidden *equality fruits* from the civil rights tree. The outcome has been a *civil-rights fixation* and a failure to confront our three major demons. Rather than confront them, our recourse has been to forge our second bondage, Victimology. To Victimology we can trace our widespread lack of a positive core identity, which lies at the root of AMSAC and its inseparable social problems.

Admiration of Washington

I have always admired Washington. It started when I was a junior high school teacher of social studies in Buffalo, New York in the 1950s. The textbook I used said Washington was born a slave, but upon being freed had become a teacher, founded Tuskegee Institute, and wrote a famous book, Up from Slavery. I was amazed that an ex-slave could write a book and do what he did. So I read the book, and as I did, my heart throbbed. It was as if his story set a receptive soul ablaze.

The flame still burns, and Washington's story evokes the throbbing of my heart never more so than after writing this byproduct book. And never more so because, never before, had I fully realized the extent to which the fate of the race rested on him. From the literature, one might get the impression that the establishment of Tuskegee Institute was his great contribution – and indeed it was at the backbone of his contribution – but at its center was his foundation-building philosophy of brains, property, and character, of which Tuskegee was a model and instrument. His standing rests, not so much on what he did for Tuskegee, but, inseparably, on what he did for the race. He gave us the Age of Booker T. Washington, which lasted almost two generations, from 1880 to 1915, his power and influence during at least most of this period leading Florida A&M University historian David H. Jackson Jr. to call him "the virtual boss of black America" (132:177). His accomplishments earned him world-wide fame -- including including the embrace of our native home, Africa – a fame which, except perhaps by President Barak Obama, has not been equaled by any other black leader. Yet, as his revisionist (my designation) biographer Norrell puts it, "history [has]brought Booker so low" (192:438) or -- as his definitive biographer, the late University of Pennsylvania historian Louis Harlan, describes the outcome, "It is ironic that Booker T. Washington, the most powerful black American of his time *and perhaps of all time*, should be the black leader whose claim to the title is most often dismissed by the lay public" [emphasis added] (111:164). Norrell, moreover, counts Washington's uplifting efforts as "among the most heroic efforts in American history" – no, not just *black* history, but *American* history (192:441).

From Norrell, it became clear to me that "history [has been] brought Booker so low" due to DuBois's mindset and machinations. That Washington did not put civil rights at the center of his agenda, as DuBois came to lead others in exhorting him to do, made Washington, in his eyes, a traitor. To DuBois, civil rights was a fixation; to Washington, it was an aspiration. Of course, as well, factors of power and ambition were key in Dubois's assualt, but, directly and indirectly (his education differences with Washington having civil rights implications), civil rights dominated his public agenda – and thus became dominant in the public mind. The late Yale historian, C. Vann Woodward, and his student, Harlan – Norrell argues – embraced and engraved DuBois's mindset, thereby giving imprimatur to **DuBois's Washington Demonization**. The vanguard of the Black Power phase of the Civil Rights Movement of the 1960s came along and enshrined that demonization. The result is that in our approach to adaptation, we have come to deify the route propagated by one and denigrate that demonstrated by the other – a show of ingratitude bordering on the unforgivable. Washington's infamous Atlanta Compromise of 1895, not only memorialized his Age, which was marked by dramatic black progress, but, I argue, it also gave us our own black Gettysburg Address. Insofar as known, not recognized, I contend, in a contrary interpretation, that his Compromise also gave us our black Declaration of Independence. As the Declaration of Independence provides the spiritual foundation for equality in American life, Wasshington's Atlanta Compromise Address provides the spiritual foundation for an *equal* place for blacks in American life – entitled, as other Americans, to "Life, Liberty, and the pursuit of Happiness."

Dr. King: from respect to some admiration

Though not an African American Garden of Eden participant, our beloved Martin Luther King Jr. has a consequential and, to most I am sure, a surprising connection to the story. I have always respected Dr, King, but I have not always admired him, because I cannot admire a black leader who is not committed to self-help, which I had always thought Dr. King was not. I was wrong. I discovered that, to King, Washington was not an Uncle Tom, but a hero. Dr. King embraced self-help and Washington's Self-Responsibility Tradition. However, in pursuit of that embrace, King was shackled by the young black radicals of his day and by what I call civil-rights cure-allers, who feel that civil rights is the answer to all our problems. Their criticism and nonsupport kept, and have kept, Dr. King in their civil-rights straitjacket. They would have us believe that King belongs in it, so, we do not hear about his self-help legacy, it is hardly written about, and it is not celebrated as part of his holiday. I tell the story of this shackling of Dr. King, and try to make the case that he can be regarded as the successor to Washington, enabling us to draw upon his name and self-help legacy in addressing our crisis and problems.

Our African American Garden Eden: endless reflection

As I read and studied, I kept seeing a replay of the DuBois-Washington contest. It was as if I were opening time capsules. I could see that, still, adaptation is the challenge, and that, still, the same two doctrines to its attainment evoke a war of sorts. I took the bits and pieces of those doctrines -- scattered throughout the literature -- and brought them together so as to see each doctrine, not only in its parts, but in its whole as well. When we are able see both, we are likely better to understand and to analyze.

Our Self-Responsibility Tradition tends to focus on the masses with the intent of making us a self-made people essentially through, as Washington put it, an emphasis on brains, property, and character, with civil rights pursued in the context of compromise and conciliation, hope and optimism being its underlying spirit. In Washington's mind -- as he stated it in an address before the Afro-American Council in July 1903, "an inch of progress is worth more than a yard of complaint" (168:107). In contrast, our System-Responsibility Tradition tends to focus on a middle-class agenda with the intent of making us a self-made people essentially through an emphasis on civil rights, the outcome sought being equal access and equal opportunity, anger and protest being its underlying spirit. In DuBois's mind -- as he put it in his <u>The Souls of Black Folk</u> -- "manly self-respect is worth more than lands and houses...." (64:41).

How well each tradition has served us must be measured by its success in enabling us to meet our **Adaptation Requirements**. As with other immigrant groups, voluntary or involuntary, those requirements are for us to get the education, get the jobs, and establish the stable families and neighborhoods which will enable us to enter the mainstream. Seven socioeconomic variables can be used to measure success on these requirements: (1) intact homes; (2) basic education; (3) postsecondary training; (4) employment; (5) home ownership; (6) poverty; and (7) crime.

My argument is that the doctrine pursued by Washington's Self-Responsibility Tradition has been eminently more successful in enabling us to do well on these variables – and thus better adapt – than DuBois's System-Responsibility Tradition. Its self-help emphasis fosters the success on these variables which is essential to building the foundation from which **"average expectable environments"** ensue, such environments serving to nurture a positive core identity, so vital to school and life success.

DuBois's System-Responsibility Tradition, on the other hand, minimizes self-help and emphasizes civil rights, leaving success on these variables more open to chance. When DuBois refused the official request of the NAACP board that he use the <u>Crisis</u> to acknowledge and condemn black *crime*,[6] he can be said to have laid the self-help posture for his tradition: we will not confront our major demons. Guided by his declaration in the Souls of Black Folk that the "burden belongs to the nation,"[7] in less forthright fashion, he said the same with regard to our to other two demons: *IQ lag* and *fatherless families*, which – like crime – to some degree we have had all along. He attacked Washington's emphasis on industrial education and he emphasized, not manhood (to which familyhood can be said to be intrinsic), but "manly self-respect." I make his astonishing refusal to acknowledge and condemn our crime problem and its mindset our first mnemonic: **DuBois' refusal to use Crisis to acknowledge and condemn black crime / "burden belongs to the nation."** Throughout, I will use mnemonics to remind us of some of the key factors in understanding and solving AMSAC and our inseparable social problems. This mnemonic reminds us that, from the outset, DuBois's System-Responsibility Tradition, minimizing self-help, has historically failed to confront our three major demons: *IQ lag-fatherless families-crime*.

Consequently, dominant for nearly a century, our System-Responsibility Tradition has left one-fourth of our people to system care and to community care (underground economy and the mother-grandmother female family structure). As David Kennedy proclaims, "The decades after the civil-rights victories should have been a celebration," as in fact "acial segregation declined; the black middle class grew dramatically," but "both the absolute number of blacks living in poverty and their concentration in poor neighborhoods increased" (144b:142). Hardly support for an endorsement of DuBois's System-Responsibility Tradition. Rather, alone, a justification for its replacement and a return to Washington's Self-Responsibility Tradition, which I call **The Tradition of Choice**.

Like Dr. King did, we must heed a hero who was a pragmatist and foundation-builder versus one who was an ideologue and activist. "Think white" must replace "think black." To "think black" is to think the DuBois way and the way so many in our community demand, a way which honors victimhood – a mental state which keeps us mired in

---

[6] See Norrell, 192:416.

[7] 64:46.

Victimology. To "think white," on the other hand, is to think the way Washington would have us think, a way which honors brains, property, and character -- assets which, for people of every color, lead to success.

A Unified Theory of Black America?

As might be evident, in addressing our black male school crisis, I have been forced to think broadly about our plight. That broad thinking has led me to the formulation of a theory. I call it the **Core Identity Theory of Disproportionate Maladaptation Among African Americans**. Essentially it is this: we blacks can explain our disproportionate maladaptation primarily as a function of our core identity and character, both flawed, and the associated lack of a "series of average expectable environments" wherein, foremost, family life is valued and our children provided a "hallowed presence" (security and love).

What I Have Said so Far

Let me bring together some of my main points, and then indicate what I propose. The African American Male School Adaptability Crisis (AMSAC) is caused mainly by the fact that so many of our black male students do not possess the character traits required to succeed in school, or in life; and they do not have those traits because they lack a positive core identity. Their IQ is a factor as well, but home-student-school factors are more decisive. Whatever the influence of IQ, evidence offers little hope that much can be done *directly* to enhance it, and therefore we should instead focus on achievement, which is far more malleable. *Indirectly*, however, we can and should focus on IQ through prenatal care and an enriched home, community, and school environment -- the possibility being that, over time, we can raise it.

Even if we cannot thereby raise our IQ, such a focus addresses the two factors most responsible for the crisis: our students' character and identity. For such a focus means providing our children and students **"average expectable environments,"** starting at the prenatal stage. And it is from such environments that we are likely to get the sound character traits and positive core identity on which school and life success depend.

Joe L. Rempson

Required: Child Family Rights Movement

Having attributed the fact that we have a black male school crisis and associated problems due to our African American Garden of Eden, I call for a **Child Family Rights Movement** to redeem ourselves. The few efforts that I have come across to address the crisis do not parallel what I propose in that they do not represent a comprehensive self-help solution -- nor for that matter a limited one (for example, see 84, 127, 129, 152a, 152b, 162, 177, 207, 208a, and 212). A notable exception is Jawanza Kunjufu's book, Reducing the Black Male Dropout Rate (148a). Refreshingly, he examines causes and solutions as pertains to all of the involved parties: school, parents, community, and students. However, I proceed from a different premise and offer a different approach. Let me explain.

To garner the kind of energy needed to do something significant about the major demon responsible for AMSAC and its inseparable social problems, *fatherless families*, we need a **movement**. Various programs and initiatives, of themselves, however meritorious, will not alone suffice to effect the systemic or massive change needed. As suggested by Thomas Rochan in his book, Culture Moves: Ideas, Activism, and Changing Values, systemic change requires movements -- collective action of various types (for example, demonstrations and discussion groups) which direct attention to the problem and convey a determination to do something about it (228).

To generate a movement around fatherless families, I am suggesting that we recast our civil rights movement into a child family rights movement. Rather than continue to focus on the civil rights due us by society, now largely won, we focus, instead, on the civil rights due our children by us. Like segregation as an obstacle, our family breakdown as an obstacle involves *rights*, in this case rights due, not to us adults, but to our children – and due them, not by society, but by their families. As suggested by the United Nations Declaration of the Rights of the Child, for example, children have what we can call (inclusively) family rights – the right to an intact family, security, love, and school and life preparation. Pope Francis as well has endorsed the concept, reportedly acclaiming "the right of children to grow up within a family, with a father and a mother able to create a suitable environment for their development and emotional maturity" (426d) The breakdown of the black family results in a massive and gross violation of such a right, about which we blacks have done little or nothing. To end that violation, a **Child Family Rights Movement** is required. The Movement needs a message and an agenda, which, in my last chapter, I recommend.

Should no one, such as, desirably, the National Association for the Advancement of Colored People (NAACP), emerge to lead the Movement, as a secondary and default goal, depending on its progress with AMCAP (discussed below) and on its resources, my foundation, the Rempson Foundation, would attempt to assume the lead. A Coordinator would be appointed to provide it. Even, however, if it did not led the Movement, many of the activities conducte by it in its implementation of AMCAP would help to generate and support the Movement.

The initiation and success of the Movement depend on our Self-Responsibility Tradition, whose dominance it must seek to restore. Under our current and dominant civil rights-fixated System-Responsibility Tradition it could never get off the ground. Parallel, therefore, with its impact on fatherless families (a reduction, say, from 72 percent of out-of-wedlock births to under 50 percent) and other adaptation variables, a major and symbolic measure of the success of the Movement would be the establishment of a joint **Dr. King-Washington holiday**, just as we have what some states designate a Washington and Lincoln Day (commonly called Presidents' Day). The change, energy, and drive which this accomplishment would require could spark the kind of reawakening on which success would depend. No doubt involving a long struggle, its achievement can be foreseen as a turning point in the Movement, signaling the return to dominance of our Self-Responsibility Tradition. I call it the Gettysburg of the Movement, since, like the real Gettysburg was a turning point in the Civil War to end our first bondage, it would likely be the turning point in our cultural war to end our second bondage. A monumental milestone in the war could be the creation of a **Booker T. Washington (BTW) Library and Self-Help Center**, a task which might possibly interest Tuskegee University.

To address AMSAC, I have designed and seek funding for the aforementioned **African American Male Career Pathway Program (AMCAP)**, which can also be a catalyst in promoting a **Child Family**

Rights Movement. I have written a draft guide for it, <u>AMCAP (African American Male Career Program) Task Guide</u>, and fully describe it in Chapters 13-15. Conceived as being funded by my private foundation, it is a proposed three-hour after-school program to enable African-American male high school students to achieve career success through an increase in the number who graduate from high school and then go on to attend and complete college or other postsecondary training. As part of a mixture, it would inclusively target as a majority those whom Writer and Speaker Paul Tough terms the "the deeply disadvantaged," those from families who earn under $11,000 a year and with whom we have had the least success. It would utilize DISCOVER, an internet-accessible career discovery exploration program, and it would be conducted by African American male counselors who, in addition to guiding the students in career discovery and pursuit, would address their daily and developmental needs as well as provide them academic support. The environment provided would be characterized by the **practice of the art of loving (Care, Responsibility, Respect, Knowledge**) and would promote autonomy and a positive core identity. It is based on student-centered principles of counseling and education and reflects evidence-based knowledge.

As progress warrants, the plan is to expand AMCAP to include a yet-to-be designed school-hour (versus afterschool) component for grades K-8. The vision is that through an AMCAP Resource Room, staffed mainly by black male paraprofessionals, appropriate components and modifications of the program would be conducted on a scheduled basis for the black male students in those grades. That would make AMCAP a grade K-College program which supports black male students throughout almost the entirety of their educational career. Guided by a no-dropout expectation, students would graduate from elementary or middle school with an **AMCAP High School Transition Plan**. Approved by the student and his parents, and formulated in a joint AMCAP-school-parent/student conference, the plan would provide the students a number of viable options to achieve career success and avoid dropping out, including the use of Job Corps, which is thought to be an undervalued resource.

The program is not envisioned as a permanent part of the public school structure, but rather as an experimental program. Its various components would be evaluated for practicality, effectiveness, and dissemination.

As Washington used students in building Tuskegee, in the dissemination of AMCAP, students are envisaged as playing a major role through **Student AMCAPs**. Student AMCAPs would be high school student clubs whose purpose would be to encourage and assist their classmates in the discovery and pursuit of their career pathway. Collaboration with the BTW Society might be the ideal way to pursue this goal, and the support of our black male athletes and entertainers would be a big boost. Given the resources, the Rempson Foundation would provide coordination and, perhaps, part-time paraprofessional advisement and assistantance, along with equipment and materials, but the clubs, just as other student clubs, would otherwise be self-operating.

Successful, AMCAP can help to end our black male school adaptability crisis. It would likely produce black males who have the means, inclination, and character required for a strengthened black family. But for such a family to emerge, as Enola Aird of the Motherhood Project emphasizes, community support is also required. That is why the call for a **Child Family Rights Movement** is so critical. It can generate such support where it counts most: in our black neighborhoods.

Practice of the art of loving

I consider the **practice of the art of loving** the soul of the proposed movement. It is borrowed from the late world famous psychoanalyst Erich Fromm's <u>The Art of Loving</u> (98). Fromm says loving is a skill, and that, as is the case with any skill, with due diligence and the exercise of certain attributes, we can all learn it. He defines love as **Care, Responsibility, Respect,** and **Knowledge** [emphases added]. It is considered the soul because, more than any other single initiative, it can lead to the creation of **"average expectable environments"** wherein we provide our children security and love, and it can foster the development of that positive sense of core identity and those character traits on which school and life success depend, especially if, from infancy through childhood, we make our children its target. The values and enrichment of the human spirit which ensue from its practice, and the energy and drive from that enrichment, can make it all possible. Each of us already engages in the practice; it is a matter of elevating it into a *conscious, constantly practiced skill*. To promote the practice, resources permitting, the Foundation proposes to fund the writing, publication, and distribution in selected poverty areas (it would also be made generally available) of a pocket-size guide, **Practice of the Art of Loving Guide**, to provide an understanding of its meaning and application.

Character

Character development or emotional intelligence (EI) is a major focus. Emotional intelligence can be defined as the "ability to monitor one's own and others' feelings and emotions, to discriminate among them and to use this information to guide one's thinking and actions" (102:36; 438c). Research by psychologist Daniel Goleman and others suggest that, as Goleman asserts, it can matter more than IQ and, further, that it is malleable. There is controversy about how malleable it is, but less so about the decisive role it plays in school and life success.

From the many character traits that might represent EI, I tried to identify those revealed in the literature as possessing the potential to make a large-scale decisive difference. I ended up with five: **mindset (MS)**, **time perspective (TP)**, **willpower (WP)**, **grit (GR)**, and **love (LO)**. Controlling for IQ, each alone is powerfully related to outcomes. For example, a study by Angela Duckworth and Martin Seligman found that "self-discipline [willpower]... predicted academic performance much better than did IQ, and the researchers estimated that self-discipline accounted for twice as much variance in GPA [grade point average] as did IQ" (393b). At the same time, each is a trait which represents a devastating weakness among a disproportionate number of African Americans and has research evidence to support (not establish, but support) its malleability. Moreover, the five traits are overlapping, interactive, and mutually reinforcing. Focus on any one of them can, therefore, have a multiplier effect and optimize results.

A couple of recent books have powerfully reinforced in my mind the critical role of EI or character. One draws on neuroscience and other disciplinary research, while the other one was written by a neuroscientist.

The books: <u>The Social Animal: The Hidden</u> <u>Sources of Love, Character, and Achievement</u> by <u>New York Times</u> columnist, David Brooks, and the other, <u>Incognito: The Secret Lives of the Brain</u> by Baylor College of Medicine neuroscientist, David Eagleman (23, 73). Both make the point that to a far greater extent than we are accustomed to thinking, we are hardwired -- in fact, almost entirely so. However, though a function of that hardwiring, how we turn out is not necessarily determined by it. To quote the Commission on Children at Risk (discussed in Chapters 12 and 14), drawing upon the same body of knowledge as Brooks and Eagleman: "**SOCIAL CONTEXT CAN ALTER GENETIC EXPRESSION**" [emphases added]. In my mind, this reality magnifies the role of EI, that executive part of our chemical-electrical network called the brain which enables us to be relatively good self-managers.

Focus on the System -- Not Letting the School "Off the Hook," but *a* Cause, not *the* Cause

Although I have talked entirely about our internal problems as the cause of AMSAC and its inseparable social problems, that should not be taken to mean that I exonerate either the system or the school. However, rather than the blanket, racial condemnations of the schools which we so commonly voice, we need an affirmative school agenda. Washington had one for his time, and we need one for our time. And not one guided by racial or political sensibilities, but by accepted principles of teaching and learning. In Part III, I offer one. It, or some modification of it, can become the school agenda of the **Child Family Rights Movement**.

The school is *a* cause of our students' poor school performance, but not, as so much of the prevailing attention suggests, *the* cause of it. The research shows that only about 20 percent of the variance in our students' performance can be attributed to the school. That is no small percentage, but it is not 100 percent, nor the 80 percent which can be attributed to non-school factors, including 49 percent to home and family. For our students, in particular, however, the research shows that individual teachers can exert a powerful, and perhaps decisive, influence, which, of itself, gives us a reason not to let the school "off the hook." In fact, I take it to be self-evident that we cannot be successful if both the system and the school do not play their part.

As regards the school's role, the conclusion of Christopher Jencks and Meredith Phillips in their book, <u>The Black-White Test Score Gap</u>, is something to keep in mind. Jencks is a Harvard social policy professor and Meredith a University of California at Los Angeles policy studies professor. They say that "changing the way parents deal with their children *may be the <u>single most important</u> thing we can do* to improve children's cognitive skill" because "the cognitive disparities between black and white preschool children are currently so large that it is hard to imagine how school alone could eliminate them" [emphases added] (136: 45-46).

Accordingly, my belief is that those who place blame on the school are wrong. So is their remedy: teacher accountability and school choice (privatization), which gets translated into elaborate teacher evaluation schemes, charter schools, and failing school policies. Those are the trends of the moment, their origin being the subject of an informative analysis, discussed in Chapter 17, provided by highly regarded educational leader and historian Diane Ravitch.

The centerpiece of my remedy is what I call **Art of Loving (AOL) Schools**. They would be so called because, in them, the **practice of the art of loving** would be ubiquitous (by students and staff); and they would employ what I call a bread-and-butter curriculum whose gold standard would be not to leave any child behind based, rather than just on standardized test results, also on opportunities for them to develop their abilities, and-- in response to their dropout problem and to their iidentity and character deficits -- on their identity development, their persistence, and their acquisition of the basic emotional, relationship, job, and everyday living skills necessary for them to live valued and self-reliant lives. Their classrooms would be *family-oriented*. My other school proposals constitute what I call **Black Advocacy of School Do's and Don'ts**.

To solve AMSAC, and generally improve our students' school performance, we must not let either party "off the hook" -- neither the school nor us. Here is the imperative: both parties, school and home, must do their best, rather than one putting responsibility on or blaming the other. Perhaps neither can be expected to be above average, and we cannot continue to afford for either to be below average.

Success and Our Self-Responsibility Tradition

The dysfunctional and self-sabotaging life led by so many of our males has come to be accepted as normal, at least ostensibly (David Kennedy has found a silent moral rejection), but we functional African American males must prevent it from becoming permanent. As black educator and charter school founder, Steve Perry, exclaims in his book title, <u>Man Up! Nobody is Coming to Save Us</u> or, as I put it, we must **"Take Arms Against [our] Sea of Troubles,"** otherwise, without end, we will "suffer the slings and arrows of [our] outrageous fortune." The taking of arms requires us to confront and exorcise our **three major demons**, *IQ lag--fatherless families--crime*. As our arms, I propose a **Child Family Rights Movement**, a distinct part of which would be my proposed experimental program, **AMCAP**. Both are grounded in our **Self-Responsibility Tradition** and are dependent on it for their success.

Organization of Book

In four parts, I have tried to make my case. Often, I have gone into considerable detail, but have tried to provide summaries and thereby obviate the need for more detailed reading if not desired or necessary. For me, the details have enhanced my understanding and perhaps forced me to gain insights that I might not have otherwise acquired. The details may or may not do the same for you, but you must bear in mind that I speak to a range of audiences. It is not expected that every reader is going to be, nor necessarily should be, interested in every part or chapter of this book, or in many of its extended explanations. Yet, all of the content is intended to provide the kind of contextual understanding which anthropologist John Ogbu emphasized as essential to formulating solutions to our school crisis.

This introductory chapter attempts to cover the main content in the book and, read in conjunction with the last chapter, gives the reader the essence of my thesis and proposals, thereby permitting a more selective reading of other chapters.

In Part I, in one chapter only, I document and discuss our African American Male School Adaptability Crisis (AMSAC) and its inseparable social problems, give them some historical and contemporary context, and convey my thesis.

In Part II, in nine chapters, I discuss the causes and context. The topics are: the role of home and school, the culture of our students and community, IQ, "acting white," core identity, and Victimology. I also examine the origin of our two traditions and, throughout, give attention to their influence, one chapter being specifically devoted to their contribution to our identity formation.

In Part III, in five chapters, I grapple with school solutions. I discuss those solutions and their shortcomings, beginning with an examination of what we can learn from our own two traditions and -- most important -- about what we can do about our IQ lag. More broadly, I offer my own thoughts about how our public schools might be improved, advocating what I call Art of Loving (AOL) schools. Addressing the particular needs of our African American male students, in two chapters, I describe the experimental program which I propose and, in a separate chapter, make the argument that my proposal can succeed only if the program uses African American male counselors.

In the final part, Part IV, in four chapters, I grapple with African American solutions -- what we ourselves must do if our crisis and problems are to be solved. I begin by making a case for the tradition which is better suited for the task, and then turn to the need to renew what I call **The Tradition of Choice**, our Self-Responsibility Tradition, through a Child Family Rights Movemen to replace our Civil Rights Movement, or, should I say its remnants. Next, I take up the shackling of Dr. King and give perspective to his possible role in the proposed Movement. I conclude with some specific proposals as to what, with the help of the nation, we African Americans must do.

A Handbook and an Experimental Program (AMCAP)

Please bear in mind that I started out to write a handbook to accompany my proposed program, AMCAP. The intent was to provide the staff, along with suggestions on how to conduct the program, some background information. Although this byproduct book far exceeds that goal, and while it serves multiple purposes, I still regard it has a resource for the program staff, only much more of a reference and resource book than a handbook. It gives the staff context and grounding for its task. My hope is that, as a result, the staff executes the program with greater clarity and perspective, enhanced inspiration, and a firmer and shared sense of purpose. The handbook per se is still in the works.

Peer Review

Although self-published, I consider this book a traditional scholarly publication. At least an attempt has been made to meet the standards of such a publication. Whereas editorial assistance was obtained, it was not sent to experts in the represented disciplines for critique and review, something highly desirable but precluded by a number of practical considerations. But my area of training is education, a professional and applied science whose body of knowledge entails the use of knowledge from a range of disciplines, inclusive of the humanities and the social sciences, and which employs tools of research and study common to most disciplines. You might say it is an interdisciplinary discipline. In large measure, the extent to which one capitalizes upon the entailed exposure to various disciplines is a function of the required courses taken and the elective courses chosen.

An additional consideration is topic identification. Immersing oneself in that which is native to one's heritage and history can enable one to feel the unfelt, see the unseen, and say the unsayable. As a result, the scholarly can be enhanced and amplified.

I say the foregoing because a frequent refrain one hears when one writes about a given topic is whether one is an expert in that field. I say it also because of what is said to be a proliferation of questionable journal publications which fail to meet traditional journalistic standards (393c). As regards the former, if one is writing something about history as I am, for example, an expected question is likely to be whether I am a historian. It is a fair question. The answer is no. Further, nor am I a psychologist or a sociologist, other disciplines on which I have drawn heavily. As stated, I am an educator. But being none of these other disciplinarians does not preclude me from making use of, or applying, content from other domains. Such is the nature of an interdisciplinary discipline. Moreover, history, for example, is written, not just for consumption and use by historians, but for and by anyone who reads it. And anyone who reads it is scholarly justified in making whatever use of it which is deemed reasonably warranted. Of course, doing so would not make one a historian, just one who has engaged in historical reading or research and put what was learned to use. Consistent with my training, that is what I have done with the disciplines which are represented herein, making every attempt to differentiate the knowledge of specialists in these disciplines from my use and application of their knowledge. Albert Einstein is quoted as saying that "A little knowledge is a dangerous thing. So is a lot." Similarly, I say, "A lot of knowledge is fruitful. A little can also be." My hope is that I have given a fair response to an anticipated fair question.

Part I
The Crisis

2

The African American School Adaptability Crisis (AMSAC): Present and Past

Proverbs, 16:22 - "Understanding is a wellspring of life unto him that hath it: but the instruction of fools is folly."
Galatians, 6:5 - "For every man shall bear his own burden."

Present

We know that most of us African Americans are like all other Americans. We go to school to get an education, work to earn our living and raise our family, and live by the rules, like them or not. But for many it is a struggle. Based on the 2010 census, the following data suggest why.

- Females, with no husband present, head 30.1% of black households [almost one- third], while the comparable percent for Latinos is 19.2%, and for whites is 9.9% (400a).
- For these black female-headed households, with no husband present, 17.4% have children of their own, while the comparable percent for Latinos is 12.1%, and for whites is 5.2% (400a).
- The poverty rate for all female-headed families is 46.9% versus 11.6 for married couples, while the poverty rate for black female-headed families, no husband present with children, is 47.5% [almost one-half] (433a, 459e).

- Overall, the poverty rate for blacks is 27.4%, while for Latinos, it is 26.5%, and for whites, it is 9.9% (459e).
- The black unemployment rate is 13.4% versus 10.8% for Hispanic, and 7.5% for whites (459f).

If we want an easier way to capture or visualize our struggle, the number **72** might do it. That is the percent accurately publicized by CNN's black anchor Don Lemon in a commentary on our black problems, Lemon pointing out that this is the approximate percent of our children who are born out-of-wedlock (433c). In one of his chapter titles in his heralded book, Tally's Corner (1967), the late anthropologist and sociologist Elliot Liebow provided a poignant way of thinking about this plight: "Fathers without Children" (154d). Lemon's mention of it is noted because it drew the usual firestorm when any perceived negative about us is expressed. The consequences of this percent are manifold, and, perhaps, it is our most important mnemonic. We, therefore, want to remember the number **72** as a reminder of the black out-of-wedlock birthrate and, thus, the family breakdown from which our personal and social problems originate and which prevents the race from having a positive core identity and the self-pride associated with it.

The percent **59** might also help. Based on a 4-year graduation rate, this is the median black male dropout rate for the 56 highest black male enrollment districts, compared to a median white male dropout rate of 42% for these districts.[8] Consideration was given to using a national dropout rate, as is customarily done, but since our problems arise primarily from the dropouts which occur in our large urban areas (Chicago, Milwaukee, New York City, Newark, Detroit, Philadelphia, Los Angeles, and so on), it is the black male dropout rate in these areas which more realistically conveys the problem.

If a national dropout rate were used, one option would be **52** percent. That is the national black male dropout rate for the class of 2003 versus a national white male dropout rate of **26** percent for that class, the source for these data discussed in Chapter 13. Support for these national

---

[8] These percentages are based on data contained in the following publication: Black Lives Matter: The Schott 50 State Report on Public Education and Black Males 2015, Table 9, p. 26-27 (440b).

rates was provided by the Schott Foundation for Public Education, a private foundation engaged in public education advocacy, which since 2004 has published biennial reports on black male 4-year graduation rates. Based on 2007/8 Grade enrollments, its data revealed a **53** percent national dropout rate for black males versus a **22** percent dropout rate for white males (440). Its estimated 2012-13 graudation rate shows a noticeable improvement, however: a **41** percent natonal dropout rate for black males (down from 53 percent), **35** percent for Latino males, and **20** percent for white males (440b: 6-7). On the surface, the 12-point rate drop is impressive, but the report explains that black males are still at the bottom of the 4-year graduation rate, and, moreover, that the graduation rate gap between black males and white males *continues to widen*. The report also provides the data on the 56 highest black male enrollment districts, on which the above 59 percent dropout rate is based. Again, it is reasoned that, compared to these national rates, the 59 percent dropout rate based on the largest districts is probably a better indicator of the dimension of the black male dropout rate problem.

Let the percents **72** and **59** serve as mnemonics to remind us of our crisis. They make the fact that we have problems understandable. In the absence of cultural constraints, such percents, and the impoverishment which their consequences signal, are more likely than not to breed problems-- and not always ordinary ones, but those that, as in the case of our African American male students, can reach a crisis proportion. To us, and to society at large, the cost is considerable -- disproportionately, for example, draining our public resources, putting our neighborhoods in disarray, contributing to substandard schools, and curtailing our sense of racial pride.

Fathers and faith

But we must not despair. Booker T. Washington never did, and he had to struggle on two fronts: to uplift us, his own people, and to hold off Southern white opposition. With no need to hold off anyone, except perhaps some from within as Washington also had to do, our challenge, nevertheless, not only is far less, but our resources to meet it far more abundant. With Washington's kind of faith and determination, like him, we can energize our people, uplift our impoverished, and, thereby, instill in ourselves a sense of *genuine* racial pride. Things do not have to be the way they are, and when it comes to our African American male students, it is up to us, their collective fathers, to see that they do not continue as they are. As Steven Ivory says, "...all [of us black] men shoulder some responsibility in how children turn out" (131: 247). As an attribute of manhood, we must accept and perform that responsibility. As an article of faith, we must embrace the sentiments expressed by retired educator, Edwin Farrell, of the City College of the City University of New York, who, in his book, <u>Hanging In and Dropping Out: Voices of At-Risk High School Students</u>, writes:

> That certain students have not experienced academic achievement is obvious, but it strains credibility to say that when 40 percent of students have dropped out of a certain school, they have all done so because of a lack of innate ability. By the time the prospective dropout arrives in high school, she usually has a history of poor academic performance, has not developed a positive attitude toward schoolwork, and may have one or more serious skill deficiencies in the three R's. This might be the result of cultural, socioeconomic, instructional, familial, emotional factors, or even innate ability, but I take it as an article of faith that the vast majority of children start kindergarten with the intellectual wherewithal to complete high school twelve years later (81:2).

This author, an African American male, shares Farrell's "article of faith." Our students can do much better, and should be doing much better, and, as their collective fathers, we African American males have it within our power to enable them to do so.

Are we all *really* responsible?

Farrell justifiably believes that our students start kindergarten with the intellectual wherewithal to complete high school twelve years later. But we know, as Farrell acknowledges, that it takes *more* than intellectual wherewithal to complete those twelve years. Unfortunately, our children often do not possess the *more*. So twelve years later, the number **59** reminds us of the percent of our male students who end up short of the journey, to say nothing about those who, though they complete the journey, do so in mediocre fashion.

No, not all of us African Americans are responsible for their failure, nor even most of us. Some of us, in fact, are quite adamant in our refusal to accept such responsibility, so reports Ellis Cose in his <u>The Rage of a Privileged Class</u> (47: 93-110). But accept responsibility or not, we are faced with a race problem, and, our posture aside, the data can only arouse our discomfort. The fact is that enough of us are responsible to make the behavior and values involved seem to represent more the rule rather than the exception. So much of what occurs seems to be a normal and accepted part of life in many of our neighborhoods and among our people. To others, it appears that "they" do not finish school, "they" kill one another, "they" father children all over, and so on.

So responsible or not, enough of us are responsible to make all of us suffer along with those who are actually responsible. Fair or not, the image projected is not limited to the perpetrators, but is cast as well over those who share their identity -- which is to say, all of us who are African American males. We must, then, remember the words of Dr. King: "the relatively privileged Negro will never be what he ought to be until the underprivileged Negro is what he ought to be. The salvation of the Negro middle class is ultimately dependent upon the salvation of the Negro masses" (147:140-41). The import here is that when all is said and done, however removed we might be, there are factors which impel us to *accept* responsibility even though we may not be *really* responsible. Those factors include its race effects, Dr. King's concept of middle-class duty, and Ivory's notion of collective fatherhood. What we cannot expect is what human nature precludes: for others to be more responsible for us than we are for ourselves.

If not us, who?

If we do not assume responsibility for the masses, broadly, we leave that responsibility in the hands of the system and, from a community vantage, we leave it in the hands of the underground economy, the mother, and the grandmother. That is, we leave it to system care and to community care (underground economy, the mother, and the grandmother). The former tends automatically to come to mind, but not necessarily the latter. However, when we abandon our responsibility to the masses, we need to remind ourselves that we leave it, not just in the hands of the system, but also in the hands of the community itself. In effect, we say to the system, "You take responsibility," and we say to the community, "You have to make do." In our poor communities, "You have to make do" too often boils down to an underground economy (especially drugs) and the mother and grandmother along with other female family members. And we know that when it comes to the mother, so often alone and unready, she has to turn, like others in the family, to the grandmother who, traditionally, is the backbone of the family.

But notwithstanding the strength of the grandmother, this "best" is not enough to enable its inhabitants, particularly its males, to fulfill their needs and wants. Hence the drug dealing and the preying on one another -- stealing, robbing -- and the host of problems which plague our inner cities. It is beyond the scope of this book to elaborate on this familiar community care scenario. The point is that, not only have we abandoned the poor to our governmental system (and this includes the school), but we have abandoned them to their community care system as well, which is often dysfunctional or cannot cope. One wishing to know more about it might turn, for example, to black Yale sociologist Elijah Anderson's <u>Code of the Street</u> (5). Based on his ethnographic study, as well as on the literature on which he relied, Anderson provides an informative portrait.

Our African American Male School Adaptability Crisis (AMSAC)

At the core of our problems is the **African American Male School Adaptability Crisis (AMSAC)**, as it is herein called. The **African American Male School Adaptability Crisis (AMSAC)** is defined as *the failure of our African American male students, as a group, to adapt to school requirements, consequently, resulting in their exceptionally poor school performance, catastrophic high school dropout rate, and markedly lagging college attendance and graduation rates – adaptation being the attribute which has made possible human survival and progress, its failure producing such results as these*. Nevertheless, reflecting many of us in their adult African American male world, for adaptation, our students substitute opposition and separation (their "cool-pose culture," as sociologists term it), yet, aspire to and demand – certainly expect -- the rewards of adaptation (the culture of the school). Of course, the two cannot be reconciled, but, too often destructively, their quest to make them reconcilable goes undaunted, creating in the process the array of social problems which overextend our police forces and social service agencies. In AMSAC, then, inseparably, each as cause and effect, we have a school crisis and an array of social problems.

But, as the saying goes, "wonders will never cease." Some of us blacks do not see it as a crisis. Prominent Yale University professor emeritus and Teachers College, Columbia University professor emeritus, Edmund Gordon, provides a case in point. He calls the attention to the problems of our black males a "generalized distortion," taking the position that "the African American male condition is not one of universal failure," their failures and dysfunctional behaviors being "an artificial or at best a manufactured problem" (104a: ix-x). He argues that the distortion results from the focus being on the pathology of the minority instead of -- in the context of an array of social, economic, and geographic differences -- on the range of adaptive and maladaptive behaviors of the majority, acknowledging, however, that "some African American males are in trouble." The argument embodies the same kind of diversity, small percentage defense that is variously made by many of us in response to other perceived negatives as, for example, when it comes to the issue of "acting white," the black family, and black self-hatred.

On the other hand, while not denying the problem, John Jackson, black President & CEO of the private foundation, Schott Foundation for Public Education, a la William Ryan of "blame the victim" fame, turns it around and changes the focus. In his introduction to the Foundation's 50 State Report, he refers to our black males, not as dropping out of school, but of "being pushed out" (440). That change-around translates into a *pushout* rate of 52 percent, Jackson arguing that such a rate will continue so long as "Black male students continue to be concentrated in schools and classrooms where there are few opportunities for them to succeed." But Jackson is by no means the first to use the term. Over the years, one has heard the pushout description from time to time -- and even Jackson's rationale for it --only it is somewhat surprising to see that Jackson gives it such currency.

In addition to the **59** percent dropout rate for the 56 highest black male enrollment districts, the facts tell a different story. Since specific data about black males are frequently not disaggregated, those facts are not easy to come by. As Sharon Lewis and her colleagues at the Council of the Great City Schools observe, "while much work over the years has gone into addressing the challenge of the Black-White achievement gap, there has been no concerted national effort focused on the education and social outcomes of Black males specifically" (398:2).

Nevertheless, there are disaggregated data and Lewis and her colleagues, among others, have undertaken an attempt to provide some of it. Theirs is among the most recent data found and is based on information gathered from 18 big city school districts. From an array of their findings, the following seven findings illustrate the nature and dimensions of AMSAC:

1. "In 2009, the average reading scale score of large city ... Black males *without Disabilities* ... was only two points higher at grade 4 and five points higher at grade 8 than the score of White males nationwide ... *with disabilities* ...." [emphasis in original] (398:4)
2. In most districts, at least 50 percent of fourth and eighth grade black males scored below Basic levels in reading and mathematics (398:4).
3. In 2008, the high school dropout rate for black males was 9 percent versus 5 percent for white males (398:5).
4. "In 2009, the average SAT scores of Black males were lower than those of White males in critical reading, mathematics, and writing. The gap between White and Black students taking the SAT was 104 points in critical reading, 120 points in mathematics, and 99 points in writing" (398:5).
5. "In 2006, Black students were three times more likely than White students, two times more likely than Hispanic and American Indian students, and five times more likely than Asian American students to be suspended from school" (398:6). [Note: black males are not disaggregated, but data show that males compose most of those who are suspended.]
6. In 2001, the college graduation rate for white males was 50 percent higher than that of black males (398:6).
7. In 2008, black males, age 18 and over, were 5 percent of the college population, but 36 percent of the prison population (398:6).

When we compare black males with black females, two percents highlight the discrepancy crisis: **11** and **30,** giving us additional mnemonics. Eleven is the number of percentage points separating their high school graduation rate. In contrast to the 48 percent national graduation rate for black males, for black females it is 59 percent, meaning that the national high school graduation for black males is 11 percentage points *below* that of black females; for white males, theirs is only 5% percentage points below that for white females (74% versus 79%). Thirty is a percent which provides a more telling story of the problem. Such a story is often provided when we look at the overall in microcosm, in this case, that microcosm being the inner-city predominantly black four-year Medgar Evers College of the City University of New York. Of its 6,500 undergraduates, only 30 percent are males, its President, Rudy Crew, confiding that "it is an indicator of the perilous state of many young African-American men" (365b).

Journalist, Paul Schwartzman, of the Washington Post, responding to an email inquiry, also provides a specific and striking example of this disparity in regard to a situation to which one might think it would not apply. Schwartzman spent nearly one year tracking down the 59 fifth-grade Dreamers (as they came to be called, 80 percent being African American), who, while in the fifth grade in 1988, were promised a paid college education upon their graduation from high school (440a). The promise, which, at the time, got a lot of publicity and stirred a lot of excitement, was made by two wealthy businessmen, Abe Pollin, owner of the Washington Bullets and Washington Capitals, and Melvin Cohen, owner of the film processing company District Photo. The two set up the I Have a Dream Foundation to carry out their promise, and hired Tracy Proctor as its coordinator and counselor for the students. Schwartzman reported his findings in an impressive and informative three-part series.

In his report, there was no indication of any male-female differences in outcomes. So, emailed and asked, Schwartzman responded that "on an impressionistic level, it seemed that the academic stars tended to be the girls. They seemed to be less drawn to the street life that lured the guys. Not that they didn't get into some trouble. A number of the girls had issues with fighting, for example."[9] An impression is not the same as hard data, but read his series and one can sense how he derived it, for it enhances one's understanding of how the social world of our black male students, even under relatively ideal external circumstances, contributes to our male-female gap (something that shows up, as already cited, in the differential effect, on each gender, of early educational intervention).

There are, however, hard data which do support Schwartzman's impression. Jensen cites the late Russian American psychologist, Eric Bronfenbrenner, as providing evidence showing that black boys perform less well in school than black girls to a greater degree than between white boys and white girls, and that the gap tends to increase with age, and, for both Southern and Northern blacks, across all socioeconomic groups (139:87). This difference would appear to reflect, at least in part, an IQ difference between the two. Sowell reports research which, contrary to national sex patterns, shows that high IQ blacks are predominantly female, and Richard Nisbett alludes to the same research (241:40; 188a:103; 399c). In general, one study showed the IQ of our black males to be 2.4 points lower than the IQ of our black females, 85.7 versus 87.25, whereas for our respective white counterparts, it was 102.7 versus 103.6, for a difference of 0.8 (399c, 438c).

Table 1

Black Male, Comparative, College Enrollment and Graduation Rate

	Percent of high school graduates who enrolled in college the following October	Percent of 2006 cohort who graduated within 6 years
Black males	57%	35.2%.
Black females	69	43.6
White males	62	59.8
White females	72	64.9
Hispanic males	62	47.7
Hispanic females	76	54.9

Source of enrollment data: Pew Research Center analysis of the October Supplement to the Current Population Survey

---

[9] Personal email, January 2, 2012.

(400b). Source of graduation data: National Center for Education Statistics, U. S. Department of Education, Institute of Education Sciences (420b).

Not surprisingly, as the 30% black male enrollment at Medgar Evers College suggests, the gap persists at the college level. As evident from Table 1, noticeably fewer black male high school graduates enroll in college than their black female counterparts (57% vs. 69%), as well as their white female and Hispanic female counterparts (57% versus 72% and 57% versus 76%, respectively). The enrollment gap is far less, however, when they are compared to their male counterparts, the entering gap separating them from each, white males and Hispanic males, being the same: 5 percentage points (57% vs. 62%).

Far more bleak is their college graduation rate. As calculated from Table 1, black males graduate at a rate which is:

- 8.4 percentage points below their black female counterparts (35.2% versus 43.6%),
- 19.7 percentage points below that of their Hispanic female couinterparts (35.2% versus 54.9%),
- 24.6 percentage points below that of their white male counterparts (35.2% versus 59.8%), and
- 12.5 percentage points below that of their Hispanic male counterparts (35.2% versus 47.7%).

To our **59** mnemonic for our black male high school dropout rate, we can then add **57** for the percent of black male high school graduates to enroll in college, and **35** (rounded number) for the percent who graduate from college within six years.

To be sure, the male-female divide is not just a black problem; it is a national and world problem (233, 259, 311). In the words of Pulitzer Prize-winning social trends and education writer Peg Tyre:

> The gender imbalance in education is not only an American problem. Almost everywhere in the industrialized world, in places where boys and girls have equal access to education, the underperformance

of boys is not just an uncomfortable fact but a real and pressing problem (259:33).

Reflective of the problem is the male proportion of students enrolled in four-year colleges and universities in the United States. In <u>Boys Adrift</u>, family physician, psychologist, and single-sex public education advocate Dr. Leonard Sax, reports the proportion as follows (233: 8-9):

1949: 70%
1959: 64%
1969: 59%
1979: 49%
1989: 46%
1999: 44%
2006: 42%

These data show a drop of nearly 30 percentage points in the proportion of males over roughly the last fifty years.

According to Heckman and Lafontaine, the decline in the high school graduation rate is due almost entirely to male dropouts. Their longitudinal study revealed that, from the first cohort examined [1946-50] to the last cohort examined [1976-80], the overall male graduation rate fell 7 percentage points, while the female graduation rate fell by only 1 percentage point. "The forces affecting the increasing high school dropout rate," they posit, "operate more strongly on men than on women" (368:20).

Sax attributes these declines and our "boys adrift" problem to five such forces: video games, teaching methods, prescription drugs, environmental toxins, and devaluation of masculinity. Whatever the reasons, our black male students are disproportionately affected; they are simply more adrift than other boys, perhaps primarily because, from the outset, they are handicapped: disproportionately fatherless and disproportionately poor.

As a specific case in point, the datum by Lewis and her colleagues pertaining to the minimal reading score differential between our *normal* black male students and *disabled* white male students exerts a Richter-scale jolt. The score for "Black males *without disabilities* [emphasis in original] ... was only two points higher at grade 4 and five points higher at grade 8 than the score of White males nationwide ... *with disabilities* [emphasis in original] ...." This datum provides us another mnemonic: **disabilities differential of 2-5 points**.

The problem for black males begins in kindergarten, with a sharp downturn occurring in grade 4, followed by dropout in grade 9, the pivotal dropout grade as discovered in research conducted in formulating MCAP (the experimental program, mentioned in Chapter 1, conducted by the author). As black educator Jawanza Kunjufu explains it, "Boys don't drop out in the 12th grade. They physically drop out in the ninth grade, but they emotionally and academically drop out in the fourth grade" (148a: 9). It does not appear that the most recent effort to address the problem, and the overall black-white school achievement gap, the No Child Left Behind law, is meeting with success in solving the problem (327). Since it does not address the major underlying cause, student and community culture, nor does President Barak Obams's Race to the Top offer any more hope.

While we think of the problem as limited to the poor, the experience of Joseph Hawkins reminds us that it is not. Hawkins, an African American, is an evaluation specialist for the Montgomery County Public Schools (Maryland). Montgomery County is one of the wealthiest in the nation and, as Hawkins says, "...it is extremely common to find Black students coming from homes where both parents are present and employed." "It also is rather common," he adds, "to find Black parents who are college graduates" (118:109). "Nevertheless," he later continues, "the right social and economic conditions do not translate automatically into the right outcomes." Then he comes to his punch lines:

> If it is a *good* [emphasis in the original] academic thing--Scholastic Achievement Test (SAT) scores, grades, honors course work--Black students generally come in last place. If it is a *bad* [emphasis in original]--suspensions, special education placements (i.e., overrepresentation)--Black students generally come in first place. When academic measures and outcomes are disaggregated further by gender, the picture worsens, with Black males nearly always coming in dead last (118:109).

From Hawkins' punch lines, we have this mnemonic: **academically good -- dead last; academically bad -- first**. This mnemonic directly captures what AMSAC is all about: our African American male students coming in last when it comes to that which is *academically good*, but first when it comes to that which is *academically bad*. Nor can it escape our notice that Hawkins is not even talking about the poor or the Abandoned, the focus of AMCAP and of the discussion on these pages; he is talking about those whom Ellis Cose terms "the privileged" and whom Eugene Robinson terms "middle-class mainstream majority." No surprise, we can be sure, to John McWhorter, for example. Hawkins merely affirms the import of McWhorter's research and analysis: the black first-last inverted academic status, while commonly a concern as pertains to the poor, permeates almost the entirety of our black student population, our black male students occupying, almost alone, the lowest rung. While, then, we are talking about the poor, it is not just the poor "Standing in the need of prayer," for our mainstream we can add: "But it's me [too], oh Lord."[10]

This refrain occasions another mnemonic: **MSAN**. This mnemonic may help us to remember that although the crisis centers on the poor, the problem is social-class inclusive. The Minority Student Achievement Network, started in 1999, consists of the superintendents of fourteen urban and suburban school districts located, not in poor communities, but in affluent communities. They got together, black Hispanic New York University sociologist Pedro Noguera tells us, "for the purpose of providing the districts with strategic support in tackling a common problem: the racial gap in student achievement" (191:133). The white students in these districts were doing fine, so given their affluent status, the superintendents figured that our black students could do the same. But so far they were wrong. Noguera concludes that "after nearly three years of meetings and conferences," "there is still no sign that the districts in MSAN have discovered ways to close the achievement gap or to reverse these disturbing academic trends" (191:135-36).

In general, then, our African American students are not doing as well as they can and should be doing. Only our males from our poor

---

[10] Source: http://www.gospelsonglyrics.org/songs/its_me_o_lord_standing_in_the_need_of_prayer.html. 25 November 2014.

neighborhoods are the worst off -- too many causing trouble while in school, disproportionately failing, and disproportionately dropping out. The only saving grace is that, unlike the poor, the mainstream is more connected, has more of a safety net, and has fewer social problems.

With the poor, we are at a time when action must be taken (1) to avoid our school failure from becoming a permanently accepted norm, not just by the larger society, but also by our own race and (2) to avoid the consequence of that failure leading to the permanently accepted isolation of the failed, and again not just by the larger society, but also by our own race -- at least its more mainstream element. That could mean the abandonment of special remedies at resolution, the status quo resulting in a permanent and sizable African American male underclass. In fact, one can only hope that such is not already the case, as alluded to black Pultizer Price-winning <u>Washington Post</u> journalist, Eugene Robinson, who describes them as "the Abandoned."

The stain on the race would thus be permanent -- our progress stifled, our fragmented identity perpetuated, our standing hopelessly subordinate. For the absence of a strong and positive male presence can only mean what we already know and what, for example, psychoanalyst, Alexander Mitscherlich, tells us in his <u>Society without the Father</u>: chaos, aggression, and regression (180).

The black male underclass and its social structure would likely continue ad infinitum to make up "The Other America" about which Michael Harrington wrote a little over two generations ago, and "the Abandoned." about which Eugene Robinson writes today, in 2010. Harrington had this to say about the poor:

> The other Americans feel differently than the rest of the nation. They tend to be hopeless and passive, yet prone to bursts of violence; they are lonely and isolated, often rigid and hostile. To be poor is not simply to be deprived of the material things of this world. It is to enter a fatal, futile universe, an America within America with a twisted spirit (114:120).

Robinson's updated commentary is no less bleak. He sees the poor as standing alone and apart. He says they resent the recent emerging immigrants, mainstream do-gooders, and the black elite (227:236). As DuBois saw the problem of the 20th Century as the color-line, Robinson sees the problem of the 21st Century as that of the Abandoned.

Past

We cannot say that we have had no warning. Some of us in the field of education, for example, might remember James Conant. In his famous report on his visits to large city slum schools and to suburban schools nearly a half century ago [c1960], <u>Slums and Suburbs</u>, the late renown former Harvard President sounded the alarm. Conant concluded, "*Social dynamite* [emphasis added] is building up in our large cities in the form of unemployed out-of-school youth, especially in the Negro slums" (42:146).

He cites the report of a principal of one of the schools in his study. In part, the report said the following:

> The parents of at least one-third of the children are either in penal institutions, are on probation, or have prison records. At least 100 children are on probation to the Juvenile Court. There has not been a day since I've been at the school that there has not been one or more children in detention at the Juvenile Court…(42:16-17).

Referring to another principal, this time by way of interview, Conant writes:

> He [the principal] went on to say that the area had a set of social customs of its own. The women, on the whole, work and earn fairly good wages, but the male Negro often earns less than the woman and would rather not work at all than to be in this situation. As a consequence, the streets are full of unemployed men who hang around and prey on the girls. The women are the centers of the family and as a rule are extremely loyal to the children. The men, on the other hand, are floaters, and many children have no idea who their father is. Similar reports from principals and teachers can be heard by the attentive and sympathetic visitor to the Negro slums of any one of several cities. Racial discrimination on the part of employers and labor unions is certainly one factor which leads to the

existence of so many male Negro floaters. What is terrifying is that the number of male *youth* [emphasis in original] in this category is increasing almost daily (42:19-20).

Conant compared the situation to "the piling up of inflammable material in an empty building in a city block. Potentialities for trouble--indeed possibilities of disaster [that is, social dynamite]--are surely there" (42:18).

If Conant, who died in 1978, were alive today, he would see the accuracy of his prognosis—and, to an extent, he had already seen it. The social dynamite was indeed there, and, as reflected in "Figures, and More" (Chapter 17), has exploded --sometimes with the bangs of big city riots and continually in the form of disproportionate crime, delinquency, and disorder.

That explosion has resulted in the *prisonization* of our black male culture. Conant alludes to it when he cites the report of a principal that, "The parents of at least one-third of the children are either in penal institutions, are on probation, or have prison records." Remember, this was back in 1960. That fraction would likely be larger today, for we know that "at any given time, as many as one in four of all young black men are in the criminal justice system -- in prison or jail, on probation, or on parole" (46: 9); and that "one of every 14 black children has a parent in prison" (245: 239). The effect is what sociologists are calling the *prisonization* of our culture: antisocial norms, hostility to authority, normalization of crime, and commodification of prison life (for example, prison-style clothing and gangsta rap) (39:92-94).

Around the same time that Conant issued his warning, another national figure, Daniel Patrick Moynihan, did the same -- and in no less dire terms. In his infamous 1965 publication, The Negro Family: The Case for National Action (published under the authorship of the United States Department of Labor), sociologist and then Assistant Secretary of Labor Moynihan under President Lyndon Johnson, described the disintegration of the black family and is said to have elsewhere offered this analysis:

> From the wild Irish slums of the 19th century Eastern seaboard, to the riot-torn suburbs of Los Angeles, there is one unmistakable lesson in American history: a community that allows a large number of young men to grow up in broken families, dominated by women, never acquiring any stable relationship to male authority, never acquiring any set of rational expectations about the future--that community asks for and gets chaos. Crime, violence, unrest, disorder--most particularly the furious, unrestrained lashing out at the whole social structure--that is not only to be expected; it is very near inevitable. And it is richly deserved (184:254).

The social dynamite that Conant saw through his study of the schools, Moynihan thus saw in his study of the families that provided the school their students. The consequences which both authors foresaw back then have turned out to be what we see today, only expanded.

That our own black leaders (among others) ignored these warnings and denied the existence of the conditions on which they were based, in the case of Moyniha, for example, attacking him for making a case for national action, is one of the most tragic episodes in the history of our race. On a watershed issue, the inherent self-retarding nature of our dominant **System-Responsibility Tradition** was revealed. Through such aggressive denial of the role of internal factors in causing our problems, that tradition has undermined our progress and left one-quarter of our people Abandoned, as Eugene Robinson terms them -- more or less left to fend for themselves and what they can wrest from one another and from the system. The problem of our new century might indeed be, as Robinson suggests, the problem of the Abandoned, but it is one that, in this instance, we can hang more on ourselves and our leaders than on the system, which so commonly and immovably is our leaders' object of fixation.

The Haitian earthquake in 2010 should have been a traumatic reminder to all of us, our black leaders in particular, of what happens in the absence of an emphasis on adaptation and self-help: degradation and helplessness. After over 200 years of freedom, in the wake of the worst natural disaster in human history, they could do practically nothing to help themselves. Booker T. Washington had foreseen it. In one of his famous **Sunday Evening Talks** to his Tuskegee students, staff, and others he told them about his European trip, expressing regret that while in France he was not able, as intended, to visit the tomb of Haiti's liberator, Toussaint L'Ouverture. Then he went on to make these observations about Haiti:

> ...there are a good many well educated and cultivated men and women of that nationality in Paris. Numbers of them are sent there each year for education, and they take high rank in scholarship. It is greatly to be regretted, however, that some of these do not take advantage of the excellent training which is given there in the colleges of physical science, agriculture, mechanics and domestic science. They would then be in a position to return home and assist in developing the agricultural and mineral resources of their native land. Haiti will never be what it should be until a large number of the natives receive an education which will enable them to develop agriculture, build roads, start manufactories, build railroads and bridges, and thus keep on the island the large amount of money which is now being sent outside for production which these people themselves could supply (275:276).

New York Times columnist David Brooks called the Haitians the victims of "progress-resistant cultural influences" (312). So are our Abandoned, thanks to the civil-rights fixation of our national black leaders since our African American Garden of Eden and the Age of Booker T. Washington. Let, then, the **Haitian earthquake of 2010** serve as a mnemonic to remind us, traumatically, of AMSAC and its inseparable social problems and the price we pay, helplessness, for maladaptation and a failure to cultivate a culture of self-help.

Thesis

In our adaptation to American life, we African Americans have been guided by two traditions, the Self-Responsibility Tradition of Booker T. Washington and the System-Responsibility Tradition of W.E.B. DuBois – these two leaders herein depicted as having fathered these traditions during the early stage of our freedom when we were in our own African American Garden of Eden. With the death of Washington in 1915, DuBois's System-Responsibility Tradition became dominant, replacing

Washington's Self-Responsibility Tradition, which had been dominant since around 1880. Under it, our adaptation has been fostered through increasingly sufficient opportunities for advancement, together with increasingly sufficient support to enable us to avail ourselves of those opportunities. But the opportunities and support have not been accompanied by the internal adaptations required to translate them into outcomes that would normalize community life among the poor. The reason can be attributed to the failure of the System-Responsibility Tradition to emphasize the necessity of such internal adaptations, and even its devaluation of that necessity through defamation of Washington and his Self-Responsibility Tradition. With its reliance on direct action, the Black Power phase of the Civil Rights Movement of the 1960s popularized that devaluation, further diminishing Washington's influence and even bringing him into disrepute. Only, however, through a renewal of Washington's Self-Responsibility Tradition can we solve the African American Male School Adaptability Crisis (AMSAC) and its inseparable social problems, a renewal which can be accomplished through a Child Family Rights Movement with the herein proposed African American Male Career Pathway Program (AMCAP) as a mainspring. Through the Movement, we can bring an end to the second bondage in which our civil-rights fixation has ensnared us, Victimology, and in its place create the "average expectable environments" out of which we can forge a positive core identity and a sound character, which are the foundation of school and life success.

Part II

Causes and Context

3

To Blame or Not to Blame Ourselves: Cosby Versus Dyson / Loury versus Ferguson

>*Proverbs, 16:22 - "Understanding is a wellspring of life unto him that hath it: but the instruction of fools is folly."*
>*Galatians, 6:5 - "For every man shall bear his own burden."*

Fixing The Blame (Self-Responsibility)

"To be or not to be--that is the question," goes the famous line from William Shakespeare's Hamlet.[11] As can be applied to the African American School Adaptability Crisis (AMSAC), it might be rephrased, "To blame or not to blame ourselves--that is the question." Of course, the kind of life versus death meaning that the line holds in Hamlet does not apply to AMSAC, but it does invoke, as in Hamlet, the image of action or inaction and confronts us with the implications of that choice. "To blame ourselves" -- herein meaning to accept responsibility ourselves --requires us **ourselves** to "take arms against a sea of troubles." "Not to blame ourselves" leaves us to "suffer the slings and arrows of [our] outrageous fortune," in this instance, **others** being left to take up any arms -- in fact, exhorted and pressured to do so.

---

[11] Quotes from play and references to it based on the following source: http://en.wikipedia.org/wiki/Hamlet 11 November 2014.

To be clear, when we say blame, we mean responsibility; and when we say responsibility, we do not necessarily mean cause. What we do mean is the *acceptance* of responsibility for our condition, whatever its cause, together with the need for the self-effort intrinsic to that acceptance. And such acceptance is less about philosophy or belief than about the proven imperatives of survival and progress.

The choice of that acceptance, and its consequences, permeates the controversy that surrounds AMSAC. Leave that controversy unresolved, or deficiently resolved, and the crisis will go unsolved. Only if we know who must fight this battle -- who must "take arms" -- can we win it. There are some battles which others cannot fight for us. The African American Male School Adaptability Crisis and its inseparable social problems is one of them, for it requires doing something that only we can do: confront and conquer our **three major demons**, *IQ lag-- fatherless families—crime*.

To become victors in this confrontation, we are required to do something different: to renew **The Tradition of Choice** (the Self-Responsibility Tradition of Booker Taliaferro Washington). The dominant System-Responsibility Tradition of William Edward Burghardt DuBois, responsible for the existence of the demons in the first place, has not acknowledged that responsibility, nor made any credible internal attempts to do anything about them.

For an overview of the controversy, we turn to the crossfire between two media personalities and two academics: black comedian, actor, and author, Bill Cosby, versus black Georgetown University sociologist, Michael Eric Dyson, on the one hand, and black Brown University economist, Glenn C. Loury, versus black economist at the Harvard Graduate School of Education and the Harvard Kennedy School, Ronald F. Ferguson, on the other hand. Their crossfire personifies and articulates the controversy while leading us into the causes and context of AMSAC and its inseparable social problems.

Cosby versus Dyson

Cosby was invited to Howard University by the National Association for the Advancement of Colored People (NAACP) and the NAACP

Legal Defense Fund to be the featured speaker, on May 17, 2004, at their celebration of the fiftieth anniversary of the United States Supreme Court decision in *Brown v. Board of Education of Topeka*. The decision desegregated our public schools, declaring separate schools for the races to be "inherently unequal." Cosby had a prepared speech for the occasion, but scraped it and delivered instead an impromptu message. In blunt language, he exhorted the poor among us to exert effort and initiative on their own behalf, "to accept personal responsibility and embrace self-help" (46: xviii). Later, in 2007, together with renown black Harvard Medical School psychiatrist and author, Dr. Alvin Poussaint, he communicated his thoughts in book form, writing <u>Come on People: On the Path from Victims to Victors</u> (46).

Somewhat like Charles Murray, a generation earlier, Cosby's call was provocative, for he was treading on similar philosophical grounds as Murray. Paul Tough, in telling the story of Goeffrey Canada's Harlem Children's Zone, recounts how social scientist Murray of the Manhattan Institute had stirred the same encompassing hornet's nest as Cosby with his book <u>Losing Ground</u> in 1984 (258: 28-29). Like Cosby, his topic was poverty and what to do about it. Murray's analysis and prescription provoked harsh criticisms, most notably from renown black University of Chicago sociologist, William Julius Wilson, in his book published three years later, <u>The Truly Disadvantaged</u>. Their confrontation is discussed in Chapter 17. The point here being, as Paul Tough notes, Cosby was taking sides on an issue which had been taboo before Murray openly questioned the then current wisdom that the plight of the poor was due, not to any fault of their own, but to faults in the system.

Cosby's speech was an unsparing, gloves-off reaction that can easily be interpreted, as some did, not only as advocating personal responsibility and self-help on the part of the poor, but as an assault on the poor (306b). Citing a 50 percent dropout rate, Cosby termed *Brown v. Board of Education* an empty victory. So using the humor, wit, and sarcasm that are his trademarks, he expressed his disappointment and pain, albeit in the form of anger, and enlisted his audience to share it. Among other things, he decried:

- the outcome of Brown v. Board of Education, which "paved the way," asking, "What did we do with it," asserting, "The White

- Man, he's laughing -- got to be laughing. 50 percent dropout -- rest of them in prison."
- "These people are fighting hard to be ignorant. There's no English spoken, and they're walking and they're angry. Oh God, they're angry and they have pistols and they shoot and they do stupid things. And after they kill somebody, they don't have a plan. Just murder somebody. Boom. Over what? A pizza? And then run to the poor cousin's house."
- "People putting their clothes on backwards. Isn't that a sign of something going on wrong? Are you not paying attention? Pople with their hat on backwards, pants down around the crack. Isn't that a sign of something, or are you waiting for Jesus to pull his pants up. Isn't it a sign of something when she's got her dress all the way up to the crack ...and got all kinds of needles and things going through her body."

One can see this outpouring as an "assault" on the poor or as the cry of a caring, emotionally invested, disappointed man, feeling let down by his race and suffering from the pain of that letdown. It is as if his "cup runneth over,"[12] not with joy or plenty, but with disappointment and pain. Throughout, however, given his humorous expression of it, he drew laughter and applause.

To Dyson, it was worthy of neither, however. In his book, Is Bill Cosby Right? (Or has the Middle Class Lost Its Mind?, in equally unsparing, gloves-off fashion, he responded. To him, Cosby's speech was the performance of a "rhetorical gun slinger," firing "vicious," "mean-spirited," "ill-informed," "vulgar" charges. As the title of his book implies ("...with only half my tongue in cheek," he says) Bill Cosby and other middle-class blacks who share his views have lost their mind. He grants Cosby the "right to speak his mind," but it is his mind that is the problem, plagued as it is by "poor comprehension" (70:16).

He further grants that Cosby's views are widely shared (though not in public) in the black community, especially among what he calls the *Afristocracy*, the upper-middle-class blacks, and even among the black poor and members of the working class. However, he declares that

---

[12] From Psalms 23:5

in our quest for social justice, of necessity we have not neglected the pursuit of self-help (70:10-11). Only Cosby, he contends, overemphasizes personal responsibility since the suffering of the poor is not of their own making, but rather is due to the structures of society (70:5). Not that there is anything wrong with personal responsibility, he says, but by assuming personal responsibility, the poor cannot "*in any significant way* alter their social plight" [emphasis added] (70:215). Insistence on their doing so, Dyson believes, "lets society off the hook" (70:219-20).

There we have it, a reflection of the essence of the broader controversy of which the approach to solving AMSAC represents and which spans the history of the adaptation demands we have historically faced. Following the adoption of the Thirteenth, Fourteenth, and Fifteenth Amendments (1865, 1866, and 1870, respectively), which gave us our freedom, citizenship, and right to vote, respectively -- and especially since the end of Reconstruction in 1877 when federal military and political control of the South was ended -- we can be said to have been on our own, at least on paper or in theory. In any instance, now free and American, we have had to adapt to our new circumstances and meet the demands of that freedom and the Americanization which it required. The issue, then and now, has been how successfully to achieve that adaptation.

President Johnson's War on Poverty represents the most ambitious effort to assist us in making that adaptation. It was based on the assumption that through job, income, and education initiatives, the government could make that adaptation achievable, an assumption disputed by Murray but endorsed, and even extended, by Wilson in his proposals. In Cosby and Dyson, we see a continuation of the Murray/Wilson divide, a difference of particulars only. At issue still: what is the best approach to ending poverty, which is, effectively, the same as asking what is the best approach to enabling the poor to adapt. In Cosby and Dyson, we get an overview of how we ourselves, the ones who are its subjects, have responded to the issue. The thesis herein is that our response has taken a twofold tradition: the Self-Responsibility Tradition of Booker T. Washington and the System-Responsibility Tradition of W. E. B. DuBois. In Cosby and Dyson, we see a manifestation of the two.

In assessing the efficacy of these traditions, the contention herein is that our Self-Responsibility Tradition is **The Tradition of Choice** because our System-Responsibility Tradition contains an intrinsic fatal flaw. As represented by Dyson, that intrinsic fatal flaw is system-centered thinking in disregard for the law of diminishing returns, or for the principle that a continual increase in system support does not lead to a continual increase in intended results; as Murray suggests, there is a point when, in fact, system inputs become counterproductive. Personal responsibility and self-help have no significant role in such thinking, no less a central role; these attributes are instead subordinated or minimized. Dyson, as a system proponent, stipulates that we never neglected self-help. He is corrent, but never to neglect something is quite different from emphasizing it. Emphasizing it, Dyson insists, lets "white and black elites off the hook" (70:11). Of course, many in this tradition, like its father, DuBois, fall sway to trying to have it both ways; their *two-ness* (discussed in Chapter 18) or ambivalence is on constant display.

The case has to be made to the Invisible Man of today, and those who identify with the Invisible Man, that the veil is "really being lifted," not "lowered," and that any ambiguity about what is being done derives (to borrow Cosby's language), not from "what they're doing to us," but from "what we're not doing" (306b).

In his <u>Up from History: The Life of Booker T. Washington</u>, aforementioned University of Tennessee historian, Robert J. Norrell, tells us the story of the lifting of the veil. It follows:

> This demonization [of Booker T. Washington] took place even in Tuskegee. In the mid-1960s students at the Institute challenged older civil-rights leaders because they were advising blacks to share power with whites as the best means to build a truly democratic community, even though blacks now had enough votes to take every office. In 1966 a student who had grown up in Tuskegee dismissed one leader's call for moderation by likening him to the most famous local Uncle Tom. The young man

Figure 2. Statue of Booker T. Washington "Lifting the Veil of Ignorance," by Charles Keck. Located at Tuskegee University in Tuskegee, Alabama; courtesy of the Library of Congress, Carol M. Highsmith Archive.

had read *Invisible Man*, the brilliant modernist novel by the former Tuskegee student Ralph Ellison about a young man who goes to a grand, all-black school in the Deep South. Ellison portrays the school's leaders as harsh and indifferent to students, indeed to all blacks beneath them. The protagonist, the Invisible Man, describes a sculpture depicting the school's now-dead founder in front of a kneeling slave. Just such a sculpture, *Lifting the Veil of Ignorance*, has been the focal point of the Tuskegee campus since 1922. The Invisible Man describes the founder's 'hands outstretched in the breathtaking gesture of lifting a veil that flutters in hard, metallic folds about the face of a kneeling slave; and I am standing puzzled, unable to decide whether the veil is really being lifted, or lowered more firmly in place; whether I am witnessing a revelation or a more efficient blinding' [footnote number omitted].

In 1966 the very visible Tuskegee Institute student angrily declared: 'We got this statue out here of that man who's supposed to lifting up the veil. Man, he's putting it back on.' Other interpreters of Booker T. Washington would take the same stance for at least a generation (192:14).

This story symbolizes the fundamental fissure in African American thinking that is under discussion and is evident in the Cosby/Dyson divide. It underlies the student/home-centered versus system-centered approach to AMSAC and its inseparable social problems which the divide reflects. It reflects the Self-Responsibility Tradition of Washington at war with the System-Responsibility Tradition of DuBois.

And a war it has been. Dyson's attack on Cosby is indeed reminiscent of the attack of DuBois on Washington. Norrell tells us that even in his eulogy of Washington, writing in the <u>Crisis</u>, DuBois could not muster for Washington any measure of regard. He wrote that Washington "'never adequately grasped the growing bond of politics and industry; he did not understand the deeper foundation of human training and his basis of better understanding between white and black was founded on caste,'" adding that "Booker's failing ... went beyond ignorance: 'In stern justice, we must lay on the soul of this man, a heavy responsibility for the consummation of Negro disfranchisement, the decline of the Negro college and public school and the firmer establishment of color caste in this land'" (192:421-22). Is this any different, in sum, as Dyson does, asking whether and implying that Bill Cosby and those who share his views have lost their mind? In the next chapter, we will dig deeper.

Loury versus Ferguson

In Cosby versus Dyson, we see our African American Male School Adaptability Crisis (AMSAC) in its broader social context. In Loury versus Ferguson, we see it in the microcosm of our school crisis.

The home versus school controversy which Loury and Ferguson personify reminds one of the subtitle of Steven Pinker's <u>The Blank Slate</u>, namely, <u>The Modern Denial of Human Nature</u> (210). That is analogous to what we have in this controversy: the modern denial that the home has a major responsibility for our school crisis. A case in point is provided by Steve Perry. In his most recent book, <u>Push Has Come to Shove: Getting Our Kids the Education They Deserve -- Even if it Means Picking a Fight</u>, Perry makes this assertion:

> Nothing improves student performance as much as the quality of instruction. The lion's share of the blame must rest squarely upon

the shoulders of educators like me. No, parents are neither the cause nor the solution for the problems in our schools. Teachers and the amount of time that students spend on instruction are what improve student performance (209a:87).

However, apparently without realizing it, Perry himself refutes his own assertion. Take a look at his list of five things parents can control and five things for which parents are blamed but cannot control (209a:95-96).

Five Things Parents Can Control	Five Things for Which Parents are Blamed but Can't Control
1. Early reading	1. Test scores
2. Early numeracy	2. School violence
3. Setting high expectations	3. Dropout rates
4. Curiosity	4. Truancy
5. Discipline	5. The condition of the schools [quality of teachers and administrators]

Based on *his* list, contrary to what he asserts, one would reasonably conclude that, to quote him, "the lion's share of the blame must rest squarely upon the shoulders," *not* "of educators" but of parents. Both experience and research, cited below, suggest that the five things which he cites that parents can do are the things which mainly determine school success.

But never mind logic or consistency when it comes to this issue or some other race-associated issues. Even if one thinks the home bears responsibility, it is politically incorrect, if not punishable, to say so. The popular refrain is, "we have failing schools," a refrain that gets translated into a teacher evaluation craze, schools being closed, and states taking over local schools (480). To focus on our home, to quote black Harvard School of Education sociologist, John Diamond, is to "barking up the wrong tree." But Diamond and others seem to forget that upon gaining increasing attention since the school desegregation decision in Brown vs. Board of Education in 1954, our schools have been the object of a lot of barking, but, as the Loury/Ferguson debate makes evident, apparently not enough to satisfy him and some others, Steve Perry among them.

The home and student context

In his informative book about black educator Geoffrey Canada's Harlem Children's Zone (HCZ), Tough, in telling the story of Loury versus Ferguson, takes us back to what can be considered the historical origin of their dispute, the Moynihan Report and the late John Hopkins University sociologist James S. Coleman's <u>Equality of Educational Opportunity</u> (which came to be called the Coleman Report). Both came out at about the same time -- the Moynihan Report in 1965, the Coleman Report in 1966 --and both were about the *decisive* role of the home in black wellbeing, specifically school achievement in the case of the Coleman Report (258:26-28).

The Coleman Report (1966). Under mandate from the Civil Rights Act of 1964, Coleman and his colleagues were commissioned to undertake a study of educational equality in the United States. Their Report turned out to be one of the largest studies in history (involving some 650,000 students and teachers in over 3,000 schools) and, in the eyes of some (due largely to its school integration implications), one of the most important studies of the century. Of interest here are its findings relative to the home versus school controversy. The Report concluded the following:

> ...schools bring little influence to bear on a child's achievement that is independent of his background and general social context; and that this very lack of an independent effect means that the inequalities imposed on children by their home, neighborhood, and peer environment are carried along to become the inequalities with which they confront adult life at the end of school. For equality of educational opportunity through the schools must imply a strong effect of schools that is independent of the child's immediate social environment, and that strong independent effect is not present in American schools (40:325).

In particular, the Report points to the strong influence of student variables. Three were examined -- interest in school and pursuit of reading outside school; self-concept as pertains to learning and success in school; and sense of control of the environment. Of all the variables examined, including family background and all school variables, these three student attitude variables "showed the strongest relation to achievement, at all three grade levels [grades 6, 9, and 12]" (40: 319). The latter of the three -- sense of control of environment -- was found to be most strong for our students and, unlike for Oriental and white students, persists through the grades. "It appears reasonable," the Report interjects, "that these attitudes depend more on the home than the school" (40:324).

Here was conventional wisdom being turned upside down: if we were to close the black/white achievement gap in our schools, we had to seek a remedy, not primarily through the school as had been and still was the case, but primarily through the home (inclusive of students).

Subsequent confirming research: Marzano. In his informative book, What Works in Schools, Robert J. Marzano reviewed studies which have analyzed the Coleman Report's ten-percent-school-effect finding. In addition, he reviewed other studies that have broadly addressed the issue of factors which influence student achievement. An internationally known educational researcher and trainer, Marzano is an advocate of and leader in evidence-based education (a la the evidence-based approach in medicine). He runs his own research laboratory, and has authored numerous books. A tabularized summary of his review is shown below.

Based on data he assembled, Marzano concludes that Coleman underestimated the role that schools can play, as "research in the last 35 years demonstrates that effective schools can have a profound impact on school achievement" (164:8). "The schools that are highly effective," he adds, "produce results that almost entirely overcome the effects of student background" (164: 7). Marzano details what research suggests would characterize such schools, while conceding that to produce such schools "requires a powerful commitment to change the status quo" (164:10). He is not denying the pivotal role of what he calls student-level factors (home environment, learned intelligence and background knowledge, and motivation), even observing, "Both research and theory indicate that student-level factors account for the lion's share of variance in student achievement [80 percent]," but his evidence-based thesis is that "the negative effects of these factors can be overcome" (164:123-25).

Teacher qualifications (years of experience, level of certification, and pedagogical knowledge), which account for 43% of the variance in school achievement, help to support Marzano's thesis, as well as the position of those who place responsibility on the school. *But*, reviewing the various factors in their totality, Marzano has underlined where the evidence shows "the lion's share" resides: student-level factors. The home and family account for 49 percent of the variance, and home atmosphere for 33.29 percent of it.

Table 2

Factors Found to Account for School Achievement

Factor	Percentage of variance accounted for in school achievement
School – Coleman Report	10%
School – Other studies	20%
Non-school factors	80%
Home and family	49%
Teacher qualifications	43%
Class size	8%
SES indicators	
Income..................................	9.92%
Education.............................	3.24%
Occupation...........................	4.04%
Home atmosphere only..............	33.29%
(e.g.: read to children, help with homework, take them to library and to cultural events)	
Intelligence (fluid)	
American Psychological Association Task Force................................	25%
7 research studies	
Median among them.................	24%

Range among them...................	11% - 50%
Intelligence (crystallized)	
8 research studies	
Median among them.................	42%
Range among them...................	4% - 55%
Student motivation	
8 research studies	
Median among them.................	12%
Range among them...................	4% - 37%

Source: compiled from data in Marzano's book, <u>What Works in Schools</u> (164: 6-7, 63, 123-25, 134-35, 145).

Subsequent confirming research: Wang, Haertel, and Walberg. In a far more comprehensive review in <u>Educational Leadership</u>, Wang, Haertel, and Walberg of the National Center on Education in the Inner Cities undertook a funded study to "identify and estimate the influence of educational, psychological, and social factors on learning" (263, 462a). They surveyed 61 educational researchers, compiled 91 research

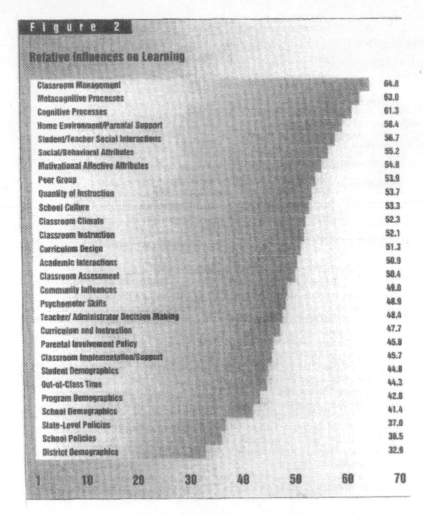

Figure 3. Relative influences on learning. Reproduced with permission of the Association for Supervision and Curriculum Development (ASCD). Learn more about ASCD at www.ascd.org (462a).

syntheses, and analyzed the content of 179 handbook chapters and narrative reviews. They used meta-analyses statistically to aggregate and to quantify their results, shown in Figure 3, which yielded 28 variables. They ranked the 28 variables by their T scores, a statistical test used to determine the relative effectives of different factors, the higher the T score the greater the influence.

Of the 28 variables derived and ranked, classroom management emerges with the highest influence ranking, with a T score of 68.4, the lowest T score being 32.9. However, of the ten top variables, seven pertain, not to school factors, but to home and student factors (e.g.: home environment, student aptitude, and student behavior and motivation). Like Marzano's review of the evidence, Wang, Haertel, and Walberg's review likewise shows that the "the lion's share" resides in student-level factors. Like Marzano's analysis as well, their analysis points to the significant impact that the individual teacher can exert -- an impact, however, which can be neutralized or nullified by a number of equally, and in totality, more powerful student-level factors.

Parenting. The evidence of Wang, Haertel, and Walberg, likewise, point to strong influence of parenting on learning (a T score of 58.4). The research of several others also underlines the critical role of parenting. In his book about Geoffrey Canada, <u>Whatever It Takes: Geoffrey Canada's Quest to Change Harlem and America</u>, Paul Tough reviews research done by Betty Hart and Todd R. Risley, Bettye Caldwell, Martha Farah, and Annette Lareau which answers the question: what makes the student/home variable, as shown by the research above cited, such an influential, if not decisive, factor in student achievement and success (258:41-52). The research has focused on parent-child interactions and practices, finding that poor children are hindered in their development, not by their material disadvantages, but by these interactions and practices. Their poor performance is associated with parents who, as a group, in contrast to middle-class parents, tend to be as follows:

1. sparse in the frequency, number, and kind of words and statements used
2. insensitive
3. not socially and emotionally nurturing
4. not stimulating as regards their children's cognitive development
5. negative in their feedback rather than positive and encouraging
6. intrusive or detached
7. more reliant on their children than on themselves as regard their children's use of their free time (do not plan activities to cultivate their children's development, leaving the children to plan for themselves)

8. authority-oriented, erecting a line between the adult world and their children's world

These interactions and practices, also observed by Silverstein and Krate in their study of Harlem preschool and elementary school children, are associated with deficient cognitive skills as well as with the lack of the attitudes and the emotional and social skills required for school and life success. To quote Wang, Haertal, and Walberg, "… the home functions as the most salient out-of-school context for student learning, amplifying or diminishing the school's effect on learning" (263:278). Although a recent study by Keith Robinson and Angel Harris showing that, in general, parental involvement does not affect academic success one way or the other might seem to contradict their assertion, Wang, Haertal, and Walberg are not referring to parental involvement per se, but to the role of the home. And as regards the role of the hone, Robinson and Harris declare, "We believe that parents are critical to how well children perform in school, just not in the conventional ways that our society has been promoting" (227a; 438g).

Jencks and Meredith Phillips, who in the words of Tough, undertook "the first serious and comprehensive effort to engage the achievement gap as a subject of scientific inquiry" provides a no less convincing case for focus on parenting (258:41). In the introductory chapter of their highly acclaimed, The Black-White Test Score Gap, they examine a variety of family and background variables believed to explain the gap, including single-parenting, and conclude, "Although we believe that improving the nation's schools could reduce the black-white test score gap, we do not believe that schools alone can eliminate it" (136:45). What else can make it possible? They say "changing the way parents deal with their children may be the *single most important thing* we can do to improve children's cognitive skill," and that is because "the cognitive disparities between black and white preschool children are currently so large that it is hard to imagine how school alone could eliminate them" [emphasis added] (136: 45-46).

In his recent book, How Children Succeed: Grit, Curiosity, and the Hidden Power of Character (2012), Tough makes the single most convincing case. To answer the query suggested by the title, Tough conducted interviews and classroom observations, and he mined the extensive work and research of economists, educators, psychologists, and neuroscientists. He learned that the latest experiences and research show that the skills which determine success have been found to be, not the traditional cognitive skills which we have emphasized, but the soft character skills which we have not emphasized, such as grit, curiosity, and character. These soft character skills are "rooted in brain chemistry, and they are molded, in measurable and predictable ways, by the environment in which children grow up" (258a: 196). The home (consisting, Tough says, of "at least… one parent and ideally two") is the foundation of that environment, and if it provides the child a secure and nurturing relationship, Tough explains that the research evidence indicates that the child's brain chemistry is likely to function so as to enable the child to persevere and to succeed (258a:181-82).

The foregoing thus makes it evident that the Loury-Ferguson debate takes place in the research context of student-level factors, which include the home, which has been shown to account, in the words of Marzano, "for the lion's share of variance in student achievement," and for skills, attitudes, and behaviors deemed essential for school success. Yet, evidence points to the school being able, under certain circumstances [early intervention and possibly highly effective schools], to overcome home factor deficiencies. What it does not point to is the feasibility of duplicating those circumstances on a scale commensurate with the problem.

The school context (urban school reform)

In addition to this research context pursuant to the Moynihan and Coleman Reports, the Loury-Ferguson debate has a parallel school context. Research shows that when it comes to our students, school characteristics, in particular teacher characteristics -- whether they can overcome home deficiencies or not -- make more of a difference than they do for majority students [for example, see the Coleman Report (40:316-19), Wang, Haertel, Walberg (263), and Ferguson (346)]. Consistent with this evidence, to close our achievement lag, Diamond and others have called for barking up, not the home tree, as the weight of the research directs, but the school tree. Their bark has so far prevailed, so now we take a look at what it has yielded.

Title I. In <u>Title I: Compensatory Education at the Crossroads</u>, editors Borman, Stringfield, and Slavin (all of John Hopkins University) tell us about the history of Title I of the Elementary and Secondary Education Act (ESEA) of 1965, "the cornerstone of the federal commitment to equality of opportunity" (17: ix). "Funded at more than $8 billion per year," they say, "and serving more than 10 million students, the program is the federal government's single largest investment in America's schools ..." (17: ix). These extra funds have been distributed to districts and schools based on poverty data for children and on the education needs of their poorly performing peers who do not meet poverty criteria. They have made possible an array of instructional practices and parent programs which the authors describe and analyze. The early results, during the 1970s and early 1980s, were promising as there was evidence of positive Title I effects, but since the late 1980s, studies show that the effects have plateaued. Overall, the editors conclude, "Title I has had a modest positive impact on student achievement, but we argue ... that it can and should do much more" (17: ix).

In her book, <u>The Culture of Education Policy</u>, Sandra Stein (Academic Dean of the New York City Leadership Academy) supports the overall assessment of Borman, Springfield, and Slavin. She sees Title I as having created a *culture of policy*. Her conclusion is that the way funding is provided under the act leads to certain school language and practices that come to constitute a culture of policy devoted to meeting compliance standards and preserving Title I infrastructure. As a result, students get labeled, expectations get lowered, instruction becomes fragmented and ritualized rather than responsive, failure gets rewarded with funding, and creativity and innovation are stifled.

Seven large cities. In <u>Race Against Time: The Crisis in Urban Schooling</u>, Cibulka and Boyd (the former, a University of Kentucky professor and dean, the latter, a Pennsylvania State University professor) make the point that reform efforts in seven large cities -- Baltimore, Boston, Chicago, Los Angeles, Philadelphia, Washington, D.C, and New York -- "have not led to significant and sustained urban education renewal" (36: 223). The efforts have focused on system reform, increased mayoral influence, and external intervention. They cite a fourth reform effort that is in its infancy: school choice and privatization. Studies have led them to conclude that to be successful such efforts -- contrary to those so far -- must be comprehensive, with particular attention to the ability of schools to make improvements and to the teaching-learning factors that account for the problem. They say the same when it comes to funding. Adequate funding, they explain, deemed by many to be the answer to the problem, is not in and of itself the case, citing (from Paul Ciotti of the Cato Institute) the following description of what happened with the Kansas City, Missouri, school system that was able to spend $2 billion over 12 years to improve its schools:

Kansas City spent as much as $11,700 per pupil--more money per pupil, on a cost of living adjusted basis, than any other of the 280 largest districts in the country. The money bought higher teachers' salaries, 15 new schools, and such amenities as an Olympic-sized swimming pool with an underwater viewing room, television and animation studios, a robotics lab, a 25-acre wildlife sanctuary, a zoo, a model United Nations with simultaneous translation capability, and field trips to Mexico and Senegal. The student-teacher ratio was 12 or 13 to 1, the lowest of any major school district in the country. The results were dismal. Test scores did not rise; the black-white gap did not diminish; and there was less, not greater, integration (36:ix, 316:1).

No Child Left Behind Act, 2001 (NCLB). In an ambitious attempt to make Title I work better, President George W. Bush got NCLB enacted (471j). Through setting high standards and using standardized tests to see that students meet them, the premise was that this would close the black-white achievement gap. Federal funds were made available to support the needed teacher and school improvements. Accountability was made central, schools being required to make Annual Yearly Progress (AYP) in test scores. Fail to make progress and the schools were required to submit plans for improvement, and if, after five years, sufficient improvement were not made, the school was closed and declared a failing school. Research results show that it has made only "minimal headway in closing the achievement gap" (323b). Substantial gains are reported for students in math, but none in reading, those gains being only modest, however, for the disadvantaged.

Stein's assessment is that President Bush's redesign did not significantly change the culture of policy. Still, she argues, the spotlight was on failure, as standards were lowered to meet NCLB requirements and the concept of failing schools operationalized. Nor from her perspective have data been meaningfully used, which would be to examine the teaching-learning process so as to connect input with results. Instead the focus has been on poverty and performance (248:137).

Every Student Succeeds Act, 2015 (ESSA). These NCLB outcomes, and the federal control and intrusive testing entailed, finally led to its revision and replacement, in 2015, under a new name, Every Student Succeeds Act (ESSA). Its discussion is left to Chapter 16, where school reform and parent involvement are examined.

So Much Reform, So Little Change: The Persistence of Failure in Urban Schools. Of the literature reviewed, this book by aforementioned black University of Chicago sociologist and professor Charles M. Payne provides one of the most recent (2008) overall assessments of school reform efforts --and one of the best. Payne has done a balanced analysis and seems a little more optimistic than some (208a:191-205). He finds fault with both liberals and conservatives, yet conveys a sense of hope. At least he sees the beginning of change. He feels that, finally, much has been learned and the effect of that learning can be seen in improvements here and there, but only here and there. "What is happening now," he concludes, "is as if the most determined activists and educators have seized parts of the system by the throat and are beating some sense into it. It's improvement, but it's not stable" (208a:9).

As these lines are being written, a headline from The New York Times, however, underlines the overall impression with which the literature leaves one and which is conveyed by the Kansas City school system $2 billion failure. The headline reads: "Willie Brown Academy, Born in 1992 with High Hopes, Will Close in May, a Failure" (359). Opened in a predominantly black San Francisco neighborhood, the academy is described as once part of a "Dream Schools program that brought millions of dollars in special aid, along with school uniforms, longer school days and Saturday classes." But now plagued by "chronic student underachievement and high truancy," with students roaming "the hallways during class time," it could not stand the scrutiny of No Child Left Behind Act and had to be closed." No doubt the case of the Academy represents the extreme, but it is often through the extreme that we can get a better sense of the mean.

Face off

That sense of the mean suggests that we are putting money and effort (and a lot of both) into closing the black-white academic achievement gap with little or nothing to show for it -- money and effort directed at system change. Yet, think about what the research shows about the *decisive* role of home factors versus what it tells us about the resources-without-results initiatives that have gone into the school factors, such as, in the case of the Kansas City school system and the Willie Brown Academy. That contrast provides the context for the Ferguson-Loury face off.

Battle time. As Tough tells it, and as Ferguson himself tells it, apparently, the aforementioned black Harvard economist Ronald Ferguson has done a lot of thinking about this issue. As a result, based on his own research and that of others [which he details in his policy paper, "Toward Skilled Parenting & Transformed Schools Inside a National Movement for Excellence with Equity" (347)], he has concluded that, along with other efforts to address our achievement gap, there must also be efforts to enlist the support of black parents and communities. In his words:

> ...the impact that any particular public discourse will have on societal support for the black poor or for racial equality more generally is quite uncertain. I believe that notification and mobilization of black parents and communities to address parenting practices, youth culture, and other lifestyle issues can foster important progress, even as the struggle continues for a more just policy mix and a less racially biased collective consciousness. Indeed, these various efforts may be mutually reinforcing. There is no necessary contradiction between addressing the lifestyles issues ...and larger efforts to enlist the nation-at-large in living out the full implications of the idea that there should be no 'them' in the United States (347: 25).

Ferguson was both responding to Glenn Loury, his "friend and colleague" as he terms him, and stating his own position. Ferguson was quoting Loury as opposing such "notification and mobilization" on the ground, in effect, that it would take the system "off the hook," a familiar and historic refrain of system-centered thinkers. As Ferguson describes Loury's position, putting the home agenda "near the center of an explanation for inequality reinforces stigmas and may help solidify what is already an abdication of responsibility by national leaders." As already cited, responding, Ferguson expresses uncertainty as to whether such would be the case; rather, he asserts that it could "foster important progress" and, in the context of other efforts, "may be mutually reinforcing." Tough, in an elaboration of Loury's position based on Loury's presentation at the 2006 conference at Harvard University on the achievement gap, quotes Loury as saying that the conferees were "'engaged in a construction of a narrative'-- and if they chose to make it a narrative about problems in black homes, rather than inequities in the economic structure of the country, they would in effect be giving comfort to the enemy and ignoring the true problem." "'What's really going on,'" Tough goes on to quote Loury as saying, 'is that society as a whole has failed to commit itself to the development of the human resources of all of its people'" (258:102).

Siding with Ferguson

Personified by this Loury-Ferguson exchange, the home versus school controversy that overlays our African American Male School Adaptability Crisis (AMSAC) occurs in the context of the lesson of experience and the legion of research. One might think, therefore, it would be less one-sided, that Ferguson, rather than expressing a minority view, if not expressing a majority one, would at least be expressing a widely accepted and vocalized one. But despite all the "barking up the school tree," we hear calls for even more such barking [the wild and blanket variety, incidentally], Ferguson being among the few notables who, looking at the research and the record, publicly assert: there is another tree which can be productive, and up which, therefore, we need to bark, the home tree -- and to put that assertion at or near the top of the public agenda.

Among the other few who call for "barking up the home tree" are previously discussed Charles M. Payne and just mentioned Paul Tough

-- Jencks and Phillips, Ogbu, and Cosby elsewhere cited. In particular, Tough stands out.

Payne. But first, Payne. In addition to his training, professional experiences, and research, Payne has the advantage of insight gained from having worked with low-income youth and their parents. Thus, rather than being shocked by what Cosby said, Payne asserts that "the heart of what he was saying was not only true but unremarkable." Asking, "Is it possible for inner-city parents to do a better job of supporting their children's education?," he answers, "Indeed it is, and we really shouldn't have to have a debate about it. Almost anyone who works with urban children [as he has], no matter how sympathetic to parents [as he appears to be], can recite the litany of counterproductive parenting habits" (208a:199). Payne goes on to add, "Of course, it does make sense to speak to The Man, to challenge dominant ideology, but sometimes it makes sense to speak to The People too, and doing that usually requires more than telling them that nothing is their fault" (208a:200). Whether we should be speaking to The People just "sometimes" is subject to question, but "sometimes" is better than "no times."

Tough. Because his research for his recent book led him to the home as the key to how children succeed, Tough urges that we go against the grain in our effort to help the children of the poor succeed. Rather than so commonly focusing on out-of-school factors which tend to have little to do with family functioning, we should, instead, focus on those factors which have a lot to do with school success, however politically delicate or otherwise difficult the undertaking. For, Tough argues that "the biggest obstacles to academic success that poor children, especially very poor children," face is "a home and a community that create high levels of stress, and the absence of a secure relationship with a caregiver that would allow a child to manage that stress" (258a:194-95).

To recap, Tough's position is based on the finding of the new generation of neuroscientists (which he sees as their most profound finding) regarding the infant's hypothalamic-pituitary-adrenal axis (258a:181-85). ***Their finding is that, if during infancy (roughly through age 3) the chemical interactions involved in the infant's*** *hypothalamic-pituitary-adrenal axis function well, the infant is likely to acquire those character skills which are more decisive than IQ in determining school and life success, such as conscientiousness, grit, resilience, perseverance, and optimism.* How do we get these chemical interactions to function well? Neuroscientists say: provide the infant security and nurturing (or love). As Erik Erikson might put it: provide the infant a "hallowed presence." Provide the infant a "hallowed presence" and the infant grows to become successful in school and in life because the infant's brain chemistry (specifically, the hypothalamic-pituitary-adrenal axis) will function well, as a result of which the infant -- due to his or her well-functioning brain chemistry -- is likely, naturally (in the process of daily living), to develop the character skills on which the infant's school and life success decisively depend.

Tough's position gives us another mnemonic, **infancy**. The recommendation herein is that we **practice the art of loving**, and Tough makes a compelling case for adding **infancy** to it, thereby emphasizing the imperative to engage in the practice during a child's infancy, a time when its practice will stimulate the child's brain to function in a way that will foster the development of success-required character traits. Our expanded mnemonic thus become: **practice of the art of loving (infancy).** Later, we will expand it further to include **black males** and **career**. The completed mnemonic which directs attention to the recommended solution to AMSAC and it inseparable social problem: **practice of the art of loving: infancy - black male - career and character**.

Verdict

These home-focused proponents are not necessarily saying that the schools are doing a fine job and do not need to be improved; for the most part, just the opposite. The fact is that to fare well, it appears that our students typically need above-average schools. However, given the theory of normal distribution, it is going to be difficult to get such schools on a scale commensurate with the problem. Nevertheless, the attempt has to be conscientiously pursued, but with the understanding that we must do our utmost to optimize that which the attempt yields, which could fall short of what is needed or expected. The implied imperative is a two-party approach: both parties, school and home, must do their best, rather than one putting responsibility on or blaming the other. Perhaps neither can be expected to be above average, and we cannot continue to afford for either to be below average.

It is not a matter of "constructing a narrative," as Loury is said to have depicted it, but of accepting the reality that we have done a lot of barking up a lot of school trees with -- the evidence indicates -- little more to show for it than the predominantly black (over 70%) school district of Kansas City or the Willie Brown Academy has been able to show. By one count, in 2004, we had already spent $9 trillion on the War on Poverty, with some counterproductive results, which is Charles Murray's thesis in <u>Losing Ground</u> (479). When it comes to closing the black-white academic gap, the prey seems as elusive as ever. Former New York City mayor, Michael Bloomberg, and his former schools chancellor, Joel I. Klein, for example, thought they had found the answer through centralization and concomitant curriculum and other school changes, only to discover that the earlier gains they touted evaporated, leading to the <u>New York Times</u> headline, dated August 16, 2010, "Triumph Fades on Racial Gap in City Schools" (429). Some five years later, on August 12, 2015, a news website headline about the City Schools told the same story; it read, "Racial Gap Persists as School Test Scores Edge Up" (480a).

4

The Crisis as an Outgrowth of Our Two Adaptation Traditions: Washington Versus Dubois In Our African American Garden of Eden

Proverbs, 16:22 - "Understanding is a wellspring of life unto him that hath it: but the instruction of fools is folly."
Galatians, 6:5 - "For every man shall bear his own burden."

The maladaptive behavior which the African American Male Career Pathway Program (AMCAP) addresses is deeply rooted in a fundamental fissure which spans our history as free black Americans. This chapter addresses that fissure. It does so with the understandilng that history is a discipline whose subject matter lends itself to understanding and interpretation by those willing and able to use its tools. It is also a discipline whose understanding and interpretation may be enhanced by having "*stepped* within the Veil," as DuBois reveals he did in writing his classic, <u>The Souls of Black Folk</u> [emphasis added]. In some ways, to have "*lived*" within it, as applicable to this author, is more enhancing. So, what DuBois says of himself applies to the words written on these pages, "I who speak here am bone of the bone and flesh of the flesh" (60:3-4). So speaking, and so drawing upon historians and upon the tools of their trade, as it were, the alluded to fundamental fissure is herein described as the **Self-Responsibility Tradition** versus the **System-Responsibility Tradition**.

Booker Taliaferro Washington (1856-1915) is viewed as the father of the Self-Responsibility Tradition, William Edward Burghardt DuBois (1868-1963) as the father of the System-Responsibility Tradition. They are the most prominent and famous symbols of each tradition, as well as its most influential representative, yet, lest it be misunderstood, neither was its initiator; both were the product of their time, reflecting prevalent and previous modes of thought (see especially, Meier, 168: Chapters III and VI). Under their then and now famous names, however, they popularized and propagated that thought.

This interpretation is based on the late Kent State University historian August Meier's classic, <u>Negro Thought in America, 1880-1915: Racial Ideologies in the Age of Booker T. Washington</u>. Meier's acclaimed account of social thought during the period has led historian, Robert Norrell, to assert that he "mastered the sources of black thought in the age of Booker Washington more completely than any other historian, black or white" (192:434). Meier saw a dichotomy in black thought during this period (168:161-189). It was conservatives versus radicals, that is:

- accommodation vs. agitation
- self-help, racial pride, and solidarity vs. assimilation and integration
- moral and economic improvement vs. agitation, political action, and civil rights
- laissez-faire individualism vs. economic radicalism (for example, interracial trade unionism and socialism)

Washington came to be the voice of the conservative faction (the **Self-Responsibility Tradition**), DuBois the voice of the radical faction (the **System-Responsibility Tradition**).

Joe L. Rempson

In the Beginning:
Our African American Garden of Eden

That to Washington and DuBois can be traced the fissure might be better grasped if viewed allegorically, in this case, in a biblical context. In the Garden of Eden, Adam and Eve had instructions, which, disobeyed, has left us in a state of sin -- goes Christian thinking (Genesis: 2-3). Upon emancipation, we African Americans were in our Garden of Eden, so to speak -- not "so pleasant to the sight," to be sure – but, nevertheless, our beginning as free Americans. Ours, however, is an adaptation story versus a creation story. This is how that story can be imagined.

> **Somewhat like Adam and Eve in the Garden of Eden, we African Americans began our life of freedom in our own African American Garden of Eden. In its midst were planted trees which were good for foundation-building: a tree of brains, a tree of property, and a tree of character. Also in its midst was planted a tree that was good for acquiring equality: a tree of civil rights. From among us in the garden arose a leader, Booker Taliaferro Washington, and an aspiring leader, William Edward Burghardt DuBois. So that we would surely prosper, Washington, a self-help apostle, commanded us to eat freely from the *foundation* trees, but not from the *equality tree* of civil rights. Although he himself ate from it, he did so mostly secretly and seductively, fearing that, otherwise, Southern fury would provoke further turmoil and derail our progress. While the equality tree was the most alluring among the trees, Washington felt that we were unready to eat from it, as the enchanting and blinding powers of its fruits would cause us to fix our hunger on it, and surely to suffer due to neglect of the other less attractive, but *foundation trees*. He acknowledged the value of "sane agitation and criticism," which the civil rights tree triggered, "but not to the extent of having our race feel that we can depend upon this to cure all the evils surrounding us." At first, BuBois more or less echoed our great leader. But after a time, he himself came to eat freely from the forbidden civil rights tree, and to declare that if we did not do the same, we would never prosper, it being futile for Washington to urge us to eat freely of the foundation trees but not from the most important one among them, the *equality***

tree of civil rights. "Mr. Washington's programme," BuBois proclaimed, "practically accepts the alleged inferiority of the Negro races." During his lifetime, Washington was heeded, but upon his death, DuBois, a civil rights apostle, took his place in the garden, and it was his command which came to be heeded. Years later, Martin Luther King Jr. led the successful movement to secure the civil rights so paramount to DuBois. At the same time, as an admirer of Washington, King tried to renew the self-help legacy so paramount to Washington, shackled, he failed, and his attempt goes unrecognized. That is the story of the origin of our continued suffering as a free people: the fruits of the alluring, but forbidden, *equality tree* of civil rights, with its enchanting and blinding powers, came to be too freely eaten, leading -- as Washington warned – to the neglect, by our leaders, of the *foundation trees* of brain, property, and character, the result of which is a *civil-rights fixation* and a failure to confront our three major demons: *IQ lag-fatherless families-crime*. From that *civil-rights fixation* and failure, Victimology has emerged as our second bondage. Our first bondage, slavery, bounded us physically; its replacement, Victimology, binds us psychologically. Victimology inhibits and vitiates our manhood and, thus, produces fathers without children and family dysfunction. As a result, many of our children grow up in unstable homes, prevented thereby from acquiring a positive core identity, which they must possess if they are to forge the sound character on which school and life success depends. That they – and their family members – do not possess sound character lies at the root of AMSAC and its inseparable social problems. Thus is the price we pay for our *sin*.

But it is not a sin without grace. We must do what Christians believe must be done: repent and atone. As in the biblical story, we cannot recreate our Garden of Eden, but, like DuBois in his fading years, nothing prevents us from seeing and acknowledging that our great leader in the Garden "believed that we should get what we could get." So seeing and acknowledging, maybe, in repentance and atonement, we can make Washington a kind of Prodigal Son, cast out by us but welcomed back because it is *we* who have been lost (due to DuBois,

Woodard, Harlan, and the Civil Rights radicals) but now we are found. Through understanding, being founding is possible, understanding being something which this chapter is intended to promote.

A National Perspective and an Introductory Snapshot

We African Americans have had four national leaders (241: 31-34). They were: *Frederick Douglas (1865-95), Booker T. Washington (1880-1915), W. E. B. DuBois* (1915-34, when he resigned from the NAACP), and *Dr. Martin Luther King Jr.* (1954-68). Of abolitionist fame, upon emancipation, Douglass, though an advocate of industrial education, gave emphasis to civil rights. DuBois did likewise. Dr. King, too, stands out for his emphasis on civil rights, but, although not commonly recognized, he also emphasized self-help. Washington, on the other hand, stands out for his emphasis on self-help, but unrecognized in his case, he also emphasized civil rights.

Of the four, it can be said that Washington and DuBois, the rivals in our African American Garden of Eden, were the two who exerted the most powerful formative influence. We can think of all four, however, as our Adaptation Fathers, much in the same way as we think of the founders of our nation as our Founding Fathers. Our Founding Fathers gave us the Declaration of Independence and the Constitution, setting this new nation on a course that has led us to become the preeminent country in the world. Similarly -- to focus on our two most powerful formative leaders -- Washington gave us the Atlanta Compromise Address and Tuskegee Institute, along with the Washington gospel of brains, property, and character; and DuBois gave us The Souls of Black Folk, and, in part, the National Association for the Advancement of Colored People (NAACP), along with the gospel that the "burden belongs to the nation." At issue is where what each gave us has led us.

Division and differences marked both the founding of our nation and the adaptation of our people. However, the fathers of our nation's founding were able to compromise and overcome their differences. Not so of our African American Adaptation Fathers. As was later to be the case with our nation, our Adaptation Fathers early on – in our African American Garden of Eden -- got involved in a North versus South war, the relatively free and urban North versus the newly freed and agricultural

South. The war can be viewed as the interests of the middle-class versus the needs of the masses. DuBois spoke for the former, Washington for the latter. It was like the Civil War being replayed, however, this time not over slavery, but rather between ex-slaves over our adaptation. During his lifetime, Washington prevailed, but without having ever reached the kind of compromise with DuBois and his New England opposition which the Founding Fathers of our nation had been able to reach. They produced the Declaration of Independence and the Constitution. But Washington and DuBois, together, never produced a single document or message, at least none which DuBois honored. Instead, from them, we inherit two very different documents and two very different messages.

Washington: establishing Tuskegee

Until his death in 1915, Washington's Self-Responsibility Tradition, though challenged by DuBois, almost exclusively dominated African American life. From roughly 1880 until his death in 1915, he was "the central figure -- the dominant personality -- in the history of African Americans," leading black historians John Hope Franklin (Duke University professor emeritus) and Alfred A. Moss, Jr. (University of Maryland associate professor), to call those years, as others have, the Age of Booker T. Washington (92: 306).

Tuskegee Normal and Industrial Institute (commonly simply referred to as Tuskegee Institute and now renamed Tuskegee University) stands as the most preeminent symbol of his Age. Now designated a National Historic Site, the only black college so designated, it is ranked as the top black college in Alabama, and the sixth best black college nationally. It owes its origin to Lewis Adams, an ex-slave and a leader in Macon County, who, in return for delivering black votes to Wilbur F. Foster (a white Democrat and an ex-Confederate colonel who was seeking reelection to the state senate) asked for legislation to establish a school for blacks in the county. Foster won and delivered, securing the passage of legislation providing $2,000 annually to pay for teacher salaries in the county -- and nothing more; other resources were to be provided by the county. This accomplishment, incidentally, won Foster the reputation of being a "nigger lover" and ruined his political career (234:2).

To establish and administer the school, Adams and the other two members of the board chose, upon recommendation of General Samuel C. Armstrong, young, untested, twenty-five-year-old Booker T. Washington. Six years earlier, in 1875, Washington had

OUR AFRICAN AMERICAN GARDEN OF EDEN RIVALS

Figure 4. Booker T. Washington, 1908; courtesy of the Library of Congress.

Figure 5. W. E.B. DuBois, 1909; courtesy of the Department of Special Collections and University Archives, W.E.B. Du Bois Library, University of Massachusetts Amherst.

graduated from Hampton Institute, which had been founded by Armstrong, who was also its principal. Washington had greatly impressed Armstrong, a Civil War veteran from the Union Army and member of a missionary family, and Armstrong, in turn, had made an imprint on Washington. The result: a principalship for Washington and, as it turned out, a normal school established by Washington fashioned after the industrial education of Armstrong's Hampton Institute and, beyond that, a life acknowledged to have been lived in accordance with many of Armstrong's principles.

At the time, however, Washington had a principalship in name only. Or, more accurately, it was a principalship of $2,000, the amount of his salary. The $2,000 was allocated for teacher salaries, but Washington was the only teacher. There were no buildings or supplies or students. Through a month of foot travel and recruiting throughout the county, Washington was able to open the school on July 4, 1881, with thirty students in a broken-down shanty, part of a nearby Methodist Church. "Whenever it rained, one of the older students would very kindly leave his lessons and hold an umbrella over me while I heard the recitations of the others," reveals Washington in his classic autobiography, <u>Up from Slavery</u> (265:273).

Twenty years later, he goes on to recall in <u>Up from Slavey</u>, from this beginning, he had built Tuskegee into an institution with the following: 2,300 acres of land, 700 used for cultivation with student labor; 40 large and small buildings, all but four erected by students -- and most multistoried built from red bricks *manufactured on the campus*; 28 industrial departments; 1,100 students from twenty-seven states and territories, as well as from Africa, Cuba, Puerto Rico, Jamaica, and other countries; and 86 officers and instructors (265:381-82). The expansion continued beyond those twenty years. Before Washington's death in 1915, annual enrollment had grown to around 1,500, surpassing that of nearly *all* other Southern higher education institutions, Norrell tells us. With some 10 new buildings being added, the campus became, in Norrell's words, "an architectural showplace" (192:197). Its endowment reached over a million dollars (192:9).

Not only is the Tuskegee accomplishment the preeminent symbol of the Age of Booker T. Washington, it logically and simultaneously stands also as the signature of Washington's Self-Responsibility Tradition -- and by deliberate intent, not by chance. In describing Washington's use of students to construct most of the campus buildings, Norrell tells us why:

> He was not just training teachers but enabling those men and women to replicate what they were now doing--to build their own schools. The Institute construction experience would be as valuable as their academic work. And building the school themselves would make Tuskegee Institute an exclusively African-American achievement. It would prove to blacks that they could accomplish a large, complex task, and would demonstrate to whites that blacks were capable of running a large enterprise without white help or interference. Almost all other black institutions of higher education had been built and run by whites--including Booker's model, Hampton Institute. Tuskegee would be different (192: 61-62).

And it was not just that we blacks ourselves constructed the buildings, but -- as Norrell's passage implies -- we ran the school. Black Florida A&M University historian, David Jackson Jr., points out that "At a time when most black colleges were still run by white missionaries, Tuskegee had an all-black faculty and virtually an all-black student body," adding, "... some of the leading black scholars in the country wound up teaching at Tuskegee." "Washington," he reveals, "boasted that Tuskegee employed the largest number of black college graduates in the country" (132:2).

What Washington had in mind for Tuskegee he had in mind for all his race. Through the Tuskegee model, he envisioned what might be termed a self-made race. That would be made possible through the establishment of "Little Tuksegees" throughout the South, set up and run by teacher corps which would help to lay the foundation for blacks in American life.

DuBois: establishing the NAACP

Upon Washington's death, the nascent System-Responsibility Tradition of DuBois gained ascendancy (92:395-97, 465-66). That ascendancy was led, however, not by DuBois, who never became a leader of the masses, but by the National Association for the Advancement of Colored People ((NAACP), which had been formally started in 1910. Though not its official leader, DuBois might be said to have been its intellectual and ideological leader, thanks to the <u>Crisis</u>. Historian and sociologist, he was the first African American to get a doctorate from Harvard (1895), and his research, writing skill, and activism earned him a national standing. That standing got translated into his being elected to the Board of Directors of the new organization, its only black member; and it earned him appointment as the organization's Director of Research and Publicity. In the latter position, he created and became editor of its official monthly publication, the <u>Crisis</u>. The <u>Crisis</u> gained wide circulation and made DuBois an influential national intellectual leader. By about 1920, some five years after Washington's death, thanks to the NAACP and DuBois's <u>Crisis</u>, the System-Responsibility Tradition had taken center stage and Washington's Self-Responsibility Tradition had receded into the background.

Joe L. Rempson

The Instructions and Anointment:
Washington's Atlanta Compromise Address of 1895

The Self-Responsibility Tradition of Washington, and the broad framework of his commandment (to stick to the Garden of Eden analogy), are memorialized in his famous -- and today infamous and grossly unheralded -- Atlanta Compromise Address in 1895 (see Appendix A). Norrell gives an excellent historical account of the address, as does Harlan, the pertinent factual details of which are relied upon in the interpretation and casting given it herein (192:115-35; 108:204-32). The address is also variously called the Atlanta Exposition Speech, the Atlanta Exposition Address, the Atlanta Compromise Speech, the Compromise of 1895, and the Tuskegee Compromise. It can be viewed as the "Gettysburg Address of *African* American History," deserving of as much attention, study, and reverence, especially by us African Americans, as Lincoln's famous address.[13]

Like the Gettysburg Address, it can be argued that, combined with the relevant record, it gives its author a hallowed place in our nation's history -- a place that makes him, too, deserving of a national holiday. While Lincoln fought to keep the union united, Washington fought to unite the races. In any era, his in particular, this was a forbidding and formidable undertaking, but as Norrell observes, "In Washington's view, his life was not just a struggle up from slavery but also a great effort to rise above history" (192:16). Washington's germinal effort, and its imprint, gives him Lincoln-like standing. His Atlanta Compromise Address symbolizes that effort and its intrinsic focus, not just on black foundation-building, but, equally, on nation foundation-building. Of course, we blacks lobbied to create *our* national holiday, not, of course, for Washington, but for Dr. King. His deeds and popularity made Dr. King an understandable choice, but Washington presents an equally, and arguably even more, compelling choice.

Although Washington's Address marked a watershed moment in our history, one hardly sees it in the literature or being posted. The "Father of Black History," the late Howard University historian Carter G.

---

[13] Source for Gettysburg Address data: http://en.wikipedia.org/wiki/Gettysburg_Address Retrieved on 26 November 2014.

Woodson, for example, gives it only brief mention in his The Negro in Our History (1922), and neither of two of our notable self-histories contain it or give it much attention, the aforementioned late Howard University sociologist E. Franklin Frazier's The Negro in the United States and Franklin and Moss's From Slavery to Freedom. The most recent self-history examined, black Harvard University historian Henry Louis Gates Jr.'s Life Upon These Shores: Looking at African American History, 1513-2008, represents a refreshing departure. Gates devotes practically one and one-half pags to it, with pictures, detailing its content and giving credit to its place in black history (99a:201-02). He says this about the address: "Washington's speech that day not only defined the rest of his career but helped shape the very direction of African American history for decades to come" -- and it can be added: including the present one.

Washington's address embodies one of the great compromises in American history – and maybe in all history -- providing a formula for relative racial peace during a time of severe racial strife. Its acceptance puts Washington in the company of the likes of our Founding Fathers and Henry Clay. Think, too, for a moment: in one address, Washington laid out an accepted framework for racial peace which, in South Africa for example, required a mandated Truth and Reconciliation Commission that had to undertake years of work (471). While not exactly comparable, the two situations bear similarities. That Washington's compromise was spelled out in one of the great addresses in American history only enhances its stature.

To continue its equation with the Gettysburg Address, relatively speaking, it has the brevity and beauty of that address, was delivered on a decisive historical battlefield, laid out what was at stake, saw a new era in the making, and exhorted a divided people to dedicate themselves to the unfinished task of ensuring liberty and equality. As with Lincoln's address, Washington's address distills the element of struggle and the spirit which drove it. Both addresses seize on a moment in time and, within it, give meaning to the struggle at hand, define its spirit, and capture the engulfing issues that were the driving and entangling forces at a watershed juncture in the destiny of their people. Both addresses remain as relevant today as then, even -- due to the African American Male School Adaptability Crisis and its inseparable social problems -- more so in the case of Washington's address. A fundamental difference is that, at the time, Lincoln did not have to chart a course for the future; Washington did.

Having been previously prohibited from participation with whites in Southern events, we got our chance in 1895. It was during the same year that our leader, Frederick Douglass, died and we were left with a leadership void. It was at a time when the black condition in the South was deteriorating, as the few rights we had were being eroded. We were at a crossroads and the Exposition provided us an opportunity to be heard. Washington was invited by the Exposition planners to be our voice, and when he stepped onto the stage of the Exposition, he was indeed stepping onto a battlefield of sorts. His very presence, as a black man, reflected the battle being waged between the Southern forces of oppression and disintegration and those on the side of survival and uplifting. No less than Lincoln, Washington was cognizant of the historic nature of the moment – for the first time, a black man being given a symbolic seat by Southern whites at their table (something which some felt that not even the North had done). He seized moment to steer our course. In the fashion of Lincoln, he can be interpreted as holding that the outcome would determine if, for us blacks, the Civil War and the freedom that it brought was "in vain" or whether our people in the South would "have a new birth of freedom." How that outcome would be achieved was in Washington's hands, as it had been in Lincoln's hand.

And like the Gettysburg Address and other great speeches or documents, Washington's address has its historic line. Few, if any, have gone through our schools (although one never knows about the schools of today) who are not familiar with the line, "Four scores and seven years ago our fathers brought forth on this continent, a new nation, conceived in Liberty …." The same can probably be said, for example, of, "We hold these truth to be self-evident, that all men are created equal, that …," or "We have nothing to fear but fear itself …," or perhaps, "I have a dream that my four little children will one day…." But how about, "In all things purely social we can be as separate as the fingers, yet one as the hand in all things essential to mutual progress?" Given the demonization of Washington, his historic line is probably not as recognizable, yet this famous line from his address, in its inspiration and impact, can be said to be of equal rank with any of these, including the above quoted line from the famous address under discussion, "Four scores and seven years ago...."

The speech was thunderously received and won Washington instant national fame (anointment, as it were). In fact it may well rank as one of the most electrifying speeches in American history, if not world history. Harlan and Norrell provide us a sense of the moment (108 :216-22; 192:123-28). Harlan says that Washington had worked hard on the speech, getting feedback from his wife, Margaret, and, on the day before its delivery, he reading it to his Tuskegee faculty for its input. Escorted from his hotel in a procession of carriages occupied by black dignitaries, he made his way to the overflowing Exposition grounds and eventually marched onto the stage, evoking a cessation of applause by the whites in the auditorium, who started asking what a nigger was doing on the stage. After a number of preceding speeches, they found out. In "quiet but perfectly distinct tones," Harlan recounts, Washington began his delivery and, "Whatever his inner turmoil, his outward manner was easy and natural, with nothing of either timidity or bravado" (108:217). Harlan's description elsewhere continues:

> Washington' voice rang out loud and clear, and it had a remarkable range of tone as he moved from humorous story to admonition to lofty sentiment, and paused impressively as he made a point. 'Within ten minutes the multitude was in an uproar of enthusiasm, handkerchiefs were waved, canes were flourished, hats were tossed in the air. The fairest women of Georgia stood and cheered. It was as if the orator had bewitched them' (108:219).

In part Harlan is here quoting a reporter who was there, James Greelman. Harlan goes on to say, "Greelman had heard great orators in many countries, but not even Gladstone [Gladstone (William), being the British leader famous both as statesman and orator] could have pleaded a cause more powerfully than 'this angular negro standing in a nimbus of sunshine surrounded by the men who once fought to keep his race in bondage'" (108: 220; also see 363a). Harlan writes that a scientist who was there representing the Smithsonian Institution, W. J. McGee, later recalled, "'By and by there was more applause and louder, extending amongst the audience, and when the Negro finished such an ovation followed as I had never seen before and never expect to see again'" (108: 216-17; 402b). (Apparently, Booker T. Washington had his "I Have a Dream" Speech, too.)

Our new leader to replace Frederick Douglass thus emerged, and with his address our Self-Responsibility Tradition had been enshrined undet the rubric, The Age of Booker T. Washington. To bridge the racial divide, Washington invoked the strategies of accommodation and de-politicization. "In all things that are purely social," he declared to his white audience, "we can be as separate as the fingers, yet one as the hand in all things essential to mutual progress." Indeed, he proclaimed, any agitation for social equality was folly, observing that any privileges which we were to enjoy must be achieved through "severe and [constant] struggle, rather than *artificial forcing* [emphasis added]...." And while asserting that we were due all of the privileges of the law, he emphasized that it was "vastly more important that we be prepared for the exercise of these privileges."

To us, his own race, he urged further, "Cast down your bucket where you are" -- "in agriculture, in mechanics, in commerce, in domestic service and in the professions." In other words, rather than looking for some enticing escape from the burdens of the past, dig in and exert the effort and hard work required to take advantage of the opportunity at hand. If, for example, it is tilling the soil, then till the soil. For, he declared, "No race can prosper till it learns that there is as much dignity in tilling a field as in writing a poem." Nor, he further declared, were we to forget that "It is at the bottom of life we must begin and not the top." And should we harbor grievances, he counseled that we should not "permit our grievances to overshadow our opportunities."

He said something else of historic significance which, insofar as known, never gets attention. It was this: *"There is no defense or security for any of us except in the highest intelligence and development of all. If anywhere there are efforts tending to curtail the fullest growth of the Negro, let these efforts be turned into stimulating, encouraging and making him the most useful and intelligent citizen."* Hardly is this declaration one of surrender or subservience, as DuBois would have us believe about the Washington way. Rather, as discussed in Chapter 17, this declaration could even have been used to provide the spirit for our Civil Rights Movement. There, in the maligned Atlanta Compromise, was planted the roots to black civil rights, secretly and seductively nourished by Washington – and even publicly nourished by hm during his last three years -- but left fallow by his race.

Washington had spoken for our people -- issued his commandments -- and provided what was immediately accepted by blacks and whites alike as the blueprint for our adaptation. Not until 1901, Norrell explains, was there any noticeable black opposition. As discussed below, then William Trotter went on the attack, to be soon eclipsed by master nemesis, DuBois, surrounded by a small group of educated black New Englanders (192:6-7). To maintain his dominant position in our imaginary Garden of Eden, DuBois's rise forced Washington into action. The Washington-DuBois war followed, the seeds having been sown by Washington's Atlanta Compromise of 1895. As a reminder of this imaginary beginning, this is our mnemonic: **Washington's Atlanta Compromise of 1895: our African American Garden of Eden**.

The groundwork which made possible Washington's invitation to speak at the Atlanta Exposition had been laid by his founding of Tuskegee Institute in 1881 and his success in making it a premier institution. The fame brought by his speech and success was immensely enhanced with the publication of his classic, Up from Slavery in 1901. Though not having the *enduring* influence of The Souls of Black, the comparable notable work of his arch foe, DuBois's Folk, Washington's Up from Slavery has had a profound and prolonged influence, and continues to have a valued place in American and, in particular, African American life (see for example, Harlan, 109: 130-31; and Norrell, 192: 216-24). Unlike The Souls of Black Folk, it does not, however, make literary writer and academic Jay Parini's list of the thirteen books that changed America, but it is on his one hundred list. Of its influence, he writes, "Washington supports the idea that African Americans must make their own way, by themselves, not asking for help from white society" (206:358). That characterization somewhat misrepresents Washington's views, for whereas he preached self-help and preparation, he, likewise, saw our relationship with whites being "one as the hand in all things essential to mutual progress." That is hardly the same as making our own way "by themselves."

Yet, Parini has underlined the essential thesis of <u>Up from Slavery</u>: self-help and preparation (113a). Further, whereas it does not fall among Parini's 13, nevertheless, on the Modern Library Board's list of the "100 Best Nonfiction" books of the 20th century, it ranks #3; <u>The Souls of Black Folk</u> #31. Neither, however, makes the comparable Reader's list of the 100 Best Nonfiction books. <u>The Autobiography of Malcom X</u> does, which perhaps says a lot about the racial passions of our time. It is noteworthy being noteworthy that, until Malcom's autobiography, it was Washington's <u>Up from Slavery</u> which, from the outset, had been, and remained, the most popular African American autobiography (471t).

The Disobediance and Declaration:
DuBois's <u>The Souls of Black Folk</u> (1903)

As the Self-Responsibility Tradition of Washington is memorialized in his Atlanta Compromise Address, DuBois's System-Responsibility Tradition -- and the disobedience which it embodies -- is memorialized in his 1903 classic, <u>The Souls of Black Folk</u> (64). Parini includes it among the thirteen books which, in his assessment, changed America. The thirteen were chosen from among an exhaustive list of possibilities which Parini assembled. "By books that 'changed America,'" he says, "I mean works that helped to create the intellectual and emotional contours of this country." "Each," he goes on to say, "played a pivotal role in developing a complex value system that flourishes to this day" (206:2). On <u>The Souls of Black Folk</u>, he offers this assessment:

> More than a hundred years after its first appearance at the turn of the twentieth century, this book--a medley of essays and meditations on the meaning of race in America--has become a touchstone, offering a road map for those who wish to travel to freedom (206:185).

In its chapter, **"Of Mr. Booker T. Washington and Others,"** DuBois made his public break with Washington, painting him both politically and educationally as selling out the race and relegating us to an inferior, caste-like status (64:35-47). This portrayal, Norrell points out, was reinforced in his 1940 memoir <u>Dusk of Dawn</u>, published after Washington's death (192:425-26). The break demonized Washington and marked the disobedience in our imaginary African American

Garden of Eden, wherein DuBois partook of the forbidden, though alluring civil rights tree, as a result fathering our system-help tradition and its civil-rights fixation, which in turn has led to our second bondage, Victimology. To remind us of DuBois's disobedience and its consequences, our mnemonic is his classic, **The Souls of Black Folk**.

DuBois begins with a historical observation, declaring, "Easily the most striking thing in the history of the American Negro since 1876 is the ascendancy of Mr. Booker T. Washington." The very tone of DuBois's declaration suggests that there was something unsavory about Washington's ascendancy. He goes on to credit Washington's agenda as having won over the South and North alike, adding, "… and after a confused murmur of protest, it silenced if it did not convert the Negroes themselves." The implication is that blacks went along with Washington, though not necessarily subscribing to his views. Then, he turns to qualified praise. For example, DuBois:

- describes Washington as "the most distinguished Southerner since Jefferson Davis, and the one with the largest personal following" while implying that it was at the price of the "Atlanta Compromise" and, most important, notes Norrell, "The comparison to Davis was a not-so-sly jab: Du Bois had earlier called the Confederate president a morally obtuse Teutonic character" (192: 277);
- says that "he intuitively grasped the spirit of his age" while implying that his grasp was possible because he was a man possessed of the kind of "narrow" vision which makes it possible for one to fit in, so to speaks; and
- while proclaiming that "Mr. Washington's *cult* [emphasis added] has gained *unquestioning* [emphasis added] followers, his work has wonderfully prospered, his friends are legion, and his enemies are confounded," he goes on to declare the necessity of speaking "of the mistakes and shortcomings of Mr. Washington's career."

For the rest of his essay, the gloves were mainly off, except to interject:

> It would be unjust to Mr. Washington not to acknowledge that in several instances he has opposed movements in the South which

were unjust to the Negro; he sent memorials to the Louisiana and Alabama constitutional conventions, he has spoken against lynching, and in other ways has openly or silently set his influence against sinister schemes and unfortunate happenings (64: 46).

In DuBois'a mind such instances were overshadowed, however, by Washington's "mistakes and shortcomings." Declaring that Washington "represents in Negro thought the old attitude of adjustment and submission," he spells out those mistakes and shortcomings (64):

1. Washington is so concerned about our economic wellbeing, preaching the "gospel of Work and Money," that his emphasis "apparently almost completely ... overshadow[s] the higher aims of life" (p. 41)
2. At a time when prejudice against our race has intensified, calling therefore for the traditional Negro tendency to react self-assertively, Washington advocates submission, something that other races and people have not done since "manly self-respect is worth more than lands and houses" (p. 41)
3. Washington's "propaganda," though not having caused, has accelerated Negro disfranchisement, legal inferiority, and diminished support for institutions of higher training of the Negro (p. 42).
4. Without the right to vote, workingmen and property owners, whom Washington was urging our people to become, could not "defend their rights and exist." (p. 42)
5. Although our voting, civic, and educational rights could not be expected to come immediately, the way to gain them "is not by voluntarily throwing them away and insisting that [we] do not want them; that the way for a people to gain respect is not by continually belittling and ridiculing themselves." (p. 44)
6. While Washington teaches thrift and self-respect, his counsel of submission, by its very nature, undermines those manly attributes (p. 46).
7. Washington advocates common schools and industrial education but opposes higher training institutions to provide qualified teachers for them, his position, he implies in another chapter ["Of the Training of Black Men"], consigning the Negro in the South to life "as an ignorant, turbulent proletariat" (p. 78).

8. The feeling privately expressed by some in the North, such as himself it must be noted, was that "Mr. Washington's counsels of submission overlooked certain elements of true manhood, and that his educational programme was unnecessarily narrow"(p. 37)
9. Washington's position that we must uplift ourselves primarily through our own efforts leads whites to place the burden on us and avoid any responsibility themselves "when in fact the burden belongs to the nation," without whose help and encouragement we could not "hope for great success" (p. 46) [This position has come to be expressed as not letting the system "off the hook."]

Later, DuBois concludes by declaring, a la our Declaration of Independence, *his* Declaration of Independence. That, in fact, is what his The Souls of Black Folk amounts to: *his* Declaration of Independence from Washington. As with the Founding Fathers, who with our Declaration of Independence broke from their own, England, so with The Souls of Black Folk, did DuBois break from his own, the Age of Booker T. Washington of which, more or less, he had been an inseparable part. Intended or not, in style and substance, his closing makes that comparison unmistakable.

- He speaks of "the black men of America" of having a "duty stern and delicate" to oppose Washington.
- He declares that so long as Washington "preaches Thrift, Patience, and Industrial Training for the masses," that is, pursues these "self-evident" worthy goals, then we must support him, "rejoicing in his honors and glorifying in the strength of this Joshua called of God and of man to lead the headless host."
- On the other hand, he stipulates that insofar as Washington engages in behavior destructive of our inalienable rights -- "apologizes for injustice, North or South, does not rightly value the privilege and duty of voting, belittles the emasculating effects of caste distinctions, and opposes the higher training and ambition of our brighter minds" -- he must be "unceasingly and firmly" opposed.
- Then, using language from the Declaration of Independence, he makes his declaration:

"By every civilized and peaceful method we must strive for the rights which the world accords to men, clinging unwaveringly to those great words which the sons of the Fathers would fain forget: 'We hold these truths to be self-evident: That all men are created equal, that they are endowed by their Creator with certain unalienable rights; that among these are life, liberty, and the pursuit of happiness'" (64:47).

The battle lines are evident, and, thereafter, observes Samuel R. Spencer Jr., DuBois became less restrained, contesting Washington on almost every issue (244:151).[14] But to be sure, though perhaps more restrained, in his Declaration (<u>The Souls of Black Folk</u>) -- and even before -- he had already begun that departure. For example, as Norrell notes, in 1900, three years earlier, racial nationalism began to emerge in his work. "After 1900," Norrell says, "the main expression of, and motivation for, his racial nationalism became his opposition to Washington's racial leadership" (192:232). We will examine the beginning phase, after which we will turn more broadly to Spencer's point that DuBois became less restrained.

Taking issue with Washington his Declaration (<u>The Souls of Black Folk</u>)

That Spencer refers to DuBois's tone in his Declaration as more restrained than in his later writings only underlines the vile and vitriolic nature of his later attack, for there was nothing meek about his tone in this initial thrust. He not only breaks with Washington, he demonizes him, depicting him as silencing his race and representing "in Negro thought the old attitude of adjustment and submission." What must be understood is that, at the time, this was a radical reading of Washington. Washington was part of, and leader of, the black mainstream, a point repeatedly made by Meier. In Meier's words, "It cannot be overemphasized that Washington's philosophy represents in large measure the basic tendencies of Negro thought in the period under consideration" (168:102). That mainstream thinking includes the thinking of DuBois's Talented Tenth, the group from which the

---

[14] The late President of Davidson College, Spencer wrote a biography of Washington, the details appearing in the References.

"radicals" drew most of their support; they (the radicals), too, while inconsistent, tended -- says Meier -- to embrace Washington's ideas over those of DuBois. While there appears initially to have been scattered opposition to Washington, that opposition seems to have soon disappeared. The "new attitude" of which DuBois speaks appears to have been more a product of his desire, and that of a small group of his black New England activists, than a reflection of a new reality.

Therefore, however valid Du Bois's condemnations, he was representing a tiny minority. It was a minority that, in the interest of its own middle-class oriented agenda, was seeking to wrest from leadership and power from Washington. It is not as if Washington had devised some alien strategy whose pursuit was commonly deemed tantamount to surrender and submission. Rather, Meier tells us that it was a strategy that most endorsed and whose pursuit most thought would ultimately yield black integration into American society. It was only DuBois and his few fellow radicals who thought otherwise. Yet, DuBois would have us think -- and has succeeded in having most of us think -- that Washington's agenda represented betrayal and was opposed by his own people, among whom, though confused and silent according to DuBois, he had "encountered the strongest and most lasting opposition" (64:36-38).

The image painted by DuBois is that of Washington on a course to ruin the race -- "insisting," as he painted it, on throwing away our voting, civic, and educational rights -- while DuBois pictures himself as coming to the rescue, of course, creating his own calling rather than responding to the will of the people; the people, after all, supported Washington. Though he and others were justified in responding to their own intellect and conscience, such justification is not to be confused with responding to some external cry for racial rescue. Back then, to most, Washington was doing just that, rescuing the race; DuBois was the renegade, himself seeking to seize the reins.

To DuBois's claim that Washington's "own people" opposed his agenda, since most did not, we must ask: who were these "own people." We have somewhat answered the query in saying that it was DuBois and a small group of educated black New Englanders. Meier describes them further:

> The radicals were not evenly distributed among all groups in the population. They were more numerous in the North than in the South. Ray Stannard Baker characterized the Northern radicals as being highly educated individuals who held themselves aloof from the masses and tried to avoid or deny the existence of the color line. 'Their associations in business are largely with white people and they cling passionately to the fuller life,' he observed. Though the whole matter is extremely complicated, it appears ... that many radicals belonged to the older upper class which believed in immediate integration because its roots were to a large extent in the white community (168:179-180).

Given Meier's assessment, these "own people" to whom Du Bois alludes, then, might mainly have been, not just college-educated professional men, but, at the same time, men with minimal ties to the masses and whose "roots [lay] to a large extent in the white community." We know, in fact, that when it comes to the NAACP, the preeminent instrument of DuBois's tradition, its roots were in the white community in the person of a few Northern liberals. It was white-founded, white-funded, and white-dominated. With the Crisis as its mouthpiece, it propelled DuBois, its editor, into national standing and gave his tradition national status. It thus seems safe to say that DuBois and the "own people" who opposed Washington were in a world of their own, not their own people's world. Their world, created with "outer pressure" and ends-oriented (equality-oriented) versus means-oriented (adaptation oriented), was fixated on its own success symbol, civil rights, which it mistakenly equated with the survival struggles of our people.

Moreover, it is plausible to argue that DuBois and his allies themselves constituted "outer pressure." Washington was an indigenous leader. He was a slave, now free, leading slaves, who were also now free -- all inhabitants of the Southern soil. He and they were indivisible, except that he was fortunate enough to have worked his way up and land a position that enabled him to reach out to the others and lead them along the kind of pathway that he had traveled. DuBois and his allies, on the other hand, as Meier describes, were from a different world -- the Northern world, a middle-class, educated world of relative privilege and power. As a territorial matter, here was an outside group (carpetbaggers we might call them) trying to weaken a local leader and wrest control from him. While, as members of the same race, they had a right to try -- and apparently felt impelled to do so -- the right does not alter their outside status. Their right is not in question; their comparative suitability is.

Put the shoe on the other foot, of course, and it can be argued that Washington was speaking for them. A Southerner, he came to speak for the entire race, South and North. Just as DuBois and his allies were not indigenous sons of the South, neither was Washington an indigenous son of the North, even though he came to speak for it. The difference: the role was somewhat thrust upon Washington and, further, 85 percent of our race -- which is to say most of us -- lived in the South. That he thus came to be recognized as leader of his race, not just in the South, but also in the North, is more or less a matter of arithmetic. With his role came the function, and rather than work with him in its fulfillment, DuBois and his circle chose to work against him.

Nevertheless, one reads in some of the literature that Washington and DuBois agreed on most things. True, they did -- until, that is, DuBois disobeyed. Meier tells us what those "most things" were the two agreed upon prior to then:

> Both tended to blame Negroes largely for their condition, and both placed more emphasis on self-help and duties than on rights. Both placed economic development before universal manhood suffrage, and both were willing to accept franchise restrictions based not on race but on education and/or property qualifications equitably applied. Both stressed racial solidarity and economic co-operation. DuBois was, however, more outspoken about injustices, and he differed sharply with Washington in his espousal of the cause of higher education (168:196)

In his own words, from an address before the American Negro Academy in 1897, entitled "The Conservation of Races," DuBois had this to say:

> We believe that the first and greatest step toward the settlement of the present friction between the races--commonly called the Negro problem--lies in the correction of the immorality, crime and laziness among the Negroes themselves, which still remains

as a heritage from slavery. We believe that only earnest and long continued efforts *on our own part* [emphasis added] can cure those social ills (65:47).

This is vintage Booker T. Washington spoken by *then* obedient and true believer, W. E. B. DuBois -- before the fall.

DuBois: two divisive issues

Two issues emerge from DuBois's list of Washington's "mistakes and shortcomings" which seem, to the extent to which issues were a factor, to have underlined the fall: voting rights (encompassing civil rights generally) and higher education. On the voting rights issue, it is clear that the two *came to differ*. One would never know from DuBois's castigation of Washington, let alone from the Civil Rights Movement radicals who came to deify him, that at one time Washington and DuBois agreed. While Washington did not change his mind, it must be noted that he secretly fought against disenfranchisement, and on the few occasions when he addressed political issues, Meier tells us that he supported the preservation of our constitutional rights, although DuBois's point is that Washington's customary silence amounted to surrendering them (168:109-10). Of course, if you were not publicly "striking blows," you fell short of DuBois's test for the duty of the oppressed.

On the higher education issue, we may have more of a distortion than a difference -- a misrepresentation by DuBois in the interest of accenting his own views and differentiating himself from and denigrating Washington's. His claim was that Washington was, more or less, opposed to higher education for us. In his The Souls of Black Folk, DuBois asserts, "Mr. Washington distinctly asks that black people give up, at least for the present, …higher education of Negro youth…" (64:41). In another of his other signature works, "The Talented Tenth," published in the same year, 1903, he argues that "the demand for colored-bred men by a school like Tuskegee ought to make Mr. Booker T. Washington the firmest friend of higher training." In support of his argument, he cited the college credentials possessed by a number of those recruited by Washington. Despite Washington's reliance on such higher-education trained blacks, however, DuBois concludes, "One of the effects of Mr. Washington's propaganda has been to throw doubt upon the expediency of such training for Negroes, as these persons have had" (331).

Contrary to the impression that he apparently hoped to convey, these positions do not indicate that DuBois is literally accusing Washington of outright opposition to higher education for blacks; they merely indicate equivocation. The equivocation is seen in DuBois's phrasing as follows:

- says that Washington "asks that black people give up ... higher education," but adds "at least for the present;"
- says that Washington should be not just a "friend of higher training" but its "firmest" friend; and
- says not that "Washington's propaganda has been to throw doubt upon the expediency of such training of Negroes," but that the "the effects of" his propaganda has been ....

This phrasing represents what Norrell points out DuBois knew to be the fact: that Washington, rather than being outright opposed to higher education for us, *conditionally* supported it in contrast to DuBois's *unconditional* support. In reverse, DuBois conditionally supported the self-burden approach to adaptation while Washington unconditionally supported it. For Washington, industrial education would have priority because our need was for education that could be put to practical use. Reflected are two mindsets: one focused on the needs of the masses, the other on the aspirations of the higher classes; one focused on adaptation, the other on equality; one grounded in gradualism, the other in immediacy; one set on foundation-building, the other on status-building; one with a progressive time perspective, the other a regressive one. Understood in the context of these mindsets, their higher education controversy is less about higher education per se than it is about the broad fundamental approach to our uplifting. Higher education was not to be separated and treated apart from that approach but a reflection of it.

Seizing upon a specific issue, however, DuBois's apparent goal was to cast himself as a supporter of higher education for blacks and Washington, in contrast, as an enemy of it. Being an enemy would put Washington in the position of keeping us in a servile and subservient state. He sketched the state which *he* had in mind in the last paragraph of his chapter, "Of the Training of Black Men," describingm as follows, what it means to be a black man with an expanded, liberal education leading to a cultivated, self-developed "sovereign human soul":

> I sit with Shakespeare and he winces not. Across the color-line I move arm in arm with Balzac and Dumas, where smiling men and welcoming women glide in gilded halls. From out the caves of evening that swing between the strong-limbed earth and the tracery of the stars, I summon Aristotle and Aurelius and what soul I will, and they come all graciously with no scorn nor condescension. So, wed with Truth, I dwell above the Veil. Is this the life you grudge us, O knightly America? Is this the life you long to change into the dull and hideousness of Georgia? Are you so afraid lest peering from this high Pisgah, between Philistine and Amalekite, we sight the Promised Land? (64:81).

A reminder of the lyrics, "I can dream, can't I,"[15] DuBois's egalitarian musing embodies that refrain. In this picturesque fashion, he paints the picture of the kind of "broad-minded, cultured men and women," "sovereign human soul[s]," as he puts it, that he felt were needed to "scatter civilization among a people whose ignorance was not simply of letters, but of life" (64:73). This process for him entailed "the loftiest of ideals and seeks as an end culture and character rather than breadwinning," which, though deemed "the privilege of white men and the danger and delusion of black," must apply equally to both (64:71). The egalitarian picture painted is one whose production, he argued, Washington "distinctly" opposed, which brings us to Washington's views.

"Not so," said Washington. "This is an error. I do not oppose college education for our people, but I do urge that a larger percentage of our young men and women, whether educated in college or not, give the strength of their education in the direction of commercial or industrial development, just the same as the white man does" (264:105). He went on to point out the 15-20 college educated teachers he employed at

---

[15] Source: http://en.wikipedia.org/wiki/I_Can_Dream,_Can%27t_I%3F 11 November 2014.

Tuskegee and to suggest that having something for graduates to do is the best way of approving of college education.

Having something for graduates to do held great meaning for Washington. As Norrell observes, his position was that " 'an academic education was entirely appropriate for blacks who could put it to use.' " (192:279). Booker was not about knowledge for the sake of knowledge, but, given our condition at the time, he was about knowledge for the sake of its practical use in building a foundation for the race. As Washington went on explain, "for the next fifty or one hundred years," the need of our people would be in the industrial or hand training," pointing out that "the young white man who graduates at college, in nine cases out of ten, finds a business waiting for him that he can enter into as soon as he gets his college diploma," but "the black boy graduating from college finds no business waiting for him; he must start a business for himself; therefore, it is important, in our present condition, that the Negro be so educated along technical and industrial lines that he can found a business for himself" (264:105).

Washington's denial has support. The Father of Black History, Carter G. Woodson, wrote the following:

> Washington's advocacy of industrial education…in spite of all that has been said, was not a death blow to higher education for the Negro. That movement has lived in spite of opposition, and Washington himself frequently stated that industrial education, as he emphasized it, was for the masses of the people who had to toil. He did not object to higher education, knowing that the race had to have men to lead it onward (290:279).

Specific instances of Washington's support include being a trustee of two of the leading black universities, Howard and Fisk, and of his having successfully lobbied Andrew Carnegie to fund a library for Fisk University (109:176-77; 192:312). However, as Norrell observes, DuBois never acknowledged such instances (192:279). Nor did he acknowledge a number of other considerations which, according to Norrell, weighed on Washington (192:93-99). Among those considerations were: practical knowledge as emphasized by Washington was a nationwide trend; he would not have obtained the funding for Tuskegee had he not marketed it as a trade school, even though it mostly trained teachers; and a focus on liberal education would have been opposed by whites who did not want any classical education for blacks. To fend off Southern white opposition, Washington even wanted them to think as many thought: that he was preparing students for housework and other manual, subservient labor. So each year, Harlan reports, scores of letters arrived requesting domestic servants. Washington replied that Tuskegee was preparing students to serve their own people (109:172). Such deft handling of delicate situations, of course, helped to earn him the moniker of Wizard.

Further, DuBois ignored the fact that Tuskegee had an Academic Department which, in Washington's words, "offer a thorough course of instruction, nearly, if not quite, equal to high school courses of Northern and Western States" (264:178). As Henry Louis Gates Jr. specifically points out, in addition to industrial education, Tuskegee "taught the so-called higher subjects like literature, geography, and the sciences," something, incidentally, which a teacher training institute would do. However, for the reasons stated, Washington knew that, more or less, he had to mask that component of his curriculum (99a: 88; 109:143-73).

Harlan perhaps best sums up Tuskegee. Having asked the questions of whether it represented progressive education, a trade school, a black man's dream of achieving self-sufficiency, or a white man's dream of preparing blacks for subordinate roles, he answers, "Perhaps the best answer is that Tuskegee was none of these abstractions, but an amalgam of parts of each, with a predominance of intense desire for racial progress through self-help" (109:144). Harlan goes on to add, "The Tuskegee curriculum ... was ... clearly centered on self-help, and on a greater flexibility than the term industrial education suggests." "The higher students progressed ... into the junior, B middle, A middle, and senior years," he goes on to point out, "the broader the academic training. Many of those who survived the sifting and winnowing of Tuskegee to graduate, went on to college, and into the professions of the Talented Tenth" (109:144-45).

But such differentiated training apparently was not enough to satisfy DuBois since it would not enable most Tuskegee students to "sit with Shakespeare," "move arm in arm with Balzac and Dumas," or "summon Aristotle and Aurelius and what soul I will." As for the other considerations, to an activist and ideologue, what does practicality or reality mean, especially if either stands in the way of your ambition, which was to replace Washington?

DuBois/Washington: time perspective and core identity

With regard to their two major divisive issues, as well as to other issues, Scott's psychological explanation (lack of a positive core identity) of the pronounced dysfunction which we see in our poor black neighborhoods invites consideration of its relevance here, as well as the relevance of another psychological explanation encountered, time perspective. For, as David Brooks proclaims in his The Social Animal: The Hidden Sources of Love, Character, and Achievement, it is the psychological explanation -- that which occurs in our hidden, unconscious depth -- which (as his subtitle suggests) reveals the true story (23). We humans advance issues and fight for them because of who and what we are -- and who and what we are, we are increasingly finding out, is largely a product of what occurs in our hidden, unconscious depth. To identify what that is gives us understanding and instruction. Alone, an examination of differences on the issue could not give us the same understanding and instruction. It might be said that in these matters full vision requires bifocals: a look at both content differences and psychological differences. In this instance, it is argued that not only is Scott's thesis applicable, so is another psychological explanation encountered in our research: *time perspective* (the psychology of time, as it were) -- time being such an important factor in the historical assessment of the differences between Washington and DuBois, and in the fate which Washington has suffered. We will look at both.

Time perspective. Based on psychologists Philip Zimbardo and John Boyd's book, The Time Paradox: The New Psychology of Time That Will Change Your Life, it is argued that the evident differences between Washington and DuBois in time perspective may help to explain the reason for their differences, not only on the issues cited, but on the range of other issues which they confronted. Not that the matter of time does not explicitly or implicitly surface in a discussion of their differences, but it does not appear as an object of psychological analysis, as Zimbardo and Boyd have made it, and as they say few others have. In Chapter 14, in our discussion of our AMCAP hypotheses, we talk more about their analysis. Here, we simply emphasize their thesis -- based on over 30 years of research involving over 10,000 people around the Western world -- that largely unconsciously and subjectively our time perspective influences our thoughts, feelings, and actions. They say that "Ernest Becker won a Pulitzer Prize for arguing that a universal fear of death is at the heart of the human condition" – in Becker's words, "'a mainspring of human activity.'" Their own point is that this "human activity" which emanates from the fear of death is influenced by our time perspective (294: 21, 6c). That is, as fear of death is a mainspring of our life activities, our time perspective is a mainspring of their harvest -- of how well these activities turn out.

Zimbardo and Boyd have identified six time perspectives used in the Western world. They are:

1. **Past-negative**: hold negative memories of the past
2. **Past-positive**: hold positive memories of the past
3. **Present-fatalistic**: feel that what will be will be and own personal actions will not make a real difference
4. **Present-hedonistic**: place interest and energy on having fun and pleasure in the here and now
5. **Future**: have realistic approach to life, set goals, and willing to sacrifice to achieve goals
6. **Transcendental-future**: are future-oriented *and* believe in life after death

Of the six, their conclusion is that the optimum time perspective profile is high past-positive, moderately future, and moderately present-hedonistic combined with a low past-negative and low present-fatalistic. Being high past-positive, moderately future, and moderately present-hedonistic, they conclude, gives us *roots*, *wings*, and (constructive) *energy*. If, on the other hand, we are high rather than low on past-negative and present-fatalistic, we have a problem because, as Zimbardo and Boyd declare, "Our research suggests that nothing good comes out of them" (294:298). They go on to explain that studies reveal that "emphasizing a negative past or a fatalistic present put people at risk for both mental and physical illness" (294: 298). Here is a list of those illnesses (294:298-99):

- lack of self-control
- lack of personal responsibility
- difficulty in interpersonal relationships
- low sense of self-actualization
- low levels of positive outlook and expectations
- anxiety
- depression
- anger

Since our time perspective, like death, plays a mainspring role in human activity – per se, not civil rights, not higher education, not any other issue, or combination of issues -- puts time perspective itself at the center of the explanation for the Washington-DuBois divide. For the issues themselves, though of obvious importance, perhaps reflect something even more important: the psychological attitude toward time from which the issues ensued. The issues emanated from conflicting time perspectives-- those perspectives having to do with more than the fact that one focused on gradualism and the other on immediacy, but with psychological attitudes about time which led them to their positions. The gradual versus the immediate was simply one aspect of that attitude -- the aspect on which all the attention commonly centers. But when we expand our concept of time, as Zimbardo and Boyd have done, to include the psychological along with the temporal, we tap into a deeper, *hidden* meaning – the meaning by whi, the new research suggests, we are almost entirely driven.

The question for both of our two famous leaders is what was the deeper, *hidden* meaning of time for each of them. Not being able to give them The Zimbardo Time Perspective Inventory (ZTPI), we can only infer an answer. For Washington, it is inferred that he approximated what Zimbardo-Boyd conclude to be the optimum time perspective profile [herein referred to as *progressive time perspective*]: high past-positive, moderately future, and moderately present-hedonistic combined with a low past-negative and low present-fatalistic. For DuBois, it is inferred that he, on the other hand, approximated what the authors conclude to be a worst time perspective profile [herein referred to as *regressive time perspective*]: high past-negative and high present-fatalistic combined with a low past-positive, low future, and low present-hedonistic. In one case, we discern what Zimbardo and Boyd's research indicates we get from those with a *progressive time perspective profile*: *roots, wings,* and (constructive) *energy* while, in the other, we discern what their research indicates we get from those with a *regressive time perspective profile*: problems, inclusive of mental and physical illnesses. What we got from them, we have gotten from their traditions! Of course, it is not a black and white picture, all peach and cream on one side and vinegar on the other. Instead, we are talking about, not total, but predominant profiles.

Core identity. It is not a stretch, in turn, to trace their different time perspectives to something equally as deep and hidden, and no less fundamental: their different core identities, core identity being at the heart of our explanation for AMSAC and its inseparable social problems. Core identity is explained and discussed in Chapter 8. Zimbardo and Boyd's research link time perspective and health; the more optimal our time perspective profile the more optimal our health and vice-versa. In Washington's case, arguably, we have the approximation of an optimum profile -- and thus a healthy personality. In DuBois's case, arguably, we have the worst profile and, thus, an unhealthy personality. A healthy personality, in turn, may reflect a positive core identity while an unhealthy personality may reflect a negative core identity. Throughout their war their personality is markedly on display. For DuBois, that display shows a personality which largely reflects the above list of illnesses (if we wish to call them that) associated with his inferred time perspective profile (lack of self-control, difficulty in interpersonal relationships, low levels of positive outlook and expectations, and so on), Washington's personality standing in contrast.

Whereas, then, voting rights (and civil rights generally) and higher education were the two major issues which provoked the disobedience, an explanation of why lies beyond the particulars of these issues. It extends to the hidden forces largely responsible for their thoughts, feelings, and actions -- as they largely are for the thoughts, feelings, and actions of all of us. Those forces, arguably, were their contrasting time perspective profiles and sense of core identity. Of course, we do not engage in a public contest, or for that matter in any other contest, over time perspective or sense of core identity; we contest the concrete. So it is with the two divisive issues and others, and as we continue our discussion of the Washington-DuBois war, we must do so cognizant of the deep, hidden forces which drives those issues and all else which comprises their war -- a cognizance which enables us to understand better what happened and to decipher its lesson.

DuBois: taking issue with Washington, thereafter, "on almost every point of his program"

Now let us turn to Spencer's point that DuBois's tone was less restrained -- or, if you will, more vile and vitriolic -- after the forbidden fruit had been publicly eaten, thereafter taking issue with Washington "on almost every point of his program." Let us examine those points, of necessity including points made in his Declaration since there is continuity and overlapping.

Self-help versus System-help. We begin with the philosophy of their traditions: self-help versus system-help. Self-help is the core philosophy of Washington's Self-Responsibility Tradition. We have quoted Norrell as stating that Washington believed that "self-made people were more likely to succeed" (192:74). Whites had some responsibility and should exercise it, but the major responsibility belonged to us, Washington feeling that we could not succeed unless we had "a certain amount of groundwork and foundation…" (165:29).

To Washington, struggle was a condition for success. In his mind, all his race, like his students, had to work hard to get ahead. From Washington's <u>The Case of the Negro</u>, Meier quotes him as saying, "'No race of people ever got upon its feet without severe and constant struggle, often in the face of the greatest disappointments'" (168:105). Rather than a hindrance, paradoxically, Meier observes, Washington saw such struggle as more of a help than a hindrance, "for under pressure the Negro had put forth more energy which, constructively channeled, had been of untold value" (168:105).

DuBois, on the other hand, had a different perspective. He looked, not at the struggle, but at the subservience -- the wrongs and injustices which were part of it. That look led him to focus, not on the self, but on the system -- on making system-help the core philosophy of his System-Responsibility Tradition. Like Washington, DuBois saw us as having a role in our making, but unlike Washington, his emphasis was, not on our role, but on the role of the system. In DuBois's words:

> ... while it is a great truth to say that the Negro must strive and strive mightily to help himself, it is *equally true* [emphasis added] that unless his striving be not simply seconded, but rather aroused and encouraged, by the richer and wiser environing group, he cannot hope for success (64:46).

DuBois goes on to say that "His [Washington's] doctrine has tended to make the whites, North and South, shift the burden of the Negro problem to the Negro's shoulders and stand aside as critical and rather pessimistic spectators; when in fact the burden belongs to the nation...." (64:46). That is, to him, Washington was placing too much emphasis on our role. The problem must not be shifted to our shoulders while the system stands by, but the system must play, not just a supportive role, but a leading one. Since we also must "strive and strive mightily," DuBois thus strikes the semblance of a meet-us-at-least-halfway approach. However DuBois and his tradition emphasize just one half: the system half -- expanded!

Instruments of self-help: brains, property, character (civil rights, Southern residency). In Washington's translation of his self-help philosophy into practice, he placed priority on activities which emphasize brains, property, and character, along with secret and seductive civil rights activities, as means to create a self-made people. His brain or education activities are represented by the aforementioned Tuskegee Institute and by the some 16 Little Tuskegees established by his Tuskegee graduates. His property or industry activities are represented by his crusade for property ownership, by his establishment of the National Negro Business League (now National Business League), and to a lesser extent by his participatory role in the founding of the National Urban League. His character activities are represented by his 37 addresses to students, faculty, and Tuskegee guests -- copies of which were distributed to the Tuskegee community and others. In his **Thomas**

A. Harris Rescue and his **Birmingham Letter** (yes, he, too, had a Birmingham letter) we have symbols of secret and seductive civil rights emphasis.

Above all, it is Tuskegee which stands as the preeminent symbol of Washington's philosophy and its practice. Through Tuskegee, Washington demonstrated his wizardry and, thereby, gained access to the levers of power that made possible the Age of Booker T. Washington. But credit goes not just to Tuskegee per se. The gospel of brains, property, and character which he so tirelessly preached, and on which he so tirelessly worked, permeate the range of his endeavors. Whether through the school, through other means or agencies, education *for the masses* was a common thread, as was property and character. Not only were students to be educated, but, for example, through more informal means, so were farmers, businessmen, and ministers as well. This community-oriented concept of education anticipated the progressive education movement of John Dewey and others at the turn of the twentieth century. As the late Teachers College, Columbia University president and historian, Lawrence A. Cremin, put it in his prizewinning The Transformation of the School: Progressivism in American Eduation, 1876-1957, progressive education "meant broadening the program and function of the school to include direct concern for health, vocation, and the quality of family and community life" (52:viii). That is what Washington did; he broadened "the program and function of the school."

That program and function centered on industrial education (only, as will be discussed below, somewhat more broadly conducted than many perceived). Washington's preoccupation was preparation for "the things of real life." At the same time, he felt that, "No race can be lifted until its mind is awakened and strengthened." Therefore he declared that "By the side of industrial training should always go mental and moral training, but [that] the pushing of mere abstract knowledge into the head means little." "We want more," he asserted, "than the mere performance of mental gymnastics." What is that more? Washington's answer: "Our knowledge must be harnessed to the things of real life" (270:357).

Washington's preoccupation with "the things of real life" – industrial education – was historically rooted. It was not just something for us blacks; it was something for any similarly situated people – people who were starting from the bottom and wanted to rise (244:156). As he proclaimed in his Atlanta Compromise Address of 1895, "It is at the bottom of life we must begin and not the top." You rise from the bottom by building a foundation through industrial education. That, for example, is what our Pilgrim fathers had done. Of them, he said the following:

> We forgot the industrial education that was given the Pilgrim Fathers of New England in clearing and planting the cold, bleak, and snowy hills and valleys, in the providing of shelter, founding the small mills and factories, in supplying themselves with home-made products, thus laying the foundation of an industrial life that now keeps going a large part of the colleges and missionary effort of the world (165:20).

So for us blacks to do as the Pilgrims and other similarly situated groups have done, like them, we too must first build a foundation. "On such a foundation," he declared,

> will grow habits of thrift, a love of work, economy, ownership of property, bank accounts. Out of it in the future will grow practical education, professional education, positions of public responsibility. Out of it will grow moral and religious strength. Out of it will grow wealth from which alone can come leisure and the opportunity for the enjoyment of literature and the fine arts (270:357).

Moreover, Washington felt that we must prove ourselves. To him, therefore, in contrast to DuBois, our education was not about "intelligence, broad sympathy, knowledge of the world," or being concerned with "what Socrates and St. Francis of Assisi would say," but with the pressing needs of the present. Tuskegee stood for "an integrated training of head, heart, and hand" that would produce concrete results -- get done what, at that time and in that place, we needed to do, and what needed to be done for self and community in order to uplift ourselves (244:53). He felt that the "doubt in many quarters as to the ability of the Negro unguided, unsupported, to hew his own path and put into visible, tangible, indisputable form, products and signs of civilization…" could not "be much affected by abstract arguments, no matter how delicately and convincingly woven together." Rather, "Patiently, quietly, doggedly, persistently, through summer and winter, sunshine and shadow, by self-sacrifice, by foresight, by honesty and industry, we must re-enforce argument with results" (270:360).

Washington apparently saw those results mainly in the form of an agricultural base. He told his students that "during the next fifty years," he would have "every colored minister and teacher, whose work lies outside the large cities, armed with a thorough knowledge of theoretical and practical agriculture, in connection with his theological and academic training." For he saw our race as "an agricultural one." "Upon this foundation," he proclaimed, "almost every race in history has gotten its start. With cheap land, a beautiful climate and a rich soil, we can lay the foundation of a great and powerful race." "The question that confronts us," he declared, "is whether we will take advantage of this opportunity?" (272:343)

Even though committed to our agricultural grounding, for those of us who lived in the city, Washington told his students that the same work ethic applied. "Show me," he told them, "the race that leads in work in the wood and in metal, in the building of houses and factories, and in the constructing and operating of machinery, and I will show you the race that in the long run molds public thought, that; [sic] controls government, that leads in commerce, in the sciences, in the arts and in the professions" (272:344).

Attention to Washington's character emphasis as symbolized by his 37 addresses to students, faculty, and Tuskegee guests is given in Chapter 12 in our discussion of amplifying IQ, with attention now turning to that aspect of his philosophy and practice which has so devastated his standing: his secret and discrete civil rights activities as symbolized by his **Thomas A. Harris Rescue** and *his* **Birmingham Letter**.

As told by Harlan, Thomas Harris was a black lawyer in Tuskegee (108:171-75). He had let an itinerant white clergyman stay at his home for several days, during one of which he was seen going to Harris's home in the rain after church accompanied by Harris and holding an umbrellas between two sexually mature daughters of Harris. Threats of a white mob forced him to leave town. Later, the mob ordered Harris to leave town, and when he did not, the mob descend upon his home to kill him. In his attempt to escape, he was wounded, his son later in the night taking him to Washington's home for help. Harlan describes Washington's response as "characteristically devious," appeasing whites by seeming to turn Harris's son away while privately providing Harris safety and the care of a doctor.

Harlan reports that Washington explained to a confidante that he could not take Harris into the school and risk the lives of students whose parents had entrusted them to his care. He felt no obligation to have his home serve as a sanctuary for those in personal trouble. Instead, Washington explained, he helped to get Harris to a safe place and, out of his own pocket, paid for his comfort and care. Harris did recover, expressed his lasting gratitude to Washington, and kept in touch with him.

In 1914, when the Birmingham board of commissioners proposed a segregation ordinance, Washington wrote them suggesting that the ordinance would create racial strife and discourage leading blacks (109:428-29; see also 112:124-25). He stressed the need to maintain the harmony and friendship between the races that had been made possible through the influence of leading black citizens working in cooperation with the best citizens among whites, suggesting that the harmony might be disrupted because sensible and conservative black leaders might be offended by the ordinance. Then he went on in this **Birmingham Letter** to suggest an alternative whereby, if the commissioners made their wishes known privately to some of the leading blacks in the city, the matter could be settled without the passage of an ordinance. They could rely on custom alone. The officials acquiesced, and Washington, through savvy and seduction, achieved -- in the context of the times -- what might be called a civil rights victory, preventing custom from becoming law and perhaps avoiding a counterproductive racial conflict in favor of a battle that could be fought under more favorable circumstances (109:428-29).

Instruments of system-help: civil rights and protest agenda (higher education, urban residency). In DuBois's translation of his system-help philosophy into practice, he placed priority on civil rights and on a protest agenda which would lead to their acquisition and, consequently, to the equal status on which -- along with our self-help emphasis on higher education -- was dependent our ability to uplift ourselves. His civil rights and protest agenda are represented by the Niagara Movement, the NAACP, The Crisis, and The King Years or the Civil Rights Movement (1954-68). His self-help agenda is represented by his emphasis on higher education and the "Talented Tenth."

Above all, it is the NAACP and the Civil Rights Movement which can be said to be the preeminent symbols of DuBois's philosophy and practice. Both encompass his interrelated emphasis on civil rights and a protest agenda. Though formally organized by white liberals in 1910, DuBois, as indicated, was a founding member of the NAACP and, until his resignation in 1934, its leading voice. He was its Director of Publicity and Research, board member, and editor of its official publication, Crisis. It is through the Crisis that he exerted national influence and contributed to the organization's growth and influence, which became extensive and considerable (92: 352-54). During its first fifteen years, it won a number of important court cases and grew from one branch in Chicago to some 400 branches throughout the country. Its flagship legal victory was to come in 1954 with the Supreme Court school desegregation decision in *Brown vs. Board of Education*. Today, it remains our premier civil rights organization, fighting for our civil rights on a variety of fronts, with its website indicating some 2200 member units spread throughout the country -- considerable credit going to DuBois for his formative role. His role in the Civil Rights Movement, on the other hand, was less direct, but it was around his name that the radicals of the movement rallied.

In his famous essay, "Talented Tenth," DuBois made *his* self-help case, urging an emphasis on black higher education as the way to develop the Talented Tenth, since "The Negro race, like all races, is going to be saved by its exceptional men." So we can say that, in his dual approach, DuBois's efforts were mainly in the system domain -- as symbolized by the NAACP, Crisis, and the Civil Rights Movement – and, secondarily, in the self-help domain as symbolized by his essay, "Talented Tenth."

Region of residency might also be considered a self-help emphasis of DuBois. As elaborated, Washington thought that we should stay on the land. DuBois, however, thought we should migrate to the urban areas of the North, away from Southern whites. To him, the South, rather than having agricultural land that provides the "foundation of a great and powerful race" -- as Washington saw it -- was instead "largely... an armed camp for intimidating black folk" (64:79).

As for the Niagara Movement, it is a testimony to how DuBois, in contrast to Washington, often dealt with the practical. The Niagara Movement was set up to pursue his protest and civil rights agenda -- and, more important perhaps, to compete with and replace Washington. It had its beginning in 1905 when 29 blacks from among the Talented Tenth of New England and the Midwest [note, not the South] responded to his (and William Trotter's) invitation to meet in Niagara Falls to undertake an organized effort to secure full citizenship (92:351-53; 164a:281-82; 192:321-22, 337-38; 244:157-58). Norrell's analysis is that it "represented DuBois's open, concerted challenge to Washington and the beginning of his campaign for recognition as the leader of his race" (192:321).

After a couple of meetings, lack of funds and internal dissension are said to have led to its dissolution, its members later being invited to join in starting the NAACP, most of whom accepted. That acceptance might have been its most important contribution to its cause. However, for a period of five years, it was a thorn in Washington's side, wresting control from him of the Afro-American Council, our first national civil rights organization and eventual successor to the Convention Movement (1830-1893) wherein, from time to time, black leaders met at state and national conventions to address our problems (168:178-84 and throughout). That control, however, did not turn out to make the Council any more consequential than the Niagara Movement; it, too, faded away.

One incident provides some insight into DuBois's leadership and the group's approach. It occurred at their three-day meeting in 1906 at Harpers Ferry, Virginia (now West Virginia), the site of John Brown's Raid. In an effort to get arms to free the slaves, Brown raided the United States Armory there in 1859, but was captured, found guilty of treason, and hanged. DuBois and Niagara Movement members visited the site of the armory and engaged in a ceremony whereby, in commemoration, they pulled off their shoes and socks and walked around the site singing "John Brown's Body" (244:157-58)., hey wanted to leave no doubt about the spirit of anger and protest that motivated the movement; it was about confrontation, not compromise.

It is this same spirit, "strike the blow," that DuBois had conveyed in the opening of his attack on Washington in his The Souls of Black Folk in 1903 (64:35). He begins with this quote from Lord Byron:

> From birth till death enslaved; in word, in deed, unmanned!
> Hereditary bondsmen! Know ye not
> Who would be free themselves must strike the blow?

It is the "strike the blow" spirit that became a hallmark of his tradition.

It was his "strike the blow" call that made DuBois the hero of the Civil Rights Movement. To the Movement, the NAACP was fine, insofar as it went, but that was neither far enough nor soon enough. Its legal and political approach did not offer immediacy; that was offered only by direct action, the striking of blows. So the marches, the sit-ins, the boycotts, and other activities. The epicenter remained the same, our civil rights, but our civil rights here and now, not later (92:522-61). Dr. Martin Luther King Jr., as a founder and president of the Southern Christian Leadership Conference (SCLC), became the Movement's leading voice, leading historian Taylor Branch, in his award-winning trilogy of Dr. King's life, dubbing the Movement "The King Years" (1954-68) (20b). Other leaders and organizations played a role as well. In particular, there was the Student Nonviolent Coordinating Committee (SNCC) and the Congress of Racial Equality (CORE). The NACCP also made contributions.

The War

In DuBois's **The Souls of Black Folk**, the "more subtle than any beast of the field" had spoken, triggering a public contest between him and "the Lord"[16] -- a contest which, in various forms, lasted until "the Lord" departed the earth in 1915. Until then, Washington remained the

---

[16] Based on Genesis 3:1.

dominant figure of his Age; DuBois did not destroy that dominance, only tested, taunted, and diminished it (109:359-360; 192:403-420; 244:144-161).

One often hears or reads about Washington and DuBois's crossfire as a "debate," but Norrell more accurately captures their rivalry in his chapter title, "The *Warring* Ideals" [emphasis added] (192: 263-87; also see Spencer, 244:144-61). For a war of sorts it was, not just a debate -- an unrelenting attack on Washington by DuBois in alliance with William Monroe Trotter (whom DuBois had met at Harvard) and a small group of educated black New Englanders. Trotter began the challenge through his newspaper, the Boston <u>Guardian</u>, which he started in 1901. With his publication of <u>The Souls of Black Folk</u>, DuBois publicly joined forces with Trotter, helping him to edit the paper, and intensifying the battle. DuBois gave the fissure a kind of imprimatur, lifting it to a more credible, newsworthy status, at least as pertains to our black decision-makers. Now it was DuBois, the preeminent scholar and the leading activist, versus Washington, the Wizard of Tuskegee. Below we recount some of the major encounters in their (and their factions') war.

The Boston <u>Guardian</u> assault (1901-10, its most influential years)

As stated, Trotter began the challenge through his Boston <u>Guardian</u>. Norrell reports that it conducted an assault on Washington "in every issue from its inception" (192: 278). "In the view of Trotter and a few like-minded men," Norrell explains, "he [Washington] had sold out black political rights, capitulated to Jim Crow discrimination, and promoted inferior education for blacks" (192:6-7). In Norrell's words:

> Among the epithets applied [to Washington] were "Pope Washington," "the Black Boss," "the Benedict Arnold of the Negro race," "the Great Traitor," "the Great Divider," "he miserable toady," "the Imperial Caesar," and "the Heartless and snobbish purveyor of Pharisaical moral clap-trap." A Guardian reporter described his features as monstrous: 'Harsh in the extreme,' marked by 'vast leonine jaws into which vast mastiff-like rows of teeth were set clinched together like a vice.' His forehead was 'a great cone,' his chin 'massive and square,' his eyes 'dull and absolutely characterless, and with a glance that would leave you uneasy and restless during

the night if you had failed to report to the police such a man around before you went to bed' (192:264).

Even Washington's unfriendly definitive biographer, Louis R. Harlan, characterized the <u>Guardian</u> as being on the border line between personal journalism and libel (112:118).

Norrell documents its resort, and that of other Washington enemies, to slander and misrepresentation in an attempt to sabotage Washington's leadership, including attacking his children (192:263-310). At times, they apparently attacked Washington more ferociously than they did the system itself. In one editorial, Trotter proclaimed that "'Tuskegee has proved the most deadly enemy of Negro liberty, more deadly than the south itself, because it comes in the guise of a friend'" (192:278).

The "Boston riot" of 1903 (early turning point)

The "Boston riot" of 1903 saw Trotter's verbal assault result in violence (192:282-84; 109:32-62). Trotter co-led, with Granville Martin, a disruption of Washington's speech to the Negro Business League at a Boston church. Their group baited the podium with cayenne pepper, shouted out at Washington and hurled nine questions at him upon his ascent to the podium [including, for example, one about whether the lynching rope was all the race is to get under his leadership], and in the process caused a riot among the 2,000 present. Police had to restore order and Trotter and Martin were arrested, convicted, and had to spend 30 days in jail. DuBois was not there and did not approve of the antics employed, but – since he also strongly objected to Trotter being arrested -- in the weeks following the riot, and during the trial, he lived with Trotter in his Boston home and later wrote a letter defending and extolling him while demeaning Washington (192:290, 164a:281).

As not unusual for events in Boston, the riot turned out to have a significant outcome. Being a man of reason, restraint, and conciliation, Washington was not given to verbal warring, but the riot went beyond the verbal to the violent (244:158, 161). As a result, Norrell writes, "The public battle in Boston induced Washington and his allies to engage all their enemies, thus matching the total-war attitude of Trotter's group"

[Vengeance *belongeth* unto me, I will recompense, saith the Lord"[17]] (192:283).

Compromise attempt: The Carnegie Hall Agenda (January 1904) and the Committee of Twelve

Seeing the "total-war attitude" as detrimental, Washington's requested DuBois to convene a meeting of prominent black men at Carnegie Hall to consider "'quietly all the weighty matters that now confront us as a race'" (192:293-94). "The meeting called for the creation of a Committee of Twelve to coordinate future action, with DuBois and Washington as its conveners and about nine of the members mostly friendly to Booker" (192:294-95). However, seeing that the Committee came to reflect Washington's wishes over his own, DuBois dropped out, and Harlan says that the Committee became mainly a paper organization (109:81-82, 63-83).

The Niagara Movement (1905-10)

As it turned out, while Washington had in mind an organization to unite the factions, DuBois had in mind just the opposite. He wanted an organization to strengthen his own faction and weaken Washington's, or, more accurately, to replace Washington's -- something which, Norrell notes, had been his passion since around 1900, in effect publicly saying so in 1903. Accordingly, he founded the aforementioned and discussed Niagara Movement, which Harlan says was his brainchild (not Trotter's or any of his other anti-Bookerite allies, but his), but -- as discussed -- it failed (109:84-106). The ostensible management reasons have been discussed, but the deeper reason (and herein our search is for the deeper and hidden – the root factors) may be in the social-psychological domain. From late Kent State University sociologist Elliott Rudwick's description of what occurred, we get an understanding of why – and the description is worth quoting in full because of what it tells us about DuBois himself and because of its reinforcement of Meier's similar analysis.

---

[17] Hebrews 10:30.

Du Bois, as general secretary of the Niagara Movement, simply could not match the skill and resources of Booker Washington. He 'hated the role' of being a social action leader. His personality was aloof and many Negroes considered him conceited. He never attempted to appeal directly to large numbers of colored people, although he said that he represented the race. He was satisfied to assemble a small group of educated men and he assumed these people would carry his message to the masses. However, most of the Niagara men were psychologically isolated from average Negroes. Many regarded the masses as inferiors and considered their own college diplomas as symbols of social prestige instead of tools to raise the race (229e:311).

Thus a deeper insight, not only into why the Niagara Movement failed, but further and more fundamentally, into the seeds of Victimology sown by DuBois and his allies, who saw themselves in a separate world from those for whom they spoke. That the masses were of the same race as they, it might be argued, was palatable so long as their condition could be attributed to victimization. Norrell observes that Washington "thought they were embarrassed by the ignorance—the lack of respectability and "civilization," in the vernacular of the day—of southern blacks" (192:150).

Founding of the NAACP (1910) -- the decisive turning point

DuBois was not the only one who wanted to replace Washington; so did Oswald Garrison Villard and a few of his fellow white Northern liberals (even call them radicals if you will). Unlike DuBois, they succeeded in setting up, in 1910, an organization to do so: the previously discussed NAACP. Harlan and Norrell point out that several factors made that success possible. Two stand out: the decline of Washington's political influence with President Theodore Roosevelt and his successor, William Howard Taft and three racial flareups which he did not publicly protest: the Atlanta riot of 1906, The Teddy Roosevelt Brownsville decision of 1906, and the Springfield Race Riot of 1908 (109: 295-337, 360; 192:340-58, 380-81, 386). A third gets frequent attention: the Ulrich affair in 1911 (109:379-404; 192:393-402).

Three racial flareups. In the *Atlanta riot of 1906*, white mobs, reacting to rape allegations, white mobs went on a rampage over a five-day period. Better-off blacks were especially targeted. The mobs destroyed black property and probably killed as many as 30 blacks, while 2 whites were killed. A few weeks earlier, a bartender had been killed and a policeman injured by shots fired on a *Brownsville*, Texas, street. Soldiers from the mostly black 25th United Infantry Regiment. which three weeks prior had arrived in the area, were blamed. Pleas from Washington to the contrary, President Theodore Roosevelt ended up disbanding the entire unit. In the *Springfield*, Illinois riot, white mobs reacted to two blacks suspected of violent crimes against whites. They destroyed 40 black homes, several black businesses, killed six blacks, and drove 2000 others from the city. These racial flareups were seen as dramatic and galvanizing evidence of white oppression and injustice. While Washington was outraged and fought back, he did not do so publicly, exhibiting in Harlan's words, the "lack of one essential attribute for the leader of an oppressed minority—the capacity for righteous public anger against injustice" (109:323).

In particular, President Roosevelt's *Brownsville disbanding* dealt Washington a severe blow. It was betrayal by the very man whose support had enabled Washington to wield such power. In this case, however, the President is said to have acted more or less arbitrarily, scorning Washington's plea for delay and reconsideration. As Norrell puts it, "... what Teddy had given Booker, he took away with Brownsville" (192:357). At the same time, the Brownsville disbanding provided anti-Washington ammunition which strengthened DuBois and his enemies in their leadership displacement drive. Washington's political power taken away and his reputation under siege, the *Springfield* riot occurred and led Villard and his Northern allies to start the NAACP. They created it to do what Washington did not do: *publicly* lead the "righteous anger against injustice." As a reminder of Washington's failure to express public outrage over racial injustices and the contribution of that failure to the decline of his power, as well as to **The BTW Meme**, our mnemonic is **Washington's public silence: Atlanta, Brownsville, Springfield**.

The Ulrich affair. The Ulrich affair occurred as the NAACP was emerging. While further undermining Washington's reputation, neither Harlan nor Norrell concludes that it meaningfully affected Washington's standing. Both, however, suggest that it traumatized him. Henry Ulrich, a white New Yorker, accused Washington of peeping through a keyhole at his girlfriend's apartment house and responded by beating him with a heavy walking stick causing sixteen stitches. Washington brought charges, and in the trial that resulted, although his name was cleared of Ulrich's accusation, Ulrich was acquitted on the ground that "his vicious motive was not proved beyond a doubt" (192:399). The problem, however, turned out to be that Washington did not convincingly answer the question of why he was at the apartment house in the first place, as a result of which, it became widely believed, that he was there for an extramarital affair. DuBois even spread a rumor that Washington was there to meet a white prostitute and had gone there previously.

Given a weakened Washington, DuBois and the NAACP made headway. DuBois's editorship of the <u>Crisis</u> gave him the base he needed to wage his unrelenting war. Like Trotter, he now had his own mouthpiece -- and standing among the leadership class to go along with it. Reference to his popularization of the <u>Crisis</u> and the growth of the NAACP has been made. Washington, like DuBois, had been invited to participate in its founding by its organizer, Oswald Garrison Villard, journalist and grandson of William Lloyd Garrison of abolitionist fame. But, says Norrell, Washington declined, writing to Villard that "he knew the value of 'sane agitation and criticism, but not to the extent of having our race feel that we can depend upon this to cure all the evils surrounding us'" (192:389). He thought Villard to be well-meaning, but as having surrounded himself with bitter and resentful Northern blacks, and with idealistic and impractical whites who did not understand the South (109:359, 164a:281-91).

Norrell explains that Villard, a onetime Washington supporter, had come, however, to believe that "protest was the only means for black uplift" (192:387). Not only that. Given Washington's contrary view, combined with Washington's loyalty to the Republican Party, Villard had come to feel that Washington had to be replaced as leader of the race. His new organization, of which he became chairperson, was borne then, not just to uplift us through a "protest agenda," but also -- *in the person of Villard* -- to replace Washington as our leader. Of course, he did not succeed, just as DuBois himself did not succeed. Disgruntlement with Villard's paternalistic and autocratic leadership led to his replacement, and the later appointment of black lyricist, novelist, diplomat, and Bookerite, James Weldon Johnson, as secretary in 1916 led to the organization becoming, by 1920, black-run rather than white-run (192:386-393, 414-416).

But what Villard and the NAACP did succeed in doing is challenging Washington's leadership and forcing him to contend with organized opposition which, inevitably, weakened his power. Each perceived the other as enemy, and Harlan and Norrell alike give details of their acrimony, and of the failed attempts at cooperation (109:359-437; 192:380-429). After the NAACP's official start in May 1910, Washington and the NAACP's mutual agreement to refrain from publicly airing their differences almost immediately (in the Fall) turned to "open, deep, and permanent rupture" due to public criticisms by NAACP ally, civil rights leader, John Milholland, and by -- who else? -- DuBois (109:367-78; 192:389-93). The occasion: a speech by Washington in London to the Anti-Slavery and Aborigines Protection Society. Miholland sent out a circular letter criticizing the speech and airing the customary castigations of Washington and, through the National Negro Committee, DuBois -- going further -- sent out a letter "To the People of Great Britain and Europe." The Committee was composed of a number of DuBois's prominent black allies, and while it was a Committee letter (really a DuBois letter), it used the original stationery of the NAACP, giving the impression that it was NAACP endorsed. The letter pictured Washington as beholding to his rich supporters, his report on black progress being, not the entire truth, but the part of the truth which these supporters wanted him to tell (109:359).

In the midst of the open rupture -- and during what would turn out to be his last few years -- Washington underwent a major change: he began to go public. "By 1912," Norrell says, "a change could be detected in the way Washington talked and wrote about the wrongs done to black people." Norrell continues:

> He had always spoken out against discrimination and exploitation, but he had usually done so with extreme care--the restraint he

thought necessary given the complete intolerance of white southerners for criticism of their racial practices. But about 1912 his language began to show more assertiveness, more emphatic rejection of injustice, and he would maintain that new tone for the rest of his life. He admitted no change, because he said little that he had not said before, but now he placed less blame on blacks for their conditions and more on whites for their unfairness (192:407).

One possible factor in this change, which Washington never explained, is, as both Harlan and Norrell cite, the Ulrich affair. Harlan saw it as forcing him to recognize that even he, Booker T. Washington, was subject to racial attack, just as was the case with any other black man (109: 404). Or, as Norrell puts it, "The humiliation of the Ulrich affair may have so personalized the injustices of being black that he shed some of his natural caution" (192: 407). Given the attention herein to the inner, psychic forces which explain our feelings and actions, such speculation is warranted. Not subject to speculation is his open embrace of a protest agenda, in the BTW style, versus the DuBois style, or as Harlan terms it, in a persuasive way versus a challenging way (109:404).

That embrace was apparent in his article in the Century magazine in 1912, "Is the Negro Having a Fair Chance?" (279; 192:408-410). As usual, Washington pointed out the fair chances which he thought we were given, but at the same time, the unfair ones as well, including the following:

- lack of job opportunities as skilled laborers or workers in such special industries as bricklaying and carpentry
- lack of representation and grievance mechanisms in the South
- substandard and unequal railroad accommodations in the South
- injustice and inequality in the funding of public schools in the South -- in several states "an effort ... being made to give immigrant peoples special opportunities for education over and above those given to the average citizen" -- the South accused of not giving our race a "square deal" in education
- all-white juries
- unequal application of voting restrictions

Having publicized his "grievances," Washington concluded:

> I am aware of the fact that in what I have said in regard to the hardships of the negro in this country I throw myself open to the criticism of doing what I have all my life condemned and everywhere sought to avoid; namely, laying over-emphasis on matters in which the negro race in America has been badly treated, and thereby overlooking those matters in which the negro has been better treated in America than anywhere else in the world.
>
> What has been accomplished in the past years, however, is merely an indication of what can be done in the future.

Norrell observes that even DuBois, in an issue of the Crisis, acknowledged a different Washington, writing, "'We note with some complacency that Mr. Booker T. Washington has joined the ranks'"(192:409). Norrell goes on to add, however, "DuBois knew that the article reiterated what Washington had said many times earlier, but he correctly perceived the change in tone" (192:409). But, DuBois and the NAACP were really not interested in his message, but in his replacement. "Is the Negro Having a Fair Chance?" was an olive leaf of sorts, but in Norrell's words, "His 1912 assessment of the unfair treatment of blacks overall apparently counted for nothing with the organization" (192:414).

It ought, however, to count for something in our assessment of Washington's place in black history. It is testimony to the *public* side of his fight for our civil rights. Of course, it can be argued, as DuBois did, that Washington was late in joining the fray, but this is a misleading argument. It is misleading because, as Norrell notes, it ignores Washington's lifelong secret and seductive, or *private*, fight, something which DuBois deliberately did. It also ignores the fact that there is no one way to fight for, or achieve, our civil rights. After all, as discussed below, by DuBois's own admission, his *public* fight bore meagre results, so it is not as if the public fight waged by him and others was that worthy of joining, especially as they conducted it. The need publicly to have pursued our civil rights is indisputable, but so, it can be argued, is the need to have done so judiciously. By that measure, the verdict goes to Washington.

As a reminder of this *public* side of Washington's civil rights fight, while his "Fair-Chance" article has substance and serves the purpose, a story told by Spencer might more memorably do so. Though citing no date, Spencer relates the story in the context of discussing Washington's new public posture. When he took the stage in a Tampa theatre to speak to those gathered, he found blacks and whites separated by a row of sheets down the aisle. Visibly irritated, Washington did not begin his remarks, but instead said to the audience that in all his travels, he had seen nothing like it before, and that before he began, "'I want that thing taken down from there'" (244: 191). It was taken down, and then Washington began his remarks. Thus our mnemonic to remind us of Washington's *public* fight for us during the last three years of his life: **Washington's public protest: "'I want that thing taken down from there.'"**

The "Treaty":
Unity Platform of the Amenia Conference of 1916

Nevertheless, all wars come to an end, and with the death of Washington in 1915, ostensibly, so did the war between Washington and DuBois. The end of a war is often marked by a treaty, which, tantamount in this case, was the "Unity Platform" arrived at by the conferees at the Amenia Conference of 1916. Held near Amenia, New York, on August 24-26, at the estate of NAACP head, Joel Spingarn -- and upon invitation from him and DuBois -- a group of over 50 white and black leaders across the ideological spectrum, including, for example, Emmett Scott [Washington's secretary and alter ego] and Trotter, met to reconcile their differences (295; 229e:184-207). The outcome was the "Unity Platform," a number of resolutions supporting "the desirability of all types of education, the importance of the ballot, and the necessity of replacing ancient suspicions and factions with respect for the good faith and methods of leaders in all parts of the country" (168:184). In what can be taken as an implementation of the "treaty," later in the year, a Bookerite, the aforementioned James Weldon Johnson, was appointed as NAACP secretary. The deal was thus sealed, so to speak; in principles and personalities the Washington-DuBois forces were joined – at least that was the hope and the hype.

The results justified neither. Rudwick contends that the "Treaty's" success was overrated. Although the goal had been to achieve something sought since 1904, racial harmony, it failed. They did not achieve racial harmony because, as Rudwick puts it, "The conferees did not hammer out 'a practical working understanding' in Myrdal's sense of a functional interacting division of labor." "For example," he goes on to add,

> such an 'understanding' would have permitted Southern leaders to stress industrial education while Northerners like Du Bois could have emphasized secondary-college education. Neither group would have tried to demolish the other but simply would have attempted to push its own program. Thus, the race would have achieved as much as possible. But old animosities did not die and old dogmas prevailed (229b: 189).

As for why "old animosities did not die and old dogmas prevailed," Rudwick gives an answer we have come to expect:

> Probably Du Bois more than any other racial leader violated the Amenia principle of peaceful co-existence. He minimized the social pressure which was placed on Southern Negro leaders and still blamed them for failing to propagandize on behalf of reforms he favored. Therefore, he continued to deprecate their projects and programs (229b:187).

To remind us of DuBois's violation of the Amenia Conference of 1916 "treaty" and his repeated sabotage, even after Washington's death, of agreements reached to achieve racial unity: **Amenia Conference of 1916: DuBois's sabotage**.

While the "Unity Platform" did not mean death for the Self-Responsibility Tradition, it did, as an active movement, leave it comatose. The black agenda became the "protest agenda" of the System-Responsibility Tradition -- *absent* brains, property, and character. As Norrell puts it, "Washington's departure from the scene allowed the already-existing consensus on a protest agenda to emerge fully" (192:422). The voice of the "more subtle than any beast of the field" prevailed.

No ignominious ending

One can read into the treaty an ignominious ending for Booker -- his political power eviscerated and his leadership contested and weakened. Only the record suggests otherwise. Washington was displaced by the NAACP, but its agenda -- absent brains, property, and character -- is pretty much what Norrell tells us that, for years, Washington had advocated and secretly fought for. In Norrell's words:

> The irony of Washington's displacement by the NAACP was that he had anticipated almost all of the NAACP's civil-rights agenda. Over the previous two decades he had protested discrimination on railroads, lynching, unfair voting qualifications, and discriminatory funding in education. He had organized and financed court challenges to disfranchisement, jury discrimination, and peonage. The NAACP likewise focused on segregated public accommodations, lynching and the criminal justice system, and disfranchisement. It would eventually echo Washington's concerns about economic discrimination and equal educational rights. Its efforts to lobby Congress for legislation against lynching and for civil-rights protections closely resembled Washington's pressure at the Capitol to confirm William Crum [a black physician whom President Theodore Roosevelt, upon the recommendation of Washington, appointed to the prestigious position of revenue collector for the Port of Charleston, he and Washington overcoming determined white opposition to secure, after three years of effort, Senate approval of his appointment]. The NAACP would also regularly condemn the ugly stereotypes prevalent in American life. Indeed, a consensus on the measures needed to protect black rights had emerged as early as 1900. By 1910 there was little debate among African Americans about the necessity for direct challenges to discrimination. The argument was whether they should be mounted aggressively and defiantly, or carefully and indirectly. There was a case for each method, but any rational discussion of strategy and tactics was made subordinate to the personal acrimony that had emerged between Washington and anti-Booker groups. The personal hostility to Washington--more potent from powerful whites than from blacks in 1909 and 1910--made the method of racial uplift the overriding issue (192:392).

Although Washington publicly moved towards the embrace of a protest agenda, he never moved away from his commandment. Norrell, like Harlan, observes that in neither words nor deeds did he ever falter from his gospel of brains, property, and character (for example, see Harlan, 109:202-237; 405-406). Nor did his embrace of a deft approach to the acquisition of our civil rights versus a confrontational one ever change. Although his leadership came under increasing challenge from blacks and whites alike, he remained the unquestioned leader of our race. In particular, Harlan's chapter in his second volume on Washington, Booker T. Washington: The Wizard of Tuskegee, 1901-1915, "Outside Looking In," makes for informative reading in this regard (109:405-37).

One example will serve to underline his continued standing. In the interest of promoting black health, Harlan reports Washington's initiation of National Negro Health Week, March 21-27, 1915, some six months before his death (109:235). The climax of the week was his address at the Bethel A. M. E. Church in Baltimore. About 3000 people are said to have crowded the auditorium, thousands of others having been turned away after waiting for two hours. Described as eager and enthusiastic, the assembled represented both races.

More broadly, Washington's continued national standing was evident from his Southern Educational Tours, 1908-1912, chronicled by Jackson in his informative book, Booker T. Washington and the Struggle Against White Supremacy (132). The tours covered ten states, in order, Mississippi, South Carolina, Virginia, West Virginia, Tennessee, Delaware, North Carolina, Texas, Florida, and Louisiana. Largely under the aegis and participation of the National Negro Business League (NNBL), of which he was founder and President, the tours reached an estimated 1 million black and white people. Through his speeches in a variety of settings, his intent was to aid them in their "industrial and moral life," everywhere his basic message, self-reliance through brains, property, and character, being the same (132: 4,82).

Along with his continued standing, Washington also maintained continued national influence. As an example, when, in January 1915, Congress, during the Woodrow Wilson administration (famous for its segregation policies), attempted to enact a bill to exclude from the country all immigrants of African descent, including those from the

West Indies and elsewhere in the Americas, Washington was alarmed and went into action, calling into battle his Tuskegee Machine (109:413-16). He had less than a week to stop it, but stop it he did. He mobilized a successful newspaper, letter, and lobbying campaign. The Senate had passed the bill, but even with Southern Democrats in control of the House and also expected to pass it, Washington got it soundly defeated 250 to 77 -- and again, with less than a week to do it. Harlan reports that Washington received many congratulations for his success, even winning over Monroe Trotter who thought it would be a fine thing for Washington, DuBois, and himself to appear in Washington, arm in arm, fighting against the bill (109:413-16).

That was BTW to the very end. He remained the recognized leader of his race, immensely popular, and a tireless crusader on behalf of the welfare of the black masses. And, Norrell writes, the defeat of the immigration bill showed that though "Booker may have been powerless at the White House ... he still had real influence in the country at large" (192:405).

No such continued standing was enjoyed by those in Washington's leadership circle. But to be fair to them, to thrive, a cause needs a leader and their leader had been taken away. Norrell observes that there was no one of the stature and will to take Washington's place. Amid contending voices, to come up with someone at all was apparently quite a challenge to the Tuskegee decision-makers, as is often true in the case of replacing a towering leader. Moreover, one gathers from Norrell's informative discussion of the succession issue, to galvanize their now leaderless forces and continue to wage war against a now formidable foe, the NAACP, which embodied the DuBois challenge, probably would have meant almost certain defeat (192:421-23). Meier, too, points to the inevitability of the outcome (168:184).

Affixing Blame

The fixing of blame for the Washington-DuBois war in our African American Garden of Eden has had a profound impact on African American history. In contrast to the biblical Garden of Eden, it lead to "the Lord" becoming Satan, and to Satan becoming "the Lord."

Following is an attempt to make the case that this reversal has been a tragic mistake -- and a rather obvious one at that.

The core question is whether, of themselves, the Washington-DuBois differences over the issues were of such magnitude as to occasion Dubois's "disobedience." Norrell has made it clear that they were not, that their differences were in regard to strategy and tactics. More relevant -- believe it or not -- DuBois himself did not believe his differences with Washington were major. Meier points out that DuBois later recalled that he was probably less disturbed by his ideological differences with Washington (which he remembered mainly as a matter of emphasis) than with his political power difference with him. He was apparently disturbed, says Meier, by Washington's "immense power over political appointments, over philanthropic largess, and over the press wielded by what DuBois has labeled the 'Tuskegee Machine'" (168:98; also see Norrell, 192:293-296). His friend, Trotter, and his other close allies had the same response (192:288-296). And Spencer, for example, makes the same point (244:161). Their warring was really not over substance, but power; even DuBois confided as much.

It is argued, therefore, that those who deify DuBois and defame Washington give more weight to their ideological difference than DuBois himself did. For what DuBois publicly espoused was apparently not consistent with what, in his heart, he thought -- or might have thought, which brings up the next point.

DuBois was a man with a divided mind. In fact, Meier observes, "In W.E.B. Du Bois ... the most distinguished Negro intellectual in the age of Booker T. Washington, we find explicitly stated most of the threads of Negro thought at that time" (168:204). His attack on Washington has to be considered in that context -- and further, in the context of a divided mind seeking Washington's power. He differed, not just with Washington, but with himself as well. He was indeed, Meier tells us (as do others), a man of paradoxes.

> Scholar and prophet; mystic and materialist; ardent agitator for political rights and propagandist for economic co-operation; one who espoused an economic interpretation of politics and yet emphasized the necessity of political rights for economic advancement; one who

denounced segregation and called for integration into American society in accordance with the principles of human brotherhood and the ideals of democracy, and at the same time one who favored the maintenance of racial solidarity and integrity and a feeling of identity with Negroes elsewhere in the world; an equalitarian who apparently believed in innate racial differences; a Marxist who was fundamentally a middle-class intellectual, Du Bois becomes the epitome of the paradoxes in American Negro thought (168:206).

Of course, his tradition has ignored the paradoxes, as it has his early agreements with Washington and his later changes of mind. With civil rights as its epicenter, Washington and DuBois's political disagreements, to whatever extent a matter of emphasis, trump all else and result in the demonization of Washington.

But why should DuBois's followers be any different from him? Though confiding in later life that his differences with Washington were a matter of emphasis, he himself, nevertheless, made those differences historic. Washington's "mistakes and shortcomings" led him to declare himself, along with other blacks that he names and describes, independent of Washington.

Having, in 1903, publicly declared his independence, he publicly did what Norrell says he had privately started doing in 1900: went on an attack-and-destroy mission which, though enormously successful over time, was not successful during Washington's lifetime. Decades later, the more radical leaders of the Civil Rights Movement came along and, taking their cue from DuBois, practically read Washington out of the race – found him to be a lackey and an "Uncle Tom" rather than a champion of freedom as they saw to be the case with DuBois in particular (239:xi). It is doubtful if they knew anything about Washington's "secret life," as Harlan terms it, and there is no reason to believe that they cared. Nor, apparently, did they know or care about a couple of his co-credentials dear to some in their ranks: Pan-Africanism and Black Power.

While DuBois's Pan-Africanism (he, for example, renounced his American citizenship and became a citizen of Ghana) reinforces his image of being "for us" -- making him kind of a gold standard of what it really means to be black – they did not know or acknowledge that Washington was not so provincial himself. Harlan devotes an essay to Washington's "substantial" involvement in African Affairs (110). Although he never visited Africa, he "and other Tuskegee's [including Tuskegee students] were actively involved in Togo, Sudan, South Africa, Congo Free State, and Liberia" (110:69). They introduced cotton culture into these countries, and Washington consulted extensively with various African leaders on racial and educational policies. Washington even helped to plan one Pan-African Conference and held one at Tuskegee in 1912. A planned follow up meeting three years later was derailed by the World War and Washington's death (109:274-76). Harlan notes that he played his greatest role in Liberia, managing to get a commitment of American aid (110:77).

Perhaps less obvious, Washington's Black Power credentials, too, are a matter of record. The late black University of Michigan history professor and author, Harold Cruse, makes the argument that those in the Black Power vanguard were so fixed on vilifying Washington, however, that they – unlike one of the most famous among them, Marcus Garvey -- failed to recognize or acknowledge the debt they owed Washington. Garvey even came to this country to see Washington and lamented the fact that "'Since the death of Booker T. Washington, there was no one with a positive and practical uplift program for the masses—North or South'" (52b:78). In part, that program was about self-help through the amassing of black wealth and economic power (translatable into political power), which is what, in part, Black Power was about. The difference, Cruse argues, lies in the militancy of the Black Power approach versus Washington's moderate approach. In Washington's "five fingers, yet one as the hand" call, Cruse even cites the origin for the nationalist-separatist doctrine espoused by elements in the Black Power ranks. In sum, Cruse argues, *"Black Power is nothing but the economic and political philosophy of Booker T. Washington given a 1960s militant shot in the arm and brought up to date"* (emphasis in original) (52b:177).

It was not, however, just the "more militant black leaders and their white allies" who did Washington in; it was also historians. In his chapter, "The Veil of History," Norrell recounts how historians, "even more than activists," he says, "disparaged Washington's historical reputation" (192:433, 433-38). Maybe this is because their assessment -- much like those who founded the NAACP -- was conditioned *even more* by their own station in life and by a perspective shaped by factors and forces far removed from those which confronted Washington and the civil rights activists. Their groundwork was laid and disseminated by the late Yale historian, **C. Vann Woodward**, who, according to Norrell, in 1951, published "the most influential book on the post-Reconstruction South," Origins of the New South. One of his students, the late University of Pennsylvania historian, **Louis R. Harlan**, followed his lead, becoming "the biographer [of Washington] almost universally regarded as definitive." His two-volume biography of Washington, Booker T. Washington: The Making of a Black Leader, 1856-1901, and Booker T. Washington: The Wizard of Tuskegee, 1901-1915, were prize winners -- the former winner of the Bancroft Prize in 1972, the latter of the Pulitzer Prize in 1983 -- cemented Woodward's negative portrayal. We need only cite some of the references to Washington in Harlan's Preface to his first volume to get some sense of the ingredients in the cement, laid by DuBois and spread by Woodward, was made (108:preface):

- made by white authors a "token Negro in company of white heroes"
- "outward humility"
- "changed roles with skill of magician"
- "his methods were too compromising and unheroic to win him a place in the black Pantheon"
- "power was his game"
- "used ideas simply as instruments to gain power"
- "mind as revealed in formal public utterance was a bag of clichés"
- "his psyche…was a kaleidoscope of infinitely changing patterns"
- "benevolent despot"
- "his economic program was peasant conservatism"
- "used ruthless methods of espionage and sabotage against his black critics, tactics that stood in sharp contrast to his public profession of Sunday-school morality"
- "he paradoxically [secretly] attacked the racial settlement that he publicly accepted"
- "a personality that vanished into the roles it played"
- "he seemed to lose sight of his original purposes of his dance"

As Norrell argues, combine this kind of reputable academic portrayal with **DuBois's Washington Demonization**, then throw in the inflammatory rhetoric of the radical elements among the civil rights activists, and "... little wonder that history brought Booker so low" (192:438). Seldom, if ever, does one hear our leaders invoke his name, to say nothing of acknowledging his accomplishments. Our leaders want no part of what Smock terms "Washington's outmoded social philosophy and program for race advancement" (239:x). Rather, we have recently ended what might be called the Century of W. E. B. Du Bois, a designation that might please him, especially since his rival commands only an Age. Who knows, the time might have to be extended. Though not, as Washington, a leader of the masses, in the fashion of a Karl Marx (and he would probably not object to this comparison either), he has become the ideological and inspirational leader of the political and intellectual vanguard whose System-Responsibility thinking has come to dominate African American thought. As testimony to his standing, we have the W.E.B. Du Bois Institute for African and African-American Research, established at his alma mater, Harvard University, in 1975, and, less prominently, the W.E.B. DuBois Scholars Institute at Princeton (92:142-77, 350-56; 192:419-42).

Washington -- fighting back

Descriptions of the war between the two sometimes read like a gangster novel (192:263-310; 109:359-78; 239:110-51). As the DuBois forces might script it, Washington had a power thirst and could not stand criticism, gang warfare resulting (yes, quite some Garden of Eden).

Power thirst. "From 1903 on [after DuBois made his disobedience public]," writes Meier, "Washington found himself increasingly under attack. He used every means at his disposal to combat his critics--his influence with the press, placing spies in the opposition movements, depriving their members of church and political positions" (168:115). Meier goes on to add:

> His attacks upon 'the opposition' suggest that something more than tactics or ideologies was at stake. It appears that Washington feared the effect of his critics on his personal power and prestige. He did not object to protest too much as long as it was not aimed at

him and his policies. As he wrote R. C. Ogden, 'wise, conservative agitation looking toward securing the rights of colored people on the part of the North is not hurtful' (168:115-16).

There we have a sample of his critics portrayal (DuBois foremost among them): a personal-power-thirsty Washington resorting to devious and diabolical schemes to undermine and destroy his black enemies, perceived or real, while being accommodating and subservient to whites. Do they have a point? Meier offers this intriguing response:

> It would appear to this author that a large part of Washington's motivation was his desire for power. To a large extent he had to be satisfied with the substance rather than the symbols of power. His desire for power and prestige, however, does not necessarily indicate insincerity or hypocrisy. It is usually hard to distinguish where altruism ends and self-interest begins. So thoroughly and inextricably bound together in Washington's mind were his program for racial elevation and his own personal career, that he genuinely thought that he and only he was in the best position to advance the interests of the race (168:116).

The rebuke: the man and his cause. Meier's central response -- and the central response to be made to the DuBois forces and others -- is Washington's inseparable identification, in his mind, of his success with the success of his race. That inseparability was not a delusion. Washington felt that his failure to make Tuskegee a success would be interpreted as a failure for the race, and Tuskegee came to mean, not just the institution, but also its associated activities -- educational, social, economic, and political. For blacks and whites alike, he was the accepted and recognized leader of his people. That, then, he saw his success and the success of his race as inseparable was not the product of a daydream or narcissism. Sociologist Charles Cooley's concept of the *looking glass self* suggests that he would tend to see himself as he pictured himself from his interactions with others and from his perceptions of him held by others. The historical record is indisputable: the message of those interactions and perceptions was that the fate of the race was in his hands.

To say, therefore, that a "large part of Washington's motivation was his desire for power" and leave it at that is falsely to characterize him, which Meier has not done, but which DuBois and his critics did. Did he seek and prize power? Of course, he did. If he were powerless, how would he be able to lead our uplifting? How would he have been able to attract the support of the rich and powerful? Otherwise stated, the more power he possessed, the greater his chances of success in acquiring the resources to uplift his people -- not himself, but simultaneously and inseparably, himself *and* his people. It is not unusual for great or famous men and women and their cause to become inseparable -- Nelson Mandela, Jackie Robinson, Sojourner Truth, Rosa Parks, and Dr. Martin Luther King Jr. immediately coming to mind. Booker Taliaferro Washington is among them. Meier is right. In his war against his enemies, "something more than tactics or ideologies was at stake," and that "something more," as validated by history, was the inseparable fate of his race. It is only fair that we let him speak for himself:

> I knew that, in a large degree, we were trying an experiment--that of testing whether or not it was possible for Negroes to build up and control the affairs of a large educational institution. I knew that if we failed it would injure the whole race. I knew that the presumption was against us. I knew that in the case of white people beginning such an enterprise it would be taken for granted that they were going to succeed, but in our case I felt that people would be surprised if we succeeded. All this made a burden which pressed down on us, sometimes, at the rate of a thousand pounds to the square inch (265:292).

The rebuke: critics' tactics. As for his critics' portrayal of his tactics against his opposition, his opponents were not exactly among the meek. They were relentless and ruthless -- out for the kill. They (with DuBois in the vanguard) said so in Trotter's <u>Guardian</u> and elsewhere and translated their words into actions -- from the Boston riot of 1903, to the Niagara Movement of 1905, to the establishment of the NAACP in 1910.

Washington, therefore, waged a *defensive* campaign against his opponents, not because (it is argued) -- as suggested by Meier -- he "feared the effect of his critics on his *personal* [emphasis added] power and prestige," but because he feared its effect on his *public* power and prestige, on which he felt the fate of his race depended. One can question whether it was rational for him to think, as Meier suggests he "genuinely" thought, "that *he and only he* [emphasis added] was in the best position to advance the interests of the race," but we must consider the context of that thinking. When your opposition is led by unstable personalities like DuBois and Trotter, what else are you to think? Keep in mind some of Washington's cited characterizations of his opponents:

- "They know books but they do not know men."
- They are "ignorant in regard to the actual needs of the masses of colored people in the South today."
- "There is another class of colored people who make a business of keeping the troubles, the wrongs, and the hardships of the Negro race before the public."
- "Some of these people do not want the Negro to lose his grievances, because they do not want to lose their jobs…."

Norrell also points to "the resentment he felt at their refusal to stand with him against the attacks from the white South since he dined with the president" (192:322). To Washington, Norrell indicates, his black critics did not seem to realize that in attacking him they (DuBois and Trotter, in particular) had, in effect, joined hands with the white nationalists. The white nationalists, in attacking him, were also attacking the race. In joining the white nationalists in their attack against him, DuBois and Trotter, were at the same time joining them in attacking the race (192:327-28). DuBois and Trotter no doubt saw the situation differently, though, it is argued inaccurately. Such is the likely outcome of a regressive time perspective and a flawed core identity. Moreover, having no leadership responsibility, they could be indifferent to the consequences of their actions.

The rebuke: gradualism versus immediacy. In contrast to these characterizations, Washington, an ex-slave himself, apparently felt that he knew the needs of our people and, in responding to those needs, unlike his opponents, was guided by this maxim which he proclaimed in an address before the Afro-American Council in July 1903, "'**An inch of progress is worth more than a yard of complaint**'" [emphasis added](168:107). As a reminder of

Washington's emphasis on gradualism and his support of "sane agitation and criticism" in contrast to DuBois's doctrine that we "must strike the blow" and "must insist continually, in season and out of season," (64:35,44) our mnemonic is **Washington (1903): "An inch of progress is worth more than a yard of complaint."**

While, on the other hand, acknowledging that the rights and results sought would not "come in a moment," DuBois, nevertheless – in a typical DuBois paradox -- championed and undertook unceasing agitation, observing in his Declaration, "Negroes must insist continually, in season and out of season, that voting is necessary to modern manhood, that color discrimination is barbarism, and that black boys need education as well as white boys" (64:44).

But Washington, a son of the South, knew that it was just such aggression – even, for that matter, anything which might be interpreted by whites as a sign of aggression – that would likely mean death and defeat. He knew that he had to be delicate in his relations with whites -- that he had to "wear the mask," as black Florida A&M University historian, David Jackson Jr. tells the story, and exercise delicacy and circumspection in what he said and wrote (132:31-52).

The rebuke: accommodating and subservient versus realistic and savvy. Being accommodating and subservient in his relations with whites, as Norrell points out, was, therefore, a forced choice. We are talking about black life in the South during the post-Civil War period. It is in this context the charge against Washilngton has to be weighed. In particular, as a sociologist, one might expect DuBois to have weighed it quite differently, but that would be to forget that we are talking about, not his expertise, but his thirst for power. Norrell points out that another black sociologist, Charles S. Johnson, in a 1928 article in the black journal, <u>Opportunity</u> -- in publication from 1923-49 -- indeed weighed the situation quite differently, making what Norrell calls a "sophisticated defense" of Washington's forced choice (192:424-25). As Norrell sums up Johnson's defense, "Washington saw that white fears were a threat constantly on the verge of explosion, and they had to be abated or at least controlled if blacks were to make progress."

But remember how easy it is to forget – or, more applicable to DuBois -- to engage in fabrication. To accuse Washington, as DuBois did, of "voluntarily throwing them [our civil rights] away and insisting that ... [he does] not want them..." is to do just that (64:44). The realities which Johnson saw were there for DuBois and others – past and present – to see. Compromise has historically proven to be a wise way to deal with such realities. It served the cause of the Founding Fathers quite well, as it did, for example, the cause of Jackie Robinson in breaking the color barrier in baseball and the cause of Nelson Mandela in stabilizing South Africa as it emerged from apartheid. Henry Clay's fame in American history rests on his reputation as a "Great Compromiser." Yet, we have allowed DuBois – along with Woodward, Harlan, and the Civil Rights Movement radicals -- to brainwash us into thinking that what is regarded as a virtue in these famous figures is a vice when it comes to Booker T. Washington – even though it was a *forced* choice.

So when DuBois refers to Washington's Atlanta Exposition Speech as the "Atlanta Compromise," it is taken as pejorative. Yes, it was a compromise, and there is nothing wrong with calling it just that. Harlan reminds us that it occurred at a time when Southern whites were waging a campaign of war and terror against blacks and Washington's compromise offered a peace (112:110-11). Though that peace was glaringly deficient, because of that peace -- thanks to the Age of Booker T. Washington – we were able to make great progress.

Norrell, and far less so Harlan, writes extensively about the hostile Southern white supremacist environment in which Washington had to function (192:185-339; 108:288-324; 109:238-65). Just to fend Tuskegee itself against white attack and enable it to survive and prosper was itself a miracle – accomplished only through his ability, among other things, to compromise. The fact is that to put the compromise or accommodation label on Washington puts him in some pretty good company, helping to make him deserving of his moniker, the Wizard of Tuskegee. Even DuBois, while condemning Washington, acknowledged as much, writing in his classic, <u>The Souls of Black Folk</u>:

> It startled the nation to hear a Negro advocating such a programme [industrial education, conciliation with the South, and deferral of civil and political rights] after many decades of bitter complaint;

it startled and won the applause of the South, it interested and won the admiration of the North, and after a confused murmur of protest, it silenced if it did not convert the Negroes themselves.

To gain the sympathy and cooperation of the various elements comprising the South was Mr. Washington's first task; and this, at the time Tuskegee was founded, seemed, for a black man, well-nigh impossible. And yet ten years later it was done in the word spoken at Atlanta: 'in all things purely social we can be as separate as the five fingers, and yet one as the hand in all things essential to mutual progress' (64:36).

What a tribute! Yes, this romanticist was capable of at least perceiving the real. Only he would have us believe that the reality that he acknowledges, and which, in effect, he describes as miraculous, is, at the same time, malevolent, indeed traitorous. Of course, DuBois is not the first to attempt to square a circle, only he is among the first to have so many believe that he actually succeeded. Ironically, chief among those who believed he succeeded -- historian Norrell tells us – was influential historian, C. Vann Woodward, and his student, Washington's prizewinning, definitive biographer, Louis R. Harlan, both of whom have been so instrumental in spreading his feat.

Whether we are talking about the famous or the multitude, the fact is that accommodation is a staple of everyday living, not a character or leadership flaw as fabricated by DuBois, validated by Woodward and Harlan, and glorified by the Civil Rights Movement radicals. Accomodation enables us, not just to co-exist, but to prosper. When made to appear otherwise, as DuBois and the like-minded have done on a historic scale in the case of Washington, though at the same time explicitly acknowledging his accomplishment of the "well-nigh impossible," it might not be too much of a stretch to say that we are being somewhat delusional.

As to the twin charge of subservience, history is clear: Washington was not subservient. As he urged his students, he conducted himself in a "manly way." No screaming activist, he put into practice the adage that "you catch more flies with honey than vinegar." Witness, for example, his aforementioned **Birmingham Letter**. The point: to accuse

Washington of being subservient is to confuse subservience with savvy – or, as Norrell puts it, "style with the substance."

Nor was Washington nearly as accommodating as he projected himself to be, as he was perceived to have been, or as he is accused of being. Harlan's essay, "The Secret Life of Booker T. Washington," by its very title, suggestively underlines the point. That secret life shows, not an accommodating Washington, but, in the words of Harlan, "his complexity, his richness of strategic resources, his wizardry" (112:110). Washington was no wall flower, shrinking vine, spineless spectator -- or, if you will, Uncle Tom -- but apparently one of the most deft operators, black or white, to appear on the American scene. The many among us, particularly our leaders, who condemn his accommodation are no doubt guilty of a lack of knowledge, however willful. The fact is that Washington's secret life, like his public life, is a classic study in the acquisition and use of power to achieve group goals, there being abundantly more to learn from it than to condemn. His accommodation/subservience attributes served him, his race, and his nation extraordinarily well, and could, to this day, similarly serve us, the nation, and the world. He functioned, not necessarily as he wished, but judiciously and surreptitiously, as necessary and prudent, in the interest of his people – us, we blacks.

One is reminded of Jackie Robinson, in 1947, breaking the color barrier in baseball. During the first few years after 1947, he was on a leash, so to speak, sucking it in and keeping his cool. But once he got established and the color barrier diminished, he became more outspoken. Similarly, Washington was on a leash. It can be argued, though, that when, like Jackie Robinson, he felt relatively more secure (around 1912), he emerged from his secret life, "Underground Railroad" status, to a more public protest mode. Maybe, too, like Jackie Robinson, to some extent at least, he was responding to the wounds of battle – in his case, in part, the Ulrich affair.

Washington "set us back"

One often hears today what DuBois essentially alleged back then: that Washington "set us back." As DuBois's expressed it, he sewed "the inevitable seeds…for a harvest of disaster for our children, black and white" (64:45). The invalid import is that we were at some advanced stage, actual or prospective, from which to be "set back." A more consequential concern: what if Washington had failed.

Interesting itself, what makes this query all the more provocative is the chance circumstances that led Washington to become who he was instead of who he might have been. In his <u>The Social Ideas of American Educators</u>, late University of Wisconsin pioneering social and intellectual historian, Merle Curti, describes those circumstances:

> The elementary schools for freedom established in some places in the South by the missionary societies of Northern churches and by the Freedman's Aid Bureau had apparently not penetrated the mining region where he lived. It was consequently not his fortune to learn his three R's from any of the courageous Yankee schoolma'ams who had gone South to educate the Negro. Had he come under the influence of one of these teachers, who were regarded by Southern whites as obnoxious and who sometimes saw their schoolhouses burned by the Ku-Klux, his later social philosophy might have been very different. If it was true, as Southerners insisted, that these Yankee teachers were inculcating in the blacks pernicious ideas of racial equality and hatred toward their former masters, Booker T. Washington might have developed a militancy which would have altered his outlook on life (53:288-309).

That is, if Washington had been exposed to Yankee influence, so to speak, he too -- like DuBois and his coterie -- could have turned out to be an activist and ideologue, his identity and time perspective differently forged. So if he had failed, we would have only the Yankee, System-Responsibility Tradition, the same potentially being true if he had been taught by "Yankee schoolma'ams." The possible meaning of these imagined scenarios, while somewhat unsettling, is instructive. Our tradition might be a one-imprint tradition: the System-Responsibility Tradition; there likely would be no defined and personified Self-Responsibility Tradition upon which to draw. Civil rights would likely have dominated our agenda, not for most of our history, but for all of it, and personified self-help leadership for none of it.

What if that had been the case? What would have happened to our race in the absence of the kind of self-help imprint left by Washington and the total domination of a civil rights imprint? We do not have to imagine an answer; we can turn to history. Consider what happened during Reconstruction and what has happened after the Civil Rights Movement. Consider, too, what has happened in Haiti, and throw in Liberia, and, upon independence, the countries across the African continent. Until now, we have had an inordinate combination of political enmeshment and social and economic entropy. That is the price that we pay when we do not, as Washington did, preach "brains, property, and character"; disproportionately, we get, not uplifting, but material and moral impoverishment. Therein lies the "setback."

Ponder for a moment: To what national institutional black accomplishment -- at that time, or even now for that matter -- could we (if we choose to do so) point with such great pride and proof of our constructive nature, of something black-built, black-staffed, and black-administered? Or, in this era of post-Civil Rights gains disappointment, to what proven black unifying creed could we turn, if we chose, to energize and uplift our race?

Washington's critique of this "set us back" camp

These questions bring us to Washington's critique of this camp – a critique as relevant now as then. It expands on Meier's above-cited description. Washington made the point that he had mainly gotten his education, not from books, but from actual contact with things – in the fashion, for example, of a carpenter, blacksmith, or farmer; whereas those whom he said described themselves as "The Intellectuals" or the "Talented Tenth" [the core of his small group his critics] had mainly gotten theirs from books (244:140).

In his My Larger Education, Washington pictures his critics, therefore, as being unprepared to perform useful and productive work or to solve real problems. Rather, they had emerged from college with "the idea that the only thing necessary to solve at once every problem in the South was to apply the principles of the Declaration of Independence and the Bill of Rights" (265a:428-29). Further, he alleges, they have the idea that if they were black they were "entitled to the special sympathy of the world, and they have thus got into the habit of relying on this sympathy rather than on their own efforts to make their way" (265a:428).

However, it was not just the intellectuals of whom he took measure. In his My Larger Education, he characterizes, as follows, those others who, in the spirit of DuBois, were habitually "striking blows":

> There is another class of colored people who make a business of keeping the troubles, the wrongs, and the hardships of the Negro race before the public. Having learned that they are able to make a living out of their troubles, they have grown into the settled habit of advertising their wrongs--partly because they want sympathy and partly because it pays. Some of these people do not want the Negro to lose his grievances, because they do not want to lose their jobs.

> I am afraid [he continues in a subsequent passage] that there is a certain class of race- problem solvers who don't want the patient to get well, because as long as the disease holds out they have not only an easy means of making a living, but also an easy medium through which to make themselves prominent before the public (265a:430- 31).

An attempt at compromise over combat

Notwithstanding his grasp of his small group of enemies, on at least three occasions, Washington reached out his hand to them, but, absent the Zen koan of "one hand clapping," it takes two hands. Had they returned their hand with a shake and the respective forces had been able to come together and pursue a unified, integrated course, how different would be the legacy of our African American Garden of Eden. Instead, they returned it with a slap, not a shake, telling him, after one meeting, in effect, to go back to the South and take care of his educational business and leave the politics to them (109:16-17). An attempt at compromise through the Carnegie Hall Agenda has been discussed, as has been the attempt at compromise during the early years of the NAACP, which was sabotaged when DuBois and his committee authored the aforementioned open letter, signed by 31 other prominent blacks, "To the People of Great Britain and Europe" accusing Washington of misrepresenting the facts about black life in America in his tour of continental Europe in 1910 (109:367-376; 112:124). Those facts pertained to the progress which Washington said that we were making, something which could not be denied. However, it was not progress that the bitter DuBois and his activist ideologues wanted highlighted, but instead -- being in a 24/7 victim mode -- pain and victimization. Nothing Washington could have done would have satisfied them, their implacable hostility to Washington having been noted by Norrell and others. Nothing! Absolutely nothing! At issue, was not an agenda, but a person, power, and a propensity; it was DuBois versus Washington, possession of power versus desire for power, and anger and emotion versus reason and reality. As we are reminded by the mnemonic **Amenia Conference of 1916 "treaty" sabotage**, DuBois did not honor any of the agreements he and others reached in an attempt to achieve racial unity, not even after Washington's death.

Did he *have* to do it -- to go after his enemies?

Since Washington's attempts at compromise were rebuked by DuBois and his allies, DuBois in particular, one might conclude that Washington was justified in going after him, as Meier has described what occurred. But Norrell dissents, making the case that rather than getting "down into the mire" and getting up "bruised and dirty," Washington "might well have ignored Trotter and the others and lost little influence" (192:284). Norrell argues that Washington's support was overwhelming, while DuBois, Trotter, and his other adversaries constituted a tiny opposition.

Conceding Booker's attack on his enemies to be defensive, Bookerites must, nevertheless, concede that Norrell has a point. Any of us who might, to some degree, have been in Washington's shoes know -- and as the Boston riot demonstrated -- such opposition as he faced can be provocative and exasperating. The opposition members typically are immune to logic and reason; their mind is set -- against you. They are out to destroy, not debate or cooperate. And if they destroy you, they also jeopardize the larger purpose to which you dedicate your life. Often, they are ill informed, if at all informed, about what you are doing and they have little or no desire to understand or work with you; their consuming passion is to harass and work against you. They are destroyers, not builders -- and their fight is often more about who and what they are than about what the problem or issue is. Typically, they are the problem or issue, driven, as John McWhorter argues, by therapeutic alienation -- and who knows what can be said about their core identity or time perspective.

The substance not being central to such opposition, to engage its members, as Washington did, can exact a price. One price that Washington paid, Norrell contends, was a "reputation damaged once and for all" (192:284). Nothing read, however, suggests that the damage translated into a damage to Washington's program. Nevertheless, while Proverbs tells us that "the instruction of fools is folly," another scripture tells us that if we are wise -- as many think Washington was -- we "suffer fools gladly, seeing ye yourselves are wise."[18] Perhaps we would all like to have untarnished heroes, but the fulfillment of that desire would require an eternal wait.

The Legacy: Our Two Traditions

Through the words and actions discussed above, both men left us a legacy which has become embedded in our culture and, more or less, serves us African Americans as guides in the pursuit of our adaptation and uplifting. Following is the interpretation herein of those legacies.

> **Washington's <u>Self-Responsibility Tradition</u> is masses-oriented and responsibility- receptive. It seeks to cultivate a self-made people through an emphasis on self- help and preparation made possible by reliance on brains, property, and character. It seeks to live in harmony with whites through an emphasis on compromise, cooperation, and a common humanity. Its guiding spirit -- due mainly to its progressive time perspective – is underlined by hope and optimism.**

> **DuBois's <u>System-Responsibility Tradition</u> is middle-class oriented and responsibility-resistant. It seeks to cultivate a successful people through an emphasis on system-help, equal opportunity, and equal outcomes made possible by reliance on protest and civil rights. It perceives whites as the opposition**

---

[18] Corinthians 11:19

whose domination must be fought through separatism and siege. Its guiding spirit -- due mainly to its regressive time perspective – is underlined by anger and anxiety.

Neither tradition is without elements of the other. However, we are talking about, not just what each tradition embraces, but rather about what constitutes its distinctive, central, driving force -- the essence from which it mainly derives its direction, power, and energy. Of course, the elements and interpretations herein ascribed are subject to dispute, but, in this chapter and others, an attempt is made to demonstrate their justification.

Legacy Survival

While DuBois's System-Responsibility Tradition thrives, since its tenets do not command the headlines, the very existence of Washington's Self-Responsibility Tradition may be in question. But the point has been made that, whereas Washington's tradition does not thrive, nevertheless, it is still alive – and very much so, just nationally leaderless.

Moreover, it must be again emphasized, as Meier does, that although it is Booker T. Washington who is herein cited as the father of our Self-Responsibility Tradition, Washington did not initiate its self-help core and other tenets; he only propagated and popularized them, and has come to personify them. The tenets which he espoused preceeded him, starting to take root before the Civil War and gaining a firmer foothold during the travails of Reconstruction in the 1870s. When, thus, we speak of the survival of his Tradition, we are talking about something "more than" that which came down from him; we are talking about something which, thanks to various personalities, is deeply rooted in our culture and history, only it is Washington, thanks to his accomplishments and acclaim, who has memorialized it.

So, given its germinal roots, it is not so surprising that Washington's legacy survives, even without national leadership. Even nationally, however, if it had not been for the shackling of Martin Luther King Jr., we would have a different story to tell. King can be regarded as the successor to Washington, not just by embracing his tradition, but, doing so by explicitly invoking Washington's name. *Yes, in what might come as a surprise to most of us, Dr. King attempted to renew Washington's Self-Responsibility Tradition by invoking Washington's name.* However, the same forces arrayed against Washington went on the attack and shackled him, and, by ignoring his attempt, these same forces have shackled this leg of his legacy. They, and we, celebrate his civil rights legacy, and, to a lesser extent, his economic justice legacy, but ignore his self-help legacy and his explicit association of it with Booker T. Washington. More to come in Chapter 19. Now, we turn to other evidence to support our case.

Harlan calls our attention to an easily overlooked fact: Washington's classic autobiography, <u>Up from Slavery</u>, is still in print – and selling! In comparison with DuBois's <u>Souls of Black Folk</u>, following is its Seller Rank on Amazon for the Dover Thrift Editions Series:

<u>Up from Slavery</u>	<u>The Souls of Black Folk</u>
# 2,762 among Books	# 1,072 among Books
# 6 among Educators	# 1 in American literature
# 15 in African-American Studies	# 7 in African-American Studies
# 49 in Historical category	# 7 in Classics category

There is, moreover, a **BTW Society** – an organizational entity dedicated to the propagation of the Washington gospel (308a). Founded by Boston University graduate and Vietnam veteran, service-minded Ronald Court, the Society was started in 2005-06. In various ways, it seeks to foster what it calls the Booker T. Way, which comprises seven personal values: initiative, commitment, hard work, ownership, organization, service, and endurance (summed up in the motto: I CHOOSE). The story of how Court started the society, however, underlines Washington's demise. Browsing the internet, Court just happened to browse to a webpage discussing Washington's birthday. The date (1856) suggested to him that the next year would be Washington's Sesquicentennial (150th) birthday. So he googled to see if he could find anything about it, but found nothing. Soon thereafter, attending a college event, he heard the speaker, Reginald Jones, enthusiastically mention Washington. The two spoke after the event and agreed that Washington's Sesquicentennial birthday should be remembered. That marked the origin of the BTW Society. Among its activities is promoting the founding of BTW Society chapters in schools and cities throughout the country.

Then there is the **Booker T. Washington High School** in Memphis, Tennessee, winner of the 2010 Race to the Top High School Commencement Challenge. Not only does it bear Washington's name, it too, like the **BTW Society,** explicitly embraces his philosophy (308a). More will be said about it in Chapter 12.

While, further, lacking a recognized national leader, the Washington tradition is embraced and propagated by any number of local and widely-known black leaders, one singled out by Norrell in the Acknowledgements section of his book, is Lee Walker. **Lee Walker** is black founder and President of **The New Coalition for Economic and Social Change** and a senior fellow at The Heartland Institute. Like the Booker T. Washington High School which bears his name, the commitment of The New Coalition to Washington himself is no less explicit. Inclusively, a la Washington's Negro Business League, it seeks to increase black economic independence, and it attacks black social problems (see its website). Among its activities is "Presenting the Booker T. Washington "New Citizenship" Award annually to Americans who have succeeded against the odds." An excellent esample of succeeding against the odds, in Walker's view, was Barak Obama quest for President in 2008. In these words, he connected it to Washington:

> When the history texts are updated, they should strongly reflect the contributions of Booker T. Washington and Sen. Barak Obama as blacks who could lead both blacks and whites at challenging times in American history when race relations were at a critical turning point. Barak Obama's presidential candidacy is powerful confirmation of the truth of Washington's vision of hard work and self-reliance as the route to success for blacks as for all Americans (462c).

Another Bookerite is **Rev. Jesse Lee Peterson**. Rev. Peterson is founder and president of **BOND** (Brotherhood Organization of a New Destiny) (see the website). Like the Rempson Foundation, BOND focuses primarily on "rebuilding the family by rebuilding the man." A perusal of its website shows a number of self-help initiatives to accomplish this goal, including business consulting, an Entrepreneur Program, and a Leadership Academy. Like the Booker T. Washington High School and Lee Walker, Peterson's Washington connection is explicit. In his book, <u>Scam: How the Black Leadership Exploits Black America</u>, he confides that Washington is one of his heroes and reveals that one of the primary textbooks in his After School Character-Building Program is Washington's autobiography, <u>Up from Slavery</u> (209c). Read Peterson's book and you can imagine Washington saying most of what he says.

As for Washington's Self-Responsibility Tradition itself, there have been what is herein considered to be three major mainstream attempts to renew it, not in his name or memory, but in their self-help focus. The first is the **Moynihan Family Initiative** of 1963, the second is termed **Fordham-Ogbu's "acting white" Thesis** of 1986, and the third is the **Bill Cosby Brown Anniversary (Pound Cake) Speech** of 2004. To be discussed in Chapter 18, due to its focus on our Achilles heel, the black family, the **Moynihan Family Initiative** especially stands out. Each attempt emphasized black self-responsibility and ignited a national debate centered essentially around our two traditions. At the same time, amid these three reminders (and others), there has been what is herein considered to be one major mainstream reminder of the demise of Washington: **President Obama's Washington Omission in His First Inaugural Address** in 2009, to be discussed in Chapter 18.

For additional Washington reminders, we can go further back – to the New Negro proclaimed by black Harvard Ph.D. and Rhodes scholar, Alain Locke, in his edited book (1925), <u>The New Negro</u> (154a). This is the Negro of our pre-Civil Rights Movement and the product of the Age of Booker T. Washington. In the words of Meier, "He owed an equal debt to Howard, Fisk, Lincoln, and Atlanta and to Hampton and Tuskegee; to the Niagara Movement and to the National Negro Business League; to Booker T. Washington and W. E. B. Du Bois" (168:278). Although Washington died in 1915, we see his influence cited in the forging of the New Negro of the pre-Civil Rights Movement. The point is that the "tendencies," as Meier puts it, which he represented, helped to fashion, and got rooted, in our culture -- and remain so. However, since the Age of Booker T. Washington, they have not been nourished, but instead, stifled by the magical civil-rights fixation of our System-Responsibility Tradition.

While evidence of that rooting is readily seen in the concrete examples cited above, such as the BTW Society, evidence also exists of the continuation of Washington's legacy among us African American males ourselves and among African Americans in general. The <u>Washington Post</u> survey of 1,328 black males in 2006 (no distinction being made between African American and other black males) found that "The majority of black men in the poll...said the group's problems stem from its own failures. Black men were *more likely than whites* [emphasis added] to express such sentiments. And while such negative views were held across the board, better-educated, affluent black men were most likely to criticize black men for not taking education seriously enough" (245:20). One respondent expressed such views as follows: "They [young black men] tend to goof off, and very few are going to college. I don't see in them a will to succeed. They don't see the point of using good language. They emulate who they see on TV or on videos or who they hear on the radio." He went on the add: "That's the reality. The ones that sit back and blame things on other people, they're the ones who don't go very far. They just want sympathy and handouts."

These are some of the same views which Cosby expressed. But Dyson would have us think that Cosby -- and the black middle class along with him -- has lost his, and its, mind. But the <u>Post</u> survey found that this sentiment was held "across the board." So maybe if we are to believe Dyson, the majority of black men, "across the board," have also lost their mind. In a biblical sense, however, it could be that whoever loses his mind for the sake of black male self-help will find it, for in that loss lies the hope for the renewal of our Self-Responsibility Tradition.

As for such sentiment among African Americans generally, a PEW Research Center survey one year later (2007) revealed the self-help ethos (432a). The Center surveyed a total sample of 3,086, blacks comprising 1,007 of it. The results showed that a majority of blacks (53%) "believe that blacks who have *not gotten ahead* in life are *mainly responsible for their own situation* [emphases added], while only a minority (30%) blamed "racism for failures to advance." As previously cited, even Dyson, despite his criticism of Cosby, concedes that Cosby's views are widely shared (though not in public) in the black community, especially among what he calls the *Afristocracy*, upper-middle-class blacks, and even among the black poor and members of the working class (70:xiii-xiv). In his 2008 speech on race, President Obama offered one clue as to why, in part, that may be the case (426b). On the topic of self-help, he observed that "Ironically, this quintessentially American -- and yes, conservative -- notion of self-help found frequent expression in Reverend Wright's sermons" [Rev. Wright was the President's pastor, his sermons containing racial content which caused controversy in the President's election bid in 2008]. Experience suggests that the same might be said of many other black pastors as well as of other black community leaders -- those in contact with our people's daily needs and, therefore, see those needs, not from an ideological or political perspective, but from a daily living one.

No less compelling is the evidence that one finds in the works of those who can be considered critics of various aspects of black life. Toure¢ and McWhorter (Toure¢ discussed in Chapter 9 and McWhorer discussed throughout) provide examples. Toure¢'s plea, despite what he sees as racism, is for us to become part of the system and, rather than fighting it, get what we deserve from it (258b: 201). It is clear from Ellis Cose's The End of Anger (variously cited herein) -- as well as, for example, from the surveys cited -- that Toure¢ speaks for many, especially many of the young. That, too, was the sentiment of Washington: rather than futilely fighting the system, become part of it and get what we can ("... one as the hand in all things essential to mutual progress").

McWhorter addresses the kind of leader we need. He does so by devising an assessment scorecard, which he entitles "Black Leader A and Black Leader B: A Scorecard" (161: 359-60). It follows:

1. Black Leader A unabashedly celebrates our victories.
   Black Leader B celebrates our victories only in parentheses, under the impression that trumpeting our failures is more important because it lets whites know they are "on the hook."
2. Black Leader A is committed to eventually getting past race.
   Black Leader B is committed to delineating us as a race apart, seemingly hoping that whites and other races will blend together but blacks will remain a separate group, since we were brought here against our will.
3. Black Leader A is interested in cultural hybridity as evidence of progress.
   Black Leader B is interested in cultural hybridity as evidence that whites "appropriate" blackness "and sell it back to us."

4. Black Leader A identifies racism and discrimination after careful consideration.
   Black Leader B identifies racism and discrimination as the cause of all statistical discrepancies between blacks and whites.
5. Black Leader A is interested in blacks succeeding in the system as it is and considers us capable of doing so.
   Black Leader B is interested in blacks succeeding in a system transformed by a revolution and considers us incapable of doing so otherwise.
6. Black Leader A considers the equation between alienation and black identity a problem.
   Black Leader B considers the equation between alienation and black identity a "wake-up-call" to a benighted white Establishment by a people "denied love."

Choosing between the two, McWhorter says, "Some will prefer Black Leader B, but people of this kind will have no influence on the future of black America." "This version of activism," he adds, is "an unwitting lapse into self-indulgent cruelty," holding out the promise of a "second revolution [that] will never occur" (161:360-61). It is evident that the choice McWhorter presents is essentially a choice between a Washington and a DuBois, for Leader A embodies that for which Washington stood while Leader B represents that for which DuBois stood, and McWhorter's preference -- like that of a majority of blacks -- is Leader A, a Booker Taliaferro Washington.

Amid the survival of this Washington self-help ethos, however, is the feeling among us blacks that when it comes to job opportunities we are discriminated against. A Gallup Poll in 2013 revealed that, "While 60 percent of African-Americans today say whites have better opportunities than blacks to get jobs, just 39 percent say they believe whites and blacks have equal opportunities to get jobs for which they are qualified" (462b). But that belief changes when it comes to educational opportunities, the poll showing somewhat the opposite. The majority (56 percent) of us say that blacks and whites have equal educational opportunities, while those who say that we do not are in the minority (43 percent). So from this poll, and from the polls cited previously, it appears safe to say that the majority of us do not automatically resort to the race card to explain our plight, but rather invoke it selectively, with the emphasis being on self-reliance.

While we understandably attribute our gains from the Civil Rights Movement to our System-Responsibility Tradition, it can be argued that, in considerable measure, those gains can be attributed as well to our Self-Responsibility Tradition. For it was the embrace of values preached and propagated by Washington -- brains, property, and character -- which have been essential to the gains attributed to civil rights; they enabled us to take advantage of the opportunities which those rights opened up. The situation is analogous to that described by Norrell in assessing Washington's impact on the immediate domain of his influence, the town of Tuskegee. In what will later be discussed, Norrell points out that while black economic success did not automatically lead to civil rights in Tuskegee, it made possible significant political progress. Washington's self-help gospel led to the economic independence of many blacks in Tuskegee, as a result of which, later they were able to win voting rights and gain more political power. That same gospel, it is contended, also made it possible for many of us to take advantage of the our civil rights gains -- something which is inferentially argued by Glenn Loury and William Julius Wilson, both of whom point out that more so than the disadvantaged, it is those who hold middle-class values (have internalized the brains, property, and character message) who have most benefited from our civil rights advances.

So while the core of our Self-Responsibility Tradition, espoused from our early beginning in the 1870s, is still very much alive among black people, since the Age of Booker T. Washington, except for Dr. King's shackled attempt, we have not had a national leader to give it vibrancy. The Garvey Movement of Marcus Garvey (1916-25) and the Black Muslims (1930-present) might be considered in that tradition, but neither occupies a prominent place in the mainstream African American story (92:395-98, 465-66). As a reminder of its persistence, our mnemonic is **The Booker T. Washington Society (BTW Society)**.

The Veil of History

Court's founding of the BTW Society reminds us, too, of something else: of what, in his last chapter, Norrell terms "The Veil of History"

(192:421-42). The Society was founded because that veil -- reinforced by our civil rights radicals and civil rights cure-allers -- has "brought Booker so low," as Norrell laments. It brought him so low that, on that seemingly limitless source, the internet, Court found no mention of his Sesquicentennial (150th) birthday. Not even a mention! That being the case, while we clamored and got a holiday for Dr. King when, in fact, it can be plausibly argued that Washington did as much for us African Americans as Dr. King did -- in fact, even more, much more! However, the intent here is not to pit one against the other (something which, it can be surmised, both men would denounce) -- far from it, for both belong to the same tradition and we are indebted to both. That is the point: we African Americans, in particular, and the nation, in general, are indebted to *both*, something which Norrell argues is negated by the veil of history. That veil, which has "brought Booker so low," would have us think that it is he who was the serpent's voice in our African American Garden of Eden.

Veil lifted from Washington

So we would be well served if we lift that veil. For that purpose, we turn to the "Father of Black History" and to the two authoritative sources on which we have most extensively drawn: Norrell and Harlan.

The "Father of Black History," late black Howard University historian, **Carter G. Woodson**, put Washington's realities and challenges in this context:

> Washington's long silence as to the rights of the Negro…did not necessarily mean that he was in favor of oppression of the race. He was aware of the fact that mere agitation for political rights could not *at that time* [emphasis added] be of much benefit to the race, and that their economic improvement, a thing fundamental in real progress, could easily be promoted without incurring the disapproval of the discordant elements in the South. He may be justly criticized for permitting himself to be drawn into certain entanglements in which he of necessity had to make some blunders (290:278-79).

Elsewhere, Norrell quotes Woodson as having proclaimed of Washington: "'no president of a republic, no king of a country, no emperor of a universal domain of that day approached anywhere near doing as much for the uplift of humanity as did Booker T. Washington'" (192:424).

Norrell reflects:

> Booker Washington's emphasis on educational, moral, and economic development became [after the 1960s] a lost artifact for most American thinking about how to integrate minorities and any other disadvantaged group in the modern world. This outcome is especially ironic given that in the twentieth century Washington's ideas inspired and instructed struggling people throughout the Third World. Washington's style of interracial engagement has been all but forgotten, and when remembered, usually disparaged: he put a premium on finding consensus and empathizing with other groups, and by his example encouraged dominant groups to do the same. He cautioned that when people protest constantly about their mistreatment, they soon get a reputation as complainers, and others stop listening to their grievances. Blacks needed a reputation for being hard-working, intelligent, and patriotic, Washington taught, and not for being aggrieved. The main lesson that people around the world took from Booker Washington was that hope and optimism were crucial ingredients in overcoming the obstacles of past exploitation and present discrimination. Indeed, the ability to imagine a better future was what African Americans needed most in Washington's time. That may be true at all times, for all people, and yet the dismissal and misapprehensions of Washington's message have obscured it in the society he worked so hard to improve.

> Booker Washington's response to his circumstances reflected a sophisticated mind that had contrived a complex means for achieving what, by any standard, were high- minded goals. But this was an awful time that set narrow and unjust limits on what he could do to pursue his ends. In Washington's view, his life was not just a struggle up from slavery but also a great effort to rise above history (192:16).

Finally, notwithstanding his criticisms of Washington, **Harlan** offers this assessment:

> Washington's power over his following, and hence his power to bring about change, have probably been exaggerated. It was the breadth rather than the depth of his coalition that was unique. Perhaps one Booker T. Washington was enough. But even today, in a very different society, Washington's autobiography is still in print. It still has some impalpable power to bridge the racial gap, to move new readers to take the first steps across the color line. Many of his ideas of self-help and racial solidarity still have currency in the black community. But he was an important leader because, like Frederick Douglass before him and Martin Luther King after him, he had the program and strategy and skill to influence the behavior of not only the Afro-American one-tenth, but the white nine-tenths of the American people. He was a political realist (111:179).

So this is some of what we see when we lift the veil of history from Washington – unless we are like the Tuskegee student who interpreted the statue of Washington's *Lifting of the Veil of Ignorance* as his really covering us up instead. Thus, maybe, for example, his being a "political realist," as Harlan describes him, is being a traitor -- or that his being "aware of the fact that mere agitation for political rights could not *at that time* [emphasis added] be of much benefit to the race," as Woodson says was the case is the same as surrendering them, as DuBois alleged. Who knows? When possessed of a civil rights fixation, and under the bondage of Victimology, distortion trumps reality, facts become fiction, and stories replace evidence -- such being the legacy of our African American Garden of Eden.

Veil lifted from DuBois

Now let us lift the veil of history from DuBois -- the heroic veil of history with which so many have covered him, turning, in his case, not to notables, but to the record, as will be done more fully for both Washington and DuBois in Chapter 17.

Dismissive of, while disconnected from, the reality of readiness, the fact is that our great hero and his cadre were out for the quick fix, via the system route. Early in his career, Spencer says, DuBois had declared that he had set out for the quick fix, apparently feeling that he and those like him had a leadership calling (244:145). Nothing about his later career suggests a change of mind. He and his fellow activists scorned "'**the philosopher of the possible**' who believed in '**reaching the ideal by gradual approximation**'" [emphases added], as an earlier critic, late black Howard University professor Kelly Miller, posthumously described Washington (192:424). Over a century later, we see the reverberations in the African American Male School Adaptability Crisis and its inseparable social problems.

We see today, too, the same kind of response to AMSAC from a likeminded intellectual cadre, the example of Michael Eric Dyson having been cited. Educator Steve Perry's description of Dyson is applicable to a number of others and is reminiscent of how Washington saw DuBois and others in the same category over a century ago:

> Most of us don't have the luxury of pontificating about the fate of the Black community from an Ivy League skybox. From up there, where most of the students are White or Asian and extremely wealthy, the struggle looks different. The rest of us see what happens when we praise negativity. Kids get hurt. Our community crumbles. Our future dims.
>
> When you are on the dirt floor of the coliseum with the lions, there is no time to turn away the support of the likes of Dr. Cosby for the promised doom that thugs bring. Visiting college campuses for $10,000 per hour can create a cognitive dissonance, which could lead to cultural dementia. This is the condition in which the enemy becomes the hero. From Dyson's lofty perch, it does not matter what happens to the community that you misrepresent, you're still getting paid (209:44-45).

The parallels between then and now are unmistakable. With his book, Dyson makes himself a standout, but his company is considerable, from Cornell West and Tavis Smiley, for example, on the national stage to James Ainsworth-Darnell and Douglas Downey on the academic platform. They are on the attack, just like the father of their tradition.

In view of his singular contribution to the cause of our civil rights, the view which many of like mind hold of DuBois is understandable, as is his standing in our race. Something we hold dear, he fathered. But to assess his place based solely on his civil rights contribution represents a restrictive and misleading reading of his legacy. While he can be considered the father of our civil rights agenda, at the same time DuBois was an attacker and a divider who devalued foundation-building. Perhaps the main reason that we do not have an African American infrastructure today (a viable home life being at its epicenter) is his failure, and that of his tradition, to prioritize its building. He attacked Washington, the NAACP, the white race, and, ultimately, his nation. At least when it came to Washington, that attack was, on occasion, characterized by outright lies and calculated misrepresentation. In the process of his attacks, he divided the race and fostered racial animosity. And all to what end? To champion a civil rights crusade at a time when we were preoccupied with survival? To champion higher education at a time when our crying need was for basic literacy? To replace Washington at a time when, in his own words, Washington was "the most distinguished Southerner since Jefferson Davis, and the one with the largest personal following"? Outside of his small group, DuBois himself had no following and, moreover, neither the leadership skills nor the charisma to garner one. The pursuit of such ends is dumbfounding. Yet, that pursuit has brought DuBois veneration, only at a crippling price: our second bondage, Victimology.

At a time when the race needed unity and a singular sense of direction, DuBois spread discord and did his utmost to seize the reins. At the very outset of our adaptation, he undertook a civil rights crusade. Under normal circumstances, Ray Stannard Baker's position -- Baker considered an astute and fair-minded social and political analyst -- that both men were needed makes sense. But, neither then or now, was there anything normal about our circumstances. We were "down in Egypt's land" and needed someone to lead us out, something which Thomas Fortune realized and proclaimed and which Frederick Douglass approved. Under the circumstances, public quarreling over marginal and practically insignificant differences [insignificant because black freedom of action was severly limited by both Southern oppression and black unpreparedness] as to how we were to get out was a luxury that we could not afford. Responding to those circumstances required the harnessing of our energy, not its dispersion. Moreover, to differ with someone is one thing; to engage in a relentless and ruthless campaign to ruin and replace someone quite another. There is nothing to suggest that it is the latter that Baker had in mind.

The fact is that Washington had us on a pathway that was leading to pride and progress during times of peril. Call it the Pathway of Adaptation. Why alter it when it was succeeding? Why engage in a campaign to destroy success? We were *working* -- not imploring, not demanding, not protesting, but *working* -- our way out. As Washington himself declared:

> 'Tell them that the sacrifice was not in vain. Tell them that by the way of shop, the field, the skilled hand, habits of thrift and economy, by way of industrial school and college, we are coming. We are crawling up, working up, yea, bursting up. Often through oppression, unjust discrimination, and prejudice, but through them all we are coming up, and with proper habits, intelligence, and property, there is no power on earth that can permanently stay our progress!' (234:51-52)

After being the first black to receive an honorary degree from a prestigious university, he was speaking, in 1896, to Harvard's at an Alumni Dinner. That was his message from his race to Harvard for its deceased alumni who had fought for our cause.

Washington was telling the Harvard alumni that their sacrifice had not been in vain, that we were coming. And coming we were. At the time, we therefore needed internal dissension and attack about as much as we needed the Ku Klux Klan. On that note, was not the opposition of some Southern whites enough of a battle for Washington? Did members of his own race have to pile on? "To every *thing there* is a season…" indeed.[19] And this was a season for one man, Booker Taliaferro Washington.

Differences with Washington's approach could have been addressed privately rather than publicly. As Norrell points out, it was expected

---

[19] Ecclesiastes, 3:1

that there would be some who would not agree. Nor was the Tuskegee Machine power inclusive (is that not true of any such machine?). But, at issue, was not inclusiveness, or any of the other politically correct demands of our own time, but survival. The fact is that Washington responded audaciously, creatively, and successfully to the exigencies of the time; and, in time, as necessary and advisable, his approach could have been modified – and, in his later life, modify it he did. Only possessed of a regressive time perspective -- to say nothing of power deprivation -- DuBois, ideologue and activist that he was, could not wait for that time and disregarded what Washington was doing in the present. But, the fact is that Washington's time found him and he responded to it with an unmatchable command. That DuBois chose to do everything he could to sabotage that response and replace him – trailing and attacking him even on European soil and undermining all attempts at compromise -- makes him, not a hero, but a villain. In him, we had in our African American Garden of Eden a Brutus on our hand (the serpent, after all, wears many guises), not a Mark Antony. Accordingly, we might be reminded that, "The evil that men do lives after them; The good is oft interred with their bones." And yes, in this case, "So let it be with DuBois."[20]

But, easier said than done with such a towering figure as DuBois. No quick or easing turning the crowd against him. His tradition has sapped the will and motivation of his adherents to change course. They are on automatic pilot, fueled by therapeutic alienation (to use John McWhorter's analysis). Civil rights has become their fixation, any perceived deviation from its focus eliciting the kind of reaction shown by Dr. King's widow, Coretta Scott King, when, in an address to the National Urban Coalition in 1984 (discussed in Chapter 7), Glenn Loury declared, "The civil rights movement is over." Her reaction: tears -- not of joy, but of sorrow. Former NAACP head, Benjamin Todd Jealous, even sought to *expand* the movement. Their battle cry is apparent: the struggle goes on and will not end until we rid ourselves of the last vestiges of racial injustice – conceivably, therefore, forever.

---

[20] From and based on William Shakespeare's play, "Julius Caesar." Source: http://en.wikipedia.org/wiki/Julius_Caesar 26 November 2014.

Meier paints the picture of the man responsible for this battle cry as one of paradoxes and changes who marched to the beat of his own drum. Thus his followers, as his critics, have much from which to choose in support of their posture. However, his paradoxes and changes suggest that the choice might best be tempered. It may be praiseworthy that he marched to the beat of his own drum, but, if in lock-step fashion, we ourselves march to its selected sounds -- as so many are doing -- we could find that we have made a bad choice. That being the case, though perhaps seeming an act of rejection, to change our mind would be to follow in his footsteps, which would merely free us up to march to some of the other beats that he has sounded. Perhaps with no less conviction, just with a different mindset, maybe even an adaptation one, as DuBois himself earlier possessed, and with a different time perspective, maybe even one closer to the progressive time perspective of Washington, just like a younger DuBois.

Most relevant, it is in regard to Washington that we see on display the DuBois paradox and change of mind. Harlan reports that near the end of his life, in 1954, in an oral history memoir at Columbia University, DuBois, looking back, said the following of Washington: "'Oh, Washington was a politician. He was a man who believed that we should get what we could get'" (111:177). And he was speaking, inclusively, from first-hand experience. Harlan reveals that before his break with Washington in 1903, Washington had assisted DuBois in a challenge to the Georgia law segregating sleeping cars and that the two were secretly cooperating to test the Tennessee Jim Crow law (112:115). While in his The Souls of Black Folks, he acknowledged "several instances" of such acts, DuBois, nevertheless, painted the overall picture of a Washington who "on the whole [left] the distinct impression ... that the South is justified in its present attitude toward the Negro because of the Negro's degradation..." (64:46). That he waited until his fading years to admit what he *knew* from first-hand experience -- never mind his "distinct impression" -- to be the truth is a failure which has been historic in its outcome.

The same applies to DuBois's acknowledgement of the near futility of his aggressive protest agenda. He is said to have privately admitted to NAACP board chairman, Joel Spingarn, that the "'direct frontal attack' did not pay off too well" and even that "true equality' would not be achieved 'for several generations'" (229e:185). As pertains to NAACP court victories, he is quoted as saying "'We continued winning court victories and yet somehow, despite them, we did not seem to be getting far'" (164a:293). Not only, then, did DuBois admit that Washington got what he "could get," he further admitted that out of his protest/civil rights agenda what he and others "did get" did not make much of difference. Yet, he rested the progress of the race on that agenda and failed to admit what he was, *at the time* realizing: that in pursuing it we were not "getting far" and, in any instance, "for several generations" we would not get far.

That failure of admission has allowed us African Americans to fall under the sway of **DuBois's Washington Demonization**, brainwashing us into a false understanding of the man and his legacy. As a result, DuBois has arguably deprived us of our one hero who can connect us African Americans to our roots and provide the inspiration and pathway to the continued pursuit of our destiny. Such a hero is hard to come by and failure to recognize him once he does can become a curse that endures. That is a lesson from divine life that we can apply to earthly affairs.

Washington's demonized choice was a strategy of accommodation and self-help, and it is that choice, along with his masterful skills and unfathomable determination and drive, which enabled him to bear "a burden which pressed down ...at the rate of a thousand pounds to the square inch" and thus "to build up and control the affairs of a large educational institution," something that whites did not think we could do [and maybe neither did many blacks] and that stands today as a monument to black achievement. For that achievement and the Age of Booker T. Washington which it gave us, we owe him our gratitude. In our childhood stage, so to speak, he took us unto his care, nurtured us, and put us firmly on our path to the mainstream.

Early on, Andrew Carnegie -- after reading Washington's Up from Slavery – saw his place in history, and, to free him to fulfill it, he donated $150,000 to Tuskegee to be used by Washington for the duration of his life to meet his personal and family needs. "'I wish this great and good man,' he wrote, 'to be free from pecuniary cares that he may devote himself wholly to his great mission'" (234:384-85). He elaborated:

'To me he seems one of the foremost of living men because his work is unique. The Modern Moses, who leads his race and lifts it through Education to even better and higher things than a land overflowing with milk and honey – history is to know two Washingtons, one white, the other black, both Fathers of their people' (234:385).

Father of our people he is, only, in the climate of the day a neglected and discredited one. Nevertheless, what Carnegie saw is there for us all to see. We can look back and criticize some perceived faults of Washington, but from these pages it will be evident that those criticisms are little more than sound and fury; his actual deeds – the source from which gratitude derives -- dwarfs them all. As Norrell so aptly argues, "Led by Du Bois...many have confused the Washington style with the substance" (192:439). Washington's transformative deeds are a matter of record. Our failure to recognize and honor those deeds borders on the unforgivable. Cicero is said to have declared gratitude to be, "'not only the greatest of the virtues, but the parent of all others'" (471r). Recent research studies give some support to his declaration. They show that the possession of gratitude increases individual and group wellbeing (471r). For us African Americans, nothing has decimated that wellbeing more than AMSAC and its inseparable social problems, and nothing can lead the way to its restoration more than our collective due show of gratitude to BTW through a revitalization of the pathway on which he set us.

Figure 6. Tuskegee Norman and Industrial Institute, 1916; courtesy of the Library of Congress.

Figure 7. The Oaks, Washington's home at Tuskegee Institute built in 1899 with bricks made by faculty and students; courtesy of the Library of Congress.

Figure 8. Cotton States Exposition, 1896; courtesy of the Library of Congress.

Figure 9. Interior of Negro building, Atlanta Exposition, 1896; courtesy of the Library of Congress.

Figure 10. Tuskegee faculty, 1897; courtesy of the Library of Congress.

Figure 11. George Washington Carver, center front, with staff, ca. 1902; courtesy of the Library of Congress.

Figure 12. Theodore Roosevelt visit to Tuskegee in 1905; courtesy of the Library of Congress.

Figure 13. Booker T. Washington Silver Anniversary lecture at Carnegie Hall, 1906; courtesy of Wikimedia Commons and the New York Times Archives.

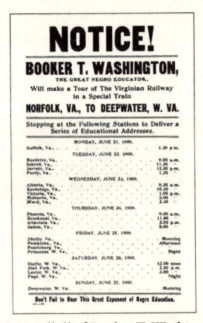

Figure 14. Handbill of Booker T. Washington 1909 Virginia Tour, part of his Southern Educational Tours, 1908-1912; courtesy of Wikimedia Commons.

The African American Male School Adaptability Crisis (AMSAC)

Figure 15. Booker T. Washington speaking in New Orleans, 1915, the year of his death; courtesy of Xavier University of Louisiana Archives and Special Collections.

Figure 16. Interior view of library reading room at Tuskegee, Tuskegee students seated, ca. 1902; courtesy of the Library of Congress, Frances Benjamin Johnston Collection.

Figure 17. History class at Tuskegee, ca. 1902; courtesy of the Library of Congress, Frances Benjamin Johnston Collection.

Figure 18. Chemistry laboratory at Tuskegee, ca. 1902; courtesy of the Library of Congress, Frances Benjamin Johnston Collection.

The African American Male School Adaptability Crisis (AMSAC)

Figure 19. Studying botany—Tuskegee students, between ca. 1910 and ca. 1915; courtesy of the Library of Congress.

Figure 20. Upholstery (tailoring) class at Tuskegee, between ca. 1910 and ca. 1915; courtesy of the Library of Congress.

Figure 21. Students working in print shop at Tuskegee, ca. 1902; courtesy of the Library of Congress, Frances Benjamin Johnston Collection.

Figure 22. Roof construction by students at Tuskegee, ca. 1902; courtesy of the Library of Congress, Frances Benjamin Johnston Collection.

The African American Male School Adaptability Crisis (AMSAC)

Figure 23. Field work by Tuskegee students, between ca. 1910 and ca. 1915; courtesy of the Library of Congress.

Figure 24. Outdoor work at Tuskegee, between ca. 1910 and ca. 1915; courtesy of the Library of Congress.

Figure 25. Tuskegee students cutting sugar cane, ca. 1902; courtesy of the Library of Congress, Frances Benjamin Johnston Collection.

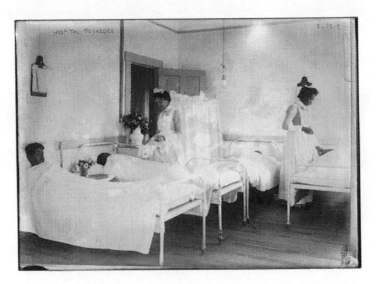

Figure 26. Hospital at Tuskegee, showing patients and staff, between ca. 1910 and ca. 1915; courtesy of the Library of Congress.

Figure 27. Commencement day parade at Tuskegee, 1914; courtesy of the Library of Congress, Arthur P. Bedou Collection.

Figure 28. Booker T. Washington's coffin being carried to his grave site at Tuskegee Institute, 1915; courtesy of the Library of Congress.

Figure 29. Langston Hughes, with Jessie Fauset and Zora Neale Hurston, at Tuskegee, 1927, standing in front of statue, "Lifting the Veil of Ignorance"; courtesy of the Langston Hughes Estate, Victoria Sanders &Associates, LLC and the Yale University Library, the Beinecke Digital Collections, the Langston Hughes papers.

Figure 30. Booker T. Washington 1940 post stamp; courtesy of Wikimedia Commons.

Figure 31. SS Booker T. Washington, 1942, first Liberty Ship named for an African American, christened by Marian Anderson shown (the taller of the two females), at launching of ship, in photo with Mary McLeod Bethune and black ship construction workers; courtesy of the Library of Congress.

Figure 32. Booker T. Washington National Monument, Hardy, Virginia, between 1980 and 2006; courtesy of the Library of Congress, Carol M. Highsmith Archive.

5

Why the Crisis?
The Maladaptation of Our Students:
Cool-Pose Culture versus School Culture

Proverbs, 16:22 - "Understanding is a wellspring of life unto him that hath it: but the instruction of fools is folly."
Galatians, 6:5 - "For every man shall bear his own burden."

There is a divide between the street and peer culture of our black students and the culture of the school (22; 45:81; 82; 127:72-82; 229; 235:40-60, 212-19). The values of our street and peer culture include fun and excitement, physical and verbal prowess, and style, or a "cool image" as manifested in dress, walk, speech, posture, and manners. That is, those in our peer culture tend to value freedom and fun. The values of the school, on the other hand, include hard work, cooperative behavior, and task achievement. Differently expressed, the school has created a "little world," as Washington once described the school to his Tuskegee students, which values work, rules, and rewards. Sociologist and Director of Group Dimensions International, Janet Mancini Billson, reminds us that, on the other hand, our "black males have created their own world to salvage their pride" – no doubt copying, it should be added, their adult world, which has done the same. This is another and perhaps more memorable way of saying what John Ogbu says, which is that they have created an oppositional culture, a culture in which they are comfortable and of which they take pride.

In pursuit of their values and of the pride which it bestows, our students rebel against the values of the school. They seek the approval of their peers, not that of their teachers or of the school. They bring to the school a peer-status achievement-oriented culture whereas the school requires an academic-status achievement-oriented culture. The concern of our students -- which kicks in at an early age -- is about their status or standing among their peers, which calls for being tough, streetwise, and cool. It is not about meeting the approval or expectations of teachers and school authorities, whose "little world" calls for achievement striving and behaviors that get you good grades and praise. More often than not, that kind of striving is a negative, earning disapproval from peers, as, for example, in the case of the sixth-grader, Lenox Robinson, in an Ossining, New York, school who reports having "stopped trying after his friends made fun of him" (385: 2-3).

Barry Silverstein and Ronald Krate provide a vivid picture of the kind of classroom environment in which a Lenox Robinson might find himself. They write about the students in the black elementary schools of Harlem in the early 1970s. They each taught for 5-6 years in these schools, did research-based substitute teaching in many of them for one year, conducted classroom observations, undertook interviews with teachers, principals, and other school personnel, and held individual and group discussions with teachers in developmental psychology classes which they later taught. They observed how peer-group dependency came to determine student behavior, noting the following: :

> By the upper elementary grades, the behaviors supported by peer groups in many Harlem classrooms included continuous talking and socializing as opposed to any individualized, sustained work effort; responding to difficulty or frustration by leaving the room, tearing up papers, or throwing away books; arriving at school with no concern for the hour; and demonstrating skill in putting down children, parents, and teachers.

> The conflictful nature of street peer-group relations was not filtered out by the walls of the school. Fighting was so much of a norm to the children that one sixth-grade boy was annoyed when he was prevented from boxing with his friend in a classroom to determine,

then and there, who could beat whom. He shouted at his teacher, 'Dam, man! You can't even fight in peace around here!' (235:118).

This is the same kind of behavior which apparently was being described some generation later (in 1993) by a school secretary who had worked five years in the public school system. Interviewed by black Norfolk State University educator Ronnie Hopkins, he quotes her as telling him that "'Black males were some of the most devious acting kids in the entire school system.'" She recalled constantly seeing them in the principal's office, some acting "'out so bad that they had to participate in partial-release prison programs.'" (127:68). They listened, she said, neither to parents, teachers, or principals.

Most notable about such behavior is how deeply rooted it is in peer culture. Black educator, Geoffrey Canada, of Harlem Children's Zone fame, who grew up on the streets of the deprived South Bronx, gives us a sense of the pull in Paul Tough's book, <u>Whatever It Takes: Geoffrey Canada's Quest to Change Harlem and America</u>. Speaking of his attendance at his junior high school near the same time that Silverstein and Krate were undertaking their study, he told Tough:

> 'My body was at JHS 133, but my heart was on Union Avenue. If I failed a test in school, I was hurt about that, but not nearly as hurt as if I failed a test on Union Avenue. The set of values and standards that I learned there became so important to me that I would do anything to keep from being pulled out of touch with them' (258:112).

Canada was echoing a sentiment that so many of his peers took even further, as do our young blacks males today. That sentiment is captured furher in this <u>New York Times</u> headline, in 1997, "Academics Lose Relevance for Black Boys" (341). The story reports Jason Osborne's study in which he examined the link of self-esteem to academic success as shown by 15,037 black, white, and Hispanic teenagers moving from 8th to 12th grade. He found that over the 4-year period the link dropped slightly for all groups, except that it rose slightly for Hispanic girls, but dropped dramatically, to no link at all, for black boys. Black boys, in fact, were the only students whose self-esteem was increasingly tied to athletic skill and popularity.

In a similar large-scale study, the Steinberg, Dornbusch, and Brown study (1992) revealed similar results (450). From a sample of 15,000 students in nine high schools that included roughly 1500 African American students [along with an approximately equal number of Hispanic and Asian American students and over 10,000 White students], they found that "Even when African American students have parents supportive of academic success, these youngsters find it difficult to join a peer group that encourages the same goal." They go on to conclude with regard to African American students:

- "Peer support for academic success is sometimes so limited that many successful African American students eschew contact with other African American students and affiliate primarily with students from other ethnic groups."
- "African American students are more likely than others to be caught in a bind between performing well in school and being popular among their peers."

This stifling peer influence is given perspective by John Ogbu. Based on his analysis of black history and on studies conducted by him and others, he postulates that the peer culture of our students is characterized by a *low-effort syndrome* wherein "they do not work hard or persist long enough in academic tasks and do not maintain serious attitudes toward their schoolwork" (195:452). He attributes this syndrome to "community forces" and our adaptation to those forces, which he cites as follows:

> ...black folk theories of getting ahead under a castelike stratification, disillusionment over the job ceiling which gives rise to ambivalence about schooling, ambivalent or oppositional group identity and cultural frame of reference, and conflict with anddistrust of the public school and white people who control them (195:452).

In Chapter 6, the role to which Ogbu attributes castelike stratification will be elaborated.

In essence, he sees that castelike role as the transmission and perpetuation of caste-induced attributes which cause black students' poor school performance. That is, the "community forces" to which he alludes are caused by the castelike nature of the system. That castelike nature produces, in response (coping mechanisms), community adaptations which result in child rearing practices which foster the attributes of dependency, compliance, manipulation, and associated behaviors. That is the way you "get over" or survive. Open social mobility for whites, on the other hand, leads them to foster in their children the attributes of independence, initiative, and industriousness. One set of attributes curtails academic achievement, the other fosters it. One can dispute Ogbu's rationale, but hardly in dispute are the attributes which he cites.

We thus get the picture of our academically adverse peer culture, not as just a peer culture, but a people culture as well. That picture is reinforced in a survey of how we black males view ourselves based on a Washington Post survey of 1,328 black males in 2006 (no distinction being made between African American and other black males), 3 of 4, or 75%, say they value success in a career, more than either white men or black women; however, a *majority say that "Black men put too little emphasis on education and too much on sports and sex"*[emphasis added] (245:19). And in Losing the Race, McWhorter makes the case that "… black students do so poorly decade after decade not because of racism, funding, class, parental education, etc., but because of a virus of Anti-intellectualism that infects the black community," later adding, "it… permeates the whole of black culture, all the way up to the upper class" (160:82-163, 83). He elaborates: "… the appearance that black students do poorly in school because the System does them in is an illusion that denies these students' basic humanity …the actual determining factor is a culture-internal legacy" (160:84). So viewed, we have a continuation and reproduction, as it were, of the evolved culture of a portion of our people adapted, as Ogbu saw it, in response to slavery and post-slavery conditions and lived out in home, community, and school.

As it particularly pertains to our males, the nature of that culture is memorably captured by Geoffrey Canada, who, as a teenager in the South Bronx, was part of it -- indeed a leader of it, although (fortunately) he himself did not wholly abide by what he preached. In his book, Reaching Up for Manhood, Canada gives an insight into the mindset of the culture.

To be a man, Canada tells us, you were taught to "create an emotional distance between yourself and the rest of the world." In this way, and only in this way, could you maintain your manhood because it would enable you to endure the "constant barrage of hurt from life--racism, poverty, violence, disappointment, failure, and betrayal" -- that were the inevitable fate of the "poor black man." In summary, he says:

> We were taught, and many boys are still taught, a way of thinking that can be summed up in two words: "fuck it." If you failed your English class, "fuck it." If the boys from Home Street were after you, "fuck them." If one of your friends stole your girl, "fuck him." If you hurt someone's feelings, that was "too fucking bad." Living life with this as your prevailing philosophy gave you a way to emotionally distance yourself from the hurt, the fear, the pain. And if in our daily choices we disappointed our girlfriends, or teachers, or peers, "fuck it." To care about someone, anyone except your mother, more than yourself was a sign of weakness that could and would be used against you, making it a potential threat to your manhood. Teenage boys today wear their pants so that you can see their underwear: "fuck you." You tell them if they dress like that and talk like that they will never get a job: "fuck it." (26:50-51).

Canada goes on to observe that this mindset is understandable given the context of his life then, and their lives now. That context: death from handguns, AIDS, generational unemployment, inhabitable buildings, no fathers, and broken dreams. Add the following to these factors, he says: "… boys are taught that sex, not a relationship, is what to want from girls," and "… girls… more willing to have sex with boys after shorter period of time." Often, he explains, the sex produces babies with the boys, and often the girls, having no intention of partnership to raise a family. The result: fatherless families and a perpetuation of the culture that is being described. However inelegant, it is not inaccurate to describe that culture precisely as Canada has (forgive the language): a "fuck-you, don't care" culture, in which the school is as much an object of rejection as anything else, mothers excepted, Canada says.

Black Harvard economist, Ronald Ferguson, calls attention to another factor that might be added to Canada's list: popular culture. In discussing the school versus home issue, reference has been made to Ferguson's research regarding this factor. He sees popular culture -- less leisure-time reading, hip hop, rap music, and "acting white" -- all probably contributing to youth "disengagement from academic endeavors."

We know from the data that, for males, their academic disengagement far exceeds that of our females. This is the core problem which AMCAP addresses. In an informative article, Ron Matus, a staff writer for the St. Petersburg Times, drawing upon the literature, speculates why it exists (406). As discussed, there is a growing worldwide male-female gap in educational attainment, but the gap is much more pronounced for us blacks. The gap, in part, Matus writes, is attributed to better female preparation in reading, communication, and social skills in the early grades. Also, males' predisposition makes them less willing than females to endure difficulties and obstacles (remember the "manhood thing" which Canada describes). To these factors can be added a major premise of AMCAP, which is that boys lack suitable male role models at home and school whereas girl have their mothers.

Matus also cites the previously cited description of Billson that "black males have created their own world to salvage their pride." That pride serves as immunity to their school adaptation. For many, the alternative way to a good life, Matus observes, is through "sports, music, and drug dealing." In the words of one Florida State University student, as quoted by Matus, "'When you're in the 'hood, you don't look at school as the way out.'"

Left unaddressed, as Ogbu's work suggests, and as the classic Paul Willis ethnographic study (1977) reminds us, this culture will keep reproducing itself with the same results (284). Willis's subjects were working class high school boys in England (15 comprising the main group) whom he followed their last two years in high school and their first six months on the job ("the lads," as they and the members of their counter-school culture called themselves). In his book, Learning to Labor, he reports his findings. His subtitle captures the relevance of his study, how working class kids get working class jobs. How do they? *They reproduce themselves.* Because of their anti-authority, anti-school attitude and behavior, the school had no effect on the boys in his study. They left as they entered, shaped in the process, not by the school, but by themselves and their own peer counterculture. So they qualified, as they left, for the same jobs for which they qualified at entry, working class jobs, not middle class jobs for which the school sought to prepare them.

The same outcome applies to the Jocks in the Solomon study (1992). The Jocks were an extensive social network of black high school seniors of West Indian ancestry and culture centered around a core of eight, high-profile athletes at Lumberville High in Ontario, Canada (240). Like "the lads," they had their own separatist culture and created and lived by their own code of behavior, which was anti-authority and anti-school. Opposed to the school culture, like "the lads," they left school influenced only by their own counterculture, their dreams of athletic fame and fortune having faded or vanished.

It was a revelatory moment to read what the aforementioned Silverstein and Krate had to say about cultural reproduction in the black elementary schools of Harlem. Their analysis led them to the belief that the children had more influence on the school than the school on them (235:217). Not only does this conclusion support the cultural reproduction findings of Willis and Solomon, it extends it. In the process of reproducing their own peer culture, the authors speculate that they ended up changing the school because the school adapted to accommodate them, rather than vice-versa.

The lesson seems evident. Leave our students alone and fail to focus on their culture, focusing instead on the system, and the students will simply reproduce their culture. Like "the lads" in Willis's study, they have made the school a battlefield. We can engage them on this battlefield -- and it is a cultural battlefield -- or we can surrender and let them continue to reproduce themselves. The choice is between reproduction or adaptation. It is their cool-pose culture versus the dominant school culture. The outcome is mediocrity, failure, and regression versus success and progress.

As previously quoted, Noguera has taken cognizance of the problem, in part observing that "Black males are not merely passive victims but may also be active agents in their own failure …." So has aforementioned Bob Herbert, formerly of the New York Times and now with the think tank Demos. Focusing, too, on black males, these are his thoughts:

> The effort to bolster the educational background of black men has to begin very early. It's extremely difficult to turn a high school dropout into a college graduate. This effort can succeed on a *large scale* only if there is a *cultural change* in the black community -- a powerful change that acknowledges as the 21st century unfolds that there is no more important life tool for black children than education, education, education [emphases added] (377).

Again, left unaddressed, our student culture, as memorably captured by Canada, alluded to by Noguera and Herbert, and variously depicted by others, will continue to reproduce itself. The remedy is adaptation, which requires that, with equal energy, we expand our efforts beyond the academic domain to the cultural battlefield. School and community must attack those attitudes and behaviors which too often leave our students in charge and our schools constantly struggling to regain charge. We are talking, not just about a battlefield made up of students from poor families, though primarily about them, but -- as black linguist and bestselling author John McWhorter emphasizes -- also, to some degree, on some variables, made up of students from the middle class as well. What is the nature of the battlefield, of the attitudes and behaviors that confront the school? Canada has provided a useful overall description, and from him and the other sources cited, we can derive a list of some inclusive and overlapping descriptors of it -- of the attitudes and behaviors of our black male students, those attitudes and behaviors constituting what John Ogbu calls an *oppositional culture*. The list follows:

- lack serious attitude toward school work
- fail to work hard in school or persist long enough in doing school work
- do not complete or do homework
- do not identify with school (disidentification)
- place value on having a cool image
- place high value on toughness (an extraordinarily prized manhood trait)
- emphasize sports and popularity at expense of education
- present disciplinary problems
- have anti-authority attitude
- play around in class

- arrive late for school
- are often absent from school
- use verbal insults (sounding)
- will often resort to fighting
- have strong peer group culture (compensating for weak family ties)
- do not have peer support for academic striving
- subscribe to academically and intellectually-alienating popular culture

One descriptor not on the above list is "acting white." The academic and public attention given to "acting white" has catapulted it to what, herein, is considered the second major attempt to revitalize the self-help core of our Self-Responsibility Tradition. The attempt is called **John Ogbu's "acting white" Thesis**. Because of what the controversy surrounding the thesis tells us about the dynamics involved in AMSAC, it is treated separately in the next chapter.

6

Why the Crisis?
"Acting White" as a Cause

Proverbs, 16:22 - "Understanding is a wellspring of life unto him that hath it: but the instruction of fools is folly."
Galatians, 6:5 - "For every man shall bear his own burden."

To say that there is a cultural divide that contributes to the African American Male School Adaptability Crisis (AMSAC) and its inseparable social problems is to enter into a crossfire ignited over twenty years ago (1986) by Signithia Fordham and the late John Ogbu with their article in the <u>Urban Review</u>, "Black Students' School Success: Coping with the "Burden of 'Acting White'" (89). The crossfire centers on this issue: what is responsible for our black students' poor school performance, the culture of our students and community -- OR -- the structures of school and society.

These choices correspond to the traditions from which they derive: the **Self-Responsibility Tradition** of Booker T. Washington and the **System-Responsibility Tradition** of W.E.B. DuBois. The crossfire ignited by Fordham and Ogbu provides a replay of the war that took place between these two adversaries; only the particulars differ. One ignited a struggle in the public arena -- our African American Garden of Eden -- the other in academia. The basic arguments are parallel; so are the animus and some of the tactics. It has never reached the "war" stage of the Washington-DuBois face off, but the heat of the crossfire is palpable. The personalities in this case are not comparably towering, but they draw attention, boiling down to the more established author of the article, John Ogbu, and a number of academic critics, notable among them sociologists, James W. Ainsworth-Darnell and Douglas B. Downey, both then at Ohio State University. They, along with Cook and Ludwig, are said to pose the primary challenge to the Fordham-Ogbu theory.

The crossfire lightning rod is the epithet **"acting white"** which Fordham-Ogbu conclude is one major cause of black students' poor school performance. "Acing white" is a trigger because it connotes an attitude which devalues academic striving and success and which opposes a white life style. While some oppose their conclusion on scholarly grounds, others oppose it from the kind of opposition impulse which characterizes the System-Responsibility Tradition. Not only do they say the conclusion is wrong, they further assert that the focus on the culture of the students is misguided. In their mind, the culture of the students is not contributing to the crisis; rather, the system is responsible. So they dismiss, not just the conclusion of Fordham-Ogbu, but any focus on the culture of the students as responsible for black students' poor school performance as well.

In so doing, the System-Responsibility Traditionalists commit a fatal mistake. Herein, an effort will be made to show that the conclusion of Fordham-Ogbu has merit. While research and experience do not justify the conclusion that "acting white" is *one major reason* for the crisis, nevertheless, an attempt will be made to show that they validate its existence, but that it is more a *symptom* than a cause. As a symptom, it merits attention in its own right, but, even more important, it exposes and directs our attention to the underlying issue that *is* the *main cause*: **a devaluation of academic striving and success as manifested in their character traits.** Disproportionately, black students exhibit character traits which lead them not to work hard enough (in John Ogbu's terminology, they have a low-effort syndrome) and, too frequently, to engage in disruptive classroom and school behavior. Thus, to dismiss the "acting white" thesis and, at the same time, denigrate or minimize a focus on the culture of the students, as the System-Responsibility

Traditionalists do, is to ignore the underlying main cause of the problem and, therefore, make it unsolvable.

We all understand that the system -- home, school, neighborhood, and societal conditions -- influences the lives of our students. That is Education 101, indeed, Life 101. But that is all the more reason to focus, rather than not to focus, on students' culture. To the extent that resources and responsibilities permit, we want the school to do for students what is not done -- or what is done adversely -- by other responsible agencies, including the home. Insofar as possible, we want to compensate for those shortcomings in their life that are likely to diminish their school success. We cannot do so by denying the indisputable role of culture in that success. We can only do so by recognizing and appropriately responding to it. That is what the Fordham-Ogbu article suggests that we do. The contention here is that their article, rather than diverting our attention from the cause of our black-white achievement gap problem, points, instead, to a cultural asymmetry which exposes its main cause: the character traits of our students as manifested in their maladaptive school attitude and behavior, described in the previous chapter.

Their Study

The article, summarized below, was based on an ethnographic study conducted by Fordham for her doctoral dissertation. For over a year, she intensively studied 33 juniors at Capital High School, a predominantly black (99%) high school in a relatively low-income area in Washington, D.C. (89; 90:593-627; 390). To write the article, she teamed up with Ogbu, an established researcher and writer (and her mentor) in the field of minority education.

Ogbu's Explanation of Black Students' Poor Performance: OCF

To explain minority school performance, Ogbu had earlier developed a framework or model based on school and society attitudes and behaviors and minority responses to them (171). He called it the Oppositional Cultural Framework (OCF), since he saw those responses as constituting a black *oppositional culture*. The essence of his oppositional culture theory is that, in response to white denigration of black intelligence, exclusion from assimilation, inferior schools, unequal rewards for acquired education, limited job opportunities, and the job ceiling (limit to upward job mobility), blacks have developed opposition through "a sense of peoplehood" ["we-feeling" or "belonging"] with various devices used to protect black group identity and maintain a boundary between them (whites) and us (blacks).

Teaming Up with Fordham, Ogbu's Expanded Explanation: CEM

Utilizing the data gathered by Fordham at Capital High School, he teamed up with her in an analysis which showed the use of "acting white" as such a device -- but, as they theorize, one that harms rather than protects. The device (inclusively) led Ogbu, in addition to its existing school and society component, led Ogbu to add to his model a community component encompassing fictive kinship and cultural frame of reference. He then called it a Cultural-Ecological Model or Cultural-Ecological Framework (CEM).

With his CEM, Ogbu believed that he now had a framework composed of the complete range of diverse interlocking factors essential to a credible explanation of minority education and performance (90: chapters 1, 6, 16). He describes it as a model which "includes a wide range of interlocking factors, each of which may independently influence the school performance of all, many, or just a few students in a given minority group" (197:11). "Acting white," he argues, is *one* of those factors.

He does not contend that any one factor, including "acting white" in particular, explains the poor performance of black students, but that each factor, independently, exerts some influence, be that influence on few students, on many, or on all. "Acting white," he argued, is *one* of those factors. One can then say, for example, that "acting white" affects only a few students, but Ogbu's point is that some components in his model may influence just a few students, but, nevertheless, in his interlocking model help to explain black students' poor academic performance. His intent was to capture the range of factors which permits a more or less complete explanation of the problem.

Oppositional Culture

The *oppositional culture* which the black community creates in response to society and school forces is at issue in "acting white" because *acting white* is one of its five components. Frequently, however, the literature does not specify the components being addressed and treats "acting white" as if it were the only component. In his "acting white" study, black Princeton University sociologist, Angel Harris, provides one of the clearest statements of the five components (367a). They are:

1. Black children perceive fewer returns to education and more limited opportunities for upward social mobility than white children.
2. Black children have less favorable affect toward school than whites.
3. Black children exhibit greater resistance to school than whites.
4. **High-achieving black children are negatively sanctioned by their peers to a greater degree than high-achieving white children: The "acting white" hypothesis**. [emphasis added]
5. The peer groups of black children have a greater counter-educational culture than those of white children.

"Acting white" is one component among the five and, as Ogbu states, like the other components in his model, it can be studied independently. Thus to find, for example, that "acting white" has no significant influence on black students' school performance is no basis for claiming that oppositional culture does not exist. At the same time, however, all five components constitute oppositional culture, one, "acting white," serving as its sanctions component (device), while the other four are its approved behaviors, deviations from which are labeled "acting white," and are punishable.

Where "acting *w*hite" exists, so does its source, one or more of the other four oppositional culture components. Depending on the situation, the reverse does not necessarily true: where oppositional culture exists "acting white" exists. It is therefore possible for oppositional culture to be one reason for black student underachievement without "acting white" also being a reason; it may not show up as a component which, independently, contributes to the underachievement.

The African American Male School Adaptability Crisis (AMSAC)

CEM in Context: Ogbu's Earlier thinking

Ogbu's early work (1978), <u>Minority Education and Caste</u>, gives context to his attempt, through CEM, to explain black students' poor academic performance and the role which system-oriented thinking plays in it (194). It is worth attention because it goes beyond the typical surface charge of system sins into how those sins translate into poverty outcomes which are manifested in the school performance of black students. In it, Ogbu argues that while we think of America as stratified along social class lines, which is true, it is also stratified by a parallel race-based caste system. As with any caste system, membership is based on birth; it is, therefore, ascribed rather than achieved. However, our race-based caste system does have social classes based on achievement. But those race-based social classes are not on par with their parallel white social classes because they, too, are subject to the same race-based caste criteria. This birth-determined, race-based caste system is defined by (1) its near exclusion of blacks from professional and skilled job and their relegation to low-skilled, low-wage jobs, and (2) its failure to reward blacks in terms of jobs and pay even when they possess qualifications and skills commensurate with whites. So, rather than America being a country of upward mobility open to all, these birth-based stratification features make it a country with a castelike minority. This designation is given credibility by the fact that our black minority shares the same castelike features of other castelike minorities in this country and elsewhere. Ogbu provides details about these other castelike minorities.

This caste system (or castelike system as he interchangeably refers to it), Ogbu's reasoning continues, produces in blacks a set of attributes different from those which the class system produces in whites. Because the class system permits whites upward mobility, it fosters their the development of such personal qualities as independence, foresight, initiative, industriousness, and individualistic competitiveness. Because the race-based caste system denies blacks upward mobility and access to resources owned by whites, except on a limited competitive basis, it encourages black reliance on white patronage and, increasingly, on organized civil rights efforts. Black reliance on white patronage, in turn, has led blacks to develop such personal qualities as dependency, compliance, and manipulation -- adjustment behavior qualities which stand in contrast to the qualities of independence, initiative, and industriousness developed by whites.

These divergent racial-attribute outcomes of the caste system are propagated and perpetuated by the school as well as by black parents and community. Schools perpetuate the outcomes by providing inferior education. Black parents transmit them to their children through the normal socialization process, and the community transmits them through the development of parallel institutions (home, church, community organizations) which reflect the kind of adaptive behaviors (the "make it" type behavior) deemed needed in the caste system.

As observed in Chapter 5, **Ogbu hypothesizes that the transmittal and perpetuation of these caste-induced attributes -- dependency, compliance, manipulation, and associated behaviors -- causes black students' poor school performance**. Our children are socialized, consciously and unconsciously, in accordance with them in order to enable them to "make it" in the world. Accordingly, they bring to school those "skills" taught them -- as well as "caught" by them, as we sometimes say in education -- which will enable them to adapt to their castelike status, a status which excludes them from professional and skilled jobs and, even if they get an education, will not reward them with the job or pay which it merits. Their status does not call for independence, foresight, initiative, industriousness, and individualistic competitiveness (attributes required for school success). Instead, it calls for dependency, compliance, manipulation, and associated behaviors (attributes which lead to school failure).

As Ogbu back then hypothesized, our children's school failure, therefore, can be attributed to caste system-induced incongruent adaptation contrasted with an ability or cultural deficit. Why, nevertheless, some children do better than others, was something that Ogbu said exceeded the scope of his study (but he later felt that his CEM provided the answer). As for solving the problem, Ogbu back then offered familiar system thinking. "To change this situation--to eliminate black academic retardation--," he wrote, "requires, first a total destruction of the caste system--that is, the creation of a new social order in which blacks do not occupy a subordinate position vis-à-vis whites." "If we destroy the caste system," he continued, "both schools and blacks will begin to manifest changes compatible with the new social order, and academic retardation will disappear." "Under the new social order," he reasoned, "schools have no choice but to change their policies and practices and train blacks as effectively as they train whites because the new society will demand the same degree of competence from both" (194:359).

Their Study: the Fordham-Ogbu thesis

Turning to the Fordham-Ogbu study, they observe that, previously, they had devoted attention to the historical and structural factors. They label these the *external* factors (school and society). But, in this article, they explain that they confined their focus to cultural factors only: the *internal* or within-group factors. These internal factors, they say, had not yet even been "generally recognized, let alone systematically studied" (90:617, 621). Their data led them to this conclusion:

> **Our main point in this paper is that *one major reason* [emphasis in original] Black students do poorly in school is that they experience inordinate ambivalence and affective dissonance in regard to academic effort and success** [emphasis added] (90:594).

To get good grades would mean that they would be "acting white" and thus betraying their peers because, to black students, academic striving, perhaps unconsciously, has become something that historically white people do (it is a "white prerogative") -- and white people's way of living is the opposition culture.

This ambivalence about getting good grades creates stress and anxiety, or affective dissonance. If black students strive for academic success, they probably fear (again perhaps unconsciously) that they are "acting white" and, thus, betraying their peers (who do not strive); and, if they succeed, there is the anxiety that white society may not accept them either. Even if they do not fail, ambivalence and affective dissonance probably cause them to perform below their potential.

In this adverse environment, Fordham-Ogbu cite student profiles of how "acting white" causes students to underachieve and how it causes them to use camouflages if they are high achievers (90:604, 622). The underachievers mainly use *avoidance* to keep from being seen as "acting white." For example, they may not do their homework or conform to classroom expectations. On the other hand, the high achievers resort to *camouflage*. They do not want to attract attention to themselves, so, for example, they do not brag or clown around. That is, two words can be used to explain the effect of "acting white": *avoidance* (resulting in underachievement) and *camouflage* (resulting in lower achievement due to the time and energy used to divert attention from their academic effort and success).

Because of what he felt had been so much misrepresentation of their conclusion, Ogbu later denied what he felt to be the wrong interpretation of what Fordham and he were saying: That because of oppositional culture, black students do not want or strive for academic success. Rather, he asserts, their contention was that some students – not the majority or all -- do not engage in the behaviors which lead to get good grades because, to do so, would be "acting white" (197:16).

The role of fictive kinship. The role of fictive kinship in this process is pivotal, explain Fordham-Ogbu. Fictive kinship, found in a number of societies, is a kin-like relationship which is not based on marriage or blood but, instead, commonly on a limited reciprocal social or economic relationship. As applicable to black Americans, however, it has taken on a broader meaning. It describes -- not a limited reciprocal or economic relationship -- but a "mindset" or "worldview" of what it means to be black (90:601). It does not, as customary, describe just color or other physical race characteristics. In black fictive kinship, it is not enough to be black in color or race, one must be black in mind as well.

It is through fictive kinship, Fordham-Ogbu say, that black collective identity and cultural frames of reference (the cultural components that they added to Ogbu's original structural framework) get expressed. The relationship might be viewed thus: collective identity (sense of peoplehood based on shared experiences) + cultural frame of reference (correct way of behaving or talking) = fictive kinship system (group mind set). The system has evolved over time and, in the process of interacting with parents, peers, and others as they grow up, children, consciously and if unconsciously, learn its prevailing norms. The system has its own criteria by which blacks are judged, quite apart from white society. These criteria are held in high regard by the black community and, if violated, can produce sanctions. Loyalty to the group is expected, as is opposition to the dominant group, whites. But the system is not ironclad. Some blacks reject the system and others identify with it only to varying degrees. Black fictive kinship in the school setting is characterized by certain academic norms. "Acting white" is the sanctions used to enforce those norms.

Deviancy or adaptation. What fictive kinship makes evident, to continue the summary, is that "acting white" is not a phenomenon limited to the school setting, an assertion which Ogbu expands in a subsequent publication (196:chapter 2). Nor is it deviance or pathology. Rather, it is historical, reflecting a black fictive kinship (group mindset) that has evolved over time as an adaptation. Black fictive kinship, or group mindset, is the blacks' evolved cultural answer to our oppression (90:594-95). It represents historically evolved black adaptation to white prerogatives in the education and employment domains. This makes education -- a domain where blacks have historically felt denied equal access, not respected, not recognized, and not rewarded -- part of that oppressive white society. As such, behaviors associated with education or school are to be opposed. This includes learning because learning, as whites go about it, is one of the behaviors which represens oppressive white society.

Oppositional culture behaviors. Fordham-Ogbu provide the following inclusive list of "acting white" behaviors found at the school where Fordham did her research:

- speaking standard English
- listening to white music and white radio station
- going to the opera or ballet
- spending a lot of time in the library studying
- working hard to get good grades in school
- getting good grades in school
- going to the Smithsonian
- going to a Rolling Stones concert
- doing volunteer work
- going camping, hiking, or mountain climbing

217

- having cocktails or a cocktail party
- going to a symphony orchestra
- having a party with no music
- listening to classical music
- being on time
- reading and writing poetry

Thus, as Fordham-Ogbu explain it, to engage in such a "white behavior" as getting good grades is to cross the boundary of fictive kinship (learned from childhood) and to enter (consciously or unconsciously) another world. In that crossing, the student leaves part of himself or herself behind, which produces in the student ambivalence and affective dissonance. In fictive kinship thinking, then, the crossing is seen as "subtractive," not "additive," making the student less, not more.

Cross cultural. Such a response to white society, or any other dominant society, is not unique to black Americans, explain Fordham-Ogbu. Other subordinate minorities in this country (for example American Indians and Mexican Americans) and minorities in other countries (for example Australian Aborigines and Buraku Outcastes in Japan) show a similar pattern. That pattern is resistance to the dominant school rules and practices and, consequently, minority students tend to have lower academic achievement.

In his cross-cultural analysis, Ogbu distinguishes *involuntary minorities* from *voluntary minorities*. Involuntary minorities, such as black Americans and American Indians, are here as a consequence of slavery or conquest and, through oppression, are relegated to a castelike, subordinate status. Voluntary minorities, on the other hand, are here by their own volition, seeking a better life for themselves. It is among those minorities that face similar structural and cultural barriers -- the involuntary, subordinate minorities -- that we find similar adaptations. So the adaptations of American blacks to the American way of life, *including school life*, are the adaptations that, in this country and in other countries, are common to subordinate minorities.

Rejection of genetic and cultural deficit explanations. Fordham-Ogbu see their enhanced cultural-ecological framework [which embraces the historical as well] as an alternative theory for explaining black academic failure. Ogbu explains that he originated his search for an explanation of black academic underachievement as an alternative to the genetic explanation offered by Arthur Jensen and the cultural deprivation rationale advanced by Benjamin Bloom and others. While, by no means, the entire alternative explanation, "acting white' is, nonetheless, a part of it, the main part theorized to be the opportunity structure which, until their joint article, was considered by Ogbu to have been the *only* explanation (90:622). Still, both contend that, as a condition for improving the academic performance of black adolescents, it is necessary to change the opportunity structure -- but not sufficient! To reach sufficiency -- through their enhanced cultural-ecological framework – they argue that students' own oppositional culture must also change, inclusive of "acting white," one ot its five components.

Solutions. Fordham-Ogbu offer the following suggestions (paraphrased and put in outline form) for what to do about this unaddressed problem (90:623):

1. Open the job opportunity structure to change black adolescents' negative perceptions and incentive to strive for academic success
2. Eliminate educational practices that treat black and white students differently, creating equalized educational opportunities
3. Schools and black community should recognize and respond to "acting white" A. Schools
   (1) Seek to understand influence of fictive kinship system on students
   (2) Develop programs, including counseling, to help students differentiate between academic success and "acting white"
   (3) Expose students to success stories in Black history
B. Community
   (1) Reexamine own attitude towards school learning and teach children that academic striving does not mean group betrayal
   (2) Publicly recognize and celebrate academic effort and success as is done for those who succeed in field of sports and entertainment

Summary. Fordham and Ogbu's thesis, and Ogbu's elaboration of it, can be summarized thus:

"Acting white" is the exhibition of learning values and lifestyle behaviors associated with whites, and conscious or unconscious fear of rejection by their black peers because of "acting white" is *one major reason* black students underachieve or *avoid* academic effort and success or, if they are high achievers, often engage in *camouflage* to divert attention from their academic effort and success. Rather than being a pathology, however, "acting white" is an evolved cultural adaptation of blacks to white oppression and prerogatives as manifested in white denigration of black intelligence, exclusion from assimilation, inferior schools, unequal rewards for acquired education, limited job opportunities, and the job ceiling -- an adaptation no different from the kind of adaptation made by similarly situated involuntary immigrants in five other societies studied by Ogbu. Not unique to the school setting, consciously and unconsciously, "acting white" has been historically preserved and transmitted through black fictive kinship or group mindset. That mindset dictates, with sanctions, that one oppose rather than embrace white values and lifestyles, inclusive of those which pertain to academic striving and school success.

The Publicity

As documented by O'Connor, Horvat, and Lewis (193), the Fordham-Ogbu article still reverberates -- at least its "acting white" attribution. In addition to persistent scholarly interest, the national -- and even international -- media interest has been no less, with references to it having been made in over 150 articles. Perhaps the most famous of these references was made by then Senator, President Barak Obama, in his keynote speech at the Democratic National Convention in 2004. "Go into any inner-city neighborhood," he declared, "and folks will tell you that government alone can't teach kids to learn. They know that parents have to parent, that children can't achieve unless we raise their expectations and turn off the television sets and eradicate the slander that says *a black youth with a book is acting white* [emphasis added]."

The color of Ogbu's critics

In her Foreword to Ogbu's last book, <u>Minority Status, Oppositional Culture, & Schooling</u> (2008), Roslyn Arlin Mickelson (University of North Carolina sociologist) reveals that the controversy that accompanied his (and Fordham's) "acting white" thesis "at times ... threatened to overshadow the impact of the scholarship itself" (172: xvi). As a friend and colleague, she describes his frustration at what he saw to be misinterpretations of his work. He even wondered if some of his critics had even read it. Whether they had read it or not, when he attended conventions, some of them were vocal and, sometimes, she says, vicious -- attacking him, for example, because he was a Nigerian immigrant. Here is Mickelson's description of them:

> After observing various versions of these interactions for several years at professional meetings of several disciplines, I realized that John's public critics were more likely to be African Americans or Latinos, while Whites, members of voluntary minority groups, and scholars from abroad were more likely to find his theoretical work highly insightful and compelling (172: xix).

Not enough anger

Mickelson suggests that the reason for the difference in response may lie in what black theologian, Cornell West, Professor Emeritus at Princeton University and Professor at Union Theological Seminary, said of President Barak Obama regarding the President's reference to America as a "magical place" in his aforementioned keynote address at the Democratic National Convention in 2004. On the "Tavis Smiley Show," National Public Radio, August 4, 2004, Professor West said, "'So there is a sense in which, as brilliant as he is and as wonderful as he is, he tends to lack a certain kind of rage connected to what is meant to be an involuntary immigrant as opposed to a voluntary one'" (172: xv). That is, the voluntary minorities might have responded to Ogbu the same way as the African-American and Latino involuntary minorities responded if their experiences had imbued them also with "a certain kind of rage."

No doubt Ogbu did not see himself as taking up the Self-Responsibility Tradition of Booker T. Washington and, as such, was equally as subject as Washington to attack from the same System-Responsibility forces. In his case, those forces were represented by a small group of educated black and Latino colleagues, apparently filled with enough simmering anger to meet Cornell West's anger bar for blackness. With Washington, it was displayed, for example, by Trotter and his fellow protestors in disrupting Washington's speech before the Negro Business League in 1903.

Adaptation versus pathology

But the die had been cast. Fordham-Ogbu had made the point that while system change is a prerequisite to significant improvement in black student school performance, alone, it is not enough; changes in the attitudes and behavior of the students and their communities themselves is a co-requisite. That was more than the System- Responsibility Tradition adherents could bear. Their thinking could be summed up as follows: How dare you blame the students; they are the victims. Sophisticated as they were, seemingly quite innocently they (and in particular Ogbu, the target because of his national standing) had sounded a call to arms. The boundary of fictive kinship had been crossed. "Acting white" had to be discredited, and Ainsworth-Darnell and Downey stand out among those who set out to do just that.

In the fight which ensued, "acting white" came to connote, not so much an adaptive behavior as Fordham-Ogbu saw it, but deviant or pathological behavior as they did not see it. It came to mean blacks giving less importance than whites to education, academic striving, and intellectual pursuit. That "acting white" also means an anti-white life style as well is not controversial, as it does not suggest deviancy or pathology but merely a plain and, apparently, socially acceptable cultural difference.

Other Studies: Testing Their Thesis

Studies to test the Fordham-Ogbu thesis have been both qualitative and quantitative. The qualitative studies, similar to the Fordham-Ogbu study, have relied on ethnographic or interview data. Some of the studies are listed below, with the level of support provided. The number following each study is the number of its listing in the References section.

Little /No Support
Cousins study (1994), 50

Akom study (2003), 3
Carter study (2006), 28
Bergin and Cooks study (2002), 7
Tyson study (2002), 260
Horvat and Lewis study (2003), 384

Partial/Complete Support
Mickelson and Velasco study (2006), 173
Neal-Barnett study (2001), 423
Solomon study (1992), 240

The quantitative studies, by sample category and support provided, are listed below.

	Little/No Support	Partial/ Complete Support
National Representative Sample		
Ainsworth-Darnell and Downey study (1998), 298	X	
Cook and Ludwig study (1998), 43	X	
Farkas, Lleras, and Maczuga study (2002), 343		X
Fryer and Torelli study (2005), 354 *and* Fryer Study (2009), 353a [same study, two reports]		X
Flashman study (2008), 350		X
Farkas study (2008), 80		X
Local or Regional Sample		
Kao, Tiender, and Schneider study (1996), 391	X	
Tyson, Darity Jr., and Castellino study (2005), 457	X	
Ferguson study (2001), 345	X	
Harris study (2006), 367a	X	

Steinberg, Dornbusch, and Brown study   X
(1992), 450
Witherspoon, Speight, and Thomas study   X
(1997), 289
Taylor study (2008), 253   X
Irving and Hudley study (2008), 130   X
Mickelson study (2008), 171   X

Qualitative studies

As can be seen, results of other qualitative studies tend *not* to support the Fordham-Ogbu thesis of "acting white" being one major reason for black academic underachievement. Rather, several (Mickelson and Valesco; Carter; Tyson et al.; Bergin and Cook) do not cite academic achievement as a factor in "acting white." Instead, they cite white behavior and life styles. Only three of the nine studies cited, however, found *no* evidence of "acting white" as pertains to academic success: Cousins (1994), which was conducted in a high school where Black Muslim influence existed, Akom (2003), whose subjects were, in fact, Nation of Islam students, and Bergin and Cooks (2002). The others, while not supportive of the Fordham-Ogbu thesis, did find *some* evidence of "acting white." In her study, Tyson, for example, though finding little such evidence, reports that she found some evidence of it "in situations where none or very few other Blacks were in the more rigorous courses and programs" (260:82).

As for the two studies in the support category, Neal-Barnett (2001) appears to have found considerable support for it, as did Mickelson and Velasco (2006). At the same time, however, Mickelson and Velasco found partial support for the critics. They conclude that the "acting white" epithet can cause some students to respond by excelling academically instead of retreating from academics as the thesis postulates. They also found that school organizational features, such as tracking, contribute to the achievement disparity, something later acknowledged by Ogbu but omitted from the Fordham-Ogbu thesis. Additional qualitative support for the thesis is provided by various anecdotal reports (see, for example: 160:89-100; 161:278-82; 376; 385).

Quantitative studies

Unlike the qualitative studies and anecdotal reports, the quantitative studies provide the generalizable hard data customarily thought to be needed for reliability. Of the 15 studies cited, a majority (9 of 15, or 60%) found statistical evidence of "acting white," and of the six national studies an even a larger majority (4 of 6, or 67%) found statistical support for it. Further, all of the national studies -- including the Ainsworth-Darnell and Downey study, notwithstanding the authors' interpretation to the contrary, as well as, on one variable, the Cook-Ludwig study — found some support for one or more of Ogbu's other five oppositional culture components. None of the studies concludes that "acting white" is one *major* cause of black students' poor academic performance. Farkas expressly said that it explains "only a modest proportion of the achievement gap...," adding that "... it may be more a consequence than a cause of poor achievement" (80:344).

Criticisms of Fordham-Ogbu Study

Most of the studies are critical of the Fordham-Ogbu study and its "acting white" thesis. The researchers say, inclusively, that it:

- is based on a small and unrepresentative sample (Ainsworth-Darnell and Downey; Cook and Ludwig; Fryer and Torelli),
- ignores the range of variables which influence identity, such as time, place, community, individual adaptations, gender, social class (Cousins; Hemmings; Carter),
- does not account for variation in response to group pressure and oppositional culture (Bergin and Cook; Irving and Hudley; Akom),
- does not give enough attention to system forces that impact student learning (Foster, Ainsworth-Darnell and Downey; Weis),
- sees culture as static rather than dynamic, leading to labeling of groups (Foster),
- omits comparison with white students (Ainsworth-Darnell and Downey; Tyson et al.; Cook and Ludwig),
- applies to white behaviors or lifestyles, not to academic striving (Mickelson and Valesco; Carter; Tyson et al.; Bergin and Cook),

- overlooks cultural diversity within black communities (Akom; Cousins), and
- fails to measure resistance across involuntary, dominant, and immigrant groups (Ainsworth-Darnell and Downey).

The main criticisms among these have been the use of a small and unrepresentative sample and the lack of across-race comparisons.

Testing Their Thesis: The Primary Challenge by Ainsworth-Darnell and Downey and Cook-Ludwig

Although broadly criticized, the primary challenge to the Fordhan-Ogbu "acting white" thesis and Ogbu's OCF has been provided by the first two national statistical studies to examine their work: the Ainsworth-Darnell and Downey study [at the time, the former a black doctoral student in sociology at The Ohio State University and the latter a sociology professor there] and the Cook-Ludwig study [Cook a Duke University sociologist and Ludwig a Georgetown University public policy professor].

The Cook-Ludwig study tested the "acting white" component and collapsed the other four components into what they termed "alienation from school." Except for one variable, they did not find support for either the Fordham-Ogbu "acting white" thesis or its OCF. The one variable pertained to time spent on homework, the hardest-working black students spending statistically significant less time on it than the hardest-working white students.

It is Ainsworth-Darnell and Downey who seem more determined to undermine the Fordham-Ogbu thesis and its OCF. They take it on component by component, collapsing its five components into four and stipulating that "lack of support for any of these claims is cause for skepticism." They say their findings reject all four components, except, in one instance, the rejection was partial. That instance pertains to greater black student resistance to school, for which they found mixed support. Based on students' **skills**, **habits**, and **styles** (classroom effort, disruptive behavior, doing homework, and being in trouble), they found support for it, whereas, based on what they term students' **concrete attitudes**, they did not. The skills, habits, and styles were based on teacher assessments, while the concrete attitudes were based on student self-reports. The items which comprised the self-report form are shown below.

As regards "acting white" – and this is what perhaps, most of all, makes their study stand out -- they say their data support an opposite finding: **that high-achieving black students are more popular than their white counterparts and that, generally, black students have *more* pro-school attitudes than white students**. Contrary to Fordham-Ogbu and to traditional thinking and research, then, they argue that their data show that there is no oppositional culture problem or black student attitude-achievement paradox; and that, therefore, rather than focus our remedies on the culture of students and community, those remedies should instead focus on the system.

In the fashion of DuBois's "Of Mr. Booker T. Washington and Others" in his <u>The Souls of Black Folk</u>, Ainsworth-Darnell and Downey thereby declare war on the Fordhan-Ogbu thesis and its implicit Self-Responsibility Tradition. We, therefore, examine it in some detail so that, in the academic domain, we can see the legacy of the System-Responsibility Tradition which it represents. So often when it comes to our plight, it is the tendency of that legacy, not to seek truth or foster understanding, but to excuse, deny, and distort in the interest of victimhood and Victimology.

Meaningful pro-school attitudes and higher esteem of education.
Not only do these researchers say black students have significantly more pro-school attitudes than white students. They further contend that, rather than being meaningless, which they say Ogbu and others suggest, their pro-school attitudes are significant predictors of grades, with our students holding education in higher esteem than white students. The authors further defend their findings in a later joint article as well as in an article by Downey alone (60:298-311;330). They respond to the skepticism of their finding of more pro-school values held by black students than white students, presenting attitude-behavior correlations and other arguments to support their finding's validity. Downey goes so far as to exclaim,

"Proponents of oppositional culture theory impugn Blacks' cultural values as part of the problem; I see them as part of the solution" (60:309). He makes the point, for example, that it is, in part, the pro-school values of African-American students which explain the decline in the black-white achievement gap during the 1980s. What, among other things, he fails to mention is that, since then, a plateau has occurred, and maybe the gap has even begun to widen again (18: ix). Jointly, Ainsworh-Darnell and Downey challenge those who maintain that there is no relationship between our students' attitudes and their behavior, posing three questions (330):

(1) Why are attitude-behavior correlations among blacks consistently in the expected direction?
(2) If the argument is that blacks' attitudes are meaningless because their attitude- behavior correlations are slightly smaller than those of whites, shouldn't we also dismiss the attitudes of Asian Americans and Hispanics? Their attitude-behavior correlations are also typically smaller than those of whites.
(3) What more must black students do before we believe they mean what they say?

Failure of others to find pro-school attitudes due to an unrepresentative sample. To explain why they were able to discover pro-school attitudes while other researchers have not, Ainsworh-Darnell and Downey contend that, if Fordham-Ogbu and other ethnographers had used a national representative sample, as they did, instead of a sample from a poor neighborhood, they too might have found the same pro-school attitudes. Ferguson's Shaker Heights study provides some support for their claim (346). Ferguson examined the black-white achievement gap in the Cleveland, Ohio suburb of Shaker Heights based on a survey of 1699 students in grades 7-12 at the end of the 1999 school year. Shaker Heights is regarded as a model community consisting of a stable mix of middle-class blacks and whites and, reportedly, having one of the best school systems in the nation. Nevertheless, the proportion of black students from one-parent families and families with a lower educational background significantly outnumber white students who fall into these categories.

Ferguson found that pro-school attitudes differentiated black high achievers from black low achievers, and that black males showed more interest in school than white males. However, Ferguson is much more cautious than Ainsworth-Darnell and Downey in interpreting the role of attitudes, asserting, "The impact that particular beliefs, attitudes, and behaviors might have on achievement is more difficult to determine than one might initially expect." He adds: "causation operates in both directions and is cumulative over time. Unfortunately, for most, if not all, of the attitude and behavior variables in the analysis, the magnitude of causal effects in each direction are difficult, if not impossible, to sort out" (346:20).

On the basis of the research, Ferguson's caution is well warranted and might have served Ainsworth-Darnell and Downey equally as well. The previously cited author of the renown textbook, <u>Social Psychology</u>, David Myers, tells us that forty separate factors have been counted which complicate the attitude-behavior relationship (186:136), elsewhere observing, "We are likely not only to think ourselves into action but also to act ourselves into a way of thinking" (186:150).

Farkas responds. George Farkas, a sociologist at The Pennsylvania State University, responded to the challenge. He and others had previously challenged the authors, asserting that their conclusions are invalid; this time Farkas alone responded (80; 343). He accused the authors of shifting the debate from one of *discrepancy* between black student attitudes and their performance to one of *correlation* between the two. His point was that the debate is not about correlation but about discrepancy, and that discrepancy derives from a variety of forces, including oppositional culture. Fargas argues that if you separately correlate the attitude-performance of each group -- black, white, and Asian -- you could end up with similar correlations since correlations show, not discrepancies between variables, but whether the variables increase or decrease at the same time. Whether the discrepancy is small or large, the variables can, nevertheless, increase or decrease at the same time, that increase or decrease telling us nothing about the size of the discrepancy between the variables. Therefore, Farkas contends, although Ainsworth-Darnell and Downey can claim that they have proven that there is no black attitude-behavior discrepancy gap

-- given that the correlation is no different from that for white and Asian students -- Farkas's interpretation is that their claim is based, not on discrepancy as he and others base their claim, but on correlations, on which they do not base their claim. Those correlations, he assert, do not reflect those factors on which he and others base their claim of a gap and, moreover, are relatively modest anyway.

Farkas is the technical expert here and we will leave it to his fellow technical experts to weigh in on his response, but there is a constant in the Ainsworth-Darnell challenge that is subject to non-technical examination: African American students show high pro-school attitudes while having the lowest grades. That these pro-school attitudes, nevertheless, mean something constitutes the core of their challenge. What more, they ask, must black students do before we believe they mean what they say.

Why make such a big deal of black pro-school attitudes and esteem of education? If our students have more pro-school attitudes than white students and, thus, esteem education even more than they do, yet have lower grades than both white and Asian students -- as the Ainsworth-Darnell and Downey study shows -- then it is logical to ask why they make black students' pro-school attitudes and esteem of education such a big deal. They respond, in effect, yes our data do show that our students have lower grades, but they also show that, notwithstanding, their pro-school attitudes (the importance they place on education) *still* leads to their getting good grades. That is, contrary to previous research and conventional wisdom, it means that African American students with pro-school attitudes (like white students with pro-school attitudes) get good grades and African American students who get good grades (like white students who get good grades) are rewarded, not punished, by their peers. Ogbu and others, they say, are, therefore, wrong in asserting that the positive attitude that our students consistently express towards education does not translate into good grades. Not true; it does, just as it does for white students.

Logically, then, since our students have more pro-school attitudes than white students, and these attitudes translate into good grades, then the grades of our students should be higher, not lower, than those of whites and/or Asians. True, Ainsworth-Darnell and Downey, in effect, argue, but what happens is that the grades of our students are depressed by their lack cultural skills -- skills, habits, and style (classroom effort, cooperative behavior, completion of homework, and staying out of trouble). That is, the grades of our students are depressed, not by their attitudes, but by their lack of cultural skills. So it is possible, on the one hand, to get good grades when you look at attitudes alone, which is what they have done, and poor grades when you look at behaviors alone (skills, habits, and styles), which is also what they have done.

So, in the eyes of Ainsworth-Darnell and Downey, the big deal is that it is "misplaced" to make the attitudes of our students the focus in our attempt to bring them up to par; instead, we must focus on their cultural skills. We should focus on their behaviors (with which there is something wrong) rather than on their values (with which nothing is wrong; indeed it is their strength). One might readily think that this would still mean that we focus on the students, but on their behaviors instead of on their expressed values. But that is not what Ainsworth-Darnell and Downey have in mind. Rather, they think it is best to focus on the system.

Their logic for focus on the system is that the behavior problems of our students (their lack of cultural skills) does not derive from what they are doing -- since our students have pro-school attitudes and are more likely than whites to esteem their high-achieving peers -- but, a la Ogbu in his early years, from the material conditions under which they live. Those material conditions contribute to these behavior problems, to a cultural deficit -- to skills, habits, and styles (lack of classroom effort, disruptive behavior, not doing homework, and being in trouble) which are not "rewarded by teachers"; as a result, our students perform poorly. The best way to remedy those conditions, as they see it, is through an emphasis on "policies that reduce economic inequality and residential segregation." An emphasis, instead, on the behavior of our students -- on their cultural deficits or their skills, habits, and styles -- would be "misplaced."

Where they say Ogbu and others have gone wrong. So, their view is, that while Ogbu and the oppositional culture proponents are right to specify the behavior of black students as an impediment to their academic achievement, they are wrong in the remedy which they prescribe. They are wrong because they have not understood that these behaviors do not reflect the values of our students, but, instead, their material conditions. Ainsworth-Darnell and Downey have, accordingly, used their research findings to challenge Ogbu, along with the "acting white" thesis and its connotations, and to justify an emphasis, not on the self, but on the system. Flashman, Fryer and Torelli, and Farkas have all drawn attention to the flaws in their use of survey data (as with other studies using survey data) and to other problems with their data. Ainsworth-Darnell and Downey seem confident, however, that they have discovered something that other researchers have not: that the documented discrepancy between black student values and their performance is a myth; that discrepancy is no more than the discrepancy for any other group. So all is well on the attitude front; indeed, to reiterate, they ask, "What more must black students do before we believe they mean what they say?"

Accounting for the black attitude-behavior paradox: begging the question. Ainsworth-Darnell and Downey, unavoidably, acknowledge the attitude-behavior discrepancy since their data, like other data, document it. But, in their words:

> ...by simply noting that a given attitude is rarely the only independent variable predicting a behavior, we can understand how blacks can have more positive attitudes (valid ones) and poorer behaviors (valid ones) than whites. In a multivariate model, if blacks are disadvantaged on other independent variables that predict behaviors, (e.g., material conditions and other unmeasured variables) then they could easily have a higher group mean on attitudes but a lower group mean on behaviors. There is no need to invoke an attitude-behavior inconsistency argument (298:549).

In other words, the paradox exists, but there is a valid reason for it to exist, and because there is a valid reason for it to exist, it really does not exist; so no reason to invoke "an attitude-behavior inconsistency argument."

Ainsworth-Darnell and Downey are right. There is no need to invoke it, merely to describe it. Their research findings, as the research findings of others, are there for the reading, so to speak. As the proverb goes, "If it walks like a duck, quacks like a duck, looks like a duck, it must be a duck." Only having acknowledged the discrepancy, they introduce the issue of validity to declare it non-existent. In so doing, they resort to what is in dispute (the validity of the behaviors) to declare the outcome (that the behaviors are valid). *It is called begging the question and is a logical fallacy.* That they see these behaviors -- lack of classroom effort, uncooperative behavior, homework deficiency, and being in trouble -- as valid does not make them so. Nor should it.

No doubt system factors contribute to those behaviors, as they do for all of our behaviors, but, as with all of our behaviors, they are a product of multiple interacting factors. Even so, in the end, students (and we) own the behaviors and the students (and we) must be a party to their alteration. Our students can and must meet higher standards; to accept less is to render them devoid of the qualities on which the survival and progress of humankind have always depended: the ability to adapt and, through intelligence and will, to cope with the exigencies of life. To contend otherwise is to treat them unrealistically and condescendingly. We understand that there are multiple causes for these behaviors, but these are *their* behaviors and they are *accountable* for them, however we go about getting them to exercise that accountability. They are just as accountable for them in logic as, at some point, in law.

Taking responsibility for oneself begins at an early age and insanity comes to be about the only basis of escape from it. That Ainsworth-Darnell and Downey immeasurably expand that escape is testimony to the kind of victim syndrome which permeates this issue and so many other issues which we blacks confront. It is vintage System-Responsibility Tradition thinking and vintage victimhood. This mindset, in which we are eternal victims of a vicious, racist system in constant need of a fix helps to make the African American Male School Adaptability Crisis (AMSAC) unsolvable and renders a sizable portion of our people to a life of permanent impoverishment. As McWhorter argues, Victimology condones weakness and failure and hampers performance (160:41-49). In "validating" our students' behaviors, Ainsworth-Darnell and Downey, not unlike so many others, make our students helpless victims, no more able to control their behaviors than robots because they are under siege from the system. But our students' behaviors are what they are and cannot be "validated" away. What Ogbu and others have shown is that, historically, there is the inconsistency which Ainsworth-Darnell and Downey deny. But there is nothing uncovered, or logically contended, by them which refutes it; rather, they confirm it by engaging in logical fallacy which undermines their attempt to support their denial.

No paradox, if.... Mickelson does agree with them that there is no paradox, but she interprets her study as showing that there is no paradox only *if* you change how importance placed on education is measured, which she did (170). If you measure it the traditional way, based on students' abstract attitudes (their embrace of the American Dream), the paradox persists. If, on the other hand, you measure it based on what she terms students' concrete attitudes (their everyday life experiences), the paradox disappears; their academic achievement is impacted by those concrete attitudes. Ainsworth-Darnell and Downey say, yes, you are right about the concrete attitudes but wrong about the abstract attitudes because *they (the abstract attitudes) also* impact their grades. Other research, they say, supports their contention, citing the study of Alan Kerckhoff and Robert Campbell, at the time both sociologists at Duke University (392).

But did Ainsworth-Darnell and Downey measure the same attribute measured by Mickelson, or by Kerckhoff and Campbell? Did they measure abstract attitudes the Mickelson way and the Kerckhoff and Campbell way (which is also the Ogbu way and the traditional way) -- or some other way?

Measuring attitudes. At the heart of the Ainsworth-Darnell and Downey challenge to the cultural gap implicit in the 'acting white" controversy -- and that lies at the premise of AMCAP -- is the assertion that there is no culture gap because black students "mean what they say." Rather than their culture being a problem, their pro-school attitude is "part of the solution." So, if they did not measure abstract attitudes as Mickelson and Kerckhoff and Campbell measured them, but, instead, measured them some other way, then their data provide no basis for that assertion. An examination of the questions used in their respective studies enables us to decide if they did.

Questions used by Ainsworth-Darnell and Downey to measure concrete attitudes

1. Treatment by teachers. Do you agree: (a) When you work hard on schoolwork, your teachers praise your effort; (b) In class you often feel "put down" by your teachers; (c) Most of your teachers really listen to what you have to say.
2. Attitude toward teachers. Do you agree that: (a) The teaching is good at your school; (b) Teachers are interested in students.
3. Discipline is fair. How much do you agree with the following statement about your current school and teachers? Discipline is fair.
4. OK to break rules. How often do you think it is OK to: (a) cut a couple of classes; (b) skip school for a whole day; (c) disobey school rules?
5. Doing what I am supposed to do in class. Do you agree with the following statements about why you go to school? I get a feeling of satisfaction from doing what I'm supposed to do in class.
6. OK to cheat. How often do you think it is OK to: (a) cheat on tests; (b) copy someone else's homework?
7. Good student. Do you think that other students see you as a good student?
8. Troublemaker. Do you think that other students see you as a troublemaker?
9. Tries hard in class. How often do you try as hard as you can in math, English, history, and science?

Questions used by Mickelson to measure concrete attitudes

1. Based on their experiences, my parents say people like us are not always paid or promoted according to our education.
2. All I need to learn for my future is to read, write, and make change.
3. Although my parents tell me to get a good education in order to get a good job, they face barriers to job success.

4. When our teachers give us homework, my friends never think of doing it.
5. People in my family haven't been treated fairly at work no matter how much education they have.
6. Studying in school rarely pays off later with good jobs.

Questions used by Mickelson to measure abstract attitudes

1. Education is the key to success in the future.
2. If everyone in America gets a good education, we can end poverty.
3. Achievement and effort in school lead to job success later on.
4. The way for poor people to become middle class is for them to get a good education.
5. School success is not necessarily a clear path to a better life.
6. Getting a good education is a practical road to success for a young black (white) man (woman) like me.
7. Young white (black) women (men) like me have a chance of making it if we do well in school.
8. Education really pays off in the future for young black (white) men (women) like me.

Questions used by Kerckhoff and Campbell to measure attitudes

1. How much more schooling do you really expect to get?
2. How much more schooling would you get if you could do what you *really want* to do?

Comparing the measurement: school experiences versus family and community experiences. Ainsworth-Darnell and Downey claim that their finding that black students' pro-school attitudes are good predictors of grades contradicts the finding of Mickelson that black students' absract attitudes are not good predictors of grades. Their claim is false. Their finding does not contradict Mickelson's finding because, contrary to what Ainsworth-Darnell and Downey *imply*, their questions, listed above, do not measure abstract attitudes. Instead, their questions measure concrete attitudes. If they had measured abstract attitudes, their questions would have been similar to the questions, listed above, used by Micdelson to measure abstract attitudes, but they are not. Rather, their questions are similar to the questions used by Mickelson to measure concrete attitudes. In one of their footnotes, they themselves even say that this is the case. Here is how they express what they did: "... we borrowed Mickelson's *concrete* term to highlight the way in which our attitudinal indicators measure students' views of their own everyday school experiences" [emphasis in original].

In sum, Ainsworth-Darnell and Downey borrowed Mickelson's term, concrete (attitudes), and used questions similar to those employed by her to derive the concept, but, nevertheless, proceed to claim that what they measured is different from what she measured. By all logic, however, since their questions were equivalent to the questions used by Mickelson, what they measured was equivalent to what Mickelson measured, which was concrete attitudes. But that is not what they claim. They claim that they measured abstract attitudes. Based on this claim, Ainsworth-Darnell and Downey contend that their finding that black students' pro-school attitudes predict their grades contradicts Mickelson's finding that black students' abstract attitudes do not predict their grades. They trumpet this finding as tentatively upending previous research, along with convential wisdom, which holds that the high esteem blacks place on education does not translate into positive educational outcomes.

But there is a twist to their claim. It is implied rather than stated. Nowhere in the report do Ainsworth-Darnell and Downey *literally* say that black students' abstract attitudes are good predictors of their grades. Here is what they do say:

- "... in our study African Americans reported more pro-school attitudes for nearly all of our attitudinal measures, and these same indicators were meaningful predictors of educational success above and beyond the effect of behaviors."
- "... we contend that students' preferences, when measured as concrete attitudes regarding specific issues, also can be good predictors of grades...."

These excerpts show that what Ainsworth-Darnell and Downey do say is that black students' "pro-school attitudes," or "preferences," are good predictors of their grades.

But, as argued, their list of questions tap, not into abstract attitudes, but into concrete attitudes. So, while Ainsworth-Darnell and Downy claim that Mickelson is wrong, they fail to use parallel language back up their claim. Nowhere do they say: *Black students' abstract atttitudes are good predictors of their grades.* Instead, they say: *Black students' pro-school attitudes, or stated preferences, are good predictors of their grades.*

In their analysis, however, they treat "pro-school attitudes," or "stated preferences," *as if* they were abstract attitudes.

Furthermore, Ainsworth-Darnell and Downey claim that the data of "many others" support their finding, specifically citing Kerckhoff and Campbell. But the Kerckhoff-Campbell study supports their finding only if their study is interpreted as measuring concrete attitudes. It is evident from the questions, listed above, used by Kerckhoff-Campbell that they, like Ainsworth-Darnell and Downey, measured concrete attitudes based on students' school experiences, not -- as Ainsworth-Darnell and Downey would have us believe – on students' abstract attitudes. So, if there are "many others' whose data support their finding, from among them, Ainsworth-Darnell and Downey chose those whose finding does not support their interpretation of it.

In this play on terminology, Ainsworth-Darnell and Downey have done something similar to what Farkas accuses them of doing in regard to the attitude-behavior relationship being addressed: shifted the grounds of the debate. In their controversy with Farkas (and others), they shifted the ground of analysis from discrepancy to correlation. In this case, they shift the ground of definition by making concrete attitudes mean the same as abstract attitudes. Only, to be fair to them – and for what it is worth -- they do so implicitly, rather than explicitly.

To turn to their critique of Ogbu, Ainsworth-Darnell and Downey's claim that their finding contradicts Ogbu's analysis is based on outright misrepresentation. They contend that their finding that pro-school attitudes predict grades "disputes Ogbu's ... claim that African Americans' responses to survey questions represent mere 'wishful thinking,'" citing Ogbu's 1991 article, "Minority Coping Responses and School Experience." Ogbu makes no such claim in this article. Beginning one paragraph with, "I attribute the lack of seriousness and effort to disillusionment over dismal future job opportunities ...," Ogbu goes on to say the following:

> Although blacks express high educational aspirations when asked, this may be more of a wishful thinking. They "wish" they could get ahead like white people through education; but they "know" that they "can't" from their historical encounter with the job ceiling. Therefore, they "attack" the tests and/or credential requirements rather than prepare for them; or they go to the tests with ambivalence, or they simply do not match their aspirations with effort (195:446).

This hardly sounds like, as Ainsworth-Darnell and Downey portray it, an outright dismissal of "African Americans' responses to survey questions." Rather, it is a description of African Americans' abstract attitudes, on the one hand, and their concrete attitudes (they "know" that they "can't"), on the other hand. Their finding, rather than contradicting Ogbu's "wishful thinking" reference, supports it, for Ogbu is saying, in effect, that it is the concrete attitudes which really count, since the expressed high educational aspirations get altered by "material conditions," as it were, and, therefore, *may* be [not are] no more than wishful thinking. But, again, Ainsworth-Darnell and Downey treat their finding *as if* it reflects abstract attitudes when, in fact, it reflects concrete attitudes – the attitudes which, like them, Ogbu sees as having predictive value.

Orwellian presentation? Sounds confusing? Well, it is because the authors are doing what Farkas accuses them of doing with regard to their attitude-behavior correlations, shifting the grounds of the debate. The debate, inclusively, is about the validity of the "acting white" connotation that black students place less importance on education than white students. Ainsworth-Darnell and Downey say their data reject this connotation, showing, instead, that black students have *more* "pro-school attitudes" than white students. To fortify their case, in sum, they use the devices which follow.

- They shift the language from "importance placed on education" (or some equivalent customary phrase) to "pro-school" (a new descriptor).

- They then use a different metric. They switch from abstract attitudes to concrete attitudes, yet apply the same meaning to both: stated preferences or attitudes (not distinguishing one set of attitudes from the other). *Their* concrete attitudes thus become simply attitudes.
- They assert that Mickelson is wrong to conclude that "concrete attitudes predict students' grades, while abstract attitudes do not" as if their data provide contrary proof when, in fact, their data are based on concrete attitudes and therefore support, not contradict, Mickelson.
- They cite the Kerckhoff-Campbell study as supporting their case, which it does, but only if it is interpreted as measuring concrete attitudes, which they do not; they interpret it as measuring abstract attitudes and cite Ogbu as not supporting their case when, in effect, he does.
- They argue that there is no black attitude-achievement paradox even though their data show that there is, but which they say is not because there are "valid" reasons for it.
- Above all, they separate culture into two parts: cultural attitudes and cultural skills [cultural attitudes as manifested by concrete *attitudes*, and *cultural skills* as manifested by skills, habits, and styles (classroom effort, being in trouble, and homework)]. Having made the separation, they show that, for black students, the attitudes are better than those of other groups while the skills are worse. They, nevertheless, conclude that it would be "misplaced" to focus either on the attitude part of their culture because their attitudes are above par, or on the skills part because students are not responsible for that part; so let it be. As for who is responsible, beyond citing economic inequality and residential segregation, they seem as well to implicate the teacher reward system since the students' cultural skills are not "rewarded by teachers."

If all this strikes one as somewhat Orwellian, it might be because it is.

The race card. In case this were not enough, Ainsworth-Darnell and Downey resort to one other weapon that is common to System thinkers, the race card. In asking, "what more must black students do before we believe they mean what they say," they shift the attitude-achievement paradox issue from one of evidence to one of belief. Their question suggests that, rather than the paradox being based on what the *evidence* has shown, it is based, instead, on the *belief* that researchers and others have in what black students say. Their refrain goes: you believe white students and Asian students, so why not believe black students.

Giving us something to think about: dual belief system. All considered, if we were to apply the same standard to our analysis of the Ainsworth-Darnell and Downey findings as they apply to Ogbu's oppositional culture model, namely, that "lack of support for any of these claims is cause for skepticism," we would not only have to be skeptical about their findings but outright dismissive of them. But that would be a mistake. The authors have helped to call our attention to an important variable in trying to decipher the black attitude-achievement paradox and in understanding the African American Male School Adaptation Crisis (AMSAC), namely, the dual belief system factor.

Abstract beliefs versus concrete beliefs. Insofar as known, Mickelson (drawing upon previous research pertaining to the concept) was the first to draw attention to the paradox by separating abstract beliefs from those based on practical, concrete, everyday experiences. Her data show a different result for each of the two sets of beliefs. Ainsworth-Darnell and Downey acknowledge having "borrowed Mickelson's *concrete* [italics in original] term" and, having applied it to their parallel data, discovering -- like Mickelson -- a meaningful outcome. Without factoring the dual belief system into their design, Kerckhoff and Campbell found implicit evidence of it anyway. Their findings showed that while, as an independent variable, high expectation (based on the two concrete questions listed above) was not predictive of success, it was "more important for blacks [than whites]" in contributing to it. It can even be argued that Ainsworth-Darnell and Downey's declared target, Ogbu, recognized the two. Ogbu made it clear that his ethnographic studies showed that students want to get good grades (give abstract or theoretical importance to education, as it were), but he indicated that his studies, likewise, showed that "what the students reject that hurt their academic performance are "White" attitudes and behaviors conducive to making good grades ...," that is, they exhibited concrete attitudes at variance with their abstract attitudes.

Really more pro-school attitudes? The question of what Ainsworth-Darnell and Downey have discovered remains: do our students *really* have more pro-school attitudes than white students and do these attitudes reliably predict good grades. Over all these years, have we been deceived by experience and research? How can we explain their finding that "Blacks' pro-schooling attitudes exhibited predictive validity on par with Asians' and Hispanics' and only slightly lower than that of Whites" (60:307). The answer appears to lie in the way they have measured pro-school: as concrete attitudes based on students' *school* experiences. So measured, contrary to the impression that Ainsworth-Darnell and Downey repeatedly and misleadingly convey, we are not even talking about the conversation and research that we have had over the years. As Mickelson points out, that conversation and research have been about abstract attitudes -- about, as it were, our students' subscription to the American Dream. Nevertheless, Ainsworth-Darnell and Downey might have highlighted another means of assessing our students' attitudes towards education: their everyday school experiences rather than their internalized (and Americanized) view of the appropriate.

The one question of the nine in the Ainsworth-Darnell and Downey study that did not predict success, discipline is fair, provides further support for this possibility. Why would this be the only one of the nine variables without predictive power in the same direction as the others? Two studies provide a clue: the Kerckhoff-Campbell study and Ferguson's Shaker Heights study. Kerckhoff and Campbell found discipline, along with IQ, to be the only significant independent variables in predicting grades, pointing to the power exerted by discipline (staying out of trouble) on black school success -- a power that it was not shown to exert on white school success. It could be, then, that discipline, unlike the other eight variables, uniquely impacts African American students (especially males) whereas our students are more similar to the other groups on the remaining eight variables. On a variable similar to those eight, educational expectations, Ainsworth-Darnell and Downey found that although it was not a significant predictor, for black students it did have a grade impact, suggesting that although it might have impacted black students more, still black students were similar to the white students. Ferguson, too, found a related variable -- inclined to act tough and get into fights -- to differentiate black from white students while finding no significant difference between the two on other school attitude variables, especially when controlling for socioeconomic background.

So, based on the three studies -- by Ainsworth-Darnell and Downey, Kerckhoff and Campbell, and Ferguson -- one might infer that, as a group, except for discipline, African American students share with other groups similar, if not more favorable, attitudes toward their school experiences. For many, the school environment, indeed, may be more hospitable than their home or neighborhood environment. As Noguera observes, "Urban schools are increasingly the most reliable source of stability and social support for poor children" (191:231). And, based on his ethnographic study, Elijah Anderson has this to say:

> The school is a microcosm of the community in a sense. Although police and disciplinarians are on patrol, kids are parading up and down halls, socializing, even buying and selling drugs. The same things are going on inside the school as outside it. Yet it remains a haven, a place where one can go and expect relative order (5:98).

Further, it is reasonable to assume that these concrete attitudes impact their grades, and, contrary to what Ainsworth-Darnell and Downey would have us believe, Ogbu, Mickelson, and others are not contending otherwise. Their position is simply that the research evidence shows that black students' abstract attitudes do not. While Farkas appears to attribute their pro-school attitudes to exaggeration, there could be less exaggeration than might first appear. Maybe -- and only maybe -- many of our students *really* have more pro-school attitudes [attitudes based, not on their practical, concrete, everyday non-school life experiences, but on their school experiences] than white students and these attitudes may reliably predict good grades. In view of the research showing the major role played by student attitudes in their achievement, discussed herein in connection with the home versus school controversy, such would not be surprising.

Adding the pro-school variable -- and predicting educational outcomes for black students. A clue to the prediction puzzle is provided by Kerckhoff and Campbell. With regard to the model they used to study the educational attainment of the 503 boys in their sample -- 390 white and 113 black -- they observe that "The model is generally much 'looser' or less coherent for blacks," the results for the whites appearing "to be much more "rational" or "orderly." They add, "Perhaps even more striking, nothing in the model helps us very much in explaining black expectations whereas white expectations seem to be based on such "rational" antecedents as SES, IQ, and junior high school grades" (392: 25). In concluding their study, Cook and Ludwig raise a somewhat similar conundrum in citing the experience of two top graduates from DuSable High School in Chicago who ended up dropping out of college. Journalist Paul Schwartzman did likewise in his previously cited investigation of what happened to the 59 fifth-grade "Dreamers." Of the 59, he reports that "It was often difficult to predict who would make it and who wouldn't. One kid who looked hopeless might end up graduating from college.... Another kid who got A's and scored nearly 1200 on his SAT might drop out ...." (440a). In sum, it could be that because of the uncertain role which the concrete plays in their life, assessing their fortunes does not lend itself to customary formulations. When all is said and done, maybe Ainsworth-Darnell and Downey's most important contribution is to have underlined this probability.

As for why the unpredictability, it is herein surmised that it has to do with our students so often not being the product of "**average expectable environments**," thanks, in no small part, to issues of racial identity and the kind of associated emotional upheaval which Scott theorizes comes with it. What so frequently ensues is a failure to develop a positive core identity, a **"subjective sense of an invigorating sameness and continuity."** Without that **"subjective sense of an invigorating sameness and continuity**," it can be argued that predictability becomes more problematic.

Conclusion. Ainsworth-Darnell and Downey have used their black students' pro-school finding as an affirmative basis for rejecting Fordham-Ogbu's oppositional culture thesis and, therefore, for minimizing direct attention to the cultural needs of our students. All of the studies, however, theirs included, document the low achievement level of our students. And not just our students from poverty neighborhoods. Ferguson's research reveals that even in the model middle-class community of Shaker Heights, our students have a grade point average one letter grade below white students (roughly C+ for blacks and B+ for whites), and our seniors there score 200 points below whites on the Scholastic Aptitude Test (SAT). The failure of the aforementioned The Minority Student Achievement Network (MSAN) is evidence that this low achievement of our black middle-class students is not limited to Shaker Heights.

The studies show, too, that the *behavior* (used interchangeably with *character*) of our students undermines their achievement. Their pro-school attitudes touted by Ainsworth-Darnell and Downey notwithstanding, there is, therefore, more reason than not to focus on their behavior as a remedy. However, Ainsworth-Darnell and Downey choose to label that behavior "cultural skills" and absolve our students of responsibility for lacking them, shifting it to the system. Their own evidence reveals though, *that because of their behavior* (in their language, lack of "cultural skills"), those pro-school attitudes do not translate into their getting good grades. To then proceed to ignore that behavior, as they recommend – other than through a focus on the system – is no different from ignoring the callus on one's foot on the premise that the shoe is responsible, so we must, instead, focus on the shoe. Not both, just the shoe, since, after all, though having a callus, there is nothing wrong with the foot – leave it alone; the shoe is the problem, and the sole solution.

That black students -- and black people -- hold education in high expressed regard is not really in dispute. In her study of the attitude-achievement paradox, Mickelson, for example, begins her report:

> Education has had a special place in the hearts and minds of black Americans since the era of Reconstruction. Although public schooling was not widely available until over 100 years after the demise of slavery, blacks held fast to their faith in education as one of the few institutions that could lift them from poverty and oppression (414:44).

She goes on to cite various ethnographic studies which support her contention. Quantitative research by her, Tyson (2001), Ferguson (2005), Cook-Ludwig (1998), and others, likewise, support it. In maybe the most massive study in our educational history, the Coleman Report supports it, showing "Negroes even more interested in learning than white" (40: 320). Most noteworthy, Ogbu's research supports it. In short, it might be said that friends and foes alike do not differ on this issue, that blacks expressly place great importance on education, often even greater than whites place on it. But Fordham-Ogbu's "acting white" thesis challenges this belief, in response to which many go to great length to fend off their challenge. For example, in her Foreword to Horvat and O'Connor's <u>Beyond Acting White</u>, black Northwestern University education professor, Carol Lee, cites 1,500 Sabbath-day schools established by blacks, on our own, after the Civil War as evidence of our educational regard (151:x). Maybe she is correct, but it is a considerable stretch to attribute to Sabbath-day schools an educational function as contrasted with a religious one. One is reminded of the saying, "grasping for straws in the wind."

Having acclaimed the high value we attach to education, the divergence occurs on the contention by Mickelson in her very next sentence: "Even so the rhetorical importance that blacks place on education has rarely been matched by their scholastic performance." In its massive study, the Coleman Report makes the same point, as has so many other reports and studies, including Ogbu, the Report stating that their "reported interest is not translated through effective action into achievement" (40:320). Even if their grades do not reflect their reported high interest, one would expect -- taking that interest at face value -- that their "cultural skills" would reflect it. However, notwithstanding the excuses offered by Ainsworth-Darnell and Downey, as well by Cook and Ludwig, for example, their own research shows that not to be the case.

Here is the point: there is a difference between feeling or *thinking* that something is important and placing a *value* on it. The research shows that our students, like our people, think education is important; that is their opinion or belief. When it comes to the *value* they place on it, however, that is another matter. The *value* placed on education, consistent with how the scholarly literature defines the term value, is more than just whether students (or others) *think* education is important, praiseworthy though that may be. It is inseparably linked to their translation of their *thinking into action* in a way that, according to Louis Raths (late New York University pioneer of the Values Clarification approach to character development), has pattern, consistency, and repetition (216). Otherwise, their thinking is not a value; it is just that -- thinking, hardly removed from daydreaming.

Too frequently missing from the importance that our students place on education is the translation of that thinking into action which has pattern, consistency, and repetition. They do not exercise the appropriate classroom and school behavior, nor do they put in the time and hard work required. What they do (their values) does not reflect what they say or think (their belief or opinion). That could be because their thinking, as so often is the thinking of so many of us, emanates more from the head than from the heart, but it is thinking *in one's heart* that makes the difference. Or, as Mickelson might put it in their case, it is their *concrete* thinking, rather than their *abstract* thinking, which makes the difference.

Study Support for the Challenge

To get a sense of the academic mindset which Ainsworth-Darnell and Downey, as well as Cook-Ludwig, espouse, we can turn to Tyson and Lewis for examples. Based on her studies, black University of North Carolina sociologist, Karolyn Tyson, concludes:

> ...to truly understand the burden of acting white with respect to academic achievement, we must begin in the schools, for that is where the association between whiteness and achievement originates for many children. As students mature, they increasingly perceive the lack of minority students in rigorous courses and programs as embarrassing and insulting. They then use the cultural tools [like "acting white"] available to them to understand why such disparities exist and to maintain a positive perception of themselves in the face of this insult. With each succeeding generation, American schools help perpetuate inequality and group animosity (260:86).

In discussing her research findings, black Emory University sociologist, Amanda Lewis, asserts:

> Not only are there many reasons for questioning the explanatory value of Fordham and Ogbu's acting-white hypothesis ... ; the very fact that it has become so popular is illustrative of the exact dynamics that facilitate the perpetuation of the larger racial hierarchy--that we continue to successfully blame the subjects of racial exclusion for their own situation. Not until African American students have equal educational opportunities--including such things as access to preschool, schools with highly qualified and culturally competent teachers, all necessary instructional supplies, functional technology, and safe facilities--can we begin to talk about blacks' attitudes as relevant for explaining their overall school performance. Until then, such conversations serve as ways to avoid having to make tough choices about how to fundamentally change social and school arrangements more generally (153:198).

The mindset is evident. In both instances, as with Ainsworth-Darnell and Downey and Cook-Ludwig, we see a data perspective which conforms with our System-Responsibility Tradition.

The Challenge Rejected

Unlike in the public domain of the Washington-DuBois war, however, the studies of the System-Responsibility academics are subject to objective scrutiny. Under that scrutiny, the conclusion of Ainsworth-Darnell and Downey and Cook-Ludwig have been rejected by two comparable national statistical studies, therefore, leaving partly standing the Fordham-Ogbu thesis. The rejecting studies were conducted by Fryer-Torelli [Fryer, the previously mentioned black Harvard economist; and Torelli, a Harvard graduate and a leader in Quantitative Social Science] and Flashman [Postdoctoral Associate at the Center for Research on Inequalities and the Life Course, CIQLE] (353a; 353b; 354; 350).

Fryer-Torelli study

To overcome one of the major shortcomings of the Ainsworth-Darnell and Downey study as well as the Cook-Ludwig study, reliance on self-reports, Fryer-Torelli devised an index of social status and, to overcome another shortcoming, they used same-race, rather than across-race, peer popularity. They also formulated an adjusted definition of academic achievement.

Fryer-Torelli's adjustments led them to find that "acting white" *did exist* in their national representative sample and, rather than being concentrated in low-income minority schools, was "robust across many alternative empirical models, subsets of data, and definitions of both social status and academic achievement." In general, for whites, higher grades were associated with higher popularity; whereas for blacks and Hispanics, higher grades were associated with lower popularity. However, they found this popularity drop to be more salient in schools under 20 percent black than in schools over 80 percent black, where it was hardly discernible. But a high-achiever popularity drop they did find, and, therefore, they reject the Ainsworth-Darnell and Downey and Cook-Ludwig study findings, which do not show a drop – Ainsworth-Darnell and Downey even finding the opposite.

At the same time, however, in a dubious interpretation, Fryer-Torelli declare their agreement with Ainsworth-Darnell and Downey and Cook-Ludwig on their rejection of Fordham-Ogbu's oppositional culture thesis. While concluding that *much of the data supports the Fordham-Ogbu thesis*, specifically including the data showing the nonexistence of "acting white" in private schools, Fryer-Torelli nonetheless say that Fordham-Ogbu's oppositional culture thesis "does quite poorly in explaining why 'acting white' is more salient in schools that are less than 20 percent black relative to those that are greater than 80 percent black." That is, as they interpret it, if the Fordham-Ogbu thesis were valid, it should apply in both situations, and Fordham-Ogbu fail to explain why it does not, something which they themselves do not do either, but, as we shall see, Flashman perhaps does. In view of the fact that much of their data support the Fordham-Ogbu thesis, its ostensible failure satisfactorily to explain diverse scenarios would not appear to be a sound basis to reject it *completely*. Rather, as is typically done, their finding might be more soundly interpreted as providing mixed support. Their questionable interpretations have come in for criticism from Kitae Sohn, referenced below, who has reviewed the "acting white" studies (446b). Not in question, however, is their rejection of the findings of Ainsworth-Darnell and Downey and Cook-Ludwig.

Joe L. Rempson

Flashman study

In the most recent (2008) national "acting white" study reviewed, Flashman rejects not only the Ainsworth-Darnell and Downey and the Cook-Ludwig challenge to the Fordham-Ogbu thesis, but also Fryer-Torelli's challenge to it as well (350a, 350b). Stating that the findings of qualitative and regional studies cannot be generalized beyond the study population, she confines her focus to the three national studies under discussion. Her own study came from a data base of 89,940 seventh through twelfth graders compiled by the National Longitudinal Study of Adolescent Health.

Of the Ainsworth-Darnell and Downey and Cook-Ludwig studies, she says that they are based on the bias inherent in self-reports and, consequently, that while at first glance they appear to "contradict the argument that blacks under-achieve in order to avoid social punishment," the "results…cannot differentiate between popularity among blacks, popularity among whites, and popularity among the whole school populations." As a result, they do not provide a valid test of the same-race sanction factor hypothesized by Fordham-Ogbu.

As for the Fryer-Torelli study, while commending its correction of the self-reporting bias in the other two studies and for using same-race criteria, Flashman offers a possible contrary interpretation of the results. She argues that the approach they use "confounds opportunities for friendships and preferences for friendships," and, therefore, the results may be interpreted as either supporting the "acting white" taboo or as a case of high-achieving black students rejecting low-achieving black students instead of being rejected by them.

In her study, Flashman corrects the flaws she cites, controlling for race/ethnic homophily and academic homophily, and factoring in *opportunities for friendship*. Her goal was to determine if opportunities for friendship, not considered by Fryer-Torelli, would yield results consistent with or different from their results. The answer is that her results can be interpreted, not so much to be a contradiction of their results, but as an extension and clarification of them. This is how she sums up her results:

I find some support for the hypothesis (Fordham-Ogbu's oppositional cultural hypothesis]. The implication of this result is that the peer environment of black adolescents is *not* [emphasis in original] hostile to high academic achievement when black adolescents make up less than 50% of the school population. When black students make up more than the majority of a school, high academic achievement among black students *can* [emphasis in original] be a detriment. In these schools there is a strong stigma against friendship groups that are, on average, high-achieving.

Like Fryer-Torelli, in her analysis, Flashman also discovered a statistically significant "acting white" effect based on the percent of blacks in the school population, for her, that percent being 50, whereas, for Fryer-Torelli it was 20. Maybe the opportunities for friendship factor helps to explain the difference. Their findings suggest something similar to what, in the housing domain, is called a "tipping point" whereby when a residential neighborhood reaches around 13% blacks, whites begin to leave it. In this instance, to use Flashman's finding, when a school population reaches around 50% black, "acting white" begins to exert a statistically significant influence. Call it the "'acting white'tipping point," keeping in mind (for those who deny any meaningful existence of "acting white") that just because "acting white" may not exert a statistically significant influence when the black student population is under 50% does not mean that "acting white" does not exist in those situations – and, further, that in those situations it does not exert some influence, especially since, as Fordham-Ogbu argue, the the influence may be conscious or unconscious. Thus, another way to view their *"acting white" black-student- percentage effec*t might be as follows: as the percent of black students in a student body increases so does the effect of "acting white" – a proposition which must be quite tentative, however, since it is based on just two national studies.

Status of Challenge Following Rejection

The research evidence provides qualified statistically significant support for Fordham-Ogbu's "acting white" thesis that high-achieving black students are negatively sanctioned by their peers to a greater degree than high-achieving white students. Based on two national studies so far, the qualification is that the sanctioning appears to be dependent upon the percentage of black students making up the student body, the higher that percentage the more likely there will be sanctions. However, that the sanctions is "*one major reason* Black students do poorly in school" [emphasis in original], as Fordham-Ogbu contend, is not confirmed. With one exception found, the studies, in fact, do not even address this issue, but rather limit their inquiry to whether "acting white" exists. The one exception is Farkas's study, in which his statistical analysis of its influence led him to conclude that oppositional culture explains "only a modest proportion of the achievement gap…," adding that "… it may be more a consequence than a cause of poor achievement."

Based on the same foregoing research, others might summarize the status of the challenge to the Fordham-Ogbu thesis differently, but, unlike the review herein, no scholarly review of the research which includes the Flashman study was found. However, scholarly reviews that include the other national studies were found, and their interpretations differ. In their review, **Starkey and Eaton**, for example (both of the Harvard Law School's Institute for Race and Justice), conclude that "acting white" "could be one factor affecting some students some of the time and, considering the research as a whole, the problem may be more prevalent in diverse schools" (447:10). They add, "However, proceeding as if this is the only cause or the primary cause of the achievement gap would not be sensible either," for to do so "may obscure other important, more complex, less "sexy" explanations for the gap" (447:10). They see "acting white" and other factors as constituting a "complex web of often confounded factors," suggest a number of ways to respond to "acting white" as *one* of those factors, and conclude, "Ignoring and denying the "acting white" phenomenon will hurt children. At the same time, placing too much emphasis on the phenomenon, and failing to see it in the larger context of the inequality and discrimination in which it lives, will also harm our children" (447:12-13).

In her more extensive, detailed, and comprehensive review, **Kitae Sohn** (economist at the Korea Institute for International Economic Policy), on the other hand, while not completely rejecting the Fordham-Ogbu thesis, since, she says, it offers a valuable conceptual framework for understanding the black-white school achievement gap. She concludes that the empirical evidence, from either a cultural or an economic perspective, provides little support for it (446b). She discusses why she regards Ogbu's assumptions as invalid and cites the Fryer-Torelli study as being impressive, but her assessment is that their findings are inconsistent and their explanation of their findings "conceptually unclear and historically incongruous."

Whether the Flashman study would change the review of Starkey-Eaton, Sohn, and others is unknown, but Flashman's study sets a new paradigm for "acting white" research. Reviews which do not take it into account would be remiss.

Ogbu's Response to the Challenge

Ogbu answered his critics in an article for the <u>The Urban Review</u> in 2004. The article is a chapter in the last book that he wrote (above referenced) before his death in 2003. The book was finished posthumously for him by University of North Carolina sociologist, Roslyn Arlin Mickelson, from his drafts (172:foreword; 201:chapter 2).

What he says. Ogbu's main point in the article is that his critics had reduced his cultural-ecological framework to a "single-factor hypothesis of *oppositional culture*" [emphasis in original] and then gone on to construct and study "a different problem than the one we laid out in the joint article" (196:29). They ignored, he felt, his framework from its diverse perspectives. So, in his last book, in addition to a reproduction of his article, he adds another chapter in order more fully to explain his framework and, at the same time, to elaborate on his response to his critics (196:3-28). Following is some of that response.

- He asserts that his critics lack knowledge of the historical and community genesis of the "acting white" phenomenon and of the fact that it still exists in the black community. They treat it, he argues, as something limited to the interaction among students in the school setting when, in fact, the students are reflecting what they learn from the community and what has been historically transmitted. In his last book, he uses part of a chapter to report one of his ethnographic studies which supports the student-community linkage (200:112-29).

- To the claim that their thesis did not account for variation in response to "acting white," he gives accounts of how blacks in different periods in our history have coped with it, and how the students of today variously cope with it in school, which, he says, is the same way which adults cope with it in the community.
- He does not argue with those who say that our students want to get good grades, something that other studies by him also reveal. But he indicates that his studies also show that what prevents them from doing so is their rejection of the attitudes and behaviors ("acting white") required to get good grades (196:57). In addition to making this point in his article, he devotes part of a chapter to the issue in his last book (200:112-29).
- He acknowledges the existence of peer pressure *unrelated* to "acting white" which contributes to the low school performance of black students. In his last book, he allocates an entire chapter to a range of such pressures (199:89-111).

In the final sentence of his response, Ogbu responds to what seems to have most bothered his critics. He writes: "Lastly, other and even more important contributors to their low school performance are societal, school, and other community forces that discourage academic engagement ..." (196:59). To be fair to him, as noted above, Fordham and he had made the same point in their 1986 article, suggesting that if opportunity structures were not opened up significant changes were unlikely to occur. So this was not a new position. What is different in this article, though still not a new position, is his in-depth treatment of the pervasiveness of "acting white" in the life of black people. The one new element was his declaration that peer pressure unrelated to "acting white" also contributes to the low school performance of black students. His declaration was added perhaps because he relied upon, not just the study at Capital High done by Fordham, but also on ethnographic studies done by his students and him in Stockton, Oakland, and San Francisco, California, and Shaker Height, Ohio. One could have inferred from his 1986 article with Fordham that he saw the detrimental peer pressure was solely a function of the "acting white" sanction -- which he denies.

The small-sample allegation. One major criticism left unaddressed in Ogbu's response is the charge of his (and Fordham's) use of a small, unrepresentative sample. But, in his last book, he sets aside one full chapter to defend his ethnographic methodology, gives a detailed description of it, and compares it to other methodologies, including the statistical approach used by many of his critics (198:64-88). He specifically cites the two studies which have provided the primary challenge to his findings, the Ainsworth-Darnell and Downey study and the Cook and Ludwig study, calling their reliance on self-reports a "serious problem." He summarized his ethnographic methodology thus:

> ...ethnography is rigorous, scientific and a more appropriate methodology for studying school engagement and community forces than other approaches. Some attitudes and behaviors simply cannot be captured through surveys or interviews. The ethnographic methodology as described here allows the researcher to understand the "lived" experiences of the people they are studying and the nuances of everyday living, to compare verbalized attitudes and actual behaviors, and to see community dynamics in action (198:85).

The Traditions React: Representative Voices

Having examined the "acting white" research and presumably disinterested scholarly reviews of it, we now turn to two representative views of "acting white," one from the traditions which interpretations of it tend to fall. For one, black Harvard sociologist, John Diamond, the other from black Columbia University Professor, John McWhorterr. both previously referenced. Diamond represents the System-Responsibility Tradition, McWhorter, the Self-Responsibility Tradition.

John Diamond: System-Responsibility Tradition. Diamond review is comprehensive, including, except for Flashman's study, all of the national studies. His review leads him to pose the question of whether the cultural explanation is "barking up the wrong tree." He answers, yes, seeing "no consistent support for oppositional orientations being pervasive among, or unique to, African American peer groups." "At best," he avers, "oppositional orientations impact some small segment of the African American student population" (325:14). His conclusion: "There are tangible structural, institutional, and symbolic consequences to being African American that have educational implications for students. This unequal educational terrain has more powerful implications for the Black/White achievement gap than the much more illusive and less prevalent oppositional culture" (325:17). What really makes the difference, Diamond says, are the following:

- less qualified teachers
- concentration in lower educational tracks (meaning less qualified teachers, less challenging course work, and less learning)
- lower teacher expectations (resulting in fewer opportunities for classroom learning and teacher abdication of responsibility for student learning)
- school segregation (results in lower outcomes and depresses teacher expectations and sense of responsibility)
- poor households
- fewer assets possessed by black families (unlike whites, no money for tutors, educational materials, private schools, and more expensive colleges)
- segregated neighborhoods (as a result, they pay more for housing, have less property appreciation, live further from employment opportunities, and attend more segregated schools)
- more difficult neighborhoods (even the middle class is more likely to live in or near high poverty areas with higher crime rates, poorer city services, and less effective schools)
- symbolic meaning attached to race suggesting blacks less intelligent than whites (negatively affects teacher expectations and may lead to "stereotype threat" whereby students underperform due to fear of confirming the stereotype)

John McWhorter: Self-Responsibility Tradition. McWhorter similarly reviewed the research, and, in his mind, the cultural explanation is the right tree to bark up. In Winning the Race, he argues that "acting white" is part of a new black teenage culture that had its advent in the late 1960s, even -- based on testimonials received since the publication of his Losing the Race -- pinpointing its emergence to around 1966 (161:61-82). In his words, "… it is, quite simply, a familiar and deeply entrenched part of black American teen culture" (161:270). It is not just the culture of the poor, but of the middle class as well. Citing the MSAN (Minority Student Achievement Network), he observes that "In one place after another, educators are baffled as even middle-class black students perform much more poorly than we would expect year after year. And reports are rife with such teens recounting having been teased for "acting white" when they embraced school and often even checking out of scholarly achievement to have friends" (161:267).

McWhorter sees a *therapeutic alienation meme* at work. Therapeutic alienation is alienation that occurs, not in response to a real-life situation, but rather unconnected to a real-life situation or disproportionate to it, but, nevertheless, is maintained because it gives one a sense of psychological security and satisfaction as it reinforces identification from and opposition to the enemy (161:1-14). When the alienation gets passed along from mind to mind, much in the same fashion as genes are passed along, we have the existence of what McWhorter points out is a *meme* (161:172-74).

In "acting white," we thus have, in McWhorter's interpretation, something which is passed along without thought, question, or examination from generation to generation -- a *meme*. You will recall that a meme is not taught, but automatically picked up in the course of everyday living. In the case of "acting white," therapeutic alienation embodies, on the part of black teens, the sense that to perform well in school is to engage in white behavior in contrast typically to "getting by," which engenders a feeling of belonging to the race and differentiating oneself from the enemy or "opposition."

Having criticized Ainsworth-Darnell and Downey and others (on essentially the same bases as others have criticized them), McWhorter -- in support of his own stance -- points to the anecdotal evidence he presents in <u>Losing the Race</u> and cites a number of sources that provide similar evidence. His emphatic conclusion is that "People who treat studies like this as showing that there is an "acting white myth" reveal themselves as placing alienation over reality" (161:282).

Joe L. Rempson

Making Sense of It All

Undermining "acting white"

Most striking in reading the literature, especially when it comes to us blacks and those who share our mindset, is the common inclination to dismiss or undermine "acting white." In the fashion of Dyson, who labeled it "the academic equivalent of an urban legend," black psychologist Margaret Spencer (then a Professor at the University of Pennsylvania) and Vinay Harpalani (then law student at the New York University School of Law with a doctorate in Education), for example, went so far as to declare that "acting white" is not a cultural reality. Rather, they describe it to be an "in the moment" coping mechanism.

> Overall, the "acting White" phenomenon, as it occurs, is not responsible for Black academic underachievement, nor is it reflective of a broad frame of reference, as Fordham and Ogbu (1986) suggest. It is simply of many possible reactive or "in the moment" (see Stevenson 1998) coping responses; these reactions are most often utilized by Black youth in response to inferred but unacknowledged encounters of academic devaluation, perceived social inequities and rejection. These experiences, given normal developmental processes, occur in varying social contexts as youth broaden their social experiences and represent what Chestang (1972) describes as individual character formation efforts occurring in hostile environments (243:35).

The research proves that Spencer-Harpalani are wrong, as is Dyson. It is more than an "in the moment" coping mechanism and is not just "the academic equivalent of an urban legend." It is, in fact, rooted in black history. Ogbu traces "acting white" from slavery to the present. Particularly informative is a passage from E. Franklin Frazier's previously cited famous and controversial study of the black bourgeoisie in the 1950s, <u>Black Bourgeoisie: The Rise of a New Middle Class</u> ((201:29-63). It reads:

> When a Negro is competent and insists upon first-rate work it appears to this class that he is trying to be a white man, or that he is insisting that Negroes live up to white standards. This is especially

true where the approval of whites is taken as a mark of competence and first-rate performance. In such cases the black bourgeoisie reveal their ambivalent attitudes toward the white world. They slavishly accept the estimate which almost any white man places upon a Negro or his work, but at the same time they fear and reject white standards. For example, when a group of Negro doctors were being shown the modern equipment and techniques of a white clinic, one of them remarked to a Negro professor in a medical school, 'This is the white man's medicine. I never bother with it and still I make $30,000 a year.' Negroes who adopt the standards of the white world create among the black bourgeoisie a feeling of insecurity and often become the object of both envy and hatred of this class (94:217-18).

How Fordham-Ogbu broke rank

In singling out "acting white" and urging that it be made "a target of educational policies and remediation effort," Fordham-Ogbu made it a prominent factor in the discussion of what to do about black students' poor school performance. Their particular concern – based, it should be emphasized, on intensive study of 33 students over a one-year period -- was the plight of high-achieving black adolescents who, their study revealed, because of their effort and success, were often sanctioned by their lower-achieving black peers. As a result they had to resort to *camouflage* [or use an *alternative identity*] in order to persist, in the process (Fordham-Ogbu reason) using time and effort which would have enabled them to do even better. Not only did the high-achievers suffer, they say, so did the underachieving students who, because of conscious or unconscious fear of sanctions *avoided* putting forth the effort.

To those in the know, so to speak, there is nothing shocking about their finding. But it is not those in the know who command the black public agenda, but rather those (black and white) who weave a narrative which places our plight at the feet of the system and leave no burden for us to bear. Long among them, with his "acting white" thesis, Ogbu, as did Fordham, broke ranks. Ogbu (the more established of the two) was no conservative academic or right-leaning reformer, but a reputable and severe critic of the system, out to dismantle it. But when he teamed up with Fordham to analyze her Capital Hill data, he found them so compelling that he modified his previous scholarly work which laid the blame *entirely* on the system. It was not some discourse or chance event which changed his mind, but the *evidence*. The evidence trumped his ideology, if only partially; he accepted and confronted what their data yielded. He, as Fordham, still laid the plight of our students mainly at the feet of the system. However, as he said, his (and Fordham's) critics made it appear that Fordham and he were offering a "single-factor hypothesis of *oppositional culture*" to account for black students' poor school performance, ignoring the historical and community context – and the interlocking factors which compose his Cultural Ecological Model (CEM).

What seemed to have escaped Ogbu's awareness, however, is that, like the high-achieving students in their study, Fordham and he were violating the boundary of fictive kinship. As the students were "acting white," Fordham and he were "thinking white." Like the students, Fordham and he, therefore, were subject to sanctions. It is indeed Ogbu who draws attention to the fact that "acting white" has its roots in black community life – that community including the black academic community, and in placing blame on students and community -- *any blame at all* – they were violating its boundary, a boundary which until then Ogbu had famously honored. So Mickelson points out that he was heckled by fellow minority group members at conventions, and the likes of Ainsworth-Darnell and Downey were determined, not only to discredit their "acting white" thesis, but the totality of Ogbu's OCF. In the process, they triggered another clash of the two traditions that have shaped African American history: the Self-Responsibility Tradition of Booker Taliaferro Washington and the System-Responsibility Tradition of William Edward Burghardt DuBois. The foregoing research review and discussion are intended to convey a picture of that clash.

Where they went wrong

Their break was justified, but not their conclusion. Both the subsequent qualitative and quantitative studies reviewed predominantly confirm that "acting white" exists, and the most credible of them all, the Flashman study -- since unlike all the other studies it is a national study which controls for both same-race effect and opportunity for friendship – shows that "acting white" is statistically likely to be found where black students make up over 50 percent of the student body. So it appears widespread. But the Flashman study does not show that its *effect* is widespread – that it significantly affects black students' school performance. Although she cites a "strong stigma against friendship groups that are, on average, high-achieving," that does not mean that the "strong stigma" significantly affects the students' grades. In fact, in the one study which has sought to quantify its grade impact, Farkas, as noted, concludes that the existence of "acting white" has only a modest effect on grades. Fordham-Ogbu's conclusion, therefore, that "acting white" is *"one major reason* Black students do poorly in school" is not justified either by their study or by the only other study reviewed which quantifies its effect. Without such quantification, Fordhan-Ogbu had no way of reliably assessing the performance of the sanctioned students; they could, as they did, only theorize about it, and so far, there is no statistical evidence to support their theory.

The lack of statistical support for Fordhan-Obgu's thesis, however, does not undermine their impactful contribution. Given their data, "acting white" would appear to affect students' academic striving and success. Their study, together with other subsequent studies, reveals that students' response to "acting white" exacts a price in regard to their time, drive, and lifestyle choices – factors which *can* affect their grades. Relevant support for that possibility is provided, for example, by the stereotype studies of Steele and Aronson, discussed in Chapter 12. Steele, drawing upon their studies and related studies involving a range of life situations, concludes that threats derived from being perceived a certain way adversely affect and impair human functioning and interactions. In the academic domain, he and others found that negative perceptions adversely affect the performance of high-achieving college students, the academic subgroup of particular concern to Fordham-Ogbu. Low-achieving students are not affected. So how we are perceived by others, to say nothing about how we are treated by them, influences our performance, academic and otherwise (186:285-327).

That the effect of "acting white" on grades might not be as significant as Fordham-Ogbu's thesis suggests finds support, not just in Farkas's study, but, as well, in the responses of students. Fordham-Ogbu, and others, report students' successful use of *camouflage* or *alternative identity* to cope with "acting white." Some studies conclude that its impact is social rather than academic. They point to students being accused of "acting white," not on the basis of their academic achievement, but on the basis of their social behavior and lifestyle. Often, they point out, black students' feeling seems to be that it is OK to be a high achiever, but is is not OK to be a high achiever who in behavior or lifestyle acts white -- through speech, manners, musical tastes, or friendship choices, for example.

The admission from their recommendations

But the most important factor pertaining to the effect of "acting white" is suggested by Farkas's observation that "… it ["acting white"] may be more a consequence [or symptom] than a cause of poor achievement." If that is the case – and the interpretation herein is that it is – then logically no significant grade impact would be expected. The impact on grades would come, not from the symptom, "acting white," but from what the studies suggest is the cause of poor grade performance, the oppositional culture of which "acting white" is both a part and a symptom. Their quest to refute the Fordham-Ogbu thesis notwithstanding, even Ainsworth-Darnell and Downey explicitly conclude: "When we focus on students' skills, habits, and styles, our results are consistent with the oppositional culture model…." (298: 541). Their results showed that black students put forth significantly less effort, were more frequently disruptive, and did less homework – and, therefore, performed poorly. Implicitly, and ironically, the most convincing support for this interpretation comes from Fordham-Ogbu themselves. Although their study addresses "acting white," as *one major reason* for black student poor school performance, Fordham-Ogbu's above cited recommendations for its remedy focus, not on "acting white," but on oppositional culture. That is, although they document and declare "acting white" to be a cause, their remedial recommendations treat "acting white," not as a cause, but as a symptom. Those recommendations do not attack "acting white"; they attack its incarnation, oppositional culture.

Where they went right

Though not having been shown to have the impact of a cause, as indicated, the Fordham-Ogbu study, as other studies, still suggests that, as a symptom, "acting white" can have an independent effect. It may reduce the number and achievement of the prospective Talented Tenth on whom, as DuBois declared, the progress of the race rests. Our history is instructive. E. Franklin Frazier points out that "...middle-class Negroes who have made real contributions in science and art have had to escape from the influence of the "social" life of the black bourgeoisie (see Chapter 7). He was referring to the 1950s, but John McWhorter makes essentially the same point with regard to our time, citing the cult of Anti-intellectualism. Our students' attitude towards their higher achieving peers, then, merely reflects the attitude transmitted to them by the community from which they come – just as Ogbu emphasizes. Studies cited in this chapter, and in Chapter 5, show that this attitude typically punishes, rather than fosters, students' academic striving and success. In singling out "acting white," Fordham-Ogbu have brought this phenomenon to our attention. That they might have overstated its effect does not undermine their contribution. In general, they have brought to our attention what can be called the **"acting white" effect**, which can be defined as a black mindset (fictive kinship) which sanctions black divergency and, therefore, confines black thought and behavior, with the result that, among other things, it curtails the cultivation and creativity of our Talented Tenth

Summary and conclusion

In sum, the evidence does not support Fordham-Ogbu's thesis that "acting white" is *one major reason* for black student poor school performance. Rather, their data, together with the data of others, suggest that it is a symptom of an underlying oppositional culture which is *the main reason* for black student poor school performance, "acting white," however, possibly having the effect of reducing the number and attainment of prospective Talented Tenth black students. Support for oppositional culture as *the main reason* derives, not just from the studies reviewed, but also from the discussion of the culture of our students and community (Chapters 5 and 7, respectively). It is a culture which devalues academic striving and success, traits which dominantly influence school achievement since they better predict grades than IQ scores (350c). The previously cited research of Marzano reveals that student motivation can account for as much as 37 percent of the variance in school achievement. Among Wang, Haertel, and Walberg's

28 variables found to influence learning, student motivation ranked seventh (7th) on the list at 54.8 percent influence. Behavior came in sixth (6th) on their list at 55.2 percent influence. Combine such influences on learning with what experience and research show about the attitude and behavior of many of our black low-performing students and we can declare those factors to be *the main reason* of their poor school performance, which Ogbu himself expressly argued but placed the blame and remedy mainly of the system.

In Our Court: The Family Right of Our Children

Those who disparage the Fordham-Ogbu thesis and dismiss "acting white" disregard the evidence, which validates its existence. Its very existence can be said to violate a child's family rights, as herein designated. Our children do have child family rights, among them, the right to strive for academic success. Their families, in conjunction with our educational agencies, have the responsibility to secure for them that right. Any curtailment of it must be condemned and eradicated. "Acting white" is such a curtailment – self-imposed, as it were, but, nevertheless, a curtailment. Never mind how many students it affects. If it affects just one, and that one is our son or daughter, would we regard it as negligible and dismiss it? Individual rights is the distinguishing hallmark of our country. It took only one person, for example, to bring about the Supreme Court decision to outlaw prayer in the public schools. That one person (the Supreme Court ruled), like every other person, had the right not to have religion imposed imposed upon her. It is no different in this instance, and although no "acting white" case could be expected to reach the Supreme Court, or any other court, it is in the court of black culture, and we can decide whether to undertake a movement to cease and desist.

Listening to the "acting white" stories

The experiences of Alicia, a black female high school senior, and Marc, a black seventh grader, remind us what our ruling should be. Alicia was a high achiever, and Marc engaged in "white" behaviors. Both were interviewed in the Tyson and Darity study (2005), both black, Karolyn Tyson a sociologist at the University of North Carolina, and William Darity Jr., an economist, with positions at both Duke University and the University of North Carolina. Reminders, too, come in the stories, for example, of two black authors, one, black Harlem Children's Zone director Geoffrey Canada, and the other, black Hispanic New York University urban sociologist Pedro Noguera, and from the ethnographic study of black Yale University sociologist, Elijah Anderson.

This is part of what Alicia told the interviewer:

> If you make all As, you're white. If you're not coming in here with Cs and Ds and Fs, then something's wrong with you. You don't have a life--that's what it was. They thought I didn't do anything else but study.... You are called a betrayer of your race, and then you start questioning your blackness as I did. And I was like, 'Well, what *is* wrong with me? (457:595).

This is part of what Marc told the interviewer:

> *Interviewer*: What about different racial groups in this school? Are there, is it integrated, do black and white students hang out together all the time, or are they more separate? How does that work?
>
> *Marc*: Most of the time, but a lot of the black people think that they're better than the white people, or vice versa. Or the black people will always pick on the white people about what they do [inaudible], and if you're black and you act like you're white, then they would hold it against you. The black people would not like you as much .... Well if you're black and you act like you're -- you do stuff that the white people do, then, then, like skateboarding and stuff like that, then they say that you're white and that you, I don't really know how to really say it, they just say that you're really white and that you don't care about everybody else that's black. And stuff like that. Like if you surf or if you talk differently, like "dude" or something like that. 'Cause sometimes I say that (457:596).

Canada describes what happened to high achievers who grew up in urban poverty neighborhoods like the South Bronx where he grew up. In telling the story about a high-achieving young man, Scott, who had been lured into a coat-taking scheme, Canada reflects:

Scott was in the predicament that many young men find themselves in if they are academic achievers and live in inner-city neighborhoods. Other boys are always testing you to see if you think you are better than they are. If they believe that you think so, then watch out: you become a target and might be jumped, robbed, threatened, humiliated, or ostracized. So if you're a boy like Scott, you walk a thin line. You try to be friendly and hang out with boys that provide you with social cover; the more friends you have who are known as tough kids on the block, the better your chances of not being targeted for abuse (26:90).

Noguera puts the spotlight on his son and himself. In his book, <u>The Trouble with Black Boys</u>, he tells the story of a crisis in the life of his son, Joaquin. When in the 10th grade, Joaquin turned from being an excellent student and athlete into a failing student exhibiting anger and rebellion at home. He did not recover until he was in the 12th grade. Noguera figured out that Joaquin was struggling "to figure out what it meant to be a young Black man": to be respected by his teachers and value academics as he always had -- or instead -- to be respected by his peers and value, as they, hanging out and being cool and tough. Then Noguera puts the spotlight on himself, revealing that, as a high school student in advanced classes, he had to camouflage his achievement by playing basketball, hanging out, and fighting when necessary – feeling, in fact, forced to act one way in class, another way among friends, and still another way at home (191:4-5).

In his ethnographic study, <u>Code of the Street</u>, Anderson describes a similar camouflage. He tells of the code switching in which decent kids, contrasted with the street kids, must engage in order to survive. They must show, as Geoffrey Canada says he had to show, that they share their street culture. In that culture, Anderson reports, "For many alienated young black people, attending school and doing well becomes negatively associated with acting white" (5:93). To illustrate his point about code switching, Anderson cites the story of a 15-year-old boy he observed. He says that the boy "typically changed his "square" clothes for a black leather jacket (thereby adopting a street look) after he got around the corner from his home and out of his mother's view." "In order to preserve his own self-respect and the respect of his peers,"

Anderson continues, "he would also hide his books under his jacket while walking to school, bidding to appear street" (5:95).

What the "acting white" stories are telling us

To pursue Alicia's thought pattern, we might ask ourselves whether there is something wrong with *us* if we dismiss her query, or if we dismiss the ruminations of Marc and other black students, the life experiences of Canada and Noguera, or the ethnographic findings of Anderson. Does it bother us that they have to lead a "double life? Does it bother us if, among our own, they are not accepted if they do not fit the mold -- that is, come in, as Alicia said, with Cs and Ds and Fs?

These stories are telling us something, and whether we share Fordham-Ogbu's formulation of what that something is, it is self-evident that they are telling us something about ourselves -- about how, if you are a high-achieving black student, you might pay a price from deviating from the norms of your lower-achieving peers. Fordham-Ogbu saw those norms as part of an *oppositional culture* which takes the form of a devaluation of academic striving and success -- of seeing education as something that whites do, and thus, when we blacks strive for academic success the same way whites do, we are "acting white." The same dynamic applies to our students' social behavior and lifestyle, but in these domains the norms are not so restrictive, nor, obviously, so consequential.

The lesson of "acting white" is that many of our black students show a disidentification with school success. If we are not good at something, we tend to come to disidentify with it. We withdraw our psychic energy from it and make it unimportant to us. We do so because, in what is called stereotype threat, we fear failure. If our peers join in to support us, the disidentification can become a group norm. Thus, members of our stereotype threatened group, through disidentification, thereby establish a norm which protects the group from a common threat. The norm is then transmitted culturally. This is the situation for so many of our students. They exhibit a culturally transmitted disidentification with school and learning. Arguably, their disidentification stems from the same kind of situation which, as above cited, Frazier attributed to the black bourgeoisie of his day: fear and rejection of white standards. However explained, at question is the attitude and behavior of our students. Their attitude and behavior leads to the kind of stories cited above. "Acting white" is the headline for those stories; the students' underlying oppositional culture is the content.

Alicia and Marc, and those for whom they speak, to say nothing about those who are unaware that they need to be spoken for, are not voices out of the wilderness. Nor are they speaking with the tongue of whites, or of "black traitors" like Ogbu, Cosby, and McWhorter; they *are us*, our daughters and sons revealing *to us* what is in their heart. Do we turn a deaf ear to their complaints -- or -- as herein proposed, do we go to their rescue by examining why they are made targets of sanctions by their black peers and what we can do about it? They are voicing reactions to *learned* dispositions -- dispositions learned from family and community, *from us*, that is, through a process of cultural adaptation and transmission which, for example, Ogbu chronicles and which Frazier captures. Their voices are directed, not to the system, but to us, the ones who cause their anguish. We can turn our backs, but in doing so we nullify their child family right to strive for academic success. As a result, we contribute to the possible curtailment of, or even prevention of, their success and to the success of an unknown number of others who feel the pressure and are the victims of the underlying syndrome. It is a syndrome marked by disidentification with, if not disdain for, academic effort and success. Its "acting white" sanctions especially victimize our prospective Talented Tenth. It is, therefore, this syndrome which is the main story because it is the main cause of our students' academic lag. But if we turn our backs, we will not discover their story, nor honor their child family right; the "acting white" headline would have deceived us.

7

Why The Crisis: The Adaptation Of Our Community, A Window Into The Adaptation Of Our Students

Proverbs, 16:22 - "Understanding is a wellspring of life unto him that hath it: but the instruction of fools is folly."
Galatians, 6:5 - "For every man shall bear his own burden."

John Ogbu stands out in being emphatic in his insistence on the need to understand our community culture if we hope to understand our student culture, since the latter reflects the former. So that will be our task in this chapter. We will look at our two-culture legacy, the cultural legacies of slavery, our middle-class culture, our externally adapted culture, the culture of poverty, and finally – to lend more perspective – the traits of successful immigrant cultures in American life. The attempt will be, not so much to come up with a consensus portrait, but instead, to come up with relevant cultural snapshots which can provide instructive insights into black student-community culture.

Two Cultures from Slavery

The late sociologist, Jessie Bernard of Washington University, tells us that slavery yielded two cultures. Drawing upon the work of others, particularly Drake and Clayton (1962) and Lewis (1955), she labels them the *acculturated* and the *externally adapted* (8:27-66). Both are acculturated, says Bernard, "but to different aspects of the larger culture" (8: 33). The acculturated "have internalized to a greater degree the moral norms of Western society as these exist in the United States," whereas the externally adapted -- rather than having internalized these norms -- have "adapted themselves to their demands superficially" (8:33). Neither culture, she explains, is based on socioeconomic status, but on ethos. For the acculturated, that ethos is the Puritan work ethic and the Puritan family and sex ethic; for the externally adapted it is "essentially hedonistic and pleasure-loving" (8:33).

Role of education

The role of education in these two cultures, Bernard tells us, like the cultures themselves, is divided. While both cultures endorse its importance, it is primarily the acculturated who are willing to make the sacrifice and do the hard work it entails (8:135-37; 94:146-49). Not that the externally adapted are not willing to work hard, Bernard says, but hard work to them does not mean the pursuit of a stable, steady, and secure job [or cracking the books and doing homework] but rather "the externally adapted like adventure and risk --"hustling" or "cashing in" or "boosting." To pursue such likes, we should remind ourselves, one does not have to go to school, but to the streets.

Such likes say nothing about the ability of the externally adapted, Bernard argues. The issue is not ability or class, but ethos. Bernard observes that their penchant for adventure and risk notwithstanding, they "sometimes show the enterprise, the initiative, the entrepreneurial skills, and the innovative talents traditionally associated with the original bourgeoisie" (8:56-57). She admits, however, that "All too often their activities are illegal," though "in them they may exhibit the same kind of talents as those involved in legitimate enterprises" (8:56).

Those talents, Bernard explains, often lead to creative outcomes. Illustrations are provided "by their contributions to music and dance, and by the eagerness of the avant garde to imitate their speech, their clothing, and their art forms" (8: 65-66). "Perhaps," she suggests, "young, externally adapted Negroes might be offered--rather than economic security and middle-class values [wherein education would be valued]--the prospect of excitement and adventure in the creative arts, *their* [italics in original] creative arts" (8: 66). Today, a little over forty years after her suggestion, perhaps that is precisely what the hip-hop culture exemplifies, their love of excitement and adventure more or less productively channeled. The street culture, however, remains evident, even magnified through its subgenre, gangsta rap.

Splintering and persistence

In fact, we probably would be mistaken to think that, in view of the Civil Rights Movement and our subsequent advances, Bernard's two culture analysis is outmoded. One might, for example get that impression from Robinson's <u>Disintegration: The Splintering of Black America</u>. Robinson, previously cited, sees his alluded to splintering as yielding, in essence, four current cultures: the majority Mainstream, a large minority Abandoned, a small Transcendent elite, and two Emergent groups of mixed-race and recent black immigrants (227). As evident from the African American Male School Adaptability Crisis (AMSAC) and its inseparable social problems, however, the Abandoned one-fourth is testimony to the persistence of the externally adapted. The other three groups logically fall into the acculturated category. We have even seen it, for example, in the "acting white" controversy and in the attitude-achievement discrepancy. Both highlight the discrepancy between what those of us among the Abandoned say and what we do -- between our internalization of mainstream American values and our vocal espousal of them. Both further suggest that, although herein the Abandoned one-fourth are the target of concern, other African Americans often share some of their externally adapted behavior. A specific case in point is provided by black evaluation specialist Joseph Hawkins' meeting with twenty black male students (fifteen of whom were seniors) in the wealthy school district of Montgomery County. Hawkins tells what took place:

> When I asked how many planned to attend college, every hand in the room went up. When I asked the seniors how many had actually applied to a college, just six hands went up. It was late March. Typically, by late March or early April many seniors have already been accepted to college. Of the six seniors in the room who had

applied, only one had been accepted to college and was willing to give its name (118:117).

Identity

The very process of acculturation -- of adapting to the culture of another people, in this case, our former masters -- raises the question of identity. Our former tribal life had been virtually uprooted and destroyed, and now we were forced to seek a new identity, one appropriate to our new circumstances. Bernard says that our response was the adoption of two cultures. But regardless of which culture we adopted, we could not share the identity of whites; we had to fashion a culture from the fabric of our own subordinate and marginal existence, cutoff from the mainstream, and branded inferior. Nor could we share a naional identity. White men and women were Americans while we were savages from the jungles of Africa. Time and suffering, however, have done much to erase Africa's cultural imprint -- whatever that imprint might have been. So our identity quandary was twofold: who were we as a people, and as persons, and with what nation could we identify or feel at home.

For us males, this identity quandary was compounded. Bernard tells us that the externally adapted culture appeared especially pronounced in African-American males as contrasted with African-American females. "Even after emancipation," she contends, "most Negro men have, in effect, lived in a social and mental concentration camp" (8:75). To a much greater extent than African-American females, she argues that African-American males have been the victim, not just of prejudice and discrimination, but also of the isolating and dehumanizing influence of an "inimical environment" (8:73-76), an environment that might be characterized by love and good intentions, but which nonetheless is dehumanizing. She cites the crippling, dependency-inducing benevolence of Southern whites, the lower standards of expectations resulting from being romanticized by Northern whites, and the isolation from and lack of interaction with the larger society and its acculturating influences.

Acculturated or externally adapted, for us males there was -- in addition -- the interwoven and inherent animating drive for manhood identity. Remember, as a near universal proposition, anthropologists tell us that manhood -- unlike womanhood -- must be earned; it is not a birthright, but a rite of passage that somehow must be acclaimed or recognized by community and society (101). That was what we had to do, then as now: get our manhood acclaimed or recognized. There we were in an oppressive environment, stripped of human and national identity, yet faced with the natural and irresistible urge to satisfy this powerful manhood need. It is not hard to imagine the difficulty, nor perhaps, the various means used to surmount it. The personality imprint of slavery did not help.

Sambo personality?

For many of us that personality was a Sambo personality. The very mention of the term will understandably cause many of us to recoil, yet -- recoil or not -- we know that there is something called Sambo personality. Historians agree that it existed and, a la "acting white," *may* in some forms still exist. Sambo derives from the name given to the typical plantation slave (Sambo meaning black), with Sambo personality describing the kind of personality of such a slave. What kind of personality was it? Here is a list of some of the ascribed traits (8:72; 76:81-139, 82, 111; 393; 467).

- docile
- indolent
- faithful
- humble
- humorous
- silly
- playful
- cheerful
- dishonest
- steals
- superstitious
- improvident
- musical
- clownish
- childlike
- irresponsible
- fights

From slavery, these ascribed traits carried over into our subsequent life in freedom. We African Americans have been labeled as follows (144a:3):

- dirty
- shiftless
- lazy
- happy-go-lucky
- smelly
- ignorant
- treacherous
- superstitious
- cowardly

The dispute arises over the prevalence of this personality and whether it was innate or the result of slavery. We draw mainly upon Wikipedia to summarize the dispute (467). Late Yale historian, Ulrich Phillips, in the first study of the subject (1918), is said to have seen it as the dominant slave personality that could be attributed to innate slave characteristics. In 1959, late Smith College historian, Stanley Elkins, came along and, while accepting this dominant personality profile, rejected Phillip's innate interpretation of it. He attributed the Sambo personality, instead, to the slave system as it operated in this country. He saw that system as equivalent to the Nazi concentration camp, producing a similar childlike personality. He contrasted it with the slave system of Brazil where the slaves were treated more humanely and did not, consequently, develop such a personality. Then, in 1972 and 1979, late black Yale historian, John Blassingame, offered his interpretation, rejecting both the thesis of Phillips and Elkins. He saw their studies as relying too much on the accounts of slaveholders and not enough on the accounts of slaves. Rather than the Sambo personality being the dominant personality, Blassingame saw it as one of three. The other two he called Jack and Nat. Jack was the hard working and faithful slave who would rebel if mistreated while Nat was the runaway and rebellious type. As with "acting white," in these interpretations, we can sense the nature and intensity of the debate.

Unlike with "acting white," however, we will not explore any of the details in the debate. The point has been made: Sambo personality existed and *may* in some forms still exist, affecting our sense of identity and our quest for manhood. One final reference will serve to support this conclusion.

Late University of Rochester historian, Eugene Genovese, in reviewing Elkins's work in 1967, submits that the personality described by Elkins does indeed result from slavery, but all slavery, not just American slavery. In his words: "On close inspection the Sambo personality turns out to be neither more nor less than the slavish personality; wherever slavery has existed, Sambo has also" (100:297). "Elkins has not described to us the personality of the southern slave," he continues, "nor, by contrast, of the Latin American slave; he has instead demonstrated the limiting case of the slave personality. Every slave system contained a powerful tendency to generate Sambos, but every system generated countervailing forces" (100:313). "Neither slavery nor slaves," he tells us, "can be treated as pure categories, free of contradictions, tensions, and potentialities that characterize all human experience" (100: 312). In other words, we African American males emerged from slavery, not exclusively with Sambo personalities, but with a range of slave-related personalities that defy any one characterization. Blassingame would obviously agree, but neither he nor Genovese, while not seeing a dominant Sambo personality, sees a non-existent one either.

Family

Whatever the state of our personality, we know that it was hardly fully developed, the product of established mores and folkways; it represented, instead, as Bernard suggests and as Ogbu elaborates in his signature contributions, our adaptation to the dominant culture and to our oppressive circumstances. We know as well that the natural desire and search for identity which confronted us, somehow, had to be satisfied. Such satisfaction, if fulfilled, had to have a grounding -- fertile soil, as it were -- to provide sound root and direction. That fertile soil is provided by the family. Wholesome personality and identity development depend primarily on a wholesome family life. That is a point which, in essence, as previously quoted, Lee Rainwater makes. In his "Foreword" to <u>Black Families in White America</u>, Billingsley more directly does the same in these words: "The family is the most basic institution of any people, the center and source of its civilization.

Within the intimate context of the family, individuals develop their concept of themselves, their values, and their worth in relation to others in the world" (9). In regard to the welfare of us blacks, in particular, Dr. King had this to say: "The shattering blows on the Negro family have made it fragile, deprived and often psychopathic. This is doubly tragic because nothing is so much needed as a secure family life for a people seeking to rise out of poverty and backwardness" (147:114).

Yet, for many of us -- goes **one school of thought** -- the family was deficient from the outset. Though the foundation to our development, for most of us, it was too weak to provide a foundation (8; 9; 183; 241: 7-28). Such a family could not provide us that which is deemed essential to the unfolding of a positive core identity: a **"subjective sense of an invigorating sameness and continuity,"** as psychoanalyst Erik Erikson describes it, and the kind of **"average expectable environments"** from which such a sense is derived. The result is that our need and search for livelihood and manhood too commonly went awry, lacking in the required boundaries and guidance that comes from a stable home life.

During slavery, typically, our women and their children were the most stable and protected family members. We men were subject to separation for sale or other reasons. Nevertheless, during slavery, some form of family life existed. Frazier even concludes that "under the most favorable conditions of slavery the Negro family did among certain elements of the slave population acquire considerable stability" (93:309). However, sanctioned institutionalized family life with the male as household head did not exist, the exceptions being in the case of benevolent slaveholders, household servants, and free blacks; instead, the practice of prizing our women and their children helped to lay the roots of the maternal family while. de facto, making us males subordinate.

Of course, emancipation made change possible, and, indeed, it was accompanied by the development of a more traditional family life. But the development was not uniform. It varied in accordance with economic status, economic arrangements, rural and urban environments, and social standards. The result was that, while after emancipation we developed into the family and manhood role of provider and protect, we also, simultaneously more or less, floundered into the role of what might be called wanderers. Unfettered and without stable attachments ("rolling stones," as it were), along with grandparents and other family members, our women were often left alone to bear the primary family burdens. Frazier points out that the mass migration to the cities only compounded the problem (93:313-32).

This picture of family dysfunction is in dispute, however, for there is **another school of thought**. Black Hoover Institution economist, Thomas Sowell, cites research which reverses this portrait (241:28-29). Rather than our slave families being fragmented and female-headed, instead, they are depicted as normal two-parent families with the father as household head. It is said that slaveholders felt that such families served their best self-interest. That, incidentally, was certainly the case with sharecropping, which for many replaced slavery. The landowners wanted intact families to provide reliable "hands" to farm their land and provide them a source of produce and income. The fragmentation occurred, Sowell argues, after slavery when adjustment to urban life resulted in family disintegration, just as had been the common pattern among European immigrants. Sowell's thesis has partial support form Frazier, except that Frazier sees other disorganizing forces as well, specifically citing the Civil War itself and the reorganization of the South after Emancipation (93:332-333).

It is the late City University of New York historian, Herbert G. Gutman, however, who is most often cited in refutation of the typical slave family portrait (105a). Based on data about black families in Buffalo, New York, and New York City, together with data from the Freedmen's Bureau, he concludes essentially what Sowell -- not based on a study of his own, but upon the work of others -- has concluded. Gutman saw an adaptive slave family that had developed its own standards and rules of conduct, not one ensnared by a "tangle of pathology" (Moynihan's phrase). He attributes the rate of family breakup from 1950 to 1970, not, therefore, to some pathology inherent in black family life and traceable to slavery, but to pressures and dislocations caused by the mass migration to urban areas and to unemployment and underemployment which -- with several exceptions -- had more or less existed since the Great Depression of 1929 (105a:461-75).

Over the years, a number of other historians and sociologists have joined the controversy (for example, see 38:Clayton, Mincy, and Blankenhorn,

Black Fathers in Contemporary Society). Enola Aird, affiliate scholar and director of the Motherhood Project at the Institute for American Values (New York) points out that their argument revolves around external versus internal factors. As she puts it, referring particularly to out-of-wedlock births: "Much of the argument has been focused on placing blame on racism and on discrimination by those who attribute the problem to external factors, and on individual fathers and mothers and the black community by those who focus on internal factors" (2: 157). She goes on to add, "By now it should be clear that external and internal forces are inextricably intertwined and that all these factors must be addressed with equal force and equal urgency" (2:157). Whether, at this juncture, they need to be addressed *equally* is another matter, but it is a fact that, whatever and whenever its origin, black family disintegration among the poor has been an undisputed and stark fact of life. Especially since the 1970s, black males hav grown up paying the heaviest price.

The Acculturated: Middle-Class Culture

It is to the middle class that we turn for a second source of our cultural legacy. That is the class that sets our standards and provides our leadership. Frazier's classic, Black Bourgeoisie: The Rise of a New Middle Class, anchors our discussion of its culture.

Education

In his classic study of our middle class culture, Black Bourgeoisie: The Rise of a New Middle Class, conducted in the 1950s, the late black sociologist, E. Franklin Frazier, of Howard University gives a picture of its education component.

Making a living versus learning. He reports that with the advent of the rising black middle class in the 1920s and 30s, the aim of education for blacks [and for the larger society as well] began to change. It went from an emphasis on the Puritan virtues of piety, thrift, and respectability to emphasis on social and economic mobility – from making men to making money (94:78). The black middle class and the students who were seeking an education were not interested in learning, Frazier's reports, but in making a living so they could "maintain middle-class standards and participate in Negro "society" (94:81).

Their real interests. Frazier paints their real interests as having been in recreation and participation in Negro "society" [Negro being the description in vogue at that time] --rather than in learning or in their profession (94:195-212). Many of the professionals spent their time playing cards, drinking, and going to movies and parties. Their conversation was not about books, art, literature, or culture, but about sports (baseball and football) and the material things in their life, such as cars, furniture, and household appliances. Extolled by the Negro press, Negro "society" – lavish houses, cars, parties, clothes, jewelry, food, and so on – was their preoccupation. Fraternal orders and Greek letter societies were central in that "society," serving, in addition to social goals, economic and political goals as well (94:90-95). They were instruments for acquiring power and influence, making money, and even serving the race as, for example, in undertaking health projects or promoting Negro business. Business, professional, and community life were centered around "society" life. Frazier's interpretation is that this "society" preoccupation assuaged their feelings of inferiority both by earning them identification with and (hopefully) acceptance by whites and by earning them ingroup status.

Making contributions. Frazier observes that Negroes who had made bona fide contributions in science and art had to escape Negro "society." Its "spirit of play and lack of serious effort," he states, "has permeated every aspect of the life of the Negro community" (94:237). Given this analysis, the acculturated might be said to have bequeathed a legacy that embraces education as a status value but not necessarily its companion or outgrowth, which is interest in learning or intellectual pursuits.

Legacy. In this schismatic legacy we then have a huge, though partial, positive. Education is embraced as *essential to our material success, but not necessarily at the same time for the sake of learning or for the pursuit of knowledge.* It is seen, disproportionately by blacks compared to whites, as a means of getting ahead in life than about getting more life into the head, so to speak. Nevertheless, the value placed on education has been a critical factor in getting us to attend school and to strive to succeed, but whether, in the absence of a corresponding respect for knowledge and a desire to learn, it is sufficient to sustain that attendance, to enable us to perform satisfactorily, and to persist is another matter.

By chance, insight into the issue is provided by DuBois in his <u>The Souls of Black Folk</u>. In discussing the increase in the number of blacks attending college, he observes that the increase had occurred "despite the active discouragement and even ridicule of friends" [maybe because they were "acting white"?] (64:78). This was around the turn of the 20th century. So, even then, although basic education apparently had great support, it was different when it came to higher education. The former was an instrument to our wellbeing, the latter, perhaps, not so perceived. Apparently learning itself did not commonly hold an equivalent value.

The question raised is whether this learning-adverse legacy serves to stifle our desire and drive to do our best and to perform on a reasonably comparable level with other groups. McWhorter suggests that it does. To model the possession of diplomas and degrees, as Frazier says many of the black bourgeoisie did, is one thing. To model the possession of knowledge and exhibit a lust for learning quite another. Given a culture which values learning for its own sake, one could reasonably anticipate much higher attendance, persistence, and graduation rates, as well as more success across a wider range of disciplines -- and for a much larger segment of the population. Such is the nature of group influence (186:285-327), and such is what the performance of other groups tell us (160:86-100). That is, in effect, the point McWhorter is making. He is saying that, disproportionately, we do not value knowledge and learning for their own sake. Dyson, on the other hand, contends that we are no different from mainstream society.

In <u>Losing the Race</u>, McWhorter makes a detailed and comprehensive case for the role of anti-intellectualism in African American culture (160:82-163). He postulates: "Black students do so poorly decade after decade not because of racism, funding, class, parental education, etc., but because of a virus of Anti-intellectualism that infects the black community," later adding, "it…permeates the whole of black culture, all the way up to the upper class" and "the appearance that black students do poorly in school because the System does them in is an illusion that denies these students' basic humanity...the actual determining factor is a culture-internal legacy" (160:83, 84). He captures their motivation in a number of memorable descriptions, among them the following under the chapter sideheading, "Walking Against the Wind":

> As students today, young black people are walking against the wind. Even when trying to stride ahead with all of their efforts, the message their culture inculcates that "books are not us" is a wind blowing at them from the opposite direction. This wind keeps them from getting as far as the white, Asians, Indians, and even Caribbeans and Africans who stroll along opposed by no such wind. The aggregate effect of this wind is the direct cause of the scarcity of black students in the sciences, the rarity of black students at the top of any class, and the strikingly low test scores one sees on college applications even by earnest middle-class black students year after year.
>
> The saddest thing is that the anti-intellectual cultural inheritance hobbles even the great many black students who are trying their best. As often as not, they are less participants in teasing black nerds than observers, and regardless, by high school or college, the schoolyard and the driveway are distant memories. Yet their culture, their inalienable comfort zone, now handicaps them in subtler but equally powerful ways, as often as not in what is not done or said as in what is. Rarely will they meet a black student as besotted with a class or subject as many white students are. Rarely will they see a black student using every possible strategy to do well in a tough class (160:161).

Among others, Dyson takes exception to this anti-intellectual label, asserting that black communities are not "any more anti-intellectual than the mainstream" (70:84). Citing Richard Hofstadter's <u>Anti-Intellectualism in American Life</u> and other source materials, he argues that anti-intellectualism even precedes the origin of our nation, going back to Victorian times and extending worldwide (70:84-85). So anti-intellectualism does exist, he says. Only, unlike McWhorter, he thinks that its existence among black youth is no more than its existence among other youth groups, past or present.

Joe L. Rempson

The world of make-believe

Defined. Frazier saw the black bourgeoisie as having created for itself a world of make-believe in which its members sought to escape from a feeling of inferiority and from rejection by white America -- a rejection which left them with no meaningful role in American life, a role (one might say) which was not in substance radically different from that performed under slavery. In its created world, the black bourgeoisie made-believe that the activities of its world made a significant contribution to the welfare of the race and of the nation, thereby earning it an important role in American society. But Frazier analysis is that this was not the case. A prime example of such a world was their faith in "Negro business" ("the business enterprises owned by Negroes and catering to Negro customers"). Contrary to the social myth, it did not make a significant contribution to either; rather, he argues, its impact on the race and on the nation was negligible (94:43-59).

Origin. Frazier contends that the fact that whites did not take us seriously, but rather viewed our activities as inconsequential in American life, tended to encourage among Negroes irresponsibility and a spirit of "play" or make-believe (94:195-212). So "Negroes," he declares, "have "played" at conducting their schools, at running their businesses, and at practicing their professions." "The spirit of play or make-believe," he goes on, "has tended to distort or vitiate the ends of their most serious activities" (94: 204-05).

It was through this make-believe world, Frazier tells us, that the black bourgeoisie sought something which the real world denied its members: status. Status, for them, meant prestige among their fellow blacks and recognition by whites, and they strove to gain it through an emphasis on their wealth, possessions, and especially on their "society" life.

Separation from masses. It also meant separating themselves from the masses -- the externally adapted, as it were -- and opting, instead, for identity with white America. Whereas the black educated classes that preceded them had a sense of responsibility toward the masses, their concern was their status. Many teachers, for example, rather than being devoted to their students as teachers in the past had been, instead, looked down on their students and up to the income that would anchor them in "society." Given the opportunity, the masses were more likely now to be exploited than assisted by teachers and others in the educated class. In sum, as Frazier saw it, the black bourgeoisie failed in its responsibility to the Negro community (94:235). The poor, on their part, were no more endeared to it.

Outcome. The make-believe world of the black bourgeoisie, Frazier explains, did not, as intended, provide its members an escape from their misery and insecurity, or from the feeling of inferiority which many felt -- which, incidentally, paints a picture of them which is reflected in the contemporaneous psychodynamic study of Kardiner and Ovesey, reported in their book, <u>The Mark of Oppression</u>, discussed in Chapter 11. Fear of competition with whites, particularly for jobs, added to their misery. As a result, many of them turned for escape to sex, alcohol, and such games of chance as playing the "numbers" and, especially, poker. Keep in mind that he is talking about the professional class, not the masses. Generally, as Frazier sums it up, the lives of its members were without "content and significance" (94: 238).

Portrait. Frazier's analysis suggests a black bourgeoisie of his era (the 1950s) as disproportionately:

- status-seeking
- social/recreation-centered
- lacking in learning orientation
- frustrated and miserable
- lacking in seriousness
- possessed by a sense of inferriority
- fearful of competition with whites
- exploitive of the poor
- responsibility shirking in regard to the poor
- and generally living a life devoid of content and significance.

Reaction to the world of make-believe

Substance accepted; otherwise flawed. As might be imagined, Frazier's characterizations caused an intellectual storm, much in the fashion of Fordham-Ogbu's "acting white" thesis of our time. But it earned Frazier a celebrity status that far exceeds that of Fordham-Ogbu. The criticisms, likewise, were similar. Black Boston University sociologist and Professor Emeritus, James Teele, recounts the reaction in the introduction to his edited book, E. Franklin Frazier and Black Bourgeoisie (2002)(256). Frazier was accused of "washing dirty linen" in public, exaggerating, using a flawed sample, and relying upon questionable conclusions from secondary sources. But while critical of his portrayal, Teele writes, most did not deny its substance. In Teele's words, "… most of the reviews presented here accepted the substance of his charges, and some applauded Frazier for his courage in publishing *Black Bourgeoisie*," adding, "… it should be emphasized that these observations apply to nearly all the reviewers, whether journalists or academics, black or white" (256:9).

Dr. King's echo. Fast forward to a decade later (the 1960s) and we can count among their company none other than Dr. Martin Luther King Jr. He was not responding to the furor, but, in his last book, Where Do We Go From Here: Chaos or Community, he takes the middle class to task. While acknowledging the contributions of some, he is critical of many, accusing them of having forgotten their roots and being more concerned about material things than about justice (147:140).

The world of make-believe today (the interpretation)

Few have looked back to assess whether Frazier's characterizations still apply, which led Teele and a number of his colleagues to do so in his aforementioned edited book. As it turns out, however, their look back is more limited than might be expected or hoped for. Nevertheless, two of the contributors undertake the task.

Bracey and Kilson. John H. Bracey (black University of Massachusetts Amherst professor and chair of the Department of Afro-American Studies) sees, since 1964, "a virtual repudiation in significant, intellectual, cultural, and political ways of the middle-class hedonism that Frazier so lamented," adding:

And the constant talk now among black intellectuals is of their responsibility and what their responsibility should be. And I don't think you'll find a single member of the black intelligentsia in any field who will not acknowledge that he or she has come in contact in some relationship to the larger black population and shares its experience in values and its responsibility (19:100)

Martin L. Kilson (black Harvard University political scientist and professor emeritus) thinks Frazier exaggerated the "social pathologies" and did not provide "direct evidence" of their existence. His perspective of the middle class of the post-Frazier era is, not of a group living in a world of make-believe, but one that has become part of the economic and political mainstream. This situation, he argues, is made possible through their professional organizations (which are instruments for the process of status-deracialization, whereby race becomes less of an exclusionary factor) and a stronger middle class. As a result, citing various data, he sees the post-Frazier black bourgeoisie as exerting "power-mustering" influence versus the "high-society" type influence for which Frazier had disdain; and as exerting a liberalizing mainstream political influence, rather than being excluded, as Frazier thought would continue to be the case (145).

Lacy. Though not responding to Frazier, Karyn Lacy (black University of Michigan sociologist), in her study (2007) of three middle-class suburban communities consisting of upper-middle-class blacks and lower-middle-class blacks, provides support for Kilson's mainstreaming analysis (149). She describes a process of what she calls *strategic assimilation* whereby middle-class blacks do, indeed, become active participants in the American mainstream. However, that assimilation is intentionally on a selective and limited basis, since, at the same time, they opt to maintain strong ties to the black world. That is, her *strategic assimilation* thesis is that the black middle class, while choosing to mainstream, does not select mainstreaming over racial identity, but undertakes it in a way that assures that its racial identity is maintained. But, as Frazier observed for his era, Lacy found that this racial identity excludes the black poor; it is limited to blacks of their own kind (other middle-class blacks). They separate themselves from the black poor and, in their social and residential choices, from the middle-class white world as well.

Dyson. In his attack on Cosby and the middle class, Dyson, two years earlier, in 2005, had somewhat foreshadowed Lacy's characterization (70). He, too, had cited a distinctive segment of the black middle class as having distinctive attributes. He calls its members the *Afristocracy* and accuses it of detesting and attacking the values of the poor, who make up what he calls the *Ghettocracy*. Membership in either class, he points out (as others have), is not just a matter of economics; style and behavior also count. So one can be a rich athlete, for example, and still be a member of the Ghettocracy, as style and behavior would come into play (factors other than money, incidentally, also enter into class membership for whites). While Dyson cites neither Bernard nor Frazier, his analysis suggests a current black middle class that still reflects the historical two-cultures described by Bernard and others, and that still reflects having little sense of responsibility for the poor as described by Frazier.

Robinson. In his book, <u>Disintegration: The Splintering of Black America</u> (2010), Eugene Robinson provides further insight into our black middle class (227:77-106). He sees it as living a double life: one life in integrated settings wherein blacks are unsure of where we stand and the other life in black settings wherein a sense of solidarity, and shared history and experience exists. Most of their life is spent in black settings, Robinson confides, indicating that, although perhaps race should not matter, it does. As Cose's survey reveals, Robinson points out, among the young, race matters less. Robinson's current picture, however, somewhat like Kilson's, is one of a prosperous black middle class, with highly accomplished individual members, which cherishes its own self-segregated life and, in this instance somewhat like Bracey observes, is involved in helping the poor through the efforts of its individual members.

Bart Landry study and Myers and Margavio study. Other studies also provide support for Bracey's conclusion of a less social-oriented and a more civic-oriented black middle class. In his study (1987), black sociologist and University of Maryland Professor Emeritus,

Bart Landry, found that most of those in his national sample had been involved in some kind of protest and many had been directly involved in civil rights activities or belonged to civil rights groups (150). In their analysis of 525 articles from the black magazine, Ebony, Myers and Margavio, in a similar vein, inferred a more civic-minded black middle class (416).

Civil rights and collective self-help

Civil rights versus social needs. Whereas the studies cited reveal that in the post-Frazier era, there has been a more civic-minded versus social-minded middle class, at the same time, they show a civil-mindedness that emphasizes civil rights, not social needs, as its primary focus. Where the social needs of the poor do constitute the emphasis, nothing has been located to indicate that the scale and scope of the effort is anywhere near commensurate with that of the crisis. That even applies to the activities of the National Urban League, whose inclusive mission is to address those needs. On this front -- our obligation to the poor front -- our approach lacks the kind of energy and drive that has gone into the civil rights movement; rather, it is limited, sporadic, and piecemeal -- thanks to the weak self-help ethos of our middle class and the System-Responsibility Tradition responsible for it.

Local efforts. The fact is that, unlike other ethnic and racial groups, as Dinesh D'Souza declares, we have failed to advance "collectively ... by setting up ladders of opportunity for [our] less privileged members" (62:243). The forementioned black economist Ronald Mincy, for example, provides the following analysis with reference to our at-risk males: "Churches, fraternities, independent community-based agencies, and civil rights groups provide culturally sensitive programs but have few resources." More to the point, he adds: "Although minority agencies affiliated with national fraternities, church denominations, and civil rights groups address a variety of minority concerns, the needs of high-risk youth are given a low priority" (175:191). And, of course, what applies to at-risk males applies generally with regard to our social problems. True, resources are meager, but it is the priority factor which may be most determinative.

The charitable work of Ulric Haynes, African American Dean of Hofstra University's business school, appears to reflect D'Souza's analysis and, at the same time, conveys a picture of the kind of local efforts which do exist (47:95). Haynes would appear to be among the black intellectuals, all of whom Bracey asserts have "some relationship to the larger black population." In any case, Cose, in his previously cited book, <u>The Rage of the Privileged Class</u>, quotes Dean Haynes as telling him the following:

> 'Among my circle of black friends, who by anybody's standards would be overachievers, every one of us is concerned for the so-called underclass and, in some way or another, is involved in helping.... I have gotten our school of business involved in a partnership relationship with the Hempstead school district--which is overwhelmingly black and Latino, and is horribly poor in terms of quality--in curriculum redesign, in trying to get them computer equipment or upgrade their business education program, in one-to-one relationships.'

However, in response to the idea of the middle-class being responsible for the wellbeing of the underclass, he goes on, in part, to add: "'In every society there are the underdogs and there is an underclass. *And I am not going to take on the black underclass as a special burden of mine as a black man, although I am concerned. And I will demonstrate my concern. But don't hang that one on me*'" [emphasis added].

Dean Haynes is expressing, not just a personal ethos -- or an ethos of "all the Black intellectuals" -- but what appears to be a cultural ethos as well. Through our actions, if not our words as in the case of Dean Haynes, we are saying: "Don't hang that one on us." We go even further, of course, -- we in the middle class, in politics, in academia -- adding: "Hang it on the system; it is responsible." As the aforementioned survey of black males by the <u>Washington Post</u> suggests, perhaps it is only the larger African American community that may demur. Its ears are closer to the ground, so to speak -- as were Washington's, incidentally.

Past examples. We do, however, have past examples of collective self-help. Thomas Sowell provides this description of collective advancement of "free persons of color":

> Unlike some European minorities, or later generations of Negroes, the "free persons of color" were seldom recipients of public charity. They "cared for their own poor" [footnote omitted] through numerous mutual aid organizations which sprang up in communities of free Negroes from the earliest times. The first recorded mutual aid society among free Negroes was formed in Philadelphia in 1787; [footnote omitted] by 1813 there were 11 such organizations in the same city, and by 1838 there were a hundred mutual aid organizations among the free Negroes of Philadelphia [footnote omitted]. In Baltimore, there was a mutual aid society in 1821, and by 1835 there were 30 such organizations among free Negroes [footnote omitted] (241:18-10).

Frazier documents the role of mutual aid societies (which provided help in times of sickness and death) and secret fraternal organizations dating back to "free persons of color" and going through their period of growth in the 1920s (93:367-86). With Frazier, as with Sowell, the reference is to the past, not the present.

Meier gives an account of such efforts during the Age of Booker T. Washington. He observes the following:

> ...in all phases of life, behind the wall of segregation, the majority of Negroes had come to believe in the necessity of banding together and building counterparts to white institutions--whether cultural, welfare, religious, educational, economic, or purely social--though a very vocal minority still opposed them (168:138).

Activities, he points out, included the following: general charity, women's clubs, old folks' homes, orphanages, hospitals, social and literary clubs, libraries, day nurseries, kindergartens, and settlement houses. Old folks' homes and orphanages are said to have done the most successful work, black churches having played the primary role prior to the 1890s, only, thereafter, to be surpassed by these secular organizations. Though largely white supported, these activities were promoted and conducted by blacks and were regarded as self-help activities (168:130-38).

Middle-class exodus. Like the white middle class, the black middle has sought a better environment by moving to the suburbs -- away from the crime, disorder, and substandard schools and services that typically characterize poor urban neighborhoods (218: 102-17; 286). Eugene Robinson captures what has happened in his description of the transformation of "U St. NW" in Washington, D.C., once a hub of sophisticated black culture and class. He cites the story of an art dealer who told him that on his block they had had school teachers, a mail man, a retired garbage man, and a registrar at Howard

University. But by the late 1960s, many, if not most of the educated professionals had moved away. A community that once had been racially segregated but economically and socially integrated had become, no longer just segregated, but isolated and poor as well (227:57).

The exodus means that the Abandoned have been left to fend for themselves. The help they get from the middle class is individualized and otherwise primarily in the form of protesting and pleading on their behalf versus collective outreach. However, as pointed out in the last chapter, the exodus has not been on the scale that has, heretofore, been thought, many from the middle class still living in lower, if not low, income neighborhoods.

Middle-class intentions. D'Souza even contends that "What E. Franklin Frazier wrote of the black bourgeoisie in the 1950s is even *more true* [emphasis added] of the civil rights establishment: 'The lip service which they give to solidarity with the masses very often disguises their exploitation of the masses.'" (62:241). Absent the exploitation charge, Loury makes the same point, concluding, "A broad array of evidence suggests that better-placed blacks have been able to take better advantage of the opportunities created since the early 1960s than have those mired in the underclass" (155:48). William Julius Wilson makes the case that if the middle class disproportionately benefit -- or differently put, if advantaged minority members (to use his description) benefit more -- it is because they are positioned by such factors as family stability, schooling, and income to be able to take advantage of the opportunities created (285a:146-49). Therefore, call the outcome an unintended consequence.

The world of make-believe and modern middle class culture

When it comes to social consciousness, reflected in collective self-help, these three cultural tests suggest that the world of make-believe which Frazier said we middle-class African Americans created for ourselves in the 1950s lives on. Although Bracey and Robinson, along with the studies cited, point to, at present, a less social-minded and more civic-minded black middle class, that civic-mindedness is about *individual* outreach and contributions; it is not the same as collective self-help, the kind of self-help which Dinesh D'Souza points out has enabled other minority groups to uplift their poor. That we have not provided collective self-help, but, nonetheless, defend, even tout, our civic-mindedness and contribution to the poor by citing individual efforts qualifies as make-believe. For those random individual efforts are, in fact systemically inconsequential, and further bring into question another attribute cited by Frazier: our seriousness. Are we in the black middle class serious about helping the poor, or does the fact that we tout our individual contributions suggest otherwise -- that, as Frazier observed of the black middle class of his time, we "play" at it. We are not really serious, rather acting out of a "spirit of play" – making-believe?

Furthermore, as Frazier said of the black middle class of his day, the black middle class of our day has escaped from the masses -- gone to the outlying areas and left them in the inner city. Whether, in addition, it has exploited them as Frazier said was done by the black middle class of his day, can be argued, but what cannot be argued is that it is those of us in the black middle class, not the masses, who have mainly benefited from our civil rights gains. Eugene Robinson alludes to the tension, noted by Frazier, which still exists between our black middle class and the poor (227:236).

No indication was found that belief in the important role of black-owned businesses -- a central part of Frazier's black middle class world of make-believe -- holds the same place in the black middle class mind today as in Frazier's era. More than anything else, a perusal of the topic on the internet suggests more of a concern about their problems and failure to measure up to white businesses. It is informative, in fact, that Kilson, in refuting Frazier's make-believe characterization, does not cite the importance of black-owned businesses, but rather focuses on the increase in black mainstreaming through what he terms status-deracialization and power-mustering influence. That refocus can be considered counter to Frazier's analysis, a turn from the world of make-believe to the world of reality. For those of us who might think these businesses hold an important place in the wellbeing of the race or the nation, we are -- as during Frazier's time -- engaged in make-believe. Consider, for example, the following: for 2012, the top 100 black-owned industrial/service companies employed 53,866 people and the 60 largest black-owned auto dealers employed an additional 8,415 people for a combined total of 62,281 people, whereas the total for Chevron alone in 2011 was 61,000, considered low for the oil and gas industry (433d; 471j). These figures hardly point to a significant role by black-owned businesses.

At the heart of Frazier's middle class depiction was a status-seeking, insecure, hedonistic black middle class living a life devoid of content and significance with no serious commitment to learning and scholarship. Bear in mind, though critical of these characterizations, Teele points out that neither black nor white reviewers basically refuted their validity. As evident, for example, from Bracey and Kilson -- and from the reaction of the black intelligentsia to McWhorter's Losing the Race -- that is not the case as regards our black middle class today; refuters abound. Yet, a case can be made that Frazier's characterizations still hold. Indeed, McWhorter's two books, for example, Losing the Race and Winning the Race, can be said to make the case. Only Robinson's Disintegration: The Splintering of Black America suggests that the hold is not as firm as during Frazier's time, as does, for example, Cose's The End of Anger. The hold is certainly not as firm among the younger generation and, most probably, neither among those engaged in bridging or strategic assimilation.

Of course, hedonism, status-seeking, and commitment to learning and scholarship are issues of concern among whites and other groups as well, but Frazier was talking about their disproportionality, if not dominance, among our black middle class of his time. Most striking is Frazier's observation that middle-class Negroes who had made bona fide contributions in science and art had to escape from the influence of Negro "society." In his Disintegration, the splintering notwithstanding, Robinson provides a glimpse of that pull today. He confides the pull of "racial affinity" and its associated social life, painting a somewhat mesmerizing and idyllic picture of it in his description of a Sigma Pi Phi fraternity (popularly called Boule) get-together attended by him and his wife. Boule is an invitation-only African American fraternity composed of diverse prominent black professionals, including college professors, former campus radicals, doctors, lawyers, and financers. Here is Robinson's description of the gathering:

> The only items on the agenda were food and fellowship. There was talk about the recession and its impact on the California real estate market. There was a certain amount of networking, I suppose, although these were men and women who had known one another long enough to have already made all the possible connections. The real point of the gathering was to gather--to laugh, commiserate, solve the problems of the world, debate the prospects of the Sacramento Kings, and agree on tee times for the coming week. There was something warm and almost womb-like about the afternoon--easy comfort in a house full of total strangers. There was so much we knew about one another's lives without even having to ask.
>
> Everyone present was black. This slice of Mainstream black life--like so much of the cake--is for us. Not for anybody else (227:102).

Implicit in Robinson's description is what Frazier saw in his time: the preoccupation of the black middle class with its social life or "society." The preoccupation, too, is implicit, for example, in the attention Robinson devotes to its sorority and fraternity connections. Whereas this is just one anecdote, and the life and connections of just one person, to those of us who are participants in the middle class life of our time, as Frazier was a participant in the life of his times, we know that, in essence, it is not isolated, but rather typifies so much of black middle class life. But we know, too, as Robinson goes on to observe, that life is indeed changing -- thanks mainly, as stated, to the younger generation, and perhaps as well to bridging or strategic assimilation. We are no longer relegated to a black social life; integration might be said to have afforded us the utmost of two worlds: our own black world and the white world.

As for Frazier's characterization of the content and significance of black middle-class culture, Robinson laments the inattention to its successes. However, it could be that such successes as he cites -- for example, black professors studying international relations, black scuba clubs, and black motorcycle clubs -- are too few and far between to generate an overall impression. That learning holds a more central place in middle-class culture is certainly not evident from black achievements cited by black Harvard historian, Henry Louis Gates Jr., in his recent voluminous look backward at African American history, 1513-2008, nor by co-founder of the National Black Women's Justice Institute and former NAACP Vice President, Monique W. Morris, in her compilation of black statistics in the 21st century. The achievements cited by both fall disproportionately in the fields of entertainment and sports (99a:407-42; 181a). When it comes to ideology, in fact, Martin Luther King Jr. alludes to the fact that few black thinkers have influenced American thought (147:146). And, as discussed above, McWhorter makes the argument that anti-intellectualism has become part of the bedrock of black identity (181a; 99a).

There might well have been a diminution of the feelings of inferiority and insecurity discerned by Frazier and found by Kardiner and Ovesey in their classic study, <u>Mark of Oppression</u>. However, our second bondage, Victimology, and its many manifestations, Affirmative Action being maybe the most notable among them, attest, in whatever degree, to its persistence. In fact, the frequency with which one can detect it is somewhat surprising. For what Kardiner and Ovesey saw in their 25 black subjects back then (and what in essence Frazier saw) -- their being "constantly ill at ease, mistrustful, and lacking in confidence" -- is not uncommon today. Eugene Robinson seems to put his finger on why, asserting that one important way in which Mainstream black experience differs from that of other middle-class American groups is that, "Despite all the progress that's been made, there's still a nagging sense of being looked down upon, of being judged, of being disrespected" (227:81). To trace that "nagging sense," however diminished, to the same feeling of inferiority and insecurity seen by Frazier and by Kardiner and Ovesey is not unreasonable.

As for a make-believe world, it is argued that many of us in the black middle class still live in one, anchored not so much by our society life as in Frazier's time -- and certainly not by black businesses, but by

Victimology, our second bondage. We make-believe we are victims, and, as victims, we make-believe that, but due to our color, our life would be the same as that of other Americans -- the same educational level, the same economic success, the same proportion of significant contributions, and so on. We make-believe that civil rights is still a major concern. Above all, we make-believe that our full acceptance into the American mainstream rests on *feeling equality*, herein defined as the notion that whites are obligated to *feel* that we are equal to them.

Robinson tells the interesting story of a television encounter with conservative commentator, Pat Buchanan, wherein he lost his cool, as he puts it. "My eyes got round and crazy, friends say," he confides, "and apparently I looked as if I were about to smack him--was when he adamantly, even aggressively refused to acknowledge my point that Sotomayor's personal history was every bit as American as his own" (227:98-99). The idea that our American experience (and to some degree we somewhat tend to make a minority person like Sotomayor the equivalent to one of us) is not equal to that of a white person of traditional American heritage, like Buchanan, was apparently more than Robinson, probably like so many of the rest of us, could bear.

The point here is not that Robinson is thought to have been wrong, for the American story is one of a melting pot -- or at least a mixing pot. The point is to illustrate the powerful need we blacks have for total white recognition, something more than just recognition of our civic equality, but, as Lasch-Quinn detects, personal acceptance of us as well -- that personal acceptance herein called *feeling equality*. It is a quest for civic equality, plus feeling equality, which equals total equality ("race-egalitarianism" is what Loury calls it). Robinson, after all, says that he had appeared dozens of times with Buchanan and managed to keep his cool, but this time, his eyes got round and crazy and he almost lost it. The raw nerve of *feeling equality* had been touched. It was not enough for the Supreme Court nominee to be civically accepted; in addition, she must also be personally or feelingly accepted. Seemingly not doing so, maybe Buchanan deserved to have been smacked, but the consolation would have been illusory. Robinson and the rest of us can make-believe that the smacking would have gotten the message across, but there are some things which must emanate from within -- and how others feel about us is one of them. However, in a world of make-believe, it is an unaccepted reality.

In addition to Victimology, there is another reason we blacks are still in make-believe mode. We had believed that the civil rights gains of the 1950s and 60s would transform our status from subordination to equality -- or at least to a greatly diminished prevalence of black social problems. That simply did not happen. Our situation even worsened, causing black disillusionment in the 1960s and 70s. In some quarters, that disillusionment caused the failure to be attributed, in so many words, to white racism. White racism, in turn, gave rise to what can be termed escapist solutions -- escapist because the solutions did not address our own demons, responding instead to perceived white demons. Remedies were devised which have emotional appeal but little or no chance of meaningful acceptance or of making a difference. Just as Frazier said we thought our business and society life in the 1950s gave us status and importance, since the 1960s we have thought that these escapist solutions would do likewise. Perhaps enhancing that belief is that, for some escapist solutions, we have gotten substantial white support, Black Studies departments being one example.

But it must be kept in mind that our status in American society rests on "results" (to borrow Washington's word and thinking) which contribute to our wellbeing as well as the nation's. From such black solutions as herein singled out -- the Black Power movement, nigrescence, Afrocentrism, and critical race theory, in particular, along with Black Studies departments, black caucuses, black professional organizations and publications, and continual complaints and protests -- we have not gotten, nor is there any reason to believe that we will get, such results. Rather, one can, instead, sense in them Frazier's "spirit of play" and McWhorter's therapeutic alienation.

So our modern world of make-believe has a dual foundation: Victimology and escapist solutions -- solutions which, as in Frazier's time, provide us an escape from a feeling of inferiority and from rejection by white America. Disillusioned with our lack of post-civil rights gains, we make-believe that the reason for our lack of gains lies in our continued victimization. We make-believe that the solution lies in remedies which have not shown, nor can be expected to show, "results." It is not that we blacks have not made significant gains in the post-civil rights era, for indeed we have. However, it is the distribution of those gains and the persistence and aggravation of an array of social problems which constitute our quagmire. Of course, racism, our security blanket, externalizes the quagmire and provides us a measure of comfort amid our discontent.

The Externally Adapted: The Poor or Underclass

When we focus on the poor, or underclass, we focus on the Abandoned, as Eugene Robinson labels them, the subgroup on which this book mainly focuses. As Paul Tough points out, from them come the students who have proven the most difficult to reach. Tough cites, in particular, those from families earning under $11,000 a year. But as Elijah Anderson's study (reported in his book, Code of the Street) documents, their culture is not homogenous (5). We have the working poor, and decent families along with street families. Most of them, Anderson reveals, "are decent or are trying to be" (5:36). Nor are they isolated from middle class values. As Bernard postulates, and as Anderson reveals, it is a matter of degree of internalization. These considerations notwithstanding, the literature suggests that we do have what has come to be termed a "culture of poverty" (471u).

As previously observed, Michael Harrington depicts that culture as consisting of those who are isolated from the rest of the nation. "They tend," he says, "to be hopeless and passive, yet prone to bursts of violence; they are lonely and isolated, often rigid and hostile." Drawing upon the research, he further says that they:

- exhibit frequent mental and physical illnesses,
- are suspicious,
- are fatalistic,
- lack feeling of belongingness,
- lack friendliness,
- lack trust in others,
- lack affiliation,
- lack gratification postponement,
- tend to "act out,"
- are not well informed, and

- live a somewhat open and chaotic life among themselves – fighting, loud noise, loud radio and television all part of their shared existence (114:130-33).

He could have added to this enumeration: use flagrant vulgarity routinely and indiscriminately.

The male-female relationship in this culture is commonly contentious and acrimonious (285:11-21; 209c:178-81; 46-127-43). Each views the other unfavorably, and confrontation and violence is more common among them than among other races. The men tend not to want to be tied down, to have multiple female relationships, to be unfaithful in marriage, and to spend more time in the streets than at home. The women, consequently, do not trust them to be dedicated husbands. The men, however, blame the women, accusing them of being difficult and demanding, bossy, and having an "attitude." Fifty percent of them, in fact, say that they cannot find a suitable mate, while black women often prefer to remain alone, there, in any instance, being only five suitable black marriageable males for every ten black females.[21] Rev. Jesse Peterson depicts the relationship between the two as "The War Between Black Men and Women" (209c:178-80). The war (combined with other factors) has resulted in increasingly lower marriage rates and in marriages which increasingly do not last. Their children are the war's most tragic victims. They carry its imprint and bear and its consequences. As Lee Rainwater declares, they leave the homes of this war prepared to function in the ghetto world, but not in any other world. They are not provided the safety and love on which, Paul Tough points out, the new research shows school and life success largely depend.

If this deprivation were not enough, the work of child psychiatrist and trauma specialist, Dr. Pamela Cantor, reported in a <u>The New York Times</u> article, compels the addition of another malady to their plight: trauamatized (309a). After 9/11, Cantor was hired by the New York City Board of Education to assess its impact on its school chidren. To her and her team's surprise, the trauma they uncovered was concentrated among children in poverty area schools, and their trauma symptoms were

---

[21] See Chapter 8 for research revealing 1.5 million missing black males.

caused, not by 9/11 or by living near Ground Zero, but by shock from their home environment – exposure to violence, inadequate housing, sudden family loss, addicted or depressed parents, and so on. Cantor, whose Turnaround for Children organization is discussed in Chapter 16, estimates that one-fifth of the children had "full-blown psychiatric disorder," and that 68 percent had learning impairment due to prior home-inflicted trauma.

Support for the possibility of home-inflicted trauma comes from a surprising source: Dr. Martin Luther King Jr. In his last book, <u>Where Do We Go From Here: Chaos or Community</u>, King refers to the ghetto as "an emotional pressure cooker" (147:122). His reference is to the experience of their children, over the summer in 1967, living with him and his wife in the ghetto of Lawndale in Chicago, Illinois. After only a few days, he says, their behavior changed. "Their tempers flared and they sometimes reverted to almost infantile behavior." King attributed the change to the hot, crowded flat and, due to limited space and traffic-filled streets, to the lack of recreational, or play, outlets.

Neuroscience, the article explains, is coming to understand better the consequences of the stress which such trauma produces. In the words of New York University Applied Psychology Professor C. Cybele Raver, stress disrupts "higher order cognitive functions," thereby curtailing the child's ability to learn. Further, Cantor explains that the prevalence of stress among children in a school also contaminates the school climate and disrupts school learning as well.

Alarmingly, the stress can apparently be so severe as to jeopardize the very life of some children. In a new finding, researchers reveal that, *for the first time*, the suicide rate among black children, ages 5 to 11, is higher than the suicide rate among white children (451e). In fact, the researchers explained, it is the first time that, *for any age group*, any national study has found a higher suicide rate among blacks than suicide rate among whites. The researchers were so surprised by the finding that they waited a year to get additional data to confirm their finding, which the additional data did.

In sum, the culture of poverty leaves many of our African American children doubly unprepared. They lack both cognitive readiness and emotional readiness. Only, as Tough's review of the research, Cantor's investigation, and the rising suicide rate of black children show, it is the lack of emotional readiness which is so devastating. To remind us of both lacks, our mnemonic is **68 / suicide rate of black children, 2015** – the percent of black children in poverty areas found in one study to be learning impaired due to home-inflicted trauma and, *for the first time*, suicide rate among black children exceeds the suicide rate among white children and, moreover, the first time, *for any age group*, that black suicide rate has exceeded white suicice rate.

We Black Males: In the Spotlight

It is we black males, in particular, who are in the spotlight in this book and in this cultural vortex. In our quest for manhood, which must be earned (manhood is not inherited; society must bestow it), we have created a subculture of our own. As previously quoted, Janet Billson declares, "Black males have created their own world to salvage their pride." From the research and literature, some of which is discussed in Chapter 5, that black male world can be described as one in which many among us disproportionately value toughness, style (speech, walk, dress, manners), sex, sports, and hanging out. To us, too often recreation trumps responsibility, and pleasure trumps parenthood; we let our hedonistic impulses prevail over our restraining instincts (see, for example, following references: 5, 10, 26, 38, 113b, 178, 212b, 245,285).

Cross-Cultural Perspective

The question often arises as to why our black culture cannot be like some other minority group cultures, particularly the same-race West Indians, who have thrived in American life.

West Indians

Seen as a race success story, some look at West Indian culture and, given that we are of the same race, ask why we cannot be like them. Most notably, Thomas Sowell addressed the issue in his comparative study (1978) of black subgroups. His study revealed that West Indians are similar to whites on a range of socioeconomic variables and free of many of the social and economic woes which plague us African Americans

(241:7-64). Sowell attributes their success to the self-management and occupational exposure black West Indians experienced under British slavery, in contrast to the more repressive elements of American slavery. The former produced a more autonomous (self-reliant and enterprising) personality, the latter produced a more Sambo-like personality, as Stanley Elkins argues (76).

However, in a recent study (2008), retired University of Massachusetts sociologist Suzanne Model dissents (181). Putting Sowell's explanation through a variety of statistical tests, Model declares it false. She says her data show that West Indians are not endowed with some autonomous attributes lacking in African Americans; rather, West Indians immigrants are a *select* group -- the more educated and ambitious. Therefore, she concludes that the West Indian success story is not a *race* success story, but an *immigrant* success story, not unlike the story of other successful immigrant groups (181:3). Thus, to treat West Indians as a subpopulation equivalent to native blacks (African Americans) is a mistake; they are not. They are *immigrants*, a select group composed of a subpopulation equivalent to other immigrant groups, not to us African Americans, who are former slaves and their descendants.

Other recent immigrant groups: The Triple Package

In an even more recent study (2014), Yale professors Amy Chua and Jed Rubenfeld, provide support for Model's thesis (34a). Based on their study of eight successful immigrant groups – Mormons, Cubans, Indians, Jews, Iranians, Lebanese, Chinese, and Nigerians -- in their book, The Triple Package: How Three Unlikely Traits Explain the Rise and Fall of Cultural Groups in America, they say that *The Triple Package*, not IQ, explains the success of these groups. The three unlikely traits are: *superiority* (an internalized feeling of being special), *insecurity* (feeling that what they have done is not good enough), and *impulse control* (especially including persistence in the face of hardships). These three traits, they theorize, give these immigrant groups the *drive* responsible for their success. With respect to blacks, the authors' focus is not on West Indians, but on Nigerians, although she also cite West Indians and Ghanaians. Chua and Rubenfeld's point is that, ethnicity or IQ notwithstanding, it is culture which accounts for immigrant success.

Not that the authors dismiss IQ, only they consider drive a better predictor (34a:194-95).

Baumeister-Tierney offer a noteworthy illustraton of Chua-Rubenfeld's thesis. In contrasting the IQ of Chinese and Japanese Americans with white European Americans, Baumeister-Tierney write:

> ...the Asian-Americans' IQ is slightly lower, on average, although they do show up more at both the upper and lower extremes. **The big difference is that they make better use of their intelligence** [emphasis added]. People working in what Flynn calls elite professions, like physicians, scientists, and accountants, generally have an IQ above a certain threshold. For white Americans, that threshold is an IQ of 110, but Chinese-Americans manage to get the same elite jobs with an IQ of only 103. Moreover, among the people above each threshold, Chinese-Americans have higher rates of actually getting into those jobs, meaning that a Chinese-American with an IQ above 103 is more likely to get an elite job than an American with an IQ above 110. The pattern is similar for Japanese-Americans. By virtue of self-control--hard work, diligence, steadiness, reliability--the children of immigrants from East Asia can do as well as Americans with higher IQs (6b:195).

That is, in the terminology of Chua-Rubenfeld, by virtue of The Triple Package, with lower IQs, East Asian immigrants can do as well as Americans with higher IQs. Thus, Chua-Rubenfeld give a nod to drive over IQ, and consider the past, and continuing, failure of the country to extract the Triple Package from us blacks to be an important factor in explaining our lower overall socioeconomic status.

Early European immigrants

European immigrants who came here during the third immigrant wave from 1890-1914 (Italians, Poles, Greeks, Slovaks, Spanish, Portuguese, Irish, Germans, Jews, and others) provide another relevant comparison. Sowell states that during the period of their poverty and dysfunction, their status was similar to ours (242). That they rapidly transformed their status is commonly explained as a function, not of their IQ, but of economic opportunities and hard work (223a, 240a).

Discussion

When we consider the cultural traits which have enabled other groups -- early Europeans, West Indians, and more recent immigrant groups -- to become successful in American life, we African Americans fall short on those traits. Our drive, ambition, and hard work are not sufficiently pervasive. Those are the traits which Washington so tirelessly labored to instill in, and extract from, us – and with considerable success, only to have DuBois and his tradition undermine his labor. Even, however, if not undermined, that the ultimate outcome of Washinton's labor would have yielded in us African Americans the Triple Package possessed by these successful immigrant groups is debatable since, as John Ogbu argues, we are involuntary (forced) immigrants while they are voluntary (selective) immigrants. No doubt, we have to consider other factors as well. Steven Pinker's book serves as a reminder that neither we nor the successful immigrant groups have undertaken our American journey with a "blank slate" (210).

Conclusion

If we better understand ourselves, we can better understand our students, since, as John Ogbu so scholarly detailed, they reflect us. That is what this chapter is intended to help us do: to understand ourselves better so that we can understand our students better. Its data make possible the cultural profiles assembled below. Some of the profiles have no validity, while other profiles have varying degrees of validity. Of itself, the process of deciding their validity can enhance our self-understanding. Perhaps there is no need to be that definitive in our profiling, instead, there is just a need to be more aware so that we can be more perceptive.

Bernard's Acculturated	Bernard's Externally Adapted	Frazier's New Black Middle Class
·have Puritan work and sex ethic	·hedonistic ·pleasure-loving ·adventurous	Disproportionately: ·status-seeking ·social/recreation-centered ·lack interest in learning ·frustrated and miserable ·lack sense of seriousness

Joe L. Rempson

Culture of Poverty Traits
- passive
- hopeless
- violence prone
- rigid
- hostile
- unfriendly
- unaffiliated
- ill-informed
- cannot postpone gratification

- often mentally ill
- often physically ill
- suspicious
- fatalistic
- lack a feeling of belonging
- mistrust others
- "act out" Value:
- chaotic home/community life

- exhibit sense of inferiority
- fear competition with whites
- exploitative of the poor
- do not accept responsibility for poor
- live life devoid of content and significance

Some Ascribed Black Male Traits
- toughness ·sex ·sports
- style (speech, walk, dress, mannerisms)
- hanging out

Ascribed Cultural Traits of Our Students
- lack serious attitude toward school work
- fail to work hard in school or persist long enough in doing school work
- do not complete or do homework
- do not identify with school (disidentification)
- place value on having a cool image
- place value on toughness (an extraordinarily prized manhood trait)
- emphasize sports and popularity at expense of education
- have disciplinary problems
- have anti-authority attitude
- play around in class
- arrive late for school
- are often absent from school
- use verbal insults (sounding)
- will often resort to fighting
- have strong peer group culture (compensating for weak family ties)
- are irresponsible
- do not have peer support for academic striving

Ascribed Sambo Personality
- indolent
- faithful
- humble
- humorous
- silly
- playful
- cheerful
- dishonest
- steal
- superstitious
- improvident
- musical
- clownish
- childlike
- fight-prone
- docile

·subscribe to academically and intellectually-alienating popular culture

Ascribed Sambo Personality Carry-Over Traits
- ·dirty
- ·superstitious
- ·shiftless
- ·lazy
- ·happy-go-lucky
- ·smelly
- ·ignorant
- ·treacherous
- ·cowardly
- ·superstitious

8

Why the Crisis?
The IQ Factor: Adaptation as a Function of Our Innate Ability

Proverbs, 16:22 - "Understanding is a wellspring of life unto him that hath it: but the instruction of fools is folly."
Galatians, 6:5 - "For every man shall bear his own burden."

In this chapter, we address one of our **three major demons**: our *IQ lag, fatherless families* and *crime* being the other two. The question of its role in influencing our adaptation has been given special prominence by two publications (62:431-76): Arthur Jensen's (1969) article in the Harvard Educational Review, "How Much Can We Boost IQ and Scholastic Achievement?" (139) and, more recently, Richard Herrnstein and Charles Murray's (1994) book, The Bell Curve (121). Jensen makes a comprehensive and documented case for the role of IQ in black school performance. Herrnstein and Murray make a similar case for its role in both school and life performance, not only for blacks, but for all Americans. Inherited intelligence, in their view, affects what we can and should do in regard to our school and national policies and practices. Our failure to recognize and respond to that reality, they contend, has doomed, and will continue to doom, our remedies.

Some of their key relevant data are outlined below, followed by an exploration of some of the issues they raise, especially as they pertain to racial IQ differences. In the outline, the numbers in parenthesis are the page number in their respective publications cited above. It is realized that it is unusual to have such an outline in a book, but the reason for the outlilne is that, practically speaking, and to some extent, these publications have been censored. They have been so maligned that many people just refuse to read them, that politically correct and therapeutically sensitive professors omit them from their reading list, and that some librarians skimp on the number of copies ordered; those which they do order often being confiscated. In the era of what Lasch-Quinn calls "race experts," such is the nature of open debate and the status of liberty and justice for all, to say nothing of the viability of the First Amendment.

Jensen: Some of His Key Data

1. Role of IQ
   A. "'In the actual race of life, which is not to get ahead, but to get ahead of somebody, the chief determining factor is heredity.' So said Edward L. Thorndike in 1905. Since then, the preponderance of evidence has proved him right, certainly as concerns those aspects of life in which intelligence plays an important role" (28).
   B. "Most geneticists and students of human evolution have fully recognized the role of culture in shaping 'human nature,' but also they do not minimize the biological basis of diversity in human behavioral characteristics" (30).

2. IQ versus mental ability: *Intelligence* and *mental ability* are not the same. Intelligence [as used in the technical literature] refers to the capacity for abstract reason and problem solving that is measured by standardized tests whereas mental ability refers to the totality of a person's mental capabilities.

3. IQ variance and malleability
   A. IQ is determined mainly by hereditary rather than environmental factors.
   B. IQ is variable in early life, but after age 4 or 5 becomes predictably stable, much as in the case of the development of most strictly physical characteristics.

C. Nutritional therapy (proteins, vitamins, and minerals) in the case of *severe* undernutrition has a beneficial effect on IQ, the earlier instituted the greater the benefit, but even as late as two years of age, one study showed a gain of 18 IQ points while another, however, showed no significant gain after age 4. Rare cases of extremely deprived environments have shown gains of as many as 60 or 70 IQ points. Disadvantaged children, however, do not typically fall into the severe deprivation category, generally showing no early deficit.

4. Role of the environment
   A. Environment serves as a "threshold variable" in that extreme deprivation can keep a child from performing up to the child's genetic potential, but an enrichment program cannot push the child above that potential.
   B. Environment contributes more to the IQ of children who are above the mean IQ than it does to those who are below it.
   C. There is relationship between socioeconomic status and IQ, the mean IQ difference between groups ranging from 15 to 30 IQ points.

5. Racial differences in IQ
   A. According to geneticists, "Any groups which have been geographically or socially isolated from one another for many generations are practically certain to differ in their gene pools, and consequently are likely to show differences in any phenotypic characteristics having high heritability" -- and this includes IQ as well as behavior (80-81).
   B. The IQ variance among black children has been found to be less than that among white children; otherwise stated, black children have been found to have about 60% as much IQ variance as white children.

6. Boy-girl differences
   A. "It has long been suspected that males have greater environmental vulnerability than females, and Nancy

Bayley's important longitudinal research on children's mental development clearly shows both a higher degree and a greater variety of environmental and personality correlates of mental abilities in boys than in girls ..." (32).

B. Black boys have been found to perform less well in school than black girls to a greater degree than between white boys and white girls. The gap tends to increase with age -- and across all socioeconomic groups.

7. Compensatory education
   A. Compensatory education (Headstart and enrichment programs) have failed to close the black-white achievement gap or the IQ gap since the programs have not adequately addressed the needs of disadvantaged students, which should be based, not just on environmental differences, but on IQ differences as well.
   B. "...despite all the criticisms that can easily be leveled at the educational system, the traditional forms of instruction have actually worked quite well for the majority of children," only they have not adapted to the learning abilities that more typically characterize the disadvantaged (7).

8. Raising scholastic achievement versus raising IQ
   A. In general, scholastic achievement is less heritable than IQ, possibly less than half as heritable (58-59).
   B. "...it seems likely that if compensatory education programs are to have a beneficial effect on achievement, it will be through their influence on motivation, values, and other environmentally conditioned habits that play an important part in scholastic performance, rather than through any marked direct influence on intelligence per se" (59).
   C. Enrichment and cognitive stimulation programs have produced IQ gains ranging from 5 to 20 IQ points (but typically from 5 to 10) and scholastic achievement gains ranging from one-half to two standard deviations for such specific achievement measures as reading, arithmetic, and spelling. The amount of gain is related to the intensity, specificity, cognitive emphasis (especially in verbal skills),

and home extension of the programs. The IQ gains, however, appear to be gains in *crystallized intelligence* versus *fluid intelligence*, and educators might more justifiably focus on achievement gains rather than the small gains to be made from attempting to boost IQ scores.

Fluid intelligence [called the Gf factor] involves the capacity for new learning and problem solving whereas *crystallized intelligence* [called the Gc factor] derives additionally from prior learning and past experience.

9. IQ and patterns of learning ability
   A. Intelligence is postulated to be two-dimensional rather than (as traditionally conceived) one-dimensional, one dimension characterized by associative ability (Level I intelligence) and the other characterized by conceptual ability (Level II intelligence).
   B. Associative ability entails outputs which derive from the formation of associations from stimulus inputs with little manipulation of those inputs whereas conceptual ability entails outputs which derive from self-initiated elaboration of inputs with personalized transformation of those inputs.
   C. Level I ability is distributed about the same in all social classes, but Level II ability is distributed differently in lower and middle socioeconomic (SES) groups, that difference increasing with age--and in favor of higher SES groups.

   The point to be emphasized is that lower-class children -- whether black, white, or Mexican-American -- perform as well on tests of this ability as middle-class children up to an IQ of 100, even higher.
   D. This basic ability of the disadvantaged to learn through the pattern of abilities which are exhibited through Level I intelligence (associative learning abilities) has not been tapped through traditional instruction, which emphasizes learning through conceptual ability, that is, through a unidimensional concept of learning.

10. Conclusion

"If diversity of mental abilities, as of most other human characteristics, is a basic fact of nature, as the evidence indicates, and if the ideal of universal education is to be successfully pursued, it seems a reasonable conclusion that schools and society must provide a range and diversity of educational methods, programs, and goals, and of occupational opportunities, just as wide as the range of human abilities. Accordingly, the ideal of equality of educational opportunity should not be interpreted as uniformity of facilities, instructional techniques, and educational aims for all children. Diversity rather than uniformity of approaches and aims would seem to be the key to making education rewarding for children of different patterns of ability. The reality of individual differences thus need not mean educational rewards for some children and frustration and defeat for others" (117).

Herrnstein and Murray: Some of Their Key Data

1. IQ versus environment
   A. "Cognitive ability is substantially heritable, apparently no less than 40 percent and no more than 80 percent" (23).
   B. There is no easy way to raise IQ -- not through formal schooling nor, by any sizable and sustainable number of points through Headstart or other preschool programs -- though (a) improved nutrition and (b) adoption at birth from a bad family environment have been found to result in higher scores, ranging from 4 to 8 points (389-416).

2. Black-white IQ differences
   A. The black IQ mean is about 85, the white IQ mean about 100, with a standard deviation of about 15. Differently viewed, the average white person tests higher than 84% of blacks and the average black person higher than 16% of whites (269,276).
   B. Black-white IQ differences occur at every level of socioeconomic status, but the difference is greater at higher SES levels than at lower SES levels (269).

C. Even in view of IQ mean difference between blacks and whites, there is considerable overlapping in IQ when comparing an equal number of blacks and whites; however, although there are approximately equal numbers of blacks and whites at the lower half of the IQ range, throughout the upper half of the range whites outnumber blacks in large numbers (278-80).
D. The last few decades have seen a narrowing of the black-white IQ gap by about three IQ points, perhaps due to a reduction in low scores rather than an increase in high scores (269-70)
E. Both genes and environment contribute to black-white IQ difference; it is not just the environment alone, the percentage of each being indeterminate (280-315)
F. The limited available data comparing the IQ of African Americans and black Africans show black Africans to have a lower IQ than African Americans (288- 89)

3. Social significance of IQ
   A. Individual's IQ scores are useful, but have limited meaning except in combination with other information whereas group IQ scores, in contrast, have considerable meaning in relation to predictable average outcomes (19-20).
   B. There is a positive association between IQ and such demographics as children born out of wedlock, high school dropouts, males ever interviewed in jail, and poverty, with higher IQs related to more positive outcomes (341-68). On these same indices, most of those who exhibit social problems are in the bottom half of the IQ range, accounting, for example, for 82% of all children in single-parent homes (369-86).
   C. Notwithstanding the predominant makeup of those who have social problems, "Most people in the lower half of the cognitive distribution are employed, out of poverty, not on welfare, married when they have their babies, providing a nurturing environment for their children, and obeying the law" (385). "By the time people were even approaching average IQ, the percentages of people who were poor, had

babies out of wedlock, provided poor environments for their children, or exhibited any other problem constituted small percentages of the population" (536).
D. A small shift in adult group IQ, even as little as three points, can have significant social consequences. A drop of three points shows an 11% rise in overall poverty rate, a 13% rise in children living in poverty during the first three years of their lives, an 8% rise in children born to single mothers, a 13% rise in men interviewed in jail, an 18% rise in men prevented from working due to health problems, and a 14% rise in the proportion of children living with nonparental custodians, women ever on welfare, and high school dropouts.

Viewed from the perspective of a rise in IQ, a 6-point rise reduces by 43% the proportion of people who never get a high school education, by 36% those who live below the poverty line, by 38% the number of children living in foster care or with noparental relatives, by 31% women ever on welfare (364-68).

4. Social implications of IQ (527-52)
   A. General goal: to replace the current reign of the cognitive elite, fashion society wherein all the functionally intelligent find, and feel that they have found, a valued place for themselves so that they would be missed if they were gone
   B. Policies
      (1) Restore, where possible, a wide range of social functions in neighborhoods or municipalities to restore their former interconnected and diverse services and functions wherein there was a place for everyone.
      (2) Make it easier to make a living by, for example, simplifying rules and eliminating some of the credentialism.
      (3) Make it easier to live a virtuous life by simplifying the rules and consequences. For example, delineate the major crimes and provide certain and quick verdicts, and return marriage to status whereby you have the obligations of marriage, if married, but none (such as child support) if not. married

(4) Explore ways to replace the social welfare system with cash supplements for low-wage earners.
(5) End policies that subsidize births by low-income women or any other category of women.
(6) Shift the flow of immigration from mainly those admitted under nepotistic rules to those mainly admitted under competency rules.

5. Educational implications of IQ
   A. Limits on general improvements in education
      (1) Student success and expectations must be reexamined in context of cognitive distribution, with realization that many students will not achieve the expected basic level of education.
      (2) Most parents do not want a drastic increase in student work load.
      (3) The average student does not have the incentive to work harder in high school since it does not pay off in better jobs or wages, or unless the student wants to go to a Yale.
      (4) Employers are unlikely to place an emphasis on high school performance and colleges are not inclined to shrink their student body through higher admission standards.
      (5) Reform at the national level is compromised by political forces that, for example, make it difficult to raise teacher certification standards or national educational standards, which means reform must originate at the local level from parents and teachers.
   B. Recommendations
      (1) Federal support of parental school choice
      (2) Establish a federal prize scholarship program competitively based on standardized test performance, for example, granting students $20,000 to $25,000 on top of any other aid they might receive.
      (3) Reallocate some federal money from the disadvantaged to the gifted so as to bring about a better balance, and rescind regulations that might discourage localities from doing the same.

(4) Revive the concept of the "educated man" or "educated person" whereby our most gifted students, from elementary school through the university, are trained in the classical sense of what it means to be educated, being able, for example, to write and argue logically, and to know history, literature, arts, ethics, the sciences, and so on. The future of our society rests on this group.

The Fiery Furnace

These scholarly works documenting black-white IQ differences as a factor in our school and life performance force us to face the issue. The fuse, Of course, is the claim of heritable racial IQ differences. Most in academia, as elsewhere, fiercely dispute it. However, the issue is raised by serious scholars and, automatically, even scornfully, to reject their contributions -- and further excoriate them for making them -- could deprive us of invaluable insights. Yet, on our part, and on the part of many in the larger society, more or less, that is what has happened, their works igniting a fiery furnace.

Stoking

Thomas Sowell. Thomas Sowell, making an informative case, is one of the cooler respondents, however. Sowell does not dispute the notion that IQ is partially heritable; his point is that there is no racial difference in that heritability (242:229). Statistically analyzing mental test data for a variety of groups and subgroups -- including Mexican American, Puerto Ricans, Polish Americans, Irish Americans, Oriental Americans, Italian Americans, European immigrants, blacks, black females, black males -- his findings lead him to conclude that black IQ scores are not unique, neither in level nor pattern. Rather, both the level and pattern are similar to other groups in similar socioeconomic circumstances -- a mean of around 85-90 and test scores that are low on abstractions and higher on the concrete. And, he argues, as the socioeconomic status of those groups has risen, so have their IQ scores, by as much as 20 points or more. We must note that the time period (around 1920) during which their mean IQ score was around 85-90 for some of those groups, Sowell says their circumstances were similar to ours.

> However, some forty or fifty years later (roughly two generations), their scores were at or above the national average of 100. Sowell does not set a time period for an equivalent rise for us. However, Harvard psychologist, Steven Pinker, in personal agreement with Sowell's thesis, somewhat does, explaining that, due to slavery and segregation, the experience of African Americans is not comparable to that of immigrants or rural isolates, and, thus, the rise would probably take longer (210:144).

On the other hand, whereas Sowell himself does not set a time period, he does set the criterion of a rising socioeconomic status. Clearly, in the environment-predominates camp with which Jensen-Herrnstein-Murray are at odds, given Sowell's thesis, as our socioeconomic status rises we would expect our mean IQ, likewise, to rise -- *and* to a level comparable to other groups, including whites of the same socioeconomic status. However, Herrnstein and Murray's data show this not to be the case (121:286-88), suggesting, in Jensen's formulation, the role of the environment as a "threshold variable" whose adverse effect can limit IQ potential but whose positive effect cannot exceed that of its inherent potential. In sum, in their view, we are not born with a blank IQ slate which can be environmentally and potentially limitlessly filled with the ability to think, reason, problem-solve, and otherwise perform mental functions. That slate, they argue, contrary to the claim of Sowell and others (and Pinker's personal opinion), differs, by race.

William F. Brazziel. The late professor emeritus of the University of Connecticut, William Brazziel, departed from the reasoned response of Sowell. He wrote in reply to the invitation for letters in reaction to Jensen's article in the <u>Harvard Educational Review</u>. Brazziel fulminates:

> Fortunately, doubts about the ability of black and yellow people to master war, finance, science and technology are waning rapidly in both white and black minds. The imprecision of standardized testing is now clear to most literate people and the criminal use to which they are put in schools is also becoming clearer. Black history has made people aware that white people did *not* [emphasis in original] give America such things as the spotlight, the shoe last [sic], heart operations and sugar refining but that black people did

this. That John Smith did not develop corn and tobacco but learned to grow these crops from the Indians. And the beat goes on. People are now witnessing with their very eyes the fact of black youth finally given a half of a chance at education and jobs and being able to make exotic formulas for bombs and napalm as well as anyone else. As a result of all this, I think the present set-to might be the last go-round for white supremacy psychological theory (21:349).

In his conclusion, Brazziel expresses the belief that "the most potent strategy in the end will prove to be a combination of early stimulation and imprinting, and integrated schools with teachers who are free of racial and social class prejudices. IQ test will also be eliminated from the schools" (21:256).

Glenn Loury. We can also turn to the aforementioned Brown University black economis, Glenn Loury. Somewhat more measured in his response -- but only somewhat -- he still ends up calling Herrnstein-Murray's Bell Curve a "condescending apologia" and accuses them of "engaging in the crudest of racial generalization" (155:303-09). Yet, he concedes that they have "stated the facts of this matter." What bothers him is their belief that there is nothing that can be done about these facts, that is, the black-white IQ differences, a position which he declares to be a "posture of resignation." Having so declared, one reads further to find out what *he* would do, but in vain -- almost. One infers he thinks that "intelligence isn't everything" and that, rather than focusing on racial IQ differences, we ought to be "stressing individualism." Only when we stress individualism, we stress differences and reasonable acceptance of and respect for those differences. So one gathers that Loury thinks it is okay to recognize individual differences but, apparently, not group differences.

Squelching

Brazziel and Loury alike indeed illustrate the emotional power of the racial IQ issue. It seems to touch the essence of our sense of self-worth. Much too hot to handle, their suggestions steer clear of the IQ gap, except in the case of Brazziel, who would put the matter to rest: just abolish IQ testing. No shock or surprise, however. As Pinker tells us in the subtitle of his best-selling book, <u>The Blank Slate</u>, we live during a time of <u>The Modern Denial of Human Nature</u> (210). It is not the everyday, routine kind of denial; it is of the quasi-religious variety -- a kind of blind faith that "the human mind has no inherent structure and can be inscribed at will by society or ourselves" (210:2-3).

"Heretics and infidels!" That is what they -- Jensen-Herrnstein-Murray -- are: heretics and infidels who are proclaiming, in Brazziel's words, "white supremacy psychological theory" -- or who, as seen by Loury, have written a "condescending apologia" and are "engaging in the crudest of racial generalization." And that is why so many have not stopped stoking the fire, least of all, we African Americans for we *know* that when we make measured intelligence (IQ) a factor, we are going to come out on the short end. We know that we do not measure up to the dominant group, notwithstanding the fact that, to repeat Brazziel:

> Black history has made people aware that white people did *not* [emphasis in original] give America such things as the spotlight, the shoe last [sic - lace?], heart operations and sugar refining but that black people did this. That John Smith did not develop corn and tobacco but learned to grow these crops from the Indians. And the beat goes on.

But Brazzie, presumably, well knew that "the beat goes on" for only a short time and its sounds are relatively muted and confined; inspirational history is not to be confused with factual history. For what Washington biographer, Spencer, says about the status we had achieved by the midpoint of the last century is still basically true, which is that "he [the Negro] earned a name for himself in the fields of entertainment, athletics, and the arts, but had produced only a few men and women of national stature in such areas as statecraft, industry, scholarship, and law" (244:200). That is, just as there is an indisputable IQ gap, there is an indisputable corresponding contribution gap in fields which require higher IQs. Maybe someday we will measure up to whites, just as Sowell predicts, but that day is not at hand. The black-white IQ gap reported by Jensen-Herrnstein-Murray is an open secret, quite removed from "white supremacy psychological theory" or "condescending apologia." Jensen- Herrnstein-Murray did not discover it; they derived it from the scholarly literature, an analysis of existing data, and from a review of the accumulated and extensive research findings based on the use of diverse instruments. Only they were "heretics," "infidels," and "white supremacist" enough to come out, proclaim it, and make it a matter of policy and programmatic discussion. No sweeping it under the rug.

At the very least, as Pinker declares, "A conventional summary is that about half of the variation in intelligence, personality, and life outcomes is heritable --a correlate or an indirect product of genes" (210: 374). He declares it to be a "stable property" which can be linked to such features of the brain as its "overall size, amount of gray matter in the frontal lobes, speed of neural conduction, and metabolism of cerebral glucose" (210:150). He notes, further, that "it predicts some of the variation in life outcomes, such as income and social status" (210:150). And on the possibility of racial IQ differences, his personal opinion aside, Pinker indicates that the research evidence suggests that the inbred nature of the different races has produced a "somewhat different distribution of gene frequencies," which makes racial genetic differences "biologically possible" (210:144).

Going further, what Jensen-Herrnstein-Murray, have said yes, not only are racial IQ differences "biologically possible," there is evidence for their heritable existence. We must bear in mind Pinker's point that scientists have linked IQ to such features of the brain as overall size and amount of gray matter in the frontal lobes and, if IQ *potential* is to be altered, it is logical to assume that these features must be altered and, further, to assume that such alteration is possible only through evolution. In effect, Jensen-Herrnstein-Murray argue that these features largely determine our IQ.

Still simmering

Therefore, the controversy goes on. The Jensen-Herrnstein-Murray attribution of the black-white IQ gap being due mainly to genetics rather than to environmental differences remains very much on the burner (58a; 471a). Of the several books that have kept it aflame is one by University of Michigan psychologist Richard Nisbett, Intelligence and How to Get It: Why Schools and Cultures Count, which is considered by Rushton and Jensen to be the most comprehensive and encompassing (471b). Nisbett sets out to refute Jensen-Herrnstein-Murray as well as a more recent research update by Jensen as junior author in collaboration with late University of Western Ontario (Canada) psychologist, J. Philippe Rushton, in their joint article in 2005, "Thirty Years of Research on Race Differences in Cognitive Ability" (438b). The article reaffirms Jensen's earlier research interpretation as to a hereditary explanation for the black-white IQ gap.

Nisbett, however, sees no hereditary basis for the gap. He does not question what Pinker points out to be conventional thinking that IQ is about 50 percent heritable, but he takes the position that 50 percent is probably the maximum, the rest due largely to the environment and to a small amount to measurement error. As for the black-white IQ difference, Nisbett asserts that "Genes account for none [yes, none!] of the difference in IQ between blacks and whites; measurable environmental factors plausibly account for all of it" (188a:118). To make his case, Nisbett relies on an array of data, including racial ancestry data and data showing a closing of the gap over the past 30 to 60 years. His case boils down to this: the heritable IQ of blacks and white is the same, the difference we measure is attributed to environmental factors. Make their environments equivalent, and you make their IQs equivalent. In Nisbett's mind, what clinches his claim are the "IQ gains in the past generation or so." Blacks have gained "about 5 points on whites over the past thirty years," Nisbett points out, and, further, "blacks of today [have] higher IQs than the whites of an earlier period in our history" (188a:232-33).

In a 2010 article entitled, "Race and IQ: A Theory-Based Review of the Research in Richard Nisbett's *Intelligence and How to Get It*," Rushton and Jensen extensively responded, finding, they said, "Nisbett's errors of omission and of commission so major, so many, and so misleading that they forced us to write a particularly long and negative review" (438c:31). And long it is, covering 14 topics of contention, debunking (among other things) Nisbett's claim of a black 5-point IQ gain over the last thirty years, and in the end declaring: "Contrary to many hopes and some claims, the narrowing of the gap in social conditions between Blacks and Whites has not led to any change in the magnitude of the Black-White IQ difference in over 100 years" (438c:32). They observe that there are two models in explaining this gap: the *culture-only model* (0% genetic - 100% environmental) and the *hereditarian model* (50%

genetic - 50% environmental), clearly casting themselves as proponents of the latter -- the debate commonly termed environmentalists versus hereditarians.

While far more heated, the acrimony reminds one of the previously discussed "acting white" controversy. Ainsworth-Darnell and Downey, notable among others, attacked Fordham-Ogbu's theories, particularly "acting white," and Ogbu responded. In this case, Nisbett is one of the leaders in the attack on Rushton and Jensen, and they responded. The reminder goes deeper. In both instances, one can discern a common tension, the one that is intrinsic to our two traditions: self versus system -- responsibility, or control, internally or externally located. The innate race factor, of course, makes a huge difference. Cut through the innate race factor, however (which often must be done to get to what is actually going on), and it can be seen that when it comes to our black problems, we have another issue whereby those problems get cast in the mode of internal responsibility versus external responsibility. The question remains: who is responsible. Is it us, or, in some way, is it the system? In this instance, the argument of Nisbett and the environmentalists seem to be: we blacks are not responsible for our IQ; historical conditions and the system-driven environment are. Rushton-Jensen-Herrnstein-Murray and the hereditarians, on the other hand, seem to argue: we blacks are responsible for our IQ because, for the most part, it is innately determined, the environment serving (in Jensen's framing) as a threshold variable which, given severe deprivation, can depress it, but, however enriched, cannot raise it above its innate potential.

Black-White IQ Differences Explained

In trying to dissect the "acting white" controversy, the research was reviewed, in particular, the Ainsworth-Darnell and Downey study, and a verdict was rendered. In this instance, the topic is far more technical, and analysis of the research requires considerable more in-depth knowledge and expertise than is herein brought to bear. Yet, in the interest of program design, in this instance too, there is a need to come up with a verdict -- of sorts. Hence, we turn to an expert, Rushton, and to others who themselves have turned to many experts.

Joe L. Rempson

How races came about and how they came to have different IQs - - Rushton

The expert is the aforementioned late J. Philippe Rushton.[22] He helps us to begin at the beginning. His name might understandably cause many of us to recoil because it is famously associated with the hereditarian explanation for black-white IQ differences. But it would be a mistake not to recognize that, controversial though his race theories are, and as some of his race activities were, they, at least, provide a basis for thinking about the issue before us: black-white IQ differences. Insofar as could be ascertained -- and no claim is being made for an exhaustive search -- no one else has produced a comparable alternative explanatory model. Applying the r/K Selection theory explained below, Rushton set forth his race application of it in his controversial book, first published in unabridged form in 1995, <u>Race, Evolution, and Behavior: A Life History Perspective</u>, reliance herein being placed on its 2nd Special Abridged Edition in 2000. The r/K Selection theory depicts two environmental extremes, each eliciting certain behaviors from its population, those behaviors, in turn, producing traits which enable adaptation to those environments. Although replaced by what is called the Life History Theory, the environmental influence which it theorizes remains a constant; it is Rushton's application of the theory to race which seems so much in dispute.

Physical differences. First, Rushton addresses physical differences among the races. He attributes those differences to climatic differences among the three racial regions: Africa, Europe, and Asia (438a:40). The human species, he notes, originated in Africa and migrated to the other two regions. Africans are black due to the melanin in the body to let in *less* of the severe sunrays, the melanin giving the skin a dark color. Europeans, on the other hand, were exposed to a climate that was colder and cloudy. As a result, they developed lighter skin and hair to let in *more* sun to provide the body the needed Vitamin D. Asians, even though they had less cloud cover and more sun than the Europeans, had an even colder climate. Therefore, they developed a thicker layer of fat to protect

---

[22] The discussion in this paragraph is based on the following source: http://en.wikipedia.org/wiki/J._Philippe_Rushton 13 July 2012.

themselves from the severe cold. The thicker layer of fact, in turn, reduces the visibility of the red blood vessels close to the skin, producing a yellow color.

Their climatic differences also produced differences in the number of children they had. Due to the warm and unstable climate which bred droughts, storms, and diseases, Africans had a high death rate and to assure survival had to have many children (r-strategy). The climate of Europeans and Asians, on the other hand, was more stable and healthier, survival being insured by having fewer children and caring well for them (K-strategy).

Mental differences. Rushton theorizes that climatic differences lead to mental differences as well.

In Africa, food and warmth were available all year round. To survive the cold winters, the populations migrating northwards had to become more inventive. They had to find new sources of food and methods for storing it. They needed to make clothing and shelters to protect against the elements. Without them, the people would have died. Both parents had to provide care to help their young survive in the harsher climates.

Whites and Orientals in Eurasia had to find food and keep warm in the colder climates. In the tropics, plant foods were plentiful all year round. In Europe and Asia they were seasonal and could not be found during many winter and spring months.

To survive the long winters, the ancestors of today's Whites and Orientals made complex tools and weapons to fish and hunt animals. They made spearheads that could kill big game from a greater distance and knives for cutting and skinning. Fires, clothes and shelters were made for warmth. Bone needles were used to sear animal skins together and shelters were made from large bones and skins.

Making special tools, fires, clothing and shelters called for higher intelligence. Moving 'Out of Africa' meant moving into a K-type life-history strategy. That meant higher IQ, larger brains, slower growth, and lower hormone levels. It also meant lower levels of sexuality, aggression, and impulsive behavior. More family stability, advanced planning, self-control, rule-following, and longevity were needed (438a:41).

In sum, as regards black-white IQ differences, Rushton, drawing upon DNA and fossil evidence, traces the origin of those differences partly to genetically transmitted adaptations in response to geographic conditions which required different mental abilities. The IQ of blacks, therefore, is what it is, not because of some pathology (or innately ordained inferiority), but -- as Ogbu argues with respect to "acting white" -- because of adaptation, in this case adaptation, not to an oppositional culture, but to a warm and stable climate with available year-round food. Survival did not require the higher intelligence needed by whites and Orientals in colder and more adverse environments. Many, if not most, in the scientific community dispute his theory, in some cases, even denying the concept of race. So, we are left to exercise our own wherewithal. Rushton has provided grist for the mill of hereditarians; environmentalists would seem to be in need of a credible competing theory. Not credible is the decisive role which many have given to the environment, leading Lasch-Quinn, for example, to call it "a new kind of determinism" and Steve Pinker, in his book title, to refer to it as "the blank slate: the modern denial of human nature" (150a:114-15; 210).

How races came about and came to have different IQs - - other experts

Harvard-trained psychologist, Mark Snyderman, and the late political scientist, Stanley Rothman, of Smith College teamed up to write <u>The IQ Controversy, the Media and Public Policy</u> (446a). In it, they report the responses of 661experts (the respondents from the 1020 surveyed) in the field of social science concerning the role of heredity in IQ. Ninety-four percent (94%) felt that heredity plays a substantial role in intelligence, and when it came to black-white IQ differences, a plurality of forty-five percent (45%), who did not want to be publicly identified, felt that these differences are due both to genes and the environment (471c). The response of the remainder was as follows: 14% did not answer, 24% said there was not enough evidence to draw a conclusion, 1% that it was entirely genetic, and 15% that it was entirely environment.

In response to Herrnstein-Murray's <u>The Bell Curve</u>, the American Psychological Association (APA) had a special task force to examine the authors' data. The Association is the scientific and professional organization that represents psychologists worldwide. Its task force, composed of 11 experts, published its findings in a report entitled, "Intelligence: Knowns and Unknowns" (424a). The report said that the authors were correct in their conclusion that IQ is substantially influenced by both genetics and the environment, but did not feel that their data provided any *direct* evidence of genetic racial differences, while, by inference, it indirectly did (471a). It felt that there was no adequate explanation for the difference.

So, based on these experts, in explaining the black-white IQ gap, we can say that while the 11 APA experts did not render a verdict, the plurality of the other experts come down on the side of the hereditarians in that they give both heredity and environment substantial roles in racial IQ differences. Snyderman and Rothman report, however, that in their study, this plurality did not wish to be publicly identified for fear that they might be subject to the same kind of attack as Jensen. Even so, we have a sample of what they *really* think.

IQ and School Success

The aforementioned task force of the APA reported that studies show a .50 correlation between IQ scores and school grades, meaning that IQ accounts for about 25 percent of grade variance, the remaining variance due to home-student-school factors. Those home-student-school factors have been variously found to be a nourishing home environment, teacher quality, high academic and behavioral demands, student interest and effort, and combined parent-peer-teacher support (208a: 93-108).

Different studies, however, have arrived at different correlations between IQ scores and school grades (164: 134). Following are some of those correlations and the percent of school achievement variance for which they account:

- **33 (11%)**
- **40 (16%)**
- **43 (19%)**

- 49 (24%)
- 60 (36%)
- 63 (40%)
- 71 (50%)

The correlations and variances do not tell the entire story. The APA suggests that the relationship between IQ scores and school performance seems to be ubiquitous, observing that "Wherever it has been studied, children with high scores on tests of intelligence tend to learn more of what is taught in school than their lower-scoring peers" (424a:82).

Further, as indicated in Chapter 3, the meta-analyses of Wang, Haertel, and Walberg revealed that two IQ-connected variables, *metacognitive processes* and *cognitive processes* rank second (2nd) and third (3rd), respectively, among 28 variables found to influence student learning [*metacognitive processes* involve a higher level of intelligence wherein there is mental awareness and the ability to employ self-regulating and self-monitoring mental strategies; *cognitive processes* involve fluid and crystallized general intelligence]. Their respective T scores were 63.8 and 61.3, 32.9 being the lowest T score. The number one rank (1st) went to classroom management, with a T score of 64.8.

Some IQ Basics

From this review and other sources reviewed, some relevant IQ basics can be derived. They are as follows:

1. IQ is correlated with a range of social and behavioral outcomes, but *alone* is not necessarily determinative of those outcomes. Factors such as emotional intelligence and career orientation also play a role in those outcomes.
2. As regards school, there is about a .50 correlation between IQ scores and school grades, meaning that IQ accounts for about 25 percent of grade variances; the remaining variance is due to such factors as student interest and effort, parent and peer support, and teaching styles and methods (424a).
3. There is a black-white IQ gap of about one standard deviation, or 15 points, black average IQ being about 85, whites about 103. At least some of the lag in black IQ is due to heritable

differences. On the Stanford-Binet IQ classification, our average IQ of 85 puts us in the *low average range* (79-88), while the average IQ of 100 for whites puts them the *average range* (89-110). Although below the average IQ of whites, our IQ is neither in the slow learner IQ range (68-78) nor in the defective IQ range (67 or below); it is in the *average* IQ range, only *low* average. That classification applies, not just to the Stanford-Binet IQ classification, also but to most of the other IQ test classifications (471m).

4. As shown by he graph which follows, there is a large overlap in black-white IQ, but at the extreme IQ ranges the differences are extreme, 20% of blacks falling in the mentally retarded category (IQ below 70) versus 5% of whites, while just 2.5% fall in the bright category (IQ of at least 115) versus 16% of whites. Throughout the upper half of the IQ range, blacks lag far behind whites at every level (393a). Similar differences at the extremes, by socioeconomic status (SES), are estimated in regard to children with IQs below 75 (139:83). For blacks at the highest SES level, the percentage with children whose IQs are below 75 is 3.1% versus 0.5% for whites, followed at the next four descending levels, correspondingly by these percentages: 14.5% versus 0.8%, 22.8% versus 3.1%, 37.8% versus 7.8%.

5. Due to whatever reasons, there are IQ differences among various racial/ethnic groups. Sources differ as to the exact magnitude of those differences, but the following average IQs of the indicaed groups, taken from Rushton and Jensen, provide a fairly representative profile from among those encountered (438c):

Jewish 113
East Asian 106
White 100
Hispanic 90
South Asian 87
African American 85
Sub-Saharan Africa 70

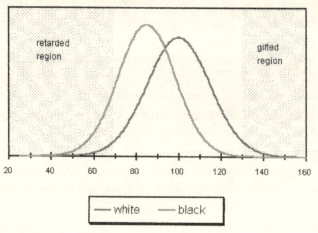

Figure 33. black and white IQ distributions. Reproduced with permission of La Griffe du Lion (393a).

6. IQ differences are driven by both heredity and environment. Heredity makes upsomething in the range of 50 percent, 40 percent being the minimum and 80 percent the maximum.
7. After about ages 8-10 [some say 8], IQ tends to be stable and, except in the case of extreme environmental deprivation, attempts to raise it have met with little success, especially with respect to reasoning and problem-solving skills [that is, to pure or fluid intelligence versus acquired or crystallized intelligence]. The extent to which IQ can be raised is a function of environmental factors, such as prenatal care, parenting, and schooling.
8. The percent of school achievement accounted for by IQ has been shown to be as low as 11 percent and as high as 50 percent, the median being about 25 percent. The remainder is attributable to home-student-school factors.
9. Two IQ-connected variables, metacognitive processes and cognitive processes, have been found to influence student learning to about the same degree as the factor which has been found to exert the most influence, classroom management.

IQ as Cause of Black Student Poor School Performance

From these basics, it can be concluded that ***IQ is a major cause of black students' poor school performance, but home-student-school factors are more decisive***. In particular, they show the following:

1. Our students fall disproportionately at the lower end of the IQ range.
2. There is a correlation between IQ and school grades, IQ having been found to account for from 11 percent to 50 percent of the variance in their grades, 25 percent being the median.
3. Students with higher IQ scores learn more than those with lower IQ scores. That is, the higher students' IQ score the more they learn, while the lower students' IQ score the less they learn.
4. Two IQ-connected variables, *metacognitive processes* and *cognitive processes*, exert a powerful influence on learning, only barely below that of classroom management, which exerts the most powerful influence.

Given this research evidence, not to address IQ as a major cause of black student poor school performance is to retreat into the kind of world of make-believe which Frazier said characterized black middle-class life during his time, the 1950s. In such a world, fear and shame lead us to pretend that our IQ is equal to the IQ of whites, or that IQ is not a factor in our students' school success, when, indisputably, the research evidence shows otherwise. The fact is that if one or more of the home-student-school factors is not in order -- which for many of our students is typically the case -- these IQ factors *can be, and are likely to be, decisive*, which makes them a major cause of their poor school performance. Based on their impressive interdisciplinary meta-analyses (discussed in Chapter 3), Wang, Haertal, and Walberg put it this way: "… the home functions as the most salient out-of-school context for student learning, amplifying or diminishing the school's effect on learning" -- and please note, amplifying or *diminishing* (462a:278). Further, as Jensen points out, in instances where students' IQ is below the mean, environment does not contribute as much to their school success as it otherwise would.

Better, therefore, to be guided by John 8:32, "and ye shall know the truth, and the truth shall make you free," than to suffer the dysfunctional and maladaptive behavior which ensues from denial and self-rejection, as well as from the negative core identity of which such denial and self-rejection are symptoms. As Shelby Steele puts it:

Fears can never be addressed and overcome when they are redefined as something else and then externalized [such as, in this instance, when we retort that the tests are biased]. For the first time in our history, we do not seem to have a clear sense of our real challenges. Only a knowledge of our vulnerabilities can give us this, and only the continued recomposing [the denial of one reality through the creation of another reality to cover over the real one] of them can hide this knowledge from us (247a:61).

Raising IQ to Raise Achievement: The Problem and the Solution

Problem: difficult to raise

Although IQ is a major cause of our students' poor school achievement, intervention results show that little or nothing can be done to raise IQ. Interventions to raise IQ have not been promising (121:403-10, 414-15; 139:96-108; 258a:97). Yet, it is far too important to do little or nothing about it for, as the correlations below from different studies show, IQ has impressively high correlations with school achievement. Marzano points out that correlations of .50 or more are rare in the social sciences (164:143-35; 133-34).

IQ and Achievement	Background and Achievement
.33 (11%)*	.21 (4%)
.40 (16%)	.46 (21%)
.43 (19%)	.46 (21%)
.49 (24%)	.64 (41%)
.60 (36%)	.65 (42%)
.63 (40%)	.66 (44%)
.71 (50%)	.66 (44%)
	.74 (55%)

*The percentages in parentheses indicate the percent of school achievement variance for which the correlations account.

Solution: focus instead on knowledge and skills to raise achievement

As it turns out, however, we do not have to settle for doing little or nothing about our students' IQ because there is an alternative: focus on another type of IQ which was identified in 1971 by the late psychologist, Raymond Cattell. It is the aforementioned *crystallized intelligence*, which is defined as the knowledge and skills acquired through our experiences, instruction, and other interactions. The original type of intelligence that we always talk about, pure or *fluid intelligence*, was identified in 1903 by French psychologist, Alfred Binet, with the help of Theodore Simon. It is defined as our natural or inherited ability to think abstractly and, without any prior knowledge, to figure out things on our own (our problem-solving skills). Put simply, fluid intelligence refers to our abstract thinking and problem-solving skills, crystallized intelligence refers to our knowledge and skills. One is more or less inherited while, to a meaningful degree, the other is acquired. That is one crucial difference between the two. The other is that crystallized intelligence, as evident from the above correlations, is more strongly associated with school achievement than fluid intelligence.

The main difference is their malleability. We can do little about pure IQ but a lot about crystallized IQ, our knowledge-based and skill-based IQ. Based on a review of twin studies, Jensen estimates that "individual differences in scholastic performance are determined less than half as much by heredity as are differences in intelligence" (139: 58). Whereas, for example, heredity might explain 50 percent of the differences in IQ scores, Jensen is saying that it would explain less than 25 percent of the differences in achievement because achievement is less than half as heritable as IQ.

A focus, then, on our other type of IQ, crystallized intelligence -- as both Jensen and Marzano, for example recommend -- means concentration on a form of intelligence about which a lot can be done and which, if done, may have a greater impact on students' achievement than is exerted by their fluid IQ. That is, our students' intelligence is a major cause of their poor school achievement, and, whereas, so far, interventions to raise IQ have not succeeded, their intelligence can be more effectively remedied by addressing it in its crystallized form, the form of their knowledge and skills. The measurement of success in addressing intelligence as a cause of school performance thus becomes, not a gain in students' IQ scores, but a gain in their school achievement, which measures their intelligence in the form of their knowledge and skills, or of their background in a given domain.

It must be noted, however, that fluid intelligence and crystallized intelligence are related. The research shows that there is a correlation between the two, between our abstract thinking and problem-solving ability and the knowledge and skill we can acquire. The more inherited thinking and problem-solving ability one possesses the more knowledge and skills one will acquire. For a given student, however, there is no way of knowing the limits imposed by inherited IQ on that acquisition, and, therefore, exploration supported by sustained work and effort are called for in enabling every student to make full and effective use of his/her inherited potential.

Solution: forget about IQ?

The knowledge and skills approach, and consequent attention to achievement, might be interpreted to mean that we should ignore IQ as we commonly think of it. But that would be a mistake. As observed, of itself, pure IQ is impressively related to school achievement, and further, research shows its indisputable association (not determination, but association) with an array of outcomes. When one reads, for example, that Albert Einstein probably had an IQ of 160 (super-genius range) we are reminded of that very fact. The two main points being made here are that, so far, interventions to raise IQ have not worked and though strongly associated with school achievement, background knowledge is even more strongly associated with it. Further, it must be observed that, notwithstanding its association with an array of outcomes, the role of IQ role in some of those outcomes is problematic. Herrnstein and Murray, for example, conclude the following as regards high school dropouts: "...the one social problem that has a widely acknowledged cause in cognitive ability--school dropout--also has a strong and complex socioeconomic link" (121:154).

Indirect focus. Most emphatically, these considerations do not justify our forgetting about IQ. The research suggests that we should forget about focusing on it *directly*, and instead focus on it *indirectly* -- as aforementioned, through prenatal care, improved nutrition, an enriched home and community environment, and – yes -- through school achievement.

The Commission on Children at Risk makes one of the best cases for this indirect approach. The Commission was composed of 33 doctors, research scientists, and mental health and youth service professionals across various disciplines encompassing diverse philosophical and political perspectives. In its publication, Hardwired to Connect: The New Scientific Case for Authoritative Communities, the Commission called for an end to the IQ debate. Its message: "The old 'nature versus nurture' debate -- focusing on whether heredity or environment is the main determinant of human conduct -- is no longer relevant to serious discussions of child well-being and youth programming" (41:19). "It is futile," it adds, "to ask which one is dominant. Instead, new scientific findings are teaching us to marvel at how wonderfully the two interact -- not like boxers, with each one trying to knock the other out, but more like dancers, with each subtle move producing a reciprocating move" (41:19). In sum, as the Commission sees the lesson of recent scientific evidence: "**SOCIAL CONTEXT CAN ALTER GENETIC EXPRESSION**" [emphases added]. As a result, the innate factor becomes tangential; the social context or environment takes center stage, inhibiting or nurturing our full IQ potential.

IQ Immutability. One is hard put to find in the literature someone who says that IQ *cannot* be altered. Seemingly, every day scientists are coming up with new information, even discovering, for example, contrary to Darwinian thinking, that some evolutionary human traits can evolve relatively rapidly rather than being drawn out over millions of years. And who knows what, over time, the effect of nutrition and other environmental factors can have on IQ, as "the Flynn effect" suggests. Even hereditarian Jensen observed that "High heritability by itself does not necessarily imply that the characteristic is immutable" (139:45). Nor, Herrnstein-Murray suggest, is the black-white IQ gap necessarily immutable, observing that:

...the instability of test scores across generations should caution against taking the current ethnic differences as etched in stone. There are things we do not yet understand about the relation between IQ and intelligence, which may be relevant for comparisons not just across times but also across cultures and races (121:309).

Moreover, they point out (as have others), in the last few decades, blacks have closed the black-white IQ gap by 3 points, which, though few, 3 points can make a significant difference in such outcomes as poverty rates and children born to single mothers (188a: 93-118; 325b).

"The Flynn effect." In fact, if "the Flynn effect" proves out, a continued rise is probable, for it is said that a rising tide lifts all boats -- and "the Flynn effect" depicts a rising IQ tide (471i). The effect bears the name of political scientist, James Flynn, Professor Emeritus, University of Otago, New Zealand, who is credited with calling attention to it, whereas it is Herrnstein and Murray who coined the phrase, "the Flynn effect." Based on an examination of standardized test results since around 1930, "the Flynn effect" posits that -- due to environmental factors -- there has been a steady and worldwide rise in both fluid and crystallized intelligence IQ scores (some say 3 points a decade). Not surprisingly, the claim is ridden with controversy, but the existence of a rise is apparently an arithmetical fact. But *interpretations* of the meaning of that documented fact are multiple and contentious. For purposes here, no need to address the issue, the only point being to indicate the existence of research which suggests the possibility that, due to environmental factors, we could raise our average IQ of 85 (that average also in dispute), which may or may not mean that we could further close the black-white IQ gap, because whites could also be raising their IQ at the same time. But even it might not close the gap, more important is that it could raise ours.

Artful dancers with our IQ nature. So perhaps the chances of our raising our IQ leaves us on the environmental stage, much like artful dancers, suggests the Commission on Children at Risk, interacting with our IQ nature and striving for a "reciprocal move," as the Commission puts it. Who knows how the dance turns out. The idea is to embrace and refine it, drawing sustenance and satisfaction from its challenge. If, in the process, our IQ is raised, good. If it is not raised, so be it; some things nature has put beyond our reach to alter. **We, therefore, *manage* our lot and move on, our wellbeing resting, not on whether we can raise our IQ, but on whether we can raise our students' achievement and, it needs to be emphasized, enable them to develop their abilities.**

Solution: nurturing abilities

On the matter of developing their abilities, we must think of those abilities in the same context that we think of IQ: as enabling students' school success. Schools have traditionally done too little to tap into our students' abilities. It is understood that the school cannot do everything, but in view of an often impoverished home and neighborhood environment, when it comes to our students, schools need to do much more in this domain. Specialized schools and programs, for example, together with cooperative relationships with various providers, can and should be means to achieving that goal.

IQ and Community Success (Adaptation)

So far, the discussion has focused on IQ and student success. We now turn to IQ and community success, or the ability of us blacks to meet what is herein termed **Adaptation Requirements**. Those requirements are for us to get the education and jobs, and to establish the stable families and neighborhoods which will enable us to enter the mainstream. The issue is whether our IQ helps to explain our failure to meet these requirements, just it helps to explains the failure of our students to meet the academic requirements of the school.

What IQ explains – in general

This is a issue famously addressed by previously discussed Herrnstein-Murray in their book, The Bell Curve (121). This is what they say regarding the role of IQ in the adaptation of the general population: "… large proportions of the people who exhibit the behaviors and problems that dominate the nation's social policy agenda have limited cognitive ability. Often they are near the definition for mental retardation...." (121:386).[23]

For those who fall throughout the lower half of the IQ range, however, they draw a more favorable conclusion. As previously quoted, they say:

> ...most people in the lower half of the cognitive distribution are employed, out of poverty, not on welfare, married when they have their babies, providing a nurturing environment for their children, and obeying the law (121:385).

> By the time people were even approaching average IQ, the percentages of people who were poor, had babies out of wedlock, provided poor environment for their children, or exhibited any other problem constituted small percentages of the population (121:536).

So, Herrnstein-Murray interpret their data as showing that, for the general population, IQ plays a role in its adaptation, but only for those with a depressed IQ.

What IQ explains – with respect to us African Americans

When it comes to us African Americans, however, perhaps surpringingly, Herrnstein-Murray did not find a relationship between IQ and the two crucial variables at the epicenter of our crisis and problems: marriage and illegitimacy. On these two variables, they say, our IQ does not explain the disparity in marriage and illegitimacy rates between us African Americans and whites and Latinos (121:329-31). For us African Americans, controlling for IQ does not meaningfully alter the disparity; for whites and Latinos, it does. That is, Herrnstein-Murray say that their data do not show that IQ helps to explains the disproportionately lower marriage rate or higher illegitimacy rate of blacks, whereas, for whites and Latinos, it does. Nor, when it comes to illegitimacy, they

---

[23] Insofar as could be ascertained, the authors do not give the definition, but do indicate that minority children in the bottom decile on one of the tests had an IQ of 80 or below. The IQ scores often cited for slow learners, as stated in Chapter 8, range from 68-78.

go on to say, do any of the other variables in their data base, or in any other data base known to them, explain the higher illegitimacy rate. The other variables which they specifically cite are socioenomic background, poverty, coming from a broken home, and education. On all of these other variables, like IQ, the proportion of out-of-wedlock births among black women is much higher than among white and Latino women. Their conclusion: IQ helps in explaining marriage and illegitimacy among whites and Latinos, but not among blacks; nor do normal socioeconomic indicators or education. As for why, they see it to be a matter not fully understood and under intense debate.

Other explanations [See also, concept of *environment-based* heritable change in gene function, Ch. 9]

The debate includes a range of explanatory factors (8, 9, 93, 96, 246). Frazier cites the following factors: strong biological sex instincts, high birth rate to enable preservation of race in face of debilitating hot climate (similar to Rushton's previously discussed r/K Selection theory), a West African culture which showed little care or responsibility for children, matrilineal African family, West African animistic and polytheistic religions which exalted sexual prowess over chastity, and mind of a "primitive man" (93:624-27). Although Frazier declared these esplanations to have been abandoned by sociologists, in his own later explanation, he discusses our African heritage (96). Surveying peoples' sex life in various African societies, he underlines sex as being part of societies' religious values. The importance they attached to sex was not for sex itself, but for reproductive purposes. Largely in the context of this value orientation, Frazier cites a range of practices and behaviors in which, as Africans, we engaged, not out of promiscuity, but as a matter of custom. Those practices and behaviors include the following: polygamy, permissive premarital and extramarital sexual relations, and permissive sexual relations between boys and girls.

In regard to our life in America, Frazier points to the disorganizing effects of slavery, emancipation, and urbanization. Those effects include the matriarchial family, the black female defined as a sexual object, and the black male's compensation for his inferior status by a demonstration of masculinity through sexual prowess. Dr. King, for example, takes notes of the hopelessness which, unconsciously, in protest, drives many of our black males to beat their wives and children (147:114). To these explanatory factors can be added the culture of poverty and, possibly, the extraverted sensation type personality of the black male, discussed in Chapters 7 and 11, respectively.

A recently discovered factor by the New York Times's The Upshot staff (Justin Wolfers, David Leonhardt, and Kevin Ouealy) can also be added: 1.5 million missing black men (474c). The researchers reveal that, mainly due to early death and imprisonment, 1.5 million of us African American men between the ages 25 to 54, considered the prime-age years, are missing from the life of our communities. As a result, for every 100 black women in this age group, there are just 83 black men; the comparable numbers for whites is 100 to 99. The numbers did not this way from birth. In childhood, they say, there are about as many boys as girls, but the gap begins to appear in the teens, widens in the 20s, and peaks in the 30s, where it persists through adulthood. According to research, the implications of the gap are disrruption, lower marriage rates, and higher illegitimacy rates.

Discussion

Chances are that if we were to do a factor analysis, at least in some way, we might find that all of these possible explanations play a role in the failure of our black community to meet Adaptation Requirements. While Frazier says that sociologists abandoned their earlier explanations cited above, the objective basis for their doing so is not clear. There seems to be an automatic tendency to dismiss any perceived unfavorable biological explanations – to say nothing of making them the subject of research -- but all of us humans are biological beings, reflecting the range of what is biologically possible. So, whereas such dismissal might be equality-reassuring, it is not necessarily justified. In any instance, it appears that we are dealing with something rather complex and perhaps not completely understandable without attention to all of the relevant variables. That we have 1.5 million missing black men provides a temping focus, but when we get into the questions of early death and imprisonment, which are said mainly to account for their being missing, we are brought back to the why question.

What seems fair to say is that marriage and family, as practiced here in America, was not practiced by us in Africa, and that our African heritage, combined with slave practices, worked against our uniform embrace of Americn family values. There was a misfit between who we were and who we had to become. Slavery aggravated the misfit. So have other factors, such as the culture of poverty and, possibly, certain personality attributes of the black male.

None of these considerations should lead to the neglect the IQ factor in community adaptation, just as we must not neglect the IQ factor in the case of our students' school adaptation. Herrnstein-Murray's finding that those who cause most of our social problems have low IQs, often even approaching mental retardation, given our disproportionate number in this category, is especially applicable to us African Americans. Only, since they did not find that IQ is a factor which helps to explain the gap in marriagte and illigetimacy rates between blacks and whites or between blacks and Latinos, we cannot, based on their study, single out IQ as an explanatory factor. When it comes to illegitimacy, Herrnstein-Murray did not find predictive any of the other standard variables either. But, obviously, in addressing the adaptation of our community, we must not ignore these other variables, for they, too, just like IQ, are associated, as Herrnstein-Murray's data show, with maladaptive outcomes.

Conclusion

The perplexity in assessing the role of IQ in the adaptation of our community leaves us, however, where it left Kerckhoff-Campbell in using their model to predict educational outcomes for the black male students (see Chapterr 6). It worked in an orderly and rational fashion for the 390 white male students, but, except for IQ, not for the 113 black male students. In Herrnstein-Murray's model, too, standard predictors of community adaptation did not work for us blacks, including IQ. So, whereas we can point to IQ as a factor in the school adaptation of our students, the data do not permit us do the same in regard to the adaptation of our community. Since, however, the APA concludes that, as our students' IQ stands, they can *substantially* improve their school performance, we can infer that, in the adaptation of both, we have more of an EQ problem than an IQ problem, especially when it comes to our community.

Joe L. Rempson

As for the failure of IQ to predict adaptation outcomes, Scott's thesis may provide a key to understanding why. Largely due to family dysfunction, we blacks have not uniformly forged the kind of "average expectable environments" which would foster in us a *"subjective sense* **of an** *invigorating sameness* **and** *continuity."* **As** argued in Chapter 9, it is the absence of such a sense of sameness, and the lack of a positive core identity which it signifies, which helps to explain why standard independent variables do not account for such outcomes among us blacks as marriage and illigetimacy rates.

Black-White IQ-Disparity Generalizations

In previous chapters (Chapters 3, 5, 6, and 7), the role of home and school in the success of black students and the culture of our students and community have been discussed. From that discussion, as it pertains to IQ, and from what has been said about IQ in this chapter, generalizations about what is known about the black-white IQ disparity have been formulated, along wth some of the major policy and programmatic implications of the disparity. Those generalizations follow.

> **Although there is a large black-white IQ overlap, blacks are vastly overrepresented at the lower extreme of the IQ range and vastly underrepresented in the upper levels of the range These disparities are associated with documented corresponding disparities in educational and social outcomes. While this correspondence underlines the importance of IQ, IQ often tends not to be the decisive factor, and on two key variables, marriage and illegitimacy, not, for us blacks, a documented factor at all. Emotional intelligence, or EQ, sometimes simply referred to as** *character,* **can be more important. Moreover, IQ tends to be stable. The extent to which it can be raised is a function of such environmental factors as prenatal care, parenting, and schooling. Therefore, for black students, since it is more malleable, academic achievement -- together with increased opportunities for ability development – is a more promising route to enhancing their school success than attempting to raise their IQ. In any case, research suggests that, as it stands, our students' IQ is not a barrier to a** *substantial improvement* **in**

their school performance. Other factors exert are more decisive influence, chief among them: teacher quality, high academic and behavioral demands, student interest and effort, and *combined* parent-peer-teacher support. Since the data suggest that IQ is not a significant factor in our community adaptation, nor is it then a barrier to a *substantial improvement* in its adaptation. In its case, too, other factors, especially character and culture, are more decisive. To the general query, can we lay the blame for the poor school performance of our students and for the social problems of the black community on our IQ lag, the research data justify the answer: as regards our students, yes, noticeably so, but not decisively so; as regards our community, no, not noticeably so.

Psychology of Black-White IQ Difference: Equality Amid Difference

Given these generalizations, it seems that the hereditarians have the upper hand in the black-white IQ controversy. However some of us may view them as "barking up the wrong tree," as Diamond puts it in the case of those giving validity to "acting white." So viewed, we can turn a deaf ear to their voices in the same way that a deaf hear has been turned to the voices of Alicia, Marc, and others when it comes to their cries as "acting white" victims. But on these pages, that will not be done.

Logically, some of the black-white IQ difference would have to be attributed to heredity. We can conjecture about how much, but not, it seems, about whether. The discussion elsewhere herein has highlighted the role of the inaccessible biological self in our thoughts, feelings, and functioning. Brooks and Eagleman, for example, devote entire books to the topic. As Pinker points out, we do not come into the world as blank slates -- not in regard to our physical characteristics, our personalities, nor any other attribute.

It is equally evident that groups differ in heritable traits, just as species throughout the plant and animal kingdom differ in heritable traits. It could be that intelligence is one of those traits to which this rule does not apply, but, so far, neither the weight of the research, nor experience and observation, justify making intelligence an exception. Individual and group IQ differences are a reality that we have to accept; otherwise, we operate on denial, wishful thinking, false hope, and make-believe -- from which, as has been the case, we can expect more harm than good.

Our challenge, as is the challenge of all humanity, is to learn to accept and respect our differences -- *all of them* -- both within and without our own group, and not to deny or to disparage those differences. That is not intended to imply an anything-goes world, but one of live and let-live, the right to life, liberty, and the pursuit of happiness being the guiding ideal. That ideal has served us African Americans, as it has the nation, fairly well so far and there is no reason to think that it will not continue to do so, whatever our IQs may be.

The inevitable outcome of acknowledging a black-white IQ gap and the herein derived black-white IQ-disparity generalization need not be a society any more hierarchical than it already is, as D'Souza, for example, seems to think is a possibility if the IQ differences are substantial, which appears to be the case (62:431-76). Nor need it mean a license for injustices. Equal opportunity and fairness, instrumental values in our society, can serve to prevent that occurrence and, where it does occur, to remedy it. More cannot be asked for or expected.

We African Americans must bite the IQ bullet. We must not see our IQ status as an obstacle or demon but as a description. Accepting it does not signify the coming end of the world; instead, it opens the door of self-acceptance to the world of self-pride -- a world in which we capitalize on our strengths and work on our weaknesses. Equal or not, if we make use of our intelligence, whatever its actual level, we can do -- as we have done (at least those of us who have put forth the effort) -- quite well in this country. **As pertains to the school performance of our students, we must bear in mind that the research indicates that it can be "substantially improved" as their IQ stands (and the reference for this IQ basic is cited above, that reference being the *American Psychological Association*)**. Problem-solving and crisis-solving require an examination of *all* of the *possible* contributing causes, however sensitive or forbidding.

If – as is the case -- intelligence is a factor in our life and schooling, we must confront and address it; it will not cease to be a factor or somehow go away, as some of us seem to think, simply because we denounce and demonize IQ testing and talk. Given that our respect is at issue, we would gain more by acknowledging and confronting the intelligence factor than by avoiding, denouncing, or demonizing it. The respect of others for us is based, not on who we want to be, but on who we are and what we make of who we are -- that is, on how we *manage* our existence. **Foremost, we do not have to be equal to the white man or to anyone else; given our citizenship equality and given equality of opportunity, we just have to feel that we are equal, "for as a man thinketh in his heart, so is he"** (Proverbs 23:7).

Perhaps **painfully and reluctantly**, that realization can allow us to *accept*, based on tests of intelligence, that so far, as a group, we African Americans have a lower level of measured intelligence than whites and some other groups. Further, the difference is due partly to genetic factors and partly to environmental factors which, if redressed, would likely make that difference at least significantly less. However, to date, whatever the explanation, consensus is that our group IQ has been shown to be 15 points below that of whites, theirs being about 103 on the IQ scale, ours about 85, with a 13.5-point standard deviation. Due to this difference, let us African Americans not be self-disparaging, self-rejecting, self-loathing, or self-deprecating. No reason to be, and let us not permit whites or others to lead us to be. We did not make ourselves, and, where lacking, let us show gratitude and pride for being members of the human family. Of course, whereas we did not make ourselves, we have to do a better job of *managing* ourselves, the reason that, herein, a **Child Family Rights Movement** is being proposed.

Our measured IQ difference is just that, a measured difference from whites. They are not superior. We are not inferior. We are always encountering those -- of whatever race -- who are smarter than us, speak better than us, look better than us, and so on, but it is doubtful if we think of them as *superior* to us -- *better* than us. Do we think of our doctor or lawyer as being superior to us? How about Michael Jordan? Or Bill Gates? Or, to recall the past, George Washington Carver or Albert Einstein? We may well see them as having (or having had) an edge on us, but *superior* to us -- *better* than us? That term covers a lot of territory and it is doubtful if we are willing to give others so much of an edge as to surrender that much territory to them. Our mindset is likely to be, and ought to be, what might be summed up as a prevailing human and cultural right: **though we may, in some ways, be different from any other, we are not less than any other, but have an equitable (fair) place in this society and in this world and that equitable (fair) place has to be respected and honored** (148:93-95). In Pinker's words:

> People are *qualitatively* [emphasis added] the same but may differ quantitatively. The quantitative differences are small in biological terms, and they are found to a far greater extent *among* [italics in original] the individual members of an ethnic group or race than *between* [italics in the original] ethnic groups or races (210:143).

In the same breath, it must be admitted that the idea that all groups are equal in their various characteristics, such as intelligence, is baseless. Social scientists have documented what we observe to be a fact of life: diversity, amid equality, is inherent in human existence and in human characteristics. That diversity places individuals and groups, not on some level playing field, but on an uneven terrain, and we do not control the evolutionary levers to make it otherwise; we can only play the hand which we have been dealt.

In chronicling the cultural history of manhood in America, sociologist, Michael Kimmel, of the State University of New York at Stony Brook, makes an applicable declaration. "Our popular impressions of equality," he writes, "have always meant the obliteration of difference--in a word, sameness--and this has fueled the anxieties of American manhood for too long." "We must," he goes on to write, "begin to imagine a world of equality in which we also embrace and celebrate difference...." (146:334). When it comes to IQ, we must do the same: "imagine a world of equality in which we also embrace and celebrate differences."

To be sure, there is something that is indeed the same, that is equal -- for all individuals and for all groups. That something is the value of our life. We know that our life is equal to that of any other human being, entitling us to "certain unalienable Rights, that among these are Life, Liberty, and the pursuit of Happiness."[24] So even if we

---

[24] From Declaration of Independence. Source: http://en.wikipedia.org/wiki/United_States_Declaration_of_Independence 30 November 2014.

take the test results to show that, to date, we are of lower intelligence, it does not mean that we are of *inferior* intelligence. To be of lower intelligence means just that: *lower* intelligence; it does not mean *inferior* intelligence, just as lower height (for example) means just that, lower height, not inferior height. Nor, in either case, would lower intelligence or lower height make one an inferior person. The term *lower* intelligence (again, as lower height, for example) makes a *descriptive* distinction; the term *inferior* intelligence makes that descriptive distinction an *invidious* distinction. That alteration, from descriptive to invidious, goes contrary to the ideal **universal norm** of respect for and acceptance of inherited and acquired individual and group differences. The Declaration of Independence enshrines the *equality of human life* as a sacred creed in American life, as does the United Nations Universal Declaration of Human Rights for life worldwide.

What the Declaration of Independence and the United Nations Universal Declaration of Human Rights do not enshrine, as no document or declaration can enshrine, is *equality of adaptation* in the way we live that life. How do we respond to our conditions and circumstances and to the imperatives of living? How do we *manage* our existence? That is a question of adaptation, which, of course, could ultimately lead us back to the question of intelligence. Be it so, adaptation dictates a different strategy, for even if intelligence lurks, we have more reason for optimism than despair. Our IQ *alone* is not the obstacle; make effective use of it and bring into play other factors, including the *range of abilities* which we possess – abilities, as Jenson notes, being something different from IQ -- and we can adequately meet our challenges. Those other factors are addressed in Chapter 12.

Neither Herrnstein and Murray nor Jensen paints a doomsday for us. As cited in the outline at the beginning of the chapter, they say the following about those of us who might be in the lower half of the IQ range (as applicable to the corresponding members of any other ethnic or racial group):

> …most people in the lower half of the cognitive distribution are employed, out of poverty, not on welfare, married when they have their babies, providing a nurturing environment for their children, and obeying the law. By the time people were even approaching

average IQ, the percentages of people who were poor, had babies out of wedlock, provided poor environment for their children, or exhibited any other problem constituted small percentages of the population (121:385,536).

Moreover, as stated, they point out (as have others), that in the last few decades we have closed the black-white IQ gap by 3 points which, though few, is enough to make a significant difference in such outcomes as poverty rates and children born to single mothers. "The Flynn effect" could bring additional raises and additional narrowing. A branch of research called cognitive neuroscience (brain science, as it is popularly called) is constantly coming up with something new. It has discovered, for example, that, contrary to traditional thinking, children can learn math before age five; and that we can accelerate the development of young students' frontal lobes, thereby improving their self-control in class (315). An intensive program for very young children with autism has been able to raise their IQ by as much as about 18 points (430). Who knows what it might come up with that will make our artful dance with our IQ nature a winning performance -- or indeed, whether the dance, in and of itself, will suffice?

Whatever the outcome, the success of our students and our race does not hinge on it. As our IQ stands, such intiatives as KIPP (Knowledge is Power Program) and the Carolina Abecedarian Early Childhood Project demonstrate that we can succeed;[25] we need only to make more full use of it and, equally, if not more important, make use of other amplifying attributes which often are more important than IQ in deciding school and life outcomes. In addition to our abilities, those other attributes pertain to our emotional intelligence or character. It can be argued that our crisis and problems are occasioned, not so much by an average IQ of 85, as they are by an equivalent average EQ (emotional intelligence quotient) which falls significantly below that number; that is, we are burdened more by a character deficit than a cognitive one.

---

[25] Discussed in Chapters 12 and 14, respectively.

Lessons to be Learned from Jensen-Herrnstein-Murray

However, the encompassing lesson, expressly intended by Jensen-Herrnstein-Murray, and with ample support from life experience, is that intelligence counts. Its role in life has profound consequences for individuals and groups. Rather than our IQ lag serving as one of our **two major demons**, then, instead, we ought, indirectly, to cast it into one of our two major challenges (strengthening our families being the other). That is what-- through the medium of education -- our tradition fathers did. Both Washington and DuBois championed the role of education in our uplifting, and we can expand upon their advocacy by coming to grips with the role of IQ as well. Jensen, Herrnstein, and Murray invite us to do so. In their messages reside a number of lessons, some of which follow.

1. While, in part, heritable, to a considerable extent, IQ can be cultivated through the environment -- from the prenatal care to the home and community environment which we provide. Due to historical inflictions and deficiencies in that environment, our group IQ is likely below what it can be. *We ought to exert every effort to improve it, not directly, but indirectly; no need to make intelligence a fetish.* But there is a need for focus on those environmental factors which foster it and which, on their own merit, deserve our care and work. The reason: "**SOCIAL CONTEXT CAN ALTER GENETIC EXPRESSION.**"
2. We ought, anyway, for example, to undertake intense activities to provide our women proper prenatal care, our children proper nutrition, and our parents proper childrearing practices.
3. We ought, as well try, to change those community standards that, for example, have come to condone teenage pregnancy, take fatherless homes for granted, and treat marriage as an inconvenience. To stand by and see the continuing and disproportionate birth of children who have little or no prospects of being properly cared for is not liberal or humanistic; it is cruel and costly.
4. Rather than waging war on our inner city schools, a refuge from disarray for many of our students, we ought to work with them to help bring about order and discipline (without which learning cannot occur) and provide the kind of support

that would encourage and assist students to do their best. No reason to prevent schools from using intelligence tests, or any other tool, that might assist them in better understanding and meeting the range of needs presented by our students. Instead, we ought instead to encourage their appropriate use, guided by Jensen's maxim that "schools and society must provide a range and diversity of educational methods, programs, and goals, and of occupational opportunities, just as wide as the range of human abilities" (see outline of his article, above).

5. We ought also to encourage, as appropriate, the kind of associative learning methodology which Jensen finds promising and which Washington practiced, not as a singular approach to teaching our students but as part of a range of approaches, their use dependent on individual and group needs.

6. We ought to encourage the cultivation of the most gifted among us, a la Herrnstein and Murray's recommendation of more support for the gifted and for a revival of the concept of the "educated man," and DuBois's advocacy of cultivating our Talented Tenth.

7. We ought to entertain the Herrnstein-Murray idea alluded to by Loury [it is not in their book, but, according to Loury, in a magazine article they concomitantly published] but dismissed by him as "errant nonsense," the idea being a vision of humanity perceived as divided into "clans" (national or race groups). Each clan could claim superiority to other clans based on the greater possession of some desirable trait, such as. long-distance running in the case of Africans, soccer skills in the case of Italians or Brazilians, or basketball skills in the case of African Americans. The self-esteem of each would be based on within-group success.

8. We ought, finally (to save the best to last), to be guided by Herrnstein-Murray's fundamental proposition that, in response to the twin realities of differences in intelligence and of the power which intelligence exerts on life outcomes, the goal of policy should be, not to equalize outcomes, but to find a valued place for everyone.

Self-Assessment: Diversified Ethnic Strengths Concept
(Lesson from Herrnstein-Murray)

Lesson #7 merits extended attention because, insofar as known, it seldom gets much attention. Yet, in the context of the IQ discussion, it merits it. To the extent he has accurately presented Herrnstein-Murray's idea, Glenn Loury seems justified to dismiss their idea of clan-based trait superiority as "errant nonsense" because, in his words, "one can make no sense of it in rigorous anthropological terms" (155:308-09). One cannot be sure of what exactly Loury means by "rigorous anthropological terms," but, in whatever terms, there is no need further to divide an already divided world, nor to legitimize claims of superiority when we should be doing the opposite: promoting humility and mutual respect. However, the *principle* involved ought not to be dismissed. That principle seems to be that various groups can derive their standing in the human family and their sense of pride and uniqueness by capitalizing upon their strengths.

For us African Americans, the thinking of some in our own race has been that our strengths lie, not in the cognitive domain, but in the emotional domain. Even with our adaptation fathers that appears to have been the case.

Washington. Norrell suggests that while Washington saw dark-skinned blacks [which in reality is who the IQ issue is about] as mentally capable as whites, he acknowledged a difference in our mental *development*. He saw whites as having developed their mental ability to a greater extent than blacks had developed their mental ability (192:231-32). Whether he was expressing his true feeling, or refraining from offending whites -- which he would have done if he had said our mental ability was equal to theirs -- is something which Norrell says we do not know. In the emotional domain, Norrell indicates that likewise Washington had a qualification. He saw no differences between the two races, except when it comes to religion, a domain in which he expressed the view that we exhibit much more emotion than whites. Relevant, too, is the statement of Scott and Stowe (keeping in mind, in particular, how closely for 18 years Scott worked with Washington) who, upon citing several of Washington's statements, conclude that the statements "show that Booker Washington had no illusions as to the ignorance and poverty of the rank and file of his people...." (234:346).

DuBois. Characteristically, from DuBois we get two views. Before 1908, Meier tells us that "while never accepting any idea of Negro inferiority, he had referred to Negroes as a backward, childlike, undeveloped race, and he had accepted the idea of inherent racial differences" (168:202). In 1908, however, DuBois attacked the Darwinian theory of undeveloped races and survival of the fittest, and in 191, he endorsed the conclusion that "there was no proven connection between race and mental or cultural characteristics" (168:202-03). But in 1913, Meier states that he took a U turn. He went back to the notion of inherent racial differences, describing the Negro as primarily an artist whose aesthetic sensitivity set its people above other races and accounted for the artistic achievements of such Africans as the Egyptians and for the "'only real American music'" (168:203).[26]

It would appear, then, to be a fair reading of their position to say that our adaptation fathers denied any inherited black-white IQ differences but acknowledged (in Washington's description) *developmental* black-white IQ differences. They saw dark-skinned black people as being (in Meier's characterization of DuBois's description) "backward, childlike, and undeveloped" – or, in a word, ignorant (as Scott and Stowe sum up Washington's view). They attributed this ignorance, not however to inherited or environmental differences (not yet in vogue), but to *developmental* differences. On its own, they saw the white race as having developed its mental capacity more than, on its own, the black race had done. Thus, even if not consistently, each acknowledged *existent* black-white IQ differences. In the emotional domain, however – the domain of the spiritual and psychical -- in whatever manifestation, or to whatever degree, each saw, not just existent differences, but inherited differences as well.

They were not alone. Meier tells us that many of their contemporaries [though Meier is referring specifically to DuBois, but, to some extent,

---

[26] The specific source of this quote of DuBois by Meier is unclear because Meier lumps the references for his discussion of DuBois's views into one citation without indicating what he obtained from each reference.

Washington as well could be included], from diverse political and ideological leanings, were of a similar mind. They shared the notion of innate racial differences, believing that black contribution to American culture would derive from our emotional nature. From that emotional nature -- the "soul of the race" as some termed it -- would emerge contributions in music, poetry, oratory, painting, literature, and the arts generally. Meier cites Benjamin Brawley, a black English professor at Morehouse College and Howard University, and an advocate of black culture and history, as pointing out the following:

> ...that almost all Negro achievements had been in the arts, in the realm of feeling—from the homes of humble Negroes who, unlike poor whites, grew flowers and hung posters on the walls, to the long line of beautiful singers, Douglass' 'fervid oratory,' Dunbar's 'sensuous poetry,' Du Bois' 'picturesque style,' and 'the elemental sculpture' of Meta Warrick Fuller (168:268).

Meier sums up their belief as follows: "Negroes could distinguish themselves in all spheres, but each race had its peculiar genius, and as far as one could predict at the time, the Negro was destined to reach his greatest heights in the arts" (168:268).

Since our "peculiar genius" has not proven to be in the IQ domain, but rather IQ has become one of our **three major demons**, it makes sense for us not to dismiss the implications of Herrnstein-Murray's notion. Nor to dismiss their research findings, which in essence reflect that which we – including at least to some extent our adaptation fathers -- admit about ourselves: that our IQ is more of a challenge than a strength. Our recourse is simply to disidentify with the cognitive domain -- not resting our laurels on it, so to speak. That disidentification does not suggest that, like our students regarding school, we exert little or no effort to raise our IQ; rather, it means that we transfer that effort to the enrichment of our environment, which would enable us, indirectly, to raise it to the extent to which it can be raised. Nor, further, does the disidentification mean that we do not value our IQ. Not to "rest our laurels on it" cannot be taken to mean that we devalue IQ. We must value every domain essential to the wellbeing of the race. Our IQ remains a domain in which we can distinguish ourselves, only not yet one in which we can see ourselves as possessed of a "peculiar genius."

The author is reminded of his years in the South. In planting crops, if the soil was good, farmers did not fertilize it, but if it was not so good, they did. Perhaps our IQ perhaps places us in a similar position. Doubt is raised as to whether it is in the best condition, so we need to fertilize it -- and that is what prenatal and parental care, along with an enriched environment, do. If a raise in IQ is a byproduct, that is a bonus; all we really require is a good crop. Of course, we are more fortunate than many of those farmers. They had to rely solely on the soil. In our case, we do not have to rely solely on our IQ; we can turn, as well, to our EQ, remembering that we are not trying to raise an IQ crop but, instead, an achievement and ability crop. In his groundbreaking work, Howard Gardner has identified a range of abilities which we humans possess (he calls them "multiple intelligences") which, like IQ, are essential to human wellbeing. From among those abilities, we must take IQ-equivalent satisfaction from that which some of our black thinkers believe to be our "peculiar genius": our contributions in athletics and in the emotional domain -- such arts as music, poetry, and oratory.

Giving such comparative perspective to our IQ has relevance for other black-white comparisons as well. Experience, history, and research suggest that the standards we employ in the management of our life in certain domains, such as the sciences and mathematics, may -- in comparison with whites -- be approximate rather than absolute. As a result, there is a need, accordingly, to assess the comparative results of some of our endeavors in terms, not of equality, but of approximation or equity.

Of course, in other domains, such as the aforementioned athletics and arts, our standards and results may be equal to or higher than those of whites. In their classic study, <u>The Mark of Oppression</u>, Kardiner and Ovesey, for example, speak of the personality profile of the black upper classes, not as the same as that of the white upper classes, but as being more approximate to that of the white upper classes than to that of the black lower classes (144). For the sake, then, of a positive core identity, we must stop chasing the rainbow and, as a group (individuals being guided by their own criteria) and as judicious, make -- not equality – but *approximation* and *equity* our goal, guided by the realization that no two people are equal (which does not imply either inferiority or superiority, just diversity). Nor, therefore, can we expect equal outcomes. In the end, what most matters is that we earn for ourselves a "valued place" in society, to borrow the thinking of Herrnstein-Murray (see below). While shooting for the stars, so to speak, in the process, we do not want to lose sight of the earth.

We can be especially well served by this diversified ethnic strengths orientation in the education of our students. As Herrnstein-Murray have provided us something to think about as regards ethnic strengths, Jensen has done likewise in regard to teaching our students. In his article, Jensen stresses as a strength of disadvantaged children associative learning abilities (Level I intelligence). He says that these abilities have not been tapped through traditional instruction, which emphasizes learning through conceptual ability. But this conclusion sent Brazziel into a rage, but the fact is that Jensen said no more than what was practiced at Tuskegee by Washington during the early stage of our freedom.

Washington was quite aware of the need to tap into our students' "untapped abilities." The idea is to focus teaching-learning, as necessary and appropriate, on the concrete, selectively moving to and integrating the abstract. Clearly, this is what Tuskegee did. Theory and practice, and the abstract and concrete were integrated (244: 81-82; 234:90-97). An English teacher would, for example, expect students to write compositions related to their shop or farm work, and might, for a spelling lesson, use a chest of drawers and the tools required to build them. Similarly, a chemistry teacher would, for example, gear lessons around the cooking done in Tuskegee's kitchen. To assist them in this concrete-oriented, learn-by-doing approach, at the end of the school day, teachers would visit different shops to get ideas and material. An attempt was made to make students' education real; school and life were to be inseparable. As Spencer quotes Washington, "**An ounce of application is worth a ton of abstractions**" [emphasis added] (244:82).

Back, then, in the 1880s, Washington used an approach which Jensen, nearly a century later, theorized would be effective today in teaching many of our disadvantaged students. According to pioneering social historian, Merle Curti, Washington's practical approach to learning also anticipated the progressive education movement that was to blossom around the turn of the century. The movement popularized the learn-by-doing approach preached by John Dewey, perhaps its most famous leader (53:291-93).

So, Jensen is not talking about something unique to the perspective of a "conservative, bigot, racist, supremacist, heretic, or infidel," but something that has grounding in our own history, specifically in the curriculum directed by the Tuskegee Wizard [a moniker for Washington which might be as applicable to his educational acumen as to his fundraising, problem-solving, and political skills]. Carter G. Woodson was ecstatic about that grounding, placing him in the company of Pestalozzi, Froebel and Herbart (290:279).

Although Woodson's reference is not to Washington's methodology but to his educational program, he, nevertheless, highlights Washington, the educator. As educator, his methodology was a distinctive component of his program. That Washington's pioneering work in industrial education -- which, incidentally, from a program perspective grew out of his tutelage under General Samuel Armstrong -- places him alongside Pestalozzi, Froebel, and Herbart is questionable. But the point is that Jensen's associative learning thesis has a basis, provided by Washington, in our own history. What both men advocate is consistent with wha, today, is commonly embraced as sound teaching-learning methodology: appropriate use of the concrete and the abstract. To ostracize Jensen and exclude from our crisis dialogue his contribution means that we also exclude the possibility of making an instructive connection to our own heritage, as well as to the more effective application of theoretically accepted methodology. We may think that we have thereby protected ourselves, which we have, but it is a protection of our bondage at the expense of our potential.

Toward a Valued Place for Everyone

Herrenstein-Murray's advocacy of the concept of diversified racial/ethnic strengths can be viewed as a corollary to their fundamental proposition, stated in Lesson #8, that, in response to the twin realities of differences in intelligence and of the power which intelligence exerts on life outcomes, the goal of policy should be, not to equalize those outcomes, but to find a valued place for everyone (Chapter 22, 121:527-54). By "valued place," they say they simply mean the following: "*You occupy a valued place if other people would miss you if you were gone"* [emphasis in original] (121:535). How simple, how profound, and how fitting! Whether it is our intelligence which is the issue, or any other attribute or behavior, we blacks could not ask for more. Nor do we have any reasonable justification for expecting more. The same can be said for any other racial/ethnic group. In a society where individual life is sacrosanct, Herrenstein-Murray's proposition is a gold standard, much as Jensen's proposition (#10, above, in the outline of his article) is a gold standard in the field of education. To remind us that it is a gold standard, our mnemonic is **Toward a Valued Place for Everyone**, a gold standard suggested by Herrenstein-Murray that can be used by us blacks, or by any racial/ethnic group, to guide our policy and program pursuits versus a standard guided by an *equal place* for everyone.

In the context of their proposition, IQ, rather than being viewed as a potential stigma or curse, simply becomes one measure, among others, which can be used to chart the pursuit of a valued place for each individual, race/ethnicity notwithstanding. Our passion aside, we can simply forget about finding an "equal place," or some semblance thereof, for all members of the human family. Equal outcome not sourced in human nature; differences in outcome are. Those differences are often consequential, as the case with IQ differences. Herrnstein-Murray have done us a service by coming out and having the courage, and undertaking the scholarship, to deliver that message. They provide the basis for us (and others) to assess IQ from a new, deeply rooted perspective (which they discuss): that of the pursuit of a valued place for everyone. They bemoan the domination of the "cognitive elite," and of a society it fashions to serve its own needs and interests, calling, instead, for a society in which there is a valued place for us all. Some of their prescriptions for creating such a society are questionable, but not their proposition. Rather, their proprosition is indeed a gold standard, and on the part of us blacks, especially, should earn their book, not condemnation, but praise. So incensed have we and some of our liberal "supporters" have been by its topic that we fail to take note of its most consequential message, delivered in its last chapter, "A [Valued] Place for Everyone."

Final Word: Fight through It

Of our **three major demons**, our IQ lag may be the most challenging for us blacks to confront. Psychologists point out that humiliation ranks at the top among the offenses which trigger the strongest responses. When we hear that our IQ is lower than the IQ whites, that can be humiliating -- seen as saying that we are *less than* whites. Neither we, nor anyone else, wants to be seen as *less than* another; it goes contrary to human nature. Thus, the attempt in this chapter has been to get the matter out into the open, discuss it, and come to grips with it at a visceral as well as at a rational level. Not easy, but all of us blacks need to do it. Do it and be open about it and we free ourselves *to be* and to *become*. Some may use it against us, but not most. Regardless, we must fight through it for our own sake so that we emerge from this second bondage and come out more confident and secure in who we are -- more comfortable in our own skin, as it were. It boils down to self-acceptance and self-pride – of being content, though not complacent, about who we are and of replacing victimhood with characterhood. IQ is not the problem; what we make of it, in combination with our other attributes, is. That is why leadership is so crucial: to provide the guidance to optimize that making -- something emphasized by DuBois in his "Talented Tenth," but not translated into practice by him and his dominant System-Responsibility Tradition. Our IQ challenge is to manage better the negative feeling which it tends to evoke, just as we must manage an array of other feelings which are part of human nature and which, left unmanaged or poorly managed, can be destructive or otherwise counterproductive. As pertains to our IQ disparity feeling, in particular, we would be well served if guided by the words of Eleanor Roosevelt, who said, "No one can make you feel inferior without your consent."[27]

Let us not give whites, or anyone else, that consent. In substance, let our response be something like the following in which we acknowledge our lag and express how we feel about it -- no further debate or discussion being necessary:

---

[27] Retrieved on 3 December 2014 from http://www.quotationspage.com/quotes/
 Eleanor_Roosevelt

For many of us, our IQ is not what we would like it to be. So we are working on things which, over time, we think are going to make it possible for us to continue the rise in it that we have seen over the last generation or so -- things like improved prenatal care, improved nutrition and, for our children, better homes and better schools. However, our IQ is not a preoccupation for us because, as it stands, we can do quite well. We just need to amplify it through the drive that we can get from emphasizing those character traits which are even more important to success, such as impulse control. We are who we are, we accept who we are, and we take great pride in who we are. Our IQ does not have to be the same as anyone else's and we don't have to be like anyone else -- and we weren't made to be like anyone else. We were made to be who *we are*, IQ and all. And as we are, we have a valued place in the life of our nation. This is a diverse world, and, whether we are talking about IQ or some other attribute, everyone is not going to be the same. Our call and challenge -- as is the call and challenge of all peoples -- is to try to be the best of who *we* were made to be. That is the real test of a people and of a person: striving to make the best of what nature has bestowed. It is the standard by which we earn our standing. Honor of that standard will enable all members of the human family to accept and respect our differences -- all of them -- and, consistent those differences, to move towards our valued places in society; and, transcending those diffeences, to move towards the realization of our underlying and unifying common humanity and its implicit moral and civic egalitarianism.

9

Why the Crisis?
The Root Cause: Lack of a Positive Core Identity

> "... that power of the mind capable of sloughing off the thingification of the past, will be the Negro's most potent weapon in achieving self-respect."
> Martin Luther King Jr., <u>Where Do We Go From Here: Chaos or Community</u> (147:131)

> "We must be as proud of being a Negro as the Japanese is of being Japanese."
> Booker T. Washington, Address before National Negro Business League, of which he was President, on August 20, 1913 (462d)

In Chapter 6, the case was made for our students' character deficits – they do not behave well enough, nor work hard enough -- as the *main* cause of our African American Male School Adaptability Crisis (AMSAC). Angela Duckworth might say they lack a certain amount of GRIT, or passion and perseverance, and John Ogbu characterized them as having a low-effort syndrome. That is, our students devalue academic striving and success. The question is why, and, in this chapter, it is proposed that the answer is that it is mainly because they lack a positive core identity. They lack a positive core identity because they do not come from **"average expectable environments,"** especially an *average expectable home environment* wherein, during the first three years of their life, in particular, they have been provided a sense of security and love.

That our students do not exhibit the requisite work ethic is seldom disputed in the literature. With their system-oriented analysis and interpretation, even Ainsworth-Darnell and Downey found, in their study, that what they call our students' *skills, habits,* and *styles* to be statistically significantly associated with their poor school performance. Of course, *skills, habits,* and *styles* -- which they define as classroom effort, disruptive behavior, doing homework, and being in trouble -- pertain to character. As previously discussed, they blame, not the students for their skills, habits, and styles, but the system – and, therefore, propose that we remedy the system, on the premise that, in turn, students will remedy their character.

Obviously, Ainsworth-Darnell and Downey and others are not totally opposed to a focus on students, but they want that focus to be on their cognitive skills, not their culture. That position reflects the generally *expressed* thinking about what to do about the problem (given the rituals of race relations which have emerged, who knows what many *really* think). As Paul Tough observes, that thinking has been that students' success depends on their cognitive skills; at least that is where the attention has been focused. Emotional skills (another way of denoting character skills), however, seem to be in the early stages of gaining traction as a focus of equal importance (258a:194-95).

Departing from the cognitive focus and breaching a cultural taboo, the thesis herein is that the *main* cause of AMSAC is the character deficits of our students and that the *root* cause, because it substantially accounts for those character deficits, is our students' lack of a positive core identity. If we can remedy our students' character and identity problems, to the extent to which they can be remedied, we can remedy AMSAC. For reborn students, so to speak, will be able to make their own way, which has already been paved.

Consistent with the thinking of the previously cited 37 experts who composed the Commission on Children at Risk, our students can make their own way, however, only if, like any of us, they become artful dancers with their behavior and IQ nature; they cannot be bystanders, enjoying the music but not taking the floor and dancing to its rhythm. This is not rocket science; it is human nature and it is social reality. It only requires that we view our students' problems, not from a racial or ideological perspective, but from a human and psychological one. That might be asking too much for many, but it is suggested that we are out of plausible alternatives.

The revelations of black activist, poet, prolific writer, entertainer, and entrepreneur, Kevin Powell, in his open letter to his father, provides an illustrative case for such a human and psychological perspective. Powell is quoted thus by Enola Aird, director of the Motherhood Project at the Institute for American Values, New York:

> 'The worst thing a child can feel is that he doesn't have a true home, a place where he feels nurtured in a way that confirms his life. I mean, if he can't trust his own parents, really, whom can he trust? Whom can that child love if he feels he has never been loved by the very people who brought him into the world?' (2:156).

Aird speaks of the "unbearable pain" and the "inwardly homeless" feeling that Powell, growing up as the child of unwed parents, conveys in this passage. As Aird suggests, Powell's pain is all too common among us African American males and, if we stop to think about it, all too applicable to our life in America. We can conceive of feeling "inwardly homeless" [bell hook's term, according to Aird] as a product of our slave legacy, and we can further conceive of the transmission and perpetuation of that legacy through the very kind of family life of which Powell is a product. It is just such a family life which gives rise to a negative core identity and the character deficits which lead to the kind of maladaptive behavior exhibited by our students.

So often, like Powell, growing up without a father presence, and in a disproportionately unfathered communities, our students need to find their place in the world of manhood. As Powell expressed the quest to his father, "I tried to make sense of my manhood and my place in the world" (212b:84). That quest cannot be satisfied by what, so often, they pick up in the streets and from their peers. A father substitute may be the answer for some, but not for enough. As a result, a void is left unfulfilled and, consequently, the emergence of a positive core identity and its associated character assets are curtailed. The deprived soul that is its outcome goes out into the world seeking fulfillment, too often finding it, not in ways which enrich it, but in ways which deprave it. Often, over time, its byproducts include, not just dysfunctional individuals, but the dysfunctional families whom the individuals procreate and from whom, in an endless cycle, emanate more deprived souls. Effective intervention requires a simultaneous humanistic attack on this dysfunctionality *and* on its root cause.

Research points to the advisability of such a dual attack. Identity and character interact; each influences the other. Summing up the research, in his popular textbook, <u>Social Psychology</u>, social psychologist, David Myers, writes, "We are likely not only to think ourselves into action but also to act ourselves into a way of thinking" (186:150). That is, as our sense of identity influences our character, so does our character or behavior influence our identity. Attack one and not the other and we reduce our chances of success; attack both and we optimize those chances.

That both identity and character also have their foundation (not necessarily their finality, but their foundation) in the parent-child relationship during the first three years of life lets us know that we are on to something meaningful and perhaps consequential -- that we have identified the problem at its origin. The basic character structure which is laid during those first three years ensues from the child's sense of identity, which, through the same parent-child relationship, is also laid during those first three years. That is, the parent-child relationship during the first three years of the child's life lays the foundation for the two correlated factors, identity and character, which experience, theory, and research show to be powerfully associated with the school and life success of the child. In sum, *more than anything else, the security and love provided the child by the parent during the child's first three years of life is the single most important factor in fostering in the child the positive core identity and the associated character assets on which school and life success depend* (21a:xiv-xvi; 79:105; 258a:182; 315c). With its varied implications, this fact serves as a guide to action, enabling the formulation of more targeted and effective prevention and remediation -- giving school, parents, and community something decisively influential on which to work in concert (keeping in mind, as Erikson points out, that, while decisive early one, security and love are lifelong requirements).

Although our discussion is about **identity**, two other related and often interchangeably-used terms enter the discussion: **personality** and **character**. It is apparent from the literature that, depending on context, the terms can mean the same thing. That is because all three refer to who and what we are, only from different aspects. That is, all are about the self, which authorities tell us has been the subject of considerable research in recent years. The research points to the complexity of the subject, a complexity evident from few uniform definitions and concepts, and, therefore, which makes the self harder to grasp (150c). Nevertheless, from the literature reviewed, applicable knowledge exists, and the discussion below draws upon it.

Personality, Identity, and Character

Personality versus character

As posted and pictured by an internet user, the distinction between personality and character is somewhat like the difference between weather and climate. Personality can be used to refer to our more variable, day-to-day, situationally modulated traits which we exhibit, whereas our character usually refers to our more stable, permanent, predictable traits which may or may not be on exhibit but which are manifested over time, especially in our response to our life encounters (thus, we can be said, for example, to have a "characteristic" response). Or, we can think of personality as meaning the impression of us held by others, whereas character refers to who we actually are. The key to determining the difference is said to be time, since time will reveal who we really are in contrast to who we appear to be (399b). Character is the term of choice herein because the focus is on **character (attitude and behavior)** in relation to school and life success as revealed in the research literature.

Identity: Erikson explains

The literature suggests that, without a sense of core identity, we live a life of confusion -- never anchored and never assured. As told by Erikson, that state is reflected in the words of Biff to his mother in Arthur Miller's Death of a Salesman: "'I just can't take a hold, Mom, I can't take hold of some kind of life'" (79:131). Nor could any of us. Not when our inner life is in disarray, which is the case, when, like Biff, we lack a positive core identity. That lack is going to lead to disarray because it is going to result in character deficits which make the disarray inevitable.

At birth, Erikson says, we begin to forge our identity and continue the process over our life span, making appropriate adaptations at various life stages. Throughout, we form and adjust our identity in our interactions with "a widening radius of significant individuals and institutions" -- family, friends, peers, neighborhood, media, and society at large (79: 93). It is through these interactions that our identity is acquired, our **identity** being a *"subjective sense* **of an** *invigorating sameness* **and** *continuity,"* as Erikson terms it [others define it differently](79:19). These "significant individuals and institutions," in effect, become what sociologist, Charles H. Cooley, calls our "looking glass," producing the "looking-glass self," in that we tend to come to see ourselves as we *imagine* others see us. That is, the picture that we *perceive* they have of us, and which, in various ways we interpret them conveying to us, is the picture that we tend to come to have of ourselves (186: 45).

The process entailed in what Erikson describes as our constantly unfolding identity is governed by the **epigenetic principle**. This principle, Erikson says, *"states that anything that grows has a ground plan, and that out of this ground plan the parts arise, each part having its time of special ascendancy, until all parts have arisen to form a functioning whole"* [emphasis added](79: 92). According to Erikson, this ground plan for us has eight stages, such as trust vs. mistrust, intimacy vs. isolation. Others in his and related disciplines cite different stages, but herein our concern is not with any of the stages, but merely to underline that social science has established the fact that the formulation of our identity unfolds in accordance with a *natural process* that, Erikson says, is common to *all human beings*. If, in our development, that process is obstructed, we are unlikely to forge a positive core identity, which will manifest itself in a maladjusted and, maybe, dysfunctional personality or character: self-loathing, anger, aggression, depression, and so on.

Amplification of Erikson: McAdams. Psychology professor, Dan P. McAdams of Northwestern University, provides another and more detailed perspective from which to view identity – and, at the same time, character, namely, as a story. In McAdams words, "One way to read Erikson's idea of identity is to see it as an internalized and evolving story of the self that people begin to construct in the emerging adult years." It becomes what McAdams calls our narrative identity, "an internalized and evolving story of the reconstructed past and imagined future that aims to provide life with unity, coherence, and purpose." "For both the self and others," he elaborates, the life story explains how I came to be, who I am today, where I am going in the future, and what I believe my life means within the psychological niche provided by family, friends, work, society, and the cultural and ideological resources of my environment. It is a story that distinguishes me from all others, and yet shows how I am connected to others as well. It is a story that narrates the evolution of a particular self, but it is a self in cultural context (156a:19).

In McAdams's amplification, we can perhaps more easily discern the challenge posed in trying to construct a positive narrative identity (or story) if one is brought up in a disadvantaged environment, as in the case of our black male and female students alike -- but especially our male students.

Other identity meanings and related terms. Social scientists say "core" identity because we have any number of identities, such as occupational identity, political identity, and sports fan identity, but these are our so-called *extended identities* or *sub-identities* and do not define our essence. In the words of world renown Florida State University psychologist, Roy F. Baumeister: "It [identity] is actually a composite definition made up of several partial definitions. The components of identity are these partial definitions. Any answer to the question "Who are you?" is an identity component, for to answer that question is to give a partial definition of oneself" (304b:269). One such partial component is our core identity.

The two other partial components are self-concept and self-esteem. The three make up what we call the *self*. This is what Baumeister has to say about it:

> The self is a large, complex structure. Self-concept [which includes identity but is not limited to it] refers to how the person thinks of himself or herself, that is, the person's own beliefs and ideas about this self. Self-esteem refers to the evaluative dimension of the self-concept--that is, how good a person one is. Identity refers to definitions of the self that are created jointly by the individual, relatives and acquaintances, and society (304b:274).

This threefold structure, Baumeister tells us, has made it "difficult for psychology to come up with firm answers about the nature of the self, for the self includes stability and change, visible manifestations of inner phenomena, ideas and feelings, and other complexities." "Even," he states, "the most stable core of the self may not be fixed and constant" (304b:247). Nevertheless, as Scott's analysis makes evident, much has been learned.

Core identity

In contrast to extended or sub-identities, Imani (formerly K.) Michelle Scott (referenced below) makes the case that core identity has a certain constancy and enduring quality that give us an unmistakable uniqueness, in our own eyes, as well as in the eyes of others. For example, more or less day-in and day-out, year-in and year-out, we may see ourselves as black man -- athletic, hardworking, and family-oriented. Such attributes give us a *"subjective sense of an invigorating sameness and continuity"* – as well as, Baumeister tells us, a sense of being different from others (304b:248). We cannot just take or leave such core attributes -- as we might do, for example, take or leave our identity, say as a New York Jet fan – for the loss of any components of our core identity can be shattering; their existence is powerful and their loss evokes a strong, pronounced reaction from within.

Example. An example in the news while these pages are being written is perhaps provided by former President George W. Bush's reaction to Rapper Kanye West's accusation that the President's slow response to the Hurricane Katrina devastation showed that he did not "care about black people" (363). In reaction, President Bush called West's accusation the most "disgusting" moment of his presidency. Why so, one is led to ask. Of all the memorable moments that must have characterized his presidency, why would the accusation of a Rapper evoke such a pronounced reaction? That is the kind of reaction that might be evoked, say, by some head of state or other dignitary, or from some notable academic or intellectual, or from some incident or event, but from a Rapper? It is proposed that the answer to the riddle is that West questioned and attacked the President's core identity. Chances are that President Bush identifies himself as a caring, racially-sensitive, prejudice-free man. West declared him to be otherwise, and, in so doing, arguably attacked the President's core identity, his sense of that which helps to give him his sense of essence or uniqueness. When that is done, any of us, just like President Bush, will not only react, but react forcefully and strongly. For, Scott argues, our core identity is our essence, the core of our existence, not something that we can easily brush off.

Factors which shape core identity and identity generally. The "Model of multiple dimensions of identity" which follows shows some of the factors which shape our

essence or core identity, followed by a number of the questions to which it gives rise, questions similar to those implied in McAdams's concept of identity as a story (432). The model was designed by Susan R. Jones and Mrylu K. McEwen [student personnel professionals, respectively, at Ohio State University and the University of Maryland] based on a study of ten women college students ranging in age from 20-24 of diverse racial-ethnic backgrounds. They stress that the "various dimensions [stemming from these factors] are present in each individual, yet experienced in different ways as more or less salient." "For example," they add, "race was found to be very salient for the

Black women in the study, and rarely salient for the White women. Similarly, culture

The African American Male School Adaptability Crisis (AMSAC)

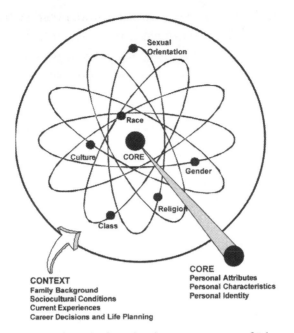

Figure 34. Model of Multiple Dimensions of Identity. Reproduced with permission of the American College Personnel Association (ACPA) (390a).

Questions to Elicit Personal Identity (432)

1. *Who are you? (What makes you tick?)*
2. *What makes you unique?*
3. *What are your values?*
4. *Your physical identity (what you think you look like to others) -- body image*
5. *Your internal identity (who you think you are in terms of your personality and character, values, and so on)*
6. *How you see yourself in relation to others*
7. *How you identify yourself in terms of your job*
8. *Your personal goals*

was salient for the Asian Indian woman and religion for the Jewish women" (390a). What becomes salient, they observe, is rooted in internal awareness and external scrutiny (e.g., race for Black women), the external scrutiny exposing differences and, in turn, the differences tending to shape identity. Since differences function to magnify phenomena, the closer the identity dimension to one's core, the more it shapes one's core identity or sense of self. That core is sensed or felt as one's personal identity or private, inner self, and, hence, something that we cannot brush off. In McAdams's conception, it becomes a story too close to the heart to ignore. Jones and McEwen suggest thinking of it (our core identity) as internalizing deeply-felt or deeply-valued personal attributes and characteristics. Attention now turns to what must happen for that internalization to turn out favorably.

The Role of *"average expectable environments"* in Identity Formation

What tips the scale one way or the other in the natural unfolding of our identity is our *perception* of the significant interactions we experience, most powerfully, in our family, and beyond our family, with our friends, peers, neighborhood, media, and society at large. For our identity to serve us well, these entities must provide us a series of **"*average expectable environments*."** If, throughout our life span, we are provided a series of **"*average expectable environments*,"** as Erikson terms it (Erikson himself attributing the term and concept to a famous colleague, Heinz Hartmann), then we can expect the scales to be tipped in favor of our acquiring a positive core identity and associated sound character traits; otherwise, we are likely to grapple with a series of crises (79:221-24). Hence we have additional mnemonics: **"average expectable environments"→ positive core identity→ sound character**. These mnemonics can help us to remember what is required to solve our crisis and problems: "average expectable environments" to produce simultaneously a positive core identity and a sound character.

The lynchpin in the process, Erikson and others tell us, is an **average expectable *home* environment**, the Achilles heel for our African American male students. Such an environment desirably has a mother *and* a father. But, Aird observes, "For fatherhood to take hold and to survive as a vital institution within a society, that society must stand solidly behind it--supporting it with norms, expectations, laws, and resources, over many generations." "Societies in essence," she goes on to add, "must help men to become good and responsible husbands and fathers" (2:160). For our African American males, that kind of society has been problematic, to say the least, not one that has stood "solidly behind" our fatherhood. Many of us, like Kevin Powell, are thus not the products of an **average expectable *home* environment** with its powerful and positive influence on our core identity. Nonetheless, Powell has overcome and thrived; the same cannot be said for many among us.

Security and love -- "hallowed presence." In the absence of an **average expectable *home* environment** during childhood, we are deprived of two ingredients deemed required for laying the foundation for school and life success: security (sense of safety) and love (nurturing). The aforementioned Paul Tough tells us that "scientists have demonstrated that [this is] the most reliable way to produce an adult who is brave and curious and kind and prudent." (258a:182). In a new introduction to his book, From Instinct to Identity: The Development of Personality, practicing psychotherapist and psychoanalyst, Louis Breger, says that the most important change since its original publication in 1974 has been "the virtual explosion of significant research on infants and young children," observing that this research has shown that "secure attachment is the bedrock for healthy personality development while the various forms of insecure attachment underlie many forms of psychological disturbance in later life." Breger goes on to add that "though it is worth noting that, while a great many variables influence the development of the person from infancy through the early adult years, the single most important factor is secure versus insecure attachment" (21a:xiv-xv). Describing what an infant needs, Erikson – in a memorable and marvelous term --says pretty much the same thing, declaring that the child needs a sense of "hallowed presence" -- a need he says which "remains basic in man" and [referring specifically to adolescents] unfulfilled impairs one's search for identity (79:105).

Implication for black students. Reference herein to a series of **"average expectable environments"** is thus referring to an environment wherein we African Americans ourselves, the school, and others provide our children and youth security and love, a goal which can be accomplished through the **practice of the art of loving**. Fail to do so and we impair their ability to forge a positive core identity and a successful life which typically ensues from it -- perhaps not necessarily success marked by the kind of exalted bravery, curiosity, prudence, and kindness to which Tough seems to allude, but, at least, success versus failure. In his reference to a *series* of "**average expectable environments**," Erikson (more broadly) is talking about the entire life cycle, our sense of identity being a dynamic product of the experiences which we encounter in the course of a lifetime.

Genetic role. To be sure, Erikson tells us, we are born with certain predispositions, but how those predispositions materialize is powerfully influenced by our home environment and our other individual and agency interactions. When it comes to identity, Erikson says that "we deal with a process 'located' *in the core of the individual* [emphasis in original] and yet also *in the core of his communal culture*" [emphasis in original]; in effect, our identity is a fusion of the two (79:22). As Pinker – like the Commission on Children at Risk -- tells us in his <u>The Blank Slate: The Modern Denial of Human Nature</u>, "genes aren't everything;" "their effects can vary depending on the environment" (210:48-49). The story he tells about Woody Allen makes the point.

Though his fame, fortune, and ability to attract beautiful women may depend on having genes that enhance his sense of humor, in *Stardust Memories* he explains to an envious childhood friend that there is a crucial environmental factor as well: 'We live in a society that puts a big value on jokes.... If I had been an Apache Indian, those guys didn't need comedians, so I'd be out of work'(210:49).

A Positive Core Identity: Personality or Character Outcome

If, then, in our natural unfolding we are to achieve a positive core identity, certain conditions are required. We need a series of **"average expectable environments," especially an average expectable *home* environment,** wherein we are provided security and love. Such environments will enable us to accrue a "a *subjective sense* of *an invigorating sameness* and *continuity*." Accordingly, we are likely to have a healthy personality, which Erikson (citing the definition of the late Austrian-British social pyschologist Marie Jahoda) says means a personality which (paraphrasing him) enables us *actively to master our* *environment, function in a unified, integrated fashion, and perceive the world and self correctly* (79:92). Psychologist and psychotherapist L. Michael Hall puts the meaning in terms of the attributes of a health personality, specifying the six (in paraphrase form) which follow (366):

1. **Acceptance**. Acknowledging reality -- what is -- without either resignation or condemnation, merely its existence
2. **Adjustment of expectations**. Adjusting expectations to conform to reality; avoiding being unrealistic
3. **Use of personal power**. Having a sense of being resourceful and powerful
4. **Flexibility and openness**. Being open to the new and willing to accept change
5. **Positive, optimistic attitude**
6. **Empowering through framing**. Framing things in such a way as to give one power over them rather than them having power over us, the locus of control being internal rather than external

These six attributes of a healthy personality essentially involve acknowledging and adjusting to reality and responding to reality with a sense of optimism and self-empowerment. In our discussion of character below, we will see how the six get conceptualized and, variously, referenced as character assets on which school and life success depend.

African American Core Identity

Our African American core identity, and its consequences, can be said to reflect a personality structure which, in part, dates back to the conceptualization of it, in 1951, by Kardiner and Ovesey in their classic study, The Mark of Oppression: Explorations in the Personality of the American Negro, discussed in Chapter 11. Drawing upon their work, and upon the subseqent literature, here is how we might conceptualize that structure:

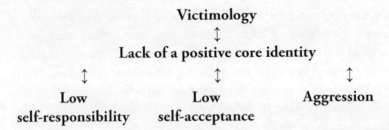

Due to our second bondage, Victimology, we can think of our personality as grounded in victimhood (a syndrome), the lack of a positive core identity being at its center, the psychological outcomes of that lack being low self-responsibility, low self-acceptance, and aggression, all associated with an array of consequences. Pronounced among our lower class, the literature suggests that, in various manifestations, it is also present among our middle class. Of course, it is equally evident from the literature that, conceivably, any number of other African American personality constructs might be possible, and defensible, but without making a specific case for this personality construct, it is contended that it, too, is defensible. The data in this chapter, and, indeed, more or less, throughout the book, are believed – directly and indirectly -- to make it so. Attention now turns to a discussion of its central attribute: our lack of a positive core identity.

Scott's thesis

In an informative scholarly paper, Imani Michelle Scott (formerly K. Michelle Scott),[28] a

Professor at Savannah College of Art and Design(SCAD), in Atlanta, makes the point that we African Americans, individually and as a group, have not developed a healthy personality, in particular, a "unified, loved self" (443). Drawing upon the theory of the transgenerational transmission of trauma developed by renowned psychoanalyst, Varnik

---

[28] Cited and quoted with permission of Dr. Scott, who formerly went under the name K. Michelle Scott. She has legally changed her name to Imani Michelle Scott. Also see her recent publication at the following link: www.crimeagainsthumanitybook.com

Vamik Volkan, she submits that, in varying degrees many, of us still suffer from the trauma suffered under enemy (Western and white) domination-- colonialism, enslavement, theories of racial inferiority, exploitation, lynchings, beatings, threats, Jim Crow laws, and so on. "There is," Scott argues, "an apparent conflict about both group and individual identity. There is, at once, a shame associated with acting black, a disdain for acting white, and an ambivalence associated with skin color." These three generational mental transmissions contribute to "the lack of a strong core identity or unified self."

Contrary to expectation, Scott contends that the Civil Rights Movement of the 1960s, and its accompanying sense of unity and themes of "Black Power" and "Black is Beautiful," did not alter these transmissions. Instead, they "only scratch[ed] the surface of a deeply rooted identity conflict." Consciously and unconsciously, the mental transmissions continue, carried through such notions as "show one's color," "act like a nigger," "act your age and not your color," and "acting white," as well as through colorism -- or different status and treatment within the African American community based on such skin designations as red-bone, high yellow, pecan tan, and black. So, she points out, do the consequences as evident in the fact that though about 12 percent of the population, when it comes to social disarray (for example, school dropouts, out-of-wedlock births, crime, and health problems), depending on the variable, we typically are in the 30-60 percent range -- "symptom[s] of the lingering pain of a collective self-esteem and identity long loss." They, too, may be symptoms of something which Scott does not make part of her discussion: family dysfunction, which herein is emphasized throughout.

In the case of poor black males, perhaps that pain is no more evident than in the homicide statistics (46:8-9). Of roughly 16,000 homicides yearly, over half are committed by black men. Black men are seven times more likely to commit murder than white men and six times more likely to be murdered. Moreover, 94% of all black people murdered are murdered by other blacks. While whites also tend to murder other whites (their rate being 86 percent), it is the proportion of blacks involved which is so alarming. Though just 13 percent of population, we blacks make up over half the homicide victims, 85 percent of those victims being young black men, 94 percent of whom are murdered mostly by other young black men (403a). As black economist, Walter Williams, of George

Mason University starkly put it, "Young black males have a greater chance of reaching maturity on the battlefields of Iraq and Afghanistan than on the streets of Philadelphia, Chicago, Detroit, Oakland, Newark and other cities" (471g). The cost to families and society is estimated to be $43 billion annually and $17 million per victim -- that cost including such factors as lost productivity, medical care costs, costs to police, courts, prisons, and social services; and costs to families of victims and suspects. As a reminder of these costs, we add another mnemonic: **young black male fratricide: 13% - 50+% - 85% - 94%.**

Optimal sense of identity. The young-black-male on young-black-male murder rate reflects the loss of self-esteem and identity to which Scott alludes, and the result of which, Scott says, is inevitable emotional upheaval and disconnectedness, out of which we get these statistics. It is inevitable because of the "innate human need to develop a positive sense of selfdom, including self-esteem, dignity, and self-respect." The inference can thus be drawn that the need for a positive identity is a basic need akin to the basic need for food, clothing, and shelter. Erik Erikson declares, as elsewhere cited, that "in the social jungle of human existence there is no feeling of being alive without a sense of identity." Maybe, too, that need is reflected in the conclusion attributed to world famous writer and art collector, Gertrude Stein, that "Negroes are not suffering from persecution they were suffering from nothingness." Erikson seems to be suggesting such nothingness can be traced to the lack of a positive sense of identity. To feel alive and to avoid suffering from nothingness, we can take from Scott and Erikson (among others) that our identity must be positive. We must have an enduring sense of sameness and continuity. This is the picture which Erikson paints when such an identity is at its optimal:

An optimal sense of identity...is experienced merely as a sense of psychosocial well- being. Its most obvious concomitants are a feeling of being at home in one's body, a sense of 'knowing where one is going,' and an inner assuredness of anticipated recognition from those who count (79:165).

Interesting, is it not, that Erikson's picture includes "a feeling of being at home in one's body," a feeling reflected by its absence in Kevin Powell's story and in the story of so many of us African Americans -- males and females alike. However, the data suggest that it is more pronounced in us males When that feeling is optimal, or at least positive, good things are likely to happen to us since, as a result -- thanks to the character assets which ensue from it -- we are more able to manage our life.

Negative sense of identity. An incident recalled by aforementioned black Hispanic sociologist, Pedro Noguera, would appear to illustrate the negative in contrast to the positive depicted by Erikson. In his book, The Trouble with Black Boys, Noguera relates the story of a playground basketball incident wherein two black males in a game in which he was a participant threatened to kill one another over a flagrant foul incident. Noguera wondered why, with so much at stake – family, job, and so on -- they would let it so escalate. What Noguera witnessed is not unusual among us African American males -- the fighting over what amounts to little or nothing -- but is, instead, somewhat common and, therefore, allows us to surmise what might have happened. It might appear that nothing is at stake in such moments when, in fact, everything is at stake, that everything being our essence or core identity -- our sense of that which anchors us in our daily living and which gives us a uniqueness and a feeling of being alive -- in this instance, that sense being our toughness.

As President Bush's reaction to the Rapper, Kanye West's, accusation might have been due to his core identity of himself as a caring, racially-sensitive, prejudice-free man. In this incident, for each player, at stake was a core identity of himself as *tough*. Any doubt cast upon that identity evoking – as in the case of President Bush – a strong and seemingly inexplicable reaction. *It be interjected that it is apparent, from life and the literature, that this toughness, along with cool-pose style and sexuality, can be said to make up part of the core identity of a large segment of us African American males, particularly the poor among us.* Scott's thesis suggests that this toughness -- this everything -- is flawed and frail, providing an answer to Noguera and to the rest of us who might likewise wonder. Being flawed and frail, it is like a house with a faulty foundation, which, understandably, is unable to hold together against a raging storm, but which, surprisingly, cannot do so even against a passing wind, to which a flagrant foul might be analogous.

Core identity and other identities. As stressed, we have other identities, called sub-identities or extended identities, but these other identities "can either be embraced or rejected," but not so with our core identity. To lose or destroy our core identity, not to have formed one, or to be in conflict about it -- as is the case with many African Americans -- "is terrifying," as Scott depicts it. Out of that terror we get the kind of disconnectedness, instability, and destruction that we see in the Noguera basketball story and in *segments* of our African American community -- just *segments*, not the entirety. Thus, in the urban riots of the 1960s, for example, we saw those segments destroy, not the neighborhoods of the perceived enemy (whites), but their (and our) own. These outcomes, Scott argues, reflect internalized aggression due to our inability – through an externalized remedy -- to repair the damage caused by the trauma inflicted on us by the oppressor. We, ourselves, now continue to inflict and sustain the trauma and the damage which result from it.

A different analysis: revisionist nigrescence (Cross)

Scott's thesis is consistent with what Erikson and others say about the pivotal role of identity in personality development and, as discussed below, gets more direct support from John McWhorter and Shelby Steele, but no such support from William E. Cross Jr., a black University of Virginia psychologist. In his book, Shades of Black: Diversity in African-American Identity, Cross gives a useful overview of what is called nigrescence, a French word which means the "process of becoming black" -- the conceptualization and study of which he initiated as a graduate student at Princeton University and, with others, subsequently popularized in the late 1960s. Nigrescence is credited with being a major force in the evolution of the "racial self" which emerged during the same period (150a:121-33).

Cross defines nigresence as the psychology of becoming black, or as a resocializing experience which seeks to transform a preexisting identity (a non-Afrocentric identity) into one that is Afrocentric. He analyzes the psychology of becoming black as a four-stage process: *Pre-encounter* (the existing identity to be changed); *Encounter* (event that provokes or triggers change toward blackness); *Immersion-Emersion* (transitional period characterized by emotional identification with blackness accompanied by serious examination of what it means); and *Internalization* (secure, at-home feeling in one's blackness). Some theorists conceptualize a fifth stage, *Internalization-Commitment,* whereby interest in black affairs in sustained over a long period of time.

Cross divides studies of black identity into two periods: the *Negro Self-Hatred* period, 1939-1960, and the *Nigrescence* period, 1968-1980. The Negro Self-Hatred period included the landmark studies of Eugene and Ruth Horowitz, Kenneth and Mamie Clark, and Abram Kadiner and Lionel Ovesy. The nigrescence studies coincide with the *Black Power phase* of the Civil Rights Movement, which began after the death of Dr. King in 1968 and continued through the mid-1970s, The rights phase of the movement covered the period 1954 until the death of Dr. King in 1968. The nigrescence studies document an increasing influence of race and culture on black *group* identity.

In a reexamination and reinterpretation of the self-hatred studies, Cross concludes that the old approach was wrong. It had been assumed that the studies from 1939-1960 showing black self-hatred were valid, but his reexamination and reinterpretation reveal that they were not. We blacks were not self-hating -- not at all when it comes to *personal identity* and only a small percentage of us when it comes to *group identity.* Cross's interpretation is that, validly interpreted, those studies which show black self-hatred instead show both a positive personal identity and a positive group identity, the exception being a negative group identity for a small percentage of blacks. Even for this small percentage – Cross's interpretation goes -- the circumstances point, not to self-rejection, but to the internalization of a Eurocentric orientation.

Cross contends that the self-hatred studies were not validly interpreted because they incorrectly assumed that which had not been validated: a high correlation between personal identity (PI) and group identity (reference group orientation, or RGO). To the contrary, he contends that "there is no overall pattern of a relationship between PI and RGO" (52a: 139). That is, the researchers' interpretation of the feelings expressed by the subjects toward the race was not necessarily an indication of their own feelings about themselves; the evidence shows that there was no "overall pattern" of such a one-to-one relationship. Furthermore, Cross argues, the researchers' interpretation was based on the study of preschool children whose preferences are formative. To justify his conclusions, Cross goes into considerable statistical and research detail.

As for the emotional upheaval addressed by Scott, Cross attributes it, and its consequent disconnection and self-destruction, not to the lack of a positive core identity, but, instead, to systemic and structural forces. Drawing upon nigrescence research, his conclusion is that "at the level of the psychology of the individual, the multilayered strengths of Black communities have afforded a successful, positive socialization of children who, as adults, have transmitted these strengths to the next generation over many generations" (52a: 186). Given this positive transmission, to explain such disconnection and self-destruction, cited by Scott and reflected in the compilation, "Facts, Figures, and More: Adapted Excerpts" in Chapter 17, Cross argues that "Only in the most recent times [his book was published in 1991] when poor and working-class Blacks have become, in economic terms, superfluous to society, has the modest level of material resources needed to continue this positive tradition been withdrawn, giving rise to the *alleged nihilism* [emphasis added] of the underclass" (52a:186). He adds:

> As an aside, my prediction is that when the research is finally all in, the "negative Psychology" of the underclass will be shown to be an exaggeration; the underclass will be revealed to be less a psychological problem than a predicament bought [sic] on by systemic and structural changes beyond the pale of any "will power" the members of the underclass are able to muster (52a: 186-87).

If, then, until recently, everything was so positive, the question arises as to why the need for nigrescence. Cross contends that it is not because of anti-blackness or self-hatred, but instead, because blackness held a low salience. Nigrescence studies, he says, convey "a picture of latent Black pride, a dormant concern for race and culture, and a general low salience for race" (52a:174). Nigrescence has functioned to awaken that dormancy and increase that salience, taking us -- as Cross views it -- through the same kind of process through which we were taken by the Harlem Renaissance or the New Negro Movement of the 1920s and 1930s, discussed below (52a:89-90). That is, we were, more or less, being born again, so to speak. Cross sees the research as showing the outcome as yielding, not everyone black being Afrocentric (as Afrocentric theorist would insist), nor everyone Afrocentric incorporating blackness in its totality, but, instead, as yielding various black identities: nationalist, bicultural, and multicultural, including Afrocentricity. That is, he sees the outcome as yielding no litmus test for blackness or "single [black] ideological" perspective (52a:222-23).

Evaluation of the two theses: "acting white" controversy deja vu

It should come as no surprise that Scott's explanation of our plight as the outcome of the lack of a positive core identity -- a unified, loved self -- occasions the same kind of self/system confrontation as the home/school responsibility debate, the IQ firestorm, and -- more directly -- the identity issue at the heart of the "acting white" controversy, a confrontation (as herein argued) that had it origin in the war between Washington and DuBois and that has only intensified since nigrescence. Like Ainsworth-Darnell and Downey in the case of "acting white," Cross is expressly intent on debunking, in this instance not "an attractive theory," but an accepted research finding: that blacks exhibit self-hatred. Likewise, in the fashion of Ainsworth-Darnell and Downey with respect to the pro-school attitude of black students, he says that our identity had been positive until recently (prior to 1991) when, in effect, the system began to deprive many of the "modest level of material resources needed to continue this positive tradition." Of course, as in the case of "acting white," he concedes that there might have been a "small percentage" who exhibited *group self-hatred* but its expression probably represented, not self-rejection, but a function of having internalized a Eurocentric culture and world view.

As for *personal self-hatred*, Cross concludes that there was never "a pattern" of its existence. Even though the often cited classic study of Kardiner and Ovesey, for example, The Mark of Oppression: Explorations in the Personality of the American Negro, documented the contrary, Cross -- as Ainsworth-Darnell and Downey have done in regard to Fordham-Ogbu's theory -- declares it invalid. As reasons for declaring the concept of notion of black self-hatred invalid, he inclusively cites its small sample size (sounds familiar?) and a reanalysis of their 25 case studies by John H. Rohrer and Munro S. Edmonson reported in their book, The Eighth Generation: Cultures and Personalities of New Orleans Negroes. In defending his reliance on their analysis, Cross argues that they "did not believe in a monolithic Black culture or Black perssonality; rather, they felt that to study Blacks was to encounter cultural and psychological diversity" (52a: 130).

Cross contends that Rohrer and Edmonson's reanalysis shows that Kardiner and Ovesey had exaggerated the evidence since as they themselves found self-hatred in only seven of their twenty-five cases. Whether Rohrer and Edmonson are right is beyond the expertise of the author to determine. But it is odd that Cross complains that their reanalysis has been overlooked by the scholarly community, including Kenneth Clark and Thomas Pettigrew. One wonders why. Could it be that the scholarly community has not found it that credible? Rohrer and Edmonson expressly set out to undermine Kardiner-Ovesey's findings. Though Cross claims that their methodology "seem[s] to have succeeded in controlling for experimenter bias, a factor they felt may well have contaminated the "mark of oppression" study," how is it that they managed to avoid bias when, as Cross states, they undertook their analysis "not believ[ing] in a monolithic Black culture or Black personality; rather, they felt that to study Blacks was to encounter cultural and psychological diversity?" If determined and delimited, one can often end up finding that which one seeks, especially if one is dealing with data which are subjective in nature and which are not so easy, years later, reliably, to reconstruct, tease out, and soundly interpret its details and nuances.

That there is no one-to-one correspondence between individual identity and group identity, as Cross presents evidence to establish, is not inconsistent with Scott's thesis. Scott's contention is that "racial identity is considered to be a powerful determinant of individual behavior." Though identity is complex and multidimensional, "racial identity", she points out, "continues to be stronger than identities based on class, gender, religion, or any other social characteristics as a predictor of attitudes." "Thus for the African American," she goes on to say, "the command of racial identity is substantial, if for no other reason than the fact that the blackness of African American skin is the single, most distinctively obvious, and thus unifying, characteristic that group members share."

Scott's point essentially echoes the same point made by retired University of California social psychologis, Thomas Pettigrew, almost forty years earlier in his <u>A Profile of the Negro American</u>. He wrote, "... the ubiquity of racial prejudice in the United States guarantees that virtually every Negro American faces at some level the impersonal effects of discrimination, the frightening feeling of being a black man in what often appears to be a white man's world" (209d:3). If that were not the case, we blacks would be an exception, for, as Erik Erikson says:

> The individual belonging to an oppressed and exploited minority, which is aware of the dominant cultural ideals but prevented from emulating them, is apt to fuse the negative images held up to him by the dominant majority with his own negative identity. [sentence omitted] There is ample evidence of 'inferiority" feelings and of morbid self-hate in all minority groups; and, no doubt, the righteously and fiendishly efficient way in which the Negro slave in America was forced into and kept in conditions preventing in most the incentive for independent ambition now continues to exert itself as a widespread and deep-seated inhibition to utilize equality even where it is "granted" (79a:155).

Cross is scathing in his criticism of the self-hatred findings being based so heavily on the study of children. However, Pettigrew has indicated that "similar studies of older Negro children find residual symptoms" (209d:8). That, too, is the implication of Billson's previously cited in-depth study of five African American males. She reports, "The strategic styles evident in early adolescence were not spurious by-products of a particular stage in the process of identity formation. The same styles are still very much operative in late adolescence--indelibly drawn, it seems, from the original portraits" (10:192). Pettigrew further points out that "confused identity in adulthood even reveals itself among the most militant and articulate Negroes." "A careful statistical analysis of Richard Wright's autobiography, *Black Boy*," he continues,

> strongly suggests this famous Negro writer lacked a basic identification with other Negroes. Four-fifths of his descriptions of Negroes are unfavorable and do not at, [sic] all coincide with his recurrent self-description. 'My life at home,' wrote Wright, 'has

cut me off, not only from white people but from Negroes as well' (209d:9; see also 281a).

It would be surprising if such residual symptoms were not present in adulthood or that, given from where they often come, many of the famous, as well, do not bear them. They, and so many of us, have come from the world of the poor -- or have in some way been affected by that world. This is Lee Rainwater's description of it:

> To those living in the heart of a ghetto, black comes to mean not just 'stay back,' but also membership in a community of persons who think poorly of each other, who attack and manipulate each other, who give each other small comfort in a desperate world. Black comes to stand for a sense of identity as no better than these destructive others. The individual feels that he must embrace an unattractive self in order to function at all (215a:205).

While Pettigrew's observations take us back to the 1960s, and while Rainwater is talking about the poor, the discussion below of nigrescence and its fallout suggests that, at least to some degree, what they say has current applicability. Here, for example, is what Kevin Powell (referenced below), writing to his cousin, has to say on the subject:

> For any children, black or white, to suffer through that kind of distortion of basic reality--that is, the notion that their culture, their way of life, is inferior and another people's is superior--is the equivalent of living a death. And die, Anthony, is something that you and I and pretty much every black boy and black girl we grew up with wanted to do. That is, we wanted, because of our self-hatred and our hatred of people who looked like us, to rid ourselves of our blackness, to jet from the ghetto, both physically and mentally, to live a life similar to what we saw whites living all around us--on TV, in films, in books and magazines. But most of us couldn't and never will, so we seek out, as I've said, escape routes: sex, drugs, alcohol, addiction to material things like clothes, cars, jewelry--anything that gives the illusion that we are somehow making it.

Then, Powell goes on to suggest the carry over into adulthood:

> Oftentimes to be "black" in America is to be in a constant state of denial: We deny our skin color, we deny our race (think of how many of us brag about being one- quarter this and one-eighth that--anything not to be black!), and we deny ourselves. And a person who denies his or her heritage, at root, is also denying his or her existence. On a basic level, this is the very reason why we black children so easily dissed each other with cracks about each other's mothers, about our skin colors, our noses, lips, butt sizes, and our hair textures. Our playin' the dozens was our self-hatred manifested (212b: 49-50).

The intent here, however, is less to examine Cross's rationale for his refutation of the popular black self-hatred portrayal and more to underline the extent to which many in the academic community go to exonerate us blacks from any responsibility for our plight, or even, in his case, to recognize that plight. Cross provides another example of our too frequent refusal to accept, understand, and realistically grapple with our problems.

The statistics cited by Scott, and which are reflected in "Facts, Figures, and More: Adapted Excerpts" in Chapter 17, can be interpreted as objective evidence which undermines his argument. So, for example, does a recent article (September 9, 2013) by the staff of the Atlanta Black Star entitled, "10 Black Celebs Expressing Self-Hate." Its opening sentence makes the point:

> Black is beautiful" is a slogan that is popular the world over and in many ways has become a maxim for black folks who love their brown skin and African features. However, some black celebrities are not as comfortable in their own skin and have either changed their physical appearance, denied that they are black, or have made statements that could be labeled as self-hating (304d).

Among the ten are Janet Jackson, Lil Wayne, Sheryl Underwood, and yes -- surprise, surprise -- the Rev. Al Sharpton ("has been wearing a perm for decades"). Of course, ten black celebrities is not the same as many or most, and it is only speculated that they "could be" seen as self-hating, but the speculation at least makes it an open question. So does the number of references to the topic which one finds as one scans the internet, and although the research points to a transformation of black low self-esteem to black high self-esteem since the 1960s, what that transformation means -- and what the research itself means -- is subject to debate (295a; 305; 446c).

Whatever the status of black self-hate, it seems not to be the topic of currency, having been replaced by the centrality of blackness as the issue – something which can be attributed to nigrescence. As Cross suggests – and as Eric Dyson, Roland Martin, and Toureȼ, for example, declare (see below) -- there is no one way to be black. What most appears to differentiate those various ways is the centrality of one's blackness -- the extent to which one defines oneself in terms of race. The interest in finding out led University of Michigan black psychologist, Robert Sellers, and his colleagues to develop The Multidimensional Model of Black Identity (MMBI), which yields a profile of what can be called diversified blackness (some of that diversity being alluded to in Chapter 1) – the idea somewhat captured by Eugene Robinson in his book subtitle, <u>The Splintering of Black America</u> (444c). Cross's point, however, is that whatever the centrality, in our blackness inheres, not as Scott theorizes, trauma producing a negative core identity, but -- until the recent assault on the underclass -- a positive one.

But Cross is wrong. The fact is that the preponderance of the literature reviewed suggests that we blacks have historically suffered from a widespread lack of a positive core identity -- a unified, loved self. This is especially true of the poor among us. It is a lack which Scott credibly argues helps to explain what Cross himself admits to be a recent "rise...[of] the *alleged* [emphasis added] nihilism of the underclass," the nihilism (to use his description) being in his eyes, please note, not a matter of statistics, but something *alleged* (get the point about recognizing and confronting our plight). Nothing need be said about Cross's idea that our psychic plight is something "recent," the product of the deprivation of "the modest level of materials resources needed." We know that for many statistics, we are talking about, not a "recent" condition but a historical one. To contribute the nihilism solely to a deprivation of material resources is a claim that one searches in vain for evidence to support. Rather, one is reminded, once again, that the world of make-believe attributed to the black middle-class of his time by Frazier still exists; only its composition has changed.

Cross has thrust himself into the black identity issue declaring that his reanalysis of the research shows that we have drawn the wrong conclusion from it: that we blacks hate ourselves. It does not show self-hate, he says, but instead shows that our self-regard is normal, only being black has held a low salience in our psyche, black salience being overshadowed by a Eurocentric perspective -- with existent black pride lying in latency, low in its salience. The prescription for him, through his four-step nigrescence – which, Lasch-Quinn says is "imbued with an adolescent tone of self-discovery" -- is to raise that salience so as to create a black identity which is Afrocentric instead of Eurocentric (150a: 123).

Revisionist nigrescence explored: a help or a hindrance

The question is whether Cross's four-step nigressence, or generally the post-1960s emphasis on blackness, helps or hinders black development of a positive core identity, a question that will be examined in the context of Scott's trauma thesis. For that examination we turn to a number of publications, several of which give us a look at the younger generation and what some call the post-blackness era occasioned by our first black president, Barak Obama. The headline, so to speak: **Panel of Publications Weigh Current Black Identity**. The panel includes:

- Steele's The Content of Our Character: A New Vision of Race in America (1990)
- Powell's Keepin' It Real (1997)
- Brown's Self Contempt (1998)
- Lasch-Quinn's Race Experts: How Racial Etiquette, Sensitivity Training, and New Age Therapy Hijacked the Civil Rights Revolution (2001)
- Dickerson's The End of Blackness: Returning the Souls of Black Folk to Their Rightful Owners (2004)
- McWhorter's Losing the Race: Self-Sabotage in Black American (2000) and Winning the Race (2006)
- Robinson's Disintegration: The Splintering of Black America (2010)
- Toure¢'s Who's Afraid of Post-Blackness?: What It Means to Be Black Now (2011)

- Cose's <u>The End of Anger: A New Generation's Take on Race and Rage</u> (2011)
- Thurston's <u>How to Be Black</u> (2012)

McWhorter's books have been previously referenced, as have those of Steele, Lasch-Quinn, Robinson, and Cose. Previously cited Kevin Powell shares intimate insights into the growing-up and ensuing experiences of a black male brought up in a low-income fatherless home who has been able to make it in the larger world. Black author, A. M. Brown, is a 47-year-old self-publisher with a social science background who reports experiences living in a variety of settings and having undertaken extensive research and interviews to write his book. Black author, journalist, and editor, Debra J. Dickerson, is part of the younger generation and draws upon a vast array of literature to make her case. Black author, novelist, and TV personality. Toure¢, draws upon interviews with 105 prominent blacks, including, using his descriptors: politicians like Harold Ford, Jr. and Sharon Pratt (first female mayor of Washington, D. C.); civil rights leaders like Revs. Jessie Jackson and Al Sharpton; visual artists like Kara Walker and Barkley L. Hendricks; recording artists Chuck D of Public Enemy and Santigold; writers like Malcolm Caldwell and Juan Williams, and academics like Dr. Michael Eric Dyson and Dr. Alvin Poussaint. Black media creator, comedian, and author Baratunde Thurston draws upon what he terms "a rock-star panel" of seven -- three black women, three black men, and one white man.

Scott's thesis. Support for Scott's thesis, as contrasted with that of Cross's, is reflected in a revealing story told by renown black Harvard historian, Henry Louis Gates Jr., as conveyed by Toure¢. This is the story:

'I give this lecture where I read quotes from people arguing over what the race should be called. They're arguing and postulating about what the race should be called and why it would be liberatory if we changed to being called 'colored.' Or why everything with the name "African" in it should be chiseled off the fucking map. Some people said Negro, some people said colored, one person said Africamericans, one person then says how about Afro-Americans? And you know when all this happened? Between the years 1831 and 1845. When I tell them that everybody in the class almost has a heart attack' (258b:203-04).

The story captures Scott's thesis that we continue our search for self-definition, Gates's students in heart-attack fashion being reminded of that reality. Toure¢'s book, as do all the others, reminds us of it too -- and engagingly so. Toure¢ concludes that "the debates over authenticity remain as passionate and pernicious as ever" (258b:154). He gives, for example, Dyson's description of three dimensions of blackness and CNN analyst, Roland Martin's description of four levels of blackness (258b:9-10, 153). Dyson names his three dimensions: accidental, incidental, and intentional. Toure¢ himself prefers to call them *introverted* (private relationship with blackness), *ambiverted* (fluid state of blackness wherein blackness is important but not necessarily dominant), and *extroverted* (a consuming, it's all about blackness). Based on proximity to the black experience, Martin names his four levels: *platinum* (authentic black, having grown up among the poor), *gold* (grew up in middle-class black neighborhood and got black experience through public school and college attendance), *silver* (grew up in mixed, educated black-white neighborhood and religious and social life middle-class oriented), and *bronze* (suburban with experiences in all-white settings with little or no black experience). Toure¢'s conclusion is that any answer that one gives as to what blackness means is valid (258b:20).

One of Thurston's panel members, Cheryl Contee (cofounder with Thurston of the *Jack & Jill Politics* blog), pus it perhaps more memorably: "'I think there is a stereotype that you're not really black unless you grew up dodging bullets, or eating food stamps, or…I don't know, actually engaging personally in rap battles or break dancing. I didn't do any of those things. I may have witnessed some break dancing and some rap battles. Okay, that may have happened. But I didn't personally do that.'" Nevertheless, her point is that "'I'm pretty black on the inside'" (257a:43).

No doubt this search for name and definition reflects an inward struggle; the question is whether to attribute it to the trauma of slavery and oppression ascribed to it by Scott. Black author, Terrie Williams (author of <u>Black Pain: It Just Looks Like We're Not Hurting</u>, published in 2008), tells Toure¢ that it is still true. She sees our people in pain – pain derived from the present and brought forth from the past through the suffering of our parents and ancestors (258b:141).

Both Steele and McWhorter agree, as does Lasch-Quinn, all seeing it as now mainly self-inflicted, self-sustained, and self-transmitted -- Steele through what he calls "objective correlatives," McWhorter through what he calls "meme," and Lasch-Quinn through the race experts.

Steele uses the term *objective correlative* to describe the process whereby an objective or random event evokes an emotionally powerful memory of an enemy, causing that event to be associated in one's mind with that enemy, and, therefore, responded to as if it were that enemy. Therefore, the objective present gets treated the same as the emotionally powerful enemy past which that objective present triggers in one's mind, although, in reality, it has nothing to do with the past. The correlatives are transmitted verbally and visually, he says, and exist everywhere – as, for example, in "you people," "credit to his race," and "one of my best friends," and the Confederate flag. From their existence, we blacks undergo pain and suffering, Steele using these terms to describe their nature: "vulnerability, self-doubt, helplessness, terror, and rage" (247a:154).

Of all the *objective correlatives*, Steele cites skin color ss the most haunting. That would appear to be Scott's thesis, too. For she contends that the themes of "Black Power" and "Black is Beautiful" (themes of nigrescence) which accompanied the Civil Rights Movement "only scratch the surface of a deeply rooted identity conflict." That conflict is rooted in color and its associated trauma, something noted not just by Steele, writing in 1990, but also, for example, by our panelist Toure¢, writing in 2011. Toure¢ reports signs of change, noting positive associations that have come to be associated with dark-skin color, specifically mentioning looking sexy and attractive.

But it is the signs of continuation which came across in Toure¢'s interviews. He asked his interviewees about the advantages and disadvantages of being light-skinned or dark-skinned. His dark-skinned interviewees groped for an answer while his light-skinned interviewees gave indications of being embarrassed by the question or voiced the advantages of being light-skinned (258b: 164-65). Dr. Poussaint told

Toureȼ that he thought dark-skinned blacks were more likely to suffer rejection by both community and family, and that he had seen families wherein the dark-skinned child would be shown favoritism over the light-skinned child because it was felt that the child's darkness would make her/his life harder (258b:162).

Powell, drawing from his experience, and writing in 1997 -- between Steele and Toureȼ -- likewise observed the color trauma. He asserts that to be black is to be in a constant state of denial – denial of our skin color, our race, and even ourselves. Many of us, he observes, brag about having some fraction of some other blood (212b:49-50). Spike Lee's film, "School Daze," coming out a year later (1988), gave credence to Powell's observation.[29] On a college campus, it revealed skin color, along with hair texture, to be a source of both identity pride and identity conflict.

McWhorter sees the trauma in our time -- which he dates from the decade 1960 to 1970, as do Steele and Lasch-Quinn -- as a "meme." as previously noted, a meme is a thought pattern "that become[s] entrenched in society via self-replication from mind to mind, along the lines of genes in organisms." Whether we are talking about the poor, the middle class, or their intellectual vanguard in the person of many academics (Cross, incidentally, being an example), the trauma (meme) does not emanate from the objective conditions imposed by whites, such as job or housing discrimination or credit denial. Improvements in those conditions no longer justify their being the source of such pain, McWhorter argues; instead, they only represent "lingering discrepancies" or "an occasional nuisance." His carefully crafted thesis is that our pain (translation: trauma) emanates instead from a *psychological* condition, that psychological condition being a lack of "fundamental self-love," or, otherwise stated, the persistence of "black self-hatred" which "after centuries of degradation…[has left] a hole in the black American soul" (160:226, 195, 163, 153-258). Scott's point is that the hole is a core identity hole whereby missing at both the individual and group level is a positive African American self-sense. She referring, more specifically, to segments of our black community wherein the hole is evident in disorder and dysfunctionality which, more or less, are the norm.

---

[29] Retruved on 4 December 2014 from http://en.wikipedia.org/wiki/School_Daze.

Prior to the Civil Rights Movement, and its Black Power phase, McWhorter argues that the hole could be filled by fighting against oppressive laws, policies, and practices. That was the source of our identity, as it were. That source, largely removed, we were left on our own, now, more or less, fully unchained, to fill that hole. We now had choices in our quest *to be* and *to become* -- of finding and defining our individuality or identity [a la Cross's nigrescence]. Drawing upon theories advanced by the great American thinker, Eric Hoffer, in his classic <u>The True Believer</u>, as well as upon Erik Erikson's theories, McWhorter points out that "The challenge was especially intimidating for a people who had had little opportunity to prepare themselves for the task" (161:166). Unprepared, we were left insecure and disconnected, needing to fill a hole that was now only half-filled, so to speak, half-filled because the filling of the hole by our civil rights successes can be characterized as physical in nature (objective, civic, structural).

The other half, the psychological half, had been left unfilled. That half is about "whites' deep-seated psychological feelings of bias against blacks." Overt white oppression had been largely removed and, thus, could no longer serve as a source of identity. But covert (inward) white oppression (the hateful feelings) had not and, therefore, could serve as the replacement identity source. Civic equality acquired, the quest became human equality [and thus, for example, attempts to get rid of IQ testing because test results can be interpreted as evidence that we blacks are not equal to whites]. The aforementioned black Brown University economist Glenn Loury would come to term it a quest for "race-egalitarianism," or the "presumption of equal humanity." With this replacement quest, "the struggle," that is the pain or trauma, was continued, "the idea that being black remains hell for all of us… [being] argued with an indignant fierceness that reveals the operations of the gut…" (161:177). In what social scientists call *path dependency*, McWhorter says that we came to depend on this idea to fill the hole in our soul even though the idea no longer reflected a changed reality. No matter, the theory continues, for in a state of disconnectedness, human beings seek a safe harbor in which to anchor their identity. We blacks found it in this idea (hateful white feelings) and have generationally transmitted it as if it were a gene. That makes it a meme, putting it at the core of our identity, for, in McWhorter's words, "The meme lives on the basis of the personally felt, the viscera, the gut. That is, the meme is a part of one's essence" (161:177).

Lasch-Quinn might well agree that our civil rights achievements left a "hole" in our soul, replaced by psychological grievances, and that, as Steele observes, objective correlatives abound. Her primary focus lies in explaining their origin. Her view is that both were avoidable, for though our civil rights were more or less won, there were abundant post-victory needs to fill the hole, needs which -- through objective correlatives -- did not have to be imagined, but that were real and fundamental -- needs, for example, as pertain to unemployment, school achievement, and gender relations.

Lasch-Quinn's thesis is that we did not avoid these pitfalls, however, because an army of race experts (educators, counselors, trainers, psychotherapists, consultants, and others), in effect, declared war on the presumed feelings which still existed in the hearts of blacks and whites. It was not enough to rid ourselves of the legal barriers which separated the races; these presumed feeling barriers must also give way. Here is her description of what, therefore, has taken place: "…nearly unnoticed, a whole army of diversity experts has penetrated mainstream America equipped with half-baked, contradictory, quasi-scientific pseudo-truths that promise to liberate whites from their alleged racism and blacks from their assumed bondage of low self-esteem" (150a:iv-xv).

Their main weapon has been sensitivity training through small-group activity, called training or T-group (or encounter group) activity, accompanied by an array of other behavior-oriented racial solutions. All have been part of the human potential movement of the 1960s and 1970s which encompassed the idea that "the personal is political" -- that through our individual growth as persons we can change the political, that is, society (150a:53-109). Lasch-Quinn's analysis is that that is exactly what has happened, but for the worse instead of the better. Steele and McWhorter have described that worse, and Lasch-Quinn concludes that one of the "main consequences was to help legitimize the notion of race-related personality traits, [and] different psychological and emotional needs and makeups." "Out of the maelstrom of racial politics in the 1960s thus crystallized," she continues, "*a newly racialized self*" [emphasis added] -- with the feelings hardened not softened but, and as both Steele and McWhorter emphasize, camouflaged behind rituals and rhetoric (150a:131-32; 110-33).

That the trauma ("thingification of the past," as Dr. King terms it) remains part of our essence is reflected, as well, by other panel members. Brown, for example, even entitles his book <u>Self Contempt: A Search for the Identity of Black America</u> and bemoans the continued existence of "a largely ominous and undignified racial identity" (23a:v). In <u>The End of Blackness</u>, Dickerson pleads for us to free ourselves of the trauma inherent in the history of our blackness, to give up "believing that … [we] are marginalized, that whites are all powerful and all evil, and that America wants to see…[us] fail" (58:49). Black Pulitzer Prize-winning author, Eugene Robinson, confides:

> …I know that the experience of Jim Crow has left me with a hard little nugget of suspicion and resentment buried deep inside, and that it gives me motivation and strength. It's the feeling that there are people out there who don't want me to succeed, which makes me all the more determined to deny them satisfaction (227:187-88).

Robinson adds that African Americans of his generation, consciously or unconsciously, pass some of this feeling along to their children.

Toure¢'s watermelon story supports Robinson's revelation (258b:112-13). Toure¢ says that, when he was young, he was taught not to eat watermelon in front of whites to avoid being stereotyped. So, when his baby son practically snatched a slice of watermelon held to his mouth by a friend, sending everyone into hysterical laughter, Toure¢ recoiled inside, possessed by the feeling that they were laughing at his little black son's stereotypical behavior. But he said he was strong enough to be able to step back and realize they were merely enjoying a baby's joy.

As Steele might interpret it, Robinson's "hard little nugget of suspicion and resentment" and Toure¢'s watermelon story represent the operation of "objective correlatives," whereas, to McWhorter, they represent a "hole in their soul," however small, and to Lasch-Quinn the camouflage of the hole to which the race experts have contributed. Perhaps harmless in the case of Robinson and Toure¢, harmless and transitory as these "objective correlatives" or "holes in the soul" might otherwise appear,

Steele, McWhorter, and Lasch-Quinn -- like Terrie Williams -- are calling our attention to the same profound consequences theorized by Scott. Steele sees them as having such a powerful hold on our psyche that it diverts and drains our resources from more productive pursuits (247a:151). Lasch-Quinn concurs, in effect, seeing the "correlatives" and "holes" as preventing "a more careful accounting of what problems we have overcome and what problems remain" (150a:xvii).

One is reminded of "acting white," of which so many of us are dismissive. As with "acting white," our panel is suggesting that the trauma is there in the form of "a hard little nugget of suspicion and resentment" which we experience and in the pervasive objective correlatives with which we live. It is a question of the solidity of its footing in our psyche. That footing is likely to be minimal if, like Toureȼ, we are strong enough, as is likely to be the case with our strong students when it comes to "acting white," or when it comes to taking a college test as in the Steele-Aronson stereotype threat studies (discussed in Chapter 12). In the eyes of most of the panel, and as documented by Ellis Cose's survey reported in <u>The End of Anger</u>, that would certainly appear to be the case with the younger generation represented by Toureȼ and by Thursten and his panel. In their case, the trauma may tarnish their core identity without producing turmoil, the solid footing of slavery and oppression replaced by the softer footing of racism. Cose captures the views of the young respondents in his survey as follows:

> Still, despite their obvious success, my respondents did not perceive a world where race no longer matters. While their take, in many respects, was decidedly upbeat, it was laced with pain and wariness. They saw a world in which race seriously affects opportunities for blacks and Hispanics, but (and this is a crucial "but") not strongly enough to prevent them from getting where they want to go (49:12).

That is, from the panel (as well as other sources) one gathers two identity footings: one in which slavery and overt oppression hold sway and the other in which its offspring, racism, holds sway. Both are traumatizing, reaping havoc on our core identity -- our unified, loved self -- that havoc evident in the dysfunctionality we see among our poor and in the pervasive dis-ease and discontent we see among the more privileged. The difference is seismic, reflective (together with other factors, of course,) of a middle-class mainstream in one case and the Abandoned in the other. We know about slavery and oppression and, equally, about prejudice and discrimination, but, as for racism, its use is thrown around so loosely that there is a need to come to grips with what it really means – or think it means.

Racism as objective correlative and recomposition. Racism can be called the problem of the mind-line versus the color-line of the past. Herein, it is being called black racism because it is based on black thinking (many whites, of course, share it). As stated, black racism can be defined as the black perception of whites as the opposition, felt to be guilty, if not of conspiring against blacks, of pervasive and persistent prejudice and discrimination against blacks, the feeling being so indiscriminate or irrational as to constitute what can be called cultural obsessive-compulsive disorder (OCD). Therefore, it might be said that it is a *psychological* thing, a *feeling*, devoid of valid objective evidence, that we have suffered a wrong due *mainly*, if not *only*, to our race. Because of the aforementioned phenomenon of objective correlative, however, the objective evidence gets transformed into a reflection of a past, still-nurtured, evil. As seen through the life of one of his interviewees, Toure¢ expressed what he learned from other interviewees as well: whatever our success, we cannot avoid racism; it is inescapable (258b:136).

Oprah Winfrey's request to see a $38,000 Tom Ford bag provides an example of Toure¢'s assertion (365c). Oprah says that when she asked to see the bag, the Zurich boutique store clerk refused to get it because the clerk felt it was too expensive and Oprah's feeling would be hurt by showing Oprah something she presumably could not afford. Oprah reports responding by thanking her and then walking out without buying it (the clerk, incidentally, denying that the incident occurred). Toure¢'s point is that we should not be surprised because elevated status, such as bestowed by her fame and estimated fortune of $2.8 billion, does not protect us blacks from racism.

Regardless of standing or fortune, the inescapable nature of racism is the operative thought here, somewhat echoing the declaration of the late black civil rights lawyer, Derrick Bell (and others who share his critical race theory outlook), that we are better off to resign ourselves to permanent racism since whites will never accept us as their equals (47:160). Touré describes it as the face of modern racism – invisible, yet omnipresent (258b: 119). It is not the trauma, for example, of slavery, Southern lynching, or Northern housing segregation, but, instead, often just transitory pain – what Touré says comedian Paul Mooney, calls "a nigger wake-up call," and Gates labels "the scene of instruction" (258b:125). Thus is the softer nature of the trauma of which Scott speaks, existing, as Eugene Robinson describes it, of "a hard little nugget of suspicion and resentment buried deep inside"-- a resentment which, as Lasch-Quinn sees it, our race experts, with declared intentions to the contrary, have not only helped to perpetuate, but have even exacerbated.

Notwithstanding our civil rights gains, racism thus conjures a race under siege, inescapably engaged in a struggle for survival and success against the omnipresent and oppressive, if invisible, evil forces of white society. It is a picture of what Steele calls *recomposition* (247a:57-75). It is a world wherein we "transform our doubts and threats into something different from what they really are" and "externalize them by seeing others as responsible for them," or, to state it differently, we "deny one reality" and "create another "reality" [security blanket, as it were] to cover over the real one" (247a:58, 60). Steele cites, as one example, the mother of a white teammate on the YMCA swimming team who would constantly correct his grammar, in response to which he told his teammate that his mother disliked black people and was taking it out on him. Told about his feeling, the teammate's mother sat him down, told him about herself and her desire for him to succeed, not giving a "good goddamn" about his race. Steele confides remorse, realizing that the teammate's mother was extending him human kindness, and that if she had been black he might not have responded as he did. But his feelings of doubt and threat had led him to recompose, creating his own "reality" in which he covered up the real one.

That is what one reads into the prevalent racism charge of our day: a cover up of the *actual realities* with *created realities*. That is what Steele is saying and that is what we can sense from our panelists. For example, Robinson's "hard little nugget of suspicion and resentment buried deep inside" is a prescription for just that. It is precisely such a nugget, for example, which led Steele and Touré to respond as each did. Both came to censor their *recomposition* and charge of racism, and to see that their correlatives were not the real thing. The panelists cry, like the cry of Scott, is for us, on a group basis, to do the same, that is, to manage productively the trauma that we continue to bear or, otherwise, continue to fall prey to its toll -- the crux of which is a flawed core identity.

In answer, then, to our question as to whether nigrescence helps or hinders the development of a positive core identity, one can conclude from our panel that the answer is that it hinders it. Instead, it reinforces the negative. Quite emphatically, Lasch-Quinn asserts that it represents, after our civil rights victories, the forces of reaction, giving "a new lease on life to race-conscious behavior not entirely unlike the double racial standard that ruled under white supremacy" (150a:xiv). Rather than moving us towards a positive black core identity -- as Cross contends is the case -- nigrescence has moved us away from such an identity, instead insulating our trauma with what McWhorter cites Erikson as calling a "synthetic identity" -- an identity with cult-like features resulting from indoctrination-like teachings. In an attempt to fill the "hole in the soul" left by our civil rights successes, such an identity, to draw upon Steele, keeps us mired in a racialized self which engages in unending recomposition and objective correlatives. It is a story which boils down to nigrescence versus Americanism.

Nigrescence versus Americanism

Although our panelists, cry for the end to our self-inflicted trauma emanates from the fallout from the decade 1960 to 1970, that self-infliction has its origin in our African American Garden of Eden. It reflects the **Self-Responsibility Tradition** of Washington and the **System-Responsibility Tradition** of DuBois.

It is herein argued that those authors like Dickerson, Toure¢, Thurston, and other panel members who want to cross the mind-line and fashion their own individual identity, fall into the Self-Responsibility Tradition. They are fighting against the pressure to "embrace an unattractive self in order to function" (as Lee Rainwater puts it) -- a self that is narrowly defined for them by other blacks, the result of which would be to deny their desire for self-definition as an American. The identity they seek is not a black identity, but an American identity. It is not about nigrescence, the process of becoming black, but about Americanism, the process of becoming an American. To become an American is to become an individual free to pursue one's passion and fulfill one's destiny. This process (embraced by Washington) is not about color, which is subordinate, but about character and completeness.

In contrast, those in the nigrescence camp engage in the process of becoming black -- of acquiring what amounts to a black world view or mindset. That mindset, as evident in the "acting white" controversy, is reflected both in one's thinking and in one's lifestyle. As Cross puts it, "Blackness is a state of mind, not an inherited trait, and its acquisition often requires considerable effort" (52a:149). One learns to become black, he elaborates, in a similar fashion as one born a Jew learns to become Jewish in one's thinking, or one born a woman learns to become a feminist in one's thinking. Only, Cross stresses, *"There is no one way to be Black"* [emphasis in original], for black encompasses multiple orientations: nationalist, bicultural, and multicultural -- including Afrocentricity (52a: 149). Consistent with the System-Responsibility Tradition of which it is a part, whatever the black way, the process of pursuing it is less about the self than about the black mind system. It is about a way of thinking and doing which stamps one as black, a blackness in which inheres an identity filled with trauma -- the trauma of which Terrie Williams speaks, that is buried deep inside us as Eugene Robinson confides, and which has even left Ellis Cose's prosperous young black respondents feeling wary and seriously affected.

One can respond that an orientation towards an American identity is also about the system, the American mind system. True. However, the American mind system is about the individual. Its boundaries tend to be broad and encompassing, not narrow and restrictive. As Dickerson declares, "Whites have at least theoretically accepted that they do not have the right to question black choices or limit their options. But blacks recognize no such boundaries." She continues:

> It is blacks who critique other blacks' choices--from styles of dress, to relationship partners, to careers, to political affiliations. It is blacks who tell other blacks what they must think about affirmative action and O. J. Simpson. It is blacks who tell other blacks that they have to belong to certain organizations and not others. It is blacks who try to control the political, intellectual, and social discourse of other

blacks. It is blacks who ostracize and denounce their brethren for disagreeing with them and who can understand disagreement only as opportunism, self-hatred, or insanity. It is other blacks whom blacks spend their lives trying to please, not whites (58:13-14).

With particular reference to the life of the poor, though not excluding blacks generally, Powell paints a similar picture (212b:48). He sees little room for individuality in their world – from how one talks, walks, dresses, and eats; to the music listened to; to how one feel about whites. There is, he contends, a with us or against us mentality.

Elijah Anderson's ethnographic study – reported in his book, <u>Code of the Street: Decency, Violence, and the Moral Life of the Inner City</u>, underlines Powell's picture. In discussing the importance of public spaces in the lives of inner-city youth, Anderson sees those places [and he is referring to street life and the places which become part of it] as shaping their identities, identities which are carried into other domains of their life – school, church, employment, and so on. Not only are the street children affected by these places, so are the decent ones since, as at some point they too must show a commitment to the street (5:99). Whereas Anderson is talking about inner-city youth, the "acting white" controversy makes it evident that such identity demands extend as well to the outer-city -- demands that Anderson notes "carry over" into later life. It can be argued that, through Dickerson, through Toure¢, and through Thurston, we see that "carry over," as we do in the case of Eugene Robinson. We have seen it, too, in the story of Glenn Loury's conversion from a black conservative to an independent liberal, for as Adam Shatz tells it, he felt a need to "display a degree of commitment" to the civil rights establishment, something about which he had left no doubt in his Harvard University W. E. B. Du Bois Lectures in 2000, published under the suggestive title, <u>The Anatomy of Racial Inequality</u>.

These descriptions depict the operation of fictive kinship in black society at large just as in the "acting white" controversy Fordham-Ogbu depicted its operation at the school level. Fictive kinship, it might be recalled, is a black group mindset wherein we blacks have our own criteria by which blacks are judged, quite apart from white society, transgressions inviting sanctions. Those criteria constitute a mind-line which blacks cannot cross and remain in good standing. Whereas Cross asserts that there is no one way to be black, or one black identity, fictive kinship, on the other hand, operates to keep the diverse ways within a narrow confine.

The point is that the evidence suggests that we blacks are born into a kind of identity vise which tends to inhibit our ability to adapt and to be, and whose grip is so firm that though some of us are able to escape it, we feel a need to demonstrate that we are still not totally beyond its confines -- as President Obama did in the Trayvon Martin case. As a result, somewhat like Erik Erikson's adolescents, many of us face -- and have historically faced -- an African American identity crisis. In our case, the crisis is not about adulthood, but about Americanhood: essentially about forging an *acceptable* black identity within American society at large. John Ogbu traces its roots back to slavery, E. Franklin Frazier discerned it in the 1950s, Fordham-Ogbu and other ethnographers see it in the continuing "acting white" controversy, and Dickerson, Toure¢, and others bring us up to date on its present pervasiveness, which, for some at least, is a challenging crisis. Put the crisis simultaneously in the context of the quest for manhood identity, and, for black males, we can see the vise exerting a compounded grip.

In his classic, The Souls of Black Folk, DuBois conceptualized the crisis as a "two-ness,--an American, a Negro, two souls, two thoughts, two unrecognized strivings; two warring ideals in one dark body, whose dogged strength alone keeps it from being torn asunder" (64:9). His insight probably deserves a standing at least equal to that accorded his assertion that "the problem of the Twentieth Century is the problem of the color-line," for it draws attention to the interconnected psychological line, which is one of inner identity. To whom is our soul (identity) to belong: to us blacks or to you Americans (that is, to you whites)? At the time, DuBois's wish was "to make it possible for a man to be *both* [emphasis added] a Negro and an American, without being cursed and spit upon by his fellow, without having the doors of Opportunity closed roughly in his face" (64:9). If that were made possible, no longer would there be "warring ideals" nor "unrecognized strivings," but a "kingdom of culture," the Negro being able "to husband and use his best powers and his latent genius" (64:9).

DuBois might have been asking for the impossible: to let the divide stand so long as the warring ceased. Scott is suggesting that a soul divided against itself, like a house so divided, cannot stand; it must be unified and loved, or else risk turmoil and unrest. Of course, DuBois was talking about two souls unified and loved, but that conception overlooks one of the two souls, our own. Signs of our "best powers" and "latent genius" to be husbanded and used did not abound. Rather, we were in search of our soul (identity), trying to self-discover and self-evolve -- in fact, forced to. The self that we knew was one that, in DuBois's own words, had been "cursed and spit upon by his fellow." As the research and literature commonly indicate, we had internalized such a self, not as a loved self, but, more or less, as a hated self, or, in Scott's term, a traumatized self. For most of us, our remedy was to seek an "inward home," not by psychologically uniting with America, but by separating from it and being in opposition to it [John Ogbu's thesis] so as to allow for the "victory" and domination of our own "warring ideals." Relevant to recall is what sociologist, Janet Mancini Billson, has observed about our black males: "**"Black males have created their own world to salvage their pride."** As can be deduced from this analysis, she is no doubt describing a dynamic that has a wider, if less pronounced, application. No doubt it was felt (consciously or unconsciously) that we would not be accepted and were, thus, in a war that we could not win; the soul of the dominant society would prevail and we would be left without the security which all humans seek.

Our "victory" in the "warring ideals" -- at least our ostensible security -- would have to come in separation and opposition. However, it did not eradicate the trauma; instead, it was tantamount to a wounded inward retreat. The mark of oppression had made and left its imprint. We had been physically freed but left in identity bondage, so to speak -- partly by choice, partly by necessity. It must be remembered that, accepted or not, there was nothing to prevent our attempt to acquire an American identity, which is exactly what Washington, in particularr sought to have us do -- and with noticeable success. The "two-ness" discerned by DuBois has, nonetheless, remained just that. Perhaps not until the twins meet will we be made whole and see the "carry over" minimized – and, as a result, along with the more pervasive identity-driven dis-ease and discontent, see the turmoil and unrest in segments of our communities subside.

Nigrescence fallout: Victimology, Separatism, and Anti-intellectualism

Nigrescence seems to have contracted and catalyzed our two-ness, making it more about blackness and less about Americanism, in fact, in opposition to Americanism. Following the Civil Rights gains of the 1960s, one might have expected otherwise, that the salience of blackness would have diminished, as Dr. King foresaw in his "I Have a Dream" speech, but, instead, with its emphasis on blackness, nigresence -- thanks to the Black Power phase of the Civil Rights Movement and to Cross and the likeminded -- has enhanced that salience. Its intent has been to fashion a new and more empowering black identity -- a transformation of Negro-to-black identity – but, instead, it can be argued that nigrescence has led to what McWhorter sees as three cults that having become "part of the bedrock of black identity": Victimology, Separatism, and Anti-intellectualism (160: xiv). (Note: although not specifically germane to the content of this chapter, with regard to the historical thesis herein, it is important to note that this enhanced salience has also contributed to the disrepute in which Booker T. Washington has come to be held, for growing into blackness not only ruled out honor of anyone perceived to have not fought for our civil rights but, also, anyone who -- like Washington -- embraced, not Afrocentrism, but Americanism.)

Victimhood, McWhorter says, has become part of our identity, not just a problem to be surmounted (which makes it Victimology instead of victimhood). Separatism, a product of Victimology, has led us to divorce ourselves from the mainstream and adopt a restricted, black way of living and thinking. Anti-intellectualism, a product of Separatism, has led us to devalue learning for its own sake and resist the rigors which it requires. This is not an identity that leads to the kind of unified, loved self of which Scott speaks. It is more reactive than self-cultivated, more compensatory or synthetic (to use Erikson's term, as cited by McWhorter) and restrictive than fostering. Iit leads to the kind of dysfunctional core personality traits that have haunted us throughout our freedom journey: documented low self- esteem and aggression evident in the disconnectedness, instability, and destruction of which Scott speaks and which statistics show.

This identity crisis would appear to be a logical outcome when our search for it has occurred in the context of what McWhorter identifies as a meme, or as objective correlatives as Steele terms it. Even though barriers to our progress have been largely removed, the barriers, nonetheless, continue to be blamed for our problems, not because they still exist in reality, but because they exist psychologically. Psychologically, we benefit from keeping them alive, deriving a sense of identity, a feeling of worthiness, self-respect, a feeling of contribution, or, overall, a sense of security (feeling "at home"). The meme or correlatives fill a hole in our sole left open by the blockage of the real. But for sake of psychological security, the hole needs to be filled, if only by a synthetic identity. To obliterate the barriers (trauma) is to obliterate me, to deny the existence of the barriers is to deny me, and to do nothing about the barriers is to neglect me. Me and the non-existent barriers, a mental reproduction of me, are so closely identified that, psychologically, the me and the meme or correlatives (the non-existent barriers) are the same. In McWhorter's words, "the meme lives on the basis of the personally felt, the viscera, the gut. That is, the meme is a part of one's essence" (161:177).

Given that a meme or correlative is our self -- our essence, our core identity -- it means that the black self which has come to be intrinsic to nigrescence is a self that, justified or not, feels victimized, oppressed, denied, "cursed and spit upon." That is, the self of nigrescence, the process of becoming a black self, ironically, seems to have led to the replacement of that from which it sought escape with an equally traumatized version of it. The idea was to replace the *old* oppressed Negro with a *new* oppressed-free Negro having a black identity distinctly grounded in the nature and history of blackness an, as such, distinctly different from the nature and history of whiteness. If an idiom is permitted, what we have gotten instead is the same-o same-o -- at least trauma wise. Nigrescence has merely moved us from the objective to the subjective, from the real to the imagined, from the fought for to the wished for. The result is that the objective factors shaping our identity have changed, but the psychology which shapes it have not just remained the same, but, as both Steele and McWhorter argue, have even been magnified -- and at its core it is a psychology of victimization and its associated trauma.

Here are a few excerpts from McWhorter which illuminate the foundation for this new black identity (161:167-68):

> ...racism had been a reality forever: It must be understood that this response to racism was in turn enabled by a particularity of the moment: whites' new interest in the black condition amid the commitments of the counterculture. This allowed a new vent for a spiritual insecurity among blacks that had existed for centuries with whites uninterested in paying it attention. After all, there are all kinds of human responses to insecurity, and black Americans had previously manifested many of them.
>
> Insecurity can make you work harder, which meant that blacks back in the day openly said, 'If you're black you have to try twice as hard.'
>
> Insecurity can make you withdraw into yourself and have as little contact with The Man as possible.
>
> Insecurity can make you just give up and while away your days in idle misery.
>
> Or--insecurity might make you dutifully protest when a white woman uses the word *nigger* [emphasis in original] in condemning it.
>
> Only in the late sixties, for example, could William H. Grier and Price M. Cobbs's *Black Rage* become a best seller, introducing the idea that blacks' problem was not only discrimination but also whites' deep-seated psychological feelings of bias against blacks. This helped usher in a keystone of therapeutic alienation, that our interest is in whether all whites esteem us in their heart of hearts.
>
> That seems so ordinary now but is, in fact, a rather eccentric fetish of ours. Blacks before the late sixties assumed that whites did not like us, and thought that sheer opportunity was what their people needed. But starting in the late sixties, endless investigations and condemnations of whites' psychological biases against blacks took center stage--even though blacks' regularly saying that they thought whites would always be racist meant that the goal was less to fix

something than to dwell in it indefinitely. As historian Elizabeth Lasch-Quinn has it,

> 'The desired goal was no longer civic equality and participation, but individual psychic well-being. This psychological state was much more nebulous, open to interpretation, difficult to achieve, and [sic] controversial than the universal guarantees of political equality sought by the early civil rights movement.'

The operative phrase here is "psychic well-being," which can be said to encompass a positive core identity. Such an identity could not be if the self were not loved, and given Cooley's looking-glass concept, the self is unlikely to be loved if it does not look in the mirror (in this case the mirror being, not just whites, but other blacks as well) and see that it is loved by what is reflected in that mirror.

Though cursed and oppressed, to use DuBois's depiction, the old Negro seems to have been laying the groundwork [the **"average expectable environments,"** as it were] for such "psychic well-being." Thanks to the Age of Booker T. Washington a new black self had begun to emerge. Meier provides this picture of that emerging new black self:

> Here...was the New Negro, resourceful, independent, race-proud, economically advancing, and ready to tackle political and cultural ambitions. He believed in collective economic effort, for the most part denied any interest in social equality, and at the same time denounced the inequities of American racism and insisted upon his citizenship rights. He was interested in the race and its past; he was becoming more conscious of his relationship with other colored peoples and with Africa--an identification which the lower classes perhaps never really lost. In fact, the Garvey Movement was in many ways the lower-class counterpart of the New Negro Movement; both held to a belief in economic chauvinism, an interest in race history, and an identification with Africa; both emphasized race pride and solidarity--though Of course, the Garvey philosophy lacked the dualistic character of the New Negro outlook. The New Negro regarded the race as a distinct group with a distinct mission, yet part of the United States [DuBois's two-ness] (168:277-78).

It is this New Negro whom McWhorter points out knew and experienced discrimination and prejudice, but, nevertheless, he sought to overcome the obstacles thereby presented, "not fetishize them" (161:172-79). He and she were forging a real "two-ness." Still, as apparent from Meier's description, we are talking about a New Negro in the making -- about an unfolding and growing process. In the main, the research shows that the process had not evolved and spread to the extent that we had not sufficiently grown out of what Cross disputes: self-rejection and self-hatred. Even if we were to accept Cross's retrospective, we would be hard put to make a case that we blacks had a unified, loved self. If that had been the case, nigrescence would, more or less, have fallen on deaf ears.

Response to nigrescence fallout

In the voices of McWhorter, Dickerson, Toureȼ, Thurston, and others, we see what McWhorter discerns to be a growing rejection of nigrescence, however, and the identity cults and their various manifestations that can be logically tied to it. To reinforce a point, it is instructive to recall black Brown University economist, Glenn Loury's, declaration that "African Americans cannot be truly free men and women while laboring under a definition of self derived from the perceptual view of the oppressor" (443:6; see also 401). For the self in search of a definition in these voices shows no concern about the "perceptual view of the oppressor," but, rather, about the perceptual view of fellow blacks. Toureȼ speaks for what McWhorter sees as their growing numbers, especially among the young, as evident from Ellis Cose's The End of Anger (49). Toureȼ argues, as does Michael Eric Dyson in the Introduction, for an identity which, like the identity of the first black President, Barak Obama, has its roots in blackness, but without restrictions (258b: 12). As Dyson's sees it, we have to abolish the idea that there is a belief prescription for blackness (258b:xv). That there is no prescription does not, however – as Toureȼ sees it – mean that we are discarding our blackness, just that we are embracing every conception of it (258b: 12). For many middle-class black Americans, this thinking translates into what the aforementioned Lacy saw in her in-depth study as *strategic assimilation* whereby we center our social life among other blacks and our work life among whites (149). Others call it *bridging* (52a:218-20). Or, we might keep in mind Dyson's three dimensions of blackness and Martin's four levels. In essence, these categories all go back to Dubois's two "warring ideals," or, differently conceived, two "warring identities."

If we are to carry our blackness with us, as Toureç advocates doing, or strategically preserve it, as many in the black middle-class do, the question arises as to what is being carried or preserved. Toureç offers his and Gates's vision of what is is being carried or preserved: something naturally recognizable and felt, as in a black church or at a barbershop (258b:12-13).

Eugene Robinson concurs that there is a recognizable (or one might say felt) black culture. He, like Toureç, Dyson, and others, contends that our black identity, rather than being objective and concrete, has always been a matter of perception and self-image – how we see ourselves and how others see us (227:225-26). As previously discussed, he sees four black Americans -- Mainstream, Abandoned, Transcendent, and Emergent – who, while black, have varied identities (227: 5).

Even so, Robinson argues that there is something that binds these four groups (227:223-24). That something is a feeling, a feeling similar to the kind of barbershop or church feeling sensed by Toureç and Gates. It is a feeling customarily nonverbally or barely-verbally transmitted in passing (a smile, a hello, a whass happenin', for example), especially in white settings -- in his case, eye contact followed by a quick nod of the head. It is an acknowledgement, Robinson feels, of shared memories and experiences, even between total strangers. That acknowledgement has been called "The nod." Toureç cites black Kent State psychologist, Angela Neal-Barnett, as seeing "the nod" as a manifestation of fictive kinship (reminiscent of Fordham-Ogbu in their explanation of "acting white") – of sharing a common mindset or worldview (258b:158-59).

Beyond "the nod," McWhorter, Dickerson, Toureç, Thurston, and the many for whom they speak, make clear that they want no felt obligatory commitment or "carry over." "Just be," exclaims Thurston, "and the blackness will follow" (257a:224). No binding Afrocentrism at the center of their life. Regarding his trip to Africa, for example, Toureç confides that, while he wanted to feel at home, at times he felt a shocking disconnect, thereby discovering that he was deeply American; so he could not make Africa the center of his life (258b:195). Teaching black history, Thurston says, should not be "simply some repackaged Afrocentric curriculum that says, 'Black people were kings and queens back in the day, and the White Man is terrible!' Instead, it's just an honest, more complete version of events" (257a:211-12). Maybe former black Tennessee Congressman, Harold Ford, Jr., captures the overall identity inclination of this younger black generation, Toureȼ citing him as saying that Post-Blackness means being fully American (258b:56). That, of course, would still leave a place for" the nod," which may be seen as an expression of "a hard little nugget of suspicion and resentment buried deep inside" us; trauma is what Scott calls it – trauma not extinguished by nigrescence but reinforced by it.

Recent research on the role of racial centrality in black identity, championed by nigrescence advocates, is intended to convey a different outcome: black diversity and black deliverance. The research has documented the diversity – the different levels and components of black identity (the MMBI inventory making it possible) – and lays claim to the deliverance power of a high level of racial centrality: deliverance from white thinking and its retarding influence. The expectation is that this is what the MMBI would show: the efficacy of high black centrality over low black centrality, for example, "thinking black," as it were, over "thinking white." Reviewing most of the few relevant studies, Kun Wang, however, concludes that – for both the relationship between racial centrality and psychological functioning and between academic achievement -- the results are mixed (474b). The Sellers-Chavos-Cooke study (1998) and the Harper-Tuckman study (2006) provide cases in point. The Sellers-Chavos-Cooke study of 248 black college freshmen showed racial centrality to have a significantly positive association with their grade point average (GPA), whereas the Harper-Tuckman study of 289 9th and 12th graders, on the other hand, showed for them just the opposite – significantly higher GPAs for those having a low level of racial centrality (444b; 367b).

The mixed results foreshadow another "acting white" controversy. So far, the limited research conducted is creating no firestorm. That may well be because it is essentially the same issue, only the firestorm has simply lost some heat. As with "acting white," we need to look beyond the headlines suggesting the positive outcomes of high racial centrality to the main story which, as with "acting white," has to do with values. In both cases, it is black values versus white values – or, as John Ogbu put it, of oppositional culture versus the dominant culture. Are we better served by making one central and the other subordinate?

When we make our blackness central, according to Scott's thesis, is that we also make central the trauma which has been transgenerationally transmitted as part of it – trauma which is limiting rather than, as claimed through nigrescence, liberating. It yields, not better performance, but poorer performance. Black centrality advocates can indeed point, for example, to the Sellers-Chavos-Cooke study to refute this claim, but it bears notice that, even in their pro-racial centrality finding, "An ideology that emphasizes the uniqueness of being Black (Nationalist) ... was associated with poorer academic performance." To paraphrase an idiom, therefore, "Let the advocates of black centrality beware!" From the few studies which have been conducted, it is safe to draw the conclusion that high racial centrality is not an unqualified positive. In fact, Sellers-Chavos-Cooke make the point that since high racial centrality showed a negative association with GPA, "Racelessness does not seem to be an effective strategy for African American college students," but, their study suggests, neither does high racial centrality.

Of course, we cannot wait for the researchers to come up with an answer. Nor do we have to. In various ways, most of the chapters herein inform this topic, Chapter 6 pertaining to "acting white" being especially relevant, as are the subsequent Chapters 10 and 11, dealing, respectively, with our identity formation and with Victimology. The answer is that we blacks have been better served when we have made the values of the triumphant dominant culture central in our identity and the values of our own traumatized black culture subordinate in it. Paramount, we are talking about *values*, not color, for whereas Sellers-Chavos-Cooke make the point that "Racelessness does not seem to be an effective strategy for African American college students," the same could probably not be said about their values.

From our African American Garden of Eden, perhaps, comes our most convincing evidence. For Washington, racial centrality was subordinate – arguably reflected in a positive core identity marked by a **"*subjective sense of an invigorating sameness and continuity*"**; for DuBois, racial centrality was dominant – arguably reflected in a negative core identity marked, not by a *"subjective sense of an invigorating sameness and continuity,"* but by **"a hole in the...soul."** As a result, from Washington, we get the foundation-building which has been the basis for black progress; from DuBois, we get a civil-rights fixated victim mindset which is the basis for our second bondage, Victimology. While we cannot pinpoint specific research to support this assertion, we can – as throughout we have -- cite something no less credible: the historical record and data which stretch over a century.

Summation

Although "the nod" is far removed from Victimology and the bedrock core identity cults ascribed to us African Americans by McWhorter, or the objective correlatives which Steele sees, Scott's thesis -- supported by our panelists -- is that the feeling of connection which it acknowledges is a feeling of racial identity rooted in consciously and unconsciously transmitted trangenerational trauma associated with our American blackness. Further, Scott is saying that segments of our African American community (not all, just segments) have disastrously failed to remedy that trauma, resulting in a fragile and flawed core identity, which, in turn, inevitably results in disconnectedness, instability, and destruction since there is an "innate human need to develop a positive sense of selfdom, including self-esteem, dignity, and self respect." Fail to fulfill that need and we suffer disconnectedness, instability, and destruction. We suffer these outcomes due to the character deficits which result from our not having developed "a positive sense of selfdom." Those character deficits are a lack of the drive, willpower, perseverance, and adaptability – attributes which, the research shows, are powerfully related to school and life success.

Although our main concern is the poor, it is no doubt evident that it is not just the poor who have a core identity problem, so do many of the more privileged, as Pettigrew argues is evident in Richard Wright's autobiography, <u>Black Boy</u>. McWhorter's thesis is that the crippling inclusive "bedrock identity" cults of Victimology, Separatism, and Anti-intellectualism, together with the *racialized self* which is intrinsic to them, pervade the entirety of African American life and thought. As shown in the aforementioned studies of Ogbu and Farrell, black high-school students in the affluent Cleveland, Ohio suburb of Shaker

Heights are just as affected by core identity issues as are their low-income counterparts in the New York City public schools. And when it comes to race issues which pertain to such problems as stereotype threat, disidentification, and teacher expectations [discussed in Chapter 12], due to the identity factor, the poor and the privileged alike are affected. Although there appears to exist the "affirming core" of which Gates and Robinson speak, of which Toureç longs to carry with him as he lives out his unrestricted blackness, of which many in the middle class strategically seek to preserve, Scott's thesis and the evidence suggest that, while affirming, that core has been traumatized, as dramatically evident in the life of the poor and discernible in the life of the more privileged. That is, the evidence points to our race identity and its associated trauma as having a widespread and continuing effect which, while often only more or less situationally discernable, for many, is functionally damaging – resulting, for example, in curtailment or mediocrity (as in the case of academic striving and success) to maladaptation or chaos (as in the case of disciplinary problems and crime).

Scott's trauma explanation for such outcomes is a rather deep one, so to speak, but we are *primarily* driven by what geneticists, psychoanalysts, cognitive neuroscientists, anthropologists, and others in the scientific and scholarly community tell us are in-depth, unconscious forces. From a mice experiment, we get a recent concrete example of just that. Neuroscientists at Emory University found that male mice taught to fear the smell of cherry blossoms passed on that fear to later generations even though those generations, unlike them, were never exposed to its smell (392b). The trait, originally not a part of their genetic code, thus became a part of it through epigenesis, or interaction between the code and the environment (smell of the cherry blossoms).

In addition to the inheritance passed along by our base or natural genetic code, the report speculates that the finding may suggest that we humans also have an inherited code similar to that shown by the mice. Our base genetic code does not intrinsically change, but -- contrary to traditional thinking -- through the environment, like what occurred with the mice, it can, perhaps, get "reprogrammed" or "retriggered" so that it functions differently -- and that different functioning becomes heritable. The experiment adds to the reportedly growing research which supports epigenesis -- or, as the Online Psychology Dictionary succinctly puts it, "occurrence of a heritable change in gene function not resulting from a change in base DNA." Scott's thesis is that we see such a *heritable change* in the transgenerational trauma we blacks experience, only her analysis is from a psychoanalytical rather than neuroscientific perspective. She deals with the trauma without attention to the chemistry.

Scott's psychoanalysis, nevertheless, takes us where chemistry also does: in-depth, below our conscious being. And rightly so since therein lies the source of our being as we are told and reminded by a number of authors, among them, David Brooks in The Social Animal: The Hidden Sources of Love, Character, and Achievement (23); Baylor College of Medicine neuroscientist David Eagleman in Incognito: The Secret Lives of the Brain (73); neuroscientist Larry Young and journalist Brian Alexander in The Chemistry Between Us: Love, Sex, and the Science of Attraction; and geneticist Dean Hamer in The God Gene. As the titles indicate, from our love and sex life, to our character and achievement, to our religious life (there is a God gene, Hamer contends) we are being controlled and propelled, not by the brain of which we are aware, but (as Eagleman puts it in his title) by the brain whose lives are secret (incognito) -- "a vast, wet, chemical-electrical network called the nervous system" permeating our body (73:2). In sum, as Eagleman wonderfully captures the point, "The conscious mind is not at the center of the action in the brain; instead, it is far out on a distant edge, hearing but whispers of the activity" (73:9).

In a directly relevant observation, Brooks declares that the failures of our officials to solve such intractable problems as AMSAC is due to their "reliance on an overly simplistic view of human nature" (23:xv). That view, he argues, does not factor into consideration the new knowledge which reveals the powerful role of our inner, unconscious life; rather, it is dominated by a rational, social-science model. Unless this model is modified to incorporate this new knowledge, he asserts that our officials will continue to fail.

This new knowledge suggests that AMSAC and its inseparable social problems can be traced to our flawed core identity. We will, indeed, continue to fail unless we integrate that story into our analysis and prescriptions. We can, perhaps, assuage the problem, or make some progress, but that is not the same as solving it. A logical question is how confident can we be that we are on the right track, that the "enhanced story" is the true story – that it corresponds with the real. Based on the evidence presented, the answer is that we can be reasonably confident. We can also be reasonably confident based on something else: collateral support.

Collateral support for thesis

That collateral evidence consists of clues encountered in the course of the research. As is sometimes the case, one comes across bits and pieces of data which tend, over time, to fit together and tell a story -- somewhat in the fashion of a detective who over the course of time gathers various clues which ultimately lead to the solution of a crime. After having identified the root cause, looking back, that was done in this instance. Having identified and worked through the cause, various pieces of data came to mind (there was no deliberate attempt to find them) which give enhanced credibility to the lack of a positive core identity as the root cause. Some of those pieces follow.

Kerchoff and Campbell provided the initial and igniting clue. Regarding the model they used for predicting educational attainment, they observed that "… nothing in the model helps us very much in explaining black expectations whereas white expectations seem to be based on such "rational" antecedents as SES, IQ, and junior high school grades." This observation raised the question of why outcomes for African American students were not predictable based on standard rational antecedents. Similarly, regarding school dropouts, Herrnstein and Murray concluded that "…the one social problem that has a widely acknowledged cause in cognitive ability--school dropout--also has a strong and complex socioeconomic link." Here too, then, a standard antecedent does not work when it comes to predicting an outcome for black students. The question: why not? Then, in the very last paragraph of their study, Cook and Ludwig observe that the problem [of black students' alienation from school] may be more fundamental than racial differences in peer group norms. To make their point, they cite the story of Scott Baylark and Telkia Steward, two of the top students in their graduating class. They say:

Both took numerous honors classes. Both were given every encouragement by the faculty. Far from being ostracized by their peers, both were elected class officers and served as class leaders. Both went on to matriculate at the University of Illinois. There, they both discovered that they were poorly prepared for the academic demands of freshman year. For that reason among others, both soon dropped out (43).

Cook and Ludwig do not attempt to answer the question they raise, but that question stands out: what is that something "fundamental" that helps to explain what happened to these two top students. Obviously their academic preparation played a part, but Cook and Ludwig say only *a part*; it was "among" other factors. Then, in his report on what happened to the 59 fifth-grade Dreamers who got counseling support and a paid college education, Paul Schwartzman found that it was not possible to differentiate those who failed from those who succeeded based on standard predictive measures, for no predictable pattern prevailed. Further, there is the disappointment which Paul Tough tells was experienced by David Levine when, after six years, only 21 percent of his high-achieving KIPP Academy graduates had completed four years of college. In search of an answer, he thinks he has found it in character, coming to the view that so few had made it because they lacked the character traits associated with school and life success.

Germane as well is the consistent finding of the importance black students place on teacher support. That importance can be interpreted as indicating that if one does not have a positive core identity as, for example, Farrell's data suggested to him that his 73 at-risk minority students did not have -- then having a teacher who is perceived as "sympathetic" and "nonjudgmental" is highly and disproportionately valued. One can surmise that academic weakness also helps to explain their attitude, as was the case with Scott Baylark and Telkia Steward dropping out of college, but as with Baylark and Steward, one must weigh the academic factor "among" other factors, it being postulated that the lack of a positive core identity is foremost among those other factors.

Outside the school domain, attention was brought to the issue by data on black marriage and illegitimacy rates. William Julius Wilson's thesis (see Chapter 17) that the dramatic rise in female-headed families from 1960-80 was due to there being fewer marriageable (employed) black men available for black women to marry has been refuted by the research which shows no significant association between employment and marriage, causing even Wilson, however begrudgingly, to attribute some role to culture. That is, Wilson's "rational antecedents," like the "rational antecedents" of Kerchoff-Campbell and others, did not adequately account for the outcome. Then there is Herrnstein-Murray's finding (see Chapter 12) that IQ helps in explaining marriage and illegitimacy among whites and Latinos, but not among blacks; nor do normal socioeconomic indicators or education. They express puzzlement as to what does, since "rational antecedent" did not.

And the use of the description "rational" is by no means intended, by implication, to stigmatize the behavior (nor is there any indication that Kerchoff-Campbell had such an intent), but merely to suggest, as Cook and Ludwig suggest, that something "fundamental" is at work, and that something calls for an explanation beyond conscious rational processes, consequently, forcing us to come to grips with the hidden, unconscious forces of which Brooks, Eagleman, and others speak.

As these clues suggest, Cook and Ludwig, indeed, are justified in speculating that, since customary formulations seem not reliably to predict selected black student and black adult outcomes, something "fundamental" must be going on which accounts for those outcomes. Except for predicting our students' academic attainment, it seems not to be IQ alone, nor grades alone, nor socioeconomic status alone, nor support and encouragement alone, nor any standard combination of such factors.

What is the answer? The aforementioned clues support the answer that, to a significant degree, theoretically and credibly, the failure can be traced to many of our black students' (and black people's) lack of a ***"subjective sense of an invigorating sameness and continuity"*** -- that is, to their lack of a positive core identity, from which ensues a lack of sameness and continuity on which predictability is based. All else being equal, no sameness and continuity, that is, no positive core identity, and little or no predictability; the associated dysfunctional character traits make outcomes hard to predict. Since he pinpoints character as the key to our students' success, KIPP's David Levine appears to have arrived at an equivalent insight, for character is closely associated with identity.

Then, finally, as evident from the chapter heading quotations, two of our famous black leaders saw our possession of a positive core identity as something which we lacked, but which was essential to our progress. To Dr. King, "… that power of the mind capable of sloughing off the thingification of the past [that is, trauma, as Scott terms it], will be the Negro's most potent weapon in achieving self-respect." As discussed in Chapter 19, therefore, King made such self-respect "the *first and most vital step* that the Negro must take in dealing with his dilemma" [emphasis added]. It is apparent that, like Scott – and, like Washington, implicitly -- King saw "the thingification of the past" as reaping havoc on the black psyche and on black functioning. How Douglass viewed the role of our identity in our progress was not come across, but DuBois's concept of our two-ness reflects the pivotal role which he gave it. It is, then, fair to say that at least three of the famous leaders on whose insight we have heavily depended to guide our destiny felt us to be lacking that which they deemed essential to our progress: the possession of a positive core identity.

Conclusion

For many of us, again particularly for the poor among us, as Scott, Ogbu, McWhorter, and others contend, we possess a flawed core identity; we lack a unified, loved self – a positive core identity or a "***subjective sense of an invigorating sameness and continuity.***" As a consequence, on the six character attributes of a personality associated with a positive core identity, disproportionately, we fall short. Rather than accepting reality, we tend to distort it; rather than adjusting our expectations to our realities, we tend to deny or avoid our realities, or try to create our own; rather than having a sense of being resourceful and powerful, we tend to glory in victimization; rather than being flexible and open, we tend to embrace fictive kinship; rather than having a positive, optimistic attitude, we tend to see the cards as stacked against us; and rather than being self-empowering, we tend to externalize power. No wonder we have such an array of social problems and, at their center, an African American male school adaptability crisis.

Footnote: Toward A Unified Theory of Black America?

Is it possible to read into this analysis a theory? The question arises from an aforementioned article about black Harvard economist, Roland Fryer, Jr. The article appeared in the <u>The New York Times Magazine</u> under the title, "Toward a Unified Theory of Black America" (330a). It reports on Fryer's interest in formulating such a theory. He is quoted as saying:

> 'I basically want to figure out where blacks went wrong. One could rattle off all the statistics about blacks not doing so well. You can look at the black-white differential in out-of-wedlock births or infant mortality or life expectancy. Blacks are the worst- performing ethnic group on SAT's. Blacks earn less than whites. They are still just not doing well, period.'

As Fryer states, he wants to "figure out where blacks went wrong," the article interpreting his desire as a goal to formulate a "Unified Theory of Black America." The progress he has made is unknown, but it could be that this chapter, together with insights from other chapters, could assist him. From them, a proposition has been derived which addresses Fryer's goal. It is called the **Core Identity Theory of Disproportionate Maladaptation Among African Americans**, which is as follows:

> **The disproportionate maladaptation among us African Americans is primarily a function of our core identity and character whose positive development, prevented by slavery and oppression, has also been curtailed by our dominant System-Responsibility Tradition which, unlike our leadership dormant Self- Responsibility Tradition, has neither enshrined the role of provider and protector as intrinsic to manhood, instead, immersing manhood in victimhood and oppositional culture, nor sufficiently conducted adaptation responsive activities, as a result of which, it has failed to foster the creation of the kind of *"average expectable environments"* wherein family life is valued and our children provided the "hallowed presence" (security and love) required if they are to forge a positive core identity and a sound character – without which they will not succeed in school or in life.**

Perhaps too simple to be true, yet one is reminded of E=mc2. One is also reminded of what Erikson said about Freud's response to the question of what he thought a normal person should be able to do well (79:136). Erikson speculates that the questioner probably expected a complicated, deep answer. But, translated into English, Freud simply said, "to love and to work." In this instance, too, we might be looking for a complicated, deep answer and, whereas, it does not come near being as simple as Freud's response, nor perhaps is it as complicated and deep as one might expect.

10

The Role of Our Two Adaptation Traditions in Our Identity Formation

Proverbs, 16:22 - "Understanding is a wellspring of life unto him that hath it: but the instruction of fools is folly."
Galatians, 6:5 - "For every man shall bear his own burden."

In large measure, our identity is the product of our two adaptation traditions: the Self-Responsibility Tradition of Booker T. Washington and the System-Responsibility Tradition of W.E.B. DuBois. These two traditions have provided much of the ethos from which the fabric of our individual and family life have been woven. We will examine their role, first, by attempting to somewhat vivify it through a snapshot of the passing of each figure, and second, by looking at what their traditions have meant in regard to four crucial factors in our identity formation: **family**, **manhood**, **race**, **intelligence**. The argument is that, as symbolized by their passing, and as evident from their impact on the four crucial identity-shaping factors, the Self-Responsibility Tradition has made a facilitative contribution, our System-Responsibility a restrictive one.

Symbolism in the Passing of our Tradition Fathers

Washington's passing

While on a speaking tour in New England in 1915, Washington became ill and was hospitalized in New York (192: 418-20). Forced to cancel his tour, and realizing that the end was near, he sent for his wife. Upon arrival, he asked that she take him home so he could die in the South of his birth. His feeble and fatal condition notwithstanding, she managed to honor his request. A day after arrival, he died in his bed. One of the largest crowds in the history of Tuskegee attended his funeral in its chapel, one of the buildings on the campus of the institution that he built from scratch. He is buried on the campus near the chapel, and, in 1922, a monument in the center of the campus, the aforementioned "Lifting the Veil of Ignorance" statue, was dedicated to him. At its base, the monument reads: "He lifted the veil of ignorance from his people and pointed the way to progress through education and industry."

DuBois's passing

DuBois was dismissed from the National Association for the Advancement of Colored People (NAACP), since he was for separate black institutions and opposed its integration policies. Subsequently, he got embroiled in a court trial over his loyalty and, in his later years, joined the Communist Party. He ended up being invited by Ghana's President, Kwame Nkrumah, to make his home there and edit the Encyclopedia Africana, a project that he never brought to fruition (though Henry Louis Gates, Anthony Appiah, and others have). He died in Ghana in1963, after having given up his United States citizenship and becoming a Ghanaian citizen. On the eve of the 1963 March on Washington, Dr. Martin Luther King led a eulogy for him. His remains are interred in the W.E.B. DuBois Memorial Center of Pan-African Culture in Accra. The Center is devoted to research into Pan-African history and culture and to the promotion of DuBois's legacy.

The symbolism

One man, in his passing, is determined to be laid to rest from whence he came, at home among his people, having spent his last days still tirelessly pointing the way, almost literally sacrificing his life in the process. The other spends his later years in a distant land, removed from his people and estranged from his country. While embarked on a meaningful endeavor, absorbed in an ideology alien to his people's toils. Two passings, two inspirations. One man's ending symbolically inspires us, arguably, to say: this is who we are; we are Americans; this is our home; we can make it; all we have to do is work at it and we will rise. And that is the stuff from which a positive core identity (a unified, loved self) is forged, which promotes a **"subjective sense of an invigorating sameness and continuity,"** and leads to the establishment of **"average expectable environments."**

The other man's ending symbolically inspires us arguably to say: we have our own culture; we are Africans and need our own separate institutions; you cannot trust the white man, for he is trying to keep us down; it is hard to make it in this country. And that is the stuff from which a flawed identity is forged, for it provides an escape from reality and promotes ambivalence, insecurity, disillusionment, anger, and incessant wavering.

Coming up from slavery and meeting the adaptation demands of the larger society was no easy task. To make the adaptation, and get there, required intense and sustained effort, in effect, the remaking of our personalithy from that of a slave to that of an autonomous person. Slavery required one type of identity, autonomy quite another. Washington knew this, and, of course, so did the intellectual superstar, Du Bois. Only Washington, the emotional superstar, knew that the positive core identity essential to autonomous functioning had to be forged -- and could only be forged -- over time [he said that it could take as long as 50 to 100 years] by building a foundation through education and industry. The intellectual, DuBois, on the other hand, seems to have thought that there could be no such foundation – and, thus, no positive core identity -- unless we simultaneously wrested our rights from the system; otherwise, we would be doomed to a duality, a "two-ness" that would prevent us from our "longing to attain self-conscious manhood" (64:9). Our sense of that duality has left us in a state of perpetual protest, a sure prescription for a poisoned core identity. We can symbolically discern their difference in approach through each man's passing. To the extent that we are influenced by our awareness of the difference is the extent to which our core identity (our unified, loved self) is, potentially, either fostered or hindered. For through a series of **"average expectable environments,"** that identity is forged and adapted *throughout our lives*.

Tradition Effect on the Four Crucial Factors: Family, Manhood, Race, and Intelligence

One can question whether the passing of each man has any meaning, symbolic or otherwise, but it is a different matter when it comes to the influence of their traditions on factors which have been so crucial in shaping our African American core identity (our unified, loved self): **family, manhood, race, intelligence**. The family factor is universal, but given our slave history, for us African Americans, the other three factors -- manhood, race, and intelligence -- have a uniqueness.

The thesis herein is that for each factor, our Self-Responsibility Tradition has played a facilitative role in its contribution to our core identity while, in contrast, our System-Responsibility Tradition has played an impedimental role. Given a family that provides a solid growth foundation (safety and love) – which, in turn, facilitates the development of a unified and loved self in regard to each of the other three factors -- we are well on the way to fashioning a normal and productive life for ourselves. That scenario would likely enable us *actively to master our environment, function in a unified, integrated fashion, and perceive the world and self correctly*, giving us "a *subjective sense* of an *invigorating sameness* and *continuity*."

But, to date, the existence of the African American Male School Adaptability Crisis (AMSAC), and of related data, indicates that for a disproportionate number of us this is not the case. It is not the case primarily because of the dominance of our System-Responsibility Tradition and the restrictive role that it has played in our identity formation since the Age of Booker T. Washington, particularly since the 1950s and 1960s. Rather than enshrine as a cultural value the near universal role of manhood as family provider and protector, it has, instead, immersed our manhood role in a civil rights fixation, with a quest for respect being a driving force. That immersion has been cast in victimhood, and victimhood has led to Victimology. The helplessness, blame, and dependency which characterize both have undermined our manhood, inhibiting and vitiating those traits required of a family provider and protector. Fighting and standing up to the white man, or for the self, has predominated over fighting and standing up for the family. It is through the latter that we forge a stable family life, and it is through a stable family life that we are more likely to forge a positive core identity and the associated character traits on which school and life success depend.

Family

The most fundamental factor on which social scientists say our core identity rests is a stable family that provides us safety and love. Our Self-Responsibility Tradition focuses *directly* on uplifting us as individuals, families, and communities, whereas our System-Responsibility Tradition does so only *indirectly*. In emphasis, the former makes us responsible for and accountable to ourselves, the latter makes the system responsible for us and accountable for us. As discussed, Washington's Tuskegee Institute, which epitomizes the Self-Responsibility Tradition, was not just about the education of its enrolled students but, through its outreach programs and activities, also about the education and uplifting of the black community as a whole.

Tuskegee's focus was on strengthening individuals and families, a stress on home ownership and character being central to its message. "Every colored man," Washington told his students, "owes it to himself and to his children as well, to secure a home just as soon as possible." "No matter how small the plot of ground may be," Washington continued, "or how humble the dwelling placed on it, something that can be called a home should be secured without delay." He went on to add: "No man has a right to marry and run the risk of leaving his wife at his death without a home" (279b:34). Further, on another occasion, he stressed to students the value of having a system in the home, such as a certain time for meals and certain places to keep things (279c). As captured by Scott and Stowe;

> There was no advice given by him more constantly or insistently in speaking to the plain people of his race, whether in country or city, than this injunction to the men to take their wives into their

confidence and make them their partners. He recognized that the home was the basis of all progress and civilization for his race, as well as all other races, and that the wife and mother is primarily the conservator of the home (234:207-08)

And nothing need be said about his emphasis on character. The title of a few of his 37 addresses to his students makes the point: "On Influencing by Example," "The Importance of Being Reliable," "Keeping Your Word," "The Gospel of Service," and "Individual Responsibility."

It is such character emphases which make a viable family life possible. Combine them, as Washington did, with the necessity of having a home as a condition of marriage – and of having men make their wife their partners -- and we have the ingredients of an average expectable home environment, from which is likely to ensue a positive core identity.

When, in contrast, we turn to the System-Responsibility Tradition, we are reminded of what is herein called the **Moynihan Family Initiative Obstruction**. As discussed, the Moynihan Family Initiative sought to address, simultaneously with our civil rights, our family needs. However, our System-Responsibility Traditionalists would have no part of it. On the other hand, they endorsed the welfare rights movement since it placed the focus on what the system needed to do for black families, not on what we black families needed to do for ourselves. Both acts exemplify the failure of the tradition to confront and address directly internal black family needs. It resisted and refused to acknowledge the existence of the needs – even while, over the years, those needs have worsened. Instead of supporting efforts to strengthen the black family, it has stood by and witnessed the black family's steady deterioration, doing nothing about the deterioration and attacking those who have wanted or sought to do something. Dyson's attack on Cosby is a case in point. Through the Office of Family Assistance, there are federal programs which (inclusively) address black family issues, such as, healthy marriage and responsible fatherhood. But these programs are limited and discrete efforts, and do not derive from, or otherwise reflect, the kind of internal cultural drive under discussion.

Manhood

Manhood is a product of family and fatherhood. While our Self-Responsibility Tradition has directly fostered both, our System-Responsibility Tradition has directly fostered neither. As suggested, family and fatherhood are part of the core message of one, but not of the other. Norrell reminds us of this fact in writing the following:

> One can imagine that if Booker T. Washington lived today, he would insist that every disadvantaged group in American society--and blacks especially--should be working *internally* [emphasis added] to improve their home lives, schools, and reputations to be ready to exploit the opportunities that arise in a rapidly evolving world (192:440).

Norrell is making the point that, although it should be, our System-Responsibility Tradition is not so insisting; and it must be added that it has never so insisted. It has not "insisted" on us blacks internally working to improve family and fatherhood, which are the foundation of manhood. That insistence would logically entail emphasis on the near universal role of manhood: that of family provider and protector. That was Washington's emphasis, but not DuBois's.

For DuBois, being a man was having self-respect. To him, "… manly self-respect is worth more than lands and houses" (64:41). Self-respect is defined as standing up to the white man and demanding our rights, such self-respect being "true manhood." If you do not strive for it, demanding your rights, or certainly not "voluntarily surrender[ing]" those rights (a swipe at Washington), you "are not worth civilizing" (64:41). To Washington, on the other hand, "A man never begins to have self- respect until he owns a home" (165: 40). What a difference!

For DuBois, at the heart of manhood is self-respect, which we acquire by standing up and fighting for our rights, whereas, for Washington, at the heart of manhood is providing for family through home ownership and partnership husband-wife partnership. DuBois puts the black man in the role of the victim of a dominant culture. He can only claim manhood if that dominant culture is at least fought. On the other hand, Washington puts the black man in the role of a man and a universal culture, who can only claim manhood if he performs the provider and protector functions which are almost universally intrinsic to manhood.

It is the victim role of DuBois, together with the oppositional culture of which it is a part, that has been internalized and which has come to dominate the black psyche – the black male psyche in particular. Family provider and protector have not been made central in our acculturation; victimization has, as has the oppositional culture of which victimization is a part -- that culture giving rise to black males who, as Janet Billson describes them, create "their own world to salvage their pride." Yet, as Enola Aird is quoted above as declaring, "for fatherhood to take hold and to survive as a vital institution within a society, that society must stand solidly behind it--supporting it with norms, expectations, laws, and resources, over many generations." "Societies in essence," she goes on to add, "must help men to become good and responsible husbands and fathers." No such help has been provided by DuBois's System-Responsibility Tradition. To its lack of support and help, and, consequently, the failure of fatherhood to take hold, we can attribute unstable families; to unstable families, below average expectable environments; to below average expectable environments, a negative core identity; and to a negative core identity, dysfunctionality and maladaptation -- witness AMSAC and its inseparable social problems. Thus, it is concluded that *the failure of the System-Responsibility Tradition to enshrine the universal provider and protector role of manhood, but rather cast it in victimhood and in its oppositional culture, is its most detrimental shortcoming, leading to an unstable family life which does not provide the foundation for a development of the positive core identity and the associated sound character traits on which school and life success depend.*

Race

The views that white society, in general, has held of our race are a matter of experience and record: inferior intellect, Sambo personality, and so on. Given Cooley's "looking glass" thesis, that these views are impediments to our core identity is a given. Not a given is the race role that we ourselves play in this impediment. But play one we do. In fact, at times, one is prone to think that the roles have come to be reversed; now -- thanks to DuBois and the dominance of his System-Responsibility

Tradition -- it is we who seemingly almost at every turn bring race into the public discourse, to say nothing of the private discourse.

DuBois's stroke of the pen. In his "The Forethought" to his classic, <u>The Souls of Black Folk</u>, DuBois gave *racial* thinking a kind of official genesis. In the very first sentences, he wrote: "Herein lie buried many things which if read with patience may show the strange meaning of being black here in the dawning of the Twentieth Century. This meaning is not without interest to you, Gentle Reader; for the problem of *the Twentieth Century is the problem of the color-line*" [emphasis added] (64:3). It is almost as if with the initial stroke of his pen, he inserted a serum into the souls of those whom he was about to write about, us blacks. In the text, he more fully describes its nature: "One ever feels his two-ness,--an American, a Negro; two souls, two thoughts, two unreconciled strivings; two warring ideals in one dark body, whose dogged strength alone keeps it from being torn asunder" (64:9).

The souls of black folk. Nevertheless, Norrell observes that he "adopted a romantic viewpoint in describing the Christ-like selflessness of African Americans." That viewpoint was that "Negro blood had a 'message for the world' that soared above the stale preoccupations of white Americans. 'We black men seem the sole oasis of a simple faith and reverence in a dusty desert of dollars and smartness'" (192:277). Norrell's summary:

> He understood blacks' religious capacity as based on their instinctive moral superiority to whites. He adopted the mantra, expressed by older black intellectuals and preachers, of the "Christ-like Negro," who had suffered so extensively in America that he provided moral authority and an object lesson of sinful and exploitative whites (192:232).

Our identity challenge, then, as DuBois saw it, was to preserve this "sole oasis". Returning to his classic, in his words:

> The history of the American Negro is the history of this strife,-- this longing to attain self-conscious manhood, to merge his double self into a better and truer self. In this merging he wishes neither

of the older selves to be lost. He would not Africanize America, for America has too much to teach the world and Africa. He would not bleach his Negro soul in a flood of white Americanism, for he knows the Negro blood has a message for the world. He simply wishes to make it possible for a man to be both a Negro and an American, without being cursed and spit upon by his fellows, without having the doors of Opportunity closed roughly in his face (64:9).

To be "*both* a Negro and an American [emphasis added]." Therein is the quandary, for history has shown that the two can be conflicting. That is what John McWhorter's <u>Losing the Race</u>, for example, is all about: that conflict as manifested in the cults of Victimology, Separatism, and Anti-intellectualism. Of course, such conflict cannot be taken to mean that in search of a positive core identity, we should not have our own subculture, that we cannot be *both* a Negro and an American; in fact, given the nature of group life, anthropologists tell us that it is inevitable. Not inevitable, however, is its maladaptive outcome and the negative core identity that the attempt to be both have wrought.

The souls of white folk. So much for the "souls" of black folk; now, what about the "souls" of white folk? Here, too, DuBois put his pen to work. In the chapter of his book, <u>Darkwater</u>, entitled "The Souls of White Folk," he poetically describes their world as one of "vermin and filth," saying about them: "All the dirt in London, All the scum in New York; Valiant spoilers of women And conquers of unarmed men; Shameless breeders of bastards, Drunk with the greed of gold," -- and then declaring "I hate them, Oh! I hate them well, I hate them, Christ!" (67b:509-10; see also Spencer, 244:154-55).

There we have it: a romantic view of ourselves, a diabolical view of whites.

Washington's stroke of the pen. Contrast this kind of pervasive racial (or is it racist?) thinking with the racial thinking fostered by Washington, a man of great race pride, but not of race prejudice. With Washington, we can also turn to the equivalent of a stroke of the pen to capture his legacy. In his Atlanta Compromise Address of 1895, he set the tone and spirit of his legacy. In his speech in Boston at the Shaw Monument Unveiling in 1897, his tone and spirit were captured in memorable words. He is quoted as saying, *"The black man who cannot let love and sympathy go out to the white man is but half free"* [emphasis added] (165:97). Later, in his famous autobiography, <u>Up from Slavery</u>, he expressed this sentiment thus:

From his example in this respect I learned the lesson that great men cultivate love, and that only little men cherish a spirit of hatred. I learned that assistance given to the weak makes the one who gives it strong; and that oppression of the unfortunate makes one weak.

It is now long ago that I learned this lesson from General Armstrong, and resolved that I would permit no man, no matter what his colour might be, to narrow and degrade my soul by making me hate him. With God's help, I believe that I have completely rid myself of any ill feeling toward the Southern white man for any wrong that he may have inflicted upon my race. I am made to feel just as happy now when I am rendering service to Southern white men as when the service is rendered to a member of my own race. I pity from the bottom of my heart any individual who is so unfortunate as to get into the habit of holding race prejudice (265:303).

Souls without malice. This conviction was a recurring theme in Washington's writings and speeches, reminiscent, one might say, of an Abraham Lincoln, "with malice toward none, with charity for all." Of course, instead, he would obviously prefer referencing, as he did, his idol, General Armstrong, but this reminiscence puts him in more historic company. Even so, parenthetically, it has not helped to spare his demise, for apparently, it is magnanimous and wise for Lincoln to exhibit such temperament, but -- by the standards of Woodward, Harlan, and our Civil Rights Movement radicals -- not so for Booker T. Washington.

This conviction, likewise, was evident in his character. One incident cited by Spencer underlines the point (244:187). Mistaken in a hallway hotel for a porter, he was asked by a woman guest for water. Unperturbed, he went to the desk and had it sent to her. Today, if this guest worked for a radio station, our leaders would demand that she be fired; or, if she owned a business, they would call for its boycott. Such is the state of our core identity, so frail as to send us into a frenzy upon such incidents, however innocent. But, in these situations, Spencer points to Washington's attributes of natural poise, humility, self-assurance, and so on, the relevant point here being that such attributes spring from a positive core identity. Washington apparently knew who he was -- and embraced it!

Making ourselves half free. Had the Washington tradition prevailed, we ourselves would not be the race revelers whom so many of us have become, resulting in such devastating consequences for our core identity and for racial unity. That we are forced to come to grips with being black and its imputed meaning is without dispute. DuBois is right to address our "two-ness," but why do so in a way which retards or fractures our core identity -- or that makes us "half free" -- instead of enhancing our freedom and our core identity? Thanks to DuBois's System-Responsibility Tradition, "half free" is what we are, our thoughts and behaviors having come to be dominated by our second bondage, Victimology. Of course, DuBois and those in his tradition argue that because of what whites do, and have done, they (whites) cause it. Their contention has some validity. However Bookerites can point to Washington as an example of the fact that we do not *have to* respond as so many of us do. We have *chosen to respond*, not as Washington taught, with forgiveness and love, but with anger and opposition. "The problem of the Twentieth Century is the problem of the color-line" has prevailed over "the black man who cannot let love and sympathy go out to the white man is but half free." As a result, the transgenerational trauma borne by our race ("the thingification of the past," to use Dr. King's description of it), as theorized by Scott, continues to play havoc with our core identity.

Intelligence

Research suggests that an environment which fosters individual and family success through an emphasis on "brains, property, and character," as our Self-Responsibility Tradition does, is likely to contribute more to the enhancement of our intelligence than one which does so through an emphasis on success based on the acquisition of civil rights, as our System-Responsibility Tradition does. The former addresses the sources of influence, while the latter addresses the opportunities afforded, leaving to chance the readiness or willingness to take advantage of those opportunities.

11

Of President Barak Obama and Others (Victimology: Our Second Bondage)

> *Proverbs, 16:22 - "Understanding is a wellspring of life unto him that hath it: but the instruction of fools is folly."*
> *Galatians, 6:5 - "For every man shall bear his own burden."*

In the previous chapter, it is argued that the pervasive lack of a positive core identity is the root cause of our African American Male School Adaptability Crisis (AMSAC) and its inseparable social problems. In this chapter, victimhood is examined as the source of the lack of a positive core identity and as a catalyst for a range of other outcomes. Undisputed is the enormous role played by slavery, oppression, and dehumanization; these external factors have made us objective victims. That is the point which Scott makes. She addresses our victimhood as "trauma," an emotional or psychological injury. Nature, as well, has played a role. From the very start, attributes with which we were born -- such as our putative intelligence, skin color, and hair texture -- have all made us victims in the eyes of the dominant society, which ascribes victimhood to them. The focus herein is on our own role and response to this victimization -- to the hand dealt us by man and by nature.

Although various factors of man and nature have made us objective and ascriptive victims, we did not have to take on the role of victims and respond as victims. We could have resisted and responded, not as victims, but as Washington urged us to respond: as people of character. Scott's thesis is that, instead, we have engaged in a transgenerational transmission of the trauma. Shelby Steele says that we have engaged in recomposition and objective correlatives. McWhorter goes further, stating that not only have we adopted and transmitted our victimization or trauma, since the 1960s, we have *expanded* it (victimhood) from a problem to be solved into an identity. McWhorter names that identity Victimology. In turn, McWhorter contends, Victimology -- which he sees as a cult -- has led to two other cults, Separatism and Anti-intellectualism. Combined, his thesis is that the three constitute part of the bedrock of black core identity.

After nearly 150 years of freedom, that bedrock identity translates among us into a still pervasive lack of a positive core identity. Those whose identity rests, in part at least, on Victimology do not have a **"a subjective sense of an invigorating sameness and continuity."** Victimology's power (it has become a cult, McWhorter says) and pervasiveness (cuts across the entirety of black life, McWhorter also says) has mde it our second bondage. Left unchained, this second bondage dooms us African Americans to a continued "half free" life (to borrow Washington's thinking) -- too many of us angry at whites, frustrated, distrustful, and disproportionately dependent and depressed. We, consequently, deprive ourselves of our potential happiness.

Research suggests that, to begin with, we control only about 12 percent of our happiness. As for the remainder, 48 percent is genetically determined and 40 percent is of the *short-duration type* which comes from events in our life, such as getting a dream job (310a). The 12 percent is said to be derived from our success (or lack of it) in pursuit of four basic values: faith, family, community, and work. In embracing Victimology, we undermine that success because victimhood, by its very nature, tends to undermine our initiative, social investment, passion, and perseverance (424b, 471l). As a result, we deprive ourselves of the drive to pursue these four basic values, thereby automatically reducing the 12-percent control that we possess over our happiness. We can debate by how much it reduces it, but not about whether it does. In sum, Victimology is a mindset and a worldview resulting in thinking and behavior which undermine, instead of enhancing, our wellbeing. As discussed, psychologically, its outcomes are low self-responsibility, low self-acceptance, and aggression, from which ensue a array of attitudes and behaviors. Some of them follow.

- Foremost, Victimology has inhibited and vitiated our universally-shared manhood role of family provider and protector.
- It has led to a civil-rights fixation.
- It has led to the false equation of equal opportunity with equal results.
- It has led to a demand for feeling equality.
- It has led to the blind characterization of normal, experience-based suspicion as racial profiling.
- And, in general, it has led to black rage, racialized thinking, and black racism.

No happiness can be perceived from these outcomes, nor from an array of others discussed, in particular, by McWhorter. Rather, however variously existent, these outcomes point to a shrinkage of the 12 percent – a shrinkage, however far, far enough to doom us to an unfulfilled life, avoidably denying ourselves much, if not most, of the happiness which is our due. To accent this curtailment, **12** is added to our mnemonics to remind us of this outcome of Victimology.

We are mired in this Victimology because our leaders, however unwittingly, have encouraged us to submit to our primitive nature, and have nurtured it. That primitive nature keeps us rooted in the rudimentary, that part of us guided more by raw emotion than by reason or reality. So guided, we disproportionately give preference to the pleasure principle over the reality principle, to put it in Freudian terms (471p). The research shows that, in doing so, we, as would be the case with any people, burden ourselves with an endless array of maladies -- from sense of helplessness, to passivity, to negativity, to loss of control, to stubbornness (471o). All are symptoms of Victimology.

As victims, our instinct habitually comes to prevail over reason, our passion over prudence. In their study of successful cultural groups in America (see Chapter 12), Chua and Rubenfeld tell us why this is a worry for the race. "No society could exist without impulse control," they say, "as Freud speculated, civilization may begin with the suppression of primal sexual and aggressive instincts." Victimology impairs or eliminates that control, as a result, curtailing our upward climb. DuBois rightly stressed the role of our Talented Tenth in that climb, but he -- unlike Washington -- failed to stress the equally decisive role of reality, instead grounding us in that which disregards and distorts reality: a victim mentality turned Victimology.

Foremost in Victimology's fallout – and in the rudimentary in which it ensnares us – is the inhibition and vitiation of our manhood, addressed in the previous chapter. That inhibition and vitiation have resulted in unstable families, unstable families in the forging of a negative core identity, and a negative core identity in widespread dysfunctionality and maladaptation, as is evident in AMSAC and its inseparable social problems.

Slavery, our first bondage, was imposed upon us, but our second bondage, Victimology, we have adopted and nurtured. Our first bondage was depersonalizing; our second bondage is paralyzing and regressing. Our first bondage was physical in nature; our second bondage is psychological in nature. We have replaced physical slavery with psychological slavery. Our physical slavery was ended through a military war and a pursuant amendment to our Constitution; we must end our psychological slavery through a cultural war and a pursuant amendment of our culture.

Our victim culture fills the media with never-ending black complaints and problems which emanate from the racialized thinking which has come to dominate our time (see Steele, McWhorter, and Lasch-Quinn: 150a, 161, 162, 247a). Possessed of a civil-rights fixation, in racialized thinking, more or less, all of our problems are attributed to our race, and, invariably, we make race a factor in addressing our life and experiences. As Victimology has spawn its web, so has its associated racialized thinking, black racism being its most extreme expression. Black racism, accompanied by black rage, can be defined as a black perception of whites as the opposition, guilty, if not of conspiring against blacks,. of pervasive and persistent prejudice and discrimination against blacks, the feeling often being so indiscriminate or irrational as to constitute what can be called an obsessive-compulsive disorder (OCD) (for a discussion of black rage, see Lasch-Quinn, 150a:23-32).

To elaborate, commonly, we are uncontrollably or clinically preoccupied, not only with what we perceive whites are doing to us, but, in addition, with the respect and regard whites accord us, or with *feeling equality* as herein labeled. More or less, we automatically attribute our life socioeconomic struggles or other misfortunes to our race. Because of our race, we are victims, and – as McWhorter argues -- victim has become as much a part of our identity as our color. To be black is to be a victim – not only, as in the past, the victim of what white people are *doing to us*, but now, also, the victim of how white people *feel about us* – both in the present and, demanding *psychological reparations*, in the past, witness the demand to de-honor President Thomas Jefferson.

Admittedly, black racism is a highly-charged allegation, but it has support in four ideologies which fully emerged in the post-civil rights era: the Black Power Movement, nigrescence, Afrocentrism, and critical race theory (CRT). Much like the Black Muslims (Nation of Islam) under the leadership of Elijah Muhammad, all have made us blacks sacrosanct and whites satanic ("blue-eyed devils" is the term sometimes heard in Black Muslim's description of them) -- we the righteous victims, they the evil oppressors. Not all adherents have subscribed to such views, but enough subscribe to give them widespread currency. Stokely Carmichael was first (1966) to use the term Black Power as a political slogan, and a segment of his Black Power Movement was expressly anti-white. William Cross Jr.'s nigrescence, for example, discussed in Chapter 11, is all about black liberation from the white oppressor (150a:57-59). Black historians Franklin and Moss give us the following description of Molefi Kete Asante's Afrocentrism:

> During the last two decades of the twentieth century, some exponents of Afrocentrism attracted widespread attention with vigorous arguments that Africa and African cultures were the original sources of world civilization, that peoples of African descent have a unique "humanistic, spiritualistic value system" unmatched by any other racial group, that European cultural and economic systems are inherently exploitative, and that blacks' high melanin content made them "inherently more creative" (92:608).

As for CRT, it probably represents black racism in its most extreme expression (209a:29; 306a; 323a; 397; 471k). First articulated in the

1970s by the late black civil rights lawyer, Derrick Bell, considered its intellectual father, and white legal scholar, Alan Freeman, critical race theory quickly gained momentum, attracting an array of lawyers, activists, and academics. (Parenthetically, this pairing and posture are reminiscent of the DuBois-NAACP alliance, in fact, more or less, a repeat of the same kind of mindset out of which their alliance emerged.) Bell and others were disappointed that the civil rights gains of the 1960s had not just come to a halt, but, as Charles Murray famously highlighted, were followed by a decline. Here are the names of some of its other proponents::

Patricia Williams
Kimberle Crenshaw
Mari Matsuda
Richard Delgado
Jean Stefancic
Cheryl I. Harris
Gloria J. Ladson-Billings
Karen Pyke
Camara Phyllis Jones
Charles Lawrence
Dorothy Brown

To illustrate the theory, unlike Murray, it would not attribute the halt and decline of civil rights gains to a failure of the War on Poverty. That would have required dealing with objective realities, and according to critical race theory, there is *no such thing as objective reality*. Rather, the theory would attribute the halt and decline, as practically all else that plagues the black poor, to the *ubiquitous and wicked influence of white supremacy*, which keeps the oppressed subordinate and oppressed. According to its dogma, this supremacy and oppression have inalterably shaped the way the two races understand and view the world -- one seeing it from a supremacist perspective, the other from the perspective of the oppressed. One perspective yields one reality -- *a white reality*, the other perspective a different reality -- *a black reality*. Thus, each race has a competing view of reality and the *two realities can never be reconciled*. So the halt and decline cannot be objectively analyzed; it can only be analyzed from a white reality or from a black reality -- and it is *always the black reality which is valid* because, unlike the white reality, it is not distorted by domination and subjugation.

Further, the crucial factor in assessing the halt and decline, some of their theorists suggest, is not any evidence that Murray might present, but the stories and personal experiences of its victims. In their mindset, *storytelling or parables and personal experiences can replace facts and evidence as tools of the poor in combating white supremacy* (some even construct elaborate fables to illustrate and authenticate their own theses). So understanding the role of the poor in the halt and decline does not lie in the facts and evidence presented by Murray, but rather, in the storytelling of the poor -- which might be said to be the equivalent of replacing English with Ebonics. Given their irreconcilable realities, then, *African Americans should pursue, not integration as in the past, but separation, the exception being integration which naturally occurs.* Although not all of these propositions are shared by all critical race theorists, they are variously shared and, in various guises, have currency.

One might think, however, that some of the ideas are too preposterous to have any meaningful acceptance. But think again. Take, for example, the notion of a *black reality* and a *white reality*. It is common to hear that in polls we blacks have one perception of something and whites quite a different perception, and in the discussion of the Trayvon Martin case below, that difference is evident. It was, likewise, evident in the O. J. Simpson case as it is in so much which occurs in the course of our daily living. Often the facts, *if known*, seem not to matter. Critical race theory validates the difference as the norm and advocates it as a way of life, subordinating the objective to the subjective and, in effect, promoting conflict over cooperation. However regressive, manifestations of this mindset do not ensue from the actions of critical race theorists, but, instead, they ensue from the everyday living which has been influenced by critical race theories – or, at least, by the thinking which critical race theories espouse (maybe critical race theorists have merely formalized existing thinking and given it a scholarly and extended casting).

Indeed, CRT, and the other three ideologies (Black Power Movement, nigrescence, and Afrocentrism) give context to Victimology and to much of what we are witnessing in black attitudes and behaviors and in black-white race relations. The never-ending black complaints and problems which fill the media are not simply the result of passing tempers, unrestrainable activists, or civil rights zealots, but reflect strands of thought that are evident in these four ideologies -- ideologies which the literature suggests variously have come to permeate the entirety of African American society, and perhaps to some extent even white society.

However, given its historical usage, one hesitates to apply the term black racism to what is observed. But it must be called what it is so that we know what we are dealing with. It is not racism in the *superiority sense* associated with whites, but racism in the *inferiority sense* associated with us blacks; call it *reverse racism*. In one case, the underlying thinking is that you are below us and must be kept separate and in your place; in the other case, the underlying thinking is that your thinking about us is simply because of our color and we are the inescapable victims of your blind prejudice and discrimination. In both senses, race becomes integral to our personality as evident in corresponding intemperate or malicious actions and attitudes. Such is another pernicious outcome of Victimology and is added to the first cited outcome, reduction of the 12 percent control over our happiness, to give us the mnemonic **black racism - 12**. This mnemonic serves to remind us of the effect of Victimology on black attitudes and behaviors and the automatic reduction of control over our happiness it exacts over the already small 12% which we humans normally exercise.

To proclaim our victim status, during the 1960s, we adopted William Ryan's slogan, "blaming the victim." Today, we have begun to reinforce Ryan's slogan with another slogan, "Black Lives Matter." This new slogan – attributed to a California-based activist, Alicia Garza -- owes its origin to the killing of a number of black males by white police officers, beginning with the Trayvon Martin case (341b). The blame is placed on the white police officers because, the "story" goes, to white police officers, black lives don't matter. On the other hand, whatever the evidence in these killings, the black males killed are held blameless. But were they?

Reflecting a critical race theory mindset, the vindicating "story" is that they were blameless because they were "unarmed." The "unarmed" is emphasized as if being unarmed made these black males harmless and, therefore, the police killing of them was blatant. That, though unarmed, they, nevertheless, could have been life-threatening is dismissed with the refrain, "they [the cops] didn't *have to* shoot them." That is, arguably, the white cops were to risk their lives to save law-breaking and police-resisting black males. That the white cops did not do so, the "story" goes, means that they were racist and, to them, therefore, black lives don't matter.

While this storyline does not apply to all of the police killings, in particular, the Eric Garner case presents an exception, it captures representative thinking. But even in the Eric Garner case, where choking him to death appears to have been indefensible, law-breaking and police-resisting by Garner were involved. Lawless and provocative behavior invites conflict, and conflict has consequences which are sometimes fatal. Like all of us, in these police encounters, our black males must bear in mind that the police are armed and have discretion in the use of their arms, or of other force. Law-breaking, confrontational, provocative, daring, and resistive behavior, such as exhibited by the black males in these killings, forces the police to exercise that discretion. The fact is that, in these killings, our black males chose, not to obey the police, but to fight or resist the police – and they came out on the short end of the stick. We can celebrate them, as the Black Lives Matter thrust shows that we are doing, but in doing so, while condemning the police, we are simultaneously condoning – even honoring -- wayward and reckless behavior on the part of a segment of our black males.

Of course, along with their family, we mourn their death, but none of us, including their families, must allow our mourning and the "story" surrounding their death lead us to misread the underlying cause, which, it is argued, had more to do with character than with color. These black males did not serve as Booker T. Washington would have had them, and the rest of us blacks, serve: as "an example for all the world in usefulness, law abiding habits and high character" (see Chapter 19). Rather, their lifestyle and behavior represented the prisonization of the values of our black male underclass and to honor them, individually or through a Black Lives Matter banner, gives those values community approval – evidence of the downward spiral in which Victimology ensares us and of the black racism which has become instrinsic to it. More realistically and meaningfully, then, the Black Lives Matter slogan might be directed, not to white police officers, or, by subtext, to whites generally, but to those of us blacks who subscribe to it, for it is we, more than whites, who, in the police killings and in other life situations, so often seem to conduct ourselves as if, *to us, our own black lives don't matter* – our Victimology, however, blinding us to this reality.

Nonetheless, no case is being made that the conduct of the police in these killings was necessarily blameless nor that the encompassing issue of mass incarceration is without validity. Experience suggests that a few police officers in these neighborhoods – and probably only a few -- can be (or, maybe, have come to be) abusive and abrasive, but two wrongs do not make a right and, though difficult it may be, we must not let the misconduct of a few police officers be an excuse for our own misconduct and blanket condemnation, nor an excuse for us, as the Black Lives Matter outcry has done, to undertake still another string of protests whereby we externalize our problems and, between police and community, needlessly create division and discord -- as in too many instances, we have similarly done with the school system -- rather than promote the kind of cooperation and harmony required to address the persistent crime problem in segments of our black community.

Killing, of course, takes police misconduct to another level. Even so, there are at least two sides to every story, and the point being made here is that Victimology prevents us blacks (and many whites as well) from seeing our side – the side of our black males -- in these police killings. Likewise, there are two sides to the encompassing issue of mass incarceration of blacks, not just a punishment-should-fit-the-crime side but also a safety-and-community-standards side – the side on which resides the originating cause. However, grounded in Victimology, the new Black Lives Matter mantra directs our focus to just one side, drawing support from none other than our (contaminated) first black President (367e).

As a footnote to the discussion, it must be observed that the Black Lives Matter movement has proliferated (341b). Under its mantra, a variety of groups with various aims and tactics have emerged, encompassing, for example, focus on criminal justice reform as well as on advocacy of anti-poverty programs, and reliance on protest as well as on political activities. In effect, however, all reflect a continuation of our never-ending

Civil Rights Movement under a different name – that Movement, unlike being based, as heretofore, mainly on the objective rather than the subjective, now firmly anchored in the bondage psychology of Victimology.

McWhorter dates the origin of our Victimology to the 1960s, however, for the victim mindset out of which it grew, we can go back to our imaginary African American Garden of Eden. In it, to be sure, the system was stacked against us, openly and officially, only DuBois made it worse. If the stacking itself were not enough, as ideologue and activist, DuBois helped to convert our subjugation into an imprint of victimhood, fostering its internalization and transmission. The system against which – with more than ample justification – he railed, he himself made worse by, in effect, making us, through his response, its psychological victims. He led us to nurture, rather than erase, its scars. As a result, in the 1960s, we saw those scars metastasize into Victimology.

From Charles Murray's Losing Ground, we can interpret why (see Chapter 17). During the 1960s, there was a popularization and institutionalization of victimhood -- the popularization symbolized by Ryan's "blaming the victim" mantra and the institutionalization by the War on Poverty and its associated incentives. The intent and expectation of program and policy makers were to reap black liberation, but, instead, the results, as McWhorter suggests, led to the emergence of Victimology. In the discussion which follows, we see its hold – the discussion centering on the Trayvon Martin case and our Talented Tenth, along with Affirmative Action and the U.S. Department of Education and the U.S. Department of Justice report on nondiscriminatory administration of school discipline.

The Trayvon Martin Case as Mirror of Our Second Bondage

Trayvon was the 17-year-old African American teenager who, while walking to from the store to his temporary home in a Sanford, Florida neighborhood, was followed by mixed-race Hispanic neighborhood watch coordinator, George Zimmerman. Zimmerman's pursuit led to a scuffle between the two in which Zimmerman shot and killed Trayvon.

Zimmerman was legally carrying the pistol and justified use of it under the Florida "stand your ground" law (471h).

The case which ensued mirrors and concretizes our second bondage. Our first bondage (slavery) is self-evident, and the Trayvon Martin case can serve to make our second bondage (Victimology) evident as well. It exposed the state of mind and emotions which characterize Victimology, a state of mind and emotions exhibited even -- and perhaps especially -- by our first black President, Barak Obama.

Trayvon's death was converted into a national racial crisis. The federal government was called upon to step in to protect Trayvon's civil rights, with pressure exerted through demonstrations, marches, and vigils -- all of which dominated the media and television screen. For their part, reporters did more side-taking, judging, and instigating than reporting (too commonly they have seemingly forgotten how to report the facts without either verbally or nonverbally editorializing). Some people interviewed even pictured the case as showing the danger to our young black males of being able to go to the store without the risk of being killed. As a result, we got a kind of fever pitch with seemingly everyone piling on in what resonated as a mob lynching -- perhaps even aptly called "high-tech lynching" as Supreme Court Justice Clarence Thomas termed a similar piling on in the Anita Hill hearing during his confirmation.

Once the jury found Zimmerman not guilty and the fever pitch spread and intensified, the President himself felt impelled to have the outcry heard through his voice, giving it a kind of official validation. So, in a surprise appearance in the White House briefing room, he offered his reaction because, together with his famous race speech, it is what can be called a smoking gun in that, even among our Talented Tenth, it credibly supports the stranglehold of Victimology.

The President's reaction was against the backdrop of the public, the black public in particular, having declared Zimmerman guilty before the trial (which is not unusual for a given trial, but there is a certain kind of zeal involved in these racial trials, a gotta-find-him-guilty craze or it is just more proof that there is no justice for blacks in this country). George Zimmerman was portrayed as a cold-blooded murderer of a harmless and innocent unarmed black teenager walking back home and minding his own business.

- Never mind, for example, that it appears that rather than simply walking home as he could have (and it can be argued should have) Martin apparently delayed his walk so as to confront Zimmerman.
- Never mind that Zimmerman's explanation that Trayvon attacked him is logical, for it does not seem that Zimmerman would have had a motive to attack Trayvon, for it was, obviously, Trayvon who felt provoked.
- Never mind whether Trayvon's actions in the ensuing scuffle were intended to harm Zimmerman (as claimed by Zimmerman), at least some credence must be given to the fact that, *at the time*, Zimmerman might just possibly have *felt* that they were.
- Never mind that though Trayvon's mother said she was certain that the voice calling for help was that of her son, under the circumstances, she might not have been expected to say otherwise -- or that originally Trayvon's father had said it was not Trayvon's voice; and that, in and of itself, the indisputable fact that Trayvon was on top of Zimmerman raises the possibility that it was Zimmerman who was yelling for help.
- And never mind, on the part of various witnesses, their contradictions and changes in testimony.

No two sides to every story here, and no such examination and consideration of the possibilities, but rather, one-sided, heart-throbbing inflammatory assertions which rule out those possibilities, declaring what Trayvon would not or could not have done. In an egregious (if not legally punishable) example, so certain of Zimmerman's perfidy and guilt, almost the minute the case went public, black producer, director, writer, and actor Spike Lee took to twitter and urged his some 240,000 or more followers to "REACH OUT & TOUCH" Zimmerman, providing them Zimmerman's address, which, incidentally, turned out to be the wrong address.

That the jury found Zimmerman not guilty expectedly only made things worse, for while asking for justice, what we really sought was vengeance. *We* had declared him guilty and that was all that mattered. So, on their

ESPN sports radio program (July 15, 2013), for example, Stephen A. Smith and Ryan Ruocco reported that both New York Giants receiver, Victor Cruz, and Atlanta Falcons receiver, Roddy White, though later apologizing, sent tweets of vengeance, Cruz declaring that Zimmerman would hardly last a year because the hood would catch up with him and White asking the jurors to go home and kill themselves.

Former Attorney General, Eric Holder, provided them aid and comfort. After the verdict, in a speech before the National Association for the Advancement of Colored People (NAACP), he addressed what he called the "tragic, unnecessary shooting," criticized the "stand your ground" laws, and lamented the "sad reality" of still having to the teach our children how to conduct themselves during police stops or confrontations (382a).

The Attorney General further championed our American right to make our voices heard through protests, rallies, and vigils "to inspire responsible debate." Why *responsible* debate? The usual call is for "open and honest" debate or discussion, he himself having used that wording in this same address. That, in this passage, he changed that wording to *responsible* debate perhaps tells us more than he realizes: that when he and others refer to "open and honest" discussion, they really do mean, not "open and honest" discussion, but *responsible* discussion – as, of course, they interpret responsible. The "open and honest" call serves to shroud the fact that any such discussion might bring one the same fate suffered, for example, by Jimmy the Greek Snyder and Al Campanis, who had their careers ruined because, on race matters, they gave their "open and honest" opinion.

The question: how might Holder and other blacks interpret either: "responsible debate" or "open and honest discussion." The answer: it would be a debate or discussion which makes us feel good about ourselves. As captured by Lasch-Quinn, since the 1960s, through encounter group therapy, race experts have promised to "liberate whites from their alleged racism and blacks from their assumed bondage of low self-esteem" – race experts, for example, being educators, counselors, trainers, psychotherapists, consultants (150a: xiv-xv). Holder and others would appear to reflect their influence, groupthink being their modality (186:11-21).

Through groupthink, we want whites to come to see why they should get rid of their prejudices and personally accept us. On our part, we want to convince them that they should do just that because they have a misconception of blacks. That is, we want *feeling equality* -- whites to *feel* that we are equal to them. So, in this story, Trayvon should not have been held suspicious or followed because Zimmerman should have rid himself of his prejudices and seen Trayvon, not through those prejudices, but as we blacks and our white supporters have idealized Trayvon to be, a young black male walking from the store and minding his own business, just as a young white male teenager would do. That is, whites should feel the same way about Trayvon as they feel about any young white male teenager.

Though calling for "open and honest" discussion or "responsible debate," we blacks, and our white allies, have created a kind of Maginot Line which discourages and penalizes both internal and external scrutiny. We want, not scrutiny, but therapy -- whites to cleanse themselves of their prejudices so they will accept and respect us as, or feel us to be, their equals. "Artificial forcing" is what, in his Atlanta Compromise Address of 1895, Washington, in essence, called such a quest; and it is what, some 100 years later, Lasch-Quinn calls "the social engineering of attitudes" (150a: xv). Washington did not think it would work back then, and even amid the changes wrought by time, Lasch-Quinn does not think it is working today, or that it can work, exacerbating black-white relations rather than improving them.

The only way the quest for *feeling equality* has worked is to put us into the kind of downward spiral which Samuel and Chiche say are intrinsic to victimhood. For "When we lose our ability to know when we are crying wolf and when our cries are based on real, actionable injustice," Lasch-Quinn warns us, "the basis for claiming legitimate redress recedes" because, she continues, "the therapeutic sensibility works against our making this vital distinction, instead leaving us mired in a generational sense of complaint and outrage that never seems to subside" (150a:xvii-xviii). That is what we see in the Trayvon Martin case -- "us mired in a generational sense of complaint and outrage that never seems to subside" -- such being the nature of the downward spiral which ensues from Victimology. To remind us of this downward spiral -- the constant and pervasive vigilant parsing of the words and actions of whites by us blacks for any sign that they do not *feel* that we blacks are equal to them, or that they treat us differently -- our mnemonic is **"leav[es] us mired in a generational sense of complaint and outrage that never seems to subside."**

Lest he be misunderstood, Holder made it clear that he was not saying that things have not gotten better for us African Americans, acknowledging, in fact, that we have made great progress (he himself, for example, a black man being Attorney General), but he cited his own personal adverse racial experiences in suggesting that "we still have much more work to do -- and much further to go." Under the circumstances, it is called pouring oil on the fire, not calming our passions, but inflaming them.

President Obama's Remarks about the Trayvon Martin Case and the Pervasiveness of Our Victimology (A Contaminated Talented Tenth)

As stated, later, the President himself stepped into the maelstrom, his thoughts serving, not to quell the fire, but to pour on more oil (see Appendix B). While accepting the verdict, he left little doubt that he did not like it either, and that whites should understand why African Americans were outraged. That outrage, he argued, stems from the association of the case with a persistent and prevalent history of blacks in America being treated differently, unfairly, and unjustly -- from, for example, the experience of being followed while shopping in a department store to racial disparities in the application of our criminal laws (as discussed in Chapter 9, these being examples of something which Shelby Steele calls objective correlatives). Though statistics, he went on, show that young black men are "disproportionately involved in the criminal justice system" and are "disproportionately both victims and perpetrators of violence," black resentment is that these disproportionalities are not considered in the context of our "very difficult history" and are used as "an excuse" to see and treat our young men differently. If Trayvon Martin had been white, he implied, "both the outcome and the aftermath might have been different." As remedies, he called for "soul-searching" "in families and churches and workplaces," for local law enforcement training, for an examination of our "stand your ground" laws, and, possibly, for the White House convening a group of diverse leaders to address the topic of "helping young African American men feel that they're a full part of this society and that they've got pathways and avenues to succeed."

The author is a great admirer and supporter of the President, having voted for him twice (and would do so again if he could run for a third term), and strongly supports his worldview and his programs and policies. On a number of counts, he is living up to his desire to be a transformative President in the mold of Ronald Reagan, but not when it comes to the plight of us African Americans. When it comes to our plight, he is wrong – dead wrong. As revealed in his remarks, and by the mindset suggested by them, rather than being transformative, the President, more or less entrapped in the civil-rigths fixation of our time, is reinforcing and perpetuating our second bondage.

The President puts himself squarely in DuBois's System-Responsibility Tradition, which is largely responsible for the black plight that we project into such incidents, and squarely out of Washington's Self-Responsibility Tradition, which likely would have prevented that plight in the first place -- and thus all of the national trauma and drama (therapy) which tend to surround these incidents. They seem to provide occasions for us to sound off and release our racialized feelings, experiencing in the process its typically transitory rewards. As discussed in Chapter 9, the more lasting reward sought, our "psychic well-being" (to use Lasch-Quinn's term) must come from within.

However, from the President's remarks, one would never imagine that to be the case. In DuBois's System-Responsibility Tradition fashion, he lays the blame on the system, inciting (it can be said), as is characteristic of our prevailing and dominant System-Responsibility Tradition, an urge to protest, demand, and racially oppose, guided by an underlying spirit of anger and distrust, instead of, as is characteristic of Washington's Self-Responsibility Tradition, a sense of racial harmony, compromise, and cooperation, guided by an underlying spirit of hope and optimism.

The President's remarks capture the essence of that which largely has come to explain our plight: an identification with victimhood which externalizes that plight and holds us blacks save harmless, often it seems, regardless of how disproportionate or maladaptive our behavior.

A double standard, as Lasch-Quinn, among others, points out. It is OK, for example, for many of us blacks, out of fear of our young black males, to cross the street to avoid them or avoid being alone with them on an elevator, but for whites to do the same is racial profiling and a failure by them to put our behavior in context. As the President suggests, if Trayvon Martin had been white, the outcome and the aftermath might, indeed, have been different, but different, not simply because of being white, but, because if Trayvon had been white, he would likely have acted differently, for example, continuing to walk home instead of showing "toughness" (a typical black male attribute) in confronting Zimmerman -- or, perhaps, more to the point, he might have continued his walk because he would not have felt the urge to confront, in Trayvon's words, a "creepy ass cracker." And, of course, in these incidents, one can reverse the *if*. The outcome, and the aftermath, might have been different *if*, for example, O. J. Simpson had been white and his wife black, or *if* (as his lawyer, Mark O'Mara, expressed) Zimmerman had been black instead of a mixed-race Hispanic.

Moreover, contrary to what the President suggests, is there not logic in our young black males being followed, or perceived as a potential threat if statistics show that they -- as he acknowledges -- disproportionately commit crimes? Why not be realistic? Are we not inclined to make initial judgments based on group information? Just as doctors, for example, want to know all about our family history to assist them in their individual diagnosis, as individuals in society, at least initially, we draw upon our knowledge of groups to assist us in making judgments about individuals within a particular group. Based on their studies, social psychologists tell us that, at least initially, black people and white people alike make initial individual judgments based on group information or stereotypes (186:331-77). In this case, just two weeks prior to the shooting, Zimmerman had spotted a young black man prowling in the neighborhood who was later arrested for burglarizing a neighborhood home and stealing a new laptop. Is it then racial profiling if he might have been suspicious of Trayvon and, therefore, followed him, especially since he said that he thought that Trayvon was not just walking home, but, like the arrested burglar, was prowling? Prowling or not, given the incident of the prior two weeks, is there anything unreasonable about Zimmerman having been suspicious -- and having acted on that suspicion? Agreed, he obviously went too far, having disobeyed instructions to halt his pursuit, but is it somewhat understandable why he might have disobeyed -- even though he should not have?

Further, we blacks make such initial judgments about whites all the time. Specifically, in this case, in her testimony, Trayvon's friend, Rachel Jeantel, testified that Trayvon said he was being followed by a "creepy ass cracker." In the cross examination of her, Rachel said that she did not find the term "cracker" offensive because people in her neighborhood use it all the time. So, here was Trayvon making and acting on an individual judgment based on group perception, but no reference by the President to such behavior on Trayvon's part -- or ours. Instead, given our "very difficult history," one takes from his remarks that for whites to do the same in regard to us is a cardinal sin which calls for "soul-searching." His remarks exhibit no realization of the fact that whites, as well, have a "very difficult history" when it comes to adjusting to and accepting black adaptation (the array of social problems with which we confront white society; and the associated programs, laws, and regulations -- inclusive of the War on Poverty -- being indicative of that history) and that, therefore, likewise, we blacks ought not to use their history as an excuse to judge individual whites (in this case Zimmerman). For the President, the *burden of understanding*, as it might be termed, rests totally with whites, none with us.

Consider, in contrast, the *burden of understanding* as Washington taught it. In one of his 37 **Sunday Evening Talks**, he said to his Tuskegee students:

> Then, too, I want you to go out in a spirit of liberality toward the white people with whom you come in contact. That is an important matter. When I say this I do not mean that you shall go lowering your manhood or your dignity. Go in a manly way, in a straightforward and honorable way, and then you will show the white people that you are not of a belittling race that the prejudice which so many people possess cannot come among you and those with whom you work. If you can extend a helping hand to a white person, feel just as happy in doing so as in helping a black person.

In, the sight of God there is no color line, and we want to cultivate a spirit that will make us forget that there is such a line anywhere. We want to be larger and broader than the people who would oppress us on account of our color (269:353).

Not only did Washington say this to his students, but, in equivalent words he said it to the entire race. And he said it not on some special occasion, nor occasionally, but repeatedly and consistently, as part of the Washington gospel. It would have been easy -- and in some quarters popular -- for him to embrace victimhood with all of its intrinsic anger and frustration, but he *chose* characterhood over victimhood. That is a choice that leads to Characterology over Victimology -- Characterology (to imitate the phrasing of linguist, John McWhorter) defined as making character a part of our core identity -- of seeing ourselves as "larger and broader than the people who would oppress us on account of our color." However, the President was not about us seeing ourselves as "larger and broader." His *burden of understanding* was laid upon whites only. That being the case, he was reflecting an outcome of Victimology: the cult of black Separatism, explained by McWhorter as "a conviction, sometimes explicit and sometimes tacit, that because black people endure such victimhood at every turn, they cannot be held responsible for immoral or destructive actions, these being "understandable" responses to frustration and pain" (160:61-62). This victim mindset adds up to the following: to be black is to be blameless. We want and demand our freedom and equality, but, consistent with Victimology, shirk their intrinsic *burden of self-responsibility*, the President providing aid and comfort.

Consider further, in contrast, another relevant Washington teaching when it comes to whites making judgments about us blacks. In one of his **Sunday Evening Talks**, he emphasized behavior on the part of many blacks which "...is very hurtful to us as a race," such as calling a teacher a Professor, something, he told them, which they should not do because it degrades the title of Professor and, consequently, the esteem of the race (279d). No such emphasis from the President. Not even a hint. Rather than, inclusively, using the case to remind our young black males that, in what they do, they represent the race, he used it to do just the opposite: to deny any such representation. He spoke as if our young black males can disproportionately commit crimes *without* *representing the race*, something not possible when the crimes occur on such a widespread and persistent scale.

The President is justified in reminding us, as he did in his speech on race in response to the Reverend Jeremiah Wright controversy during his 2008 Presidential campaign, of William Faulkner's observation that "The past isn't dead and buried. In fact, it isn't even past" (426b:5). Rather than dwelling on the positives of the past -- and at the same time those of the present -- the President, instead, dwelt on its negatives, using those negatives to validate in that speech, not just black anger, but anger in segments of the white community as well, accenting the similarities of the two -- even though, in one case, the anger can said to be grounded in the realities of the present, the other, frequently, in what Shelby Steele terms the recomposition of the present.

In their book, The Time Paradox: The New Psychology of Time That Will Change Your Life, this orientation is what Philip Zimbardo and John Boyd call a present-fatalistic, past-negative time perspective, from which they say "research suggests that nothing good comes out of them" (see Chapters 4 and 14). Although the President is neither wholly negative about the past, nor wholly fatalistic about the present, nothing good, therefore, coming from his time orientation, he was far from bringing to the case a time perspective which would better serve our race and our nation: a past-positive, future orientation. In a past-positive, future orientation, positive rather than negative memories of the past are accented, not just recalled, and the future involves a realistic approach to life wherein there is goal setting and a willingness to sacrifice to achieve those goals. A past-positive, future orientation perspective calls for remembering "by rebuilding your past upon a foundation of positive attitudes," as a result of which "you can reclaim it for yourself, and in so doing, free yourself for the pursuit of happiness in the present and the future" (294: 98). However, no such remembering took place on the part of the President.

The President, it is evident, did what our leaders in the System-Responsibility Tradition have tended to do since its origin: address the role of only one of the two parties involved, whites, while mainly ignoring the role of the other party involved, us blacks. A lot is made of what the system has done poorly, or has not done, and what it needs to do; and little or nothing about what we also have done poorly, or have not done, and what we need to do. Again, contrast this approach with the Self-Responsibility Tradition approach of Washington. In what is the most famous speech on race in our history, his Atlanta Compromise Address of 1895, Washington gave the President and our other leaders a model: he addressed both parties. He prefaced his remarks to us blacks with "To those of my race... I would say ...;" and he prefaced his remarks to whites with, "To those of the white race...I would repeat what I say to my own race," going on to do so and then adding remarks specifically intended for them. In generl, when speaking to gatherings where whites occupied the main floor and blacks occupied the gallery, Basil Mathews gives this description of his approach:

> Addressing himself to the white section of the audience he would cite examples of the way in which they had assisted his race to make more progress in half a century than any other race had done. As they glowed with satisfaction he would ask why this achievement should be marred by unjust discrimination in education, the denial of justice in courts, mob violence, and economic exploitation. Turning to the Negro group he made them swell with pride at the steps in progress made since the Civil War and Emancipation, and then lamented the blots on that record due to indolence, shiftlessness, vice, and unreliabililty. He would then rally each group to put its shoulder to the wheel of progress for the sake of both races and for the advancement of their nation as a whole (164a:202-03).

As evident, in addressing both parties, he dealt with the good and the bad on both sides, and what each needed to do for the success of its race and of the nation. His two-party approach and past-positive, future orientation helped to bring relative racial peace and saw the advent of the Age of Booker T. Washington, a period of dramatic black progress. No similar outcome can be expected from the mainly one-party and present-fatalistic leaning, past-negative approach manifested in the Trayvon Martin case by President Obama, as well as by our other leaders. When in victim mode, as they were, we tend to self-examine and forgive less, and to rationalize, resist, and blame more -- the outcome being, not relative peace and progress, but discord, stagnation, and decline.

As regards the President's future time perspective, in addition to state and local training and a review of "stand your ground" laws, he called for possibly convening a conference of leaders to address the topic of "helping young African American men feel that they're a full part of this society and that they've got pathways and avenues to succeed [something which he subsequently did]." These concrete things that we can do, as the President refers to them, are reminders of the faulty analyses and failed prescriptions which have become so commonplace -- what McWhorter calls therapeutic alienation.

One can easily deduce that to be the case with respect to the President's remarks, for his proposed remedies do not suggest a serious and concentrated attempt to solve the problem. Certainly there is no reason to believe that his "concrete things" will make a systemic difference. We have had a lot of training over the years and the laws per se do not appear to be the source of the problem. Nor is it a matter of helping our young African American men to feel anything, for therapy is not going to solve their problem; and pathways and avenues to their success abound. They have access to a free public education and, for many, more or less free higher education, augmented by an array of social programs to support them and their families. That was what the War on Poverty was about -- and what its remnants and related efforts are still about. What more can the system (private, public, or both) be expected to do to help them "feel that they're a full part of this society?" Not much more, if any more, for there is a point at which system responsibility ends and their own responsibility begins. Having provided our young men opportunities and support, the feeling which ensues from them must emanate from them. *They will come to feel a full part of this society when they do their full part in it.* It is up to us, as African Americans, in particular, our males, to see that they do their part -- the hard work and initiative which are required. Therefore, the President should have primarily directed his call to us black males and to other blacks.[30]

---

[30] It is commendable that the President his taken his own advice, subsequently announcing the creation of an independent nonprofit organization to assist black and Hispanic males, his post-presidential life to be devoted to its work (304e). One cannot be sure, however, of what, if anything, this means insofar as his leadership, broadly, in addressing our Victimology.

The "soul-searching" "in families and churches and workplaces" called for by the President needs to take place in" the souls of black folk," to borrow the words of DuBois's classic. Of course, any such suggestion might impair one's standing as a race man, the President's remarks in this instance putting him in that category, a representative of the thinking of those who make a drumbeat of his message and a furor over such incidents as the Trayvon Martin case. Their standing in the civil rights establishment (and, interrelated, in the black public) rests on it, and by implication, if you are not a race man, something is wrong; we have to check you out, or just simply brand you as "thinking white." And to have been the first, or among the first, to be "in on" these incidents is a special badge of honor. Our leaders want to be seen as being on the alert and leading the attack on racism. They want to be viewed as defending the honor and integrity of the race. Furthermor, and never mind, in contrast, no similar outcry (just as Lasch-Quinn warns) -- hardly even a murmur – can be heard when it comes to our fundamentals, such as, those which were on display in this case in the person of Trayvon having been suspended from school for cutting classes and in the person of Rachel being unable to read cursive writing, or our out-of-wedlock births and young black male fratricide; that is where the "soul-searching" stops. While customarily avoiding race rhetoric -- as he did, for example, in his famous 2008 speech on race -- in this case, the President stepped into the fray and one could not distinguish him from the "race men."

In concluding his remarks, the President observed that "... those of us in authority should be doing everything we can to encourage the better angels of our nature, as opposed to using these episodes to heighten divisions." Yet, that is exactly what the President's remarks likely did: heighten divisions. That is what you do when, instead of calling for a consideration of the facts and feelings on both sides, you do as he did: send sympathy and support only to one side and altogether ignore the other side, thereby implicitly discrediting, if not demonizing the other side.

Over one year later, amid the national controversy over two other similar racial incidents – the police shooting and killing of Michael Brown and the police chokehold which killed Eric Garner – the victim mindset of the President was again on display in an interview granted by him and his wife, Michelle Obama, to People magazine (436a). The subject was their experiences with racism. He cited having been mistaken as a waiter and as a parking valet. She, apparently not being recognized as the First Lady while shopping in the chain store, Target, was asked by an approaching woman to get something off a shelf. They did refer to these as "small irritations or indignities" and as "nothing compared to what a previous generation experienced," but added that though improvement has been made, much more needs to be done. On the same weekend of the interview, while sitting in their patrol car in Brooklyn, New York, coincidentally, two police officers were approached and ambushed by a black assassin who, then, in a police chase, killed himself. The assassin reportedly said he was avenging the police killings of Michael Brown and Eric Garner, his message being, "They take 1 of ours, let's take 2 of theirs." (325c).

It was in this context that the President and his wife were sending a message. It is proposed that the message goes something like the following: In the past we have been victims and, even now that we have reached the top, we are still victims -- minor victims, but still victims. Intended or not, their *emphasis* was on victimhood. They were saying to us blacks that, as blacks ourselves, we identify with you because, like you, we too have been, and are, victims; all of us blacks are victims because no matter who we are, at some point in our life, whites are going to subject us to "small irritations and indignities." They did not say, as they might have, that we are wrong to give such "small irritations and indignities" – or, for that matter, such occasional large ones as the Trayvon Martin case -- the kind of attention that we do. Instead, they said that we have much more to do. If they did say it, it was not reported, in which case they would have better served our cause if they had done what young Jimmy Butler of the Chicago Bulls (discussed below) did in this interview at the tender age of 21: made expressly clear that pity, sympathy, or some other form of therapy was not being sought. As reported, more or less, they exhibited a past-negative, present-fatalistic time perspective, from which – as discussed in Chapter 4 -- Zimbardo and Boyd declare their "research suggests that nothing good comes out of them."

Nevertheless, in substance, the President and the First Lady are right. History and social science suggest that the perceived racial stereotyping which they describe, not only is still with us, but always has been, and probably always will be. Regardless of how "much more we do," we are not likely to eradicate it – not even when it comes to a black President and a black First Lady. In publicly showcasing the stereotyping, they said nothing that is likely to advance an understanding and acceptance of its reality, but, instead, fed a frenzy which saw not only the customary protests, but, in addition, rioting and two ambushed and murdered police officers.

Subsequently, the President and the First Lady have seemingly taken advantage of every opportunity to show that they "are with us"-- in our bondage, as it were. In his eulogy in memory of the nine blacks murdered in the Charleston, South Carolina, church shooting, for example, the President used the occasion to call for the removal of the Confederate flag from atop the South Carolina statehouse (426e). Probably most of us would agree that the flag should have been removed, and that, in the first place, it should have been there, but, does the fact that it was there have any real consequence or significance? Moreover, could not its display symbolize something different from the subservice and slavery which we blacks saw in it? Yes, it could mean ancestral pride as some South Carolinians saw it, but, as well, could it have symbolized defeat of a lost cause and the embrace of a largely vanquished way of life? However, those snared in the bondage of Victimology, as so many of us blacks are, rather than being open to such possibilities, are fixed on the flag's perceived harm and, accordingly, expect sympathy. Giving it context, the President even went on to refer to "past injustices" which "continue to shape the present." Thanks to the President and others, the flag was removed, but the victim mindset displayed by the President in calling for its removal was reinforced by him. Instead, could he not have resisted Victimology by, for example, asking us blacks to be strong and self-assured enough to ignore the flag because we have more important things to be concerned about?

The tragedy is that, in the Trayvon Martin case, as in these other instances, the President probably truly felt that he was doing the right thing, moving us -- as he said -- towards a more perfect union when in fact he was doing the opposite. It is a tragedy compounded by the fact that he represents so many of us African Americans in the leadership class and so many who make up our Talented Tenth. Our discussion of the victim mindset of the Talented Tenth is on full display in our discussion of "acting white" in Chapter 6. To reinforce the point, however, a few examples follow.

(1) Black Harvard sociologist, **William Julius Wilson**. Here we have a world renowned black scholar. In his most recent publication, More Than Just Race: Being Black and Poor in the Inner City, he explicitly acknowledges what, in policy and political circles, previously has gone unacknowledged: we blacks have a cultural problem which contributes to the poor being poor. Therefore, Wilson argues, we must no longer restrict our policies to a remedy of the structural. From this "bold, new perspective" [his words] of his, Wilson makes the case that we should incorporate and unite into these policies remedies for the cultural as well, thereby focusing on both structure and culture (similar to the change made by Ogbu as a result of the Fordham-Ogbu "acting white" study). Nevertheless, he argues that the greater problem is the system (just as Fordham-Ogbu still argued). In his words: "…more weight should be given to structural causes of inequality, despite the dynamic interrelationships of structure and culture, because they continue to play a far greater role in the subjugation of Black Americans and other people of color" (287:135). Yet, at the same time, he admits that "… one cannot draw a simple dichotomy between culture and structure in an investigation of their relative impact. They are not mutually exclusive; in fact, they often work in concert" (287:153). He, thereby, joins the company of DuBois in attempting to square a circle. On the one hand, you can separate structure from culture, while, on the other hand, you cannot.

Nevertheless, Wilson is so committed to making the case that "… it is hard to overstate the importance of racialist structural factors" in accounting for racial group outcomes that he fails to make an unambiguous case for his own thesis that culture also is a factor (287: 152). For example, in his chapter devoted to cultural issues as pertains to our males, "The Economic Plight of Inner-City Black Males," he is unequivocal about the structural factors, but when it comes to the cultural factors, he emphasizes, for example, the shortcomings of findings showing a black male subculture of defeatism and resistance, concluding, in regard to the pertinent studies, that generally the evidence is "mixed." He even goes so far as to say that "… it is one thing to acknowledge that cultural factors ought to be included in our quest for understanding, but quite another thing to advance cultural explanations that are based on *real* evidence" [emphasis added] (287: 81-82).

One is puzzled as to what *real* evidence Wilson seeks. Acquaintance with some of the literature, especially that which pertains to the effect of absent fathers, would not suggest that evidence pertaining to cultural factors is any less *real* than that pertaining to structural factors. Nor is it any less prevalent. One is reminded of the global warming debate wherein opponents claim that no *real* evidence exists to support it. But the equivocation and ambivalence may lie less in the evidence not being real than in a failure to undertake a real examination of it, or to accept the reality of that examination. In the case of Wilson, it is apparent throughout his discourse that what occupies his passion are those "racialist structural factors" whose importance is "hard to overstate," with culture having its role, but maybe not a *real* one; at least we would not want to "overstate" it. To do so might endanger our victimhood status.

(2) Black Hispanic New York University sociologist, **Pedro A. Noguera**. In a chapter contributed to an edited publication, Noguera proclaims that initiatives must be made to rectify "institutional factors" that limit black achievement, adding, however, that "… to be effective such initiatives must also involve efforts to counter and transform cultural patterns and what Ogbu …has called the "oppositional identities" adopted by Black males that undermine the importance they attach to education" (190:56).

In his book, <u>The Trouble with Black Boys</u>, Noguera reiterates his position, and even endorses Bill Cosby and Dr. Poussaint's call for parents to take more responsibility in raising their children (191: xxii-xxv). So far, so good. Then, however, he goes on to "completely disagree with their *approach*" [emphasis added]. "I see very little evidence," he declares, "that condemning parents for doing a poor job in raising their children will improve the situation" (191: xxv). Oh? It defies logic to see how anyone who has read Cosby and Poussanit's book, <u>Come on People</u> -- which Noguera cites and at least implies that he has read -- could come away with the notion that their *approach* is to improve the situation by "condemning parents for doing a poor job of raising their children."

To distinguish his position, Noguera adds, "Unlike Cosby and Poussaint, I also believe that our society -- its schools, churches, private businesses and corporations, and local government -- must do more to address the ways in which Black boys and men are *set up* for failure" [emphasis added] (191:xxv). But, in his introduction, Cosby declares, "African Americans must never give up the struggle to eliminate the racism and classism in our society that continue to present obstacles to success for the poor" but, throughout, he and Dr. Poussaint urge persistence and striving notwithstanding the obstacles (46: xviii). Contrary to Noguera's assertion, there is no indication that they do not share his view that the agencies cited must do more. However, their exclusive emphasis is on what we should and must do for ourselves. They are not writing from the perspective of black boys and men having been "set up," as Noguera puts it, but of their need to "put up." How about Noguera? From what perspective is he writing? Where does he want the emphasis to lie -- on our black boys being "set up" or on their need to "put up?" – that is, on victimhood or characterhood?

(3) Finally, aforementioned prominent black educational psychologist, **Edmund Gordon**. While one must respect Gordon's work, for him to declare that the "generalized distortion of the conditions and status of Black males in the United States is an artificial or at least at best a manufactured problem" is nothing short of astounding (104a:x). His argument is that the distortion is based on "life in depressed inner cities where African Americans are overrepresented," the majority of residents being neglected (104a:ix). Two of our mnemonics, for example -- **72** and **59** -- tell a different story. These numbers are not about "depressed inner cities where African Americans are overrepresented," but about all African Americans – in these cities and in other cities. What they show is a *nationa*l out-of-wedlock black birthrate of 72 percent and a black male high school dropout rate of 59 percent in the 56 highest black male enrollment districts. Of course, these numbers might have been different at the time Gordon wrote his book (1999), but not materially so. Where, then, is the distortion? The answer, herein, is that it exists, not in reality, but in a victim mindset

In originating the concept, DuBois had seen the Talented Tenth as having the role of guiding us away from "the contamination and death of the Worst" towards human progress and civilization. In the person of President Obama, the Trayvon Martin case illustrates the Talented Tenth's failure to perform that role. This failure is also illustrated in examples provided by **William Julius Wilson**, **Pedro A. Noguera**, and **Edmund Gordon**. As in the case of President Obama, we see in these examples a victim mindset blinded to reality. Due to this blindness, rather than taking us away from the "contamination and death of the Worst" (Victimology), our Talented Tenth, instead, has been contaminated by the "Worst" and has put us in the shadow of its "death." It is ironic that we can lay the blame at the feet of DuBois. The concept which he authored, in laying the foundation of Victimology, he undermined. To remind us of the pervasiveness of our second bondage and the contamination of the Talented Tenth by it, this is our mnemonic: **Trayvon Martin Case - President Obama's Remarks**.

Affirmative Action and School Discipline (Contaminated Application of Laws)

Not only does our black leadership class reflect that contamination. In their application, so do some of our laws, or their components -- the Civil Rights Act (1964) and Affirmative Action (1965) providing cases in point.

Civil Rights Act (1964)

While addressing objective discrimination, at the same time, both institutionalize and enshrine victimhood because they also address ascriptive discrimination. That is, they address discrimination based on the *assumed* existence or practice of racial discrimination as determined by racial percentages, which, in effect, amount to quotas. So, for example, in their report on school discipline, the U.S. Department of Education and the U.S. Department of Justice (2014) found that though African American students made up only 15% of the Civil Rights Data Collection (CRDC),

- they made up 35% of the students suspended once, 44% of those suspended more than once, and 36% of students expelled;

- that "over 50% of students who were involved in school-related arrests or referred to law enforcement are Hispanic or African-American";
- and, further, that their "investigations...found cases where African-American students were disciplined more harshly and more frequently because of their race than similarly situated white students."

They conclude the following: "... racial discrimination in school discipline is a real problem" (459b). Thus, as applied in 2014, the report interprets the Civil Rights Act of 1964 as finding that African American students are victims of racially discriminatory disciplinary practices, the conclusion based on nothing more than the numbers and on some cases encountered, what occurred in those cases being a judgmental matter. It was *assumed* that since African American students made up 15% of the sample, they should make up 15% of the students suspended once, 15% of those suspended more than once, and so on – or, presumably, some close approximation thereof. Never mind any objective evidence that would show that the assumption did not reflect the reality -- no apparent attempt even being made to determine if it did. It was use of the law to address, not so much the objective as the subjective, which is to say, the way "victims" must be treated. One approach to the issue calls for analysis, the other for quotas. One focuses on accountability, let the chips falling where they may, while the other rationalizes and blames.

Affirmative Action

Affirmative Action is justifiably intended to redress some of the wrongs inflicted upon us in the past and to give us a chance to catch up, but that is not the same as us being victims if we cannot pass a qualifying test or get a desired promotion. It is not intended to lead to the abolition of the need to enforce defined standards and meet normative criteria. As appropriate, reasonable adjustments of those standards and criteria are in order, but to insist on customized adjustments, or quotas, is out of order. Oftentimes, to do so moves us from reasonable redress to Victimology.

On and on they go…

As somewhat of a footnote to this subsection, the urge to insert mention of Mayor Bill de Blasio's administration revision of New York City's school discipline code, announced in February 2015, could not be resisted (367d). It underlines the victim mindset exhibited in the above discussion of school suspensions under the Civil Rights Act of 1964, and is another egregious example of never-ending victim-oriented policies and practices; on and on they go. Some of us seemingly demand to be able to resist police officers without being harmed, and similarly, in this instance some seem to declare that our students should be able to engage in disruptive school behavior without being suspended. The revised policy will make it harder for a principal to suspend a student; approval of the central office will be required. Suspension ought to be a last resort, but its use should rest, not on thereaupeutic sensibility or ethnic considerations, but on educational ones. This revision addresses the former, the concern being that too many black and Hispanic students are suspended for so-called "relatively minor offenses." Never mind attention to upholding the behavioral standards on which the success of students and quality education depend, or safeguarding the authority of the principal. Apparently our students, being the victims that they are, need not meet those standards; they have an inherited status: victimhood. And never mind the authority of the principal; protection of the victim has priority. From afar, how easy it is to label an offense "relatively minor," unmindful that while distance may lend enchantment, it may also lend illusion, especially when – as in this instance – it is created by Victimology.

So through leadership and law, Victimology has been enshrined as our second bondage. To remind us of just that, we add the following to our Victimology mnemonic: **Affirmative Action - School Discipline**. We, then, come away with these mnemonics: **Trayvon Martin Case - President Obama's Remarks / Affirmative Action - School Discipline**. Now we take a closer look.

Up Close and Personal

In <u>The Power of Personal Accountability: Achieve What Matters to You</u>, worldwide personal and organizational accountability consultants,

Mark Samuel and Sophie Chiche, give us insight into victimhood -- from which Victimology has ensued (231). Although their target audience is the corporate world, what they say is applicable to any human being or to any human system. They contrast victim behavior with accountability behavior (231:xvii). They say that in *accountability behavior*, we take action, learn, self-examine, forgive, own, and recognize; while, correspondingly, in *victim behavior*, we hide, resist, rationalize, blame, deny, and ignore.

Our thinking behind such behaviors tends to be that we do not have a choice. But we do, Samuel and Chiche say, because "victim is a paradoxical word."

> Most people think they are victims when they don't have a choice. When, in fact, it is the opposite: some people *choose* to be victims. You can't always control or change the situation you are in, but you can *always* choose how you respond to the situation, and you certainly have complete control over your *attitude* about it [emphases in original] (231:4).

They go on to add:

> Some people may be born into poverty, contract a disease, or be downsized out of a job. But these events aren't what make you a victim. What makes you a victim is how you *respond* to these events. When you respond with *accountability*, you go on anyway, move forward, and achieve your goals in spite of your difficult circumstances. But when you respond *as a victim*, you begin a downward spiral that moves you further and further away from your goals [emphases in original] (231:5).

Frankl

Internationally renowned psychiatrist and logotherapy founder, Victor Frankl's, survival of Auschwitz and other Nazi concentration camps provides a prime and stark example of their point. In his bestselling, Man's Search for Meaning, the late Frankl explains how he and some of the other prisoners were able to survive under the almost impossible conditions of their daily persecution.

What was really needed was a fundamental change in our attitude toward life. We had to learn ourselves and, furthermore, we had to teach the despairing men, that *it did not matter what we expected from life, but rather what life expected from us* [emphasis in original]. We needed to stop asking about the meaning of life, and instead to think of ourselves as those who were being questioned by life--daily and hourly. Our answer must consist, not in talk and meditation, but in right action and in right conduct. Life ultimately means **taking the responsibility** [emphasis added] to find the right answer to its problems and to fulfill the tasks which it constantly sets for each individual (91:98)

Frankl's point otherwise stated: the prisoners had either to accept personal responsibility for finding a reason for living or, in the words of Samuel and Chiche, "begin a downward spiral that moves you further and further away from your goals." Frankl's point: accept personal responsibility and, like Frankl, notwithstanding the brutal circumstances, the chances are better that we can move ourselves forward.

McGill

The same lesson lies in the life of one of our own, renowned paraplegic and black artist, Jerry McGill. In <u>Dear Marcus, Speaking to the Man Who Shot Me</u>, McGill tells the story of his recovery from being shot in the back and suffering a spinal cord injury at the age of twelve while walking home at night with a friend. A six-month hospital stay and years of rehabilitation enabled him, though permanently wheelchair bound, to return to school, finish college, and become a professional artist and world renowned advocate for the disabled. His attacker, for whom he made up the name Marcus, was never discovered. McGill has written his book to let Marcus know that he overcame the anger he long harbored for so long due to so many of his dreams being by Marcus: He dreamed of being a promising athlete, musical performer, dancer, or actor. It is that overcoming, he tells Marcus (and the rest of us), that enabled him to restore his life and move forward. He says to Marcus:

> Someday I would be honored to meet you; to look you in the eyes and shake your hand. My instinct tells me that will most

likely never happen. And I'm okay with that too. It isn't absolutely necessary because here is the thing, Marcus: At some point in life all of us will be in the *wrong place at the wrong time* [emphasis in original]. At some moment we will all be "assaulted" in one way or another. For a select few, it will come early in their development, for others, it will come later in life. But be rest assured -- it will come. No one escapes the night.

And when that moment arrives it won't matter what your assailant's face looked like; whether you saw it coming or you were caught completely off guard. No, at the end of the day all that will matter is that under the dense weight of all that occurred – when all was said and done - you had the strength and the fortitude to lift yourself up, open the door, and step out into the light (157:115-16).

What enabled him to do it, to free himself of the shadow that Marcus, at times, cast over his life? He reveals that it was an epiphany that he had while watching the sunset (as best he recalls) on the beach during a visit to a friend in Los Angeles. The epiphany: "Happiness is a thing I can control if I put my mind to it. It is **my** perspective and how **I** choose to see my life that is really going to make a difference at the end of the day" [emphases in original] (157:99-100).

Jimmy Butler

That sentiment, too, is echoed by Jimmy Butler, who makes it into this publication after the completion of the first round of the 2011 National Basketball Association (NBA) draft. He was the last pick, 30th, of the first round, chosen by the Chicago Bulls [and has proven himself a worthy pick, having become an NBA star]. It was difficult to leave him out, due to what he told the interviewer and sports analyst, Andy Katz, as reported by ESPN.com's Chad Ford:

Please, I know you're going to write something. I'm just asking you, don't write it in a way that makes people feel sorry for me, ... I hate that. There's nothing to feel sorry about. I love what happened to me. It made me who I am. I'm grateful for the challenges I've faced. Please, don't make them feel sorry for me (350d).

Why might people feel sorry for him? Because his mother kicked him out of the house at the age of thirteen and he had to spend four years living from friend to friend until he was invited during his senior year in high school, by Michelle Lambert and her family (who already had seven kids) to live with them, giving him a home and an adopted mother. These hardships, however, rather than a deterrent, have apparently, as he says, "made me who I am;" and, whereas, he might welcome pity, instead, he scorns it. At the tender age of 21, he knows what our leaders and system-centered ideologues seem not to know: that victimhood is an albatross, not a lifeline.

What Frankl, McGill, and Butler show

Frankl, McGill, and Butler provide us with a mirror. They show us the dynamics of victimization, enabling us to see ourselves (we African American men) up close and personal -- if only we open our mind. We can see, as Samuel and Chiche suggest, that the key words in the mirror of victimhood dynamics are *choose to respond*. We can infer that we are in a victimization quagmire, not because of our circumstances, however harsh, but because of how we have chosen to respond to those circumstances. We can infer, then, that we have forsaken ourselves, declared ourselves victims, and have turned our destiny over to the system -- no, not altogether, but to such extent that we have created the African American Male School Adaptability Crisis and its inseparable social problems. That is what happens when we allow our locus of control to pass from us to the system or to some other external entity. No longer in charge, by choice, we become the victim of circumstances, at the mercy of default forces.

In making this case, Frankl, McGill, and Butler are cited, but we are not talking about a little-known phenomenon. Others have theorized about it, many others have told their own stories, and the chances are that most of us, too, have stories of our own that we could tell. We are talking about something called locus of control. Social psychology has validated the debilitating effect of its externality on human behavior, for example, not being accountable or not taking responsibility (186:58-62). With specific reference to school achievement, one of the hypotheses that guides our proposed African American Male Career Pathway Program (AMCAP) is that students' sense of control over their environment will enhance their achievement. Research has been cited, including the massive Coleman Report, which supports this hypothesis.

Downward Spiral and Personality Association

Samuel and Chiche proclaim, "... when you respond *as a victim*, you begin a downward spiral that moves you further and further away from your goals." Throughout, we have variously depicted that downward spiral, especially in Chapters 9, 10, and 11. Its most devastating outcome is the havoc it has reaped on our manhood, leading us to internalize victimhood as our role rather than, as nearly universally common, the role of provider and protector. We have substituted victimhood for manhood. With that substitution (victim mentality) goes a range of negatives, such as, loss of control and distortion of reality. Those negatives lead to unstable families, unstable families leading to a flawed core identity, and a flawed identity to dysfunctionality and disorder.

Such negatives are not just the product of Victimology – victimhood treated as an identity; they are also the product of victimhood treated as a problem. Due to slavery and oppression, victimhood has been a problem for us African Americans throughout our history. That is what Scott's thesis is about. It is what the dysfunctionality and maladaptation she cites as existing in segments of our black community reflect.

Low self-esteem and aggression

The toll which it has exacted has perhaps been made most evident by the classic study published in 1951, The Mark of Oppression, by Columbia University-affiliated psychiatrists, the late Abram Kardiner and the late Lionel Ovesey (144). Kardiner and Ovesey undertook a psychodynamic (insight-oriented) personality study of 25 black subjects of different age, sex, and status. On the basis of their findings, they theorized a construct of black personality, which social scientists, Robert Crain and Carol Weisman, of John Hopkins University characterize as "the most comprehensive single statement" on the subject (51:26). They gathered and analyzed data that included the Rorschach Test and psychoanalytic sessions which, over a four-year period, numbered from a minimum of twenty to over one hundred.

Kardiner-Ovesey theory. Kardiner and Ovesey's derived theory is that **low self-esteem** and **aggression** constitute the core of black personality attributes. Each, they say, produces an array of other attributes, such as unrealistic aspirations, anxiety, focus on the obvious and simple combined with fear of the in-depth, failure to meet problems head on, affective diminution and constriction, apathy, hedonism, and self-hatred projected into hatred of other blacks – some of these, as previously noted, being sociologically observed by Frazier in his <u>Black Bourgeoisie</u>. Of these other attributes, they say the following:

> The rest are maneuvers with these main constellations [low esteem and aggression], to prevent their manifestation, to deny them and the sources from which they come, to make things look different from what they are, to replace aggressive activity which would be socially disastrous with more acceptable ingratiation and passivity (144:303-04.

They add, "Keeping this system going means, however, being constantly ill at ease, mistrustful, and lacking in confidence."

Pervasiveness and currency. Like sociologist, Jessie Bernard, with her two-culture postulation, Kardiner and Ovesey draw a distinction between the lower and upper classes. Although they theorize a black personality syndrome, they see the syndrome as uneven, manifested in greater degree among the lower classes than among the upper classes; the upper classes more nearly approximate whites in their profile, but only *nearly*. They conclude:

> The chief outcome of the psychological picture is that the upper classes of Negro society have so much controlling to do of their psychic life, that they must be extremely cramped and constricted and unspontaneous. There is too little self- contentment for true abandonment, and too much self-hatred and mutual distrust for effective social relatedness. They must constantly choose the lesser evil between spontaneity and getting hurt by retaliation. Hence, they prefer not to see things as they are, or to enter too deeply into anything to the accompaniment of apathy and resignation (144:316-17).

Yes, then, Kardiner-Ovesey say, there is a black personality syndrome, with low-esteem and aggression as its constellations, and that syndrome, while most pronounced among our lower classes, is still discernible among our upper classes, notwithstanding their major differences from the lower classes and their approximation of the white upper classes. This cross-class finding parallels McWhorter's conception of our negative identity, which is that, whereas, we often think of that identity as applicable only to our lower classes when, in fact, he sees it as permeating our entire black society. Amid the class variation in identity and personality, then, there is also a degree of class commonality.

Though formulated some sixty years ago, no herein discovered subsequent research has basically altered the Kardiner-Ovesey theory -- a theory which, in essence, mirrors the sociological findings of Frazier, which were reported during roughly the same time period. In fact, an internet search did not reveal any recent research of a similar nature, perhaps due to a matter of salience and relevance, as well as to what Lasch-Quinn terms "therapeutic sensibility."

As previously discussed, however, Cross -- drawing primarily upon John H. Rohrer and Munro S. Edmonson's The Eighth Generation: Cultures and Personalities of New Orleans Negroes, in which Kardiner and Ovesey's 25 case studies are reanalyzed -- does seek to undermine their thesis as it pertains to black self-hate or low self-esteem. That Cross has made much headway is not evident, the argument having been made that he has not. It appears that more in question is why the traits exist rather than whether they do. In answer to why, various forms of oppression are cited, for example, see Crain and Weisman (51), Scott (443), Elkins (76), Patterson (208), and Bernard (8).

Extraverted sensation type personality

Another psychological outcome of Victimology, insofar as known unaddressed, can be conjectured. During a course in depth psychology, the author read an article in the New York Times reporting black out-of-wedlock births as 52.1% as compared to 17.2% for whites and 25.8% for Hispanics (yes, back then, 1984, it was only 52.1% vs. 72% today). A source of explanation was sought in Carl Jung's personality types, the query being: is there something about the personality type of black males that would help to explain why so many are out-of-wedlock fathers. The answer, written in a term report, was yes (224). Although none of the Jung material read was about the black male, one of the types he describes is *as if* he were talking about the black male, that type being the **extraverted sensation type personality**. Inclusively, Jung describes this personality type has having a weak ego and as being driven primarily by his personal and collective unconscious forces. As a result, Jung says that he dominantly lives at a primitive level of psychological existence. As the author put it in his term paper:

> In him [the extraverted sensation type personality] the attitude of extraversion is combined with the function of sensation, yielding the extraverted sensation type. In describing this type, it is almost as if Jung were at times writing specifically about the family disoriented Black male. He observes, for example, that 'his life is an accumulation of actual experiences of concrete objects, and the more pronounced his type, the less use does he make of his experience.' 'His whole aim,' he further observes, 'is concrete enjoyment, and his morality is oriented accordingly. Indeed, true enjoyment has its own special morality, its own moderation and lawfulness, its own unselfishness and willingness to make sacrifices.' 'His love is unquestionably rooted in the physical attractions of its object.' And finally, 'although the object has become quite indispensable to him, yet, as something existing in its own right, it is nonetheless devalued. It is ruthlessly exploited and squeezed dry, since now its sole use is to stimulate sensation' (224:2).

Such fixation by many black males on "concrete enjoyment" would appear to help explain our exploitation of women and derelict fatherhood. Both the exploitation and derelection may manifest, not just response to being a victim of the system, but also response to being a perceived victim, or potential victim, of women as well (see, for example, Kardiner-Ovesey, 144:348-49; Ellis Cose, 48:127-43; and William Julius Wilson, 285:11-21). If you are a black male and, more or less, can have your choice of women, exert your power over them, and father any number of children, you may not be as subordinate or helpless as you perceive society and black women are telling you that you are; instead, if successful, to both, you can prove your manhood. Jung's road to wholeness for this **extraverted sensation type personality** is an expanded consciousness and a strengthened ego, which – translated into the thesis herein – adds up to the end of Victimology and the development of a positive core identity.

Conclusion

Victimhood and Victimology have made their imprint on black identity and on the black personality. What has been done to us and our response to it have helped to shape our profile. Drawing upon this chapter and Chapters 7 and 9, which respectively deal with the culture of our community and core identity, an attempt is made to depict that profile.

AN IDENTITY VOID CREATED BY SLAVERY
-
*THE FILLING OF THIS VOID THROUGH
A TWO-CULTURE ADAPTATION*
-
*THE ACCOMPANIMENT OF THIS TWO-
CULTURE ADAPTATION
BY AN INTERNALIZATION OF VICTIMIZATION
AND IDENTITY SEARCH*
-
THE EMERGENCE OF THE NEW NEGRO
-
THE EMERGENCE OF NIGRESCENCE
-
*THE EMERGENCE OF
VICTIMOLOGY, SEPARATISM, AND
ANTI-INTELLECTUALISM
AS PART OF OUR CORE IDENTITY*
-
*INTEGRAL TO THIS IDENTITY EVOLUTION,
THE PARALLEL EMERGENCE
OF LOW SELF-RESPONSIBILITY, LOW SELF-ACCEPTANCE,
AND AGRESSION
(FOR BLACK MALE POOR: EXTRAVERTED
SENSATION TYPE PERSONALITY)
AS PERSONALITY CONSTELLATIONS,
PARTICULARY AS PERTAIN TO THE POOR*

The African American Male School Adaptability Crisis (AMSAC)

-

THE EXISTENCE OF A WHITE SYSTEM WHICH BOTH HAS HELPED TO CAUSE AND FOSTER OUR IDENTITY DEVELOPMENT AND PERSONALITY TRAITS

-

SINCE 1960s EMERGENCE OF QUEST FOR FEELING EQUATION ALONG WITH CIVIC EQUALITY

Part III

The Solution: The School "on the Hook"

12

Overcoming IQ as a Putative Obstacle to School (and Community) Adaptation

Proverbs, 16:22 – "Understanding is a wellspring of life unto him that hath it: but the instruction of fools is folly."
Galatians, 6:5 - "For every man shall bear his own burden."

Our African American intelligence quotient (IQ), discussed in Chapter 8, stands as a spoken or unspoken obstacle to the school and life success of our African American students and community. Nevertheless, efforts, to date, indicate that there is not much that we can do directly to change it -- and certainly not on a massive scale. We must, therefore, amplify our IQ -- to go beyond whatever limits it might appear to impose, just as we should do regarding any other obstacle. Such is the imperative of human survival and progress. In this instance, our challenge is manageable because we can do two things: amplify our IQ and capitalize upon our other abilities. We can amplify our IQ by enhancing our more malleable emotional intelligence, or quotient (EQ), and when it comes to our students – with home, school, and community working in concert – we can, in addition, do a better job of enabling them to capitalize upon their diverse abilities. Whatever our posture regarding the adequacy of our IQ, the fate of our students and of our race does not rest on IQ alone. Like the rest of us, our students have three other attributes at their disposal, which if nurtured and exercised, can be just as powerful, and, in some life situations, even more powerful, than IQ. They are:

1. Multiple Intelligences
2. Emotional intelligence (EQ), or Character
3. Human Spirit (and the Master Trait, Love, as Nourishment)

Before addressing these attributes, two factors will be discusssed which get somewhat frequent mention as obstacles to our students' academic success.

Two Frequently Mentioned Obstacles

Stereotype threat and disidentification

Stereotype threat and disidentification tend to get one's attention because they sometimes get thrown into the discussion, but without (as perceived herein) sufficient clarity. Left to wonder is whether they are, or are not, obstacles to be taken seriously.

The stereotype threat theory is that mistrust and concern induced by the *threat* of a negative stereotype -- the *possibility* that, in a given situation, one might be the recipient of a negative stereotype -- can lead to subconscious "stereotype anxiety" which causes one to perform in such a way as to confirm the negative stereotype (465; 449; 448). For example, if it is your perception that you *may be* seen as someone incapable of getting good grades, you may experience anxiety about your school performance. The result can be that, because of your anxiety, you end up getting poor grades. Your fear or anxiety has prevented you from performing up to par. In what is called *confirmation bias*, your poor grades confirm the negative stereotype that you are incapable of getting good grades. The stereotype *threat* -- the *possibility* that you might be perceived in a certain way -- has exacted its toll, leading you, out of anxiety, to underachieve.

Over time, the stress induced by stereotype threat can lead someone to make an adjustment to render the situation psychologically irrelevant. You make the issue or event unimportant to you. You make it something that is not required to make you feel good about yourself. It is called *disidentification*. You cease to identify with it, withdrawing your psychic energy. If your peers join in to support you, the disidentification can become a group norm. Thus, members of the stereotype threatened group, through disidentification, would have perpetuated or established a norm that protects them from a common threat. It should be noted that a stereotype need not only be negative; it may also be positive.

The theory is the brainchild of Claude Steele (twin brother of perhaps the more well known Shelby Steele, author of <u>The Content of Our Character</u>) and a colleague, New York University psychologist, Joshua Aronson. Steele and Aronson hypothesized that stereotype threat pressure could undermine black students' performance and, if chronic, lead to disidentification. To test their hypothesis, they conducted five experimental test-taking studies on ability-matched Stanford University black and white sophomores. The black students who were told they were taking a test of ability performed "dramatically less well than white students." However, the performance of the black students who were told that the test was being used to study problem solving "rose to match that of equally qualified whites" (448: 4). They concluded that "...stereotype threat lowers the performance of **high-scoring** [emphasis added] black college students on a difficult verbal test," adding, "it is not yet clear to what extent one can generalize from these findings to other kinds of students and tests" (449:424).

Working with other colleagues on subsequent studies, Steele investigated the extent to which generalization was possible. They discovered that the stereotype threat *does not affect weak academic students*, only the strong ones. Steele observes that to be affected the student must care about the domain in question, that is, identify with it. Weak students, unlike strong students, do not identify with the academic domain (448).

In his book, <u>Whistling Vivaldi And Other Clues to How Stereotypes Affect Us</u>, Steele expands upon these studies, includes others, and discusses their broader implications. He describes those implications from the perspective of "*identity contingencies* [emphasis in original] -- the things you have to deal with in a situation because you have a given social identity, for example, because you are old, young, gay, a white male, a woman, black, Latino, politically conservative or liberal, diagnosed with bipolar disorder, a cancer patient, and so on" (247:3).

Those things, Steele concludes, adversely affect personal performance and impair human functioning and social interaction.

As pertains to the performance of black students, it could be that stereotype threat enters into an explanation of their poor school performance, affecting some but not others. No research evidence was found to help answer the question. That disidentification with academic striving is a norm is well documented, and, in addition, to having its origin in oppositional culture, as posited by John Ogbu, another source of origin could be stereotype threat. Black Harvard economist, Ronald Ferguson, captures this possibility in his description of the middle-class Shaker Heights High School students he studied: "among males and females, blacks and whites, Shaker Heights has students who consider schoolwork interesting, pay close attention in class, spend a few hours each night on homework, and try to do their best. At the other extreme, students have experienced academic difficulty and lean toward disidentification as a way of coping" (345:7).

Imagine black students' entrance into the white school world. As John Ogbu argues, they do so with a historical perception of black inferiority. That perception could well translate into a stereotype threat which results in anxiety and, hence, underperformance. In the real world of today, however, one does not gather from the research that our black students are performing poorly out of anxiety. From disidentification, to be sure, but disidentification which stems more from a group norm and, as Ferguson suggests, more from running into academic difficulty than from stereotype-threat-induced anxiety. They may more often, then, have reason to disidentify, not because what they think teachers or others think about them, but because, based on their performance, what they have come to feel about themselves.

Teacher expectations

Low teacher expectations may be the most popular explanation offered for the poor school performance of African American students. Ferguson has reviewed the relevant research and does not find support for it. Rather, he finds the research to be incomplete and inconclusive. His analysis:

My bottom-line conclusion requires speculation because the research is so incomplete. It is that teachers' perceptions, expectations, and behaviors probably do help to sustain, and perhaps even to expand, the Black-White test score gap. The magnitude of the effect is uncertain, but it may be quite substantial if effects accumulate from kindergarten through high school. Unfortunately, the full story is quite complicated and parts of it currently hang by thin threads of evidence. Much remains on this research agenda (87:148).

An alternative speculation. Ferguson's speculation that low teacher expectations "probably do" have substantial effects invites a competing speculation. Given the disidentification phenomenon associated with the stereotype threat theory, an alternative speculation is that the response of the students to teachers' perceptions, expectations, and behaviors becomes self-sustaining, early on acquiring a life of its own, quite divorced from -- and even impervious to -- teachers' perceptions, expectations, and behaviors. Students disidentify early on and their disidentification becomes a norm that is not affected by teachers one way or the other, just as was the case with the weak academic students in Steele's study. As the Willis and Solomon studies suggest, more likely, these students reproduce themselves.

Support for this alternative explanation is provided by the Osborne study ((1997). Using a national representative sample from the ongoing longitudinal study of the National Center for Education Statistics (NCES), Osborne sought to determine if the African American male subjects remained disidentified from grades 8-12 and if other racial or ethnic groups disidentify as well (204). His sample consisted of 1062 African American males, 1070 African American females, 632 Hispanic males, 694 Hispanic females, 5868 White males, and 5711 White females. His finding: "In general, African-American males appear to be the *only* group that experienced serious and significant disidentification with academics. No other group evidenced of [sic] significant disidentification" [emphasis added].

An alternative target. The expectations factor is always directed at teachers. Yet, if we would pause to ponder the issue, it might be more appropriate to ask about the expectations of parents and community. Those are the expectations that perhaps most matter, but one seldom, if ever, reads or hears about those expectations. Black celebrity actor and author, Hill Harper, for example, reminds us of that very fact in his book, <u>Letters to a Young Brother: MANifest Your Destiny</u>. With regard to the expectations of his uncle Russell, Harper confides: "He expected me to get all As and instilled in me an expectation of excellence, as if it was preordained that I would earn straight As. I believe that my desire not to let him down, as well as the confidence he gave me, contributed to me being an A student" (113b:xv). Just as that desire contributed to Harper's success, it can do, likewise, for all our African American students.

Implications. The documented persistent and unique academic disidentification of our African American male students does not imply, however, that we should not be concerned about teacher expectations. The question becomes whether teacher expectations *can* influence student performance -- and research suggests that they can, especially in the case of low achievers (186:121-24). Research also suggests that expectations can also work in the other direction: student expectations of teachers can affect teacher performance as well. Students who have higher expectations of teachers have been found to perform better for those teachers and, in turn, their teachers perform better for them. As Meyers puts it, what is true in the student-teacher expectations dynamic applies similarly to everyday life: "We often get *behavioral confirmation* of what we expect" [emphasis in original] (186:126). These considerations must lead us to be concerned about teacher expectations and to act on that concern through our teacher selection practices, teacher evaluations, and inservice training programs. Given the research data available, however, to make those expectations central in our explanation of the school performance of our students is unwarranted.

Past: Learning from Our Two Traditions

In addressing our IQ as a putative obstacle to the adaptation of our students and community, we must look to lessons from our past, something which is afforded by an understanding of our two traditions. These traditions contain the variables that are an inherent part of our history and culture, and which must be dealt with because, variously, they contribute to our crisis or could aid in its solution. We need not look around for some magic solution with the idea that there must be an answer somewhere out there; just keep looking and pouring out millions, even billions and trillions, of dollars and we will find it. Typically, we have been looking in all the wrong places, to borrow words from a once popular song; the solution is right there in our own history and culture -- dating back to our African American Garden of Eden.

Booker T. Washington (BTW) High School

Principal Alisha Kiner of award-winning BTW High School apparently realizes that we must learn from our past, and build upon it. Because she does, her school was the winner of the 2011 Race to the Top High School Commencement Challenge. In addition to her aforementioned expressed indebtedness to Washington's legacy, we see that realization in the school's winning video, which features these four Booker T. Washington quotes:

> "...Success is to be measured by the obstacles you've overcome."
> "We must reinforce arguments with results."
> "Associate yourself with people of good quality...."
> "Success always leaves footprints." (412)

These BTW quotes exemplify the winning spirit that guides the school which bears his name, that served us so well during the Age of Booker T. Washington and beyond, and that, as principal Kiner demonstrates, can serve us equally as well today.

Our crisis results, not from an absence of answers, but from our failure to study, analyze, and utilize our two adaptation formulas which, to a considerable extent, contain the answers. Inspirational history, critical race theory, and Afrocentrism do not provide productive substitutes. So, we begin this chapter by looking at those formulas; then we address overcoming our putative IQ obstacle.

Inherited adaptation formulas

In promoting our adaptation, Washington's Self-Responsibility Tradition might be seen as providing what can be called a **Self-Made**

Joe L. Rempson

Formula and DuBois's System-Responsibility Tradition a **System-Made Formula**. In Washington's **Self-Made Formula,** teachers were provided industrial and basic academic training so that they could go out, provide models for the masses, and train them to do practical work, save, own property, live an upright life, and help the race -- thereby enabling us, through this self-made process, to adapt and become part of the American mainstream. In DuBois's **System-Made Formula**, teachers would be provided education equal to whites (industrial and liberal arts training) so they could go out, provide models, and train the masses in industrial education *and* the liberal arts so that they could avail themselves of the equal opportunities made possible through the acquisition of civil rights, as a result of which, they would be able to adapt and become part of the American mainstream. These formulas can be depicted thus:

$$\text{Washington's Self-Made Formula} \; \text{Self-Responsibility Tradition} = \frac{\text{indus ed + industry + character}}{\text{self-dependence}}$$

$$\text{DuBois's System-Made Formula} \; \text{System-Responsibility Tradition} = \frac{\text{equal ed (indus ed + lib ed) + civil rights}}{\text{system-dependence}}$$

The fundamental difference: in Washington's **Self-Made Formula**, *we were to make ourselves into that which we sought to become*; in DuBois's **System-Made Formula**, *we were to demand equal opportunities to become that which we sought to become.* That is, in Washington's Self-Made Formula, industrial education plus industry (hard work, land ownership, business) plus character, based on self-dependence, produce adaptation and Americanization. In DuBois's System-Made Formula, equal education (industrial education plus liberal education) plus civil rights, based on system-dependence, produce adaptation and Americanization. In our Self-Made Formula, our adaptation is more or less under our control, in other words, in our own hands. In our System-Made Formula, our adaptation is only conditionally under our control since adaptation and Americanization cannot be achieved unless system changes bring about equal opportunities.

The System-Responsibility Traditionalists might argue, as DuBois did, that industry (hard work, land ownership, and business) did not mean anything without civil rights to provide for acquisition and protection of properties and services. That is, an absence of civil rights would prevent or curtail our ability to adapt, regardless of our possessions or character. In response, Self-Responsibility Traditionalists might argue, as Washington did, that industry would put us in a better position to acquire and utilize those rights because they would provide us "intrinsic worth to the body politic" (165: 19). His repeated gospel, variously stated: "We cannot succeed unless we recognize that we must have a certain amount of groundwork and foundation, and without good foundation we shall find all our efforts largely in vain" (165:29).

Although these are different times, the adaptation issues which face us are essentially the same. Therefore, it is argued that, in substance, these formulas are as relevant today as in the past and can be used more productively. Time has tested their validity and puts us in a better position to see their merits and make adjustments. They inform, not just the content of this chapter, but, in various ways, the content of this entire book. They are our legacy from the African American Garden of Eden.

Both formulas were premised on the assumption that we African Americans had the mental capacity to adapt. Although many of us are IQ-challenged, the evidence, discussed in Chapter 8, supports their assumption. Our challenge is to exercise that capacity, as discussed in Chapter 7, that exercise being a function of our drive.

While anthropologists variously define culture, the definition herein is that culture is the "*learned* [emphasis added] behaviors, beliefs, attitudes, values, and ideals generally shared by the members of a group" (77:26). Though *learned*, similar to biological traits, culture is inherited and passed along; unlike biological traits, however, anthropologists tell us what we see (over time) with our own eyes: that culture changes all the time (77:14-28; 269-88). They further tell us that the customs that make up our culture may be adaptive or maladaptive, either enhancing or inhibiting our chances of survival and progress. We can choose or create those customs, as, for example, in our eating and reading habits and in our child rearing practices. New customs can also emerge in other ways, such as through technological changes (77:23-26).

Like the culture of any other racial/ethnic group, then, our African American culture, at least to a meaningful degree, is in our hand. We have some control over it. Whether we exercise that control depends on our drive. To meet our **Adaptation Requirements**, that drive does not have to be extraordinary, just sufficient. It has is to be enough to enable us to get the education and jobs, and to establish the stable families and neighborhoods on which adaptation depends. To meet these requirements does not require the kind of drive needed, say, to become a physician, or to be become a dominant power group -- nothing that extraordinary. Far short of the extraordinary, to meet our **Adaptation Requirements** only calls for the degree of drive required for self-care. We turn to Booker T. Washington and the **Tinkersville School Founding** to make the point, that is, we turn to our own history.

The Tinkersville school was the first school attended by Washington, the story of which is told by Harlan (108:33-39). He describes Tinkersville as a self-help enterprise traceable to the leadership of the Rev. Lewis Rice who, though illiterate, earned the title of "Father Rice" for his education and religious work in Kanawha Valley (West Virginia). Father Rice turned the bedroom in his home into a classroom, making it the first school in Tinkersville. During the daytime, he would dismantle the bed and put up from three to four hand-made slab benches, each of which seated an average of ten persons. Prior to then, he had similarly used his bedroom for church meetings on Wednesday nights and Sundays. Further self-help was extended by the community, which provided the entire support for the school. A bedroom at night, a classroom during the day, and community support all the way. That is the kind of self-care drive -- the exertion of energy and effort to acquire the essentials and make the most of the meager – which is the foundation of adaptation and which one of the students, Booker T. Washington, would later exhibit and exceed.

Conclusion

The **Tinkersville School Founding** is indicative of the kind of mindset and drive required of us African Americans to meet our **Adaptation Requirements**. Its lesson is that, given drive, we can overcome, just as drive enabled us to overcome to achieve our civil rights. We need only prove that, like in the **Tinkersville School Founding**, we can exercise drive, not only when we seek help, but, equally, in helping ourselves. It is up to us. Here is what our perspective ought to be:

> **We have proven our ability to meet the stipulated Adaptation Requirements. Our challenge is to expand the scale of our success so that such social problems as crime, out-of-wedlock births, and school failure are -- as with other groups -- at the margins of our life rather than a thriving factor in it. At such time, the question of intelligence will be no more than an afterthought, for we would have, above all, proven to ourselves that we can meet normal standards.**
>
> **That is all that really matters. No people are equal, be it with respect to intelligence or height, for example. But, as Washington so repeatedly and consistently taught, each group will respect the other group if its life and relationships are characterized by preserving norms and mutually beneficial exchanges and interactions. In effect, and to at least some extent at some point in time, our other three famous leaders -- Frederick Douglass, W. E. B. DuBois, and Dr. Martin Luther King Jr. -- taught likewise. Given such norms, questions of intelligence are likely to become, at most, matters of passing conversation or intellectual curiosity, not the subject matter of innumerable studies, detailed analyses, and endless debate. For us African Americans, as for the fellow members of our race throughout the world, this will only happen if we can adapt to the demands of this evolutionary moment.**
>
> **That is, indeed, what a solution to the African American Male School Adaptability Crisis (AMSAC) and its inseparable social problems requires of us and what the directed *use* of our intelligence makes possible. The solution is within our mental**

grasp. What we must demonstrate to ourselves, and to others alike, is whether it is also within the grasp of our emotional intelligence or character.

We must remember that the whole is greater than the sum of its parts and, potentially, exerts a force which defies the perceived power of those parts, even if one of those parts exerts the influence attributed to mental intelligence. The force exerted by that whole enables us to transcend, to go beyond limits or restrictions -- self-imposed or external, real or imagined -- and to reach out and achieve something "more than" what may seem possible. That force is called the human spirit, about which more will be said later (134). Let us, accordingly, bear in mind these thoughts from the late famous University of Frankfurt psychoanalyst, Alexander Mitscherlich, in his <u>Society Without the Father</u>: "One of the peculiarities of man is ... that he does not possess a single and definite hereditary way of adapting himself to his environment. On the contrary, he has an extraordinary ability to adapt himself to very different and changing, sometimes swiftly changing, social environments" (180: 3).

Other Attribute: Multiple Intelligences

Harvard psychologist, Howard Gardner, has introduced the concept of multiple intelligences (62:446-47; 121:117-19; 469). So far, he has identified the following 11: bodily-kinesthetic, interpersonal, intrapersonal, verbal-linguistic, logical-mathematical, visual-spatial, musical, naturalistic, spiritual, existential, and moral. However, as pointed out in summarizing Jensen's article, psychologists distinguish *intelligence* from *ability*, intelligence denoting the capacity for abstract reasoning and problem solving that is measured by standardized tests whereas mental ability refers to the totality of a person's mental capabilities. Gardner (and his colleagues), rather than making that distinction, has broadened the concept of intelligence so as to increase the personalization of the teaching-learning process and to enhance the quality of interdisciplinary educational efforts. His views have not been widely embraced, but the lesson implicit in his broadened concept has a significant practical application: the need for a teaching-learning process that meets the range of students' needs, interests, and abilities.

Gardner's concept makes for a liberal application of the term intelligence. It depicts intelligence in its various forms, and we African Americans must capitalize upon these variations. It is one of the factors which makes the family so important, for it is the family which must nurture these various forms. The school can assist but it is not set up to provide such nurturing, which begins at birth, even, in fact, during the prenatal stage, and, thereafter, must be continually provided. While some given IQ is not an imperative to a child's success, the child's success must be anchored in some form of intelligence, and Gardner provides a conceptualization of the possibilities. When we foster IQ in its various forms, we expand the child's foundation for success.

Other Attribute: Emotional Intelligence (EQ), or Character

Some of the intelligences conceived by Gardner could be subsumed under emotional intelligence (EI), or character, as it is also commonly called. Emotional intelligence is a relatively new concept, said to have been introduced as a scholarly endeavor as recently as 1985 in a doctoral dissertation by Wayne Payne. We now examine it and its role in the school and life success of our students.

Goleman's contribution

Emotional intelligence has been popularized by psychologist, Daniel Goleman, in his 1995 bestselling book, Emotional Intelligence. Goleman says that, although there is typically a balance between our rational self (our mind) and our emotions, "emotional and rational minds are semi-independent faculties, each ... reflecting the operation of distinct, but interconnected, circuitry in the brain" (102:9). On some components, there is a correlation between the two, but that correlation, he says, is slight (102:45). Thus, we can be, mentally, in the upper IQ quartile and, emotionally, in the lowest quartile, and, as a result, given the pivotal role of emotional aptitude, end up being a failure in life. "Emotional aptitude," Goleman declares, "is a *meta-ability* [emphasis in original], determining how well we can use whatever other skills we have, including raw intellect" (102:36).

While acknowledging that personality traits, like IQ traits, are inherited, Goleman's claim is that they are more malleable – in fact, *"extraordinarily malleable"* [emphasis added] (120:xiii). He admits, however, that the research has not determined how much personality traits, or EI, accounts for variation in individual outcomes, but he goes on to assert that they can be as powerful as IQ, even, at times, more powerful (102:4)

Goleman disputed

However, Goleman's analysis and interpretation are disputed by others, including the two leading researchers on the topic, Peter Salovey (Yale University President and psychologist) and John D. Mayer (University of New Hampshire psychologist) (315a; 406a; 433b; 450a; 451a; 471d). Goleman is accused of not even having consistently or scientifically defined the term and of having overstated its malleability. In fact, various EI models have been developed. As in the case of IQ, we are, therefore, left to work through the differences and derive credible conclusions.

Definition and measurement

A useful definition of emotional intelligence is provided by Goleman as well as by Salovey and Mayer. Goleman refers to EI as the ability to know and manage our own feelings well and to read and deal effectively with other people's feelings. Similarly, Salovey and Mayer define it as the "ability to monitor one's own and others' feelings and emotions, to discriminate among them and to use this information to guide one's thinking and actions" (102:36; 438d). Rather than this broad definition, which suggests one intelligence, EI is also conceived as one of three interrelated intelligences, the other two being personal intelligence and social intelligence (209b:338-39). It is evident that the broad definition incorporates all three.

Just as there are measures of cognitive intelligence (IQ), there are also measures of emotional intelligence (EQ) (209a:343-46). However, whereas IQ has been defined, tested, measured, and standardized through a process and history to yield descriptive individual and group measurements, the same has yet to be done for EQ. Some tests yield a generalized nonstandardized score, together with subtest scores, and there are numerous individual tests which assess a range of attributes which compose EI.

As object of scientific study: Peterson and Seligman

An informative source of existing knowledge on the topic is provided by University of Michigan psychology professor, Christopher Peterson, and University of Pennsylvania founder of positive psychology (1998) and Director of the Positive Psychology Center, Martin Seligman. In their book, Character Strengths and Virtues: A Handbook and Classification (2004), drawing upon numerous experts, they attempt to "start to make possible a science of human strengths that goes beyond armchair philosophy and political rhetoric" just as a science has emerged in understanding, treating, and preventing psychological disorders (209b:3-7). As their title suggests, they do not use the term emotional intelligence; instead, they use character. However, as Goleman states, "There is an old-fashioned word for the body of skills that emotional intelligence represents: *character* [emphasis in original]" (102:285). In their book, they offer no one-sentence definition that could be found, though it can be inferred that they think of it as positive individual or personality traits. Examining the research and history, and drawing upon numerous experts, they have come up with a list of 24 recognized character traits categorized under six core moral virtues: *wisdom and knowledge, courage, humanity, justice, temperance,* and *transcendence* (209b:28-31).

Malleability

Peterson and Seligman say that these traits are malleable, just as Goleman had famously contended nine years earlier in 1995. Yes, they are inherited, they say, but malleable, their malleability being conditioned by such environmental factors as educational opportunity and family support (209b:10-12). That sounds very much like an echo of the Commission on Children at Risk's research-based dictum that **"SOCIAL CONTEXT CAN ALTER GENETIC EXPRESSION."**

As previously noted, Steve Pinker would agree, putting the conventional wisdom of character or personality trait heritability at about 50 percent.

Given the most recent research findings from cognitive neuroscience and other scholarly fields, as reported by Brooks and Eagleman, that would appear to be a conservative estimate. What, in any case, warrants emphasis, at least to some degree, is the research consensus that character is malleable. Pinker says the process works something like the following: the boundaries which separate the different functions performed by the brain (seeing, hearing, speaking, and so on), with learning and practice, can move around or shift, and the moving or shifting of the boundaries produces changes in the affected functions (210:84).

The shifting among its boundaries signifies brain plasticity or malleability, Pinker argues, but not to the extent of enabling us to "dramatically" mold or reshape it, which is what Goleman claims. That is, the brain, in its original natural form, including its size (size being associated with IQ and other attributes), cannot be altered, only the boundaries among its parts and, apparently, the communication or exchange which can take place among the parts. Nevertheless, Pinker declares that, as a matter of scientific fact, experience, learning, and practice can alter, not the brain itself, but how the brain functions (210: 86-87). The "shifting" of the boundaries within it can cause it to function differently, and it is this different functioning which justifies the conclusion that EI is malleable. Whereas IQ is resistant to improvement after ages 8-10, it is this scientifically-documented brain boundary elasticity (malleability) which apparently has led Tough to conclude that EI "can be improved, sometimes dramatically, well into adolescence and even adulthood" (258a:48).

That malleability -- the boundary shifting which can occur -- apparently leads Peterson and Seligman, like the Commission on Children at Risk, to put character at the center of individual and group wellbeing (209b:95). Nevertheless, they are cognizant of the role of IQ, pointing out that many of the virtues in their classification have a cognitive component.

To whatever degree influenced by IQ, however, could it be, as Goleman suggests, that "emotional aptitude is a *meta-ability*, determining how well we can use whatever other skills we have, including raw intellect"? The research literature reviewed indicates that it could be, that possibility receiving popular reinforcement from a somewhat unexpected source, aforementioned conservative bestselling author and New York Times columnist, David Brooks. Customarily associated with the political, sociological, and cultural, in his latest book, The Social Animal: The Hidden Sources of Love, Character, and Achievement, Brooks ventures into the psychological -- the "inner or unconscious mind" as opposed to the "outer or conscious mind." Rather than focus on the "outer definitions of success," IQ along with wealth and prestige being among them, he goes beyond "the surface level of life," which they represent, to "one level down" where the inner mind lurks. To do so, he has delved into the research of numerous disciplines -- including genetics, neuroscience, psychology, sociology, economics, anthropology -- and spent an enormous amount of time in conversations, conferences, and panels with many scholars. His reinforcing message: "**The central evolutionary truth is that the unconscious matters most. The central humanistic truth is that the conscious mind can influence the unconscious mind**" [emphasis added] (23: xii). And that is what emotional intelligence is about: the conscious mind influencing the unconscious mind -- exercising self-control over the unconscious, inaccessible.

In essence, the message of the previously cited Commission on Children at Risk, writing eight years earlier, reflects Brooks's emphasis. The Comnission's diverse group of 33 children doctors, research scientists, and health and youth service professionals did not use the term unconscious mind or emotional intelligence, but the source of its recommended remedy for our ills is the same: not our IQ, but our EQ. It is the same because it relied on the same scientific body of knowledge as Brooks. As stated in connection with our discussion of the proposed AMCAP program components in Chapter 14, the Commission advocates "authoritative communities," "groups that live out the types of connectedness that our children increasingly lack." By connectedness, it means nurturing, and by nurturing it means a community which, inclusively, is warm, transmits what it means to be a good person, and embraces the principle of love of neighbor. That is, it emphasizes that which Brooks says the new science would have us emphasize: "emotion over pure reason, social connections over individual choice, character over IQ," and so on – and what Brooks, therefore, recommends that we emphasize, even though he admits being "not a touchy feely person"(23:xiii).

That, too, most recently, is the message of aforementioned Baylor College of Medicine neuroscientist, David Eagleman, in his recently released book, <u>Incognito: The Secret Lives of the Brain</u> (2011). In these words, he makes his main point:

> ...we are not the ones driving the boat of our behavior, at least not nearly as much as we believe. *Who we are* [emphasis in original] runs well below the surface of our conscious access, and the details reach back in time before our birth, when the meeting of a sperm and egg granted us with certain attributes and not others. *Who we can be* [emphasis in original] begins with our molecular blueprints--a series of alien codes penned in invisibly small strings of acids--well before we have anything to do with it. We are a product of our inaccessible, microscopic history (73:159).

How much are we "driving the boat of our behavior"? Our conscious minds, Eagleman says, "play only a *small part* [emphasis added] in our total neural function...." (73:144). Even so, by no means is Eagleman dismissive of that "small part." To the contrary, he asserts that, "it is neither biology alone nor environment alone that determines the final product of a personality. When it comes to the nature versus nurture question, the answer almost always includes both" (73:215-16).

So while scientifically recognizing the dominant role of our hidden, inaccessible, inner mind, as it were, Eagleman makes clear that our new science does not, however, grant it a monopoly over our behavior. Such a monopoly, he argues, would be dangerous to the individual and to society. That fact gives prominence to the "small part" performed by our conscious mind; it must act as supervisor. Brooks paints the unconscious as being impulsive, emotional, sensitive, and unpredictable and, therefore, in need of supervision (23:xviii). The ability of our conscious mind to exercise that supervision, Goleman contends, depends on our malleable emotional intelligence. The emotionally intelligent mind is able to optimize the hidden, inaccessible good within us and minimize the hidden, inaccessible bad. Eagleman's point is that, from the moment that sperm and egg unite, whether we are talking about

IQ or EQ, we are *who we are* and *who we <u>can be</u>*; it is set and fixed, beyond our control and inaccessible to our consciousness. *Who and what we <u>become</u>*, however, is another matter. There, nurture enters – or, as the Commission on Children at Risk might put it, our artful dance with our nature takes place, the reciprocal exchanges yielding our life performance. The point that Goleman, Peterson, and Seligman in particular, are making is that our malleable emotional intelligence plays a pivotal role in that performance [maybe the equivalent of Jensen's threshold effect when it comes to IQ].

Five success character traits

From among the 24 character traits synthesized by Peterson and Seligman, as well as from other sources, as throughout, an attempt has been made to identify the few which, conceivably, could count the most insofar as making a massively decisive difference in the school and life outcomes of African American students, along with their parents and community. The research evidence points to five such traits, herein designated **Five Success Character Traits**. To normalize their school and life success, our students must possess the five traits to a greater degree than currently: **growth mindset (GM)**, **time perspective (TP)**, **willpower (WP)**, **grit (GR)**, and **love (LO)**.

Of these five traits, as well as all the others encountered, **love (LO)** is considered the master character trait. Controlling for IQ, each trait, alone, is powerfully related to outcomes and is a trait which represents a devastating weakness among a disproportionate number of African Americans, and has research evidence to support (not establish, but support) its malleability. The five are overlapping, interactive, and mutually reinforcing. They have a common underlying dynamic: direction or purpose, self-care, and self-control. As a result, focusing on any one part of their underlying dynamic can have a multiplier effect and optimize outcome. Time perspective is the subject of Zimbardo and Boyd's book, <u>The Time Paradox</u>, and was discussed in Chapter 14. Discussion of the other four traits follows.

(1) **Growth mindset (GM)**. While one might conclude from the Jensen-Herrnstein-Murray IQ analysis that our IQ is fixed, most notably, world renown Stanford University psychologist, Carol Dweck,

argues that "intelligence is...something that can be increased through one's efforts" (68:3). Based on extensive research conducted by her and others, she concludes that, although we indeed do come with genes, we cannot find the answer to how to live our lives in our genes. Neither can we find the key to school or job success, or to successful relationships, in our genes. These, she argues, are adaptive skills which, under the right circumstances, can be taught. It is our responsibility to create those "right circumstances" (68:153-54).

Essentially, Dweck echoes the research-based dictum of the Commission on Children at Risk: "**SOCIAL CONTEXT CAN ALTER GENETIC EXPRESSION.**" Dweck's latter point -- that it is our responsibility to understand those circumstances -- is really Jensen's point also, regardless of how his IQ analysis is perceived. But to continue with Dweck's thinking, what must be emphasized is her view of the fallacy of thinking that "by measuring someone's present skills, you've measured their potential; that by looking at what they can do now, you can predict what they're capable of doing in the future ...." (68:59). Alfred Binet, the inventor of the IQ test, Dweck points out, never intended it to be so used, but, instead, devised it as a way of discovering children in the Paris public schools who needed new programs to help enhance their intelligence; he did not see IQ as a threshold indicator (69:4-5). But, again to be fair to Herrnstein-Murray, they have not contended that IQ could predict individual outcomes, only group outcomes; and Jensen looks at IQ from an abstract intelligence perspective [fluid intelligence], Dweck from a knowledge and skills perspective [crystallized intelligence].

It might be said, however, that, whereas Jensen-Herrnstein-Murray lean in the direction of the *fixed mindset* school (perhaps less optimistic than Dweck about growth), Dweck is squarely in the *growth mindset* school. Rather than things being somewhat carved in stone, a belief that characterizes the fixed mindset, the growth mindset, on the other hand, is "based on the belief that your basic qualities are things you can cultivate through your efforts. Although people may differ in every which way--in their initial talents and aptitudes, interests, or temperaments--everyone can change and grow through application and experience" (69:7). Again, however, Dweck is not talking about fluid intelligence; she is talking about crystallized intelligence. Even so, does this mean that, with effort, Dweck and other growth mindset proponents believe that people can be whatever they want? "No," Dweck says, "but they believe that a person's true potential is unknown (and unknowable); that it's impossible to foresee what can be accomplished with years of passion, toil, and training" (69:7). Again, we must keep in mind that she is talking about *a person*, not a group, and Herrnstein-Murray explicitly make the same point. Furthermore, nothing in Jensen's article suggests that he would necessarily disagree (since a number of abilities and traits, not just IQ, come under consideration).

As for the *growth mindset* that leads to the kind of "passion, toil, and training" required to realize one's potential, Dweck, among other things, has developed a "Brainology®" program intended for grades 5 through 9, although lower and higher grades have used it as well (69:213-46). Available at cost on the internet, the program is interactive, and enables administrators and teachers to involve their students in a structured, self-paced, individualized growth-mindset program. Though citing no hard data, she says it works, and information provided on the "Brainology®" website supports her claim. Some 15,000 students are said to have participated in the program. Their testimony shows that, among them, have been low-income African American students who have dramatically benefited from its use.

Emphasis must be placed, as Dweck does, on what underlines the growth mindset: "years of passion, toil, and training." That is, given a willingness to engage in the "years of passion, toil, and training," Dweck and her growth-mindset colleagues have a research-based belief in the malleability or growth of intelligence.

That is the point which is underlined further by British sports writer and three-time Commonwealth table tennis champion, Matthew Syed. In his book, <u>Bounce: Mozart, Federer, Picasso, Beckham, and the Science of Success</u>, he tells how these and other notables achieved their status, not due to innate ability, but to practice -- yes, practice, purposeful practice or work. Though he started out at the age of three, Mozart's first masterpiece, for example, was not produced until the age of twenty-one, after "eighteen years of hard, expert training" [note, *expert* training]; and the great golfer, Tiger Woods and great tennis sisters, Venus and Serena Williams, all began *purposeful* training at an early age -- Tiger at eighteen-months of ge, Venus at four years, six months and one day, and Serena at age three (251:56-57). By *purposeful*, Syed says, he means, not just concentration and dedication, but also [in the case of sports] "access to the right training system, and that sometimes means living in the right town or having the right coach" (251:92).

There is a rule involved: the *10,000-Hour Rule*. Based on extensive research on accomplished subjects from various fields, the rule derived is that for any complex task, be it in the field of art or science, to reach world-class status, a minimum of ten years of purposeful practice is required [something disputed by some]. That breaks down to a minimum of one thousand hours a year or, for a 365-day year, 2.74 hours a day.

In a far less exalted, though no doubt far more memorable way, the knife experience of former black Harlem Chidren's Zone director, Geoffrey Canada, while growing up in the slums of the South Bronx reinforces the appropriate applicability of this purposeful practice rule. Canada reports finding in the gutter a rusty and dirty K55 knife (which he could not afford to buy), refurbishing it into perfect working condition, and then learning skillfully to use it. It gave him, he says, freedom, security, and mobility. It became a friend that enabled him to roam about unafraid in the streets of his rough neighborhood, as secure in enemy territory as in his own. But it was a friend that enabled him to feel secure (perhaps even powerful) only because, with *purposeful practice*, he came to be able skillfully to use it. As he describes it:

> I spent hours trying to perfect the removal of the knife from my pocket and opening it as quickly as possible. I started off safe and careful, pulling the blade well past the halfway point to ensure that it wouldn't snap back on my fingers before I let go with my left hand to snap the knife fully open with my right. Over the months I became less and less conservative as I shaved tenths of a second off my time. Finally, after about three months of practice, I became so good with my knife that I could open it to the exact point of a hair's breadth past the place where the spring would snap it shut again. To those watching when I demonstrated my expertise my hands moved in a blur. They would hear the distinctive click signaling that my weapon was opened and ready for use even as their eyes tried to

catch up with the movements involved; the knife seemed to appear in my hand as if by magic (25:72-73).

Canada goes on to tell how, despite his expertise, in an effort to shave off that last tenth of a second, he cut his right index finger to the bone, later resulting in a crooked finger which remains so to this day. But through purposeful practice, he, nevertheless, accomplished his goal: freedom and safety through mastery of his K55 knife. Imagine what our students could accomplished if, in similar fashion, if only to an extent, they put such effort into their schoolwork.

While Canada had a specific aim, the aim of the training-advocated by growth mindset proponents is not some specific achievement, such as a tennis championship -- or becoming a K55 knife expert -- but a successful outcome, whatever that may to be. Ability or talent is never praised or prized, only effort. Disappointments and failures are neither good nor bad but opportunities for improvement. Risks are not something to be feared, but opportunities for growth. And self-esteem, deemed so central in our success endeavors, is not a feeling to be imparted but an experience continually derived from the outcomes which accrue from engagement in challenging tasks (68:127-131).

The creed of the Nick Bollettieri Tennis Academy in Florida is said to summarize much of this growth-minded thinking. The Academy has produced such notables as Andre Agassi and Martina Hingis. The is its creed:

> Every endeavor pursued with passion produces a successful outcome regardless of the result. For it is not about winning or losing--rather, the effort put forth in producing the outcome. The best way to predict the future is to create it--therefore, we believe we have the best training methods to help each athlete achieve their dreams and goals and ultimately reach their ability level in the arena of sports and life (251:133-35).

In the arena of adaptation, it is just such a mindset that, ultimately, can enable us to reach our goals -- to normalize our lives across the range of required variables. Regardless of our IQ, that growth mindset can help to assure that our efforts will produce successful outcomes. Dweck and others declare IQ not to be the decisive factor; passion, toil, and training are.

That, too, can be said to be, in essence, what Booker T. Washington taught. Tuskegee was a disciplined training camp, as it were, demanding toil and rectitude while inculcating passion. It was a further revelation to have read what Geoffrey Canada, given his own life and years of work in educating our black males, had to say on the subject. In his book, Reaching Up for Manhood, Canada remembers the lessons taught to him by his grandmother about the virtues of hard work, and urges that "We should view work, hard work, as a necessary rite of passage for boys early in their lives. We must teach them that there is nothing demeaning in working hard, whether it's for money or not (26:121}.

Dweck and others, then, in substance, are talking about decisive traits for success which two of our own, Washington and Canada, likewise, make central.

(2) **Willpower (WP)**. In their book, Willpower, Roy F. Baumeister and John Tierney refer, on its cover, to willpower as "the greatest human strength." Previously cited Baumeister is Director of Social Psychology at Florida State University and reportedly one of the world's most frequently cited psychologist, and previously cited John Tierney is an award-winning New York Times science writer. Support for their claim is provided by other evidence cited, including the Duckworth and Seligman study cited in the introductory chapter as well as the studies of Farrell and Roderick. Willpower, like time perspective, is said to determine our feelings, thoughts, and actions.

Willpower refers to self-control and self-regulation, or "how a person exerts control over his or her own responses so as to pursue goals and live up to standards" (209b: 500). Some writers, however, use the term self-control in the more narrow sense of controlling one's impulses for moral reasons. But Baumeister and Tierney are use the term in the indicated sense and as a maker of willpower. They consider it the foundation of one's character or EI -- of one's "ability to monitor one's own and others' feelings and emotions, to discriminate among them and to use this information to guide one's thinking and actions." They say that most of our major problems can be attributed to lack of self-control, citing: "compulsive spending and borrowing, impulsive violence, underachievement in school, procrastination at work, alcohol and drug abuse, unhealthy diet, lack of exercise, chronic anxiety, explosive anger" (6b:2). "Poor self-control," they say, "correlates with just about every kind of individual trauma: losing friends, being fired, getting divorced, winding up in prison (6b:2).

They also report that when, in one study, three dozen personality traits were used to predict college students' grade-point average (GPA), self-control turned out to be the only one which predicted it better than chance. It also turned out to be a better predictor of GPA than either IQ or SAT scores. While they acknowledge the advantage of IQ, they suggest that the study showed self-control to be more important because of its contribution to students' management of their behavior through, for example, reliable class attendance and spending more time working and less time watching television. They are careful to point out that some of the differences found in that study did correlate with IQ, social class, and race; however even when these variables were controlled, self-control made a significant contribution to those differences (6b:11-13).

Support for the role of self-control is, likewise, apparent in the previously cited study by Farrell of 67 successful and 73 at-risk New York City public high school students. The term "will" emerged as he combed through the data, seeing such student interview comments as a student *telling himself* that he had to change schools, another that she *came to realize* that she had to pick her own friends, and another who had to *make himself* overcome boredom. Some actually used the word "will," "willpower," or "motivation" (82:115-29). Relying upon the theory of will formulated by famed psychologist, Lee Semonovich Vykgotsky, Farrell saw in these successful students something that connected their belief with their ability, something missing in the case of his otherwise more or less socioeconomically comparable, but at-risk students. That something is what he says Vykgotsky calls "will." Will, he thinks, propelled the successful students to act on their belief and to make use of their perceived ability. Will, Farrell explains, is not conceived as some factor or real thing, such as the students' peer culture or family relationships, but rather a *process* that develops from "internalizing [from birth] the voices one hears." The successful students, he conjectures [and he emphasizes that "conjecturing" or theorizing is what he is doing] hear and have heard voices that have led them to internalize something that can be called "will," their particular circumstances making them receptive to it. On the other hand, the at-risk students may have heard the same voices, but their particular circumstances differ (their family life, for example) and so, therefore, has their receptivity also differs. That is, materially, the successful students were not essentially different from the at-risk students; it was the voices that each internalized and the "will" reflected in that internalization which explains their difference. Farrell's interpretation has support in the variations of the **Stanford Marshmallow Experiment**, discussed below. The variations point to family life stability and trust in the voices children hear as factors contributing to their willpower.

What Farrell saw in his successful students, Chua and Rubenfeld see, years later, as part of the Triple Package possessed by America's successful cultural groups, only they call it impulse control instead of willpower, but the meaning is the same. Their study does not suggest that, alone, impulse control is as powerful as depicted by Baumeister and Tierney, but the study points to its indispensable or significant role, just as appears to have been the case in the New Zealand study cited by Baumeister and Tierney in which it was not the decisive factor but, nevertheless, made a measurable contribution to the outcome. In fact, they see it as fundamental in the groups' success, declaring, as previously cited, that "No society could exist without impulse control; as Freud speculated, civilization may begin with the suppression of primal sexual and aggressive instincts." They add, however, that, in modern America the emphasis has come to be on the present rather than on suppression (34a:10-11).

Research documenting the role of willpower had its origin with the **Stanford Marshmallow Experiment** (6a:9-11; 471e). Conducted in 1972 by Walter Mischel and his colleagues at Stanford University, it sought to discover how a child learns to resist immediate gratification. One by one, they had over 600 four-year-olds brought into a room, showed them a marshmallow, and offered them this deal: they could eat the marshmallow whenever they wished, but if they held off for 15 minutes until the experimenter returned they would get a second marshmallow. Chance circumstances led them, years later (1988, 1990, and 2011), to follow up on hundreds of the children. Those who had shown the most willpower at age four had gotten better grades and test scores, and those who had held out for the entire 15 minutes scored 210 points higher on the Scholastic Aptitude Test (SAT) than those who held back for only 30 seconds. They also became more popular with peers and teachers, earned higher salaries, had a lower body-mass index (suggesting that they were less prone to gain weight during middle age), and were less likely to have drug problems (6b: 10-11).

Recent variations of the study raise a question about its prevailing interpretation as evidence of innate capacity. Not surprisingly, those variations point both to nature and nurture (392a; 471n; 460a). The studies involved show that children are able to exercise willpower, not just because it is innate to them, but also because of a sense of security due to home or other environmental factors. Children brought up in homes with absent fathers, for example, preferred more immediate rewards over larger but delayed ones, and those having trust in the experimenter were more able to delay gratification than those not having it. While supporting the role of nurturing, the studies do not, however, raise a question about the role of willpower itself

(3) **Grit (GR)**. Whether Angela Duckworth and her collaborators would agree with Baumeister and Tierney's interpretation of willpower as "the greatest human strength" is unknown. However, it may well be that, basically, her term, grit, is another name for the same trait, something herein left for the experts to determine. Aforementioned University of Pennsylvania Associate Professor of Psychology Duckworth is a MacArthur Fellows Program grantee in the amount of $625,000 for the "extraordinary originality and dedication" she has shown in her work on grit. Duckworth conceived and coined the term. Grit refers to *perseverance* [translated, willpower] and *passion* [maybe a condition for the existence of willpower] for long-term goals (332a; 332b). As applied to students, to have grit means that they must be interested in what they undertake and must be able, over time, to keep at it in the face of setbacks and obstacles. In general, Duckworth says, the gritty individual approaches achievement as a marathon, never quitting but fighting through the obstacles along the way (332a).

To measure this trait, Duckworth, working with a number of her colleagues, created the 3-minute, 12-question, self-report Grit Scale (which she has later refined). It has proven to be an exceptional predictor of outcomes. For example, it has more accurately predicted which West Point cadets persist and which ones drop out than the more complex West Point system, which includes academic grades, physical fitness, and a leadership score; and it has revealed that grittier teachers raise their students' standardized test scores more dramatically than their less gritty counterparts (332a; 332b; 455a).

In a <u>New York Times</u> article, "What if the Secret to Success Is Failure?," the aforementioned Paul Tough tells why, based on her teaching experience, Duckworth came to focus on the EI domain.

> 'The problem, I think, is not only the schools but also the students themselves.... Here's why: learning is hard. True, learning is fun, exhilarating and gratifying -- but it is also often daunting, exhausting and sometimes discouraging.... To help chronically low-performing but intelligent students, educators and parents must first recognize that character is at least as important as intellect' (455a:5).

That is what Duckworth and her colleagues, with the GRIT Scale, have demonstrated: "that character [grit] is at least as important as intellect." In fact, they found grit to be independent of IQ. Since it is unrelated to IQ, then the question arissed of how, as a predictor, it compares to other personality traits. Those traits fall into five broad domains called the Big Five (OCEAN): Openness, Conscientiousness, Extroversion, Agreeableness, and Neuroticism. Previous research had shown that of the five, if any were competitive with grit as a predictor, it would be Big Five Conscientiousness. So, they compared grit as a predictor with Big Five Conscientiousness as a predictor. They found that the two were highly correlated, but that grit accounts for more variance in outcome than Big Five Conscientiousness. So, grit has nothing to do with IQ, and has been shown to be a better predictor of outcomes than other personality traits. As pertains to AMSAC, however, there is a question of applicability. The authors point out that their findings are based on samples of relatively high-IQ subjects with a limited range of differences. Given, then, a typical group, say, of African American high school students, we would not, as pertains to IQ, have an equivalent group. They would not likely be high-IQ subjects with a limited range of diffrneces, but, instead, average-IQ subjects with greater differences. As a result, we cannot be sure that, for them, grit would be independent of IQ. Regardless of a student's IQ, however, Durckworth and her colleagues have shown that it is a desirable trait to cultivate.

(4) **Love (LO)**. Love is one of the five core EI traits, not because it appears on any list of character traits examined, but by chance. Well before AMCAP was conceived, and before the Rempson Foundation was started, love was a topic of interest and research to the author. Logic has dictated that it be made one of the **Five Success Character Traits**. And, it is informative to note, Paul Tough reports that, in creating the KIPP Character Report Card (see below), originally, love was conceived as one of the categories, but later the category was changed to curiosity, with the following three traits:

Is eager to explore new things
Asks and answers questions to deepen understanding
Actively listens to others

As will be evident, these are all traits required in practicing love and give support to the role herein accorded it.

The requirements that go into love, discussed below, and the results which can ensue from it, make love, not just one of the **Five Success Character Traits**, but the master character trait, permeating all the others and serving as the foundation of our being. Peterson and Seligman's 24 character traits, not just the 3 in the curiosity category, are all manifestations of love, and love is the catalyst to the human spirit, under which it will be further discussed.

The power of love is without dispute. Human and other animal studies attest to its power (209b:303-24; 422). Think for a moment about Christianity; it is the love of Jesus Christ which accounts for its hold on an estimated 2.18 billion people, or nearly one-third of the world's population. Of course, religion represents a particular kind of love, but love it is; and it provides a demonstration of its intrinsic potential. Most likely, we have experienced that power in our own life and seen it in the life of others. Directly or vicariously, we *know* that it can enrich and transform, and that it can be enriching and transforming. Fromm saw it as "*the answer to the problem of human existence*" [emphasis added] (98:6). David Brooks's article in the New York Times captures a core component of its power with the title, "*Stairway to Wisdom*" [emphasis added] (312a). Citing St. Augustine as his source, Brooks's thesis is that the highest form of understanding, and of the wisdom which it makes possible, is "held by those who walk alongside others every day, who know the first names, who know the smells and fears," that is, by those who, rather than standing aloof, engage in what herein is called the **practice of the art of loving**.

Teaching it: Duckworth and Washington

In a New York Times article and, subsequently, in his previously cited book, How Children Succeed: Grit, Curiosity, and the Hidden Power of Character, Paul Tough reports that, spearheaded by Duckworth, the 24 character traits synthesized by Peterson and Seligman, in modified form, have been translated into a report card. The report card, the main portion shown below, is being tried out by the prestigious private Riverdale Country School in Riverdale, New York and KIPP (Knowledge is Power Program) charter schools in New York City (455a). KIPP is a network of 125 charter schools in 20 states and the District of Columbia enrolling over 39,000 students, 85% of whom are from low-income families and 95% of whom are African American. The report card gives a concrete idea of how the term character or emotional intelligence is being used, no standardized interpretation existing.

Through Erica, one of the main fictional characters in his book, The Social Animal: The Hidden Sources of Love, Character, and Achievement, David Brooks would seem to capture, in fiction, the kind of methods used in KIPP to teach some of these traits. He says the following about the Academy Erica entered when she left eighth grade:

> …the biggest shock was the emphasis on behavior. The Academy started from the ground up. It taught its students to look at someone who was talking to them, how to sit up in class, how to nod to signal agreement, how to shake hands and say hello on first meeting. Erica

and her classmates spent the entire first session of her music class learning how to file into the room and take their seats. During the first weeks of school, they were taught how to walk down the hall, how to carry their books, how to say, "Excuse me," if they bumped into one another. The teachers told them that, if they did the small stuff right, the big stuff would be much easier to master later on. Middle-class kids may have learned these lessons automatically, but many of the kids at the Academy had to be taught (23:116)

KIPP Character Growth Card

		OVERALL SCORE	4.30	Teacher 1	Teacher 2	Teacher 3	Teacher 4	Teacher 5	Teacher 6
Zest			4.28						
1	Actively participates		4.50	4	5	5	4	4	5
2	Shows enthusiasm		4.17	5	4	3	4	4	5
3	Invigorates others		4.17	3	4	5	4	5	4
Grit			4.11						
4	Finishes whatever he or she begins		4.00	4	5	3	4	4	4
5	Tries very hard even after experiencing failure		4.17	5	4	4	3	4	5
6	Works independently with focus		4.17	4	4	3	4	5	5
Self Control – School Work			4.33						
7	Comes to class prepared		4.50	4	5	5	5	4	4
8	Pays attention and resists distractions		4.50	4	5	4	5	4	5
9	Remembers and follows directions		4.17	4	5	5	4	3	4
10	Gets to work right away rather than procrastinating		4.17	5	4	4	4	3	5
Self Control – Interpersonal			4.54						
11	Remains calm even when criticized or otherwise provoked		4.50	4	5	4	5	5	4
12	Allows others to speak without interruption		4.83	5	5	5	4	5	5
13	Is polite to adults and peers		4.50	4	5	4	5	4	5
14	Keeps his/her temper in check		4.33	4	5	4	4	5	4
Optimism			4.25						
15	Gets over frustrations and setbacks quickly		4.33	5	4	4	4	5	4
16	Believes that effort will improve his or her future		4.17	5	4	4	3	4	5
Gratitude			4.25						
17	Recognizes and shows appreciation for others		4.17	4	4	5	4	5	3
18	Recognizes and shows appreciation for his/her opportunities		4.33	5	4	5	3	4	5
Social Intelligence			4.33						
19	Is able to find solutions during conflicts with others		4.17	4	4	3	5	4	5
20	Demonstrates respect for feelings of others		4.50	5	4	4	4	5	5
21	Knows when and how to include others		4.33	5	4	4	4	5	4
Curiosity			4.28						
22	Is eager to explore new things		4.17	5	4	3	4	5	4
23	Asks and answers questions to deepen understanding		4.50	5	4	5	4	4	5
24	Actively listens to others		4.17	4	4	5	4	5	3

SCALE
1= Very much unlike the student
2= Unlike the student
3= Somewhat like the student
4= Like the student
5= Very much like the student

Figure 35. The Knowledge is Power Program (KIPP). KIPP Character Growth Card. Retrieved from and reproduced with permission of KIPP (392a).
<u>http://www.kipp.org/files/dmfile/KIPPNYC Character Growth Card SAMPLE2.pdf</u>.

Brooks goes on to describe other practices which reflect similar imprinting (if that is not too strong a word). For example, each morning, they had school-wide circle time, as they called it, during which they performed raps and chants to focus their thoughts and actions on such attributes as respect and knowledge, and on such aspirations as college attendance. And each class has its own graduation date, not from high school, but from college (23:117).

Perhaps surprisingly, thanks to Booker T. Washington, this character emphasis as a *primary* means of enabling low-income students to succeed is rooted in the history of us African Americans. Scott and Stowe, after citing several instances to show the value Washington placed on character education, conclude that he "realized that education was primarily a matter of the development of character and only secondarily a matter of the acquisition of information" (234:367). As previously stated, Washington proclaimed that Tuskegee stood for "an integrated training of head, heart, and hand." As Erica experienced what can be called a "character shock" when she entered the Academy, so did the students who entered Tuskegee Institute. In Up From Slavery, Washington gives this picture of their experience:

> It has been interesting to note the effect that the use of the tooth-brush has had in bringing about a higher degree of civilization among the students. With few exceptions, I have noticed that, if we can get a student to the point where, when the first or second tooth-brush disappears, he of his own motion buys another, I have not been disappointed in the future of that individual. Absolute cleanliness of the body has been insisted upon from the first. The students have been taught to bathe as regularly as to take their meals. This lesson we began teaching before we had anything in the shape of a bath-house. Most of the students came from plantation districts, and often we had to teach them how to sleep at night; that is, whether between the two sheets -- after we got to the point where we could provide them two sheets -- or under both of them. Naturally I found it difficult to teach them to sleep between two sheets when we were able to supply but one. The importance of the use of the night-gown received the same attention.

> For a long time one of the most difficult tasks was to teach the students that all the buttons were to be kept on their clothes, and that there must be no torn place and no grease-spots. This lesson, I am pleased to be able to say, has been so thoroughly learned and so faithfully handed down from year to year by one set of students to another that often at the present time, when the students march out of chapel in the evening and their dress is inspected, as it is every night, not one button is to be found missing (265:308).

Tuskegee students, in addition, might not have had, as Erica, "school-wide circle time," or have "performed raps and chants." Instead, they probably were too busy working with their hands. But they did have the voice of Washington to which to listen in his famous informal **Sunday Evening Talks**. Read Washington's 37 addresses to students, faculty, and guests at Tuskegee, his **Sunday Evening Talks**, and, as they, hear a voice filled with a passion for the efficacy of character (267). On one occasion, for example, he said this to his students:

> I am going to speak with you a few minutes this evening upon the matter of stability. I want you to understand when you start out in school, that no individual can accomplish anything unless he means to stick to what he undertakes. No matter how many possessions he may have, no matter how much he may have in this or that direction, no matter how much learning or skill of hand he may possess, an individual cannot succeed unless, at the same time, he possesses that quality which will enable him to stick to what he undertakes. In a word he is not to be jumping from this thing or that thing (267:97).

Scott and Stowe cite The Talks as one of Washington's most effective means of influencing the whole student body. Not only students, but also teachers, teachers' families, and townspeople would gather to hear him. They were reported and published in the school paper, which was subscribed to by graduates and others (234:341).

Teaching character, then, as a primary tool in educating the African American poor has been famously and successfully tried by Washington. Duckworth and others, therefore, might be said, in effect, to be leading its rebirth or renewal. Their drive comes with a body of knowledge and research to give it more scientific grounding and at a time when the evidence is conclusive that the cognitive skills approach alone does not work; it works in combination with a character skills approach.

Under various names (discussed in connection with the hypotheses for AMCAP in Chapter 14), historically, character education has been an integral part of American education. Different today is its role in the school success of African American students. Like Booker T. Washington, Peterson, Seligman, Duckworth and other character education advocates believe character education to be, not just a desirable part of low-income black students' education, but, given their disadvantaged upbringing, an indispensable part of it. It is essential to their school success, equaling, if not surpassing, cognitive skills in its importance.

Though not intended specifically for low-achieving African American students, we must be alert to other relevant character programs. Dweck's aforementioned "Brainology®" program is one outstanding example, as is the similar (in aim) Mind Coach by psychiatrist, Daniel G. Amen. In fact, as Tough points out, hundreds of schools have character education programs, attesting to the belief in its teachability; and one can presume these programs to be relevant for low-income black students. Attention here has been limited primarily to the successful and nationally publicized program which has evolved from the pioneering work of Peterson and Seligman, along with Duckworth.

Validating it: the research evidence

As indicated, studies support the thesis that character is just as important, if not more important in some instances, than IQ in determining school and life success. For the population, in general, the Marshmallow Study typifies the findings of these studies. For the low-income population, James Heckman's study of the General Educational Development (GED) program and the Perry Preschool Project do likewise.

Efforts of schools to teach character effectively have met with mixed results (see discussion in Chapter 14). But questions about these efforts, and about the associated research, abound. While Goleman, for example, lists six programs which claim positive outcomes, Tough reports that a national evaluation of character education programs by the National Center for Education Research "found no significant impact at all from the programs--not on student behavior, not on academic achievement, not on school culture" (258a: 60). The Center rigorously examined seven diverse school-wide, theoretically-designed programs having a sample of 6,200 students, following them from the third through the fifth grade (389b). Though the programs had no impact on the students, the evaluators cite an array of limitations and shortcomings -- such as reliance on self-reports and small sample sizes for certain individual program analyses -- which advise against giving that outcome undue weight.

The Center's evaluation underlines the problem in trying to draw empirical conclusions about the efficacy of character education based on current evidence: it is not reliable enough. If not even a rare "rigorous" study, such as that conducted by the Center, can be relied upon, what can we say about the usual ones which can lay no claim to such rigor.

A more important consideration pertains to the field itself, and to the programs themselves. Peterson and Seligman are attempting to bring structure and definition to the field, but that attempt is in its early stage and the outcome must be awaited. As pertains to the programs themselves, Tough points out that "Hundreds of American public schools now have some kind of character-education program in place, but most of them are vague and superficial" (258a:60).

Whether any of these programs can achieve the desired results is, then, more or less, an open question. As the headline of a <u>New York Times</u> article by Jennifer Kahn framed the issue, "Can Emotional Intelligence Be Taught?" (390c). The answer is that there is no body of research evidence to support that it can be. But there is some support (390c). Take, for example, the previously discussed 2011 recipient of the Race to the Top High School Commencement Challenge, the Booker T. Washington High School in Memphis, Tennessee. With character as an emphasis, since 2007, it has raised its graduation rate from 55% to 82%. Another is the KIPP charter schools. The first large-scale study of them showed a college graduation rate of 33 percent compared to an 8 percent college graduation rate among similar students nationally. More recently, that rate for some of KIPP's schools rising to 46 percent. Really staggering is their high school graduation and college matriculation rates, 96 percent and 89 percent, respectively (438e). Time will tell whether its refined character education program, being shaped by Duckworth and her colleagues, can pay off in even higher college persistence and graduation rates. There are questions about its cost, but the outcomes speak for themselves.

Whether KIPP and other programs are promising too much is a question that has been raised. Kahn quotes Yale psychologist and emotional intelligence trainer, David Caruso, as asking whether, as with the failed teaching of self-esteem, educators might be mistaken about the promise of teaching emotional intelligence. To assure that they are not, he calls for "a randomized trial that could distinguish short-term placebo effects from lasting improvements." Caruso's caution is well taken, however, for black students in our poor neighborhoods, teaching emotional intelligence can be regarded, not just as an addendum, but as filling a void left by an impoverished home and community life. As Lee Rainwater has been quoted as saying, while "the victimization process as it operates in [poor] families prepares and toughens its members to function in the ghetto world, at the same time that it seriously interferes with their ability to operate in any other world." Emotional intelligence teaching can help to remedy this handicap.

Historically, Washington's character emphasis justifies the point. Harlan reports that, "as at Hampton, there was perhaps one graduate for every ten ex-students." He adds: "There were others who received industrial certificates testifying to their mastery of their trade, but only those who proved their all-around worthiness became seniors and finally graduated." "Graduation," Harlan goes on to elaborate, "was almost an ordination as a minister of the Tuskegee gospel" (109:170). So we cannot necessarily turn to it on the basis of its contribution to the kind of academic success achieved by KIPP, but, on a number of accounts, the two are not comparable, so much being so different. But what we can turn to it for is the kind of success exemplified by the following story told by Washington in one of his 37 **Sunday Evening Talks**.

> I was in a Southern city and going about among the homes of the people of our race. Among these homes I noticed one which was so neat looking that it was conspicuous. I asked the person who

was with me, 'How is it that this house is in such good condition, looks so much better than some of the others in the neighborhood?' 'It is like this,' said the man who was accompanying me. 'The people who live there have a son whom they sent to your school, at considerable self denial to themselves. This young man came home from school a few weeks ago. For some time after he came back he did not have work to keep him busy, and so he employed his spare time in fixing up his parents' home. He fixed the roof and chimney, put new palings in the fence where they were needed and did such things as that. Then he got a stock of paint and painted the house thoroughly, two coats, outside and in. That is why the place looks so neat' (269:351).

Washington goes on to add: "Such testimony as that is very helpful. It shows that the students carry out from here the spirit [that is, character] which we try to inculcate." How common such outcomes were is unknown, but we can reasonably assume that what Tuskegee did for this young man it did for many others, including young women. It did something similar, for example, for the town of Tuskegee – its immediate sphere of influence – making it a black success story (192:428-29). So, even though, as Caruso reasons, too much promise might be tied to character education, when it comes to AMSAC and its inseparable social problems, we must weigh its value in the context of how it served us during the Age of Booker T. Washington. The culture of poverty, Rainwater, for example, reminds us that many of the social and educational problems of Washington's age are also the problems of our age. For many of our students are unprepared to function in the larger world.

Other Attribute: Human Spirit (and the Master Trait, Love, as Nourishment)

Our ability to amplify our IQ, which is afforded by our multiple intelligences and our emotional intelligence, especially the **Five Success Character Traits**, is also provided by another possibility: the human spirit. Our human spirit is omnipresent and defines our life force in its totality. Glenn Loury alludes to it in what he sees as Herrnstein-Murray's misguided emphasis on IQ. He reminds us that, rather than IQ, "human beings' possession of spiritual resources is key to the maintenance of social stability and progress." "It is," he continues, "the ultimate foundation on which rests any hope that the social malaise of the underclass will be overcome" (155:306). To that we can say, Amen!

Need and definition

In the African American Male Career Pathway Program (AMCAP), we propose to teach students that the human spirit is their "Hidden Success Center" (226). The following excerpt from our draft <u>AMCAP Task Guide</u> explains why.

> Without the energy that this Center provides, life is likely to be more passive than active, more boring than interesting, more filled with gloom and doom than with confidence and optimism. We are more subject to a lie-around, sit-around, play- around, hangout life. The likely result: frustration, anger, and despair.

> **Mind and Body Not Enough**

> From our body alone (our Physiological Self), we cannot get that energy. Our body provides us the power, so to speak, the engine on which to run our life. But having the *power* on which to run our life is not the same as running it.

> Nor, simply by adding our mind (our Psychological Self -- thinking, feeling, behavior) can we get that energy. Our mind does, indeed, give us the know-how to steer our engine (body). So now, with our body *and* mind, we have a body that *can* do things and a mind that knows (or can figure out) *how* to do things. We have the *can* and the *how*. Like a sprinter, we are at the starting line. Something more is now needed for us to heed the command: Get set! Get ready! Go! -- and then get to the finish line.

> **Need for the Urge**

> That something more is the *urge* (strong wish or need) to reach it. That urge enables us to rev up our engine (our body) and it incites and focuses our mind. Our urge energizes both mind and body, sets them in motion, and keeps them going. Otherwise, we could

GO, but without the energy needed for a proud finish. For a proud finish, we need that third part of us to kick in -- the *urge*.

The body and mind of each of us need to be energized. The *urges in us* (there is more than one urge) perform this function. We are all born with them. You might think of them as coming from a silent inner voice that exerts (pressures) us to listen to its messages. These urges/messages give each of us energy and help make us the special person that each of us is. They are intangible. We cannot see, touch, weigh, or entrap them. Nor, being silent, can we hear them. They are hidden. But they are there and we can feel them, experience them, and observe their effects. Like air, they are ever-present, active, powerful, and indispensable, yet invisible.

The Three Parts of Us

These active and powerful urges can be called our **spirit** -- that third part of us that is our Hidden Success Center. So, there are three parts of us: body (Physiological Self), mind (Psychological Self -- thinking, feeling, behavior), spirit (Spiritual Self) (225).

Only -- we go on to propose teaching them -- our spirit, while essential to our success, can also cause us to fail; it depends on what we feed or nourish it. Nourish it with love (by **practice of the art of loving**) and it will lead us to success; deprive it of love and feed it that which is negative or destructive, and it will lead us to failure. What we propose to teach our students applies to all of us and to our people. For us as a people, too, our Hidden Success Center is our human spirit which, nourished with love, can lead to success, providing us the positive energy needed to use and cultivate our multiple intelligences, including our emotional intelligence.

Sounds like pie in the sky? Well, not so fast. The mother and son team on which this proposition draws, Muriel James and John James -- both psychotherapists and clinical trainers, theologians and ordained clergy, educators, and consultants -- come to us with over twenty years of study, research, and observation. They share it in their book drawn upon here, Passion for Life: Psychology and the Human Spirit (134). The other source on which the proposition draws is the aforementioned late world renown psychoanalyst, Erich Fromm, author of 25 books. The one drawn upon here, The Art of Loving, is the bestseller among them (98). So, maybe we should not be too dismissive of the proposition.

Foremost, James and James do something novel: they define spirit. Commonly thought about in a religious context, they provide a secular or psychological meaning. That makes for more standardized communication and for more analytical and programmatic possibilities. They define *human spirit as seven basic urges: the urge to live, be free, understand, enjoy, create, connect, and transcend.*

Love defined

The love needed to nourish our human spirit is not the kind which might first enter our mind. It is not about our emotion -- how we feel about someone or something. Instead, it is about love as an art or a skill -- as a character attribute. It does not require us, necessarily, to be touchy-feely. That notion seems, for example, to have been behind David Brooks thinking in explaining why we should not ignore the emotional surges that continuously flow through us. As mentioned, he confides that he takes this position even though he himself is "not a touch-feely person." Well, the **practice of the art of loving**, or tending to those continuously flowing emotional surges does not require him or any of us to be "touchy-feely." When we think of love in this regard, this is what Deepak Chopra, famous spiritual guru and founder of the Chopra Center for Well Being, has to say about this kind of love: "… the emotional kind of love is confined, doubtful, full of fear, and driven by dreams that never get fully realized" (33:257).

We are not talking here about an "emotional kind of love." We are not talking about a kind of love that is "confined, doubtful, full of fear, and driven by dreams that never get fully realized," but, instead, about a kind of love that is pervasive, steadfast, full of confidence, the kind of understanding of which Brooks writes, and driven by dreams whose realization, though unlikely ever to be fully achieved, has a lifetime ascendancy. We are talking about love as a character trait.

We take our definition of love from Fromm, although some insights have also been derived from bestselling author Gary Chapman's Love as a Way of Life (31). Herein, love pertains to our attitude and character, not to our likes and dislikes. It is about love as a *skill* that manifests itself through our attitude and character -- the way that we *view* and *respond* to self, others, and our environment. Drawing from Fromm's bestselling The Art of Loving, we **define love as care, responsibility, respect, and knowledge** -- all of which connect us with self, others, and our environment. There are various types of love -- for example, romantic love, paternal or maternal love, agape -- but we are not talking about these types of love, but rather, again, about love as attitude and character (though when only the term character is used it is understood to include attitude as well).

CARE is *actively* looking out for our own life and growth and for the life and growth of that which we love, much in the same way as one would look out for a baby. It is actually *doing something* rather than just talking about it. To say that we want to finish school and not do our homework means that we do not really care about finishing school. Or to say that we love plants but have to be nagged to water the plants in the house means that we do not really care about plants. Care is shown through *active* concern, through what is *done*, not said, about something.

RESPONSIBILITY is responding to one's own needs and to the needs of others, even if those needs are not expressed. It is something done voluntarily or willingly. Going on a diet, staying away from certain kids, helping a disabled person to cross the street, and washing dishes for one's mother are all examples of responsibility. It is exercised with the environment when, for example, we respond to the needs of our dog or plant.

RESPECT is the desire to see self and others grow and unfold as each has come into the world instead of trying to remake another in our own image The same idea applies to our environment. Respect is the desire to see that each and everything that is part of our environment is treated as having its rightful place, just as we humans do.

KNOWLEDGE is familiarity with the behavior, feelings, and motives of self and others --and seeing things, not just from our point of view, but from the point of view of others as well. It involves not only being aware of actions, behavior, and feelings, but also of understanding what motivates (what is causing) those actions, behavior, and feelings. Further, it means looking at them from your viewpoint *and* from the viewpoint of the other person. The same idea applies to our environment. We are unlikely to understand the part that everything plays in the world, but we need to respect the fact that science has been able to explain the functions and contributions of that which makes up our environment (Excerpted from AMCAP Task Guide, 265).

Love as nourishment -- and master trait

Experience and research point to love being nearly as central to human existence as food -- and equally so if we are to enjoy our existence. Yet, we think about food, more or less, all the time, but, it can be ventured, we think about love only from time to time. In various ways, we engage in it all the time, but to engage in it is not the same as to think about it. In fact, it seems safe to say that, commonly, we do not have a thinking framework for love -- a feeling framework, yes, but not a thinking framework. When it comes to food, we think in terms of calories, starches, carbohydrates, and so on. But what commonly shared terms can we cite when it comes to thinking about love? Whereas, we do not, as in the case of malnutrition, die from a lack of love, nevertheless, we inescapably suffer -- measurably, as in the case of psychiatric illnesses, for example, and quite often immeasurably. The flip side, of course, is that with love, as with food, we grow and flourish. A few illustrations of love's power follow.

On a personal level: Jerry McGill. No doubt, for example, Jerry McGill, the previously cited black author who wrote Dear Marcus: Speaking to the Man Who Shot Me, would agree. Shot in the back and suffering a spinal cord injury at the age of twelve while walking home at night with a friend, a six-month stay in the hospital, and years of rehabilitation have enabled him to recover and become a world renown advocate for the disabled. He testifies that there is nothing "we do in this world matters more [than love]," adding, "The main ingredient that got me through this ordeal, both in the hospital and for all the years after, was the love and affection of others" (157:22).

On a person and people level: Booker T. Washington and his tradition. We African American males need only remember that we each can be a Marcus. Love can be the instrument that helps to enable us to surmount this crisis, just as it also was the instrument in enabling Washington to begin the process, only, of course, to have it truncated. While Washington was successful early in the twentieth century, likewise, we can be successful in this new century. Washington, too, faced a crisis. Southern Reconstruction (1867-77) and its aftermath had exacerbated racial conflict and left our Southern masses at the nadir of their new life -- without direction and in a search of safety and survival. Our mental intelligence, and our emotional intelligence, retarded by slavery, were still being depressed. The external forces were openly and aggressively hostile (the Ku Klux Klan, for example, had sprung up). Under these conditions, starting out alone, and with practically no resources, having brought himself up from slavery, now Washington was faced with bringing his people (us) up from freedom; and he made a successful and historic beginning. How was he able to do it?

The case is made that, as discussed in Chapter 17, he was able to do it through the **practice of the art of loving**. Only its practice enabled him to survive and prosper amid Southern hostility. A provocative incident wherein a Confederate veteran and former Congressman, who was a fan of Washington, was a speaker at a Tuskegee gathering illustrates the point. Preceded by a black notable who delivered an inspiring speech applauding black strides in education (and maybe thereby at least implying that it might put us on par with whites), the ex-Congressman was so angered that, when he took the podium, this was his response:

> 'I have written this address for you,' waving it at the audience, 'but I will not deliver it. I want to give you niggers a few words of plain talk and advice. No such address as you have just listened to is going to do you any good; it's going to spoil you. You had better not listen to such speeches. You might just as well understand that this is a white man's country, as far as the South is concerned, and

we are going to make you keep your place. Understand that. I have nothing more to say to you' (234:469-70).

The audience was stunned and indignant. While reportedly appearing unruffled, Washington stepped up, seemingly to introduce the next speaker, but, instead, he said, "Ladies and Gentlemen: I am sure you will agree with me that we have had enough eloquence for one occasion. We shall listen to the next speaker at another occasion, when we are not so fagged out. We will now rise, sing the doxology, and be dismissed."

A deft response in a delicate situation, Washington's **practice of the art of loving** enabled him to save the day, so to speak. Other possible responses could have done likewise, but only if those responses were consistent with the **practice of the art of loving**; otherwise, the incident could have had lasting and lethal reverberations. That is what typically happens when we practice, not the art of loving, but the art of anger or hate, which is too commonly the norm with our System-Responsibility Tradition -- and which, incidentally, is a norm which we see so commonly practiced throughout the world, which does not make its existence any less pernicious.

One might argue that Washington was able to respond so sanely because he just happened to have been born with a special temperament. No doubt, *in part*, that is true. However, as Merle Curti observed, if he had come under the sway of New England missionaries, he could have turned out to be a radical. Instead, he came under the sway of General Armstrong, who taught, not anger or hatred, but love (chances are that the missionaries taught it too, but, at the same time, might have instilled a victim mentality). The point is that loving is a skill which, by others and self, can be taught, practiced, and learned. At least with practice, any of us could have done something similar to what Washington did.

Amid such adversity and animosity, that Washington was able to accomplish what he did is testimony to the power of the **practice of the art of loving**. Washington was an energized and driven man -- as much determined to succeed as not to fail (to the extent that there is a difference). He was driven by love -- caring, responding, respecting, and knowing -- and love he practiced. "He practiced what he preached:," biographer Samuel Spender, Jr. tells us, "courage, self-reliance, integrity, humility, dignity, and consideration for his fellow man." His preaching and practice of love enhanced his human spirit. It did the same, incidentally, for Father Price and the Tinkersville townspeople who got Washington started on his educational journey.

Traits required. The practice of the art of loving, like the practice of any skill, requires certain traits. From the AMCAP Task Guide, here is a summary of what they are:

Like with any art, to practice the art of loving (care, responsibility, respect, knowledge), you need to exercise discipline, concentration, patience, and supreme concern. In addition, you must overcome the main hurdle that faces every human being: *narcissism* (self-love). You can overcome your narcissism by being objective, which requires that you be humble and exercise reason. You also need faith/courage and an active mind.

These requirements may make love seem almost impossible to practice, but practice it we do. Its practice is a part of our everyday living, only, as stated, the chances are that we do not think about it; we just do it naturally. Fromm tells us that to become good at it, however, is quite a challenge because it requires practicing it in all that we do all of the time. The key is lifelong practice. As David Brooks points out, this is the case with an array of character attribute. One must conceive of it as an individualized skill learned little by little, over a lifetime -- and, at least in the case of love, never completely (23:125-29).

"Authoritative communities" and neuroscience. The **practice of the art of loving** has support from the scientific community. Composed of professionals from that community, the Commission on Children at Risk makes love central in its proposal. In addressing the needs of at-risk children, it advocates what it calls "authoritative communities" to combat what it sees -- rather than typically as a health and behavioral crisis -- as a crisis of "connectedness," of "close connections to other people, and deep connections to moral and spiritual meaning." As it might be otherwise expressed, the Commission sees children's needs as a crisis of "love," of receiving care, response, respect, and knowing. David Brooks tells us that neuroscience is documenting the need which the Commission cites, finding that all of us are social animals who need, seek, and thrive on love, and Paul Tough draws our attention to its crucial role in the school and life success of our children (23:xviii, 258a:182).

Approach in proposed AMCAP. The proposal herein is that we African Americans make the **practice of the art of loving** the soul of our effort to effect a character reformation. Like what former Harlem Chidren's Zone director, Geoffrey Canada, did with his program, AMCAP would incorporate the kind of character-building features used by KIPP and depicted by Brooks (23:125-29). Only its approach would probably be more organic. The practice would be viewed as a way of life to be lived every day, all day, in all that is done. And the attempt would be to involve, not just the school, but the home as well.

Conclusion

From some sources, we might infer that AMSAC and its inseparable social problems are tantamount to an IQ crisis, and from DuBois and his System-Responsibility Tradition that the answer to solving it is civil rights and, as added in recent decades, equal results and feeling equality. But the research evidence points to a different cause and, along with Washington and his Self-Responsibility Tradition, to a different cure.

That evidence suggests that the school and life success of our African American students, like that of all students -- black or white, poor or privileged -- depends as much, and often more, on their character, or EQ, than on their cognitive skills or IQ. Over a century ago, with his Tuskegee students, Washington demonstrated the same. Yet character, their greatest need, is probably their greatest weakness -- often marked by the scars of victimhood, which have been historically propagated and transmitted by DuBois and his tradition. Those scars starkly pervade the life of the African American poor, and even contaminate the life of the more privileged. Students are merely reflectors of those scars which exist as part of, rather than apart from, the source of their being and influence. On a massive scale, to isolate them from that source and make them into something different from it is unrealistic. A better chance of success exists if -- in a somewhat "learning-to-see model," as

Brooks puts it -- students, home, and community are involved so as to provide the support, redundancy, and reinforcement on which character formation commonly hinges (23:116-32). That, too, is the lesson that can be drawn from Farrell's studies of successful and at-risk students. The "voices" which they heard and internalized -- voices which came from home and community -- are interpreted as having helped to have shaped who they became. It is for this reason that a **Child Family Rights Movement** is being proposed, with a focus on both students and community.

The Movement is based on the premise that our adaptation does not depend on any one factor, as our System-Responsibility Traditionalists seem to think. The eggs of our adaptation, so to speak, are not all in the civil-rights basket. Nor, as some others might think, are they all in the intelligence quotient (IQ) basket. We have multiple resources from which to draw: mental, emotional, and spiritual. While each is essential, the lesson that can be drawn from our African American Garden of Eden, supported by the research evidence, is that priority goes to character and the master trait of love which comprises it. Whatever our IQ, our character -- grounded in our human spirit -- will enable us to amplify it, to make it more than measured or imagined. Our character traits may not be as "extraordinarily malleable" as Goleman asserts, but the evidence suggests that -- given hard work and time -- they are sufficiently malleable to be life-shaping, and in some cases, even life-transforming.

The effort involved, while demanding, is not overwhelming, nothing even remotely like that which faced Washington. As applies to AMCAP, the core of what students are asked to do is to **discover and pursue your career pathway**. Of course, to do so, requires sustained time and work (what worthwhile endeavor does not?), and the sustained time and work needed entail energy and drive. That is where their human spirit enters. The source of that energy and drive is their human spirit -- their seven basic urges to live, be free, understand, enjoy, create, connect, and transcend. **Practice the art of loving** -- caring, responding, respecting, and knowing -- and they will nourish their spirit, their seven basic urges

Joe L. Rempson

-- to live, be free, understand, enjoy, create, connect, and transcend – and they will supply, *on their own*, the energy and drive that will make their pursuit successful. And what applies to our students applies to all of us, whatever the endeavor.

13

The African American Male Career Pathway Program (AMCAP)

Proverbs, 16:22 - "Understanding is a wellspring of life unto him that hath it: but the instruction of fools is folly."
Galatians, 6:5 - "For every man shall bear his own burden."

Historical Roots
(Recognition and Reform)

Reference has been made to James B. Conant's famous study of slum schools around 1960, reported in his book, <u>Slums and Suburbs</u>. The report came during a period of rising concern about black schools and black education following the Supreme Court's *Brown vs. Board of Education* school desegregation decision of 1954 and the Civil Rights Movement that began around the same time. That concern saw the consequent emergence of numerous policy and program initiatives. Most notably, in 1965, President Lyndon B. Johnson initiated the War on Poverty with a variety of anti-poverty programs, including the Elementary and Secondary Education Act (ESEA) and, separately, Headstart. Education reform and innovation were in ferment. Widespread initiatives were undertaken in special teacher training and in specially designed curricula and teaching methodology. Local governments, community-based groups, foundations, churches, and other non-governmental entities all joined the action. Financial and other incentives were part of the mix. These endeavors persist and, over time, have proliferated (see, for example: 17; 56; 75; 84; 87:79-116; 105; 127; 158:560-63; 159; 177; 194; 207; 212; 222; 248). In his book, <u>So Much Reform, So Little Change</u>, an excellent summary is provided by black University of Chicago sociologist, Charles M. Payne. He also provides a Program Glossary which gives a brief description of some of the popular reform projects. His summary follows.

> The late 1980s and the entire 1990s were a period of unprecedented experimentation with ways to improve schools serving low-income children. We saw the national commitment to statewide accountability systems--led initially by states like North Carolina, Kentucky, and Texas--culminating in the 2002 No Child Left Behind legislation; the closely related standards-based reform movement and the restructuring movement that preceded it; the popularity of policies calling for the end of social promotion; the transfer of authority from traditional school boards to mayors; the complete or partial reconstitution of failing schools; state takeover of failing districts; the $500 million investment of the Annenberg Foundation in improving schools; the National Science Foundation's attempt to reshape science and math education in the cities; the small school movement, freshman academies, and other forms of personalization of the educational experience; calls for much more intensive forms of professional development and instructional support, including instructional coaching; the radical decentralization followed by the radical recentralization of the Chicago school system; an arguably even more ambitious effort to transform the New York system with its one-million plus students; the attempt to duplicate the apparent success of New York old District Two in San Diego and Boston; dozens of comprehensive school reform projects, including Success for All, Accelerated Schools, America's Choice, the School Development Program (more popularly the Comer Process), the Coalition for Essential Schools and the Talent Development Program (208a:2-3)

African American Males as Target

All along, African-American males have been an inclusive target of the efforts, however, only over approximately the last twenty years have they become a more specific target (79; 168; 198; 242:210-14). But only *more* targeted; they have yet to command the kind of special emphasis reasonably warranted by the crisis which they pose. In her book, <u>Educating African American Males</u> (2005), Olatokunbo Fashola of the Comprehensive School Reform Center at the American Institutes for Research (AIR) expresses disturbance that "with the exception of a few scholars, there has really been relatively little attention given to solving this problem in the education realm" ["this problem" referring to her previous reference to the race and gender achievement disparity, that disparity (she points out) being largest for African American males] (84: xiii). There are "numerous diagnoses," she further observes, "but very few prescriptions, cures, or treatment plans" (84: xiii).

Fashola's observations are supported by later research done by Sharon Lewis and her colleagues at The Council of the Great City Schools. In their 2010 report, they state that, while a lot of effort has gone into addressing the black-white achievement gap, "there has been no concerted national effort focused on the education and social outcomes of Black males specifically." There is no Department of Education office devoted to their needs, no legislative projects, very little collection of information, and no national policy or programs. "While there are educators, researchers, policymakers, government leaders, faith-based leaders, civil rights leaders, and others intent on improving the quality of life for Black males," they say, "their efforts are often too disconnected and too uncoordinated to match the comprehensive nature of the problem" (398:2).

Precursor: MCAP (Minority Male Career Development Project)

It is against this background that the African American Male Career Pathway Program (AMCAP) had its origin. Experience, along with research and reports, all made the problem evident, only it was apparent that little was being done about it. So its founder (the author of this publication) originated and conducted an experimental program called MCAP, Minority Male Career Development Project, over a 5-year period, 1994-99, at Bronx Community College of the City University of New York, and at Taft High School in The Bronx, New York. It was funded under The Vocational and Technology Act (VATEA), a federal program administered by the New York State Department of Education. Over the 5-year period, it worked with 211 black and Hispanic male incoming freshmen and 122 minority male high school students. For one semester, twice weekly for one hour, the college students attended a freshman orientation and career development course especially designed for them with some sections of the course taught by an African-American male counselor and other sections by a black Hispanic male counselor. In addition to providing career exploration, the course dealt with topics such as self-esteem and values; and it gave students an opportunity to address issues and problems of daily concern. The students were provided out-of-class counseling, got tutorial assistance from minority male students, and were provided follow-up assistance upon request.

The high school component, far less developed, was structured around after-school workshops [sporadically held for 90 minutes, twice weekly], tutoring, field trips, and "Fridays at the College." Personnel changes, administrative matters, and getting the same group of students to meet consistently made it difficult for it to function on a firm and satisfactory basis, a difficulty augmented by its off-site status.

The results for the college participants, though inconclusive, were encouraging, despite not having the staffing, structure, and coordination deemed, then and retrospectively, to have been essential to its success. The mindset was to do as much as possible with the minimal resources available. The students had consistent and exceptionally high praise for the program, and, based on pre- and post-testing, a statistically significant increase were shown in their locus of control and self-esteem. On the crucial variables of retention and graduation rates, however, no statistically significant difference from a control group at BCC was found. Further study that might have helped explain these outcomes, such as examining certain background variables or time factors, was not possible.

The Plan: Part I (Concrete Proposal)

What is true of MCAP is also true for other programs and activities to educate the African-American male. None has yielded a template. Yet from them -- and from experience, the professional literature, and research -- the pieces can be discerned and put together to produce just that: a template. That is what AMCAP is intended to be.

The teachers and other school personnel who command our educational battlefield are in trouble and need reinforcement. But only if the reinforcement gets to the root of the problem will it make a significant and systemic difference. The African American Male Career Pathway Program (AMCAP) is designed to get at its root and provide the appropriate reinforcement to make such a difference. The proposed AMCAP staff -- its administrators and their African-American male counselors, African-American male student assistants, and African American male volunteers -- can be conceived, in military terms, as members of special forces units employed to carry out a specialized school mission to assist the regulars in getting our black male students to measure up. Whether AMCAP can make a difference requires testing. So that is what is being proposed: setting AMCAP up as an experimental voluntary program to be piloted over an eight-year year period in one predominantly African American public high school and its feeder elementary schools. The structure and curriculum of the program (which are subject to modifications as appropriate) are outlined below. Whereas, AMCAP is organized around career discovery and pursuit, it is designed to be sufficiently comprehensive to fill a void left by a disadvantaged home and community life. Although the school cannot be expected to replace home and community, in a crisis, it must explore enhancements that allow it to extend its scope.

It is a public-school centered program. Efforts by private schools, community-based groups, foundations, religious organizations, and other non-school entities are viewed as supplementary. As valuable as they might be, they cannot be expected to meet the needs on a scale commensurate with the problem. Since, in effect, we cannot afford to have two public school systems, neither can charter schools, even if some were specifically designed to address the problem. Of course, AMCAP is applicable to the initiatives of any of these entities, but it has been

Joe L. Rempson

formulated to be conducted where almost all of the targeted students are: in the public schools, which is where the 2007-08 United States Census Bureau data show about 90% of them are (420).

Target population

The majority of the target population will be African American male students with whom, Paul Tough points out, reform initiatives have had the least success: those from families whose income is less than $11,000 a year (258a: 189-94). No evidence was found, incidentally, as to whether the same lack of success applies to females from families in the same income bracket. More success, Tough adds, has been experienced with students from families whose annual income is $41,000 a year or more.

Success criteria

We can think of solving the crisis at three success levels (smaller steps make it less daunting): a **turnaround level, a moderation level, and a termination level.** The high school graduation rate can serve as a rough marker. Below are the relevant national 2003 public high school graduation rates as calculated by Jay P. Greene, Senior Fellow, and Marcus A. Winters, Senior Research Associate, at the conservative Manhattan Institute (365).[31] In considerable detail, the authors explain how they calculated the rates and examine issues which affect their accuracy. Given the acknowledged and widespread disarray and inconsistency in calculating graduation rates, one could not expect more. Rates provided by The National Center for Higher Education Management Systems Information Center (NCHEMS), which carries no ideological label, suggest the reasonable utility of the Greene-Winters rates (421). Greene and Winters report a national average graduation rate of 70% for all students versus 68.6% reported by NCHEMS, and in general their reported rates, which are based on 40 states for which

---

[31] The authors explain that their rates are based, not on 4-year, on-time graduation rates, but on the actual cohort graduation rates of the class of 2003. So, whereas the black male dropout rate is herein based on a 4-year graduation rate for the 56 largest black male school districts, as applies to AMCAP, rates are used based on Greene and Winters's cohort-derived rate.

data were available, more or less, correspond with the rates reported by NCHEMS.

To achieve the **turnaround level** would require cutting in half the 11-point gap between African American male and female students. That would raise the males' graduation rate from **48% to** roughly **54%** and would mean the achievement of a crisis turnaround.

To achieve the **moderation level** would require building upon this 6-point gain by erasing one-half of the now 16-point gap between African American male students and the 70% range of white and Asians male students, that is, reduce the gap by 8 percentage points. That would take their graduation rate from **54% to 62%** and would mean the achievement of a crisis moderation.

National Public High School Graduation Rates, Class of 2003

African American male...............48%
African American female.............59%

White male............................74%
White female.......................... 79%

Hispanic male......................... 49%
Hispanic female.......................58%

Asian male............................70%
Asian female..........................73%

Male.................................. 65%
Female................................ 72%

Total................................. 70%

Asian................................. 72%

Hispanic.............................. 53%

Joe L. Rempson

          African American...................... 55%
          White......................................78%

Table 3 source: compiled from data provided by Greene and Winters, April 2006 Civic Report, "Leaving Boys Behind: Public School Graduation Rates" (365).

To achieve the **termination level** would require closing the remaining 8-point gap between the now 62% graduation rate of African American male students the 70% range graduation rate of white and Asian male students. That, of course, takes their graduation rate to around **70%**, roughly equivalent to that of white and Asian male students, which is the ultimate goal and would mean the achievement of a crisis termination.

These three success levels represent; what is realistically possible has to be experimentally determined. But we start with the ideal, work long and hard to achieve it, but make adjustements as advisable. Whereas it is desirable for our black male students to graduate from high school at the same rate as their white and Asian American counterparts, given our three major demons (*IQ lag-fatherless families-crime*), it probably is not realistically possible, in which case, without rancor, we will have to settle for what experience shows to be possible, at some point that experience possibly being translated into some statistically estimate of what is possible.

Whole-school approach

So AMCAP projects three high school graduation success rate indicators: **54%**, **62%**, and **70%**. The indicators are to be applied both to the experimental program and to the whole school, that is, examining the direct effect of the program on AMCAP participants alone, as well as the program's operational effect (whole-school effect). Though conceived as a supplement to the regular school program, nevertheless, the intent is to treat AMCAP as an integral part of the regular school program. Not only is the idea to conduct an experiment and, at some point, possibly declare it to be a successful model which warrants dissemination, but, *in addition*, to demonstrate its school-wide efficacy and school-wide applicability. It is not expected that the success markers for its operational effect will be the same as for the experimental effect, but the emergence of a positive trend is expected. The African American Male Career Pathway Program (AMCAP) is, not just a demonstration project. It is also about an operational project, to be tested experimentally and operationally. Indicators of its efficacy, then, must reflect both conditions, experimental and operational – though not necessarily to the same degree of success.

So conceived, AMCAP is designed to have an experimental phase, which, if successful, will be followed by a school adoption phase wherein, as advisable, the school will adopt various AMCAP components into its regular operation. During the school adoption phase, the experimental program will be continued and modified as advisable and appropriate. The plan and details herein pertain only to the experimental phase, since outcomes will determine what happens thereafter. The time period for both the experimental and school adoption phases are projected for eleven years as follows:

Year 1………. Experimental program planning

Years 2 - 5…. Experimental program operation

Year 6………. Support and follow-up of AMCAP graduates
Assessment
School incorporation planning
Experimental program planning

Years 7 - 10… Continued support and follow-up of AMCAP graduates
School incorporation of experimental components
Revised experimental program operation

Year 11……. Assessment and final report

College and postsecondary phase

It will be noted that Years 7-10 include a follow-up AMCAP component. This component is integral to the AMCAP experiment, which is ultimately envisaged as extending its reach from the very early grades through college and postsecondary training. However, its initial experimental phase, represented by the content and structure outlined below, is focused on its success at the high school level.

Three-treatment design

The program is designed to test its effects in three forms: structured and intensive, structured and moderate, and independent. For this purpose, there will be three groups: a Four-Year Group, a Two-Year Group, and a Self-Paced group. These groups will permit assessing what seems to be working, or not working, under what program conditions, ultimately making it possible to formulate a program with the flexibility to meet various student needs in ways that are both productive *and* cost effective.

Career core with character (culture)

As its name suggests, AMCAP is built around black male students' discovery and pursuit of their career pathway. Research shows that discovery and pursuit are decisively influenced by character factors. Those factors include, for example, their ability to handle peer pressure, to stay drug free, to manage their female and other relationships, and to achieve their other developmental tasks. Accordingly, AMCAP has a dominant character (or cultural, if you will) dimension.

Therein lies a controversy: the addition of a cultural dimension as a requisite to solving our crisis. It is an *addition* that has traditionally drawn fire because it is seen instead as a *subtraction*. As black Harvard sociologist, Orlando Patterson asserts, "...a deep-seated dogma...has prevailed in social science and policy circles since the mid-1960's: the rejection of any explanation that invokes a group's cultural attributes -- distinctive attitudes, values and predispositions, and the resulting behavior of its members -- and the relentless preference for relying on structural factors like low incomes, joblessness, poor schools and bad housing" (431).

The dissenting mantra is that to focus on cultural explanations is to "blame the victim," a term coined by psychologist and civil rights activist, William Ryan, in response to the Moynihan Report (as discussed in Chapters 7 and 17). Patterson regards this contention as "bogus," asserting that "to hold someone responsible for his behavior is not to exclude any recognition of the environmental factors that may have induced the problematic behavior in the first place." He continues: "Many victims of child abuse end up behaving in self-destructive ways; to point out the link between their behavior and the destructive acts is in no way to deny the causal role of their earlier victimization and the need to address it." Renowned black University of Chicago sociologist, William Julius Wilson, agrees (287:20-23). As evident from the New York Times article (2010), "Culture of Poverty" Makes a Comeback," so do other scholars (317).

Wilson also dissents from a companion to this dissenting mantra: to focus on culture is to exonerate the system and let it off the hook. Wilson proclaims that "it is equally important to acknowledge that recognizing the important role of cultural influences in creating different racial group outcomes does not *require* us to ignore or play down the role of structural forces" [emphasis added] (287:21). Yet, we act as if it does. That was evident in the outcry against John McWhorter's use of the term "self-sabotage" in the subtitle of his book, Losing the Race. However, often we are our own worst enemy. The expression, "He (or she) is his (or her) own worst enemy" is common for a reason: we so often are. But the dissenters would have us believe that we are picking on the "poor" victims who could not possibly be to blame because they are the victims, ruling out, of course, the *possibility* that they are victims because, to invoke the aforementioned adage, "They are their own worst enemy." To hold the poor harmless and unaccountable for their attitudes and behaviors is tantamount to believing that, unlike the rest of us, the poor are not subject to human failings – more or less that they are infallible.

AMCAP content: tasks

Conceived as privately funded, the African-American Male Career Pathway Program (AMCAP) is an after-school program intended to enable African-American male high school students to achieve career success through an increase in the number of them who graduate from high school and go on to attend and complete college or other postsecondary training, or go into the military. The program has been laid out in an unpublished publication, AMCAP (African American

Male Career Pathway Program) Task Guide (225). The <u>Guide</u> contains 45 tasks designed to make this outcome possible. Inclusively, the 45 tasks guide students in the discovery and pursuit of their career pathway and gives them an opportunity to enhance their control over the developmental, school, and life challenges which they must meet if they want to succeed. For each task, the <u>Guide</u> list activities (not shown here) to be undertaken by students and staff to accomplish it.

TASKS 1-12: O R I E N T A T I O N T A S KS

____1. To learn more about AMCAP and what you will do as an AMCAP student.

____2. To learn about "private time."

____3. To be familiar with and follow the Rules of Conduct explained by your Career and Success Control (CSC) counselor. [These rules are subject to later review by you and your CSC counselor.]

____4. To set up your laptop computer. Your Career and Success Control (CSC) counselor will give you instructions.

____5. To provide, online (if necessary), requested background information.

____6. To complete online the inventories listed below.

____7. To learn the Relaxation Response.

____8. To participate in a preview of your AMCAP materials listed below. For the publications listed, your Career and Success Control (CSC) counselor will draw your attention to the following information:

____Author(s) and information about them

____Publisher, copyright date

____Title Page

____Table of Contents

____Appendix

____References

____Index

____Other (as appropriate)

____9. To learn about the AMCAP philosophy (belief) of SHARING.

____10. To learn the instructions to follow in performing AMCAP reading activities.

____11. To follow the record-keeping instructions of your Career and Success Control (CSC) counselor
____12. To come to understand, learn, and make wise use of the AMCAP Code.

TASK 13-15: TAKEOFF TASKS

____13. To examine your time perspectives.
____14. To learn some strategies that you can use to help reset your time perspectives
____15. To make a commitment to 100% Responsibility and 100% Effort.

TASK 16: BOOK-READING AND SUCCESS-IMMERSION TASK

____16. To engage in a *travel-reading experience*, a *spare-time reading experience*, a *scheduled-reading experience*, or from some combination of these reading experiences, to learn from the career and life success of African American and other black males.

TASKS 17-20: C A R E E R T A S K S

____17. To discover your career pathway and acquire job search skills.
____18. To perform well your job of going to school.
____19. To become aware of globalization and its possible connection to your career Pathway.
____20. To get admitted to college, to some postsecondary training program, or to the military.

TASK 21: HIDDEN SUCCESS CENTER TASK

____21. To learn how you can nourish (feed) your Hidden Success Center.

TASKS 22-42: SUCCESS-CONTROL TASKS

22-25. MIND CONTROL

____22. To learn Dr. Amen's Mind Coach system.
____23. To experience exposure to an affirmation of the mental condition necessary for you to become the best of what you can be.
____24. To learn how the mind works when we make intelligent use of it.
____25. To practice the art of loving.

26-27: HEALTH AND BODY CONTROL

____26. To learn about the changes taking place in your body and how to take care of it.
____27. To be introduced to and learn from a model of wellness.

28-29 SEX AND SEXUAL RELATIONSHIP CONTROL

____28. To learn what teenage boys want and need to know about sex and sexual relationships.
____29. To improve your ability to communicate in male-female relationships.

30-34. IDENTITY CONTROL

____30. To explore the meaning of manhood.
____31. To explore self-esteem as a factor in your life.
____32. To explore issues of race and culture.
____33. To examine your interests and your pursuit of them.
____34. To get a composite picture of your identity based on your AMCAP data.

35. COMMUNICATION CONTROL

____35. To learn what is involved in being able to communicate effectively with your peers and others and how to rate your effectiveness.

36. COPING AND RELATIONSHIP CONTROL

____36. To learn the answer to some of your questions about your feelings and problems, including peer pressure

37-38. SUBSTANCE CONTROL

____37. To become knowledgeable about the dangers of drug and alcohol abuse.

____38. To become more aware of beer, wine, cigarettes, and inhalants as factors in your life.

39. SUPPORT SYSTEM AND RECREATIONAL CONTROL

____39. To become acquainted with support systems and recreational outlets for teenage boys.

40-43. MONEY CONTROL

____40. To learn some of the basics about managing money.
____41. To learn more about the stock market -- if you wish.
____42. To hear presentation by an invited African-American male Financial Planner who will discuss The Art of Financial Planning, with inclusion of at least one success story from his experience and at least one story of failure from his experience.
____43. To weigh the ethic of personal responsibility as a factor affecting your money control.

TASK 44-45: GRADUATION TASKS

____44. To update, online, your background information so that AMCAP can stay in contact with you and provide you additional assistance.
____45. To complete, online, the inventories listed below

Joe L. Rempson

SUPPLEMENTARY ATTACHMENTS

I. Managing Stress: The Relaxation Response
II. A Simple Form of Meditation
III. Improve Your Reading Efficiency
IV. SQ3R Textbook Study System
V. SQ3R Checklist
VI. Fathering in America: What's a Dad Supposed to Do?
VII. What are Habits of Mind?

AMCAP organization

Except for the segment on structure, the following is, more or less, a duplicate of what appears in the Guide. It is the first task which the students have and provides a description of how AMCAP is organized.

___1. **To learn more about AMCAP and what you will do as an AMCAP student**

> From the enrollment process, you already know something about AMCAP. Your Career and Success-Control (CSC) counselor will take you through the outline below to make sure you understand why it exists and what you need to know for your particular group.

> A. Introduction

> Your Career and Success-Control (CSC) counselor will guide you through the reading of the Introduction, located near the front of the Guide. It explains why AMCAP exists and why you are such an important part of it. You will take turns with other students in reading it aloud and your counselor will give you, and others, a chance to react to what you read as you go along.

The structure of AMCAP:

> Three-Hour After-School Program (3:00 p.m. - 6:00 p.m., Monday Through Friday, during the school year) staffed by the following Foundation-paid personnel
> 1. AMCAP Coordinator – full-time, selected by Foundation and Principal, and designated Assistant to the Principal for AMCAP
> 2. AMCAP Coordinator's Secretary, full-time
> 3. AMCAP Career Fair and Outreach Coordinator - full-time paraprofessional (1)
> 4. Career and Success-Control (CSC) counselor - full-time professional (3)
> 5. AMCAP Resource Assistant - paraprofessional, 20 hr/wk (1)
> 6. AMCAP student tutors - 16 hr/wk (8) [high-achieving juniors and seniors from the school]

B. Staff philosophy (set of beliefs that guide the staff in working with you)

The AMCAP philosophy is to treat you as AMCAP thinks a father should treat a son. Its role is to help counsel or guide you to your manhood through the discovery and successful pursuit of your career pathway.

That discovery and pursuit requires that you ***work***. It is only through ***work*** that we accomplish anything in life. So you are enrolled in a ***workshop*** where you are going to ***work*** to discover your career pathway and pursue it successfully.

Being successful means that you need to be in control of certain tasks, such as, handling peer pressure, controlling your thoughts, and handling anger and conflict. So, in addition to helping you in your ***work*** to discover and pursue your career pathway, AMCAP is also going to help you do the ***work*** required of you so you can gain control of these tasks.

Who is going to be responsible for seeing that the **_work_** is done? Your AMCAP Career and Success-Control (CSC) counselor and the tutors who work with him and you. Your Career and Success-Control (CSC) counselor is going to be your guide, **_working_** along with you, and being like a father to you. The two of you are going to **_work_** together, and you are going to get help from your peers in the upper grades who are doing well in school. They will be your tutors if you need help -- but only if you really need help; they are not going to do the **_work_** for you. You and the others in the group are also going to **_work_** together and help each other. So, everyone in the **_workshop_**, INCLUDING YOU, will be **_working_** together and helping one another.

For the most part, you are not going to be told what to do. You, and all of the other students, are going to have an active part planning and conducting your **_work_**.

C. Three Program Components

(1) Workshop
   (a) The format for AMCAP **group** activities, contrasted with the classroom format, where *learning* takes place by havng *groups of students work and study together* in an informal (though structured) atmosphere
   (b) Staffed by a Career and Success-Control (CSC) counselor with 2 student tutors (upper-class African-American male students)
   (c) Conducted Monday through Thursday
   (d) Students do not attend on Friday; Friday is used as Staff Day to allow for preparation, planning, and outreach

(2) Resource Room
   (a) The format for AMCAP **individual** activities, similar to library Format, in which students work on their own with assistance of AMCAP staff

(b) Staffed by Career and Success-Control (CSC) counselor and 2 student tutors (upper-class African-American male students)
  (b.1) Open Monday through Friday for entire school year
  (b.2) Can be used by *all* black male students, not just African-American male students
  (b.3) Intended especially to service 2-Year students who spend 2 years in Program for 2 hours a day instead of 3 hours
  (b.4) Available for study groups and tutoring, with AMCAP students in 4-Year and 2-Year Groups having priority
  (b.5) Houses multiple copies of all AMCAP materials
  (b.6) During school days, materials must be used in Room
  (b.7) On weekends and holidays, some materials may be borrowed and returned next school day
(3) Career Fair Day
  AMCAP will sponsor, every other year, a Career Fair Day for all black male students in the school. African-American males, and other black males, *from the school community* who are employed (or were formerly employed) in the range of career fields in which AMCAP students have expressed an interest will be solicited to come to the school to be Career Speakers. They will share, with the students, information and insights regarding their respective careers and engage in discussion with them.

  In career fields where African-American males, or other black males, from the school community are not obtainable, AMCAP will solicit black male speakers from other communities and, if need be, males from other ethnic/racial groups. Students will have an opportunity to go to several rooms to hear different Career Speakers, since the day will be arranged so that (using a rotating system) each Speaker will discuss his career field with several different groups of students.

D. Three student groups

(1) **Four-Year Group** [2 sections in this category]
   (a) 15-20 students selected from feeder schools for 9th grade entry
   (b) Attend for all 4 years of high school
   (c) Enroll in Workshop (d) Workshop staffed by Career and Success-Control (CSC) counselor and 2 student tutors (who will be present and assist throughout workshop)
   (e) Attend for all 3 hours
   (f) Focus on all the TASKS
   (g) Attend study group and tutoring session
   (h) Qualify to apply for supplies and book stipend and follow-up support
   (i) Workshop procedure <u>**Until** completion of Orientation, the initial Career Tasks, and the Hidden Success Center Tasks</u>
      -- 10 minutes: Relaxation Response [Seated in circle]
      -- 20 minutes: Sharing and Discussion Time [Done seated in a circle. Sharing and discussion of work on previous day during TASK Time.]
      -- 80 minutes: Task Time [work as individual, dyad, and triad]
      -- 60 minutes: Study Group/Tutoring Time
      -- Flex minutes: Time used by Career and Success-Control (CSC) counselor for Private Time with individual students while students engage in Task/Study Group/Tutoring Time
   (j) Workshop procedure <u>**Upon** completion of Orientation, the initial Career Tasks, and the Hidden Success Center Tasks</u>
      -- 10 minutes: Relaxation Response [Seated in circle]
      -- 70 minutes: Sharing and Discussion Time/Task Time [CSC counselor and students determine time division based on interest, need, and continuity. This done each Thursday with adjustments, as

necessary, made during following week. Sharing and discussion always done seated in circle.]
-- 90 minutes: Study Group/Tutoring Time
-- Flex minutes: Time used by CSC counselor for Private Time with individual students while other students engage in Task/Study Group/Tutoring Time

(2) **Two-Year Group** [1 section for 2 years; another section for next 2 years]
 (a) 15-20 students selected from feeder schools for 9th grade entry
 (b) Enroll in Workshop
 (c) Workshop staffed by Career and Success-Control (CSC) counselor and 2 student tutors (who will be present and assist throughout workshop)
 (d) Attend for first 2 years of high school / during junior and senior years, on own time, use Workshop/Resource Room to do the college/postsecondary selection and admission Career Tasks
 (e) Attend for 2 hours / may stay additional hour for study-tutoring
 (f) Focus only on Orientation, Career, and Hidden Success Center Tasks -- *not* on SUCCESS-CONTROL TASKS (although may work on these tasks on their own with aid of counselor and tutors)
 (g) Qualify to apply for supplies and book stipend and follow-up support
 (h) Workshop procedure **Until completion of Orientation and initial Career Tasks** [on their own, will do additional Career Tasks]
   -- 10 minutes: Relaxation Response [Seated in circle]
   -- 20 minutes: Sharing and Discussion Time [Done seated in a circle. Sharing and discussion of work on previous day during TASK Time.]
   -- 80 minutes: TASK Time [work as individual, dyad, and triad]
   -- 60 minutes: Study Group/Tutoring Time for students who wish to stay

-- Flex minutes: Time used by Career and Success-Control (CSC) counselor for Private Time with individual students while students engage in Task/Study Group/Tutoring Time

(i) Workshop procedure **Upon** <u>completion of Orientation and Initial Career Tasks</u> [on their own, will do the other Career Tasks]

-- 10 minutes: Relaxation Response [Sit in circle]
-- 30 minutes: Sharing and Discussion Time [Sit in circle. Share and discuss what is on their mind, personal matters or otherwise.]
-- 70 minutes: Hidden Success Center Task / Study Group / Tutoring Time
-- 60 minutes: Extended Study Group/Tutoring Time for students who wish to stay [may, on their own, do Success- Control Tasks]
-- Flex minutes: Time used by Career and Success-Control (CSC) counselor for Private Time with individual students while other students engage in Task/Study Group/Tutoring Time

(3) **Self-Pace Group** [1 group]
(a) Use AMCAP Resource Room
(b) *All* black male students may use it, not just African-American male students
(c) Attendance is self-determined (same, for example, as use of a library)
(d) No TASK requirements -- students may choose to undertake TASK activities on their own
(e) May form study group and use available assistants
(f) Do not qualify to apply for supplies and book stipend and follow-up support

AMCAP cost

The Afterschool Alliance estimates the average per pupil cost of afterschool programs to be from $673 to $1215 compared to a cost of $10,041 per pupil for studsents enrolled in public elementary and secondary schools for the 2006-2007 school year (296, 419). That means that the per pupil cost for students enrolled in afterschool programs ranges from about 7% to 12% of the per pupil cost for regular, public school instruction.

AMCAP: 2,734,237

The experimental phase of AMCAP will cost considerably more. As conceived, AMCAP will be conducted mainly by full-time professional personnel, the necessity for which was an invaluable lesson learned from its above-described predecessor, MCAP, at Bronx Community College. The intent is to assure, insofar as possible, that the program is tested under conditions which permit a reliable determination of its efficacy, something difficult to do without committed full-time personnel. Otherwise, it is possible for the program to be sound, but not know it because it was not adequately tested due to personnel shortcomings. If the use of professional personnel indicates that the program is worthwhile, then the personnel attributes and other factors which appear to have contributed to its success can be empirically identified and, hopefully, replicated, primarily using trained paraprofessional personnel instead of professional personnel. The Foundation would establish a training unit for this purpose so that the program could be conducted on a cost-effective, yet quality basis. It is futile to develop something that "works," but is too costly to be broadly implemented, which, in effect, would make it "unworkable."

AMCAP's roughly estimated cost is based on a cohort of 80 students enrolled in four AMCAP workshops over a four-year period and an estimated 200 who will use the AMCAP Resource Room over the same period. This membership and usage can be roughly converted into an average program participation of 45 full-time equivalent students, the average used in the cost calculations.

The roughly estimated total cost for its initial experimental phase, covering six years, plus the cost of book, supplies, and stipends would be $2,734,277. That comes to an average annual cost of $455,713. Given 45 students per year, this translates into an annual per pupil cost of $10,127. Using the Afterschool Alliance 2006-2007 data, this cost far exceeds the $1215 Afterschool Alliance estimated to be the maximum cost of afterschool programs and is slightly more than the $10,041 per pupil cost for their regular public school instruction. However, given its experimental nature, the program consists of several components, such as the books and supplies fund, that are not viewed as becoming established adopted features. Moreover, when compared to high-quality preschool experimental programs, such as the **HighScope Perry Preschool Program** (discussed in Chapter 15), it would cost somewhat less: $10,127 versus $12,356.

The categorical costs, listed below, provide insight into the nature of the costs. As customary, the major cost is for personnel (76% of the budget), but attention is directed also to another major cost: books and supplies funds to support students during their college or postsecondary training (17% of the budget).

Personnel	2,028,438
(42% included for fringe benefits)	
Program evaluation	50,000
Student supplies	51,229
(laptop computers, DISCOVER, instructional, and related expenses)	
Student Information System	15,000
Books and Supplies Fund	454,800
(for income-eligible and grade-eligible students during postsecondary education/training)	
Office equipment and supplies	4,200
Travel and conferences	33,200
Indirect costs	72,370
(5% rate - maximum set by Rempson Foundation)	
Discretionary funds	25,000
TOTAL	2,734,237

AMCAP plus Foundation: $3 to $4 million

In addition to the cost of AMCAP, the Rempson Foundation would incur administrative costs as a separate entity itself. Although the program would be set up to be self-contained and self-administered, with an administrative and workshop staff to perform its functions, it requires oversight. In addition, the Rempson Foundation has responsibilities intrinsic to its existence and functions, the performance of which requires a staff of its own. Based on guidelines provided by the Council on Foundations, it is estimated that the budget involved might justify use of a consultant and secretarial help for, perhaps, two days a week (320a). That would amount to an annual general **administrative budget** of roughly **$50,000, or $300,000** over the six-**year period**. That amount is about 11 percent of the cost of AMCAP, below the maximum 15 percent which the Council says should be dedicated to small foundation administrative expenses. Of course, in experimental endeavors, there are always unanticipated costs as ideas and needs emerge which require funds. The foundation would like to be in a financial position to respond.

For the six-year period, AMCAP costs, combined with Rempson Foundation operational costs, would come to an **estimated total of $3 to $4 million**. This amount does not include costs that would be incurred if the Foundation undertakes an **African American Male Self-Advancement Project**, or **AMSAP**, as a complement to its school component, AMCAP, or if resources made it possible for it to undertake some of the activities cited in the last chapter, such as the **Practice of the Art of Loving Guide** and the book, **Black Progress The Booker T. Washington Way: Brains, Property, and Character**. Nor does it, for example, factor in the cost that would be entailed if the Foundation had to rent and equip office space. No foundation officers would be paid staff members.

These costs could be drastically altered, if, as can be dreamed, the Foundation were in a position to employ a Director who, more or less, could be another Booker T. Washington to steer the course of the Foundation for the indefinite future. The idea would be to provide the person the kind of salary and financial commitment, so as to free him up to devote his life to Foundation work, which Andrew Carnegie provided Washington. It is something which dedicated funding would make possible, an equal, in fact, more daunting challenge, of course, being to find another Booker T. Washington. But hope, indeed, springs eternal.

Cost-benefit analysis

How AMCAP would turn out is, of course, unknown, but some cost-benefit perspective is provided by data for three model preschool programs. In calculating return on investment for the threel programs, factors considered were: crime savings, education savings (less need for grade retention and special education placement), increased taxes due to higher lifetime earnings, and welfare savings (441). The returns follow:

- High/Scope Perry Preschool Program: return of $16.14 per dollar invested
- The Caroline Abecedarian Project: return of $3.78 per dollar invested
- Chicago Child-Parent Centers Program: return of $7.10 per dollar invested

Given the expected success of AMCAP, there would be an expected positive return on the dollars invested.

The Plan: Part II, K-Collge (A Vision)

Unlike Part I, Part II of the plan has not been concretized. But it has been conceptually visualized as AMCAP K-8, its broad outlines in place. It is envisioned as an integral component of AMCAP with its specifics tied to what is learned from the early AMCAP years. Its focus would be on grades K-8, the grades prior to the initiation of AMCAP's afterschool program in grade 9. The intent is to have AMCAP serve as a guide for African American male students from grades K-College.

That they will go to college is part of the culture of middle-class children. Not true of most of our poor kids, their life, instead, so often consumed by an array of survival and relationship challenges. But AMCAP would like to make it true -- to have them, too, grow up with the expectation that they are going to go to college or will pursue a career. So beginning in kindergarten, they would be exposed to career exploration. Working with one of the elementary schools -- or with one of the elementary schools and one of the middle schools -- that would be feeders to the high school where AMCAP would be piloted, a career exploration curriculum would be designed and piloted for grades K-8 in those schools.

The curriculum for AMCAP K-8 is envisioned as an adaptation of the high-school-level AMCAP. Of necessity, it would be far less intense, being school-hour rather than afterschool, but, as age-appropriate, like its parent, it would give attention both to students' career and developmental needs and interests. In each school, it might operate from an AMCAP Resource Room, staffed by two AMCAP Resource Assistants, one acting as leader, the other as his assistant, both working under the supervision of a professional counselor or some other designated school personnel. On a scheduled basis, black male students could be sent or escorted to the Resource Room.

The student would graduate with an **AMCAP High School Transition Plan.** The plan would be formulated in a transition planning conference held by the school counselor and participated in by the student and his parents or caretaker and by the AMCAP Resource Room leader. The student and his parents or caretaker would have to approve the transition plan. It would be predicated on the AMCAP dogma that dropping out of school and, consequently, lying around the house and hanging out in the street is not an option. Instead, what the student is expected to do in his transition to high school would be mapped out. Dropping out at some point would only be possible if the student were 19 years of age (not the legal age of 16, 17, or 18 as is variously the case) and had a *viable* job. This rule is not something which AMCAP can impose, but with school, parents, and community working together, it can be made a uniform *local* expectation having the force of a social norm.

If this rule and the underlying expectation are to have real meaning, the students must be given viable options. Otherwise, it becomes trying to force them into that which may or may not suit who they are, which, more or less, sets them up for failure. This is where the **Job Corps** can possibly play a significant role. It appears to do some of the things which

AMCAP proposes to do, and, in the past, this basic education and job-training federally-funded program reportedly has been effective. If AMCAP finds it so, its funding and expansion by policymakers would be up for review, desirably in the context of an overall review of the best use of federal (and state and local) resources. So, inclusive of the Job Corps, AMCAP students would enter high school with realistic options to guide them through their high school years, which would include, but would not be limited to the following options:

1. Continuing with AMCAP through its afterschool program
2. Completing some or all of high school
3. Postsecondary education
4. Military service
5. Getting a GED (General Educational Development) Diploma [all else being equal, a mandatory expectation for students who decide not to complete high school]
6. Entering the Job Corps (at some point)
7. Taking a full-time viable job

The vision is for our AMCAP students -- under the guidance of black male rolo models, the professional staff of the school, and their parents -- to have a guided and planned life and career future rather than to be the victim of default forces, something to which an expanded AMCAP could make a significant contribution. Ideally, we want them to graduate from high school and complete college or postsecondary training, but for some students these may not be realistic goals, in which case, we will not settle for dropping out as an alternative; we will work with them in the exploration and pursuit of such other viable and appropriate alternatives as listed. That mindset is not intended to convey the notion that AMCAP will attempt to do for them that which only they can do for themselves: exert the motivation and hard work which school and life success require. But AMCAP, together with the school and their parents, can attempt to provide them the kind of augmented **"average expectable environment"** (wherein they are provided a sense of security and love) conducive to such motivation and work.

The Plan: Part III, Student AMCAPs (A Vision)

To build Tuskegee, Washington relied upon student labor. In part, the plan is to have AMCAP do likewise. Student labor would take the form of Student AMCAPs. Student AMCAPs would be high school student clubs whose purpose would be to encourage and assist their classmates in the discovery and pursuit of their career pathway. They would (inclusively) use successfully-tried components of the above-described **Self-Pace Group** format. A nucleus, say, of seven or more committed male students would be needed to start a club. There would be no pay or other incentive involved. The Student AMCAPs would function just as any other student club. However, the Rempson Foundation, perhaps in collaboration with the BTW Society, would play a coordination and catalytic role. It would hope to elicit the support of black male athelets and entertainers, provide part-time paraprofessional advisement and assistance, and fund the purchase of equipment and materials.

14

AMCAP Goals, Hypotheses, Methodology

Proverbs, 16:22 - "Understanding is a wellspring of life unto him that hath it: but the instruction of fools is folly."
Galatians, 6:5 - "For every man shall bear his own burden."

Goals

The African American Male Career Pathway Program (AMCAP) has five goals:

1. To enhance students' sense of identity and emotional intelligence (EI) or character
2. To enable students to obtain at least passing grades
3. To enable students to improve their performance on standardized tests
4. To enable students to increase significantly their rate of high school graduation and college/postsecondary entry and completion
5. To foster more responsible fatherhood (as measured by out-of-wedlock births, marriage, child financial support, and child contacts)

Hypotheses

It is hypothesized that these five goals can be achieved through the accomplishment of these ten objectives:

1. To encourage and assist students in discovering and pursuing a career pathway
2. To provide students an environment conducive to their development of a positive core identity
3. To encourage students to **practice the art of loving**
4. To enable students to examine and adjust their time perspective
5. To instill in students a growth mindset which encompasses the key character traits of willpower and grit
6. To help students to achieve their developmental tasks and to cope with their daily needs
7. To enhance students' locus of control and self-esteem
8. To foster peer support and promote students' ability to manage peer pressure
9. To provide students academic support
10. To promote home-community support and school support for students

Methodology

To achieve AMCAP's goals and objectives, the methodology listed below will be used, subject to change as needed.

1. <u>AMCAP Task Guide</u> (curriculum)
2. African-American male counselors
3. Mixed professional and lay staff
4. Single gender
5. Early intervention
6. Intensive and attenuated student participation
7. DISCOVER, an internet-access computerized career discovery program
8. Staff modeling of the *practice of the art of loving*
9. Mind Coach, a system for combating Automatic Negative Thoughts (ANTs)
10. Peer support

11. Participatory, student-centered, *work* environment
12. After-school
13. School integration
14. Parent and Community Coordinator
15. Book stipend
16. College and postsecondary follow-up

Below is a discussion of the rationale for each of the ten hypotheses and an explanation of the activities which comprise the methodology. As regards the five goals, the first goal addresses the thesis for the cause of the African American Male School Adaptability Crisis (AMSAC) and is treated in other chapters. The *more responsible fatherhood* goal has no designated objectives designed to achieve it; rather, its achievement is expected to result, and is intended to result, from the combined accomplishment of all the stated objectives.

Rationale for Hypotheses

1. **To encourage and assist students in discovering and pursuing a career pathway**

This objective reflects the centerpiece of AMCAP: our students' fundamental need to be able to make a living and to forge a positive core identity. As symbolized by the AMCAP logo on the back cover of the book, students are conceived as *working* to find out what they like and what they can do. They *work* to acquire the skills and behaviors that will help them to succeed in doing what they like and can do, and in having a successful life.

This approach echoes Edwin Farrell's advocacy of creating a "meaning system" wherein learning has real-life meaning to teacher and students alike. Both have something to gain that is real to them. In his book, Hanging In and Dropping Out, Farrell tells of his experience with creating such a system in teaching the "Gang of Four," so called because they were problem ninth graders with whom the school did not know what to do (81:154-63). So, Farrell volunteered to be their teacher for one year, creating a curriculum around building himself an energy-efficient house and teaching all of the school requirements as part of the building process. It worked, and Farrell believes that it worked because all of the participants, including himself as teacher, had *something real* to gain. He had a house and the Gang of Four had a defined role in building it. For each, the result was a "meaning system" in which each had a stake.

In AMCAP, the students will not be able to undertake such a real-world project as Farrell and his Gang of Four did, yet, similar to them, they can be enlisted in a "meaning system" wherein they, like their counselor, have something at stake: a career pathway. Their career pathway is conceived as their project and, together with their counselor, their *work* will be to discover and begin its pursuit. Their tools and materials will be the various workshop, school, and community resources available to them. The ultimate tangible payoff will be a career and its rewards. It will come down the road, with the milestones along the way (AMCAP success control tasks achieved, passing grades, high school graduation, postsecondary entry, book stipends) serving as boosters and tangible evidence of *work progress*. Both counselor and students will have a stake in the milestones, each milestone signifying a tangible accomplishment for both.

Their work project addresses two of their fundamental developmental needs: the need to choose an occupation and the need to forge their identity (79:129, 117:62). Erik Erikson and Robert Havighurst stress the significant and interrelated role of both in their development. To grow up means to have a job and to have a job, at least in part, means to have an identity. As Farrell puts it, "The *primary self* that the adolescent strives for... ...can be called "self-as-my-work"; I am a (future) carpenter, lawyer, rock star. Other possible selves are self-in-family, sexual self, self-as-loyal-friend, self-in-peer-group, self-as-student, and for some, self-as-parent" (81:3). Erikson indicates that, therefore, the failure of adolescents to acquire an occupational identity is the something which most unsettles and disturbs them (79:132).

Farrell's study of high school students in New York City reveals, however, that often our minority at-risk students have not developed a self-as-my-work identity (81). They disidentify with the academic domain and, instead, cast their identity with their peer culture. Based on his study of both at-risk and successful New York City high school students, Farrell attributes at-risk students' lack of success to their lack of affiliation. The successful students, he concludes, "hear voices from many different sources--family, pastors, teachers in nonteaching roles, youth workers, and, most of all, peers, but peers who listen to and believe the same voices." In contrast, at-risk students "often hear voices exclusively of their peers; from parents and teachers they only get what they call "a speech" which they reject" (82:5). As a result of these "voices," the successful students seek to escape their limiting environment while the at-risk students get sucked into it. More generally, in their book, <u>Surprising Power of Our Social Networks and How They Shape Our Lives</u>, Christakis and Fowler's thesis is that our connections play a major role in our lives (34).

We must, then, expose our at-risk students to different voices, and, of course, they must be willing, or enticed, to listen. Hence, one method is AMCAP's use of African American mal counselors and staff. Through these connections, we want AMCAP students, like the successful students in Farrell's study, to come to embrace a career. That embrace puts them on the road to a self-as-my-work identity. That identity, in turn, can be expected to foster the motivation required for school success, just as it did for Farrell's successful students.

Citing a comprehensive review of the research by Markus and Nurius (1986), Farrell makes the point that, theoretically, there is a career and an education motivation linkage (163, 77:137). The essence of the theory that explains the linkage is that when one links an outcome to one's possible self, all else being equal, one creates motivation to become (or avoid becoming) that possible self.

Statistical evidence gives credence to this career-motivation linkage (476, 300, 329, 388, 474). The most convincing is provided by a study conducted by Mary G. Visher, Rajika Bhandari, and Eliot Medrich (461a). They expressly addressed the question of whether student participation in career exploration programs affects their high school completion rates and their preparation for college. Career programs consisted of the following: career majors, cooperative education, internship/apprenticeship, job shadow, mentoring, school-sponsored enterprise, and tech prep. To answer their question, they tracked 5,372 students from middle school through high school and into college and careers. They discovered that "neither the percentage of minority students nor the percentage of those in poverty in a school made a significant difference in the rate of participation in career exploration programs."; nor did their level of academic achievement, low-achieving students being as likely to participate as high-achieving students. These were the answers to the questions which they expressly addressed:

- **Students with career exploration experience were significantly more likely to complete high school than students without such experience, even when we controlled for other student and school characteristics.**
- **A higher proportion of high school graduates who had participated in career exploration activities enrolled in college than did nonparticipating graduates, even when we controlled for differences in student and school characteristics.**

2. **To provide students an environment conducive to their development of a positive core identity**

Erikson was cited in Chapter 9 as defining core identity as our **"subjective sense of an invigorating sameness and continuity,"** which, positively possessed, propels our success while, negatively possessed, retards it. From his study of 73 at-risk students in New York City public high schools, almost all African American and Latino from poor and working-class families, Farrell concluded that the failure of the students to integrate their different selves [self-as-my-work, self-in-family, sexual self, self-as-loyal-friend, self-in-peer-group, self-as-student, and for some, self-as-parent] into one identity was the pervasive reason for their dropout (81:8). That is, they failed to acquire a positive **"subjective sense of an invigorating sameness and continuity"** -- or positive core identity -- to sustain and guide them through their interactions, strivings, and challenges.

The intent of AMCAP is to provide its students an environment wherein, when needed, they are able to avoid this pitfall. Essential to such an environment is one wherein they are provided, as will be done, an opportunity to discover and pursue their career pathway; and, wherein, they are supported and assisted in that pursuit. Apparent from the other objectives and from the program activities, they will also be supported and assisted in a variety of other ways. The intent is to provide them, not just **"average expectable environments,"** but **above-average expectable environments** wherein they receive the f security and nurturing (love), the "hallowed presence," Erikson terms it, which characterize such environments.

3. **To encourage students to practice the art of loving**

The rationale for this hypothesis is extensively treated in our <u>AMCAP Task Guide</u> for students, and that extensive treatment is herein abbreviated in the last two chapters. Here, four points are in order.

First, below is the logo that will be used to encourage the **practice of the art of loving**. The logo will be printed on various AMCAP materials and displayed in the AMCAP workshop and Resource Room. It contains the mantra that students will be encouraged (not bludgeoned, just encouraged) to learn and use, and that all AMCAP staff will be required to learn and expected to practice in *all* of their on-job relationships, especially their student relationships.

Second, our target population typically does not come from homes which provide the security and love deemed essential for normal growth and development. Therefore, AMCAP will attempt to provide them an *authoritative community*. That is the kind of community which the Commission on Children at Risk says is essential to combating our crisis of connectedness, a science-based theme echoed by others (34, 23). The scientific, research-based message is that we are social animals, driven from within to connect with one another, and those connections powerfully influence our wellbeing. The **practice of the art of loving**, together with other program components, embodies this message and is a centerpiece of AMCAP.

The African American Male School Adaptability Crisis (AMSAC)

Figure 36. AMCAP logo: Practice of the art of loving. Copyright © by Joe Louis Rempson.

Third, the **practice of the art of loving** provides students a values framework which enables them to define or refine an ideology. It is psychologically-based, and whether religious or non-religious, students can use it as a behavioral and action guide. Such a guide can help them to fulfill their developmental need to make sense of and navigate the world about them (117:69-75). That fulfillment, combined with a career choice, is basic to their forging of a positive core identity.

Fourth, and the point that will be made with students, because of its ability to catalyze the human spirit, engagement in the **practice the art of loving** will help provide students the energy, drive, and direction which they need to achieve the five program goals. It can serve to help combat the low-effort syndrome of which John Ogbu speaks and the kind of disruptive classroom and school behavior which impedes learning and school retention.

4. **To enable students to examine and adjust their time perspective**

In their book, The Time Paradox: The New Psychology of Time That Will Change Your Life, Philip Zimbardo and John Boyd report the conclusion that **"time matters, no matter who you are, where you live, *how old you are* or what you do"** [emphases added] (294:26). It is based on over 30 years of research involving over 10,000 people around the world, and they conclude that time matters because -- without realizing it -- we think what we think, feel what we feel, and do what we do *because of our time perspective*. From their research, they have identified six time perspectives, which are shown in the logo below and which are discussed in Chapter 4.

Figure 37. AMCAP logo: time perspective.
Copyright © by Joe Louis Rempson.

A study by Mello supports their conclusion in regard to the school achievement of 310 low-income African American 10th, 11th, and 12th graders (280 males and 125 females) (408). It revealed that, controlling for socioeconomic status, grade, and gender, future orientation predicted their grade point average (GPA). Students with a high future orientation have a higher GPA.

Whatever our time perspective, Zimbardo and Boyd say that, through effort, we can change it. The goal, they state, is to have a balanced time perspective, one that "will allow you to flexibly shift from past to present to future in response to the demands of the situation facing you so that you can make optimal decisions" (294:26). It is that goal which our African American male students, in particular, need to achieve in order to adapt to the demands of the school. Making use of the logo, AMCAP will seek to help them achieve it.

5. **To instill in students a growth mindset which encompasses the key character traits of willpower and grit**

In Chapter 12, these traits are discussed extensively. The research shows that they are powerfully associated with school and life success (6b, 332a, 332b). The research also shows that they stand out, for males in particular, as glaring weaknesses of our African American students. John Ogbu characterizes them as having a *low-effort syndrome* (195:452). They do not work hard enough, nor behave well enough (43, 229, 345). That they do not work hard enough, nor behave well enough, prevents them from amplifying their intelligence. Research suggests that working hard and behaving properly behaving can enable students to amplify their intelligence. This, in particular, is the position of Carol Dweck (68, 69) [see also Casey Carter (29) and Chua and Rubenfeld (34a)]. The thesis herein is that these character deficits are the main cause of AMSAC. Therefore, in AMCAP, an attempt will be made to instill these traits, both in the way the program is conducted (learn by doing) and through individual and group activities.

6. **To help students achieve their developmental tasks and to cope with their daily needs**

Robert J. Havighurst introduced the concept of developmental task to the field of education and defines it thus:

> A developmental task is a task which arises at or about a certain period in the life of the individual, successful achievement of which leads to his happiness and to success with later tasks, while failure leads to unhappiness in the individual, disapproval by the society, and difficulty with later tasks (117:2).

For adolescents, the current focus of AMCAP, he enumerated eight such tasks:

1. Achieving new and more mature relations with age-mates of both sexes
2. Achieving a masculine or feminine social role
3. Accepting one's physique and using the body effectively
4. Achieving emotional independence of parents and other adults

5. Preparing for marriage and family life
6. Preparing for an economic career
7. Acquiring a set of values and an ethical system as a guide to behavior--developing an ideology
8. Desiring and achieving socially responsible behavior

For AMCAP, these tasks have been reconceptualized in response to certain programmatic emphases and to the pecial considerations presented by our students. Those special considerations pertain to such subcultural peer expectations as toughness, language, male-female relationships, and to home and community factors which may impede their task achievement (152). The idea was to interpret Havighurst's tasks in the context of these considerations, giving attention to the particular personal, peer, family, and community needs of our black male students – an endeavor informed by some of what we have learned from study and research, as discussed in Chapters 5, 6, 7, and 9.

The outcome is in our <u>AMCAP Task Guide</u> (225). In it, Havighurst's tasks have been reconceptualized mainly as *AMCAP Success Control Tasks*. They are:

1. Achieving mind control
2. Achieving health and body control
3. Achieving sex and sexual relationship control
4. Achieving identity control
5. Achieving communication control
6. Achieving coping and relationship control
7. Achieving substance control
8. Achieving support system and recreational control
9. Achieving money control

We want our black male students, who typically have to fend for themselves since their fathers are so often absent, to be more able to do so. We want them to come to feel that their success is in their hands and not dependent upon anyone else. Hence, the term "success control." The methodology used, though structured, will be informal and organic. In daily group discussion and individual outreach, AMCAP will draw upon resource materials listed in its <u>AMCAP Task Guide</u>.

This task is classified under what is broadly termed humanistic education. It has also been called affective education, emotional intelligence, social skills, interpersonal skills, self science, social awareness, and social and emotional growth. Content and approach vary, but the guiding philosophy of humanistic education is that "educators must assess [and respond to] the learner's needs for physical security, love, creative expression, cognitive mastery, social competency, and self-worth" to enable learning to occur and to promote "joyous, humane, meaningful living" (262:13-24; 24).

The most convincing research evidence found in support of its potential efficacy is provided by the Wellness Centers in 15 San Francisco high schools (314a). The Centers provide individual/group counseling and psychological services to teacher-referred and self-referred students. Indicative of the need, in 2010, almost half of the students, in the 15 schools of more than 7,000 students, used its services, the total usage (counting repeat visits) being 17,000 visits. A survey of teachers who made referrals showed that 75% reported improved academic success by students referred, and 86% reported an improvement in the students' emotional wellbeing. Following are findings from a survey of the student users themselves: 81 report coming to school more often and 69% reported academic improvement. Although these data fall far short of hard evidence, they provide support for at least the potential value of the services – and of a similar emphasis. Otherwise, the research evidence is mixed (308; 386; 451; 102:305-309).

Relevant, too, are such early interventions as the Perry Preschool Program and the Abecedarian Early Childhood Intervention Project, discussed in Chapter 16. In those interventions, the decisive variable in the success of the children turned out to be, not their test scores -- which in fact regressed over time -- but the noncognitive skills (emotional intelligence or character) which they acquired. And, in substance, that is what this objective addresses: the noncognitive skills (emotional intelligence or character) of the students.

7. **To enhance students' locus of control and self-esteem**

The crucial role of locus of control in school and life success is extensively documented in the literature. Locus of control refers to our perception about the underlying main causes of events in our lives -- whether we think those causes are mainly controlled by us or by external forces. If we believe that the causes stem mainly from our own decisions and efforts, we are said to have an *internal locus of control*. If, on the other hand, we believe that the causes stem mainly from fate, luck, the system, or some other external entity, we are said to have an *external locus of control*. The discussion of Victimology in Chapter 11 gives extensive treatment to this personality dynamic and presents a case for the efficacy of an internal locus of control. The essence of that case is made by social psychologist, David Myers, in his classic textbook, Social Psychology. Summarizing the research, he tells us that "Those who see themselves as internally controlled are more likely to do well in school, successfully stop smoking, wear seat belts, deal with marital problems directly, make lots of money, and delay gratification in order to achieve long-term goals" (186:59; see also, for example, 40, 229, 309).

Whether locus of control is an underlying personality trait or a learned attribute is a question raised in the literature. Some evidence suggests the latter, showing it to be a response to circumstances, and that its modification is subject to psychological and educational interventions (424). This hypotheses is based on that evidence.

Self-esteem is the regard (like or dislike) in which students hold themselves, whether, for example, they regard themselves as intelligent or attractive. The regard can be low or high. Once hailed as a kind of cure-all, its positive consequences have been challenged. From a comprehensive study of the research, Roy Baumeister and his colleagues conclude that most of the evidence indicates that it has no impact on academic achievement (305). High self-esteem, they point out, can even be a curse – fostering narcissism, self-deception, a sense of superiority, seductive pleasure, aggression, and alienation from others.

Further negating its academic impact, in their alluded to study of successful immigrant groups, Amy Chua and Jed Rubenfeld conclude that, rather than high self-esteem, these groups exhibit low self-esteem, a sense of insecurity or not feeling satisfied about themselves, versus a sense of security, or feeling satisfied or good about themselves (34a:10-11, 85-115, 212-14). The feeling of not being good enough motivates them and, consciously or unconsciously, they even promote it. As for academic achievement, they reveal that Asian American students report the lowest self-esteem while achieving the highest grades. So, they conclude, the idea that failing grades by minority students reflect their low self-esteem is not supported by the evidence.

Nevertheless, Baumeister and his colleagues conclude that the finding that high self-esteem does not translate into school success does not mean that we should not foster it. For the research shows that high self-esteem can foster happiness, initiative, and resilience. Those who possess it are more likely to use adaptive, self-regulating strategies -- better coping with adversity and persisting in the face of setbacks.

They say what we should *not* do is to foster high self-esteem as "an end in itself," which Chua and Rubenfeld also cite as the curse of the self-esteem movement. Instead, we should link it to specific behaviors and foster it as it pertains to the learning and improvement of those behaviors. Both praise and criticism, rather than praise only, would be integral to this linkage.

Carol Dweck and the growth mindset advocates go a step further (68:149-55). In their thinking, ability or talent is never praised or prized, only effort. Disappointments and failures are neither good nor bad. They are opportunities for improvement. Risks are not something to be feared. Instead, they should be viewed as opportunities for growth. And self-esteem is not a feeling to be imparted, but an experience derived continually from the outcomes which accrue from engagement in challenging tasks.

AMCAP will be guided by this new thinking. It will link self-esteem to the students' behaviors and specific outcomes, but from the perspective of the effort put into their achievement versus the achievements themselves, although that does not entirely rule out some attention to those achievements. The intent is to make the *effort* entailed paramount, serving as the main factor in praise and criticism. If Dweck and others are right, as a result the students, in turn, are likely continually to *experience* a sense of elevated esteem from the rewards they derive from their praised effort. Of course, in AMCAP, we are not talking about self-esteem, nor about any of the other program components, as an isolated pursuit, but as part of a gestalt permeated by the **practice of the art of loving**.

8. **To foster peer support and promote students' ability to manage peer pressure**

Peer pressure is a powerful force in the life of children and youth, especially our children and youth, in whose life it tends to exert an inordinate influence. It can make or break them. Steven Pinker, drawing inclusively upon the work of Judith Rich Harris (groundbreaking author of The Nurture Assumption), asserts that the behavior of adolescents is influenced more by their peers than by their parents (210:390-91;115).

The five resilient students in Roderick's study knew that peer pressure could break them. It could take them away from staying in, studying and striving, and lead them into "going out" and "hanging out" (229). So they acquired an alternate identity that allowed them to break away and find their social support elsewhere. The successful students in Farrell's study knew and did the same, and when they did keep close peer ties, they chose peers who were supportive. Farrell observes that, in comparison to students from the same socioeconomic environment who attended an elite high school on the campus of his college, these successful students "may have every positive advantage" that the students in the elite high schools have, "except for one. They do not have the peer-support system in their school that validates and maintains their symbolic universes. On the contrary, they may have to contend with deviant universes" (81:143).

Both cases provide guidance for our African American male students: to succeed, they must manage the peer pressure that will lead them into "going out" and "hanging out" in contrast to "staying in" and "hanging in." And to be able to manage it, they need the encouragement and assistance of the school. That is what AMCAP intends to provide for them, and that is what the Roderick and Farrell studies show can be a determinative factor in their success. So do an abundance of other studies, some discussed in Chapters 5 and 6 dealing, respectively, with the culture of our students and with the "acting white" controversy.

9. **To provide students academic support**

A repeated research finding is that our African American male students suffer disproportionately from disproportionate skill deficits which magnify as they move through the grades and the subject matter gets harder. In their studies, both Farrell and Roderick, for example, refer to it, and Sharon Lewis and her colleagues at the Council of the Great City School, cited in Chapter 2, devote their entire study to it. Through peer tutoring and study groups, AMCAP will address this challenge.

10 **To promote home-community support and school support for students**

The aforementioned cited qualitative studies of Roderick, Farrell, and Carter all point to the positive role of home-school-community support on student success. As factors in the success of the five resilient students she studied, Roderick cites their *strong family support* and a *high level of nonfamily support*, such as, from church and male mentors. She cites, too, school support in the form of teacher recognition and outreach. Farrell turned up similar results in his study of the 73 at-risk and 67 successful New York City high school minority students. In contrast to the at-risk students, the successful ones had positive family relationships and the support of a social network, that network for many being the church. Teacher support, too, was important to the students. Its noteworthy role in the achievement of minority students is revealed in other studies as well (40:316-19; 263; 309; 348). And Carter found that one of the seven common traits of the 21 high-performing, high-poverty schools that he studied was "principals working actively with parents" (29). All underline an observation made by Noguera, namely, that "Urban schools are increasingly the most reliable source of stability and social support for poor children" (191:231).

Statistical evidence supports these largely qualitative conclusions. Olsen and Fuller cite the analysis of Henderson and Berla (1994), encompassing 85 studies, that showthe benefits of parent involvement ranging from "better grades, test scores, and attendance" to "fewer children...being placed in special education and remedial classes" (202:129-130; see also Ronald Ferguson, 348:20, and, D'Agostino, Hedges, and Borman, 54, and Chapter 3). In regard both to home and to school support, Payne discusses research which shows that schools characterized by high-press and high-support turn out high-achieving, high-performing students (208a:96-120). High support, in addition to peer support, includes home and school support.

A recent study by Keith Robinson and Angel Harris, cited in Chapter 3, showing that, in general, parental involvement does not affect student academic success one way or the other might appear to undermine the need for parental support, but the authors say that their findings do not apply to what they term "socioeconomically disadvantaged youth," and they offer this general conclusion: "We believe that parents are critical to how well children perform in school, just not in the conventional ways that our society has been promoting" (227a:224-27; 438g).

Methodology

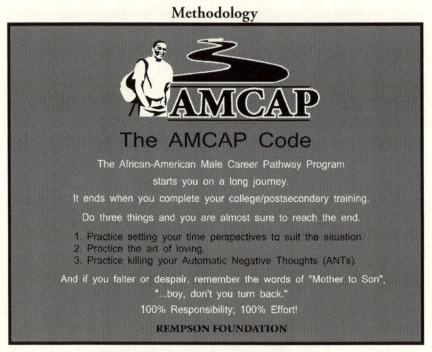

Figure 38. AMCAP logo: AMCAP Code.
Copyright © by Joe Louis Rempson.

The 16 activities which follow are those which research and experience suggest would enable the program to achieve its goals and objectives. They are expected to result in what can be called an AMCAP culture.

That culture is captured in the AMCAP Code, shown above, which will be prominently displayed in AMCAP materials, and constantly reinforced.

1. **AMCAP Task Guide** (curriculum)

One feature frequently cited as an element of successful afterschool programs is the existence of structured activities. Durlak and Weissberg's meta-analysis of studies of 73 programs, for example, concluded that all 39 which used an evidence-based approach yielded significant positive results on all seven outcomes measured, while none of the 27 which did not use an evidence-based approach yielded positive outcomes on any of the seven outcomes (334). They define evidence-based training as training that, as regards content, focuses on specific social skills and, as regards process, uses a sequenced set of activities and active forms of learning. The aforementioned AMCAP Task Guide, written specifically for AMCAP students, meets these criteria.

2. **African American male guides**

The use of African American male guides is the operational backbone of the program. The rationale for their use is presented in Chapter 15. Not only is their use the backbone of the proposed AMCAP, their use is also seen as an indispensable part of the proposed community component. With AMCAP's school component and community component, we are trying to reach and influence black males. The belief is that black males stand the best chance of reaching other black males.

3. **Mixed professional and lay staff**

Afterschool programs often do not and, maybe, in some cases, need not rely on professional personnel. However, according to Reisner and his colleagues' evaluation of 96 after-school projects in New York City, those associated with the greatest benefits had at least one staff member with a professional degree (437). Based on her extensive afterschool program research, Fashola arrives at a similar finding (83:39-40). Experience with MCAP (Minority Male Career Pathway Program), the predecessor of AMCAP, likewise, supports the need for use of professional personnel.

Reliance by afterschool programs on full professional staffing can be said to be as financially prohibitive as it is unnecessary and, otherwise, unrealistic. Beyond that, the Commission on Children at Risk deems it undesirable. It conceives the work of its *authoritative communities* being "performed largely by non-specialists" (41:37). That is AMCAP's vision as well, that particularly being the case since the program is intended to effect cultural change. That change has to emanate from within, emerging through the experiences and imprint accrued, not by professional change agents, but by those in whom change is sought. The target population must mainly do the work and carry the ball. The professional staff has an indispensable role to play, but that role is to provide certain expertise and guidance, not to be the workhorse for the program. The use of indigenous lay personnel will be incorporated from the outset and expanded as rapidly as possible.

4. **<u>Single gender</u>**

Called into question by Title IX, which, in 1972, banned sex discrimination in public schools, the legality of single-sex classes and schools is no longer a legal issue (230:150-87; 418). It was settled by an amendment in 2002 to the No Child Left Behind Act which explicitly permits single-sex classes and schools, and, in 2006, the United States Department of Education issued its newest regulations governing the Act's implementation.

Therefore, there is no legal challenge to the single-gender focus of AMCAP. Its afterschool program is seen as an integral and extended component of a traditional coeducational setting. No brief is herein being made for or against single-sex education. AMCAP reflects what an increasing number of public schools are now experimenting with during the school day: single-gender classes (55:141-42; 127:29-40; 259:201-24; 383). In fact, while in the mid-1990s, there were only two single-sex public schools, today over 500 public schools in 40 states offer single-sex academic classes, and, though rarely, some are entirely single sex (395b).

The evidence regarding the benefits of single-sex education, be it on a single school basis or an integrated basis, while mixed, does show some positive outcomes for African-American male students, as well as for

African-American female students (55:141-42; 127:15-16; 230:188-236; 259:226). Already cited are the positive locus of control and self-esteem outcomes of MCAP, the predecessor of AMCAP -- outcomes echoed in the high praise the students gave the program and the seeming therapeutic function which they felt it served. Similar social outcomes have been found in other studies. When it comes to academics, Tyre, likr Salome, concludes that, though the evidence is mixed, when wealth advantage is controlled, "What we know is that all-boys and all-girls schools seem to provide academic benefits for girls and *poor African-American boys* [emphasis added]" (259:224; see also 230:235-36). However, a recent review of existing research by Diane F. Halpern and others came to a contrary conclusion: that single-sex education does not improve academic achievement, resulting, instead, in reinforcing sex stereotypes (395b). There is no indication, however, that Halpern's review also contradicts the finding that single-sex education benefits poor black male students.

5. **Early intervention**

The African American Male Career Pathway Program (AMCAP) began with the idea of an afterschool program for older adolescents, ages 14-17, in grades 9-12. From the literature and further reflection, it became increasingly clear, however, that to be most effective, intervention must be begin earlier -- at least during younger adolescence when students are more likely to be receptive and, ideally, starting in kindergarten. So while at its outset, AMCAP will stick to its original afterschool program design, the intent is to later, guided by experience gained and by feasibility, expand AMCAP to incorporate grades 1 through 12, similar to what was done by Holland in PROJECT 2000. The conception is to have AMCAP in grades 9-12 serve as the foundation and bridge for the program, linking elementary school and postsecondary education and training.

Without any known exception, early intervention is supported, even urged (10, 75, 123, 127, 166, 235, 255, 406). Indicative of the rationale is the following observation of retired black educational psychologist, Dr. Spencer Holland, whose PROJECT 2000 was discussed in Chapter 15:

It is during the primary years that children's attitudes toward the educational enterprise are established. My experiences working with PROJECT 2000 have convinced me that many, if not most, students who eventually drop out of the educative process often do so emotionally and psychologically by the end of third grade. Further, as I have maintained for many years, students *learn to read* [emphasis in original] from first through third grades, while they *read to learn* [emphasis in original] from fourth grade through graduate and professional school (123:320).

Drawing upon the research, Silverstein and Krate quote Bloom as presenting "data showing that grades one through three represent 'the most important growing period for academic achievement and that all subsequent learning in the school is affected and in large part determined by what the child has learned by the age of nine or by the end of grade three'" (235:230).

Evidence of the effectiveness of early intervention is based mainly on three model programs, each of which was based on randomized trials: the **HighScope Perry Preschool Program** in Ypsilanti, Michigan (1962-65), the **Early Training Project** in Murfreesboro, Tennessee (1962-64)), and the **Carolina Abecedarian Early Childhood Intervention Project** at the University of North Carolina (1972-77). The evaluation of a similar regular program, the Title I **Chicago Child-Parent Centers Program** (started in 1967 and evaluated 19 years later in 1986) also gets considerable attention. Indicative of the pattern of outcomes achieved by these and similar high-quality programs are those achieved by the **HighScope Perry Preschool Program** (441, 442, 451c). Follow-up studies, through age 27, show that, in comparison to the no-program group:

- The program *group* had significantly higher monthly earnings, higher percentages of home ownership, higher levels of school completion, lower percentages receiving social services, and fewer arrests, including arrests for drug making or dealing.
- The *females* had significantly higher monthly earnings, fewer who spent time in programs for educable mental impairment, a higher level of school completed, and a higher marriage rate.

- The program *males* had a significantly lower percentage receiving social service, fewer lifetime arrests, and a higher percentage of home ownership.
- The program *group* had significantly higher IQs from the end of their first year in the program to the end of first grade (age 7), higher school achievement at age 14, higher general literacy at age 19, and fewer years in programs for educable mental impairment.

A follow-up study of the Abecedarian Project group, through their mid-30s, found still another benefit: they turned out to be far healthier (451d).

In contrast to these model programs, the research consensus is that the outcomes for the program, **Head Start,** the comparable large-scale public school program, are short-lived. Participants at the end of first grade are little different from nonparticipants (304a; 366a; 380b; 441; 459a). But, in a departure, a study by Sherri Oden and her colleagues does show similar long-term effects, *but not for males* (193a, 380b).

However, partly conflicting critiques have been made of the programs. Nobel Prize-winning University of Chicago economist, *James Heckman*, in collaboration with several of his colleagues, defends their effectiveness and makes them a factor in his advocacy of early intervention (258:188-94; 349). The other factor is his study of General Educational Development (GED) recipients (258:191). He found that, although they had a GED and scored higher on intelligence (IQ) tests, they earned no more than high school dropouts. Heckman reasoned that this is because they "lack all of the noncognitive skills [emotional intelligence] that a person must possess in order to make it through high school: patience, persistence, self-confidence, the ability to follow instructions, the ability to delay gratification for a future reward" (258:191). Since the model program participants did not retain their early IQ gains, but did retain their emotional and social gains, he reasoned that it is these factors – not cognitive factors -- which account for their success. As quoted by Paul Tough, Heckman's conclusion, in collaboration with a colleague, Dimitriy Masterovas, came to be, "'Skill begets skill; learning begets learning. Early disadvantage, if left untreated, leads to academic and social difficulties in later years. Advantages accumulate;

so do disadvantages'" (258: 193). And his research suggests that those advantages and disadvantages are more emotional than cognitive.

However, UC Berkeley economist, *Michael Anderson*, finds only partial support for the positive outcomes (301:1). He found significant short-term and long-term benefits for girls, but not for boys. Regarding high school graduation, in particular, he reports sizable and, for the Perry preschoolers, statistically significant increases for girls, while for boys the effects were "weak or negative." "Graduation rates," he, in fact, reports, "*decline* [emphasis in the original] by 10 and 6 percentage points for Abecedarian and Perry males respectively," whereas Early Training males were 10 percentage points less likely to drop out, but this outcome was not statistically significant. For boys, then, his findings are similar to the cited Head Start findings of Sherri Oden and her colleagues.

Project New Hope, however, shows how problematic it can be to try to intervene down the road, financial and other incentives notwithstanding (324). Project New Hope was a three-year Milwaukee experiment, 1995-98, that guaranteed its 678 black and Hispanic participants from its two poorest zip codes a 30-hour workweek with generous benefits. Interpretation of its success are mixed, but a couple of facts stands out: only 27 percent of participants stayed in the program and worked themselves out of poverty versus 19 percent in the control group who worked themselves out; and their high level of depression and low self-esteem upon entry remained unchanged (324, 333). The boys, but not the girls, of the participants seem to have gained more than the participants themselves, significantly improving their academic and behavior performance. Maybe structure and adult socialization were factors that affected the boys more than the girls – as the research points to boys being more influenced by environmental factors than girls. In any instance, Project New Hope reminds us of what the research evidence shows: focus on our students at an early age, even indirectly it seems, or -- our best efforts notwithstanding -- lose most of them forever.

To summarize:

Experience and research evidence suggest that early intervention, beginning at the preschool ages of 3 and 4, is essential if we are to normalize the school success of our black students, males and females alike. Success is questionable in the case of black males, however, since early intervention alone has not shown significant lasting outcomes for them. To a considerable extent, the reason might might be due to the common absence of black male role models in these programs and in their lives.

6. Intensive and attenuated student participation

Any educator knows how essential it is to be able to work with students for extended period of time to get desired results. A major frustration in working with students in the above referenced MCAP was the limitation of time and follow-up with the students, particularly at the high school level. To see them once or twice a week -- or on some intermittent basis -- does not allow for either the cultivation of more productive relationships or adequate attention to student needs. Drawing upon her extensive youth work experience, Jane Quinn of the DeWitt Wallace-Reader's Digest Fund recommends the following as one of the principles that should guide the adoption of best practices in serving young black males:, "Programs for young black males should be intense enough to make a difference in their lives." She adds: "The need for change in this direction is supported by a growing body of literature ...indicating that _sustained_ and _comprehensive_ interventions are needed to effect real change in the lives of disadvantaged youth" [emphases added] (214:139; see also Carter, 29:1, and Reisner and colleagues, 473).

7. DISCOVER, an internet-access computerized career discovery program

DISCOVER is a program of the nonprofit national and international educational organization, the American College Testing Program (ACT), started in 1959. It is internet-accessible for grades 9-12. AMCAP intends to provide students their own laptop computers to access it. Not only will it serve as a career-discovery program, but it will also be used to follow up students at the postsecondary school level. A review of 28 investigations evaluating its effectiveness shows that while it "increases users' vocational identity, level of career development, and career decision-making self-efficacy," its results are mixed when it comes to "increasing career decidedness, occupational certainty, career maturity, and career exploration." Taber and Luzzo, who undertook the review, report that it is "most effective when used in conjunction with additional career exploration and planning activities (e.g., individual counseling and group workshops)" (252:ii). That is exactly what AMCAP envisions; it is not meant to be used as a stand alone resource.

8. **Staff modeling of the *practice of the art of loving***

Mindful of the adage "practice what you preach," all AMCAP staff will be required to understand what AMCAP teaches about the **practice of the art of loving** *and* to implement it in *all* student and other in-school contacts.

9. **Mind Coach**

Mind Coach is a system developed by Dr. Daniel G. Amen, world renown psychiatrist, bestselling author, and head of his highly acclaimed brain science clinic which bears his name, Amen Clinic. *Mind Coach* is a tool for combating Automatic Negative Thoughts (ANTs). In the introduction to his book, Mind Coach: How to Teach Kids and Teenagers to Think Positive and Feel Good, Amen explains the rationale for its use:

> Everything starts and ends in your mind. How your mind works determines how happy you are, how successful you feel and how well you interact with other people. The patterns of your mind encourage you toward greatness or they cause you to flounder in mediocrity or worse. Learning how to focus and direct your mind is the most important ingredient of success (4:5).

The logo which follows will be used to help students and staff to come, over time, to master the tool.

**Figure 39. AMCAP Code: Ant Killer.
Copyright © by Joe Louis Rempson.**

10. **Peer support**

Trained upper classmen will be paid to serve as counselor assistants in the AMCAP workshops and in the Resource Room, preference being given to AMCAP graduates as the program progresses. In addition, the workshops and Resource Room will be structured so as to foster student-student interaction and the development of mutually supportive peer relationships. A major reason to have both a Resource Room and Career Fairs open to all African American and other black male students in the school, and not just to AMCAP workshop students, is to extend the reach of AMCAP to all of the black male students in the school, thereby possibly enhancing its standing among them and their support of one another in subscribing to its values.

11. **Participatory, student-centered, *work* environment**

In their child rearing, poor African American parents (in contrast to our middle-class parents) tend to be authoritarian and restrictive (46:57-97; 235:40-60; 258: 41-52). Silverstein and Krate, in particular, paint a picture the following picture of their inhibiting and controlling behavior.

> When a parent spoke to a child, it was frequently with the intent of stopping the child from continuing with an activity. Communication flowed from the parent to the child; the child was not encouraged to speak up or to answer. The inhibiting signals were frequently quite sharp if not rejecting in tone and were restricted to a small number of key words carrying maximum restrictive impact: Stop that! Come here! Don't touch that! Children were often ridiculed and shamed. We heard relatively few exchanges between mothers and children in which the children were encouraged to ask questions or to verbalize their personal concerns (235:52).

This kind of behavior results in children ill-equipped for school or life success. They tend to turn out underdeveloped, frustrated, angry, and maladjusted. Whether our prospective AMCAP students have been so reared or not, the intent is to have them participate in the management of their work environment and in the planning, conduct, and evaluation of their workshop activities. That is how we contribute to autonomous, self-disciplined, assertive, and successful adults. It is the kind of guidance that John Dewey thought the school ought to provide. As he put in in his <u>The Child and the Curriculum</u>, "Guidance is not external imposition. It is freeing the life process for its own most adequate fulfilment" (57:17).

12. **Afterschool**

With the passage of the 21st Century Community Learning Centers Act (21CCLC), in 1994, as part of the Elementary and Secondary Education Act, the federal government began funding afterschool programs. Allocated to states based on their share of Title I funds, the funding has risen from $40 million in 1998 to $1.16 billion in 2010. States competitively award the funds to schools and to community-based and faith-based organizations, the average expenditure per project in 2000-02 in New York City being $187,581 and the nationwide grant average for 2006 being $310,685 [a grant typically funding three centers] (296) States themselves also provide funding, as do private entities, which also provide other forms of support.

The Afterschool Alliance -- a partnership among the U. S. Department of Education, the Mott Foundation, and a number of industries and private foundations -- reports that "There are now [2010] nearly 3,000 grants funding afterschool programs for more than 1 million children and youth in 9,634 school-based and community-based centers [most housed in schools] across the country" (296). Still, the demand far exceeds availability, the Alliance indicating that while 8.4 million children are enrolled in afterschool programs, if they were available, parents of 18.5 million children say that they would enroll them.

While the funding emphasis is on afterschool activities which foster academic achievement, the funds are also used to support an array of social service, cultural, and recreational needs. Studies of the activities tend to show positive academic, personal, and social outcomes (296, 313, 334, 338, 437). Improved math and reading grades, along with better behavior and attendance, for example, have been found; so have higher aspirations, greater self-confidence, and a decrease in delinquency. Of particular interest, as related by Durlak and Weissberg, "One review of 35 studies reported that the test scores of low-income, at-risk youth improved significantly in both reading and mathematics after they participated in after-school programs" (334).

The foregoing suggests that the afterschool feature of AMCAP represents an established, popular, and potentially effective means of meeting the needs of our African American male students.

13. **School integration**

Unlike the typical afterschool program, AMCAP is conceived as an integral part of the school. Instead of an *extra*, it is envisioned as an *integra*l to be run as an extension of the regular school day for a subset of students. Program components -- over time – will be incorporated into the day school curriculum as advisable and feasible. The program itself will, eventually (give it a generation or so), be phased out. The idea is not to institutionalize it, but rather to use it as a bridge to regular school program.

The AMCAP Coordinator *and* the school principal would be responsible for its operation. The Coordinator would be chosen by the Foundation. Then, he would be responsible for selecting the participating school. The position would be full-time, and the Coordinator would have a work schedule adjusted to meet program needs (an afternoon-evening schedule instead of a morning-afternoon schedule). He would act as an agent of the Foundation and, on the authority of the principal, would also be the principal investigator. As agreed upon, he would participate in the same activities as other school administrators. This structure is intended (inclusively) to gain support from teachers and staff, thereby enabling AMCAP to reach more students and to garner reinforcement of program efforts. Further, the interaction between the Coordinator and school which the structure provides for should increase the chances of creating an AMCAP culture wherein its values get discussed and accepted and, wherein, its effective components get integrated.

14. **Parent and Community Coordinator**

Any number of urban schools have recognized the additional demands and importance of trying to increase parent and community involvement and cooperation, and, accordingly, have often added or designated a position to perform the function, such as parent coordinator or school-community director (222). Especially because of the cultural change it seeks, AMCAP probably will not succeed unless it is able to enlist the aid of parents and community. It is unlikely to enlist that aid without allocating – as intended -- dedicated staff (a Parent and Community Coordinator) -- to the effort. David Kennedy's Operation Ceasefire and Overt Market strategy, for example, underscores the need for, and value of, such involvement (144b).

15. **Book stipend**

Financial aid notwithstanding, many programs recognize the need to assist college students with their book costs (321c). Those costs have become astronomical, far outpacing, for example, the increased cost of medical care. Books average about $1200 a year for the typical college student (383b). Consequently, many students forgo buying some of their books, instead, borrowing books from friends or using library copies. Others, for example, are forced to take on part-time work. As a remedy, in AMCAP, for the duration of their postsecondary education, graduates who meet certain grade and income criteria will be provided a book stipend. In addition to assisting them with their book costs so they can maximize their study time, the stipend is designed – in the first place – to encourage students to undertake postsecondary education.

16. **College and postsecondary follow-up**

The research, already discussed, accents the decisive role that teachers and outside contacts can play in the success of black students, in the absence of which, students can easily succumb to the retarding and wayward forces which often surround them. Support them and you provide them that which they too commonly lack: nurturing and direction. That is what AMCAP intends to do. In addition to the book stipend, AMCAP counselors will follow them through the completion of their college or postsecondary education -- keeping in contact, providing counseling, and serving as a resource in times of need. One possible means whereby this might be done is a requirement that, until they graduate, their semester grades must be submitted to AMCAP, possibly some system being devised whereby this would be done automatically.

15

The Case For AMCAP Use of African American Male Counselors

> *Proverbs, 16:22 – "Understanding is a wellspring of life unto him that hath it: but the instruction of fools is folly."*
> *Galatians, 6:5 - "For every man shall bear his own burden."*

We African American males are responsible for our African American Male School Adaptability Crisis (AMSAC) and its inseparable social problems and it is we who bear the primary responsibility for solving it. One can dispute the truth of this proposition, but what one cannot dispute is that it is we, and a disproportionate number of our people, especially those in poverty, who, in one way or another, are suffering. And when one suffers one is obligated to do what one can to assuage the suffering. Maybe others can and should help, but quite aside from what they can or should do, one has an obligation to do for oneself. And when it comes to our school crisis, the thesis herein is that *only* we African American males can do what has to be done. The same logic applies to the social problems from which our school crisis is inseparable because to solve those problems we need to reach our black males, and it is other black males who stand the best chance of reaching them. As regards our school crisis, the case for this logic is laid out in this chapter.

The Thesis

The thesis is that **the solution of our African American Male School Adaptability Crisis (AMSAC) requires our students to make planned cultural changes, it being possible to bring about such changes, on an expansive scale, only through the use of African American males.**

Preferable but not mandatory?

Some say that it is important, or preferable, but not essential, for our black males to have African American male guides or teachers as models; all that is needed is a person, male or female, with the requisite interest and skills (85:84; 255:10). However, the goals of the African American Male Career Pathway Program (AMCAP) goes further. It is guided by the proposition that, in its program, the use of African American males as guides is not just important or preferable, but essential to its success. They are conceived as the lynchpin of the program without whose use the success of the program would be curtailed.

Why mandatory?

Only through the use of African-American male role models will it be possible to produce the kind of *expansive effect* needed to meet the current crisis -- an effect that is school-wide, school system-wide, and nationwide. Reliance upon specially qualified mixed personnel would most likely yield a *localized effect* -- an effect limited to the performance of those personnel with those students. Such an effect is no different from the effect of comparable capable classroom teachers: it is limited primarily to the students they teach. The import of Christakis and Fowler's <u>Connected</u>, of course, is that the connections of their students gives such teachers greater influence than any of us, heretofore, might have thought about. However, that influence is organic and random. With AMCAP, on the other hand, we are seeking planned and targeted change, the kind which ensues from deliberate effort.

Joe L. Rempson

The cultural change sought

The change sought is necessitated by a crisis which reflects a *cultural divide* and a *developmental rebellion* stemming from fatherless and impoverished homes. At the root of most of the crisis is the lack of a positive core identity. The cultural divide must be bridged by students' adoption of cultural norms more consistent with the academic demands of their school, and their developmental rebellion must be restrained by programs and personnel responsive to their developmental needs. The proposed cultural norm is a *career culture* that values a career self (not just in words, but in deeds as well) to replace a *street and peer culture* that devalues such a career self. AMCAP's *success-control work program* is designed to provide the students such a culture, and its use of African American male guides (father substitutes) is intended, inclusively, to help restrain their developmental rebellion. *Without such a culture, and without such a program and such personnel, the crisis cannot be solved.*

Support: Theoretical and Experiential

Imperative of "soul union" or "heart-link" -- Robert Bly and others

Traditional and contemporary belief lends support to this male reliance. In the insensitive words of the founder of the Boy Scouts, R. S. S. Baden-Powell (though the meaning is no doubt evident), "Manliness can only be taught by men, and not by those who are half men, half old women" (146:157). In his mythological classic about men, <u>Iron John: A Book About Men</u>, Robert Bly, renown poet and (among other things) a founder of the Men's Movement, put it less harshly but far more starkly, declaring that "When women, even women with the best intentions, bring up a boy alone, he may in some way have no male face, or he may have no face at all" (14:17). "Young men," he told Bill Moyers in a special production of Public Affairs Television in 1990, "A Gathering of Men," need older males "who encourages them, or holds them in their heart," thereby serving as their "heart-link through you with the male world" (182:23). That encouragement, or holding them in your heart, might mean, for example, writing him or taking him somewhere once a month. It is a role that Bly, drawing upon universal lessons from mythology, says that most young men cannot fill for one another; they do not know enough.

Second birth or soul union. Yet, it is a role that, to grow up, young men must have fufilled. Young men must experience a second birth, says Bly, this time from men -- older men. "Women," he says, "can change the embryo to a boy, but only men can change the boy to man" (14:16). That second birth is marked by separation from the feminine world of the mother and induction into the masculine world of father and, later, of other older men. Through the father, goes Bly's mythological interpretation, all else being equal, he picks up his masculine attributes, and from the intervention of older men, he gets his welcome into the male world and he gets their nurturance and guidance. When these "soul unions" are not made, the boy suffers an injury; he has no "heart-link" to the male world. Neither his peers nor women to whom he might turn, however much he is loved and respected by them (as in the case of his mother, for example), can fill the void, for it involves a universally and biologically transmitted body-soul transfer from other males -- for which there is no adequate substitute. Under these circumstances -- in the absence of that soul union -- the warrior energy which is intrinsic to his biology is likely to go unchanneled and, as a result, manifest itself destructively (for example, street gangs, crime, brutality to children) rather than constructively (for example, hard work, personal responsibility, family nurturing and protection).

The mythology and the social science. Apply Bly's insights from his Iron John story to the story of our African American males and we see suffering souls. The Iron John story, after all and above all, is a story about human nature -- the human nature of us all, especially us males. In the words of Bly, "The metaphors in the Iron John story refer to all human life, but are tuned to the psyches of men" (14:55). If, nevertheless, we are inclined to dismiss the value of such mythology, we first might want to ponder Bly's rationale for its use:

Eventually, a man needs to throw off all indoctrination and begin to discover for himself what the father is and what masculinity is. For that task, ancient stories are a good help, because they are free of modern psychological prejudices, because they endured the scrutiny of generations of women and men, and because they give both the light and dark sides of manhood, the admirable and the dangerous. Their model is not a perfect man, nor an overly spiritual man (14:25).

Drawing upon our usual source of social understanding, the social sciences, Sax puts it quite succinctly: "Human nature is gendered to the core" -- and Bly's Iron John story suggests that we are driven to seek to bond with that core (232:237).

One does not read into Bly's rationale a contradiction of the fact that anthropologists tell us that masculinity is culturally defined, no fixed and uniform trait. But that cultural definition would appear to be conditioned, typically, by form, not substance. The warrior energy, for example, is the warrior energy; how it gets expressed, suppressed, or ignored is where culture intervenes.

Application to black males. Bly's interpretation, applied to us black males, suggests a mass of father-hungry and older-male-hungry African American males, lacking a soul union, and attempts to satisfy that hunger and to find a union substitute have produced dysfunctional attitudes and behavior. In a jolting illustration, that hunger would appear to be what aforementioned psychologists, Silverstein and Krate. witnessed in their work and study in the black elementary schools of Harlem in the early 1970s (235:54-55). They report that many of the boys in preschool and kindergarten, not having yet developed the inhibitions of older boys, would trample over one another to grab hold of any adult male who entered the room.

Male hunger, confides Dr. George Jenkins, led him to scavenging – as he tells in the book, The Bond, which he co-authored with his two companions, all three now doctors who came up from poverty in fatherless homes and have told their story in two other books as well. "The older I got," he reveals, "the more I found myself scavenging in the streets to pick up the basics of male behavior." His mom, he says, "never shied away from the tough parts of parenting, but," he adds, "a woman can't show you how to be a man" (55a:15).

More telling is the story of black activist, poet, prolific writer, entertainer, and entrepreneur, Kevin Powell, who basically grew up without a father and who, in his book <u>Keepin' It Real</u>, reproduces a letter he sent him (212b:84-85). In it, he recounts his numerous pitfalls – a near nervous breakdown, homelessness, womanizing, mistreatment of mother, financial mismanagement, and so on – and then tells his father that those were the times he needed him there to show him the way. Instead, his father was adrift.

Apparently, aforementioned black celebrity actor and author, Hill, through his speaking and through his book, <u>Letters to a Young Brother: MANifest Your Destiny</u>, attempts to respond to this male hunger. "I've learned that the trajectory of a young man's life results from many social and cultural forces," he writes, adding, "one of the most important of these is the adult men in his life" (113b:xv-xvi).

When our little boys are driven to trample over one another to grab hold of *any* adult male, when Dr. George Jenkins was driven to male scavenging, and when Hill Harper feels compelled to write a book to answer their questions, then, indeed, we are witnessing male hunger. Kevin Powell provides an example of what that hunger can turn into as these little boys grow up. Most alarming is that an array of data suggest that their male hunger may never be satisfied. Kevin Powell represents the exception rather than the rule, and his story underlines why, for most of these little boys, their quest is likely to emain unfulfilled.

> **Applicability to the majority race**. To underline further the universal existence of this male hunger, we can turn for an illustration to the majority race as well. Aforementioned single-sex public education advocate, Dr. Leonard Sax, tells the story told him by a teacher about a robotics class in an all-boys school in Toronto. A retired electrician volunteered to help out, and, as Dr. Sax tells the teacher's story:

> The boys absolutely worshiped this old man. They were fascinated to hear his stories about working with high-voltage power lines. They hung on his every word about the technical details of soldering copper wire to a metal post. 'There was more going on here than just

the transfer of information,' the teacher told me. 'A *tribe* [emphasis in original] was being formed' (235:237-38).

A telling illustration, too, comes from an unexpected source: nannies. Historian and pioneer in the fatherhood movement, David Blankenhorn (author of Fatherless America), cites a New York Times report that "'men are more frequently hired as nannies by single mothers who are looking for a male presence in the children's lives'"(11:198).

Use of males from other races or ethnic groups

As for males of another race or ethnicity, Silverstein and Krate's observation is instructive, for the little boys whom they observed in the Harlem schools seemed to have been hungry for *any* male. That being the case, perhaps *any* male could help to satisfy their hunger, particularly considering that we are talking about a universal need, not a need unique to any given race or ethnicity. Maybe a male is a male, race or ethnicity notwithstanding.

However, State University of New York at Stony Brook anthropologist, David Gilmore, tells us that maleness is culturally mediated and so one would surmise that its cultural transferability is also mediated (101). For our African American male students that is not to be perceived as a negative, for, in effect, we are trying to get them to adopt the conserving traits of the mainstream male culture. The problem lies in the oppositional culture thesis of John Ogbu and the bedrock identity ascription (the cults of Victimology, Separatism, and Anti-intellectualism) of John McWhorter. Both factors serve as formidable obstacles to the use of white males. Black males of different heritages -- African, West Indian, Hispanic -- do not face these hurdles, but they are not insiders and tensions often exist between them and African Americans.

Also a factor is the externally adapted cultural status ascribed by late Pennsylvania State University sociologist, Jessie Bernard, to many of us, meaning (as discussed in Chapter 7) those who have adapted to the demands of mainstream culture, but only superficially. This is similar to the paradox between the importance we expressly place on education (often more than whites) and our poor school performance.

Words and deeds do not correspond. We risk a continuation of the same if AMCAP were to attempt to use non-African American males: external adaptation, instead of internal adaptation, and the paradox which it produces. In the words of Farrell, "they need to see people like them who are successful because they have bought into and can recreate American culture. They need to be shown by people they trust that there is a connection between school and career" (82:18).

The goal is to achieve an internalization of the adaptation required for school success, not only by the students, but also by their parents and their community. As hypothesized, parent and community support of the students is essential to the *expansive* success of the program. That means taking a comprehensive, long view, of doing that which -- over time -- takes hold, is nurtured, and gets transmitted. That will occur only if it happens with those who live in our poor communities, interact daily, share their stories, come to embrace certain common attitudes and values, and experience it from a shared sense of black pride. Only their own can make that happen, just as Booker T. Washington made it happen during his time. Males from other races and ethnicities can help, but only we African American males can assure, to the extent that it can be assured, these kind of shared and transmitted outcomes. As Holland has poignantly put it:

> ...these boys [referring to black boys living in impoverished inner-city communities] must be shown that there are African American men who love and care for them consistently and who are very concerned that they achieve success in school and life. In that setting as well, African American boys from poor urban areas must learn to dream of a better future, for if one cannot dream, the future is now. The tools that will allow these boys to look beyond the now and expand their vision of the future lie within the African American community, working and partnering with concerned citizens in other communities (123:321).

Use of females

If Blankenhorn (as indicated below) is correct in believing that much of our male rage stemming from male hunger is directed against women, females would appear to have little or no chance of being the change agents. A case in point -- at least as he saw it -- is provided by the aforementioned retired black educational psychologist Morgan State University (Maryland), Dr. Spencer Holland. While publicizing from his Project 2000 (discussed below), conducted from 1991-1994, Holland became a preeminent champion of the use of black males in the classroom (123, 446). The reason is relevant to our point about male rage against women. As he recalled in an interview with previously cited black educator, Ronnie Hopkins, of Norfolk State University (and essentially reiterated in a subsequent Journal of Negro Education article):

> I began to visit classes and stay two or three hours, not just for half an hour. And lo and behold! Things began to dawn on me. Good Lord, boys are sitting up here ignoring those women! I'd walk behind a boy and say, "Hey, don't you know how to do that? The teacher's up there demonstrating." And he'd say, "Yeah." And I said, "Let me see it, come on." And he would half-heartily do it. I said, "Come on. No, let me show you." And he would do it and the others would follow. I said, Hey! OK, OK, singing songs, playing games, the ABC song, all of these things that the boys were tagging as being sissies, girls do it. Then I began to look at the environments they were coming from--single-parent, female-headed households. Almost all of these elementary schools are female enclaves, particularly primary grade, nothing but female teachers. I said, my goodness, these boys are just ignoring women. They get tired of it, and this is seen as a female activity and they don't come to school with the kinds of behaviors the little girls come with to allow them to sit up straight and tall. We have a conflict here that is gender based. And that started the fight.(Holland, Interview, 1993) (127:60).

So the rage that Blankenhorn sees in lyrics, Holland saw at an early age in the boys' tune-out of their female teachers and in their disdain for female-perceived ("girlish") activities.

Principles from behavior change research

From the research literature examined on behavior change, five change principles were found which support the necessity of using African American males.

- Those who are the object of change must participate in bringing it about (32:32-33).
- A "person's opinions and attitudes are strongly influenced by groups to which he belongs and wants to belong" (293:22).
- Modeling is more likely than demonstration or instruction to change behavior (255:53).
- "As a general rule, people respond better to a message that comes from someone in their group…" (186:254).
- "…it is the kind and quality of the interaction between participants in the directed change process that will have the greater impact on the outcomes" (188:97).

The import of these five principles is that our African American male students are more likely to change their attitudes and behaviors under the guidance of older black African American males because the students (1) share their identity, (2) become co-participants with them in changing themselves, (3) have in them realistic models whom they can emulate, and (4) can establish more meaningful and higher-quality interactions with them. Older African American males cannot, of course, replace absent fathers, but they can serve as *psychological fathers*. Such a role is embraced by some as one answer to the absent father, the idea being that any "Nearby Guy" (as Blankenhorn terms the concept) is better than what we can call "No Guy." (11:98).

Environmental vulnerability of males

In his famous 1969 article, in these words, Jensen gives an environmental context to the behavior of boys in contrast to girl:

> "It has long been suspected that males have greater environmental vulnerability than females, and Nancy Bayley's important longitudinal research on children's mental development clearly shows both a higher degree and a greater variety of environmental

and personality correlates of mental abilities in boys than in girls ..." (139:32).

That is, in general when it comes to boys, compared to girls, environmental factors seem to have more of an effect (also see Sowell (241:40). As a case in point, although the New Hope Project goal was to improve the life of low-income adults, it turned out to have clearly significant benefits, not for those adults nor for the girls in their families, but for the boys in their families. The researchers speculate that the boys were influenced by the supervision and structured after-school activities. The import is that, since boys tend to be more vulnerable to such environmental factors as these because of the absence of a male presence in their life has a disproportionate effect on them, as, indeed, suggested by the effects of fatherless homes, our next topic.

Support: Effects of Fatherless Homes

The male soul union or heart-link hunger that Bly, Silverstein and Krate, Dr. George Jenkins (as well, incidentally, as his two doctor companions of similar background and upbringing, Sampson Davis and Rameck Hunt), Kevin Powell, Hill Harper, and Dr. Leonard Sax tell about, and which is reflected in more male nannies, is documented in the research and psychological literature. Deprived of that soul union or heart-link, unlike, for example, the Three Doctors or Kevin Powell, most males do not turn out to have success stories to tell.

Rage

According to Blankenhorn:

> Both clinical studies and anthropological investigations confirm the process through which boys *seek to separate from their mothers in search of the meaning of their maleness* [emphasis added]. In this process, the father is irreplaceable. He enables the son to separate from the mother. He is the gatekeeper, guiding his son into the community of men, teaching him to name the meaning of his embodiment, showing him on good authority than [sic] he can be "man enough" (11:30).

"Boys," Dr. Sax says, "are hungry for an answer to the question: What does it mean to be a man." "But," he adds, "the formal structures of our society--schools in particular--no longer offer any answers to that question" (232:240). When that hunger is not satisfied, and when the search and separation are not achieved, Blankenhorn asserts that there is one main result: "in clinical terms…rage." There is "rage against the mother, against women, against society." "It is a deeply misogynistic rage," he continues, "vividly expressed, for example, in contemporary rap music with titles such as 'Beat That Bitch with a Bat'" (11:30). Maybe, it is that misogyny which we saw in Kevin Powell's aforementioned revelations. Socially, Blankenhorn states, for boys the main outcome is juvenile delinquency, for girls juvenile delinquency plus out-of-wedlock childbearing -- and no doubt more attention needs to be given to its effect on girls.

Rage outcomes

A few statistics from the website dads4kids.com provide evidence of Blankenhorn's bleak picture, a picture sketched, as well, by Bly, Dr. Sax, and others (323). Except for the statistic regarding homeless and runaway children, the sources are cited on the website, though not here.

1. 63% of youth suicides are from fatherless homes
2. 90% of all homeless and runaway children are from fatherless homes
3. 85% of all children who exhibit behavioral disorders come from fatherless homes
4. 80% of rapists motivated with displaced anger come from fatherless homes
5. 71% of all high school dropouts come from fatherless homes
6. 75% of all adolescent patients in chemical abuse centers come from fatherless homes
7. 70% of juveniles in state-operated institutions come from fatherless homes
8. 85% of all youths sitting in prison grew up in a fatherless home

School outcomes

When it comes to school performance, in particular, Olsen and Fuller say that the research shows that, more than poverty alone, the absence of the father is associated with poor school performance and school dropout (202:301). They add, however, that poverty may have a significant influence on other problems, such as, delinquency. As for poverty itself, it too is closely associated with father absence, Blankenhorn even going so far as to declare that "Most scholars now agree that this link between family structure and child poverty is not simply a statistical correlation. It is a causal relationship" (11:43). How about the effect on boys in particular? A study by Sheila Fitzgerald Krein and Andrea H. Beller of the University of Illinois at Urbana shows that "the more time that children - especially boys - spend in one-parent homes, the less schooling they are likely to complete" (454).

Theory and Research: Conclusion

The theory and research cited permit the following conclusion, a conclusion which supports our thesis on the use of males: **All else being equal, as a general rule, to become the prototypical man requires that we have a soul union with older men, starting with our father, the extent to which we develop that union being perhaps the most important factor in determining a male's wellbeing.** To solve our African American Male School Adaptability Crisis (AMSAC), we must, therefore, provide our African American students an opportunity for soul union with older men who approximate prototypical African American manhood as an alternative to their reliance for soul union on peer culture and on older men who exemplify deviant African American manhood. Through this potential satisfaction of their male hunger, their longing for a soul union or heart-link with other men -- something that only older men can provide -- we can, perhaps, diminish their rage (their developmental rebellion) and redirect their warrior energy towards meeting the demands of school success. That is the requirement, and only older African American males can satisfy it. Fulfilled, it will put our students on a manhood pathway that, together with other factors, will likely result in their developing a positive core identity and the character attributes associated with it.

Prior Experiments Using Black Male Teachers

In the final analysis, the question is whether hard data exist which might directly support the hypothesized necessity of using African American males in AMCAP. Though meagre, such hard data do exist and they support the hypothesis (support, not prove). As St. John's University law professor, Rosemary Salomone, writes in her book, Same, Different, Equal, "Reports on minority males…come from isolated experimental classes," only two being found that also had African American male teachers, in addition to one project that used African American male mentors (230:221-22). These are the three: **PROJECT 2000** (1991-?) conducted by Holland, the **Wright Black-White Male Teacher Experiment** (1987-88), as herein called, conducted by the then principal of North Glade Elementary School in Miami, Florida., Willie J. Wright, and a **California Middle School Program** (c1990), as it is herein designated.

PROJECT 2000 (The Spencer Holland Project) (123, 463)

The object of considerable national publicity in the 1990s, PROJECT 2000 was designed to test the efficacy of using black adult males as role models to support and mentor black male students. It has had a two-phase life. The first phase, started in 1988, ended in 1993, and took place at Stanton Elementary School in Washington, D. C. It involved the use of mostly African American male volunteers as teacher aides to assist teachers with a group of 53 African American male students from grades 1-6, over 90 percent of whom grew up without a father figure. The volunteers were trained to provide models for them (such as in singing), emphasize with them principles which they were being taught in class (such as self-control), and, upon request, act as their disciplinarians. In addition, they provided the gamut of assistance that a teacher aide typically provides, from checking attendance, to passing out and collecting instructional materials, to helping with field trips.

The second phase, started in 1994, has continued for an unknown period of time [unable to determine, by phone or internet, its current status] after being set up in the housing project from which Stanton Elementary School draws its students. It was designed to follow up and continue to service the 53 boys as they went to different schools in grades 7 through 12 as well as to continue to service Stanton Elementary School graduating boys (but not to continue its work in the school). Daily afterschool activities as well as summer activities were provided in the areas of academic support, mentoring, personal development, and college/postsecondary preparation. Mathematics and reading skills were emphasized. Eighth graders were required to take a 10-week interpersonal skills development seminar, and students with a minimum grade-point average of 2.5 could participate in a leadership development seminar. Each year, new students from Stanton Elementary School were recruited, based on a grade-point average (GPA) of 2.0 and a C+ citizenship rating. Called "scholars," enrollees were required to maintain a 2.50 GPA. The Project operated with a staff headed by Holland and, as in its first phase, used trained peer and adult African American male volunteers.

Holland reports that, in comparison to a control group, second-, third-, and fourth-graders from the original cohort had "significantly higher GPAs and standardized test scores...in almost every subject area," and that "more than 85% of PROJECT 2000 boys were at or above grade level in almost every subject area under examination, while 85% of the boys in the control group were below grade level in these areas" (123:320). Although no formal evaluation had been done on the secondary school phase of PROJECT 2000, Holland reports that, by the end of the second year, "33 of 38 PROJECT 2000 scholars had earned GPAs of 2.00 or better and were in good standing." Moreover, "twenty-two scholars (58%) earned 'varsity scholar' status by earning GPAs of 2.50 or better. Nine (24%) earned 'first team' status by earning GPAs above 3.00" (123:320).

Wright Black-White Male Teacher Experiment (The Wright Study) (292; 230:221-22).

Wright read about Dr. Holland's PROJECT 2000 in a William Raspberry <u>Washington Post</u> article and, as a school principal, decided to try out the idea himself. So he set up two kindergarten classes, one consisting of 20 black boys with an African American male teacher and the other made up of 23 first-grade black boys with a white male teacher. All the boys in both classes were from female-headed households with no available male figure in the immediate household. African American male volunteers were recruited to serve as teacher aides in both of the classes. The results:

Black male teacher class
- 18 had perfect attendance -- 1 student absent for 2 days, 1 for 1 day, all the absences due to illness.
- Students scored 7-11% higher on standardized tests of sounds and letters than their counterparts in a regular coeducational class and their math scores were 8-9% higher.

White male teacher class
- 22 had perfect attendance -- 1 student missed 2 days.
- Students scored 4-5% higher in reading comprehension and 5-7% higher in math than their counterparts in a regular coeducational class.

Both classes (Qualitative outcomes)
- Use of dyads proved beneficial: boys learned to accept responsibility for actions and success, they got to know one another in and out of school, and their parents got to know one another.
- Students were taught and practiced social graces daily to be used in and out of School (such as saying *please* and *thank you*, and cafeteria etiquette) and learned to disagree without confrontation -- not a single fight occurred in either class.

These results suggest that black male teachers, using black male teacher aides, can have a significant positive influence on the behavior and performance of our black male students. So too, but to a slightly lesser extent, can a white male teacher using black teacher aides. The experiment was discontinued due to objections from the regional Office for Civil Rights based on civil rights violation [which tells us a lot about the System-Responsibility Tradition and its role in our crisis and social problems generally].

California Middle School Program

As reported by Salomone, 21 at-risk African American students in grades six through eight were assigned to a self-contained classroom taught by an African American male teacher (230:222). Compared to a similar group of students in the mainstream program, "the data on academic grades and days of suspension favored the single-sex program."

Cautions

Although these data tend to support the use of black male teachers in the instruction of black male students, it needs to be made unequivocal that there is no attempt thereby to support a view that the use of black teachers or black guides, per se, leads to better performance by black students. Neither experience nor research supports that view. In fact, the research is mixed, suggesting, perhaps, that the socioeconomic status of the teacher in the performance of black students may be at least as important as the teacher's racial congruence (85a:347-50).

It needs to be observed, as well, that the availability of African American males in poor communities is a perceived hindrance to their use. Holland observes that such was the case in his recruitment of a stable corps of male volunteers for his PROJECT 2000. But Holland relied on volunteers [200 in the elementary phase of his project], whereas, AMCAP is designed to use paid guides only -- and in limited numbers. Of course, whether volunteer or paid, finding quality personnel is usually a challenge. No doubt the challenge is greater in poor neighborhoods, but, maybe, not quite as formidable as we often think. In Code of the Street, Elijah Anderson identifies two family categories which those in poor communities use to describe themselves: *decent* and *street* or *ghetto*. One finds, he says, diversity among the residents – some doing fairly well and others suffering and deeply alienated and angry (5:53). His data and description support what experience suggests. So does the experience of aforementioned criminal justice expert, David Kennedy. He concludes that we underestimate the number of good people, as well as, the positive values that exist in our inner cities. The mindset which guides AMCAP, therefore, is that recruiting black male personnel from the community it services will be a challenge, but not a. hindrance.

16

Popular but Flawed Solutions to School Reform and Art of Loving (AOL) Schools as the Answer

Proverbs, 16:22 - "Understanding is a wellspring of life unto him that hath it: but the instruction of fools is folly."
Galatians, 6:5 - "For every man shall bear his own burden."

Current popular public school reform initiatives are an attack on neighborhood public schools for the poor in favor of a privatized, competitive business model. Amid the politics of it all, we seem to have forgotten that our public schools are as much a part of the foundation of our country as is our Constitution, subject, of course, like it, to timely modifications (52:3-22). But let us not confuse modification with abandonment. The damage done to dedication and professionalism in education by unions and by some teachers and other school personnel, understandably, calls for needed modifications, but these modifications must not decimate traditional neighborhood schools for the poor – or even for the better off. Nor, as argued, must we proceed on the premise that our urban school crisis is entirely -- or even primarily for that matter -- the fault of the school. Among other things, that premise ignores the lesson which, over a half century ago, James Conant says he learned from visiting and contrasting a well-to-do suburb and a slum. "*The lesson is that to a considerable degree what a school should do and can* do is determined by the status and ambitions of the families being served" [emphasis in original] (42:1).

Value-added modeling

Nevertheless, the growing popularity of value-added modeling only intensifies the teacher-school emphasis. Value-added modeling is a method whereby school systems calculate the "value teachers add to their students' achievement, based on changes in test scores from year to year and how the students perform compared with others in their grade" (328). It is used to measure total school performance as well, and is said to be exploding nationwide. Some districts have gone so far as to publish teachers' value-added ratings, reportedly possibly contributing to the suicide of one teacher who received a below average rating (402). We need to bring teachers, school, and community together, not divide and promote blame; and we need to delineate responsibilities, not distort them. Of course, we are right to demand that teachers do their job, but that demand may be better served through long-term contracts versus tenure, and through flexible evaluation criteria which can be judiciously applied by supervisors who are held accountable for school-wide processes and realistic outcomes. Obviously, as the research evidence shows, teachers influence their students' grades (that influence being most pronounced during the elementary school years), particularly the grades of our African American students, but the evidence must not lead us to confuse *influence* with *determine*.

Charter schools and vouchers

Charter schools are public schools which, authorized by the state or school district, are privately run by for-profit or nonprofit organizations. They have the flexibility to adopt staff and program changes that regular public school do not have. Unlike public schools, they are held accountable for the results they seek which are spelled out in their charter; failure to achieve them can lead to a revocation of their charter. Vouchers are government-issued certificates that can be used to pay a student's tuition at a private school, such as, a Catholic school.

Both can be said to provide a mirage, efforts which divert our attention from meeting our crisis head on and where it is (for a good discussion, see Ravitch, 217: 113-47). **Ninety percent of our students are in the public schools, and it is in public schools they are likely to remain.** In New York State, for example, Cose cites the late black attorney and New York City and State politician, Basil Paterson, as pointing out that, in the state, 30,000 kids attend charter schools while the public school population is a million-one. Those numbers leave about 97 percent of public school childen in regular public schools, leading Paterson to conclude that charter schools are fine; "'the problem is all those left behind'" (49:226). For New York State, then, call it The 3% Solution. Nationwide, the National Center for Education Statistics reports that for the 2012-13 school year, California had the largest number of students enrolled in charter schools, 8% of its student population, and Washington, D.C., had the highest percentage of its students enrolled in charter schools, 42%, followed by Arizona, which had 14%. For the nation, then, it may be a solution for a minority of its students, most being left behind, just like in New York State, if not in such numbers as New York State.

Obviously, there is practicality here. We cannot massively transport our students to charter or private schools, or create the former, just as during the school integration craze, however desirable, we could not massively transport them to achieve school integration. Let us assume that we could transport them, however, would doing so lead to their higher academic achievement? Reports of the research undertaken indicate that, in general, it would for low-income minority students in urban charter schools do, but (for whatever reasons) not for those in suburban charter schools (334a, 315e, 48:215-17, 355). Moreover, some single-gender urban charter schools show outstanding success (328a). Overall, the sense of mixed results which came from earlier reports seems to be giving way to evidence of more favorable outcomes. Even so, to champion charter schools as the solution to the low academic achievement of our black students is to believe that we can convert our public school system into a charter school system.

That the schools can and ought to do a better job is indisputable, but the fact is that the schools are probably better than they have ever been. However, they are being asked to do more than ever – and more than they can be realistically expected to do. Contrary to what so many politicians and others seemingly have come to think, school is not a panacea; it is a vehicle for transmitting knowledge and culture to our children and youth, contingent on their preparation and readiness. In the absence of such preparation and readiness, tradition holds that the school must compensate as best it can, which is historically what it has done. But there is a limit to what the school can do. That limit is tested by the cognitive skills and the character deficits with which poor African American students enter school. Paul Tough points out that, for the very poor (family income of less than $11,000 a year), we have made little or no headway in compensating for these deficits, the outcomes being better for those in the higher-income category (families with income of $41,000 a year).

What Booker T. Washington said to his Tuskegee students, basically, can be said to these and other African American students:

> Now what is true of the school is true of the world at large. This is a little world of itself. It is a small sample of civilization, an experiment station, so to speak, in which we are trying to prepare you to live in a manner a little more orderly, a little more efficient, and a little more civilized than you have lived heretofore. If you are not able to live and succeed here, you will not be able to live and succeed in the world outside. If we do not want you here, if we cannot get on with you here, it will mean that the world outside will not want you, will not be able to get on with you (234:344).

Today, however, we are not placing the responsibility where Washington placed it. To be sure, he was demanding of his teachers -- a task master, as it were -- but this message makes it evident that he was equally demanding of his students. He is telling his students that they *themselves* must be "able to live and succeed" in the "little world" of Tuskegee. To them, he emphasized their responsibility, just as to his teachers and staff he emphasized their responsibilities.

The lesson for us is that, when our students enter school, starting in kindergarten, our perspective on that entry might be enhanced if we picture it as their entry into a "little world" in which they *themselves* must be "able to live and succeed." That so many students have not been able to do so is not so much because we have poor schools, but because, as Lee Rainwater declares, "...the victimization process as it operates in [their] families prepares and toughens its members to function in the ghetto world, at the same time that it seriously interferes with their ability to operate in *any other world*" [emphasis added].

The privatization craze and teacher accountability do not address this preparedness. One is, therefore, reminded of busing to desegregate our schools in the decades following the Supreme Court *Brown vs. Board of Education* decision (1954) which made it unlawful to keep schools racially segregated. End racially segregated schools, the belief went, and we end the black-white achievement gap. In effect, institute privatization -- the current belief goes -- and we end the black-white achievement gap. In the former instance, we bused students out of our poor neighborhoods and sent them to racially-mixed schools (which the Coleman Report showed to be associated with black academic success), while in the latter instance, we put the burden on teachers and force students out of the schools in our poor neighborhoods and send them to the better schools of their choice. Call it public school decimation, a counterpart of public school desegregation. Both involve the exit of our students from toxic schools presumably to therapeutic ones.

We know that public school desegregation has not worked. Nor will public school decimation. Rather than being therapeutic, in an opt-ed article in the New York Times, black Georgetown University journalism lecturer and Interactivity Foundation fellow, Natalie Hopkinson, puts her finger on its effect. Hopkinson declares that the choice and accountability trend which underlines public school decimation, with little evidence to support its validity, "has destroyed community-based education for working-class [and poor] families, even as it has funneled resources toward a few better-of, exclusive, institutions" (383a). Apparently what we have on hand is another panacea which does not address the pivotal problem; as Hopkinson suggests, it is, in fact, aggravating it.

Let us be aware of something else. We have yet another panacea which is addressing a fetish: closing of the black-white academic achievement gap. Long addressed, the gap remains, and is likely to continue to remain. Although the evidence suggests that our black students can "substantially" improve their school performance, to quote a task force of the American Psychological Association (see Chapter 8), it does not suggest that the magnitude of the improvement would enable them to close the gap. Our three major demons – *IQ lag-fatherless families-crime* – stand in the way. Let us, therefore, not continue down this "make-believe" road, face up to reality, and, rather than expend our energy and resources in a quest for the unrealistic (such as has been done, for example, through No Child Left Behind and Race to the Top), exert them in pursuit of the goal of enabling every child to perform the basic essentials of life, defined herein as bcommonly voiced aim of enabling every child to reach her/his full potential, which, it is argued, can be done under the proposals herein.

President Barak Obama's education agenda

Race to the Top. In addressing the problem, President Barak Obama attempted to accomplish the need aforementioned Sandra Stein identifies (see Chapter 3): focus No Child Left Behind (NCLB) on teaching and learning rather than on policies and failure. Under the President's signature education initiative, **Race to the Top**, states could apply for grants to undertake relevant reforms and innovations. As regards the role of students and community, the selection criteria were not encouraging, for, whereas, they contained nothing which prohibited applicants from making student and parent-community initiatives an integral part of their relevant reforms and innovations, nor did they contain anything which encouraged them to do so. An internet search reveals that none of the selection criteria specified student and parent-community responsibility factors as a basis for awarding any of the 500 possible evaluation points. Such a focus would have had to be part of the 40 points that could be awarded to plans for "turning around the lowest-achieving school," which gave it a negligible possible impact on the total rating. In a word, Race to the Top was an attempt to shape up the public schools through privatization (charter schools) and *increased* teacher accountability, not through increased student and parent-community accountability.

In "The Billionaire Boys' Club," a chapter in her book, The Death and Life of the Great American School System: How Testing and Choice are Undermining Education, former Assistant Secretary of Education, Diane Ravitch, gives context to this mindset (217:195-222). Discussing the history of foundations in the field of education, education historian

Ravitch details the current role of three major foundations: Gates, Broad, and Walton. Her conclusion: in response to the challenge to improve our urban schools, these foundations offer a marketplace, business-oriented agenda that consists of competition (charter schools), teacher effectiveness, and test-score accountability. Through the President's Secretary of Education, Arne Duncan, a beneficiary of the foundations as superintendent of the Chicago public schools, and through the foundation officers that he has brought into the department, it is the foundations' agenda which permeates Race to the Top.

One is reminded of the war between Washington and DuBois. As elsewhere herein discussed, floundering in his attempt to form an organized opposition to Washington, DuBois was rescued by Oswald Garrison Villard and a few Northern white liberals who came along and gave him a boost. They organized the National Association for the Advancement of Colored People (NAACP), put DuBois in charge of its publicity, from which position he created the Crisis; and the Crisis brought him enhanced standing and helped to put the NAACP on the map. In the case of **Race to the Top**, we have the "billionaire boys' club," as Ravitch dubs its members, having the good fortune of having $4.3 billion Recovery Act dollars being put at the behest of its proponents, giving vitality to their approach which, though not floundering as the demise of the Niagara Movement showed DuBois to be floundering, was struggling uphill. Of course, money and connections change everything, in this case, the foothold of privatization and teacher accountability.

Not to be overlooked, however, are two Obama administration departures, or semi-departures, from this system-centered thinking. One is the **Race to the Top High School Commencement Challenge, and** the other is its **Title I parent involvement proposals**.

Race to the Top: High School Commencement Challenge. Started in 2010, the President's Race to the Top High School Commencement Challenge exhibited the privatizing and competitive elements of its parent, Race to the Top, but it had a student and parent-community emphasis. Stemming from his desire for the United States to have the highest proportion of college graduates in the world by 2020, the President launched a nationwide contest whereby high schools were invited to highlight their efforts to lead as a 21st century school (425). The reward for the winner was having the President as the Commencement Speaker at its graduation ceremony. Through the internet, the public participated in the selection process. In its first year, over 1,000 schools participated and more than 170,000 people voted their choices. Among the explicit selection criteria: "the ability of the school to engage students in learning and to foster personal responsibility and academic excellence" (464). Thus, fostering personal responsibility by students [which could implicitly involve parents and the community as well] got explicit attention and was made a selection criterion.

In the selection of **Booker T. Washington High School** in Memphis, Tennessee, as the 2011 recipient, we can get a sense of what this student personal responsibility criterion *could have* come to highlight. Immediately noteworthy is the name borne by the school, Booker T. Washington. Apparently, it is not just his name that the school bears, it is, likewise, guided by his spirit and philosophy. In the words of its principal, Alisha Kiner, "The astute wisdom [a redundancy richly deserved by Washington] of the late Booker Taliaferro Washington reminds us that *"Character, not circumstances, makes the man* [emphasis in original]." She adds, "The daily efforts of our family at Booker T. Washington High School strive to bring these words to fruition" (410). The students are from an area with 70 percent single-parent households and a median income of $10,734. Since 2007, it has raised its graduation rate from 55% to 82%. Among the stated beliefs of the school is (1) that "Given a safe, supportive and challenging environment, students will be able to accept *shared responsibility for their own academic achievement*" [emphasis added] and (2) that Teachers, students, staff, parents, and community share in site-based decision-making which establishes and sustains a culture of respectful, self-directed, life-long learners" (410). Thus, rather than the usual emphasis on just what the school must do, BTW addresses, as well, what students and parents must do.

Title I parent involvement. In the President's second Title I departure, the focus of change herein is specifically on parent involvement to the exclusion of other possible changes. Since 1968, three years after its beginning in 1965, Title I has provided for various forms of parent involvement, eventually resulting in the six provisions that we now have under a revised Section 1118 (54:118-24). These six provisions define for the LEAs (local education authorities) the meaning of parent involvement, and extent that involvement beyond the involvement required under previous provisions of the Title (54). For our discussion, the most relevant of the six provisions is the provision, in effect since 1994, which requires every Title I school to develop a **school-parent compact** that outlines how parents, the entire school staff, and students, and students will share responsibility for improved student academic achievement and the means by which the school and parents will build and develop, developed and approved by parents, that describes how the school and parents will build and develop a partnership to help children achieve the State's high standards (459g).

To put some teeth into the six provisions, districts receiving more than $500,000 in Title I funds must set aside one percent (1%) of their allocation for parent involvement activities, and 95% of this one percent must go to Title I schools.

In practice, this promising school-parent compact provision, like the others, has apparently fallen short. In their study of the compacts, Jerome D'Agostino of the University of Arizona and his colleagues found that the compacts have not made a significant contribution to student achievement. They attribute the reason, not to the concept itself, which their data showed had promise, but to implementation deficiencies (54). In her history and analysis, Karen Mapp of the Harvard Graduate School of Education arrives at a similar assessment, citing a number of weaknesses and, in general, "the relatively poor execution and oversight of the Title I parent provisions" (405:10). Rather than parent involvement activities being a core component of school improvement efforts, Mapp [quoting Gill Kressley] argues that, too often, these activities are "random acts" of parent involvement (405:10-11). This "random acts" finding, incidentally, is consistent with what has been historically true of school-parent programs in depressed urban areas (222, 205). The suggestion is that the parent involvement component of NCLB, which has typically been translated into focus on compliance and "random acts," has been no more successful, maybe even less so, than its overall academic achievement component with its focus on policies and failure as pertains to teachers and schools.

However, the Title I **Chicago Child-Parent Centers Program** would appear to be an exception.

But there was no equivalent of Race to the Top to reform this parent involvement component. Instead, there were some modest proposals, none of which appear to have been implemented. Mapp reports that Secretary Duncan has proposed to increase the one percent set-aside to two percent and to create, from existing Title I funds, an optional Family Engagement and Responsibility Fund to "launch state-run competitions to support innovative and effective local family engagement initiatives" (405:3).

History suggests caution as regards the nature of family engagement (220, 217). Herein, the concern is about our parents and our community accepting responsibility for their role in fostering student learning. It is not, as mandated by Section 1118, about decision-making participation. It is not power that we need to address our crisis; it is preparation, the preparation of our children to adapt to the demands of school success. While giving feedback, advice, and input, let us hold the professionals accountable for running our schools. That is what they are trained and paid to do; it is their job, not ours. For our part, if we manage our homes and our children well, we will have done our job.

It has been noted that a recent study of the effect of parent involvement on school achievement in the The New York Times led to the headline, "Parental Involvement Is Overrated," might raise a question about the importance herein given to it (438g). The authors of the study, sociologists Keith Robinson and Angel L. Harris, in fact, wrote the article. In the article, as well as in their book, The Broken Compass: Parental Involvement with Children's Education, the authors do make a case for the overrating description. Their findings lead them to the conclusion that most forms of parental involvement have no effect on academic outcomes, and, in some cases, a negative effect.

In essence, however, their conclusion, though recent, is not new. For example, an earlier study by D'Agostino, Hedges, and Borman of parent involvement under the Title I of the Elementary and Secondary Education Act revealed the same nonrelationship (54:117-18). They found a direct relationship between students' reading achievement and the level of their parents' *home-based* learning involvement, but no relationship between their reading achievement and their parents' *school-based* involvement activities.

Robinson and Harris emphasize that their findings are limited to what is suggested: the effect of parent involvement on *academic achievement*, not on other outcomes, such as general enrichment or social and emotional development. Further, even as regards academic achievement, the authors say that their findings suggest that "active forms of involvement at home are beneficial for socioeconomically disadvantaged youth," and that "Blacks…appear to experience gains in achievement from assertive forms of parental involvement at school" (227a:226). However, the authors do stress that these gains are minimal and fail to justify the emphasis often placed on parental involvement as a key to the academic success of black students.

Not included for consideration in their study is a form of parent involvement deemed to be fundamental in improving the academic success of black students, especially during the beginning school years: involvement which focuses on parenting skills. Whereas, in general, then, the findings appear to warrant a devaluation of the role of parent involvement as a factor in students' academic success, insofar as African American students are concerned, they support parent involvement in various at-home and in-school forms, but do not address parent involvement as that involvement pertains to parenting skills, a fundamental need of many African American parents, and for their children during their early school years, a primary object of parent involvement.

Every Student Succeeds Act (ESSA) and President Obama's education agenda

In 2015, the Every Student Succeeds Act (ESSA) was passed, replacing No Child Left Behind, in yet another revision of the original Elementary and Secondary Education Act (ESEA), enacted in 1965 under President Lyndon B. Johnson (299a, 392d, 460e, 464a). The Act marks an end, not just to President Bush's education reform attempt, but, in part, to the reform attempt of President Obama as well. It brought an end to his **Race to the Top** and its component, **High School Commencement**

Challenge, both having been acknowledged by the Department of Education as not working (446e). But, on another account, the President succeeded: under ESSA, privatization in the form of charter schools is institutionalized, as support for them is upgraded and expanded. But the President's drive for teacher accountability based on students' performance was eliminated.

In at least two ways, ESSA strengthens family involvement provisions. It sets up Statewide Family Engagement Centers to support, coordinate, and integrate family engagement activities conducted by its schools, and it requires school districts to conduct family engagement activites shown by research evidence to be effective (314c, 422a).

Some directions for change.

Although system-centered thinkers put the school "on the hook," one cannot be sure of what they would have it do. So we offer some thoughts about what they – and we – ought to have the school do.

Teacher training. The need for improved teacher training is recognized at the highest level in the person of President Barak Obama's Secretary of Education, Arne Duncan (407). Duncan calls education programs "mediocre" and called for "revolutionary changes." Former president of Teachers College, Columbia University, Arthur Levine, found that "roughly 60% of education school alumni said that their programs did not prepare them to teach" (407). Susan Engel, senior lecturer in psychology and the director of the teaching program at Williams College, gives these recommendations as to what might be done about these programs (342):

1. Get the best colleges to establish teacher training programs
2. Attract trainees who have 3.5 undergraduate grade-point average
   a. Put them through intensive application process
   b. Make tuition free
   c. Provide stipend for their first three years of teaching in a public school
3. Train them differently
   a. Have them continue studying what they will teach

b. Have them learn in same way as surgeons: intense supervision working alongside skilled professionals
  c. Have them emulate family therapy programs approach of watching videotapes of themselves and analyzing most difficult portions with senior therapists by recording their classroom encounters and analyzing them with mentors and peers
  d. Have them learn how to observe and analyze student behavior
4. Provide as many schools as possible the incentive to hire these teachers in groups of seven or more so as to create a robust community of promising professionals

One critical recommendation not on Engel's list might read: have them acquire the ability to diagnose student learning problems. Payne points out that "One important, and underdiscussed, theme in the literature concerns the power of teacher diagnostic ability" (208a:95). He cites studies showing that students of teachers able to diagnose student learning problems and adjust instruction accordingly show enormous gains, notwithstanding type of learner or situation.

Principals. Bob Herbert, former New York Tmes columnist and now Senior Fellow at Demos, emphasizes the need for "a cadre of highly skilled educational leaders" (379). He cites the Harvard Graduate School of Education as having created a new doctoral degree program to train just such leaders. The three-year program is tuition-free and instead of a dissertation, students spend their third year leading an education reform project. Although Harvard's focus is not on principals, but is seemingly on system-wide educational administrators, it appears that it could apply to principals as well. Ideally, principals would get the same kind of training that Susan Engel proposes for teachers, plus, as one example, the kind of administrative training that Harvard provides.

The total system. Turning to the system as whole, Ravitch identifies what she considers six essential ingredients for success (217: 224).

  1. A strong curriculum
  2. Experienced teachers
  3. Effective instruction

4. Willing students
5. Adequate resources
6. A community that values education

Observing that a number of other lists is possible, Payne also lists what he calls "The Big Six" (208a:94).

1. Instructional time protected or extended
2. Intellectually ambitious instruction
3. Professional community (teachers collaborate, have a collective sense of responsibility)
4. Academic press combined with social support
5. Program coherence (i.e., institutional focus; are we all on the same page?)
6. Teacher 'quality' / diagnostic ability

It is noteworthy that Ravitch includes two home-community factors among her six ingredients, and it is an implicit part of Payne's social support reference (#4). But the concern, herein, is not the details, except to portray the kind of school improvements needed to help solve AMSAC. As Herbert declares, improvements are really needed in American education generally, but more urgently as pertains to AMSAC. Too much of the literature, especially by us African Americans, is filled with general condemnations of teachers and schools, without meaningful practice or policy analyses or recommendations. Anger and vitriol are not going to improve the system or, otherwise, help our students. Nor is some form of parental or community control going to help as some politicians and activists still seem to think, such as the few who, in 2009, held up mayoral control of the schools in New York City because they wanted more parent participation in *running* the schools (444).

Black Advocacy of School Do's: AOL Schools as the Answer

We blacks need an affirmative approach to improving our schools, not a racially-charged one laden with complaints, accusations, and anger. Following is what its basic thrust ought to be.

While the school bears a major responsibility for the school success of our children, we blacks bear the major responsibility. We should not attempt to cover up our failure to perform it. We must not make the school a scapegoat and an adversary, but rather must work cooperatively with it to fashion -- not through charter schools or privatization, but at the neighborhood level where our students live -- schools which can be called Art of Loving (AOL) Schools, so called because they make ubiquitous the *practice of the art of loving* (care, responsibility, respect, and knowledge) and because they employ a bread-and- butter curriculum whose gold standard is not to leave any child behind based, not solely on standardized test results, but, in addition, on opportunities to develop their abilities and on their possession of the basic emotional, relationship, job, and everyday living skills necessary for them to live a valued and self-reliant life. Such schools are possible through *family-oriented classrooms* under the leadership of top-flight principals who have an ongoing staff and curriculum development program to assure the *practice of the art of loving* and who design and implement curricula (making use, as feasible, of African American males in various capacities, such as, teachers and teacher aides) whereby activities are conducted so as to meet the varied needs, interests, and abilities of its students and – given our students' identity and character deficits – so as to put students' identity and character development on par with their academic and cognitive development. Further, in such schools, an attempt would be made to *reduce*, perhaps within a statistically-derived range, the black-white academic achievement gap rather than to *close* it, which is an unrealistic goal in view of our three major demons, *IQ lag-fatherless families-crime*, the refocus permitting a modification of the use of the school resources.

This is a mouthful, so let the intent be clear: rather than being a burden to family and community, the core intent is to enable our African American male students, in particular -- *all* of them -- minimally, to do something which too many cannot now do, which, first of all, is to take care of themselves, and second, to take care of their loved ones. Far too many are leaving school unprepared to meet adequately the most basic life demands -- like exercising some reasonable control over their emotions, filling out a job application, getting a job, keeping a job once they are employed, and managing their money.

In AOL schools, all staff members, in all of their interactions and functions, would be expected to engage in the **practice of the art of loving** and to make it a ubiquitous part of the school curriculum and program (by, for example, having a command of basic listening and responding skills and by getting to know each student as a person). Its practice would provide students the love that they are so often deprived of and for which they, therefore, unconsciously, if not consciously, long for and need in order to foster their growth and enrich their human spirit. From that growth and enrichment, they are likely to derive the energy and drive to sustain and propel them. Students would be taught to practice the art of loving. They, too, would be expected to engage in it, and -- in and out of school -- to make it a part of their daily living.

The classrooms in these schools would be *family-oriented*. The teachers would look upon their class as a family and its students as family members. With that mindset, permeated by the practice of the art of loving, they would guide and supervise their students in a variety of structured, but informal learning activities, in the process of which, teachers and students would interact in the fashion of family members – not only listening, responding, and sharing in regard to the task activities, but at the same time, engaging in chance exchanges whereby they discuss what else might be on their mind and, as need be, the teacher engaging in follow-up. And, yes, they would have IQ scores and any other relevant diagnostic data available to assist them in better understanding each student (Alfred Binet's purpose in originating the IQ test). This classroom vision can be encouraged, and implemented, if teachers, for example, are not preoccupied with such current concerns as meeting standardized test expectations and closing the black-white academic achievement gap, rather than just reducing it.

The priority emphasis which AOL schools would give to career readiness might cause some of us to cringe -- much like it contributed to DuBois's castigation of Washington. We ought to be committed to the liberal arts, but conditionally; survival comes first. Survival is a requisite for liberation, which is what the liberal arts are supposedly all about. If this sounds like the thinking of Booker T. Washington, it is. Fixated on creating "men" rather than "workmen," DuBois, on the other hand, vilified that thinking, seemingly failing to see, like those who have followed in his footsteps, that no one shoe fits all. So concerned he seems to have been that our curriculum be equal to that of whites that he failed to see the prior demands of adaptability.

In any instance, we need to take a rigorous look at our credentialing and educational requirements -- for blacks, whites, Hispanics, and Asians alike. It is a point, for example, made by Herrnstein and Murray in <u>The Bell Curve</u> and stressed by American writer, Nicholson Baker, in an article in <u>Harper's</u> entitled "Wrong Answer: The Case Against Algebra II." Herrnstein and Murray argue that credentialing should be made easier, a lot of it currently being unnecessary or having nothing to do with one's ability to perform a given job (121: 541-42). In a similar vein, Baker argues that "life's prerequisites are courtesy and kindness, the time tables, fractions, percentages, ratios, reading, writing, some history -- the rest is gravy, really" – Algebra II included (304c:35). (Of course, if our leaders are fixated on civil rights and consumed, as Lasch-Quinn contends, by their therapeutic sensibility, they are not likely to focus on such fundamentals -- unless, that is, they can make them a civil rights or race issue.)

Broadly, this proposed bread-and-butter curriculum is guided by the maxim set forth by Jensen in his famous article, the thought being that, whatever the source, we make use of that which is going to benefit our race. When we do not, we hurt ourselves. We can benefit from the insights and prodigious work of Jensen, a very bright man. His maxim can be considered the professionally accepted gold standard of education. It follows:

> **If diversity of mental abilities, as of most other human characteristics, is a basic fact of nature, as the evidence indicates, and if the ideal of universal education is to be successfully pursued, it seems a reasonable conclusion that schools and society must provide a range and diversity of educational methods, programs, and goals, and of occupational opportunities, just as wide as the range of human abilities. Accordingly, the ideal of equality of educational opportunity should not be**

> **interpreted as uniformity of facilities, instructional techniques, and educational aims for all children. Diversity rather than uniformity of approaches and aims would seem to be the key to making education rewarding for children of different patterns of ability. The reality of individual differences thus need not mean educational rewards for some children and frustration and defeat for others (139:117).**

If students do not experience success, as typically is the case with any of us with any endeavor, they are going to get frustrated and are not likely to stick with it -- which is exactly what is happening with our African American male students. And for students to experience success, as Jensen's maxim suggests, the instruction must be responsive *simultaneously* to their diversified needs, interests, *and* abilities. No easy accomplishment, but we have put men on the moon, and if we set ideology and racial sensibility aside (likewise, no easy accomplishment; in fact Lasch-Quinn's point is that the race experts have made it even harder), we can -- as AMSAC cries out for -- design and reasonably implement AOL schools with bread-and-butter curricula. The program proposed, the African American Male Career Pathway Program (AMCAP), in fact, is designed to be such a curriculum and it would appear that the Booker T. Washington High School, discussed in Chapter 12, has many of its features, as does KIPP. George Taylor's <u>Practical Application of Social Learning Theories in Educating Young African-American Males</u> further addresses the kind of social skills which a bread-and-butter curriculum ought to emphasize (255).

Historically, schools have had components of what is being called a bread-and-butter curriculum. All schools focus on the fundamental skills and many on social and career skills as well. The proposed bread-and-butter curriculum calls for these schools, guided by the ubiquitous **practice of the art of loving**, to bring these different elements into a single, unified curriculum which -- without sacrificing the traditional academic role of the school (in fact enhancing it, which is what you do when you respond to the individual needs of students) -- has as its gold standard the ability of *all* its students to become competent in the basics and to leave being able to get and keep a job, and better able to manage their emotions, get along with others, and take care of their daily needs.

No doubt it is apparent that such schools would be person-centered rather than academic-centered, and focus would be, not just on the group, but, equally, on individuals in the group. Test results would be an outcome, not the driving force. Rather, the driving force would be career-ready, character-conscious students who **practice the art of loving** and have basic competence and cultivated interests. These factors cannot be brought together and implemented unless the following exist: principals who are highly qualified, energized, and committed, as well as teachers who are able to observe and analyze student behavior and who, at the elementary school level, are skilled in diagnostic-prescriptive teaching.

Perhaps Payne would call this description a supportive environment wherein there is **authoritative-supportive teaching** (208a:96-120). In any case, Payne says that it is this kind of teaching that we blacks remember as having worked for us -- the good old days before *Brown v. Board of Education* when we had black schools that worked. They were paragons of institutional caring where expectations were high, teachers strict, and the school met black students' academic, extracurricular, psychological, and sociological needs (somewhat like Tuskegee Institute, attention to the extracurricular being a standout exception). At least that is the selective memory. Valid or not, Payne says that it, in fact, turns out that research shows that the schools of today which have these features, summed up as high-press and high-support, turn out high-achieving, high-performing students. The features are these (208a:99):

1. High level of intellectual / academic demand
2. High level of social demand [proper behavior]
3. Holistic concern for children and their future; sense of larger mission
4. Strong sense of teacher efficacy and legitimacy

High-support, it should be singled out, comprises parent and peer support, not just support from teachers. Payne observes that a high level of performance has occurred when there has been support from all three groups; when the support of any one of the three has been lacking, student performance has been mediocre.

Joe L. Rempson

What, finally, needs to be drawn upon is New School. New School is the name given to the reported highly successful method of teaching started in Colombia and, subsequently, expanded to 19 countries (366b). Developed by Clara Victoria (Vicky) Colbert de Arboleda in the 1970s -- and designed for the children of the poor -- it uses the small-group approach to learning wherein children of various ages and grade levels work in small groups at their own pace, helping one another, with the teacher acting as a guide rather than front-of-the-classroom knowledge dispenser. The content is made relevant to the lives of students and their families; and (believe it or not) tests are given when students are ready for them. Moreover, dropouts and absent students are accommodated, since, reportedly, they can return to school at any time and continue where they left off. Not new, in its small-group and self-paced aspects, this approach is among those one learns about in teacher training courses in this country, but they are not so commonly practiced; and what Colbert has done is to incorporate these components into an overall approach which is student-centered, community-centered, and individualized. While difficult to make what works in one culture or country work elsewhere, the point is to examine New School to explore what might work in this culture. Some of its elements, in fact, quite incidentally, are part of what is suggested below -- and very much a part of AMCAP.

Some of its elements would, likewise, appear to be present in the smaller specialized high schools in New York City (446c, 460c, 461b). Between 1999 and 2010, the city closed 40 underperforming high schools and opened more than 250 small schools, so called because they enroll 110 or fewer 9th graders each year – most of the impetus coming under former mayor, Michael Bloomberg. The schools are built around various themes – such as law, environment, and sports careers – and are mostly academically nonselective. The results have been impressive. The graduation rate is 71.6 percent versus 62.2 percent for students in larger high schools, and – directly relevant – 42.3 percent of the black males who graduate enter college versus 31 percent of their counterparts in larger schools. "Teachers and principals overwhelmingly identified personalization as a key – or as *the* key – to their school's success" (461b:ES-22).

At the center of both the New School and the small schools curricula are personalization and individualization. The two go hand and hand, and the results provide empirical support for the AOL school concept herein proposed.

Thus, we have an overview of what we blacks ought to do to improve our schools, keeping in mind that if schools do what they ought to do, that will help to solve AMSAC. Some selective elaboration and some additional suggestions follow, suggestions which address specific concerns or matters which are especially germane.

Help restore discipline and order. Restoring order and discipline to the school and classroom should top the list, bringing school and community together in a concerted effort, in the process avoiding making our schools an armed camp. The KIPP (Knowledge is Power Program) national network of charter schools provides guidance for us in this regard. Geoffrey Canada's Harlem Children's Zone charter school principal, Glen Pinder, drew upon the KIPP model to help bring order and success to its middle grades (258: 155-87; 217: 135; 438e).

Turnaround for Children, a nonprofit organization run by its founder (1994) and president, Dr. Pamela Cantor, provides an example of another approach (432b). Turnaround for Children works with schools and teachers to help them create an orderly environment. Nearly all of the schools with whom it works in New York City are nearly 94 percent black or Latino. Its premise -- similar to David Kennedy's in Operation Ceasefire and in his Overt Market crackdown -- is that if you target the 5 percent of the students who behave the worst you can create an orderly environment. Failure to target them, Dr. Cantor contends, leads to their pulling "down the next 10 percent to 15 percent of troublesome students in an academic riptide." In a whole-child approach, her social workers meet with teachers and administrators to address individual cases, focusing not just on academics, but also on the student's psychological and emotional wellbeing, as needed, referring students to therapists. An independent study of effectiveness shows improved school atmosphere, sometimes dramatic, though not necessarily improvement on standardized test scores.

We might be well served, too, if we went back into our own history. Booker T. Washington's Tuskegee Institute, the preeminent symbol of race success in our history, provides a model of discipline (strict rules and regulations). Drawing upon the spirit of that discipline, we could reconnect with a revitalizing part of our past and contribute in a more transforming way to improving the attitude and behavior of our students. As exemplified by the Race to the Top High School Commencement award, that, apparently, is what the Booker T. Washington High School appears to have done.

Promote autonomy over autocracy. The need for order and discipline must not, however, lead us to advocate authoritarian schools and classrooms. Although we must first get students' attention, once acquired, we must not use it to turn them into automatons. We want our students to learn to exercise self-discipline and self-control, and to be able to be self-directed. Our guidance must not be "external imposition," as John Dewey proclaimed, but, instead, must consist of "freeing the life process for its own most adequate fulfillment." Rather than using a top-down approach, achieving these outcomes necessitates students' active involvement in the planning and conduct of practices and activities as pertain to their behavior and instruction. Such a growth and nurturing approach (versus the kind of autocratic approach that so often characterizes their child rearing) is more likely to enable them to acquire the same kind of noncognitive skills [emotional intelligence] that our children learned, for example, in the Perry Preschool Program and the Abecedarian Early Childhood Intervention Project. As discussed, in those experiments, the decisive variable in students' success turned out to be, not their test scores – which, in fact, regressed over time -- but the noncognitive skills which they had acquired.

Place emotional intelligence (inclusive of time perspective, grit, and willpower) on par with cognitive learning. The major point to be made here is that, so far, the concern of school reformers has been almost exclusively with closing the achievement gap. The research suggests that there is another gap on which we should equally focus and whose closing would likely reap far greater rewards: call it the emotional intelligence or character gap, specifically including time perspective, willpower, and grit. Research indicates that our EI or character is our executive function in that it determines how well we use the fluid intelligence (Gf), abilities, and talents which we possess. Research further shows that we can do significantly more about improving EI than we can do about improving our cognitive intelligence.

The daunting challenge that we face with so many of our students, our male students in particular, is getting them to exert the behaviors that will optimize the cultivation of their abilities and talents, whatever those abilities and talents happen to be. Those behaviors and abilities often tend to be undermined by a host of home, community, and school factors, and get manifested in a variety of anti-school, anti-authority ways. Enhance their character, and, thereby, alleviate these undermining factors, and we enable them to cultivate better their underdeveloped abilities and talents. An example of such an emphasis, as described by Cose, appears to be provided by the Perspectives Charter School in Chicago (49:216-220). It works to help its students acquire norms and values which will enable them to live a disciplined life. Twenty-six principles, as pertains, for example, to hard work and time management, serve as its guide. In his most recent book, How Children Succeed, Paul Tough cites the aforementioned (and frequently mentioned) KIPP charter schools as well as a number of other character-oriented programs. He makes a persuasive case (as attempted herein) for putting character building at the center of school reform for our African American students (258a).

Emphasize problem-solving, not rote learning. Give equal weight to emotional intelligence and simultaneously replace a drill-and-test approach to learning with an individualized, problem-solving approach, and perhaps we would have surpassed all other efforts to improve our schools (see Ratvich's discussion of the testing mania, 217: 149-67). Our students, like all students, must be taught to think, to learn skills which they can transfer to new situations and which will enable them to cope successfully with life's ever-changing personal and work challenges. Rote learning will not accomplish this goal, nor will treating all our students the same. It is a truism that instruction geared to the needs and interests of the individual student -- variously conducted on an individual, small-group, or whole-class basis -- is instruction at its best. Of course, such an approach does not preclude an emphasis on traditional basic skills, but rather should meaningfully incorporate them, not forgetting that there is indeed a crucial, though not dominating, place for test-taking skills, memorization, repetition, and drill (such as pertains, for example, to the Times Tables, poetry, and the rules of grammar, diagramming included).

Opt for cultural literacy over Afrocentrism. The latter emphasis might suggest, and correctly, an emphasis on much that is traditional which has been abandoned as we in education have become more "progressive." The author is in complete agreement with Professor Emeritus at the University of Virginia, Eric Donald Hirsch Jr., whose manifesto is in his national bestseller over twenty years ago, Cultural Literacy: What Every American Needs to Know. He makes the case for cultural literacy being an imperative, by culture meaning, not social class or artistic exposure, but "the basic information needed to thrive in the modern world." "Cultural literacy," he argues, "constitutes the only sure avenue of opportunity for disadvantaged children, the only reliable way of combating the social determinism that now condemns them to remain in the same social and educational condition as their parents" (122:xiii). A self-evident truth, one can argue, and Hirsch is to be applauded for proclaiming it. There is no place for an Ebonics or restrictive Afrocentric mindset in a world of national and global competition.

No less of a commanding reason to embrace Hirsch's advocacy is its implication for African American core identity. Cultural literacy conceivably promotes a feeling of being part of this nation, contrasted with a feeling being apart from it, or of having an identity which is without national validation (Separatism is McWhorter's description of it). The author recalls the "60 Minutes" story of a colleague, who said that, in a class of around 40, when he asked how many students had heard of "60 Minutes," not one student raised her or his hand. This was when "60 Minutes" was at the height of its popularity. The story suggests the difficulty our students have developing a part-of feeling (alluded to by President Obama in his Trayvon Martin comments, discussed in Chapter 11): they are largely insulated (absorbed in "blackness") and, as a result, probably feel a two-ness. Having a part-of feeling helps to mitigate the "two-ness" of which DuBois spoke and the Victimology and Separatism of which McWhorter speaks. That potential mitigation contributes to the enhancement of a unified, loved self -- or of a positive core identity -- the lack of which is postulated to be the root cause of AMSAC and its inseparable social problems. With a more positive core identity, we are likely to get the kind of character traits shown by research to be associated with school and life success. For that reason -- *as much as, if not more than, any other* -- as Hirsch proclaims, "Cultural literacy constitutes the only sure avenue of opportunity for disadvantaged children, the only reliable way of combating the social determinism that now condemns them to remain in the same social and educational condition as their parents."

Attend to developmental and daily needs. To return to a problem-solving approach for our students, we must apply it to their daily living as well. We must provide structured classroom time to allow for attention to their developmental and peer needs, problems, and interests. Such attention is essential to their normal development, but, in most cases, their home is unlikely to provide it. Teacher training would be required. A social-psychological support staff (for example, clinical social worker, psychologist, and counselor) would also be required. The structured classroom time could be the primary means whereby we provide emotional intelligence training, although it is essential that some of the basic elements of such training permeate the entire teaching-learning process.

Insist on early intervention. These are things that must be started at an early age, including prenatal care. The research is convincing: if we start early enough -- and only if we start early enough -- through both in-school intervention programs and parent-outreach programs, we can sufficiently compensate for our students' home deficiencies to enable them to succeed in school and in life. At least, when it comes to our girls, this holds true; for our boys what, *in addition*, must be done needs to be explored. Remember, we do not have to aspire for them to become academic stars or to be equal to whites or to any other group. We only need for them -- as a group -- to be able to take care of the bread-and-butter issues. That is, we only need for them, as a group, to perform reasonably normal. Nothing more! Let us jumpstart them right out of the box, so to speak -- in fact, before they emerge from it. Do so, and the research suggests that we stand a good chance of achieving this goal. The participation of parents on public assistance might even be made mandatory as a condition of their eligibility. In any instance, it is early intervention programs that, on a quality basis, we should be advocating -- urgently and vigorously.

As recommended by black Harvard economist, Ronald Ferguson, the advocacy should include support of parent education programs. An example of such a program is provided by the late <u>Washington Post</u> Pulitzer Prize Winning columnist, William Raspberry, whose BabySteps Project is highlighted by Eugene Robinson (227:131-32). The Project staff came to realize that, to enable the children to succeed, it was not enough to work just with the children; they also needed to work with their parents. So, they added a robust parent component which, for example, includes home visits. It might be remembered that the key to President Bill Clinton's election in 1992 was the slogan: "It's the economy, stupid!" An essential key to our success in solving AMSAC and its inseparable social problems might be phrased similarly: "It's early intervention, stupid!"

Address popular culture influences. Focus on the early years should not lead us to take our eye off our youth culture, as Ferguson emphasizes (87:58-69; 348). Ferguson sees popular culture -- less leisure time reading, hip hop, rap music, and "acting white" -- as contributing to youth "disengagement from academic endeavors." Both the home and school ought to address this disengagement, which Ferguson suggests probably helps to explain the fact that between 1971 and 1988, for 17-year-olds, the black-white reading-score gap narrowed by over 60 percentage points, but came to a halt around 1990. It may be instructive, as well. that Borman, Springfield, and Slavin's, <u>Title I: Compensatory Education at the Crossroads</u>, cited above, document a similar trend with respect to the achievement of our public schools generally: impressive achievement gains during the 1970s and early 1980s, only to have those gains stall since then. After all, our youth influence their younger siblings. Of course, changes in our popular culture may or may not explain these trends, but we must try to rectify whatever might reasonably help to account for them.

Cultivate the best and the brightest. We must not take our eye off the need to encourage and nurture the best and brightest among us. DuBois is on the mark when he opens his famous "Talented Tenth" essay with the sentence, "The Negro race, like all races, is going to be saved by its exceptional men." Let us, then, not rail against tracking and other special classes to nurture and advance exceptional students. That our students are disproportionately outnumbered in these classes has nothing to do with *racial* discrimination; it has everything to do with *academic* discrimination, as should be the case. The idea is to be *discriminating* so as to single out exceptional students for more appropriate instruction. Why begrudge any student, regardless of race, that opportunity simply because our students, disproportionately, do not qualify for it? The whole society, of which we are an integral part [sometimes seemingly hard for us to digest], benefits if the exceptional among us are appropriately encouraged and nurtured. As is too often the case, we let racial thinking blind us to our own best interest. Rather, let us do all we can to get our own students into these class. Early intervention initiatives and promoting a culture of academic striving is the means to this end. Wrath is one of the Seven Deadly Sins; envy is another.

Train our own to become change agents. While targeting the students themselves -- the ordinary *and* the exceptional -- along with their parents, we need to stress the importance of the students, in turn, upon graduation, helping our community. As AMSAC and its inseparable social problems make evident, we have not fulfilled our adaptation needs. What Booker T. Washington did with his Tuskegee Institute students, at the turn of the last century, needs to be done with our students today: preach community service and the need to put our training and skills to use helping our own people. We have had more than enough black middle-class flight from our black neighborhoods -- with the consequences that William Julius Wilson depicts in his <u>The Truly Disadvantaged</u>. We must take steps to reverse the trend. Preaching community service to our students could be one such step. Financial and other incentives might also be considered. Over time, such encouragement could measurably contribute to the completion of Washington's unfinished task that was forsaken by DuBois and the system-centered thinkers who have come to dominate the black agenda. It is, in fact, fitting to recall Washington's model and vision as related by Norrell. Tuskegee Institute was his model, and there he trained thousands of teachers to go throughout the Deep South and set up "Little Tuskegees;" and his Tuskegee board assisted black schools in the region. Through his model, he envisioned what might be termed a self-made race. As Norrell captures his dream:

> Self-made people were more likely to succeed. Washington envisioned for every black community two teachers, a man and a woman, committed to uplifting the whole community. 'Let them be teachers, not only in the school-house, but on the farm, in the flower-garden, and in the house, and we have a central light whose rays will soon penetrate the house of every family in the community.' This new teacher corps would lay the foundation for blacks 'so well that the race can stand securely thereon till it has served the great ends of our Creator' (192:74).

It is just such a model and vision that is still needed today. Rather than our constant cry about the qualifications and expectations of those who teach our students, why not, a la Washington, set about training our own to go into our poor neighborhoods to undertake the task? That would give our premier organization, the National Association for the Advancement of Colored People (NAACP), for example, something more currently relevant to undertake. The same is true for our civil rights leaders in general.

Seek and support quality leadership. Whatever we advocate, emphasis needs to be placed on getting highly qualified principals, and supporting them, since "leadership could be considered the single most important aspect of effective school reform" (164:172). If they turn out to be members of our own race, that would probably be a plus, but the determining factor must be their professional qualifications. Those qualifications should be the same qualifications, alluded to above, for the recommended AOL schools. In turn, these principals must have an ongoing inservice training program to promote teacher and curriculum development, as well as an outreach program to parents.

Black Advocacy of School Don'ts

Here are a couple of things that we should not do in an attempt to improve our schools.

Attack rather than support

Foremost, as alluded to, we need to stop engaging in a war against our schools, as so many of us do. Our activists, academics, and political leaders engage in so much anti-school rhetoric and activity that they create and perpetuate an atmosphere of school-community animosity. It was surprising and disappointing, for example, to see one of our leading black educators, the aforementioned Steve Perry, doing exactly that in his most recent book, Push Has Come to Shove: Getting Our Kids the Education They Deserve (Even If It Means Picking a Fight). Speaking to parents, he says: "You have rights. You never have to go to a meeting with the school by yourself. Bring an advocate who can help you understand and support you" (209a:93). That is shocking advice. It is divisive and irresponsibly provocative to say to parents that they cannot go to school by themselves because in effect the school cannot be trusted. While perhaps providing a sense of contribution and accomplishment [therapeutic alienation, discussed elsewhere, might be John McWhorter's description of it], the result of such commonplace rhetoric is more likely to be an atmosphere that stifles progress and success. Rather than being irritants and demonizers, we should, instead, want to be constructive partners with the one institution that offers us, through our sons and daughters, the best chance we have of uplifting ourselves and our race. We ought to be loyal supporters, doing all we can, working with the school to enable it to do the best job possible. Research shows that when we support our schools, our students do their best. When necessary, we, of course, should be critical, but constructively so, with a spirit toward helping to solve problems instead of, as is too often the case, creating them.

Put test score success over life success

Then, in our urgent need to turnaround our poor students' school performance, let us not lose sight of that which counts most: to enable them to succeed in life. That is what Booker T. Washington's Tuskegee

Institute was about, school success, yes, but school success that led to life success in the interest of self *and* community. If our students can pass all the tests and make us look good (especially our politicians) by meeting test standards, well done! But let us not drive them test crazy and consume their time with all the extras that go into the craze -- extra tutoring, extra hours, extra days, and so on. Diane Ravitch puts it well:

> Tests are necessary and helpful. But tests must be supplemented by human judgment. When we define what matters in education only by what we can measure, we are in serious trouble. When that happens, we tend to forget that schools are responsible for shaping character, developing sound minds in healthy bodies ... and forming citizens for our democracy [in our case, desirably for our community], not just for teaching basic skills (217:166-67).

Given the fade-out effect whereby our students tend, in later grades, to lose test gains made in earlier grades, the benefits of the craze are dubious. John Ogbu (among others) provides an informative review of some of the relevant research on this topic (194: 91-95). We can learn from the Perry Preschool Program and the Abecedarian Early Childhood Intervention Project that what counts more than students' test gains (not to say that test gains are not important) are their noncognitive or character gains.

Conclusion

We must strive to preserve and improve our neighborhood schools, avoiding the temptation to turn to charter schools as the answer to our students' poor school performance. We must also avoid the temptation to turn to testing and teacher accountability as the solution. The solution lies in Art of Loving (AOL) schools with a bread-and-butter curriculum which comes as close as possible to guaranteeing that *all* of our African American students will be able to meet better five core needs: basic literacy, emotional control, relationship skills, job readiness, and daily living management. Start early enough, beginning at the prenatal stage, and work with the school, rather than fight with it, and – guided by the **practice of the art of loving** – we can get our children to meet these five core needs – especially if we have top-flight principals and have student-centered curricula which inculcate in our students those character attributes on which school and life success depend.

Part IV

We African Americans "on the Hook"

17

The Case for Our Self-Responsibility Tradition as The Tradition of Choice: You be the Judge or Jury

Proverbs, 16:22 – "Understanding is a wellspring of life unto him that hath it: but the instruction of fools is folly."
Galatians, 6:5 – "For every man shall bear his own burden."

In previous chapters, we have defined and described the African American School Adaptability Crisis (AMSAC) within its social context, examined its immediate and root causes (identity and character deficits), discussed the catalytic results of its root cause (Victimology and its effects), and throughout discussed the relevant role and contribution of our two adaptation traditions, the **Self-Responsibility Tradition** of Booker T. Washington and the **System-Responsibility Tradition** of W.E.B. Du Bois. It is contended that the uplifting of the race has been better served by our Self-Responsibility Tradition, and it is only through a renewal of that tradition that we can solve AMSAC and its inseparable social problems; it is, therefore, **The Tradition of Choice**. This renewal can be brought about through a **Child Family Rights Movement**.

However, it is one thing to contend that one or the other tradition has better served our uplifting, but quite another to *prove* it. Thus the question: can you (the author) *prove* your thesis that our

Self-Responsibility Tradition has better promoted our uplifting. The answer: as in a legal proceeding, we can only offer the evidence and make the argument. Whether that evidence and argument *prove* our case is up to you to decide; you are the judge or jury.

The case is based on the premise that how well each tradition has served us must be measured by its success in enabling us to meet our **Adaptation Requirements**. Like other immigrant groups, voluntary or involuntary, we are required to get the education, get the jobs, and establish the stable families and neighborhoods which will enable us to enter the mainstream. Formulated from background knowledge, insights gained in the course of the research, and from directly relevant studies, seven socioeconomic variables were selected to measure these requirements: (1) intact homes; (2) basic education; (3) college/postsecondary training; (4) employment; (5) home ownership; (6) poverty; and (7) crime (see these relevant studies: 318a, 321b, 349b, 395c).

Judgment Guide: Meeting Adaptation Requirements

How well our two traditions have served our adaptation needs can be evaluated based on the responsiveness of their activities to these seven variables, that is, their **adaptation responsiveness**. By activities is meant, not just doing something, but also advocating or not advocating doing something, or causing something to be done, such as causing a law to be passed, a case to be adjudicated, or a school to be established. That is, we are talking about the effect on our adaptation of their deeds and ideas. We begin with their deeds.

Using Deeds to Judge Our System-Responsibility Tradition

The acts of our System-Responsibility Tradition have been mainly civil rights activities, the epicenter of its tradition. The major entity which represents the tradition, the National Association for the Advancement of Colored People (NAACP), though for most of our history, has never dedicated itself to addressing most of the variables in our adaptation index. That is why, at least in part, we have the National Urban League (started in 1911), which was started because the NAACP (started in 1910), although it had an economic component, devoted little time to economic problems per se (92:354-55). The National Urban League filled the gap; furthermore, it added a social component. We can think of it as helping blacks in the cities in a manner similar to the help which Washington, through Tuskegee, provided blacks in the South. Thus, the National Urban League can be considered to be more a part of our Self-Responsibility Tradition than our System-Responsibility Tradition. Washington, incidentally, was one of its sponsors and, later, became a member of its Board of Directors.

Beyond dispute, the System-Responsibility Tradition of DuBois has yielded impressive *opportunities*, but, along with those opportunities, uneven results. On numerous fronts, it has, for many of us black Americans, turned the dream of equal opportunity into a reality. Its accomplishments are, indeed, a matter of record. In their From Slavery to Freedom: A History of African Americans, Franklin and Moss, for example, variously cite that record, as does black sociologist, E. Franklin Frazier, in his The Negro in the United States, and more recently black historian Henry Louis Gates Jr., in his Life Upon These Shores: Looking at African American History, 1513-2008. It has brought about the desegregation of our schools through *Brown vs. Board of Education* and the end of *de jure* segregation. Under President Lyndon B. Johnson, and during the Civil Rights Movement, it brought us the *Civil Rights Act of 1964*, the *Voting Rights Act of 1965*; the *War on Poverty* (1965) and *Affirmative Action* (1965). Its goals achieved, the Movement -- as manifested through the direct-action protests of the 1950s and 1960s -- has ceased, but not the epicenter from which it derives. Most notably, through the NAACP and our leadership class, ita epicenter remains alive, as does the dominant System-Responsibility Tradition which it personifies.

The opportunities opened up by the Tradition have contributed (historians tell us that other factors were also involved) to an adaptive transformation in the lives of millions, making it possible for us, increasingly, to become part of the American mainstream and to achieve the American dream (192:421-42). In his book, Disintegration: The Splintering of Black America, Eugene Robinson succinctly captures this transformation, pointing out that, 40 years ago, in a representative sample of blacks half would probably have been poor whereas today only about one-fourth are; most, 75 percent, would be middle class (227:6-8). However, he observes that the trend stalled in the mid-'90s, leaving us with 25 percent having been left in poverty. Robinson sees this 25 percent as standing alone, and Abandoned, most of us blacks blaming them for their condition (227:227, 236).

In sum, overall, our System-Responsibility Tradition can take credit for having fostered our adaptation through gaining sufficient opportunities for us to make advancements and, simultaneously, getting us sufficient support to enable us to avail ourselves of those opportunities. No small accomplishment, but not sufficient! Is accomplishments are qualified. They benefit the acculturated, but far less so the externally adapted. Robinson makes the point that most of us might see it as their fault, but the fact is that it is our fault, our meaning the entire African American race, because the System-Responsibility Tradition which we have embraced since the death of Washington has led to the demise and disrepute of the Self-Responsibility Tradition (though its roots remain) which Washington fathered and which had as its primary target those whom Robinson labels the Abandoned.

There is another qualification. Robinson makes the point that our progress has a short history. Its origin dates back to around the middle of the past century, for it was then that World War II had given impetus to a military-industrial complex that led to an explosion in job opportunities (227:89-91). Then, in addition, there was the previous war and a vast expansion of government which, thrown into the mix, helps to explain the opportunities for progress that has occurred over the past forty to fifty years -- and only over that period (192:440-441). When, then, we talk about our progress under the Civil Rights Movement and the System-Responsibility Tradition that gave rise to it, we are talking mainly about the last forty to fifty years and the national and world economic conditions that created jobs over that span and, with the Civil Rights Movement, the vastly expanded opportunities for blacks to fill them.

It is not as if, then, the System-Responsibility has a history of success with its protest agenda. As observed in Chapter 4, DuBois admitted that neither his "direct frontal attack" nor the NAACP's legal victories had any meaningful impact. The success cited covers a relatively limited time period, has been contingent on independent external factors, and, perhaps foremost, has been selective. None of these factors minimize its significance, the point being that, to say the least, our System-Responsibility Tradition has not provided a magic formula for our uplifting. Given its condemnation of the Self-Responsibility Tradition and its glorification of its own, one might be led to think otherwise. In fact, it can be argued that without the imprint of our leaderless, though not lifeless (it has roots) Self-Responsibility Tradition, its success would have been more selective -- and more limited.

Using Deeds to Judge Our Self-Responsibility Tradition

When we turn to the deeds of our Self-Responsibility Tradition, we turn to Washington and his Tuskegee Institute because they define the tradition. Its activities are personified by those of the man and what he did, keeping in mind that he both expressed and shaped the dominant thinking of his time. The adaptation activities of the Self-Responsibility Tradition, then, are exemplified in the activities of the Age of Booker T. Washington -- of the man and his institution that dominated African American thought from 1880-1915. Some of his activities follow.

Foremost among his activities was what, herein, is being called the **practice of the art of loving**. The research suggests that Washington practiced **the art of loving**, not, of course, always (he was human), but predominantly. An explanation of the **practice** is contained in Chapters 14 and 19. Although, perhaps, not usally thought of an an activity, the discussion of it herein is believed to make it evident that, not only is it an activity, but it is a master activity on which other productive activities are dependent.

From the outset, really, its role in Washington's legacy was evident. Beginning with $2,000, and nothing more, it is his **practice of the art of loving** which enabled him to find a building for Tuskegee, recruit its first students, garner the support of the community, and, within a decade, build it into a renown institution. For example, in one of the many early obstacles, after he and his staff made three unsuccessful attempts to build a kiln for brickmaking, his staff, thereupon, urged that the effort be abandoned – and, at that point, they really had no choice since there was no money to continue. But Washington refused to give up, instead, he went to Montgomery and pawned his gold watch [a present from a New England widow] for $15 (244:76). So now a fourth try, and this time a successful one. His **practice of the art of loving**, exhibited by his **$15 Washington Gold Watch Pawning**, had enabled him to succeed.

The leadership role which ensued from such success, Scott and Stowe point out, was thrust upon him, and, as he had to build Tuskegee, he had to define, at least implicity, his leadership role – no limitation from the start, as in building Tuskegee, but with his own life and with the totality of human existence upon which to draw. In the following description, Scott and Stowe give us a sense of the definition he came up with.

> After the Atlanta speech he was in almost daily contact with what was befalling his people in all parts of the country and to some extent all over the world. Through his press clipping service, supplemented by myriads of letters and personal reports, practically every event of any significance to his race came to his notice. When he heard of rioting, lynching, or serious trouble in any community he sent a message of advice, encouragement, or warning to the leading Negroes of the locality and sometimes to the whites whom he knew to be interested in the welfare of the Negroes. When the trouble was sufficiently serious to warrant it he went in person to the scene. When he heard of a Negro winning a prize at a county fair, or being placed in some position of unusual trust and distinction, he wrote him a letter of congratulation and learned the circumstances so that he might cite the incident by way of encouragement to others (234:34-35).

At a personal level, we we see its evidence in Scott and Stowe's story about one of Tuskegee's students, Washington A. Tate. It is well worth repeating in full:

> During his early years at Tuskegee he seemed unable to grasp the most rudimentary information. His native dullness was made unpleasant and aggressive by a combative disposition. He was constantly trying to prove to his exasperated teachers that he knew what he did not know. He was almost twenty-five years of age when he reached the Institute and entered the lowest primary grade. He had the greatest difficulty in passing any examinations and

never succeeded in passing all that were required. Motions were constantly made and passed in faculty meetings to drop Tate, and were as constantly vetoed by Mr. Washington on the plea of giving him one more chance. Finally when Tate's time to graduate came the teachers in a body protested against giving him a diploma. Mr. Washington argued that a man who had made all the sacrifices Tate made at his age to stay in school, a man who had worked early and late in fair weather and foul for the school, a man who had stuck to his task in the face of repeated failures and discouragements, had in him something better than the mere ability to pass examinations. Through Mr. Washington's intercession for him Tate got his diploma. The next day Mr. Washington had him employed to take charge of the school's piggery. Because of his hard, conscientious, effective work in this capacity he was afterward recommended to the United States Department of Agriculture at Washington as the proper man to take charge of the United States demonstration work in Macon County, Ala. Tate proved to be one of the Government's most successful demonstration agents (234:365-66).

Finally, Washington was hailed for his **KNOWLEDGE** of people. In addition to his natural gift for understanding people and events, Scott and Stowe declare that "his judgments of men and events were almost infallible"(234:453). He studiously worked at that understanding. The head of his Records and Research Department, Monroe Work, is said to have provided him "startlingly accurate information about his people in every section of the United States," and Harlan points out that the son of abolitionist, William Lloyd Garrison, Francis J. Garrison, was constantly amazed by Washington's telescopic knowledge of racial matters in the South and North alike (234:38, 109:251). After hearing him speak, this is how a Georgia farmer reacted: "'I don't understand it! Booker T. Washington he ain't never ben here befo', yit he knows mo' 'bout dese parts an' mo' 'bout us den what eny of us knows ourselves'" (234:38).

These descriptions convey evidence of Washington's **practice of the art of loving: CARE, RESPONSIBILITY, RESPECT, and KNOWLEDGE**. Consider, as well, the following attributes which its practice requires (98, 226):

- discipline
- concentration → *which can be acquired through* →
- patience
- supreme concern

- objectivity
- humility
- reason

↓

Self-preoccupation or excessive self-love stands in the way of our developing these attributes and therefore we must be able to:

↓

- overcome narcissism

↓ ↓ ↓

All of which requires • an active mind complemented by • faith/courage

Throughout these pages, our discussion of Washington makes his possession of these attributes variously evident. Some of Washington's other activities follow.

- In a run-down Methodist church shanty (used as an assembly room), he started Tuskegee in 1881, and by 1900 had built it into an institution with: 2,300 acres of land, 700 used for cultivation with student labor; 40 large and small buildings, all but four erected by students -- and most multistoried built from red bricks *manufacturled on the campus*; 28 industrial departments; 1,100 students from twenty-seven states and territories, as well as from Africa, Cuba, Puerto Rica, Jamaica and other countries; and 86 officers and instructors (265:381-82). Before his death in 1915, annual enrollment had grown to around 1,500, surpassing that of nearly *all* other Southern higher education institutions, with some 10 new buildings being added, making the campus, in Norrell's words, "an architectural showplace" (192:197), one visitor calling it "Booker T. Washington city" (244: 189) [Norrell observes that the success of Tuskegee demonstrated that our race, on its own, had the ability to succeed (192:71-74]. Its endowment reached over a million dollars and it attracted prominent visitors, including two Presidents, from the nation and the world (192:9; 109:61-65)].

- Teachers trained at Tuskegee set up 18-20 "Little Tuskegees" near Tuskegee and throughout the Deep South (192:72-73, 200-01; 234:426-34).
- Tuskegee served as "a kind of informal board of education for black schools -- placing teachers, supervising curriculum, listening to complaints, and finding support for the little rural schools" (192:73).
- Enlisted philanthropic help in establishing hundreds of schools and providing our people a variety of services, from medical care, to legal challenges to discrimination, to support for black artists and intellectuals (192:368-71).
- Through Tuskegee, provided a range of services to the Tuskegede community, including:a dispensary that grew into $50,000 hospital; a Ministers' Night School, a Building and Loan Association; and a town night school and library for boys and girls in Tuskegee (244:122).
- Started Annual Tuskegee Negro Conferences in 1892, within a few years, the Confeence attracted thousands to practically-oriented proceedings, participants from the surrounding area and other states sharing information on such topics as their living conditions, landowning, schools, and moral and religious conditions (244:118-21).
- Under the initiation and direction of his wife, Olivia, conducted Weekly Women's Meetings, eventually attracting as many as 300 women each Saturday, covering such topics as morals for girls, amusements for children, and the canning of foods (244:121-22).
- Through State Agricultural Experiment Station started at Tuskegee in 1897 under George Washington Carver, brought scientific farming methods to farmers, disseminated information to them through publication of a "Farmer's Calendar," and offered a two-week Farmer's Short Course preceding the Annual Negro Conferences (244:120-21).
- Set up Southern Improvement Company, which sold graduates small farms in Macon County and provided credit and farming advice (192: 200). Apparently, due mainly to this and other efforts, by 1910, over 500 of 3800 black farmers in Macon

- County owned their own farms, and 90% of the 3800 were owners or cash renters (244:121).
- Initiated and sponsored efforts to discover and disseminate information on black progress, including the first <u>Negro Year Book: An Annual Encyclopedia of the Negro</u>, a biography of Frederick Douglass, a two-volume <u>Story of the Negro</u>, and the Southern Educational Tours, 1908-12 (192:371-75; 132).
- Organized the first statewide professional group for black teachers, the Alabama State Teachers' Association (192:73-74).
- As founder of the National Negro Business League in 1900, Washington served as its president until his death and saw it grow to 300 local affiliates by 1905, and produce such offshoots as the National Negro Funeral Directors' Association, the Negro Bar Association, and the National Association of Negro Insurance Men (244:123-24).
- He and his Tuskegee graduates exported the Tuskegee model to Africa, leading to schools and training in industrial education, the introduction of cotton, and to the spread of his self-help doctrine (192:201-02; 110:68-97).
- Encouraged and assisted in the formation of the National Urban League, and later became a board member (109:436; 192:406-407).
- Established a "Model Negro Village," *Greenwood Village*, which, in effect, residentially replicated Tuskegee (109:169-70). It consisted of 200 nearby acres of land bought by Tuskegee. Washington and Tuskegee officers arranged its layout and sale, and set up the Village Improvement Association to administer it. Mainly populated by Tuskegee faculty, by 1906, it had a population of 2,100. Under Washington's attentive eye, it was a model of cleanliness and order, its children being admitted to a Tuskegee campus model school. He demonstrated that blacks could successfully create and administer an all-black school and an all-black village as well.

In 1900, before he broke with Washington, DuBois investigated the impact of Washington's annual Negro Conferences for black farmers, surveying 200 participants (192:226). He concluded that they had brought about real progress, 30% of those surveyed being landowners of an average of 124 acres. His overall observations was that "'Here is a school planted in the midst of the rural black belt which has sought to raise the standard of living, and especially to change the three things that hold the Negro still in serfdom--the crop lien system, the one-room cabin, and the poor and short public school.'"

Nor was DuBois the only investigator to report on the "real progress" produced by Washington. By coincidence, another of his famous compatriots did likewise: leading journalist of his time (and later, among other things, Pulitzer Prize-winning biographer of Woodrow Wilson), Ray Stannard Baker. Baker was asked by Washington and Villard to investigate the causes of the Atlanta riot of 1906 which occurred in response to local newspaper reports of alleged assaults by black males on white females. Over a three-day period, white mobs killed dozens of blacks, wounded many more, and inflicted widespread business and property damage. Baker ended up extending the investigation into a nationwide examination of racial problems, doing a series of articles on what he learned and then compiling those articles in a 1908 book, <u>Following the Color Line</u>. In one of the articles, Norrell reports that he compares Washington with DuBois. At some length, we quote Norrell's description of that comparison.

> Baker witnessed support for Booker among the 'thousands of common, struggling human beings' to whom he had given hope and a plan for how to improve their lives. Booker was like Abraham Lincoln: each had 'the simplicity and patience of the soil,' immense courage and faith, and, 'to prevent being crushed by circumstances,' a strong sense of humor -- 'they laugh off their troubles.' Wherever Baker found 'a prosperous Negro enterprise, a thriving business place, a good home, there I was almost sure to find Booker T. Washington's picture over the fireplace or a little framed motto expressing his gospel of work and service.' In contrast, Baker characterized Du Bois as an intellectual with the temperament of the 'scholar and idealist--critical, sensitive, unhumorous, impatient, often covering its deep feeling with sarcasm and cynicism.' He found a parallel between him and the white nationalists: both Tillman and Du Bois exhorted their races to agitate. Washington, on the contrary, told his people to work. But Baker thought that both men were needed: Washington was the opportunist and

the optimist who did his work 'with the world as he finds it: he is resourceful, constructive, familiar,' whereas Du Bois was the idealist, the agitator, and the pessimist who saw the world 'as it should be and cries out to have it instantly changed' (192:383).

Baker's incidental anecdotal evidence supports DuBois's study, further underlining the impact of Washington's activities. The results are testimony to their uplifting role in the lives of millions, and to the fact that Washington's self-help approach, devoid of a civil rights emphasis, worked. That did not eliminate the need for us to acquire and exercise our civil rights. However, there was no need to make those rights a prerequisite for progress -- as DuBois insisted. The deeds on display add up to the building of human, institutional, and infrastructure resources ***in the absence of civil rights***.

That building adds up to something else that Norrell reminds us was wanting at the time: racial pride and favorable perception (the image problem) (192:441-42). Just out of slavery, heretofore, except for our survival, we had nothing of which to be proud and were perceived as incapable of achieving more. Against almost insurmountable odds, Washington gave us something, above all, something unique, Tuskegee Institute -- a black-founded, black-built, black-student, black-taught, and black-administered teacher training institution. In the process, he gave us capability, a black man who could accomplish near miracles and rub shoulders with the privileged and the powerful. Frederick Douglas, in part, had done likewise; he could rub such shoulders but to produce near miracles was another matter. Whether they did so or not, those who doubted that a black man possessed such capability were given reason to pause. Our own pride was evident. "For almost two generations after his death, scores of schools, parks, community centers, libraries, and streets were named for Booker T. Washington," and most of the public high schools built in the South during the 1920s and 1930s were named for Booker T. Washington or George Washington Carver (192:423).

Norrell points out, along came World War II and the deeds of Washington bore further fruits of pride and favorable perception. The nation led the way. For example, a ten-cent stamp displaying Washington's image was issued and, "In 1942 a cargo vessel was named the *SS Booker T. Washington* and given the merchant marine's first black captain and a multiracial crew" (192:427-28). To recruit its first black military pilots, the army gave a contract to Tuskegee to provide flight training for aspiring black airmen, and established a separate, segregated army base in Tuskege, called Tuskegee Army Air Field or, sometimes, Advanced Flying School. From it came the Tuskegee Airmen of World War II fame, eliciting black pride and demonstrating black ability. Such pride and favorable perception of themselves, based as they were on real accomplishments (on "results," Washington might say), can help to foster the development of a positive core identity and can translate into a positive force in helping to meet our adaptation requirements.

Though Washington dominated his age, as implied, however, he was not the only show in town, so to speak. He led his time, yes, but Meier makes clear that he also expressed it. When we talk about the Age of Booker T. Washington, it has to be kept in mind that we are talking about a period in time, 1880-1915, during which he dominated. But what he preached both lead and reflected the tenor of his time. The age is named for him, but it was not just about him; it was also about that which occurred during his reign and which represented the thinking and values which he personified. Meier captures the point being made::

> ...the roots of the New Negro, both as an artistic movement and as a racial outlook, were in the social and intellectual movements of the age of Washington. They lay in that group economy, and above all in the philosophy--itself imbedded in the social situation of the Negro group and in the institutional development of the Negro community--of race pride, solidarity, and self-help (168:259).

As for Washington's influence, Meier sees him as "reinforcing tendencies already in the foreground" (168:118). "The fact," he reasons, "that Negroes tended to see in his words what they already believed would appear to minimize his direct influence. Yet his prestige, the teachers sent out by Tuskegee and her daughter schools, and the widespread publicity generated by the National Negro Business League of which Washington was the founder and president, undoubtedly had a significant impact on Negro thought..." -- as it were, "reinforcing tendencies already in the foreground."

Those tendencies of his age -- race pride, solidarity, and self-help -- Washington lead and translated into such deeds as those cited above.

Of course, anti-Bookerites will point, not to his deeds as the earmarks of his Age, but to his lack of deeds, dwelling on civil rights. His alleged failure to "fight for our rights" serves as an albatross that, in their mind, dwarfs his deeds, making him less than a man -- certainly less than a "true man" to use DuBois's characterization, and less than black, with no place, except traitor and Uncle Tom, in the pantheon of black history. **DuBois's Washington Demonization**, depicting Washington in his classic The Souls of Black Folks as selling us out, laid the foundation for that defamation. It was reinforced by DuBois, most notably in his Dusk of Dawn. Norrell tells us that two influential historians who accepted DuBois's portrayal, C. Vann Woodward and his student, Louis R. Harlan, picked up **DuBois's Washington Demonization** and (somehow) imprinted it on the radicals of the Civil Rights Movement. Their portrayal of Washington has become so common that it can be called **The BTW Meme**, the concept of meme being borrowed from McWhorter (161: 172). **The BTW Meme** is the *thought pattern* that Washington's practice of accommodation resulted in his "not fighting for us" and his having "sold us out" – a thought pattern which, more or less, subconsciously, much like genes in organisms, has been automatically and unthinkingly been passed along over roughly the last two generations. **The BTW Meme** is one of our mnemonics, reminding us of one of the effects of Victimology and its associated civil rights fixation.

Among other things, those who subscribe to The BTW Meme fail to recognize, and to factor into their assessment, the historical circumstances. It is as if Washington lived in *their* place and time, not his own, which was the South right after the Civil War and Reconstruction. This decisive omission has been alluded to and discussed elsewhere herein, particularly in Chapter 4, which treats the Washington-DuBois war, and in Chapter 10, which treats the role of the two traditions in our identity formation. Moreover, it is really at the heart of Norrell's informative biography of him, Up from History, which has been extensively cited throughout. Why "up" from history? It is because, seeing him through **DuBois's Washington Demonization,** history has "thoroughly devastated" his reputation (to use Norrell's phrase), judging him, not in the context of his place and time, but its own. Washington was apparently suppose to disregard the danger to his race and to himself and embark, on Southern soil, on a civil rights crusade at a time when his people, barely out of slavery, were struggling just to survive and, again to quote Harlan, "A tide of white aggression was engulfing the black communities." Life there and was perilous and precarious for us. We had a "place" and to be "out of it," however slightly or perceived slightly, put us in personal danger. We had no means to "fight back." With what? There is a difference between courage and stupidity, and there is wisdom in realizing when it is better to forgo a fight so as to be able to live to fight another day. Washington knew the difference and exercised that wisdom; the same cannot be said of his critics, driven as they were by anger, a present-fatalistic/past-negative time perspective, and power resentment. As regards a present-fatalistic/past-negative time perspective, let us be reminded of what Zimbardo-Boyd tells us are its characteristic traits:

- lack of self-control
- lack of personal responsibility
- difficulty in interpersonal relationships
- low sense of self-actualization
- low levels of positive outlook and expectations
- anxiety
- depression
- anger

Still, in the relationship between the races, Washington was not, as depicted, a subscriber to surrender. As Harlan captures it, "Washington's program was not consensus politics, for he *always sought change* [emphasis added], and there was vocal opposition to him on both sides that he tried to mollify" (239:178). Please note: opposition from *both* sides: radical blacks and white nationalists (so, if we want to invoke the label, traitor, can we omit from consideration those blacks, DuBois being chief among them, who, in effect, joined forces with white racists?) Wisdom dictates that one fight from a position of strength, and through the deeds cited, Washington sought to acquire just such a position. As Meier quotes one of his friends as saying, "He was…attempting to bring the wooden horse within the halls of Troy," that is, to build that position in the unfriendly soil of the South (168:116). In the meantime, one does – as Washington did --what is practical and possible. While *publicly* conciliatory on civil rights for most of his life, he waged a lifelong underground (secret) battle against racial injustice. In his Century magazine article in 1912, "Is the Negro Having a Fair Chance?," he can be said to mark his emergence from secrecy to more openness, with the addition of a "protest agenda" -- Washington style, of course, (279; 192:407; 109: 406). Even more so was the case with his posthumous article in the New Republic, entitled "My View of Segregation Laws." Harlan writes that the NAACP was so impressed by its forthrightness that it reprinted it as a pamphlet (112:124).

Reference has been made to his mostly secret and seductive efforts. As a reminder and symbol, let us now give them a mnemonic: **Thomas A. Harris Rescue/ Birmingham Letter**. We can also give them a headline: **THE BTW MEME FALSE: WASHINGTON'S SECRET AND SEDUCTIVE FIGHT FOR OUR CIVIL RIGHTS**. Further, the aforementioned black Florida A&M University historian, David Jackson Jr., cites the **Thomas A. Harris Rescue** as an example of historians and others putting Washington into an "accommodationist box," which, for us blacks, boils down to mean that he "*did not fight for us.*" Jackson's point is that if, say, DuBois had done what Washington did for Harris, it would, for DuBois, have been a defining moment, not something that gets little or no attention, while, in Washington's case, the "fix is in," so to speak – so it gets him exactly that: little or no attention. Washington's **Birmingham Letter**, similarly, does not reflect the fervor of a "protest agenda" nor the striking of a blow.

Nevertheless, even Harlan, while observing that the **Thomas A. Harris Rescue** "deepened Washington's commitment to duplicity," also acknowledges that it was the only way that he could securely exercise power and influence (108:171). And what applies to the **Thomas A. Harris Rescue** also applies to the **Birmingham Letter**: they symbolize Washington's "fight for us," a fight which he had no choice but to wage secretly and seductively if, in the first place, he were to remain alive to be able to exercise power and influence -- this admission, not from a Washington admirer, but from one of his two most famous detractors (Woodward being the other).

But as the saying goes, "The Lord giveth and the Lord taketh away."[32] Harlan does, indeed, recognize Washington's valor, but he only gives him "some" honor for his handling of the affair (108:175). Why just "some" honor? He labels Washington's explanation of the rescue as evidence of his "genius at self-justification," contending that the secret method used by Washington was intrinsically corrupting because it "deepened Washington's commitment to duplicity" and led him to come to use such secret methods in pursuit of his other goals, such as, in war against his black enemies (108:174-75).

Given such a portrayal, what we see inside of what Jackson labels the "accommodationist box" is the portrayal of a traitor -- a man who "did not fight for us." As the saying goes, however, often, when one wants to get something done, one has to "think outside the box." In this instance, if what we want to get done is to learn whether Washington did or did not fight for us, we have to "look outside the box" -- and no further, in fact, than the **Thomas A. Harris Rescue/Birmingham Letter**. It is suggestive of Washington's civil rights leadership -- secret, selective, opportunistic, discreet, deft. Put the rescue in his adversaries accommodation box, however, and it becomes something different: **self-justification, duplicity, corrupting**. Of course, one could argue that it is all in "the eyes of the beholder," only, when those eyes are "boxed in," we ourselves have to look outside the box.

In the **Thomas A. Harris Rescue/Birmingham Letter** that look "outside the bos" reveals a man -- and reminds us of a man -- who waged a secret and seductive lifelong fight for our civil rights. His waging includes, as elsewhere cited, Harlan's own revelation that, before his break with Washington in 1903, Washington had even assisted DuBois in a challenge to the Georgia law segregating sleeping cars and that the two were "secretly cooperating as late as December 1904 in an effort to test the Tennessee Jim Crow law." Of such efforts, Harlan (though unfriendly, too good of a historian not to report the facts – and, hence, his book-winning prizes) says the following:

---

[32] Saying based on Job, 1:21: "and said, Naked came I out of my mothers womb, and naked shall I return thither: the Lord gave, and the Lord hath taken away; blessed be the name of the Lord."

> He secretly paid for an [sic] directed a succession of court suits against discrimination in voting, exclusion of blacks from jury panels, Jim Crow railroad facilities, and various kinds of exploitation of the black poor. In all this secret activism, it is clear that Washington was not merely trying to make a favorable impression on his militant critics or to spike their guns, for he took every precaution to keep information of his secret actions from leaking out. Only a handful of confidantes knew of his involvement (112:113).

Harlan goes on to describe a number of these activities -- some not so secret -- as does Norrell, as does Meier (168:110-14), and as does later referenced Scott and Stowe in their book, Booker T. Washington: Builder of a Civilization (see, for example, 192:185-20, 403-420; 234:121-56). These activities suggest Washington's use of an "Underground Railroad" when it came to civil rights. Instead of secret routes and safe houses, he used secret money (his own) and safe surrogates. However, both uses had equivalent goals, in one case, to escape capture and return, and in the other case, to escape the killing of a man and his cause. As critical as Harlan is of Washington, the accommodator, as he pejoratively saw him, he offers the assessment that "In both his secret struggle against Jim Crow laws and his espionage against his black and white liberal critics he exhibited more of what the Mexicans call *machismo* than his public role allowed" [emphasis in original] (112:127).

As a reminder, then, that Washington's defamers give him little, if any, credit for his civil rights activities – assuming, of course, that, as is unlikely, they know, or care to know, about them -- we can add the following to our **Thomas A. Harris Rescue/Birmingham Letter** mnemonic: self-justification, duplicity, corrupting. The additions yield this final civil rights mnemonic for him: **Thomas A. Harris Rescue/ Birmingham Letter: self-justification, duplicity, corrupting**. It can serve to remind us that Washington waged a secret and seductive lifelong fight for our civil rights which his defamers -- ignorant of it or not -- ignore, disparage, or minimize.

Not mentioned by Harlan, nor even by Norrell, in the context of Washington's civil rights activities is his dinner at the White House with President Theodore Roosevelt on October 16, 1901. That they have not is understandable, however, because, in itself, the dinner is not a civil rights activity. Yet, step back and put it in a civil rights context. As Senator John McCain observed in his concession speech upon defeat by President-elect Barak Obama in 2008, "A century ago, President Theodore Roosevelt's invitation of Booker T. Washington to dine at the White House was taken as an outrage in many quarters. America today is a world away from the cruel and frightful bigotry of that time." "There is no better evidence of this," he went on, "than the election of an African-American to the presidency of the United States" (402c).

Some may recall the Reverend Jesse Jackson's tears of joy on the day of President Obama's inauguration, the moment seemingly signifying for him the crowning of the Civil Rights Movement. Senator McCain reminded us that the initiation of that crowning can be said to have had its origin with the Washington-Roosevelt dinner. Washington demonstrated what foundation-building could make possible for the race: a seat and voice at the table with the dominant race, something central on the civil rights agenda. As President Obama brought tears to the eyes of Reverend Jackson, Norrell reports that Washington's dinner brought equivalent joy to most African Americans of his time. A Chicago minister hailed "the president's act as 'an omen of the coming of that day when we shall neither be favored nor hindered because of the color of our skin'" (192:246). President Obama symbolized that day and we owe to Washington the omen that set it in motion. And just as Obama has used his office for the uplifting of the race, so, through his ties with President Roosevelt, did Washington (see Harlan, 109:3-31; Norrell, 192:238-358; and Meier, 168:110-14).

As observed in Chapter 4, prior to the President's election, the connection was not lost on Lee Walker. Beyond its symbolism, he discerned the substance, demonstration of the Washington gospel of hard work and self-reliance as the route for blacks as for all others. But President Obama did not acknowledge either. That omission is herein called **President Obama's Washington Omission in His First Inaugural Address**.

It is a sad commentary that it was left to a white political leader to acknowledge and remind us of a historic part of our own black history, and to a less publicized black leader, Lee Walker, to remind us of the substance which that part of our history reflects. But that is the result of our civil-rights fixation bred by our disobedience in the African

American Garden of Eden. President Obama has been unable to escape its hold, and as discussed in Chapter 19, Dr. King was shackled. One can question why either had an obligation – or, for that matter, even a logical reason -- to connect with Washington and **The Tradition of Choice**, but leaders have a threefold obligation: to the past, present, and future. And our past is not all about civil rights; we had the Age of Booker T. Washington which also has made it about our self-responsibilities. We can ignore or denigrate that past, but we cannot obliterate it. Let us be reminded that our history is not all about civil rights; it is also about our civil responsibilities – what we owe ourselves, our loved ones, our community, and our nation. Intoxicating though the civil rights tree has been, it has not induced a coma. It is incumbent upon our leaders to recognize and draw upon the main currents which still pulsate through our culture. However, when the gospel is that someone has "sold us out," it is understandable why, in the first place, it might not be on their minds, and, in the second place, even if it were on their minds, why it might be inadvisable to make it publicly known that it is. Our second bondage, Victimology, has made any favorable Washington acknowledgement, not just unpopular, but, maybe, even punishable. To Dr. King's credit, however, when the anti-Washington tide was in its ascendancy, he took a stand against it, a story told in Chapter 19.

Otherwise, more of less, the widespread notion that Washington "sold us out" goes uncontradicted when the *facts,* inclusive of the Washington-Roosevelt dinner, suggest the contrary: Washington *fought* for our civil rights -- not as an ideologue and activist, but secretly and seductively as a pragmatist and foundation-builder.

Washington's Atlanta Compromise as Deed

It might be hard to believe that we can trace the African American *demand* for our civil rights back to Washington's infamous Atlanta Compromise Address of 1895. So civil rights consumed as were some blacks were back then, and so civil-rights fixated are so many today that, consequently, we overlook the roots of our civil rights which Washington's compromise preserved. He forbade us to eat freely the fruits from the civil rights tree in our African American Garden of Eden, but not to be denied, the Wizard of Tuskegee planted roots from it in his compromise. Those roots were reflected in his mostly secret and seductive civil-rights activities, and, quite openly, in his article, discussed in Chapter 4, "Is the Negro Having a Fair Chance?" In his Compromise, he preserved them, most notably, in these assertions (See Appendix A):

> *There is no defense or security for any of us except in the highest intelligence and development of all. If anywhere there are efforts tending to curtail the fullest growth of the Negro, let these efforts be turned into stimulating, encouraging and making him the most useful and intelligent citizen.*
>
> *It is important and right that all privileges of the law be ours ..."*

As Lincoln defined, in his Gettysburg Address, what the nation stood for, in these assertions, Washington defined our place in it. That place was not one of subservience or subordination, as DuBois alleged, but one that echoed the spirit of the Declaration of Independence: our entitlement to "Life, Liberty and the pursuit of Happiness." No small deed, and no need for our civil rights vanguard to have turned to DuBois for inspiration; they would have been better served by turning to Washington and to our African American roots which he more authentically embodies – roots which embrace both civil rights and civil responsibilities. Some might argue that, in his address -- and in the same breath -- he also sanctioned segregation, which, in all things "purely" social, he did, and that, further, he declared our need for preparation "vastly more important" than our privileges, which he did, but, as with the Declaration of Independence, the spirit of liberty which he proclaimed in these and other assertions holds for us blacks a more dominant and enduring legacy. Even at that time, contrary to whites, Meier reports that Washington's supporters emphasized the "future implications" of his remarks -- the "Life, Liberty, and the pursuit of Happiness" which, honored over time, they could bring (168:101). Our African American Male School Adaptability Crisis (AMSAC) and its inseparable social problems call for a similar current emphasis from us African Americans. The revitalization of our "Black Moses" requires us to see him, not from the perspective of what he *had to do*, but from the perspective of what, as evident from a reflective reading of his Compromise, he *sought to do*.

Joe L. Rempson

Here is the headline: **THE BTW MEME FALSE: WASHINGTON'S MOSTLY SECRET AND SEDUCTIVE FIGHT FOR OUR CIVIL RIGHTS AND HIS ATLANTA COMPROMISE WHICH PRESERVED THEM**. We can turn to his not-so-friendly biographer, Harlan, to make the case (109:244). Harlan points out that Washington was "one of a class of black leaders and spokesmen" who practiced accommodation and shunned protest. He pictures Washington as seeking to "disarm the whites by conceding what mattered least to blacks or most to whites, and then to persuade the whites to behave better by gentle rebuke, flattery, and inordinate public praise for every act of decency he could find among them in the age of white supremacy." Harlan labels him as typical rather than exceptional in this regard, exhibiting the customary behavior of black spokesmen living in the South. What made Washington exceptional, however, were "his skill in manipulating the whites, his zeal in exhorting blacks to strengthen themselves through self-help, his constant search for allies among the whites, and his deeply secret civil rights campaign through financing test cases in the courts."

Elsewhere, Harlan essentially emphasizes what revisionist biographer Norrell emphasizes: that Washington addressed many of the same issues as the NAACP addressed (109:435). Referring more specifically to Washington's later years, Harlan observes that, "Whereas the NAACP from a northern base sought to challenge racial injustice, Washington from a southern base sought to ameliorate it."

Need more be said? However, Washington's way of fighting was not the way which appeals to the "true man" image of DuBois and his System-Responsibility Tradition. That is, it was not an indiscriminate exercise in public outrage; rather, it was a calibrated exercise in action. Until those last few years, he showed little or no public outcries or condemnations or "show" of opposition. Instead, like a skillful boxer or adept martial artist, Washington's strategy was artfully defending, probing, forbearing, and taking advantage of openings and opportunities. When the circumstances changed, and the moment seemed ripe, he became more aggressive, striking the blows that he thought would earn him a victory. That is what the skillful boxer or martial artist does. He did not act from impulse, but, strategically and skillfully, from reason and reality. He balanced heart and head. That is the mark of an accomplished fighter, be that fighter a skillful boxer, an adept martial artist, or -- as in the case of Washington -- an adroit leader with the earned moniker of "*Wizard* of Tuskegee."

It might be argued that if Washington had more *publicly* displayed a willingness to "strike the blow," he might not have encountered the enmity of DuBois and others – and, thus, would have secured his place in black history. However, even if he were of such temperament, which it appears he was not, that would not have been possible in his surroundings. He would not have lived long enough, nor been able to accomplish enough, to warrant a place worthy of securing. That is another lesson to be taken from the **Thomas A. Harris Rescue/ Birmingham Letter: self-justification, duplicity, corrupting** mnemonic.

Guided by the "true manhood" motif of DuBois and his System-Responsibility Tradition, we make the mistake of projecting our manhood conception, in all its narrowness, onto the larger American stage. But that stage calls for a broader conception. Yes, it, indeed, does call for being able to "strike the blow," as DuBois puts it, but as well to retreat and defend, to deflect, to probe, to seize openings and opportunities, and to forbear. All of which require "true manhood" -- not the narrow kind that DuBois propagated and which many of us have come to prize so highly, but the broader, inclusive kind that commands the American -- and world -- stage. That we have come to judge Washington solely by the former says more about us than him.

It says that we have permitted ourselves to be brainwashed into a narrow and shallow view of our "Black Moses." Called by his definitive biographer Harlan, though no fan of Washington, "the most powerful black American of his time and perhaps of all time ...," our civil rights establishment and its kindred and its connected academics have practically exorcised him, except pejoratively, from our discourse (111:164). Our civil- rights fixation has led us to see someone who, though sharing our fight, is *not on our side* and, therefore, a traitor because he did not, in "true manhood" fashion, make a public display of it. From this mindset, we have the image of the black Tuskegee student described by Norrell as having said of Washington's statue on the Tuskegee campus, *Lifting the Veil of Ignorance*: "We got this statue out here of that man who's supposed to be lifting up the veil. Man, he's putting it back on."

It is an incredulous interpretation which defies rational understanding, regardless of what one might think about Washington's civil rights emphasis. But, when we combine the subcultural concept of "true manhood" with the psychological state of civil rights fixation, it is at least less so. For we can define *civil-rights fixation as an obsession with civil rights, regardless of context and circumstances, which leads to giving civil rights a disproportionate, distorted, or ill-founded role in black-white relationships or in black life outcomes*. In part, thus civil rights obsession probably grows out of, and is intrinsic to, the "true manhood" motif. So exclusive has become its emphasis that it is no longer just a strategy; much akin to what McWhorter calls *therapeutic alienation*, civil rights has become an animating force with a life of its own, quite apart from context and circumstances, taking on a quasi-religious quality. The Tuskegee student exemplifies such a force. And, as Norrell observes, "Other interpreters of Booker T. Washington would take the same stance [as the Tuskegee student] for at least a generation" (192:14). Yes, he said "at least" a generation. We are still counting, perhaps being reminded of Hosea 4:6, "My people are destroyed for lack of knowledge...."

Critics, too, most notably DuBois, point to Washington's emphasis on industrial education, faith in free competition and individual enterprise, and Southern habitation as misguided (see, for example, black historians Franklin and Moss, Jr., 92: 305-306). However, it is apparent from the literature that the challenge to his leadership had its origin, not so much in these issues, but in his public civil rights posture and his political power -- and it would seem to have been much more the latter than the former. In confiding that his differences with Washington were more a matter of degree than substance, DuBois admitted as much.

Overall, at stake is an approach to adaptation and race relations that, in a word, has pitted pragmatism against protest. It might even be said that one values doing good, the other values feeling good. One engages in salvation, the other in sermonizing. Or, as John McWhorter might put it, one values therapy, the other values therapeutic alienation. Or, as President Lyndon Johnson put it when the civil rights establishment and others rejected the **Moynihan Family Initiative**, one gives priority to substance, the other gives priority to symbols.

Using Hard Data to Judge Our Two Traditions

Viewed from the perspective of hard data, however, can we say that the deeds of one or the other have better served us on our seven **Adaptation Requirements** variables? Often, it gives us some level of confidence when we use hard data to make a point, so it is a tempting question to raise. If one thinks the Self-Responsibility Tradition has served our adaptation needs better than the System-Responsibility Tradition, as is the case herein, then the point is to prove it by showing that, during its dominance, we fared much better on our seven variables -- which would be proving it by association.

We take on that challenge, but not rigorously, since to do so would be beyond the expertise and scope of the author's endeavor. Based on an examination of the research undertaken, the author's presentation of the data is restricted mainly to the use to one reference source (which can be considered a primary source) and two secondary sources. The reference source is Jessie Carney Smith and Carrell Peterson Horton's two-volume Historical Statistics of Black America (238). The assumption is that differences in data outcomes associated with our two traditions would likely be revealed in a reference dedicated to the publication of an array of historical data about black Americans designed to inform rather than persuade.

The two secondary sources are Charles Murray's Losing Ground and William Julius Wilson's The Truly Disadvantaged. Murray's book is considered one of the most influential of the 20th century on policy and social science,[33] Wilson indicating that it provided the philosophical base for curtailing the War on Poverty during the presidency of Ronald Reagan, 1981-89. Both examine the outcome of the System-Responsibility Tradition for the period when it was at its zenith. That was during the period roughly from 1964 to 1980, during which the largest federal (system) effort in our history to eliminate poverty was

---

[33] Retrieved on 10 February 2015 from http://en.wikipedia.org/wiki/Losing_Ground_(book) 22 January 2015.

undertaken. That effort was initiated and labeled by President Lyndon B. Johnson as the Great Society in his State of the Union address on January 8, 1964.

Two major acts defined the Great Society: the Civil Rights Act of 1964 and the Economic Opportunity Act of 1964. The Civil Rights Act, Murray declares, marked the triumph of the Civil Rights Movement – and, thus, of the System-Responsibility Tradition of which it is the epicenter. With the power of sanctions, for the first time, it opened up the institutions of society to those of us who are black; there would be penalties for denial of black access to American institutions.

Through an array of economic initiatives which were labeled the War on Poverty, the Economic Opportunity Act was intended to complement the Civil Rights Act by the translation of the equal opportunities afforded by it into equal outcomes. Together, the two acts can be said to mark the zenith of the System-Responsibility Tradition. Murray sees the results of this zenith as producing "net harm." Responding, Wilson -- while acknowledging the data from which Murray draws his conclusion -- pins the "net harm" however, not on the self (that is, not on individual responsibility as does Murray), but on the system (that is, on an economic downturn and an adverse job market). The assumption herein is that by examining the data and the data interpretations of the two, together with the data obtained from Smith and Horton, it is possible to discover hard data that would be helpful in answering the question of whether hard data exist to prove, to some degree, the relative efficacy of our two traditions.

First, we need to have a more vivid image and a fuller understanding of what, during its zenith, the System-Responsibility Tradition entailed. University of South Carolina historian Kent Germany's following description of the Economic Opportunity Act's War on Poverty provides that image.[34]

> Begun officially in 1964, the War on Poverty was an ambitious governmental effort to address the problem of persistent poverty in the United States. Over the next decade, the federal

---

[34] Reprinted with permission of Prof. Kent Germany.

government--in conjunction with state and local governments, nonprofit organizations, and grassroots groups--created a new institutional base for antipoverty and civil rights action and, in the process, highlighted growing racial and ideological tensions in American politics and society. Marked by moments of controversy and consensus, the War on Poverty defined a new era for American liberalism and added new layers to the American welfare state. Legislatively, the first two years were the most active. Between President Lyndon Johnson's State of the Union address in 1964 and the liberal setbacks suffered in the congressional elections of 1966, the Johnson administration pushed through an unprecedented amount of antipoverty legislation. The Economic Opportunity Act (1964) provided the basis for the Office of Economic Opportunity (OEO), the Job Corps, Volunteers in Service to America (VISTA), Upward Bound, Head Start, Legal Services, the Neighborhood Youth Corps, the Community Action Program (CAP), the college Work-Study program, Neighborhood Development Centers, small business loan programs, rural programs, migrant work programs, remedial education projects, local health care centers, and others. The antipoverty effort, however, did not stop there. It encompassed a range of Great Society legislation far broader than the Economic Opportunity Act alone. Other important measures with antipoverty functions included an $11billion tax cut (Revenue Act of 1964), the Civil Rights Act (1964), the Elementary and Secondary Education Act (1965), the Social Security amendments creating Medicare/Medicaid (1965), the creation of the Department of Housing and Urban Development (1965), the Voting Rights Act (1965), the Model Cities Act (1966), the Fair Housing Act (1968), several job-training programs, and various Urban Renewal-related projects.

The Republican administration of President Nixon continued the broadly defined War on Poverty. Although President Nixon expressed dislike for much of the War on Poverty, his administration responded to public pressure by maintaining most programs and by expanding the welfare state through the liberalization of the Food Stamp program, the indexing of Social Security to inflation, and the passage of the Supplemental Security Income (SSI) program for disabled Americans. Beyond such escalations of specific programs, the Nixon administration's most noticeable contributions to the War on Poverty consisted of replacing the OEO with the Community Services Administration, redistributing control over many antipoverty programs to more traditional federal bureaucracies, and proposing a Family Assistance Plan that failed to gain congressional approval (358a; also see 100a).

Reference source data

While an ostensible logical source from which to draw hard data, Smith and Horton's <u>Historical Statistics of Black America</u> did not turn out to be as helpful as hoped, but,

Nevertheless, somewhat useful. Using sample data, the idea was to take a comparative look at what was happening during a designated period of tradition dominance in regard to the stipulated seven socioeconomic variables on which adaptation depends, intact homes being primary among the seven. Such data, however, were difficult to find -- so difficult that even the periods of that dominance had to be varied based on data availability.

Given this understandings, for our Self-Responsibility Tradition, data from Smith and Horton are used which cover the period from 1880-1940. That may not be a totally unreasonable span since it, at least, considerably precedes the heydays of the Civil Rights Movement and covers about a generation after Washington's death, over which time his tradition might have, more or less, still been dominant even in the absence of leadership. For the period of dominance for our System-Responsibility Tradition, data are used from

Table 4

Two Traditions Compared on Seven Socioeconomic Variables

1. **Intact homes** (804-805, 1895-1899)
   SYSTEM

Percentage of children living with one parent		Black	White
	1960	25	7
	1970	35	9
	1975	46	13

   SELF and SYSTEfM

Out-of-wedlock births per 1000 population:		Black	White
	1930	143.4	18.0
	1931	153.9	19.2
	1940	168.2	19.5
	1950	179.6	17.5
	1960	215.8	22.9

2. **Basic education** (520, 555-56)
   SYSTEM

Percentage completing 4 years of high school or more: 25-34-Year-Olds		Black	White
	1940	11	39
	1960	33	61
	1970	52	74
	1975	69	82

   SELF

Percentage of total population enrolled in school, ages 5-20 Male		Black	White
	890	32	59
	1910	43	64
	1940	64	72
Female 1890		34	57
	1910	46	61
	1940	65	71

3. **Postsecondary training** (624, 631)
   SYSTEM

Percentage of 18-24 year-old males: Enrolled in college		Black	White
	1950	5	15
	1960	7	19
	1970	16	34
	1975	20	30

Joe L. Rempson

Percentage of 18-24 year-old females enrolled in college	1950	4	8
	1960	7	12
	1970	15	21
	1975	21	24

SELF
Black undergraduate enrollment in public and private colleges:

	Number	% Increase
1910	2,760	--
1920	4,060	47
1930	13,572	234
1940	21,708	60

4. **Employment** (1101-1102, 1096-1097)
   SYSTEM
   Percent unemployed, 1948-1975:

	Black and other	White
1948	5.9	3.5
1949	8.9	5.6
1950	9.0	4.9
1951	5.3	3.1
1952	5.4	2.8
1953	4.5	2.7
1954	9.9	5.0
1955	8.7	3.9
1956	8.3	3.6
1957	7.9	3.8
1958	12.6	6.1
1959	10.7	4.8
1960	10.2	4.9
1961	12.4	6.0
1962	10.9	4.9
1963	10.8	5.0
1964	9.6	4.6
1965	8.1	4.1
1966	7.3	3.3
1967	7.4	3.4
1968	6.7	3.2
1969	6.4	3.1

1970	8.2	4.5
1971	9.9	5.4
1972	10.0	5.0
1973	8.9	4.3
1974	9.9	5.0
1975	13.9	7.8
Average	8.8	4.4

SELF
Percent of population employed:

		Black	White
Male	1890	80	77
	1930	80	76
Female	1890	36	14
	1930	39	20

5. **Home ownership** (from Collins and Margo (318), not Smith and Horton)
   Percentage of black male home ownership, ages 20-64

		Black	White
SELF	1900	21.84	46.16
	1910	25.70	47.11
	1920	24.64	47.50
SYSTEM	1940	20.29	42.19
	1960	39.05	66.39
	1970	46.22	69.66
	1980	53.88	73.44
	1990	52.01	71.52

6. **Poverty** (1009-10, 1016)
   SYSTEM
   Percentage below poverty level, ages 25-64

	Black	White
1959	43.3	13.3
1968	25.2	6.9

Joe L. Rempson

SELF

Paupers in Almshouses Per 100,000 Population in 1910

	Black	Native White
United States	63.9	64.7
South	49.9	40.5
North	186.3	76.2
West	159.9	61.3

Agricultural Wealth in the South
(U. S. Census Report)

	1900	1910	% change
Value of domestic animals	$ 85,216,337	$177,278,785	+107
Poultry	3,788,792	5,113,756	+ 35
Implements and machinery	18,586,225	36,861,418	+ 98
Land and buildings	69,636,420	273,501,665	+293
Total value of farm property	177,404,688	492,898,218	+177

The overall growth in Black wealth was noted in the report as increasing each year at an estimated annual rate of $20,000,00 to $30,000,000. The report concluded: "Negroes now own and operate 64 banks, 100 insurance companies, 300 drug stores, and over 20,000 dry goods and grocery stores, and other industrial enterprises" (1016).

7. **Crime** (435-436, 439)
   SYSTEM
   Blacks percentage of total arrests, 1933-70

1933 - 24	1941 - 23	1951 - 26	1961 - 30
1934 - 24	1942 - 25	1952 - 25	1962 - 30
1935 - 23	1943 - 25	1953 - 27	1963 - 28
1936 - 23	1944 - 26	1954 - 26	1964 - 27
1937 - 22	1945 - 27	1955 - 27	1965 - 28
1938 - 22	1946 - 25	1956 - 31	1966 - 27
1939 - 22	1947 - 26	1957 - 30	1967 - 28
1940 - 23	1948 - 25	1958 - 30	1968 - 28
1949 - 25	1959 - 30	1969 - 28	
1950 - 26	1960 - 30	1970 - 27	

SELF

Number of Juvenile Delinquents per 100,000 Population

	Black			White		
	1890	1904	1910	1890	1904	1910
United States	25.4	34.4	39.2	23.5	29.7	25.7
North Atlantic States	215.4	208.9	199.0	39.6	48.6	34.9
North Central States	147.4	200.7	226.0	21.8	26.9	27.6
South Atlantic States	15.7	23.9	25.1	13.9	20.9	19.2
South Central States	4.3	4.6	10.8	2.8	4.3	7.4
Western States	5.7	45.9	244.5	12.1	28.4	24.0

Table 4 data source: with one indicated exception, compiled from data in Smith and Horton's book, <u>Historical Statistics of Black American</u>, pages shown in parentheses for data cited (238).

1930-2000, beginning about a generation after the NAACP came into being and had an opportunity to have spread its influence. The idea is to try to get some sense of what has occurred during contrasting time periods when one or the other of our two traditions more likely exercised greater leadership influence. The available data influenced the choice of those time periods. It is an accept-the-data-for-what-they-are-worth approach. Since exact dates and data categories that would have been desirable were not consistently found, whatever relevant data were found have been used. After each of the seven variables, the page numbers for the data are indicated in parenthesis, except for the home ownership variable, for which the reference is cited.

Secondary Source Data: Murray and Wilson

From the hard data presented by Murray and Wilson, one set was chosen as the key to what the data tell us about the outcomes of our System-Responsibility Tradition at its zenith. It is provided by Wilson and pertains to what is regarded as the primary adaptation variable among the seven, intact homes (285a:65). For the percentage of female-headed families with no husband present, Wilson's data show that, from 1940-83:

- A modest rise for whites – from 10.1 percent to 12.2 percent, but a *dramatic rise for blacks* – from 17.9 percent to 41.9 percent,

an approximately 134 percent increase versus an approximately 21 percent increase for whites.
- For those of Spanish origin, from 1973-83 (1973 apparently being the beginning year for which data were available) there was a *noticeable rise* from 16.7 percent to 22.8 percent, for an approximately 37 percent rise, similar to the percentage point rise for blacks *during the same time period*. However, in 1983, the percentage of Spanish female-headed families was 22.8 percent versus 41.9 percent for blacks, a difference of 19.1 percentage points, which means that Spanish female-headed families with no husband present was approximately 46 percent less than for blacks.

More recent census data (2010) reinforce this picture (322a). For all racial/ethnic groups, in the 1950s, the percent of women who were married ranged from 64% to 69%, a gap of 5 percentage points. That is, in the 1950s, the marriage rate of us blacks was similar to the marriage rate of other racial/ethnic groups, including whites. Today, however, as the data below show, the percent of women married ranges from 26% to 56%, a gap of 30 percentage points, black women at the bottom (26%). This increased racial/ethnic gap of 30 percentage points represents a 21% percentage point decline for white women, 33 for Hispanic women, and 60 for black women.

```
Asian.........56%
White..........51%
Hispanic.......43%
Black..........26 %
```

Reference source data: interpretation

It might be useful just to examine these data, absent an interpretation, and draw one's own interpretation. The author's interpretation follows.

In general, these hard data do not show a marked associated difference between our two traditions on all seven variables, but they do show a difference on two of them: *intact homes* and *home ownership*. They show our System-Responsibility Tradition to be associated with a more marked decline in intact homes, the percent of one-parent families increasing nearly twofold from 1960 to 1975, going from 25 percent to 46 percent. Our Self-Responsibility Tradition is associated with significantly smaller increases in out-of-wedlock births.

As regards home ownership, the data show our System-Responsibility Tradition to be associated with a marked increase of about 156% in home ownership by black males from 1940 to 1990. During our Self-Responsibility Tradition, the percentage remained about the same, although, in contrast, in its case we are talking about a period of only twenty years (versus fifty years) and a period when economic and governmental factors were not as home-ownership favorable. As pertains to intact homes, too, it is only fair to point out that any number of non-tradition factors logically come into play as well, including increased urbanization, generally changing mores, and economic forces and factors.

Secondary source data: interpretation

Murray. Murray argues that the War on Poverty was trying to do something that, prior to 1967, had not been attempted: to assure equal *outcome* (equal results) for blacks. Prior to 1967, as most whites and most blacks thought should be the case, the goal had been to assure equal *opportunity*. However, in 1967, white confusion and guilt, he argues, led whites to assume total responsibility for black poverty -- responsibility for equal opportunity *and* for equal outcome (184a:33).

As it turned out, however, Murray's thesis is that the War on Poverty, not only failed to produce a decline in poverty, it did more net harm than good. He argues that when joblessness, female-headed families, and illegitimacy should have been declining -- due to the War on Poverty incentives -- just the reverse was true: Instead, they were soaring, the poverty rate being higher in 1980 (the end of the peak years of the War on Poverty) than at any time since 1967 (near the War's beginning). Why?

Murray theorizes that, "The changes in welfare *and* changes in the risks attached to crime *and* changes in the educational environment reinforced each other," and that "together, they radically altered the incentive structure" -- the result of which was a localized accepted and approved decline in personal responsibility [emphasis in original] (184a: 167-68). Everything, he contends, became easier – easier to: make it without working, have a baby without being able to provide care or have a husband, get away with a crime, and obtain drugs. Because of this easier life, Murray's reasoning goes, education was not necessary, nor was keeping a job (184a:175).

This easier life – made possible by policy reinforcements -- Murray concludes, led the poor to devalue striving and personal responsibility. The reinforcements reflected the belief on which the War on Poverty was founded: the poor were poor, not because of any fault of their own, but, instead, because of system failures (which the War on Poverty policies were designed to remedy). Guided by this belief, on a net basis, its policies failed to reward striving and personal responsibility while rewarding system reliance and minimizing system penalties. That the poor responded as they did was predictable, Murray argues, because they merely responded to the shared human impulse to satisfy what was in their best short-term interest (184a:176). That is, it reflects human nature, not just of the poor, but of people.

Murray's brief is that the devaluation occurred because the War on Poverty policies interacted to "produce a different short-term rationality," as "they interacted to change the very nature of the satisfactions and rewards" (184a:176-77, 154-90, passim). What was that nature? Until the War on Poverty, the poor had valued and rewarded striving and personal responsibility as routes to a better life. As the above concrete description suggests, no more. Here is his picture of what happened:

> In the day-to-day experience of a youth growing up in a black ghetto, there was no evidence whatsoever that working within the system paid off. The way to get something from the system was to be sufficiently a failure to qualify for help, or to con the system. What a racially segregated society once taught the young black about living with his inferiority was now taught by a benevolent social welfare system. The difference was that in an earlier age, a black parent could fight the competing influences. The parent could drum into the child's head the belief that he could make

it--that the people who said otherwise were racists who obviously *wanted* him to fail [emphasis in original] (184a:188).

However, the War on Poverty's "benevolent social welfare system" drummed into his head something different: the belief that his plight was due, not to his personal shortcomings, but to system failures, thereby granting him [and others in the ghetto] "the most explicit dispensation from responsibility" (184a:189). In fact, Murray declares, "For the first time in American history, it became socially acceptable within poor communities to be unemployed, because working families too were receiving welfare [Food Stamps, for example]" (184a:185). The way to a better life came to be, not so much striving and personal responsibility, but depending on and gaming the system. That is, with community approval, the satisfactions and rewards came to lie, not so much in striving and personal responsibility, but in being artful in taking advantage of the now benevolent social welfare system and its reduced social penalties.

Further, Murray argues, the War on Poverty led to "transfers" from the deserving poor to the nondeserving ones. His reference is not to money transfers, but to what might be called a transfer of means, such as eligibility for certain programs and benefits; the nondeserving – due, say, to their income or job status – would be eligible, but not those somewhat better off. The differentiation among them which had traditionally existed was disregarded, a differentiation which black Yale sociologist, Elijah Anderson, describes in his Code of the Street as decent families and street families. And, if we interject Anderson's categories (categories, incidentally, which he says the poor themselves use), he is saying that the War on Poverty policies treated them both the same, in the process requiring sacrifices from the decent families in order to assist the street families. Murray argues that those sacrifices or "transfers" inflicted needless harm on decent families simply because the policies did not differentiate them from street families, thereby diminishing the public value that should have been placed on striving and personal responsibility – and which, previously had been.

In sum, Murray says that the policy incentives violated the psychology of rewards and penalties which govern human behavior. In totality, the incentives failed to reward adequately the positive, such as, striving and personal responsibility and even punished it. The policy incentives failed to punish adequately the negative, such as, sloth and dereliction and even rewarded it. The predictable net outcome was that the policy makers got, not what they hoped for -- striving and personal responsibility, but what, in totality, their incentives produced -- sloth and dereliction. Behavior which was neglected, if not punished, diminished; that which was rewarded was enhanced.

Welfare was central in such behavior, and the welfare rights movement, spearheaded and founded by George Wiley in 1966, affords a case-specific insight into its nature. The movement exemplifies the no-personal-fault, benevolent social welfare system which Murray depicts. Murray observes that, no longer viewed as charity, welfare came to be viewed as a right -- nothing of which to be ashamed but a right to be demanded (184a: 181-84). Its enhanced benefits (from which one might gain more than from a full-time minimum-wage job), along with other policy incentives, represented short-term gains and the poor, responding much like most human beings might respond, cashed in where they could and went about, in the phrasing of the time, "doing their own thing."

Murray's thesis is that a disastrous price was paid for this behavior change: a diminution of that which lies at the core of a viable family and community life: personal responsibility. The above data on female-headed families with no husband present documents the claim, and Murray cites a number of other social indices, such as, crime and high school dropout rates, which also show dysfunction and disarray -- all adding up to "net harm" for our System-Responsibility Tradition at its zenith.

Wilson. Responding some three years later (1987), citing a number of critiques, and, presenting his own data, Wilson disputes Murray's claim. First, Wilson contends that the War on Poverty incentives failed to decrease the poverty rate, not because they encouraged system dependency and discouraged personal responsibility, but, primarily, because of the economic downturn from 1968 to the early 1980s and because of a number of adverse concomitant socioeconomic factors, including available jobs (which were moved to the suburbs) and matching skills on the part of the poor (spatial mismatch phenomenon), especially poor black males. Second, Wilson contends that Murray's thesis that the War on Poverty incentives caused the dramatic increase in social problems during the 1970s wrongly attributes that increase, which was due, not to these incentives and the associated values of the poor, but, instead, it was due to the position of the poor in the class structure and to increasing black male joblessness. In his words:

> ...cultural values emerge from specific circumstances and life chances and reflect an individual's position in the class structure. They [cultural values] therefore do not ultimately [hedging his bet] determine behavior. If ghetto underclass minorities have limited aspirations, a hedonistic orientation toward life, or lack of plans for the future, such outlooks ultimately are the result of restricted opportunities and feelings of resignation originating from bitter personal experiences and a bleak future (285a: 158-59).

Insofar as the percentage of female-headed families in particular is concerned, the sharp increase reflected no change in values caused by a change in the "very nature of the satisfactions and rewards," but rather was "directly related to increasing black male joblessness" (285a: 94-106; 104-05). Wilson based that relationship on his male marriageable pool index (MMPI), which is a ratio of the number of marriageable (employed} men to women of the same age and race. His thesis: for blacks, though not for whites, there is an association between the two; the higher that ratio, the higher the marriage rate and vice-versa. Wilson contends that the shrinkage of the index for blacks accounts for the dramatic rise in female-headed families from 1960-80; that is, there were fewer marriageable (employed) black men available for black women to marry.

Who is right: a self-answer. Looking back, each scholar has given a self-answer to the question of who is right. In his introduction to the tenth-anniversary edition of his <u>Losing Ground</u>, Murray sticks by what he wrote back then, ten years earlier, only he would make out-of-wedlock births the central focus of concern in addressing the poverty problem rather than treating it as one problem among others. Wilson, on the other hand, has made some major modifications, at least when it comes to analysis. In a new book some twenty-two years later (2009), <u>More Than Just Race</u>, while Wilson still gives no indication of subscribing to Murray's thesis, unlike in his <u>The Truly Disadvantaged</u>, however, he attributes poverty outcomes -- not just to structural forces -- but to cultural forces as well. "Culture," he argues, "*mediates* [emphasis in original] the impact of structural forces such as racial segregation and poverty" (287:133). In this turnaround, Wilson, accordingly, urges attention to both cultural and structural forces, but, primarily, the structural ones, however without any concrete indication of how he might address the "mediating" and implicitly *secondary* cultural ones.

Wilson further acknowledges that "empirical studies utilizing national data have shown only modest support for the hypothesis linking the sharp increase in poor, black, single-parent families to the declining economic status of young black men," which is to say for his marriageable (employment) pool index explanation (287:147). So, although he still rejects Murray's explanation of cultural factors playing a major role in the response of the poor to the War on Poverty, the empirical research, nevertheless, forces him, in effect, to retract his own exclusive structural explanation for it as well, although he insists that, for young black males, local data from research done by his own research unit supports his employment-based thesis – the latter claim inviting the same kind of sample-size controversy we have seen in the "acting white" controversy.

Conclusion. Murray's thesis and Wilson's response take us into scholarly territory which exceeds the scope of this endeavor and the expertise brought to it. From a number of sources read, but not cited herein, it is evident that the data and explanations get disputed and defended, requiring considerable scrutiny and some expertise fully to decipher. Even so, in the interest of programmatic guidance, we are forced to decipher and decide, and the fact that there is no dispute about the outcome makes that attempt more credible. Exemplified by the above data on female-headed households, that outcome can be characterized as disastrous, taking the poor, not forward, but backward.

The question is why. Even if we do not accept Murray's personal-responsibility reduction thesis, we cannot accept Wilson's marriageable (employment) pool index (MMPI) explanation either, for he himself later had to acknowledge that empirical national data do not support it; it reveals only a modest association between employment trends and black marriage (405a, 474a). We are then left, otherwise, to explain it, even Wilson conceding that the "otherwise," however minimally, has to include cultural factors.

Herein, it is, therefore, suggested that Murray is right. To at least some of us who have resided "within the Veil," not just stepped into it as Dubois (aloof and somewhat of an aristocrat) had to do, it has the ring of considerable truth. More than that, two items of national note, likewise, give some credence to it: William Ryan's <u>Blaming the Victim</u> and the Welfare Reform Act of 1996. So much attention has been given to Ryan's book title as a defense of the poor that we fail to see its intrinsic expose. In effect, the phrase says affirmatively that the poor are victims, and that we cannot blame them for being victims because they have been victimized. So blame the victimizers; they are *fully* responsible for the victims being victims. The phrase thus became a mantra which validates victimization and exonerates the poor from any responsibility for it.

That the poor exhibited a diminished sense of personal responsibility was not then just a Murray deduction; the mantra "blaming the victim" (in defense of the poor) declared it to be the case. To say, as Murray does, that, in their combined effect, the War on Poverty incentives caused a diminished sense of personal responsibility was merely to arrive at a conclusion about the poor which was declared on their behalf -- and which (as manifested in the Welfare Rights Movement, for example) they came to have about themselves. Murray's argument is that one can hardly imagine such an affirmation prior to the War on Poverty -- and after its beginning only because its incentives brought about an altered and community-approved sense of personal responsibility, which made the system responsible and exonerated the self. Rather than an immediate cause, the interactive and reinforcing incentives might well have been, instead, a catalytic factor, but the undisputed data (of which female-headed families is indicative) show that dramatic behavior changes occurred -- changes which the research data show cannot be attributed to socioeconomic variables, leaving a diminished sense of personal responsibility as an alternative and plausible cultural explanation.

When that culture is ensnared in what has become Victimology, as is the case, this explanation becomes even more plausible. As explained in Chapter 11:

> When we succumb to the victim mentality we burden ourselves with an endless array of maladies -- from sense of helplessness, to passivity, to negativity, to loss of control, to stubbornness (471o). These maladies immerse us in the distortion of realities and lead us to give preference to pleasure over progress -- unable to engage in the kind of reasoning that would postpone the present for the future. Instinct prevails over reason and passion over prudence.

Intrinsic to such maladies is a diminished sense of personal responsibility.

The Welfare Reform Act of 1996 has an informative official title, The Personal Responsibility and Work Opportunity Reconciliation Act. Explicitly, it addresses Murray's thesis, personal responsibility – and Murray's book is said to have contributed to it. Liberals and conservatives alike -- responding to public outcry --saw what Murray saw and, in effect, were forced to respond. What he and they saw was the System-Responsibility at its zenith, producing good, yes, but, on the whole, "net harm," that is, a transformed sense of personal responsibility which locally came to devalue personal responsibility and to value system-reliance over self-reliance.

Standout and complementary data: Self-Responsibility Tradition

In search of hard data, beyond the foregoing reference source and secondary data, relevant standout and complementary data were found.

The standout data for our Self-Responsibility Tradition is the United States Census Report for 1900 to 1910, briefly summarized above, under the title, "Property: Black Accumulations Early in the 20th Century." The report documents those accumulations for a range of variables, such as, the value of poultry, implements and machinery, and land and buildings, specifically noting that "the total value of farm property owned by the colored farmers of the South increased from $177,404,699 to $492,898,218 or 177 per cent" (238:1016). It seems unlikely that such "phenomenal increase," to use language from the Report, was natural. One would think that something must have been happening to account for it, and (given, for example, **Baker's visits**) it is not unreasonable to assume that partly the something was The Age of Booker T. Washington and the gospel of "brains, property, and character" that Washington preached and that characterized the lifeblood of his age.

Giving context to these standout data are data which are not part of the above associative data, but have relevance. They give an overall picture of our progress *before* our civil rights gains and during the period before the Self-Responsibility Tradition sank into such disrepute. As reported in Smith and Horton, over the 70-year period, 1866 to1936, the following changes occurred:

In education (328:1268):

- Percent literate: from 10 to 90
- Schools for higher training: from 15 to 800
- Students in public schools: from 100,000 to 2,500,000
- Teachers in all schools: from 600 to 55,000
- Property for higher education: from $60,000 to $65,000,000
- Annual expenditures for all education: from $700,000 to $61,700,000
- Raised by Negroes: from $80,000 to $3,500,000

In economics (328:1267):

- Homes owned: from 12,000 to 750,000
- Farms operated: from 20,000 to 880,000
- Business conducted: from 2,100 to 70,000
- Wealth accumulated: from $20,000,000 to $2,500,000,000

The point: starting from little or nothing, without our civil rights – but under our Self-Responsibility Tradition -- historic progress was made.

For the few of us who might have some familiarity with that period, it was not so much our rights which were a problem; it was trying to gain an economic footing, the means of caring for self and family. Having the right to vote, or to have equal railroad accommodations, for example, was no doubt important to some (including in the latter case, Washington himself), but one can venture that more pressing for many were such basics as food on the table, clothes to wear, and a warm house in which to live. The connection between these basics and our civil rights was probably remote, and far less germane than DuBois and other system thinkers would have us believe. That is not to deny the importance of these rights (as Washington did not), but, given such basic needs, to question their centrality (which Washington did).

Standout and complementary data: System-Responsibility Tradition

For our System-Responsibility Tradition, the near doubling of one-parent families from 1960 to 1975, the persistent higher unemployment rate relative to whites, and the poverty rate of about 25 percent in 1968 (about the same as today) all stand out. As with the Self-Responsibility Tradition, there is a context for these standout data as well that is not a

part of the associative data cited. Amid the negatives are positives, even dramatic ones. Eugene Robinson cites some of them. Although the 25 percent poverty rate in 1968 and today is high, Robinson indicates (as does the above data from Smith and Horton) that the 25 percent rate is down from 40 percent around 1960, a 38 percent decrease. Other Robinson data: three of ten households make at least $50,000 a year versus one in ten forty years ago; one of ten households make over $100,000 a year versus, forty years ago, not even two of one hundred earned the equivalent of this amount, and in a representative sample of blacks, four of five are middle class versus between two to three forty years ago (227:6-8). Like the black accumulations during the Age of Booker T. Washington, these accumulations alsorepresent a "phenomenal increase."

Exploratory data – "Facts, Figures, and More"

As explained in Chapter 1, in preparation for the Rempson Foundation's proposed program, the African American Male Career Pathway Program (AMCAP), under the title "Facts, Figures, and More," data were compiled to convey a picture of our crisis and inseparable social problems. The compilation contains 216 items, 12 of which have been excerpted and reproduced on the following page to give some sense of the overall picture. No comparable Self-Responsibility Tradition data are available, but these exploratory data give additional insight into System- Responsibility Tradition outcomes.

The tradition supported by the hard data

The hard data support the efficacy of our Self-Responsibility Tradition over our System-Responsibility Tradition. It can be argued that our strides on five of the seven socioeconomic variables -- *basic education, postsecondary training, employment, home ownership*, and *poverty decline* -- can be all attributed, at least in part, to the tradition whose activities and ideology have self-help at their core, captured in Washington's "brains, property, and character" message. Whether made during the Age of Booker T. Washington or during the subsequent dominance of DuBois's System-Responsibility Tradition, our gains required the attributes that were part of the Washington gospel, which encompassed the Puritan ethic of hard work, saving, and self-discipline. Undoubtedly, the civil rights gospel of DuBois has been pivotal in creating the opportunities which helped to make these gains possible, but without the existence of the self-help drive preached by Washington, we would not have been able to capitalize upon those opportunities and experience the gains associated with DuBois's System-Responsibility Tradition. It is the important role of that self-help drive that is underlined in the previously discussed **Bill Cosby's Brown Anniversary (Pound Cake) Speech of 2004**, which drew such a fiery response from system-thinker Dyson. Cosby was drawing our attention to the futility of having won the civil rights at the epicenter of our System-Responsibility Tradition but failing to exercise the self-help responsibilities necessary to capitalize upon them -- and which are at the epicenter of our Self-Responsibility Tradition.

FACTS, FIGURES, AND MORE: ADAPTED EXCERPTS[35]

74. Black male graduation rate from NCAA Division I colleges six years after entry in 1996 lower than rate of any other group

---

[35] Excerpted with minor adaptations from unpublished draft paper by the author, which lists 216 items.

-- 35% versus 59% for white males, 46% for Hispanic males, 41% for American Indian males, and 41% for black women (303)

77. Dramatic increase in professional black men since 1960, for example, in 2004 78,000 black male engineers, a 33% increase over the previous decade (245: 5)

86. There is "no evidence that [college] degree completion rates differ significantly for African-American students at HBCUs or TWIs [traditionally white institutions], nor were there significant differences between African-American males and females." (288: 128)

109. Home ownership rate of African-Americans 49% versus 76% for whites (237: 104)

111. Data from 2006 show that for every age group (16-19, 20-24, and 25-39), black male unemployment is double that of white males (107: 210-11)

114. "Employment rates among immigrants with much lower educational attainment and language skills are much higher than those of native-born black men." (124: 77)

140. Some black men complain that many black women prefer "niggaz" to African-American males -- the former hardcore, strong, streetwise, player; the latter safe, respectable, upwardly mobile (71: 233-34)

141. Obstacles to more love between black men and black women (71: 237)
°What makes women undesirable: failure to meet certain erotic standards of beauty; men's view of them as difficult, demanding, bossy, "attitude," aggressiveness
°What makes men undesirable: imprisonment, early death, education deficit

148. Over half of black boys, out of a total of 5.6 million, live in fatherless homes, 40% of which are impoverished (107: 209)

157. Prison data for approximately 2005 (75: 108-09)
°2 million in local, state, federal prisons, 90% men, 2/3 black and Hispanic
°average prison time -- 3 years / most not serving life sentence; means that about one-third, 650,000, released each year

⁰of those released each year, about 100,000 still in teens and about 200,000 age 24 or under
⁰about 7% of noninstutional population been incarcerated, the figure for young black males being about 30%
194. Health data
⁰One of three blacks has hypertension, the highest rate in world (237:8)
⁰Almost 70% black adults, ages 20-74, overweight and nearly half of all black women overweight (237: 8)
⁰Black women nearly 80% more likely to die of stroke than white women and 30% more likely to die of heart attack (237: 8)
⁰Over 35% of black males living in cities are drug and alcohol abusers (70: 96)

Data with respect to the other two socioeconomic variables -- *intact homes* and *crime* -- arguably underline what happens when our Self-Responsibility Tradition is neglected, as has been the case since Washington's death in 1915. Under our Self-Responsibility Tradition, the data suggest that, given our relative disproportionately high rate of out-of-wedlock births, it has nothing about which to be proud in regard to intact homes, but the data do not show the dramatic unraveling which has occurred under our System-Responsibility Tradition -- even during its zenith when intact homes might have been expected to increase but instead decreased. As for crime, the data point to its persistence and increase under our System-Responsibility Tradition. Under our Self-Responsibility Tradition, the data do not tell us much, but its existence and increase, especially in the North, are apparent. For both traditions, one can argue that the data suggest a need to more aggressively address our crime problem, something which our Self-Responsibility indirectly does through its brains, property, and character emphasis.

Using Their Doctrines to Judge Our Two Traditions

Turning from actions and data to ideas, the same adaptation variables must be applied. Again to quote black Harvard historian Gates, "Ideas are what shape and reshape our world." The question: have the ideas of our two traditions been responsive to our seven adaptation variables. One way to simplify the inquiry is to take the core of each tradition, self-help and civil rights, and try to conceptualize its relevance for each of the seven variables. Thus:

1. What does self-help contribute to *intact homes*? What about civil rights?
2. What does self-help contribute to *basic education*? What about civil rights?
3. What does self-help contribute to *college/postsecondary training*? What about civil rights?
4. What does self-help contribute to *employment*? What about civil rights?
5. What does self-help contribute to *home ownership*? What about civil rights?
6. What does self-help contribute to *fightilng poverty*? What about civil rights?
7. What does self-help contribute to *fighting crime*? What about civil rights?

This conceptualization suggests that the answer for each tradition is markedly different. One, our Self-Responsibility Tradition, exhibits direct responsiveness to our adaptation; the other, our System-Responsibility Tradition exhibits oblique responsiveness. While apparent from their very nature, when viewed from the perspective of our adaptation demands, their difference is magnified. For each, the case can indeed be made that our civil rights approach has a readily discernible responsiveness, variously contributing to meeting the adaptation needs involved, but it is the degree of that responsiveness which is so questionable. Often, one has to stop and try to figure it out. On the other hand, the same mental scan, with regard to our self-help approach, renders it unnecessary to make a case for responsiveness; the responsiveness is self-evident. No figuring out is involved. That is because, rather than a deflection of responsibility ("the burden belongs to the nation," said DuBois), these ideas embody a direct acceptance of it ("The crucial test for a race," said Washington, "is its ability to stand upon its own feet and make progress"). In one case, we are talking about becoming self-made, in the other about the *opportunity* to become self-made. In one case, we make our adaptation primarily an inside job, in the other primarily an outside job.

The same conceptualization with regard to their tactics and spirit, expectedly, reveals the same marked difference. One says we can adapt on these variables if we employ the tactics of racial harmony, compromise, and cooperation, its underlining spirit being that of hope and optimism. In contrast, the other says no, we will be unable to adapt unless we employ the tactics of protest, demand, and racial opposition, its underlining spirit being that of anger and distrust. Once more, we can do a countdown, for each variable asking whether a given tactic, and the spirit which nourishes it, is responsive to what is required.

For our Self-Responsibility Tradition, the responsiveness is again evident. On the other hand, for the System-Responsibility Tradition, we are forced to wonder. For example, take the most pivotal variable, intact homes. How do the System-Responsibility tactics of protest, demand, and racial opposition, underlined by a spirit of anger and distrust, respond to its demand? They may lead to desegregated housing, but, in the absence of the ethic of home ownership, practically speaking, what does it mean, especially when it comes to the masses? One focuses on preparing us to adapt, the other on acquiring the rights and opportunities to enable that preparation. One says, prepare and we will get the rights and the opportunities will come; the other says, without rights and opportunities, we will be unable, adequately, to prepare and the preparation undertaken will be undermined. In the entailed endeavors, the spirit of one says, we must be optimistic and cooperative; the other, we must be distrustful and demanding. In effect, we have a social and economic orientation versus a political one, each holding out the promise of our future in the American mainstream -- normal Americans living normal lives. Because of its public demise (its roots have never died), we do not know if Washington's Self-Responsibility Tradition would have fulfilled this promise, though history -- and to some extent the hard data -- suggests that it had made considerable strides. We do know, however, that its activities have responded to the demands which must be met to fulfill the promise of normalization.

As for our System-Responsibility Tradition -- dominant for most of our history -- we know that, for a disproportionate number of us, it has not fulfilled that promise. That is the reason we have the African American Male School Adaptability Crisis (AMSAC) and its inseparable social problems -- with one-fourth of our race being disproportionately ill-educated, unemployed or underemployed, and ill-acculturated. In its case, too, history -- and to some extent the hard data -- suggest that it has made considerable strides. But thanks to the low responsiveness of its activities with the prerequisites to the fulfillment of its promise, those strides have been accompanied by undue strife, setbacks, stagnation, social disorganization, and -- worse -- regression. As David Kennedy proclaims, "The decades after the civil-rights victories should have been a celebration," as in fact "racial segregation declined; the black middle class grew dramatically," but "both the absolute number of blacks living in poverty and their concentration in poor neighborhoods increased" (144b:142). Kennedy goes on to point out that:

> For these neighborhoods, those decades were a spiral of decline. The heroin epidemic of the late 1960s and 1970s, the first national wave of drug addiction and homicide, was concentrated in inner-city black neighborhoods. White flight in the face of desegregation weakened the core cities. Black flight, enabled by desegregation, took many of the better-off residents with it. School desegregation, busing, and more white withdrawal weakened school systems and eroded tax bases. The decline of manufacturing and growth of outsourcing took away living-wage jobs. The increasing education requirements of jobs in the new economy left the marginally schooled further and further behind. When I delivered the *Detroit News* in the early 1970s, only about 11 percent of Detroit blacks lived in high-poverty neighborhoods. By 1990, 54 percent did (144b:142).

Is our System-Responsibility Tradition to blame for it all? No. But its leaders must accept responsibility for it all. *If we are to hold our own in the world, and be a self-respecting race*, right or wrong, justified or not, that is what must be done. Those who lead us must accept responsibility for the Tradition'soutcomes Such are the dynamics of human nature and of the social order. System-responsibility adherents can go about saying and thinking that they have succeeded in having others think that it is the system, not us, which is responsible for our plight. But that is self-deception. Regardless of what these others say or write, *in their heart*, it would be surprising if most of them feel positively about us. Those who constantly cast themselves in the role of dependents and victims tend to be more pitied and scorned than respected.

Of course, System-Responsibility Tradition adherents are proud of their accomplishments -- and should be. Their tradition has, indeed, led to transformation and adaptation in the lives of millions. But that can give little comfort to the disproportionate millions for whom it has not. It has left them, particularly the poor, unable to adapt and inordinately more dependent on the system than on themselves. Rather than the system being a means of last resort, for them, it has been made into a means of first resort. They have not adapted and the System-Responsibility Tradition has fallen short on means to encourage and assists them to adapt. Unlike our Self-Responsibility Tradition, it has not authored activities or ideas which sufficiently generate such means through the building of our own human, institutional, and infrastructure resources. Yet, we need to remind ourselves, as D'Souza does, that this is how other ethnic groups have advanced and adapted: "by setting up ladders of opportunity for their less privileged members." Closer to home, in his exhortation, Martin Luther King Jr. does the same, exclaiming, "... oppressed as a group ... we must overcome that oppression as a group" (147:133). However, thanks to our System-Responsibility Tradition, many of our more privileged members, while often defending and providing excuses for the less privileged, have been *setting themselves up* -- in middle-class enclaves and in suburbia, away from the poor. Unfortunately, out of sight, out of mind, at least when it comes to responsive deeds versus feel-good rhetoric.

Reminiscent of Washington's aforementioned prophecy about Haiti, Ray Stannard Baker, in effect, saw the seeds of this result early on when DuBois and the nascent NAACP were getting off the ground. Harlan reports that, trying to decide between its approach and that of Washington, in 1915, he both spent an evening with Washington at his hotel and a few days later attended an NAACP meeting. In the notebook that he kept, Harlan reports Baker's impression (109:367). Essentially it was that the NAACP emphasized rights while neglecting duties, and that, while Washington's attack on the problem was probably the wisest approach from the South, theirs was a useful approach from the North. He said he tended, however, instinctively to lean towards those who taught duty and service versus those who clamor for rights, which he saw as easy to demand but hard to earn or deserve.

It is a tragedy that a century later the very same bedfellows heard by Baker back then *still* -- despite what cumulative experience and data starkly show -- do not, even today, see what, at the outset, he saw: that an emphasis on rights must be accompanied by an emphasis on duties as well. Rather than, as Baker, instinctively leaning *towards* an emphasis on duty and service, our leaders have tended, by omission, to lean, instinctively, *against* their emphasis. Even so, they become incensed when, for example, John McWhorter says we are guilty of self-sabotage. Perhaps they should not be, for there are far less charitable applicable descriptors.

Not only has our dominant System-Responsibility Tradition failed to serve the poor, but for the privileged (the more advantaged), it has been a mixed blessing. In the case of Affirmative Action, the privileged still resort to system reliance. Despite impressive advances, in The Rage of a Privileged Class, Ellis Cose reports middle-class anger, pain, and raging discontent over a range of actual or perceived wrongs at the hand of white society that include: not being able to live or work where they want, not fitting in, low expectations and limited opportunities, duplicity, and stereotyping. As discussed in Chapter 9, Eugene Robinson reports similar discontent, confiding that, despite enormous black progress, to those who have made it, the feeling of being looked down upon and of being disrespected by whites still exists (227:81)

The discontent is, indeed, pervasive and palpable. Read the literature, especially Elisabeth Lasch-Quinn's Race Experts: How Racial Etiquete, Sensitivity Training, and New Age Therapy Hijacked the Civil Rights Revolution. Turn to the media, talk to the privileged -- and you hear and feel it. The voice of the privileged is little different from that of the poor, one expressing discontent, the other deprivation. The source and target of their discontent are the same: the system -- thanks to the minimal responsiveness of the System Responsibility Tradition activities to our adaptation requirements.

But wait, an update. In The End of Anger, his most recent book, Cose's research data show change (49). As represented by his sample of 193 black Harvard MBAs and 311 ABC alumni (graduates from selective academies and prep schools who were recruited to attend and supported by the organization, A Better Chance), not only are the privileged much less angry, so are the poor. The election of our first black president, Barak Obama, has occasioned, across class lines, a surge of black optimism. Moreover, among the privileged, the younger generation is far less invested in past sins; to many of them, race is not even a primary component [not absent, just not primary] of their identity. Cose's data suggest that they, like the majority race, have a sense of entitlement, a feeling that, given hard work and credentials, opportunities will open up for them -- that being the case, maybe, even without the credentials. In general, Cose says, "With every decade since the civil rights revolution, new barriers have fallen. Each generation has fewer racial neuroses, fewer racial scars, than the generation that came before" (49:16).

What this diminution suggests, among the young, is a waning of the System-Responsibility Tradition. That is, the younger members of the race are less fixated on the epicenter of that tradition, civil rights and its associated attitudes and behaviors, than members of the older generation. They are more in touch with the roots that Washington and his generation planted, roots that are planted in the American dream and in the work ethic required to fulfill it. Although, apparently, as Eugene Robinson reports, there still remains that "nagging sense of being looked down," that sense -- as in the case of Toure¢, for example, is not so powerful as to thwart their drive or to dim their optimism. That bodes well for our future.

When it comes to the Abandoned, however, although Cose notes their historic increase in optimism, he questions its sustainability. While acknowledging that, in reality, there are always some who are left behind, he adds,. "But when it comes to black America, the numbers at risk--jobless, locked in prison, trapped in no-way-out communities--are so huge that it's hard to see, absent a social revolution, how the soaring optimism sustains itself (49:226).

"Absent a social revolution," the optimism of the Abandoned is, indeed, unlikely to be sustained. That is why a **Child Family Rights Movement** is being proposed. It can provide a realistic and sustained basis for optimism.

Requested Verdict on Our Two Traditions

To judge or jury, based on the evidence presented, it is requested that you find that the uplifting of our race has been better served by our Self-Responsibility Tradition than by our System-Responsibility Tradition, which has, in fact, been detrimental to us. In addition to examining that evidence in the context of our **Adaptation Requirements**, it is further suggested that a test be used which was employed by candidate Ronald Reagan. Some might recall the famous line to voters he used in his attempt to unseat then President Jimmy Carter in the 1980 election: "Are you better off than you were four year ago?" In similar fashion, it might be asked: **Are we better off today under our System-Responsibility Tradition than we would have been under our Self-Responsibility Tradition.**

- Or, from a different and perhaps more intriguing perspective, could DuBois have done what Washington did: built Tuskegee with a $2,000 annual salary, no land, no building, no teachers, and no supplies -- amid black skepticism and white hostility?
- On the other hand, could Washington have done what DuBois did: create the <u>Crisis</u> And, through it, enable the NAACP to ascend?

Our inquiry can even be more restrictively focused:

- What if DuBois, instead of Washington, had been invited to deliver the speech on behalf of our race at the Atlanta Cotton States Exposition in 1895? What might have he said, and might have been the consequences of what he said?

Moreover, since present perspective can be gained by looking at the future, in similar fashion, we can ask: *Are we likely to be* **better off, say, fifty years from now under our System-Responsibility Tradition than we would be under our Self-Responsibility Tradition.**

- Again, from a different and perhaps more intriguing perspective – maybe more objectified this time by turning to two previously discussed corresponding personalities, would we likely to be better off, say, fifty years from now under Cosby's mindset or that of Dyson's?

Now we summarize the verdict.

On Washington's Self-Responsibility Tradition

Washington's Self-Responsibility Tradition has demonstrably fostered our adaptation, but its dominance was too short-lived to render a verdict on its long-term efficacy. Washington said that his approach would take 50 or100 years. He himself led it for only around 30 years with no mainstream national leader having emerged after his death to lead its continuation. However its past successes, residual roots, dedication to adaptation-responsive activities, and judicious embrace of complementary civil rights activities make it the Tradition of Choice.

Our mnemonic is **Baker's visits**. Reference has been made to the request by Washington and Villard of the reputable journalist, Ray Stannard Baker, to investigate the causes of the Atlanta Riot of 1906. Baker ultimately published what he learned in <u>Following the Color Line</u>. Referring to Baker's publication, Norrell, as previously quoted, writes:

> 'Wherever Baker found 'a prosperous Negro enterprise, a thriving business place, a good home, there I was almost sure to find Booker T. Washington's picture over the fireplace or a little framed motto expressing his gospel of work and service.'

Since **Baker's visits** were made during the zenith of the Age of Booker T. Washington, they can be said to capture much of the imprint and impact of the Washington legacy, and, therefore, symbolize our requested verdict on his tradition.

On DuBois's System-Responsibility Tradition

While contributing immensely to our greatly expanded opportunities, DuBois's dominant System-Responsibility Tradition has failed to foster the adaptation required to enable us to capitalize on those opportunities on the scale needed to normalize our social problems. For those opportunities have been seized by those of us who have internalized the self-help core of our Self-Responsibility Tradition, but not by the one-quarter of us who make up the poor and who have been abandoned by our System-Responsibility Tradition to system care and to community care (underground economy and the mother-grandmother female family structure). This abandonment by the System-Responsibility Tradition, and its failure to incorporate the self-help core of the Self-Responsibility Tradition which this abandonment signifies, accordingly, requires that it be replaced by the Self- Responsibility Tradition which focuses on both system and self.

Here we need two mnemonics **U St. NW** and **"blaming the victim"**

U St. NW. Black Pulitzer Prize-winning <u>Washington Post</u> journalist Eugene Robinson's description of this street in his hometown of Washington, D.C. provides this mnemonic. The street was once a hub of sophisticated black culture and class [thanks maybe to Washington's Self-Responsibility Tradition]. But now, Robinson, recounting the story of an art dealer, paints the picture of a street once inhabited by school teachers, a mail man, a retired garbage man, and a registrar of Howard University now without them – they have departed to outlying areas – leaving behind the poor in isolation. Thus, what was once a segregated, but socially and economically integrated street, is still segregated, but isolated and poor rather than socially and economically integrated (227:57).

It shouldl be noted that Robinson is talking about the late 1960s, at the zenith of DuBois's System-Responsibility Tradition. His description captures its benefits for the acculturated and its abandonment of the poor.

"blaming the victim." Discussed above, this popular mantra captures the most pernicious imprint of our System-Responsibility Tradition: a race internalization of and identification with victimization as manifested in Victimology, our second bondage. It is an across-class imprint which, in some way or degree, has affected both those who fall in the category of those who remained on U St. NW as well those who left. Combine it with **U. St. NW** and we get **U St. NW** and **"blaming the victim"** as the mnemonic which symbolizes our requested verdict on DuBois's System-Responsibility Tradition.

Judgment

Neither tradition has fulfilled its shared promise: the normalization of our lives by making us an inseparable and equal, if distinct, part of the American mainstream through a process of adaptation. Washington's adaptation-responsive activities were a potent positive with lasting roots, but time was not on his side. DuBois did not side with time, neglecting adaptation responsive activities for the political promise.

These considerations guide our verdict and have support from Norrell. Both, Norrell contends, made an invalid central assumption: Washington that self-help and preparation would automatically lead to civil rights and DuBois that civil rights would automatically lead to social and economic gains (192:430-31). However, using Tuskegee (the town) as a test case of self-help versus political power, Norrell suggests that Washington's assumption was more valid. While black economic success did not automatically lead to civil rights in Tuskegee, nevertheless, made possible significant political progress possible. His self-help gospel led to the economic independence of many blacks in Tuskegee, as a result of which, later, they were able to win voting rights and gain more political power. Their increased political power, however, did not have the reciprocal effect assumed by our System-Responsibility Tradition adherents, namely, additional economic gains.

Norrell does not go so far as to credit Washington and his tradition with a continuing influence that has contributed to the gains made under our System-Responsibility Tradition, but there is no reason to believe that what he says about the impact of Washington's self-help gospel on Tuskegee would not apply nationwide. That is certainly what **Baker's visits** suggest, and Meier, though questioning Washington's direct influence, offers the aforementioned interpretation that he "undoubtedly had a significant impact on Negro thought, reinforcing tendencies already in the foreground." Explicit and implicit signs of its existing roots have been cited elsewhere herein as reminders of the continued existence of those "tendencies."

Whatever one might think of either tradition, however, both have unavoidably and indelibly shaped our destiny and adaptation. Their doctrines are alive in the veins of our culture, detectably pulsating in one case, pounding in the other. The imbalance translates into customs and activities which are not responsive to the adaptation requirements necessary to move us into the mainstream. Consequently, we have had an uneven and unsettling uplifting of the race. Rather than being a self-reliant, proud, and prosperous people who have a positive core identity and who derive confidence and esteem from having uplifted ourselves from slavery into the American mainstream, since the Age of Booker T. Washington, especially since the Civil Rights Movement of the 1950s and 1960s, too many of us, instead, have become mired in a debilitating and regressive quagmire that has resulted in what John McWhorter terms a "bedrock identity," in part, marked by the cults of Victimology, Separatism, and Anti-intellectualism. Together with that identity, for many of us, goes a personality structure with low self-esteem and aggression at its core. The cult of Victimology is not just part of it all, but the root of it all, thereby becoming our second bondage. The result is the African American Male School Adaptability Crisis (AMSAC) and its inseparable social problems. Drawing upon a range of sources, the above excerpts from "Facts, Figures, and More" help to depict the dimensions of that crisis and those problems.

The crisis and problems may well be due to the system, but not for the reason the System-Responsibility Traditionalists have in mind. Today, particularly, our problems arises, not from the oppressive nature of the system, but from its permissive nature. We have largely won from the system our civil rights, but, in turn, the system has not demanded from us -- and we have not demanded from ourselves -- corresponding responsibilities. It can be argued that it is guilty of what John McWhorter describes as "nurturing black self-sabotage," self-sabotage herein translated as meaning our second bondage, Victimology.

There is such a thing as individual responsibility, and the system has a role to play in demanding that it be exercised. More important, so do we. Tavis Smiley's <u>The Covenant with Black America</u> has it wrong, for "most of all" it is we, not system officials, who must be held responsible and upon whom demands must be made. If we do our job, we stand a better chance of getting them to do theirs. That, however, is a message that is not conveyed by DuBois and the System-Responsibility Traditionalists who embrace his victim-laden message. Their message is that, if individual responsibility is emphasized, we "let the system off the hook." How about the converse? Is there not a comparable danger that if the system is emphasized we "let the individual off the hook?" It is this tension that is being herein addressed and whose one-sided resolution through the dominance of our civil-rights fixated System-Responsibility Tradition and the diminution of our Self-Responsibility Tradition that has had such a devastating effect on our core identity, the consequences with which we live with daily and which one can see in the above excerpts from "Facts, Figures, and More."

Sentencing

Although our leaders have been responsible for the verdict rendered, they have committed no crime and, therefore, cannot be sentenced, but they can be assessed, their reputation and standing serving as their sentence. Contrary to all expectations, the data show a decline in the wellbeing of the poor following our civil-rights victories of the 1950s and 1960s, yet our black leaders have continued their almost exclusive fixation on our civil rights and system wrongs. In more recent times, that fixation has been augmented by charges and cries of omnipresent and oppressive racism. They appear to see themselves (and often declare themselves), not so much as *civic* leaders, but as *civil rights* leaders whose role is to see that we get what is due us. Further, because they might have spent a little time in jail, were sprayed with water, maybe attacked by a police dog, or clubbed during a protest, none of which is to be taken lightly, of course, but some seem to think that these offenses are equivalent to having spent, like the late Nelson Mandela or Josè Mujica (the austere-living President of Uruguay), respectively, 27 years or 14 years in prison. Unlike Mandela and Mujica, they insist on being victims forever, using every opportunity it seems to advertise our grievances and exploit our passions -- and to keep themselves needed and relevant.

Their shortcomings earn them failing grades from the likes, for example, of black writer, N. M. Brown, (Self Contempt: A Search for the Identity of Black America), black educator, Steve Perry, (Man Up! Nobody is Coming to Save Us), and black journalist and political pundit, Juan Williams. Brown asserts that "the most critical component to reversing the longstanding socio-economic erosion which is systematically destroying black urban communities ... is effective leadership" (23a: xii). Williams captures the situation in his book title, Enough: The Phony Leaders, Dead-End Movements, and Culture of Failure That are Undermining Black America--and What We Can Do About It. Going inside the book, Williams has this to say:

> Since the days of Dr. King, no prominent black American had dared [as Bill Cosby did] to stand apart from the civil rights groupthink and ask, 'Where do we go from here?' (which was the title of King's last book). That self-imposed censorship shows in the stagnant pool of ideas from which we black people draw when looking for solutions. It shows in the tired arguments rehearsed from the same ideological positions. It shows in the lack of energy, imagination, or vision among our most visible leaders and organizations (283:23-24).

Aforementioned black minister and Washington supporter, Rev. Jesse Lee Peterson, is far more harsh. His book title, like that of Juan Williams's, conveys his sentiment: Scam: How the Black Leadership Exploits Black America. "Over a decade ago," he confides,

> I began to realize that the so-called black leadership like Jesse Jackson, Louis Farrakhan, Al Sharpton, and others were lying about why black are in trouble today. If some blacks wonder why things don't improve despite this "leadership," they need to wake up to the fact that these leaders profit by creating hatred and animosity between the races. In fact, it is imperative for these leaders to continue creating problems even where none exists. If they don't, they're out of business (209a:xiii).

Rev. Peterson's claim may appear outrageous, but Washington, essentially, made the same claim about many of the black leaders during his time. D'Souza, Loury, and Wilson, for example, say that today, it is these leaders and their middle-class compatriots (due to their preparation, Wilson points out) who have mainly benefited from our civil rights gains.

One is impelled to ask: what is their problem. Rev. Peterson, for example, like Washington, would appear to have put his finger on the situation. But, as Cook and Ludwig ventured in the case of two top high school students in their study who ended up dropping out of college, something "more fundamental" would appear to be in play. How can they fail to see what Brown, Perry, Williams, Peterson, and some of the rest of us see? That is the question to which -- drawing from a number of sources, especially Scott, Erikson, McWhorter, Steele, and Lasch-Quinn -- an answer has been ventured in Chapters 9 and 11. The answer is the same as that for the two top high school students who Cook and Ludwig say ended up dropping out of college: Victimology and its associated lack of a positive core identity. They, like our first black President and like so many of us in various leadership positions, have been contaminated by that from which DuBois thought the Talented Tenth would save us: "contamination and death of the Worst" -- the "Worst," in this case, being Victimology. Themselves contaminated, they are ill-suited to save the rest of us from it (Victimology); instead, they reinforce and foster it. And hand-in-hand with Victimology goes the lack of a positive core identity.

Paradoxically, their failure results from that which, in the African American community, makes one an Uncle Tom and a traitor: they "think black." They "think black" when, in fact, to be effective leaders, they must "think white." Only if our leaders "think white" can they lead us out of our second bondage, for to "think black" has evolved into thinking victimhood and, therefore, to keeps us mired in it. To "think white," on the other hand, is to espouse those values captured in the brains, property, and character gospel of Washington. Those are the values which have made this nation the most powerful in the world and which propelled our black upward thrust during and following the Age of Booker T. Washington. Washington did not embrace them because they were "white" values but because they were *adaptation* values shown by whites to be the keys to success. At issue was not color, but success and how to achieve it. Nor should it be at issue today, and that so many of us in our black community have made it the issue speaks to the self-destructive effects of Victimology and the racialized thinking which it has wrought.

Not that our leaders do not, seemingly, try to rise above "think black." On the one hand, they "think black," and on the other hand, they "think white." In them -- as evident from our discussion in Chapter 11 of **William Julius Wilson**, **Pedro A. Noguera**, and **Edmund Gordon** -- one often discerns the previously discussed "two-ness" of which DuBois spoke. "One ever feels," to repeat his famous lines, "his [the Negro's] two-ness,--an American, a Negro; two souls, two thoughts, two unrecognized strivings; two warring ideals in one dark body, whose dogged strength alone keeps it from being torn asunder." However, they might derive some consolation from the fact that their quandary has historical precedent. Meier, analyzing the thinking of our leaders during the Washington-DuBois era, observes that their two-ness was not limited to different racial identities or factions, but, for individuals, was internal as well (158:168-70). Their "inconsistences, the twistings and turnings," he declares, make it impossible to make "precise generalizations" about where various individuals stood, for where they stood at some particular point in time, or on some occasion, was often a function of factors and circumstances, the practical, political, ideological, and personal variously playing a role. But of Washington, Meier notes that, "In comparison with other figures ... Washington's expressed ideology remained remarkably consistent throughout his public life" (168:103).

From "two unreconciled strivings; two warring ideals," what ensues from so many of our leaders is a failure to accept and deal with our realities. A divided soul yields a divided outcome and a recomposition (to use Shelby Steele's analysis) of the realities. Cause and control become dispersed and distorted, if not -- as in the case of Gordon, for example -- denied. Responsibility is shirked.

Here is what must be underlined in this leadership assessment: the "two-ness" so typically exhibited by our leaders prevents that which is essential to effective leadership and problem-solving: *total* acceptance of the problem and *total* responsibility for solving it. Even if not entirely responsible -- which is the case -- it would, nevertheless, behoove us to accept total responsibility -- to see ourselves as being in control, *total control*. That would more likely illicit from us our utmost effort and assure the utmost results of which we are capable of achieving. To whatever extent we are responsible, we would have done our best to carry out that responsibility – and, more likely, with appreciable success.

The research is unequivocal. Those who accept responsibility for their wellbeing are more likely to do well in promoting it -- be it, for example, doing well in school, successfully stop smoking, making lots of money, or dealing we with marital problems (186: 58-62).

The opposite is likewise true. Their leadership undermines, rather than strengthens, our belief in ourselves and in our potential, instilling in us, instead, a sense of victimhood and associated dependency and limitation -- sapping our will and motivation to persevere -- the outcome being that while our opportunities have expanded, their drumbeat, at the same time, leads to the curtailment of the very qualities required to take advantage of those opportunities. That is what happens when, rather than adopt the kind of prosperity message found in Washington's "brains, property, and character" gospel, instead, we adopt the kind of victimhood message that comes through, for example, in: "We have come a long way, but the barriers are still out there," or "There is still plenty of racism in this country." Our leaders and their allies seem unmindful of what their tradition founder, DuBois, at one time believed, as expressed in his The Philadelphia Negro: "The Negro has a right to demand freedom for self-development, and no more aid from without than is really helpful for furthering that development" (63:390). And, needless to say, they are unmindful of what Washington had to say about their role, which is, "What we want, and it is what America honors, is the man who can teach his followers to overcome obstacles, how to find a way or make one" (165:13).

We honor the valor of our leaders and the debt that so many of us owe to them for helping to pave the way for the better life that we enjoy. But that does not excuse the fact that the promotion of directly responsive self-help activities has had little or no place on their agenda. What they have done right does not absolve them from what they have done wrong, or have not done. It is not just that two wrongs don't make a right; nor do a right and a wrong make a right. As in algebra, when you combine a positive number with a negative number, you subtract one from the other. Apply the same principle to our leaders and, even if we come up with a positive outcome, that positive outcome is deeply diminished by our reflective excerpts from "Facts, Figures, and More." The data in it paint a picture of one-fourth of our race plagued by widespread dysfunctionality and maladaptation. Therefore, it does not require any extraordinary insight, nor any especially elevated social consciousness, for that matter, to conclude that the tradition which they represent and perpetuate must be replaced. That is what, in effect, for example, Rev. Jesse Lee Peterson advocates in calling for a boycott of the NAACP; and that is what some generation ago the late black Pulitzer Prize-winning syndicated columnist of the Washington Post, William Raspberry, called for in urging it to reform itself (380a).

Closing Argument

This sentencing brings us to the closing argument. You must now weigh the evidence presented and, in your own mind, decide whether the case has been won or lost. The closing argument is that the case is about more than the specifics at issue -- and certainly more than about the customary fervor over civil rights and therapeutic sensibilities; it is about ideology or a way of life. What follows is a description of that way of life.

> **Our *Self-Responsibility Tradition* is *The Tradition of Choice* because, as herein interpreted, it has a balanced approach to our adaptation, focusing *both* on what we need from the system *and* from ourselves. Its yin-yang energies are reasonably modulated. It believes that we must measure our progress as much by the steady rise of the masses as by the accomplishments of the Talented Tenth. It accepts the reality of our conditions, not by succumbing to them, but by treating them as challenges. It takes the long view that, if we use it well, time is on our side. Although it is as dissatisfied as any with so many of us living our life, materially and psychologically, on the edge, it realizes that our lot is not different from that of some other groups who, during periods of their history, have lived similarly. These groups prevailed through adaptation. This tradition knows that so must we. The means they employed were not unceasing anger, demand, protest, and supplication, but dogged, self-sacrificing pursuit and foundation-building. They prized, not victimhood, but manhood -- *real* manhood. So does the Self-Responsibility Tradition. They prized, too, not Separatism, but racial pride and racial solidarity. So does the Self-Responsibility Tradition. They prized, too, not anti-intellectualism, but**

academic striving and learning. So does the Self-Responsibility Tradition.

During the Age of Booker T. Washington, that prizing (with white assistance) led us, for example, to build our own schools; to train our own teachers; to teach our own students; to acquire our own land; to build our own houses; to establish our own businesses; to provide an array of educational, social, and economic services to our own communities; to sponsor and support publications and other efforts to promote self-knowledge and self-pride; to pursue an agenda (secretly during the early years) to secure our civil rights equivalent to the later pursuit proclaimed by the National Association for the Advancement of Colored People (NAACP); to provide assistance and support in the founding of the National Urban League to institutionalize our need for social and economic assistance; to found and administer the preeminent black-found, black-taught, black-administered higher education institution in America, Tuskegee Institute; from Tuskegee Institute, to give us, perhaps, the greatest black scientist in our history, George Washington Carver (our Black Leonardo, as dubbed by *Time* magazine); to gain pride and prominence through the Negro Renaissance; and to begin to build the foundation to put us in a position to adapt and, thereby, to escape the burdens that we continue to bear.

That prizing did not cease with the passing of Booker T. Washington and his Age -- not among the general population, only among our national leaders. As evident from surveys, the roots remain among a majority of us. Fertilize those roots with a renewed sense of dedication and, the prizing that served us so extraordinarily well during the crisis of Washington's time can do, likewise, in our time of crisis.

On the sensitive and central issue of equality, the *Self-Responsibility Tradition* is just as committed, as any among us, to equality before the law and to equality of opportunity. But that is not the same as expecting or demanding equality of results and feeling equality. For this tradition knows what experience and history teach: no persons or people are equal, for in numerous ways, though basically the same, persons and people differ and we can, likewise, expect the results of their endeavors to differ, as will their feelings towards one another. We would, thus, be better served if, in our evaluations, we were guided, not necessarily by the precepts of equality, but, also, judiciously, by those of approximation and equity, the underlying intent being to be able to earn for ourselves, as individuals and as a race, a valued place in society. Given equality before the law and equality of opportunity, what, realistically, most matters is that we truly *think* we are equal, "for as he thinketh in his heart, so *is* he."[36] That thinking, at last, can help to set us fully free and energize us. The result can be the kind of foundation-building which produces *"average expectable environments,"* home being foremost among them. From *"average expectable environments,"* we can forge a positive core identity. And, with a positive core identity, we can exercise the character attributes required to solve our African American Male School Adaptability Crisis (AMSAC) and its inseparable social problems.

---

[36] Proverbs 23:7.

18

A Child Family Rights Movement to Replace our Civil Rights Movement

> "… nothing is so much needed as a secure family life for a people seeking to rise out of poverty and backwardness."
> **Martin Luther King Jr. (147:114)**

The above quotation appears in Dr. King's last book, published in 1968, <u>Where Do We Go From Here: Chaos or Community?</u>. It expresses King's deep concern about the black family, whose fragility and deprivation, he felt, retards black progress. That same concern lies at the core of this book, and it lay at the core of the concern of the figure whoae spirit and message permeates its pages, Booker Taliaferro Washington. Dr. King reinforces that concern, which we now address in the context of our two traditions.

The argument has been made that to solve the African American Male School Adaptability Crisis (AMSAC) and its inseparable social problems, we must replace our current dominant System-Responsibility Tradition with our leadership dormant Self-Responsibility Tradition. We call it **The Tradition of Choice**. It is **The Tradition of Choice** because it embodies both traditions, since, unlike our System-Responsibility Tradition, it focuses on both the self and the system.

While our **Self-Responsibility Tradition** and our **System-Responsibility Tradition** might appear to be opposites, and, as an attempt has been made to show, in practice, they have turned out to be more or less so, nevertheless, they can be conceptualized, not as two entities, but as *one* entity existing in what Taoists call a yin-yang relationship. So seen, they are not opposites, but complementary. In our approach to solving AMSAC and its inseparable social problems, the two can be conceived as constituting a whole. Together, they make up the totality of the required response to our **Adaptation Requirements**, each being an essential and *interdependent* part of the response.

In his <u>Following the Color Line</u>, highly respected journalist, Ray Stannard Baker, at the beginning of the Washington-DuBois fissure, had essentially perceived just that. Reference has been made to Norrell's description of how Baker had seen the Washington-DuBois divide. Norrell writes that "Baker thought that both men were needed: Washington was the opportunist and the optimist who did his work 'with the world as he finds it: he is resourceful, constructive, familiar,' whereas Du Bois was the idealist, the agitator, and the pessimist who saw the world 'as it should be and cries out to have it instantly changed.'"

There is another way of looking at their difference. That way is suggested by the subtitle of the aforementioned Emmett J. Scott and Lyman Beecher Stowe's biography of Washington: <u>Booker T. Washington: Builder of a Civilization</u> (234). That is what Washington was, a *builder*. He sought the blessings of a civilization, but realized that, first, internally, we had to build one in order to enjoy its blessings. DuBois, in contrast, sought, first, to secure the blessings of a civilization, then, secondly, to build one. **One, so to speak, sought to build a house, first, by building the foundation; the other sought, first, to build a house and then to build the foundation.** Thus, in one case, we have a *builder*, in the other, an *occupant* -- predominant *yin energy* in one case and predominant *yang energy* in the other.

Although self-responsibility, then, is deemed to be the key to overcoming our crisis, it cannot be solved without corresponding system-responsibility. Tuskegee, the preeminent symbol of a black-built institution, could not have been built without system support, in search of which Scott and Stowe said Washington spent two-thirds (if not more) of his time (234:372). As the Taoist yin-yang philosophy postulates, and as depicted in its symbol, *everything* works on a **yin-yang**

principle, the energies of ostensible opposites interacting to produce an outcome, that interaction being continual and balanced (406a, 445a). Think, for example, of a battery. It has a positive pole and a negative pole, two opposites, yet they interact, come together and, as one whole, produce an outcome: energy. The yin energy (the somewhat black or dark energy – such energy never being of all existence. Here are a few examples of the two energies.

pure essence) tends to be conserving in nature, whereas, the yang energy (somewhat white or light energy -- again, such energy never being of pure essence) destructive. These characterizations (oversimplified here) have no moral implications; in Taoist thinking, they do not constitute a good and evil dichotomy. Rather, they are a description of how, by nature, things work; these energies are inherent in and intrinsic to existence -- all existence. Here are a few examples of the two energies.

Figure 40. AMCAP logo: System-Responsibility Tradition Yin-Yang. Copyright © by Joe Louis Rempson.

<u>Yin characteristics</u> <u>Yang opposite characteristics</u>

earth heaven
female male
dark light
passive active
valleys and streams mountains

To achieve the desired outcome, the challenge is to keep the two in balance and situationally modulated, dynamically *contracting* and *expanding*. In our case, the nurturing of one (the destructive energy of the yang) and disregard of the other (the conserving energy of the yin) has created an unnatural imbalance.

The unnatural imbalance is reflected in problematic or marginally adaptation-responsive ideas and activities, which, in turn, as herein described, predictably result in unmet goals, frustration, aggression, and even regression. A better balance could have enabled more of us to adapt by nurturing the productive human spirit needed to provide the energy and drive required. Instead, the basic themes of the dominant System-Responsibility Tradition have bred a spirit of victimization, which manifests itself in a sense of dependency, self-directed and system-directed aggression on the part of the poor, and a perception of unequal outcomes and system-directed anger on the part of many of the more advantaged. Largely, it is these factors which have bred the African American Male School Adaptability Crisis (AMSAC) and its inseparable social problems.

A return to our **Tradition of Choice** will enable us to remedy this imbalance by attacking AMSAC and its inseparable social problems at their origin: the breskdown of the black family. As King emphasizes, the key to solving our problems is a secure black family. Nevertheless, to target the black family as a remedy is to enter into a vortex started by the Moynihan Report.

The Moynihan Report

What it was

Daniel Patrick Moynihan undertook to understand the employment and related social issues confronting African Americans. He and his research staff compiled statistical findings and drew interpretations in a confidential report to President Lyndon B. Johnson, which became known as "The Moynihan Report" (1965). It was published by the United States Department of Labor under the title <u>The Negro Family: The Case for National Action</u> (261). In it, Moynihan saw half of our people in "desperate and deteriorating circumstances," which he traced to "the weakness of the family structure" and warned that if this weakness were not rectified, a cycle of poverty and deprivation would be perpetuated for the majority of us (183). Although making no specific recommendations, as the subtitle suggests, Moynihan called for national action.

The response

In response, President Johnson undertook his War on Poverty (summarized in Chapter 17). Loury tells us the story of our leadership class in connection with that war as pertains to the black family (155:253-60). So does James T. Patterson (Ford Foundation Professor of History Emeritus at Brown University) in his book, Freedom is Not Enough: The Moynihan Report and America's Struggle over Black Family Life from LBJ to Obama (207a). Our black leadership supported the War, but not an attack on the weakness of the black family as part of it. With support from inside and from outside the administration, the scholarly community included, they, therefore, got the family initiative focus eliminated.

As inferred from Patterson, perhaps the main line of attack came to be expressed in the title of a paper (later made into a book) written and distributed by Boston psychologist and civil rights activists, the late William Ryan (207a:81-83). Its title: Blaming the Victim. The title became the mantra for the family initiative elimination. To target the family as being "at the center of the tangle of pathology," as Moynihan had done, was, according to Ryan, to "blame the victim." Moreover, our leaders reportedly did not want to dilute the drive for integration or incur the "Uncle Tom" label. Loury quotes Moynihan as describing how their reaction affected the President: "'From being buoyantly open to ideas and enterprises, he became near contemptuous of civil-rights leaders who he now believed cared only for symbols'" (155:257).

The historic nature

At one of those potentially watershed moments in history, with federal support, our black leaders, as well as their supporters, had a chance to do something for the black masses in the form of programs to strengthen the family but, rather than seizing the moment, they deliberately set about to sabotage it -- and succeeded. Nor, subsequently, have they taken up the cause. On the other hand, Affirmative Action, which was part of the War and which they embraced, placed responsibility, not on us, but on the system.

President Johnson's Validation Omission

Rather than just being reportedly contemptuous of our civil rights leaders opposition, as Loury reports he was, President Johnson might have actually challenged them. It would have taken rare political courage and been an obvious political risk -- the same kind of courage and willingness to take political risk which, on civil rights matters, he exhibited in defying the Southern wing of his own Democratic Party. But crucial moments in life and politics sometimes require us to be poker players, and, retrospectively, it is possible to conceive of this requirement being applicable in this instance to President Johnson (someone whom one gathers, incidentally, could be quite good a good poker player). In effect, he could have said to our civil rights leaders, if you do not agree to act on the Moynihan Report, it is not going to be possible for me to act on any poverty initiatives (or on certain ones and not others); the American people will not stand for us to ask sacrifices of them and not ask your people to do their part also. That he did not do so is regarded herein as **President Johnson's Validation Omission**, and puts him in the company of another notable omission: **President Obama's Washington Omission in His First Inaugural Address**, discussed in the previous chapter.

Booker T. Washington parallel

With differences in details and degree, the Moynihan Family Initiative is reminiscent of the same situation which Washington himself faced during his time, over a half century earlier. Both men, Washington and Moynihan, saw our culture as maladaptive, education being at the core of the problem for Washington and a weak family structure for Moynihan. Both believed that, quite aside from other factors, without addressing these cultural handicaps, our situation could not be improved. Both were on stage during what can be considered two watershed moments in our history, Washington after we won our freedom and Moynihan after we won our civil rights. If our new freedom were to mean anything, Washington believed that we had to adapt our culture. Similarly, Moynihan believed that if we wanted to go "beyond civil rights" to achieve the expected "roughly equal results" from the new equal opportunities, we had to modify our culture to make those results possible. In fact, he had gotten President Johnson, more or less, to say just that in his famous civil rights agenda speech at Howard University on June 4, 1965 (207a: ix-xvii). While Moynihan might have drawn upon Stanley Elkins and E. Franklin Frazier in arriving at his insight, it is in the Self-Responsibility Tradition of Washington that his insight more fittingly commands the national agenda. And no less than Washington's initiation of that tradition, Moynihan's de facto attempt to renew it provoked fierce and unyielding opposition. That opposition, moreover, rather than being from a tiny minority, represented by DuBois, as in the case of Washington, seems to have been practically unanimous. But only "practically,"; at least one prominent exception to the unanimity was the Reverend Dr. Martin Luther King Jr.

Persistent opposition to family focus

Kay Hymowitz, Senior Fellow at the Manhattan Institute, has chronicled the persistence of the opposition to focus on the black family called for by Moynihan's Report (389). Patterson, likewise, sees continued opposition (207a:215-16). Whereas, Hymowitz explains, opposition has waned over time, nevertheless, it has been virulent and vitriolic, and still there are no certain signs of a definitive turnaround. Even the decline in opposition that has occurred, she makes evident, results, not from black leadership, but from the force of public opinion. Patterson provides this overview: "Coping with the distress of black families in the ghettos—as ever a very complicated matter to address—continues to be a relatively low priority among politicians" (207a:215). The analysis of both is underlined by the forced resignation in 2007 of Bruce Gordon as President of the National Association for the Advancement of Colored People (NAACP), which, of course, opposed the Moynihan Family Initiative. He was forced to step down because he wanted to focus more on social services and "practical solutions" to our problems (439; 452).

The analysis herein is that this persistent opposition is made, as Patterson puts it, "a very complicated matter" due to what has become our second bondage, Victimology. Victimology casts us in a status equivalent to that of slavery, and, primarily, since the 1960s, we see its manifestation in allegations of racism, just as we saw the manifestation of slavery in slave ownership. Like slavery, Victimology elicits white sympathy, especially from egalitarian white liberals. *Egalitarian white liberals*, contrasted with *equity white liberals*, tend to acquiesce to black sentiment, to see whites as mainly responsible for black wellbeing, to equate results with opportunities, to subscribe to feeling equality, and to be reluctant to blame us for our plight (they do not want to be seen as racist or in any way prejudice). On our part, our civil-rights cure-allers, responsible for Victimology in the first place, sustain it -- called cure-allers because, in Washington's words, they "depend upon this [civil rights agitation] to cure all the evils surrounding us." Fictive kindship enables these civil-rights cure-allers to hold us blacks largely blameless for our plight and, through the security blanket of racism, externalize it. Thus, to target the black family as the source of, and remedy for, our internal crisis and problems requires the kind of movement which ended our first bondage – which is what the Child Family Rights Movement is intended to be -- together with the ascendancy of the more objective and realistic equity white liberals, probably in coalition with white connservaties, over the more sympathy-driven egalitarian white liberals.

Indeed, where *do* we go from here?

If the breakdown of the black family is largely responsible for AMSAC and its inseparable social problems, and yet our leaders oppose remedies which target the black family, then, indeed, in answer to the query posed by Dr.King in his book title: where *do* we go from here? The default answer: we must do what, generally, our leaders and their allies oppose; we must target the black family – not so much, however, from a family perspective but from a child perspective.

A Child Family Rights Movement and a Renewed Message

There is consensus that our civil rights have been acquired and institutional means of safeguarding and, where needed, expanding those rights have been established, as in the case, for example, of the United States Commission on Civil Rights (1957), the Equal Pay Act (1963), the Fair Housing Act (1968), and the Equal Educational Opportunities Act (1974). No longer, therefore, is the absence of civil rights commonly perceived to be a major hurdle to our advancement. Even so, the civil rights drumbeat goes on, and on, and on.

Since, therefore, we needlessly insist on continuing to make our civil rights a passion and priority, let us somewhat hold on to the magic words, but shift their focus to where the need really exists: in regard to the family rights of our children. As defined by the United Nations, their family rights are a component of human rights, and it is possible to think of their human rights as civil rights. We adults are not the only ones who have rights; so, even before birth, do our children. Although we do not customarily think of our role relationship with our children from a civil rights perspective, our 72 percent out-of-wedlock birthrate makes self-evident our need to do so. Out-of-wedlock births tend to deprive children of their family rights -- their right to an intact family, to a "hallowed presence" (security and love), and to school and life preparation – rights which are, in essence, acknowledged and embodied in the United Nations Declaration of the Rights of the Child (458). The concept of children having rights has also been endorsed by Pope Francis. At a gathering of world religious leaders, he declared, "'children have a right to grow up in a family with a father and a mother'" (308b).

Our silence must end. Just as our lack of civil rights provoked a response, so must our family breakdown provoke a response. It is inexcusable for us to continue to protest against various deprivations of our adult civil rights while, with impunity and without social sanctions, we massively and grossly violate the equivalent family rights of our own children. Except where applicable, even though we cannot bring to bear laws and regulations in the enforcement of **Child Family Rights**, we can bring to bear the enforcement which derives from fictive kinship, or a black group mindset.

The forging of such a mindset calls for a **Child Family Rights Movement**. Consider the parallel. To remove the main external obstacle to our progress, segregation, we undertook the Civil Rights Movement – and, basically, succeeded. Since the 1960s, the comparable internal obstacle to our progress has been the breakdown of the black family, so why not a comparable response? If a movement largely succeeded in one case, why not in the other case? In both instances, we are talking about tackling entrenched forces, and – as suggested by Thomas Rochon (see last chapter) -- such forces can be made to bend to powerful assaults. Movements generate such assaults, and, hence, the call for a **Child Family Rights Movement**.

Such a movement would, indeed, be an expansion of, rather than, as might be interpreted, a departure from our civil rights agenda. It would mean a refocus of that agenda on its intrinsic other half, for it can be deduced that both Washington and, before 1903, DuBois gave a dual meaning to civil rights: what the system is obligated to do for us and what, in correspondence, we are obligated to do for ourselves. Neither of them saw the success of civil rights as resting solely with just one of the two parties, the system or us, but with both the system *and us*. To a considerable degree, one without the other negates both. The struggle was to be guided, not just by a "protest agenda," but also by a "preparation agenda," only the former came to eclipse the latter. So, Washington's Atlanta Compromise Address of 1895 laid out what both parties needed to do. Our other three famous leaders, including, before 1903, DuBois (see below), did the same.

Career and character must be at the core of the movement. It would, in addition, savor a growth mindset over a victim mindset. It would be anchored in and energized by the **practice of the art of loving**. The core message – spelled out in the last chapter -- would partly renew and update the words Washington used when he explained his philosophy in a speech before the National Education Association on July 16, 1884, in which he used the terms brains, property, and character. But, in this instance, the word career replaces brains and property while encompassing both (113a).

The renewed message is also intended to help renew Washington's missionary zeal. His **Sunday Evening Talks** to his students (inclusive of teachers, staff, and others) show that zeal. Read them and you can easily come away feeling that you have read, if not heard, the gospel: sermons infused with a call for students to love (to care, respond, respect, and know), to cultivate their emotional intelligence or character, and to be mindful of the sustained time that would be required for their own success and that of our race. One can feel the faith and sense the optimism. Unmistakable is the voice of a man on a mission. No wonder Ray Stannard Baker felt that, when he met Washington, he was in the presence of a great man, for those **Sunday Evening Talks** represent the kind of stuff of which greatness is born. Their essence can serve us as well today as they served his students and our race back then.

What DuBois and Douglass Might Say

The proposed renewed message, more or less, duplicates Washington's message. In the earlier phase of their life, during which they emphasized self-help, two of our other famous leaders, DuBois and Douglass, would likely have supported a **Child Family Rights Movement**. During their later life, however, when both shifted the burden to the nation, it is an open question as to what each might do. Since children tend to elicit adult support, it is believed, however, that a focus on the child might have their support, too, especially if the nation were somehow involved. As for our third great leader, Dr. King, the quotation cited as part of the chapter heading makes his support evident, and in the next chapter, we will address how his thinking behind that support ran into the same difficulty as the Moynihan Report.

DuBois

Its internal focus and absence of attention to civil rights would no doubt mean DuBois's disapproval. But please be reminded that DuBois was a man of paradoxes; there was the pre-1903 DuBois and the post-1903 DuBois. For support, we can turn to the DuBois of 1899. That is when he published his famous The Philadelphia Negro, a sociological study of the black population in Philadelphia in 1896-97 (63). In his "Final Word" (concluding chapter) of that study he addresses "The Duties of the Negroes" and "The Duties of the Whites." In his summation of the duties of the whites, he says:

> A polite and sympathetic attitude toward these striving thousands [of Negroes], a delicate avoidance of that which wounds and embitters them; a generous granting of opportunity to them; a seconding of their efforts, and a desire to reward honest success -- all this, added to *proper striving on their part* [italics added], will go far even in our day toward making all men, white and black, realize what the great founder of the city meant when he named it the City of Brotherly Love (63:397).

Joe L. Rempson

In beginning his commentary on the duties of the Negroes, what he says is so revealing that it is cited at length:

> That the Negro race has an appalling work of social reform before it need hardly be said. Simply because the ancestors of the present white inhabitants of America went out of their way barbarously to mistreat and enslave the ancestors of the present black inhabitants gives those blacks no right to ask that the civilization and morality of the land be seriously menaced for their benefit. Men have a right to demand that the members of a civilized community be civilized; that the fabric of human culture, so laboriously woven, be not wantonly or ignorantly destroyed. Consequently a **nation may rightly demand, even of a people it has consciously and intentionally wronged, not indeed complete civilization in thirty or one hundred years, but at least every effort and sacrifice possible on their part toward making themselves fit members of the community within a reasonable length of time**; that thus they may early become a source of strength and help instead of a national burden. **Modern society has too many problems of its own**, too much proper anxiety as to its own ability to survive under its present organization, **for it lightly to shoulder all the burdens of a less advanced people**, and it **can rightly demand that as far as possible and as rapidly as possible the Negro bend his energy to the solving of his own social problems** -- contributing to his poor, paying his share of the taxes and supporting the schools and public administration. For the accomplishment of this **the Negro has a right to demand freedom for self-development, and no more aid from without than is really helpful for furthering that development** [all emphases have been added] (63:389).

Does it not sounds more like Washington than DuBois? Well, there is more from his <u>The Philadelphia Negro</u>. Should there be a question about what he means by "**the Negro has a right to demand freedom for self-development, and no more aid from without than is really helpful for furthering that development**," he, indeed, says more. "Such aid," he continues, "must of necessity be considerable: it must furnish schools and reformatories, and relief and preventive agencies." "But the <u>**bulk of the work**</u> of raising the Negro," he goes on to say, **"must be done by the Negro himself, and the greatest help for him** will be not to hinder and curtail and discourage his efforts" (63: 389-90). He reiterates: **"Against prejudice, injustice and wrong the Negro ought to protest energetically and continuously, but he must never forget that he protests because those things hinder his own efforts, and that those efforts are the key to his future"** [emphases throughout added] (63:390).

It is as if Du Bois had in mind the following thoughts from Samuel Smiles, the author of a number of self-help books and an influential figure in the self-help movement (466, 468):

> The spirit of self-help is the root of all genuine growth in the individual; and, exhibited in the lives of many, it constitutes the true source of national vigor and strength. Help from without is often enfeebling in its effects, but help from within invariably invigorates (140:182)

Whether Smiles's popular self-help movement influenced his contemporary, the Harvard-educated DuBois, or whether DuBois's thoughts were otherwise derived, is unknown (based on the research undertaken), but the commonality is unmistakable. We see DuBois's penchant for the political, for reliance on the system, as it were. Negroes were to protest against injustice and wrong. But even more evident is his emphasis on the self, for in their protest, he urges Negroes to keep foremost in mind what the protest should be about: the removal of barriers to self-help, which he proclaimed to be "the key to his future."

Given the idolization of DuBois by our civil rights leaders, and their demonization of Washington which began during the Civil Rights Movement in the 1960s, one would never think that such thoughts ever crossed their idol's mind, but there the thoughts are in his scholarly classic, The Philadelphia Negro. And so bluntly expressed! Who would have thought it?

The point has been made. Despite all his later vitriolic denunciation of Washington, and his role in undermining Washington's Self-Responsibility Tradition, *as a scholar*, in his Philadelphia study, he embraced the fundamental tenets of the Washington tradition. His thinking was starkly in concert with it -- and it was thinking based on research and study. The values which he, thereafter, publicly espoused do not reflect this earlier thinking but reflect, instead, system-oriented thinking and power calculations quite divorced from research and study. That makes his earlier thinking no less a part of his legacy, however. He had a right to change his mind, but it is his justification for doing which is in question.

Douglass

Although civil rights was Douglass's passion, Spencer points out that he supported Washington (244:108). Because Washington, unlike himself, did not embrace a civil rights agenda, he -- in contrast to the post-1903 Dubois -- did not make Washington or his cause an enemy. Rather, Spencer portrays the two as a mutual admiration society. Washington wrote a biography of Douglass and, Spencer says, even claimed that "the essence of the Tuskegee doctrine came directly from the older man, who in later years counseled the Negro to stay in the South, develop industrial schools, and acquire property." On his part, Spencer adds, Douglass admired Tuskegee, having delivered its commencement address in 1892, and, a few weeks before his death, wrote to Washington praising his "'great and leading educational institution.'" Nevertheless, Meier points out that in his later years, Douglass departed from his earlier Washington-like emphasis on self-help and, instead, like DuBois, emphasized the burden as belonging to the nation (168:75-77).

And What Might Dr. King Say?

From the chapter quotation, there can be little doubt about what Dr. King might say, nor, had he not been shackled, by what he might have done. That is a story for the next chapter.

19

Taking Us From Here: Unshackling Dr. King

> "To be a Negro in America is often to hope against hope. It means fighting daily a double battle—a battle against pathology within and a battle against [today, negligible] oppression without."
> Martin Luther King Jr., <u>Where Do We Go From Here: Chaos or Community</u> (147:120-21)

> "While not ignoring the fact that the ultimate way to diminish our problems ... will have to be found through a government program to help the frustrated Negro male ... we must do all within our power to approach these goals ourselves."
> Martin Luther King Jr., <u>Where Do We Go From Here: Chaos or Community</u> (147:133)

To borrow a thought from Martin Luther King Jr.'s last book title, <u>Where Do We Go From Here: Chaos or Community</u>, the proposed **Child Family Rights Movement** is about taking us from here to where we must go to uplift the race. The "here" is a black family characterized by what King terms fragility, deprivation, and, often, psychopathy. The "where" is a black family characterized by what King terms a "secure family life." Or, as depicted herein, the "here" is a 72 percent out-of-wedlock black birthrate, and the "where" is the national 48 percent out-of-wedlock birthrate. The "where" thus requires us blacks to reduce the black out-of-wedlock birthrate by about 24 percentage points.

Dr. King can now do what he was unable to do during his short life: help us to achieve this goal. Deeply troubled though he was by the plight of the black family – he spent some six pages in his book discussing it -- he could not do anything about it during his lifetime because, at least partly, he was shackled. *The shackling has led us to honor Dr. King's civil rights legacy and ignore his identification with Booker T. Washington and Washington's self-help legacy.* King's identification with Washington does not exist in the public mind, nor in black fictive kinship; almost exclusively, he is identified with civil rights and, to a lesser extent, with economic justice. For example, look on The King Center website, read through Michael Eric Dyson's two books about King, read President Ronal Reagan's remarks on signing the bill, in 1983, to establish a national holiday for Dr. King, or browse through the pages of some black history books, and one finds almost nothing about King's self-help legacy. Dyson does acknowledge that "King wasn't opposed to personal initiative and responsibility," and, further, even notes King's concern about the black family, but takes the position that King "redefined it [personal initiative and responsibility] in political terms" (72:126; see also 72:105-06). However, in this chapter, we will unshackle him by removing three of the restraints which have led us to this misdeed: the BTW Meme, the System-Responsibility Tradition, and the DuBois notion that "the burden belongs to the nation." The three restraints on Dr. King are interrelated, but merit separate consideration. To remind us of the shackling, our mnemonic is **SHACKLING OF MARTIN LUTHER KING JR. as SUCCESSOR TO WASHINGTON**, the successful attempt of young black radicals and civil rights cure-allers to prevent King's renewal of Washington's Self-Responsibility Tradition and, subsequently, to prevent the celebration of King's self-help legacy.

From the BTW Meme

The Booker T. Washington Meme (BTW Meme) is the *false thought pattern* that Washington's practice of accommodation resulted in his "not fighting for us" and his having "sold us out." Previously discussed, the concept of meme is borrowed from John McWhorter (161:172-73). A meme is a *thought pattern* which subconsciously and, thus automatically and unthinkingly, much like genes in organisms, gets passed along over generations and, thereby, get entrenched in society. During King's time, thanks to the young DuBois-like black radicals, the BTW Meme had its origin, and, today, it thrives. Having opposed its origin, King would not be pleased. Although we would never know it from the public perception, King held Washington in high esteem. We will let Norrell tell story:

> At first Martin Luther King Jr. invoked Booker as a moral authority for King's ethic of love and his posture of passive resistance to white hatred. He quoted Washington's saying "Let no man pull you so low as to make you hate him" in speeches and twice in his 1958 book, *Stride toward Freedom*. But when King said much about Washington after that, he was criticized. His call for a Washington-like program of self-help was condemned in Los Angeles in 1958 as a 'dolled-up Uncle Tomism.' As direct resistance to segregation increased starting in 1960, younger blacks began to dismiss Booker as an unworthy hero, one who had sold out his people to racist white power (192:431).

Norrell goes on to explain that this emergent vilification of Booker led Dr. King to change his tune about Washington. "By 1963," Norrell writes, "King had revised his position on Washington. 'Be content . . . with doing well what the times permit,' he erroneously paraphrased Booker, which King now dismissed as cowardly resignation" (192:432). The revision, however, did not "save" him. Dr. King's revision was not enough, Norrell says, to satisfy the radicals in the Movement. They, therefore, came to demonize King in a manner similar to their demonization of Washington.

Let us now jump from 1963 to 1968, when his last book, <u>Where Do We Go From Here</u>: <u>Chaos or Community?</u>, was published. In it, we can find "his last words" on Washington, so to speak. Those "last words" show no signs of any revisions of his position on Washington. Dr. King's "last words" show a King who thought Washington was "one of America's famous leaders" – just as he did at first, at the start of the Civil Rights Movement before the radicals shackled him (147:134). In his words:

I do not share the notion that he [Washington] was an Uncle Tom who compromised for the sake of keeping the peace. Washington sincerely believed that if the South was not pushed too hard, that if the South was not forced to do something that it did not for the moment want to do, it would voluntarily rally in the end to the Negro's cause (147:137).

So, as King departed from most black leaders in not criticizing the Moynihan Report, he departed from them, too, in his admiration and support of Washington. He thinks that Washington's error was that he underestimated the "structures of evil," but, in Dr. King's mind, for Washington to error because he underestimated the "structures of evil" does not make him an Uncle Tom or relegate him to the wastebasket of black history.

By now, with the battle largely won and his standing left unvarnished by the radicals, he could return to his original Washington script, and return to it he did. Now, the shackling was unleased, at least by the radicals, and he did not have to be concerned about having to preserve and direct his Movement. He could be who, seemingly, at heart, he was: a Bookerite. In fact, he can be viewed as Washington's successor.

Both had a dream, just as both had a **Birmingham Letter**. King proclaimed *his* dream on August 28, 1963, on the steps of the Lincoln Monument, to a throng which had marched on Washington for jobs and freedom. Washington proclaimed *his* dream in his presidential address on August 20, 1913, to his Negro Business League, which was celebrating the fiftieth anniversary of the Emancipation Proclamation signed by the very same man on the steps of whose monument Dr. King stood to proclaim his dream.

Speaking at a time when President Woodrow Wilson had issued a number of segregation orders, Norrell says these were among Washington's words to the assembled:

'The morning cometh,' he said, just as the watchman had promised the Israelites. 'Those who treat us unjustly are losing more than we are. So often the keeper of the prison is on the outside but the free man is on the inside .... Let us go from this great meeting filled with a spirit of race pride, rejoicing in the fact that we belong to a race that has made greater progress within fifty years than any race in history, and let each dedicate himself to the task of doing his part in making the ten million of black citizens in America an example for all the world in usefulness, law abiding habits and high character' (192: 418; see also, 462d).

King, speaking some fifty years later amid his embattled Civil Rights Movement, uttered sentiments which basically echoed those of Washington. Among other things, he said to the assembled:

Go back to Mississippi, go back to Alabama, go back to Georgia, go back to Louisiana, go back to the slums and ghettos of our Northern cities, knowing that somehow this situation can and will be changed. Let us not wallow in the valley of despair.

I say to you my friends, in spite of the difficulties and frustrations of the moment, I still have a dream. It is a dream deeply rooted in the American dream.

I have a dream that one day this nation will rise up and live out the true meaning of its creed: "We hold these truths to be self-evident: that all men are created equal" (392c).

No wonder Norrell can conclude that, except for King being harder on whites, they had "similarities" in "purpose and appeal" (192: 432-33). We have no divergent dreams here, but rather two of our famous black leaders in a cry and call through time for perseverance in response to suffering, that perseverance to be sustained by the rewards of the freedom, respect, and equality that were deemed certain to be its outcome. We have one dream, and, for its fulfillment, one road with two tracks: a civil rights track and a self-help track (see Norrell's relevant declaration below). Both men knew, and declared, that there can be no dream fulfillment unless both tracks are pursued. It is one thing to be *created* equal and quite another to be *perceived* as equal; fair or not, like it or not, that perception requires making us "an example for all the world in usefulness, law abiding habits and high character." Otherwise, it is unlikely that "one day this nation will rise up and live out [its] true meaning."

That, like Washington, in pursuit of their common dream, King did not persevere or fight back upon being attacked is a germane concern. It invites questions of conviction. However, it is somewhat ironic that, given the available resources, Dr. King had even less freedom to pursue his self-help agenda than Washington had because his foes were far more numerous and powerful than DuBois and company, and Dr. King was far less powerful than Washington – described by historian David Jackson Jr. as "the virtual boss of black America" -- to be able to hold his own against them (132:177). Like Washington, faced with the tenor of his time, King had to make some realistic and practical decisions. Probably few men in history have had the endowment to deal with such decisions as deftly as the Wizard of Tuskegee, and there are circumstances, such as those which faced King, which may dictate caution, if not retreat, over courage.

Nevertheless, that, unlike Washington, King did not show "*machismo*," to invoke Harlan's description of Washington – even showing signs of retreat -- is somewhat disappointing. For that reason, among others, King himself – and not just the young black radicals and the civil rights cure-allers -- must also shoulder the burden for the neglect of his self-help legacy. Our disappointment at Dr. King's failure to show *machismo* must not lead us to undervalue King's self-help legacy. He took an unpopular stand on Washington and Washington's tradition, and, for the most part, stood by it, his "last words," in his last book, being his affirmation of that stand. To be sure, one gathers from Dyson, for example, that on a number of counts, King was a flawed successor (69a, 72). From Pulitzer Prize winner Taylor Branch's <u>The King Years: Historic Moments in the Civil Rights Movement</u>, we even get the impression of a man, mission accomplished, during his latter years (1965-68), in search of another project to undertake so as to remain relevant and part of the action rather than, as Lincoln put it, and as Washington lived it, being (so to speak) "dedicated ...to the unfinished work which they who fought here have thus far so nobly advanced" (20b: 151-84). However, there seems little question that, in King's mind, his stand was foremost. To make it, likewise, foremost in our own mind, would likely be what Dr. King would want us to do.

We must, finally, remember that it was not just the young black radicals who demonized King (to no avail, Norrell points out) and whom he had to fight off, let us throw in, as well, our usual suspects: the civil-rights cure-allers.

After all, they had come to dominate the black agenda. Although they might not have attacked King for his views, nor, however, is there any indication that they supported or defended him either. A foe does not have to be vocal; sometimes, silence can work just as well, maybe even better. However, we must leave the real story of the factors which influenced King's pursuit of his own self-help agenda to his biographers and to the historians.

From the System-Responsibility Tradition

We honor and have a holiday for Dr. King because of his civil rights leadership, which puts him squarely in the System-Responsibility Tradition, since civil rights is at the epicenter of that tradition. When, indeed, we celebrate his holiday, the celebration focuses on his civil rights legacy. Attention is given also, for example, to his stand on the Vietnam War and to his fight for poor people, but, in the context of his civil rights legacy. To do so is to truncate his legacy. Dr. King's life was not all about civil rights. His life was also about self-help, which is what the proposed Child Family Rights Movement is about.

Given the conceptualization herein, contrary to what is probably assumed, Dr. King belongs, therefore, not in our System-Responsibility Tradition, but, along with Washington, in our Self-Responsibility Tradition. Some of Dr. King's *major* stands puts him squarely in our Self-Responsibility Tradition.

1. As discussed in the previous chapter, Dr. King was the one of the few black leader who did not publicly criticize the Moynihan Report, which called for national action to address the breakdown of the black family. In fact, without mentioning Moynihan by name, as Patterson points out, Dr. King endorsed the Report (207a:74).
2. In a number of public addresses, he made the plight of the black family an object of concern and, while he singled out, for example, the need for jobs, education, and housing, he placed responsibility for addressing the plight internally -- on our own culture and social life (207a:74).
3. As discussed in the previous chapter, he considered the wellbeing of the black family the foundation of black progress.

Now, let us enumerate Dr. King's 5-point program for addressing our problems which he laid out in his last book, each point placing him in our Self-Responsibility Tradition (147:129-42).

1. Development of a "rugged sense of somebodyness," which he cites as "the first and most vital step that the Negro must take in dealing with his dilemma."
2. Foster group identity and unification through such community structures as churches, the press, and professional associations, to undertake programs to combat such problems as crime, family disorganization, and illegitimacy by (as the chapter quotation indicates) helping "the frustrated Negro male."
3. Make "full and effective use of the freedom we already possess."
4. Continue the kind of nonviolent and organizational activity required to complete the fight for justice.
5. Expand our struggle to focus on the need to improve our entire society and on the need for a new set of values wherein people and peace, not profit and military power, have priority.

That Dr. King made the very first remedy the development of a "rugged sense of somebodyness" is somewhat surprising -- and significant. The surprise, as well as the significance, is that, in essence, it reflects the thesis of this book, borrowed from Imani Michelle Scott, that our problems can be traced to the lack of a positive core identity. That is not the kind of thinking one tends to associate with the civil-rights fixated System-Responsibility Tradition, but, instead, we tend to associate it with our self-help-centered Self-Responsibility Tradition. But there it is, right there in King's book, and expressed with conviction: "With courage and fearlessness we must set out daringly to stabilize our egos. This *alone* will give us a confirmation of our roots and a validation of our worth" [emphasis added] (147:130). Unlike Scott, Dr. King does not go on to say that an unstable ego is largely responsible for the dysfunction found in segments of our black community, but, from his declaration, it is can be inferred that he, too, might likewise contend.

Dr. King's second point is less surprising, but no less significant. Again, he reflects a central thesis of this book, which is that if we are to solve our problems, we must address the needs of, in his words, "the frustrated Negro male." Not only, then, can it be argued that King, back in 1968, pinpointed the source of our persistent *internal* problems as lying in our flawed core identity, but he also saw their solution as dependent on helping "the frustrated Negro male." King did not, as has been done herein, elaborate on making the black male central in his solution, but, from his discussion of the breakdown of the black family and the rage and torment of the black male which is largely responsible for the breakdown, we get a sense of why he did make him central (147:110-16).

To turn to King's other three points, his exhortation for us to make "full and effective use of the freedom we already possess" echoes the spirit of Washington's exhortation to us in his Atlanta Compromise: "Nor should we permit our grievances to overshadow our opportunities." Dr. King's fourth point calls for a continuation of National Association for the Advancement of Colored People (NAACP)-type activities, the kind of activities secretly and seductively conducted by Washington during his leadership years and which, during the last three years of his life, he openly advocated. As for the last of Dr. King's 5-point program, it is consistent with Washington's **practice of the art of loving**.

These Self-Responsibility Tradition credentials notwithstanding, it can still be argued that Dr. King belongs in our System-Responsibility Tradition because it is his civil rights activities which put him in the history books, and civil rights activities fall into the System-Responsibility Tradition. True, but it is also true that the System-Responsibility Tradition is intolerant of a self-help agenda. So, if we put King in the System-Responsibility Tradition, we would have to negate his enumerated stands and his 5-point program and the self-help which they exemplify. Self-help could not be esteemed as part of his legacy. In fact, self-help as part of his legacy would have to be, as it is, neglected – and, therefore, King shackled to a civil rights legacy only. The reaction of Coretta Scott King when, in 1984, to a meeting of the National Urban Coalition, Glenn Loury began his address by declaring, "'The civil rights movement is over,'" captures the sacred and magic held by civil rights in the System-Responsibility Tradition: she cried (445). Civil rights is its tradition. Apparently, the thought of the civil rights movement being over, then, was more than Coretta Scott King could bear. While only she is reported to have cried, the other black leaders present might have had to fight to hold back their own tears.

If, then, we do not want King to be shackled, if we want to esteem, not just his civil rights legacy and, to a lesser extent, his economic justice legacy, but, also, his self-help legacy, we can only do so by placing him, by default, in our Self-Responsibility Tradition. The System-Responsibility Tradition is allergic to self-help emphases. Unlike our System-Responsibility Tradition, our Self-Responsibility Tradition, on the other hand, encompasses both civil rights and self-help. It is for that reason, among others, that our Self-Responsibility Tradition is the **Tradition of Choice**: it incorporates both civil rights and self-help.

From "the burden belongs to the nation"

DuBois's declaration that "the burden belongs to the nation" reflects the cornerstone of the System-Responsibility Tradition from which we have attempted to unshackle Dr. King. By omission and disregard, its civil-rights fixated adherents would have us believe that King shared this view. To an extent, like Washington, he did share it. As the chapter quotation makes evident, and as made evident in the last two chapters of his last book, King, simultaneously, emphasized self-help. Like Washington and the Self-Responsibility Tradition to which they both belong, King realized that, in the words of Norrell, "A rising people must operate on more than one track to lift themselves" (192:440).

Conclusion

It is that realization – that "A rising people must operate on more than one track to lift themselves" -- which enables us to draw upon Dr. King's legacy and spirit to help generate and propel a **Child Family Rights Movement**. We can, indeed, think of King as Washington's unrecognized successor, and the success of the Movement would be dependent on the revitalization of Washington's Self-Responsibility Tradition to which he was committed, but, in its pursuit, was shackled by young black radicals and civil-rights cure-allers. In celebrating his legacy, their shackling has carried the day. The System-Responsibility Tradition to which they belong would have us believe that King, too, was civil-rights fixated. The record proves them wrong. It shows that Dr. King saw our struggle as "fighing daily a double battle—a battle against pathology within and a battle against [today, negligible] oppression without."

20

Renewing Washington's Self-Responsibility Tradition: Proposals And Success Requirements

> "... let each dedicate themselves to the task of doing his part in making the ten millions of Black citizens in America an example for all the world in usefulness, law abiding habits and high character."
> **Booker T. Washington, Address before National Negro Business League, of which he was President, on August 20, 1913 (462d)**

> "This is the Negro dilemma. He who starts behind in a race must forever remain behind or run faster than the man in front."
> **Martin Luther King Jr., <u>Where Do We Go From Here: Chaos or Community</u> (147:131)**

Those of us who seek to solve our African American School Adaptability Crisis (AMSAC) through an uproot of our System-Responsibility Tradition and a renewal our Self-Responsibility Tradition, the thesis herein being that it is the only way that it can be solved, have a formidable challenge, the nature of which an attempt has been to sketch. Here is how, in recapitulation, that nature can be described.

Joe L. Rempson

Recapitulation of Book

Given an absence of an activating sense of commitment and social consciousness, our leaders typically fail to claim ownership of our problems and accordingly fail to foster self-help efforts to solve them. Instead, they espouse positions which rely on system help and which stand little or no chance of really solving our problems, but, out of therapeutic alienation, are nonetheless advocated because doing so gives these leaders a sense of satisfaction and psychological security through identification with the masses. Furthermore, espousing these positions gives them political power or academic status, and enables them to maintain that power or status by *delivering* to or *supporting* the masses.

Although their positions often lack factual foundation, creativity, or vision, race and fictive kinship, nevertheless, give them credibility, sustains them, and inhibits deviation from them, as does an underlying anti-intellectualism and sense of separatism. For even when evidence shows that their positions are invalid -- due to therapeutic alienation, anti-intellectualism, and separatism -- that evidence is dismissed and their positions maintained. Not only are these positions maintained, due to the meme phenomenon, they are passed along -- automatically and unthinkingly -- from mind to mind, generation to generation. The end which has come to be sought is racial equality as measured by equality of outcomes and feeling equality.

The process and mindset exhibited by these leaders and those of us who follow them derive from an oppositional culture and a civil-rights fixation rooted in a present-fatalistic and past-negative time perspective. The mainspring and catalyst of this process and mindset is Victimology, defined as victimhood internalized and having thus become integral to our identity rather than being a problem to be solved. This Victimology reflects a response to transgenerationally-transmitted trauma and gives rise to the root cause of our African American male school crisis (AMSAC) and its inseparable social problems: the lack of a positive core identity.

This recapitulation makes it evident that we are thus dealing with an African American cultural crisis. It is not just the culture of the students that serves as a barrier to their success but as well the culture of our community, from which they come and from which Ogbu and McWhorter (among others) tell us they derive their culture. Accordingly, to remedy the African American Male School Adaptability Crisis (AMSAC) requires an adaptation in both the culture of our students and of our community, at least to the extent of community support for the adaptation required of our students. We cannot take our students and productively do with them whatever we choose, as suggested, for example, by the 59 fifth-grade Dreamers and the 67 successful and 73 at-risk high school students in Farrell's studies. Regardless of what we do, they belong to our community, are subject to its influences (for better or worse), and its support and assistance are as essential as they are desirable. That is what David Kennedy has reportedly demonstrated in his fight against crime and drugs in our inner-city neighborhoods: involve the community, inclusive of the criminals and drug dealers, and you can normalize violent crime and eliminate the overt drug market. There is no reason to believe that we cannot be similarly successful when it comes to our school crisis.

In our search for a solution, we have now come to the end of our journey. It has taken us far and wide, looking here and there for understanding. Our mnemonics, like our recapitulation, can remind us of why we undertook it and of some of our major encounters -- and we include one which will be encountered in this chapter, the **Bill Clinton risk** mnemonic. We can get so involved in the details that we take our eye off the ball, in the process, perhaps, losing sight of the essentials. The length of this book has not made that endeavor any easier; maybe the following mnemonics summary will.

MNEMONICS SUMMARY

REMINDERS OF OUR IMAGINARY GARDEN OF EDEN: THE SOURCE OF AND SOLUTION TO OUR CRISIS AND PROBLEMS
↓
Washington's Atlanta Compromise of 1895: African American Garden of Eden

(Compromise is interpreted as originating our imaginary African American Garden of Eden, wherein Washington popularized the foundation trees of brain, property, and character, and, as a result, fathered our self-help tradition; and whereas embedded in the Compromise were the seeds of our civil rights, he forbade attention to the more alluring civil rights tree)

•

The Souls of Black Folk (1903)
(DuBois's classic, which in one essay, "Of Mr. Booker T. Washington and Others," he demonized Washington and popularized the alluring, though Washington forbidden, civil rights tree, as a result, fathering our system-help tradition and its civil-rights fixation, which in turn has led to our second bondage, Victimology)

•

Washington (1903): "An inch of progress is worth more than a yard of complaint" (captures Washington's emphasis on gradualism and his support of "sane agitation and criticism" in contrast to DuBois's doctrine that we "must strike the blow" and "must insist [protest] continually, in season and out of season")

•

Washington's public silence: Atlanta, Brownsville, Springfield (1906-1908) (Washington's failure to express public outrage over racial injustices and the contribution of that failure to the decline of his power, as well as to The BTW Meme, explained below)

•

Thomas A. Harris Rescue/Birmingham Letter: self-justification, duplicity, corrupting (1914) (Washington's secret and seductive civil rights activities in the African American Garden of Eden and their denigration or disregard, especially since the 1960s)

•

Washington's public protest: "I want that thing taken down from there."

(Washington's demand that row of sheets separating blacks and whites in Tampa theatre be removed before he spoke, exemplying, during the last three years of his life, his *public* expression of growing impatience and anger over racial injustices)

•

Amenia Conference of 1916: DuBois's sabotage
(DuBois's sabotage of conference "treaty" typifies his repeated sabotage, even after Washington's death, of agreements reached to achieve racial unity)

****

REMINDERS OF OUR SECOND
BONDAGE, VICTIMOLOGY,
and ITS PERVASIVENESS and EFFECT
↓
DuBois's refusal to use <u>Crisis</u>
to acknowledge and condemn black crime /
"the burden belongs to the nation"
(reflects, from the outset, failure of System-Responsibility Tradition,
minimizing self-help and maximizing nation-help,
to confront our three major demons: *IQ lag-fatherless families-crime*)

•

"blaming the victim"
(defense of poor which has fostered internalization of victimhood)

•

"leav[es] us mired in a generational sense of complaint and outrage that never seems to subside"
[excerpted from Elisabeth Lasch-Quinn, <u>Race Experts: How Racial Etiquette, Sensitivity Training, and New Age Therapy Hijacked the Civil Rights Movement</u>]
(captures the pervasive outcome of the quest for what is herein called *feeling equality*, wherein there is a vigilant parsing of the words and actions of whites for any sign that whites do not *feel* that we blacks are equal to them,

any indication that they do not evoking complaints and outrage)

•

Trayvon Martin case - President Obama's Remarks
(a Victimology-contaminated Talented Tenth)

•

Affirmative Action - School Discipline
(Victimology-contaminated application of laws)

•

Black racism / Security blanket / 12
(the effect of Victimology on black
attitudes, and black use of racism
as security blanket to comfort us against feelings of
inferiority and injustices often reflected by those attitudes,
and the reduction of control over our
happiness Victimology exacts
over the already small 12% control which
we humans normally exercise)

•

Separatism - Anti-intellectualism
(two of the cults which McWhorter says
have been outcomes of Victimology)

•

BTW Meme
(The *false thought pattern* that Washington's practice of
accommodation resulted in his "not fighting for us" and
his having "sold us out" – a *false thought pattern* which
subconsciously and, thus automatically and unthinkingly,
much like genes in organisms, has been passed along
over roughly the last two generations, which makes it
a meme [the concept borrowed from McWhorter])

•

Shackling of Martin Luther King Jr.
as
Successor to Washington
(successful attempt of young black radicals and civil rights
cure-allers to prevent Dr. King's renewal of Washington's
Self-Responsibility Tradition and, subsequently, to
prevent the celebration of Dr. King's self-help legacy)

The African American Male School Adaptability Crisis (AMSAC)

****

REMINDERS OF OUR SCHOOL CRISIS
↓
"acting white" effect
(black mindset, or fictive kinship, which sanctions black divergency and, therefore, confines black thought and behavior, with the result that, among other things, it curtails the cultivation and creativity of our Talented Tenth)

59:42/57:62/35:60
(respectively, percent of black males compared to their white male counterparts who drop out of high school in 56 highest black male enrollment districts, who, nationally, upon high school graduation enroll in college, and who, nationally, upon enrolling in college graduate within 6 years)

●

11 and 30
(percentage points graduation rate of
black males below black females
and, dramatically illustrative of the divide,
the percentage of black males who make
up the 6,500 student body at
Medgar Evers College of the City
University of New York - CUNY)

●

academically good - dead last / academically bad - first
(description of African American students, especially males)

●

disabilities differential of 2-5 points
(reading score point difference between
able black male students and *disabled* white male students)

●

MSAN
(failed effort by Minority Student Achievement Network to close black-white achievement gap for middle-class black students)

Joe L. Rempson

****

REMINDERS OF OUR INSEPARABLE SOCIAL PROBLEMS
↓
72
(percent of black out-of-wedlock births
and, thus, the family breakdown
from which our personal and social problems originate
and which prevents the race from having
a positivse core identity and self-pride)

•

68 / suicide rate of black children, 2015
(percent of black children in poverty areas found in one study
to be learning impaired due to home-inflicted trauma and,
for the first time, in 2015, suicide rate among black children
exceeds suicide rate among white children
and, moreover, the first time,
for any age group, that black suicide rate
has exceeded white suicide rate)

•

prisonization
(spread of prison values among black males)

•

young black male fratricide: 13% - 50+% - 85% - 94%
(blacks 13% of population,
but make up over half of homicide victims,
85% of whom are young black males,
94% of whom are murdered mostly by other young black males)

•

Haitian earthquake, 2010
(a traumatic reminder of AMSAC and its inseparable
social problems and the price, helplessness, which
ensues from maladaptation and a failure to cultivate
a culture of adaptation and self-help)

****

REMINDERS OF THE EFFICACY
OF OUR TWO TRADITIONS
↓
Baker's visits
(black homes doing well visited by famous journalist
Ray Stannard Baker had Washington's picture)
•
U St. NW
(black middle class exit from socioeconomically
mixed neighborhoods
and abandonment of the poor)

****

REMINDERS OF THE SOLUTION
TO
AMSAC AND ITS INSEPARABLE SOCIAL PROBLEMS
↓
**"average expectable environments"→ positive
core identity→ sound character**
(solution lies in "average expectable environments"
which produce a positive core identity,
and which, at the same time, produce a sound character)
•
Toward a Valued Place for Everyone
(a gold standard suggested by Herrenstein-Murray
that can be used by us blacks, or by any racial/ethnic
group, to guide our policy and program pursuits versus
a standard guided by an *equal* place for everyone)

****

REMINDER OF PERSISTENCE OF
WASHINGTON'S TRADITION
↓
The Booker T. Washington Society (BTW Society)
(founded in 2005 by Ronald Court, its president
conducts activities which promote Washington's ideas)

Joe L. Rempson

****

REMINDERS OF OUR ROLE
IN THE SOLUTION
↓
Child Family Rights Movement
(the recommended social action to strengthen the black family
so as to foster the creation of "average expectable environments,"
a key measure of success being a reduction of
72% out-of-wedlock births to under 50%)

•

**practice of the art of loving: infancy - black
males - career and character**
(ways to foster "average expectable environments"
to nurture positive core identity:
practice art of loving and
provide our children security and love,
especially through age three,
along with school and life preparation,
and support career and character education,
especially for our males)

****

REMINDERS OF ROLE AND VALUE OF WHITE SUPPORT
↓
President Johnson's Validation Omission
(did not risk acting on Moynihan Report
and thus failed to give validation to a black self-help agenda)

•

Bill Clinton Risk
(President Bill Clinton's ultimate decision, at
political risk, to enact welfare reform
and thereby give validation to a black self-help agenda)

In seeking to understand the crisis reflected in these mnemonics and the lessons from these legacies, so much has been found and read that it becomes an enormous challenge to separate the wheat from the chaff, to get at the nexus of it all. Yet, fail to do so, and our journey is rendered futile. It is for that reason that we so often have probed and pondered, working through some of the minutiae, invoking varied sources, assuming little, and questioning a lot. Thereby, to the extent possible, enhanced clarity and perspective are *forced*, for everything has to be *worked through*. Of course, by no means does that *working through* assure enhanced clarity and perspective, but, studiously undertaken, it does increase its likelihood and, minimally, it forces confrontation and justification, which are at the heart of intellectual endeavors.

The question: what has the *working through* yielded. At the end of our journey, what, if anything, from the many things, can cited as lessons learned. The journey was ultimately undertaken to understand AMSAC and its inseparable social problems and, based on that understanding, to assess and fashion solutions; and, indeed, as no doubt apparent, lessons were learned, those lessons listed below. Unheeded, their neglect will doom us to remain in our second bondage, Victimology, and, thus, to remain plagued by the lack of a positive core identity, of which AMSAC and its inseparable social problems are manifestations.

Understanding and Solutions: Lessons Learned

1. **The <u>master key</u> to an understanding of and solution to the African American School Adaptability Crisis (AMSAC) and its inseparable social problems is that, race notwithstanding, if we are to succeed in school or in life, usually we need to grow up in *"average expectable environments,"* especially in average expectable *home* environments, wherein we are provided security and love, which research shows is essential to the forging of a positive core identity and to the development of the associated sound character traits on which school and life success depend, IQ, while of major importance, ordinarily, not playing a decivise role.**
2. **The <u>auxiliary key</u> to an understanding of and solution to the African American School Adaptability Crisis (AMSAC) and its inseparable social problems is that treatment of the causes and solutions to our crisis and problems tend to fall into two historical frameworks, herein called the**

Self-Responsibility Tradition of Booker T. Washington and the System- Responsibility Tradition of W. E. B. DuBois, and that one, the Self- Responsibility Tradition of Booker T. Washington, which is in national leadership demise, is congruent with this master key while the other, the System- Responsibility Tradition of W. E. B. DuBois, which is dominant, is incongruent with it. It must be emphasized that neither, however, was an original thinker but, rather, their thinking reflects thinking which, from the beginning, has guided our uplifting, only, through words and deeds, they give it singular prominence and popularity. Therefore, to exorcise Washington from our history, as has largely been done by our black leadership, is to discredit, not just a man, but, in effect, as well, a cornerstone of our heritage.

3. We African Americans, as a group, are adaptation-challenged, failing, unlike other immigrant groups, adequately to meet the demands of adaptation due to our failure to address, internally, our three major demons (*IQ lag-fatherless families-crime*), instead, seeking adaptation through an emphasis on civil rights and a resort to opposition and separatism, means which have fallen short and which, consequently, have led to a victim mentality that is responsible for our second bondage, Victimology.

4. We African Americans will never be able, collectively, to forge a positive core identity, and, thereby, to develop a sense of genuine race pride (such as, for example – and as observed by Booker T. Washington -- that is possessed by the Japanese), unless we remedy our family breakdown (and thus the impetus for a Child Family Rights Movement) because the personal and social problems which ensue from our family breakdown -- the lack of a positive core identity being at their core – overshadow the strengths which we exhibit in various domains, especially in the domains of athletics and entertainment, self-esteem research suggesting that efforts to acquire that genuine pride through various separatist remedies to which we have resorted, such as Afrocentrism, are doomed to failure because genuine pride, as the life of Booker T. Washington demonstrates, must

stem from what we actually do and accomplish ("results"), rather than from what we idealize.

5. Our black leadership and Victimology-contaminated Talented Tenth, in concert with politicians, the civil-rights establishment, and egalitarian white liberals, use their dominance to perpetuate system-centered approaches to solving our crisis and problems and, by attacking its advocates, to prevent the rise of self- help-centered approaches to their solution, as a result of which they have kept our Self-Responsibility Tradition in national leadership demise and, thereby, they have contributed to the creation and perpetuation of our crisis and problems, rather than to their solution.

6. Due to our three major demons (*IQ lag-fatherless families-crime*), the goal of *closing* the academic achievement gap between black and white students is unrealistic and, therefore, rather than continue to make it a fetish, we must, instead, put the emphasis on its *reduction* (whose possible range might be statistically estimated) and on dropout rate, while at the same time expanding opportunites for our students to develop their abilities. Further, in view of our students' identity and character deficits, we must place their identity and character skill development on par with their cognitive skill development with the goal of contributing to their forging of a positive core identity and, overall, of enabling them to acquire, in addition to the cognitive, the basic emotional, relationship, job, and everyday living skills necessary for them to live valued and self-reliant lives. Finally, and, most important, in view of the African American School Adaptability Crisis (AMSAC) and the cognitive (IQ and academic) and character deficits of our African American males students which it reflects [on these deficits, they rank below, not only their white male, Asian, and Hispanic counterparts, but also below their African American female counterparts, that is, they are *alone* at the bottom], we must, in particular, emphasize persistence through such means as stress on their career discovery and pursuit, attention to their developmental needs, and, due

to the factor of cultural influence, the various use of black males in the teaching-learning process.

Throughout these pages, we have been talking about human nature and human behavior. That is what our crisis is about. It is not about the school or system per se, nor about race per se. Extrapolated, it is about human nature and human behavior. As Shelby Steele has put it, "… being black in no way spares one from being human." He goes on to say, "Whatever I do or think as a black man can never be more than a variant of what all people do and think. Some of my life experiences may be different from those of other races, but there is nothing different or special in the psychological processes that drive my mind" (247a:xi).

That is, it can be said that "there is nothing different or special in the psychological processes that drive" our students. Why do our students behave the way they do? How can we account for *their* response to their school and life circumstances? Robert Havighurst, a la Steele, has postulated that in so asking we are dealing with *universals*. We cannot extract our students from the forces which inhere in the immutable human nature which they share with the rest of their peers throughout the universe. They do present a crisis challenge, but that challenge derives, not from unique needs, but from a unique neglect of those needs. It is this realization which enables us better to understand the African American Male School Adaptability Crisis (AMSAC) and its inseparable social problems and the need to address remedies from such objective and behavioral perspectives as afforded by the social sciences. The challenge is indeed about the "handling of black students," black *male* students, in particular, not, however as a species apart, but rather as part of a species. Those of us who accordingly have Afrocentric or critical race theory leanings, or who otherwise engage in separatist remedies or thinking, can be said to be turning, not to a remedy, but to an escape – an escape from the challenges of adaptation.

Critical Community

It is the enumerated Understanding and Solution Lessons which are going to enable us to solve AMSAC -- not overnight, but over time. First, however, we must win over our people. How? **Through the**

existence of a <u>critical community</u> and <u>movements</u> which give life to a Child Family Rights Movement.

In <u>Culture Moves: Ideas, Activism, and Changing Values</u>, political scientist and Ithaca College president Thomas Rochon reminds us that there are times when "We must change in order to survive," "... when human communities face the need to adapt, and to do so quickly." "But," he goes on to remind us, "adaptation does not occur automatically just because it is needed" (228:3, 5). Two forces cause it to occur, *critical community* and *movements*. As Rochon puts it:

> The creation of new ideas occurs initially within a relatively small community of critical thinkers who have developed a sensitivity to some problem, an analysis of the sources of the problem, and a prescription for what should be done about the problem. These critical thinkers do not necessarily belong to a formally constituted organization, but they are part of a self-aware, mutually interacting group [footnote reference omitted]. I shall label these groups "critical communities" (228: 22).

However, Rochon elaborates, "Even when the existence and severity of a problem are matters of incontrovertible fact, naming the causes of the problem and the best solution to it are not. The facts do not speak for themselves" (228:90). For this reason, "The debate that ensues may be highly polarized between passionate supporters and equally passionate resisters to the new concepts" (228:242).

That we have a critical community composed of adherents to our System-Responsibility Tradition is no doubt evident from our discussion. John McWhorter cites names, and asserts that they see "The Man,"in his words [in equivalent terminology, "The System"], as the problem (161:3). His list:

Michael Eric Dyson
Douglas Massey
Sheryll Cashin
Elijah Anderson
William Julius Wilson
Ishmael Reed

Cornel West
Deborah Mathis
Manning Marable
Tavis Smiley
Ellis Cose
Tricia Rose
Robin D.G. Kelley
Troy Duster

Perhaps less evident is that a critical community of those who embrace our Self-Responsibility Tradition, or some elements of it, also exists. Dinesh D'Souza offers us two such lists: one composed of conservatives, the other of liberals (62:521). His conservatives list:

Clarence Thomas
Colin Powell
Thomas Sowell
Glenn Loury
Shelby Steele
Alan Keyes
Walter Williams
Robert Woodson
John Sibley Butler
Stanley Crouch
Tony Brown
Anne Wortham
Elizabeth Wright
Ken Hamblin
Armstrong Williams

On his liberals list (though liberal, he says they embrace some of the self-development themes):

Randall Kennedy
Orlando Patterson
Carol Swain
Anthony Appiah
Gerald Early
Nancy Fitch

Stephen Carter
William Raspberry
Clarence Page
Juan Williams
Hugh Price
Michael Meyers
Hugh Pearson
Mark Mathabane
Itabari Njeri

Movements

For this critical community to debate is one thing; for it to get something done is another. On this point, Rochon tells us that to enable its thinking to be translated into values that can be acted upon, the critical community requires movements. Movements -- social and political -- diffuse the ideas of the critical community, win their acceptance, and get them acted upon.

> Movements bring the issue and its value context to a wider public and to the political arena. One important part of this task is to organize demonstrations, discussion groups, petition signings, teach-ins, sit-ins, letter writing campaigns, self-help associations, and other types of collective action that draw attention to new values and show determination to act on them. While the critical community develops a language to express new values, the movement acts so as to create settings in which those values can be expressed (228:240).

Rochon includes as examples of these two forces the 1964 Civil Rights Act, the 1980 Equal Employment Opportunity Commission (EEOC) guidelines defining sexual harassment in the workplace, and various policies that have been adopted in response to alcohol abuse, such as the legal blood-alcohol content standards and severe penalties for accidents due to alcohol impairment. In each case, cultural change was made possible by the existence of a critical community and associated movements. The critical community provided the thinking (not necessarily the specific solutions) that resulted in the adoption of new values that were propagated by social and political movements. The movements in turn made it possible to translate these new values into specifics -- programs, policies, practices, and legislation.

If cultural values could be changed in those instances, they likewise can be changed with respect to the African American Male School Adaptability Crisis (AMSAC). Unlike in those instances, however, AMSAC is part of an umbrella crisis -- or at least an umbrella of social problems. Although it has received increasing single-issue treatment since the 1980s, often the critical community treats it in the context of the broader problems (212: ix-xii; 398). Unlike in the case of the Civil Rights Act of 1964, to exert a national impact, it has no Dr. Martin Luther King; or as in the case of sexual harassment, an organization like the National Organization of Women (NOW); or as in the case of penalties for drug abuse infractions, an organization like Mothers Against Drunk Drivers (MADD).

With his **Brown Anniversary Speech of 2004**, Bill Cosby appeared to have stepped into the role, but apparently he had not seen himself fulfilling it. Nevertheless, as contended, his speech has provided another sign that the roots of our Self-Responsibility Tradition are still alive. The prior **Million Man March of 1995** provided a one-day glimpse of what could be possible, and herein a call is being made for a second such march, this time to catalyze the proposed **Child Family Rights Movement**. No significant follow-up to the first one is apparent. So, missing still is a sustained Dr. King-like, NOW-like, MADD-like focus on AMSAC as a crisis in and of itself, quite apart from the larger problems from which it originates.

While the absence of such a singular focus, and of a singular personality or entity as a driving force, makes it more difficult for AMSAC to generate a movement, that difficulty should be diminished by reliance on two of our four famous black leaders as its guiding spirit: Booker T. Washington and Dr. Martin Luther King Jr. We are, after all, still burdened with the needs which Washington addressed. Something he said well over 100 years ago equally resonates today, namely, as previously quoted from his "Industrial Education of the Negro" article in 1903:

> There is still doubt in many quarters as to the ability of the Negro unguided, unsupported, to hew his own path and put into visible, tangible, indisputable form, products and signs of civilization. This doubt cannot be much affected by abstract arguments, no matter how delicately and convincingly woven together. Patiently, quietly, doggedly, persistently, through summer and winter, sunshine and shadow, by self-sacrifice, by foresight, by honesty and industry, we must re-enforce argument with results.

While, today, those doubts may be less widespread and firm, they persist, not only "in many quarters," but among us as well. And while there are many who seem still to think that "abstract arguments" will erase those doubts, experience suggests otherwise. We are being measured by, and increasingly held accountable for, "results." The body politic has grown tired of seeing millions, even billions and trillions, go down the drain with seemingly little or nothing to show for it. That is why the self-development energy bequeathed by the Washington legacy, and embraced by Dr. King, is so timely; it is about "results." It is about us getting things done by and for ourselves, applying, as he did, our imagination and our organizational and management skills in a collective and concerted push to consummate our adaptation.

Of course, it would be hard to duplicate the masterful management and organizational skills which Washington possessed, but if we are to succeed, we must recognize the need for such skills and not let fictive kinship (among other things) stand in the way of seeking and supporting those who possess them. Without skilled leaders, at best, we will tread water. As previously suggested, too often we have ostensibly well-intentioned leaders who can talk it up but who do not put up; when it comes to the management and organizational skills required to produce "results," they fall short.

Hopeful signs exist that revitalization is possible. We do have a critical community and special attention within and outside existing structures are being given to AMSAC. Although system-centered energy has so far commanded that attention, an attempt has been made to make the case that the self-help roots laid by Washington still lives among the majority of us blacks.

Joe L. Rempson

Numerous examples of life in those roots exist (for example, see McWhorter, 161:370-74 and D'Souza, 62:555-56). Some have already been cited. There is even, for instance, at least one website that provides black self-development information: http://www.blackselfhelp.info/. The information is about an array of local and national organizations engaged in self-development efforts to assist the black community. In the school domain, we have, for example:

- *AVID, Advancement Via Individual Determination* in the San Diego public schools. Through an achievement ideology which stresses self-responsibility, motivation, and hard work, it encourages and helps high-potential, low-achieving eighth and ninths grade black and Latino students to graduate and attend college; and it seeks to enlist peer and school support (167).
- *MAC, The Minority Achievement Committee Program* at Shaker Heights High School (Ohio) where, under faculty guidance, high-achieving black male high school students provide mentoring and modeling for lower-achieving black male students, a parallel attempt being made to create a community of scholars and peer support for academic striving (158).
- *Social Skills Curriculum* has been designed by George R. Taylor, Professor of Special Education at Coppin State College, to integrate the teaching of social skills (inclusive of drug intervention strategies) to African-American males throughout the school curriculum. Taylor observes that "social skills development may be necessary before academic skills can be mastered" (255:109010). It is also designed to assist personnel working in community agencies as well as parents and other family members.

Particular mention must also be made of four relevant self-help books encountered (no claim being made of having undertaken an extensive search) : Bill Cosby and Dr. Alvin Poussaint's **Come on People: On the Path from Victims to Victors**; K. Thomas Oglesby's **What Black Men Should Do Now: 100 Simple Truths, Ideas, and Concepts**; Hill Harper's **Letters to a Young Brother: MANifest Your Destiny**; and Kevin Powell's **The Black Male Handbook: A Blueprint for Life** (46, 201a, 113b, 212c). Except for Bill Cosby and Dr. Poussaint's Come on People, all are written to black males – guidebooks to help us to be better and to live better. All four can play a role in AMCAP and in the proposed Child Family Rights Movement.

Cosby and Dr. Poussaint's Come on People is more than a book. It is a self-help guide which can be considered, at once, part of and in the forefront of a **Child Family Rights Movement**. While not focused solely, or even primarily, on the African-American male school adaptation crisis, it addresses the broad range of self-help matters that can contribute to its solution -- from the choice to have a baby, to prenatal care, to sound early childhood practices, to handling teenagers, to teaching kids at home, to healthy eating. You name it. The parenting skills (and pre-parenting behaviors), applicable to males and females alike, are all there.

Oglesby's What Black Men Should Do Now can almost be regarded as must reading for us black males. In the spirit of a follow up to the Million Man March, Oglesby in effect answers the question of what, as individuals, since we have had the march, do we do now. He gives 100 truths, ideas, and concepts of what that ought to be – seemingly covering almost every conceivable topic, and with engaging conciseness and clarity. It is direct, specific, down to earth, and action-oriented.

Harper's Letters to a Young Brother is all about black males helping other black males. This book is his way of doing that. It can be called a mentoring book. Through it, he writes that he is serving in the same role to black males as his grandfathers and other adult males have served him. In his letters, in response to their questions, he is sharing with them (the them being a composite of hundreds of young men he had met over the previous five years) his life -- that is, sharing his experiences, his insights, his support and encouragement, and his advice. He is responding to their "male hunger," as it were, and doing so instructively and inspirationally.

Concerned about the "downward spiral for Black males in America," in his The Black Male Handbook, Powell has assembled the essays, in his words, of "some of the most brilliant Black male minds in America today," "all of which include concrete, step-by-step instructions on how you can heal, grow, think, and become a different kind of Black male"

(212c:xxii). How encouraging! Equally as encouraging, Powell makes reference to monthly Black and Male in America (BAMIA) workshops in New York City. Those workshops suggest signs of a movement, and those of us who count ourselves in the critical community can hope that this is, in fact, the case.

A Call to Arms:
A Child Family Rights Movement

Our crisis and problems demand more, however, than signs of self-help and individual endeavors; they cry out for a tide. That is what is herein called for: a tide in the form of a **Child Family Rights Movement**. That tide can only occur if we are able to forge a counterculture to our current dominant culture of Victimology. That can be done through a revitalization of our Self-Responsibility Tradition, which fosters a counterculture of adaptation and a growth mindset, in contrast to the prevailing culture of Victimology and a victim mindset under our current, and leadership dominant, System-Responsibility Tradition.

Leadership

If there is to be a **Child Family Rights Movement**, it must have leadership. That leadership must be provided by the establishment domain, that is, by some prominent personality or organization, or through acquired leadership, that is, by some heretofore little known, or unknown, personality or organization.

Movement or no Movement, to address our crisis and problmes, national leadership is needed, indeed required. One might think that would be obvious, but Eugene Robinson, for example, argues that, given our tremendous progress, the idea of our need for a "black leader" sounds patronizing (227: 233). In his mind, not being followers, we do not need to be told what to think. Well, let us take a deep breath. Maybe Robinson had forgotten his earlier description that, after making such great progress following the 1960s, the needle got stuck and left us with the Abandoned (227:7). So the progress which Robinson applauds, he admits has come to a halt, which would suggest that we need to do something about the halt; and further, that to do something about the halt we need a "black leader." In addition, however, to being patronizing, in Robinson's mind having a "black leader" would call for something we blacks, being splintered, do not have: one agenda, since, being splintered, we have many agendas. However, having one common agenda does not preclude the existence of discrete agendas. To be blunt, we blacks have a race problem – and a persistent one – and our splintering does not obscure or minimize it. To attack it meaningfully, rather than just "play at it" [as E. Franklin Frazier might say], we must have a "black leader." As put at the beginning of an elegy sent to Washington's family upon his death:

> Comes now the question, no dispute
> Where can we find a substitute
> To carry out unfinished plans
> And fill the stead of this "Great Man"? (109:455).

Written by a black realtor, Capp Jefferson, a century ago, the sentiment may be dormant but the question is no less pressing. Not only do we need a substitute, we also need supportive black leaders at our state and local levels (where the action is) – somewhat in the fashion of Washington's Little Tuskegees. That is, we must find a substitute for Washington at the national level and a support network of substitutes at the local and state levels. And it is being suggested that the Washington-like substitute undertake a **Child Family Rights Movement**.

Ideally, this leadership role would be a roled filled by one of our two major civic organizations, either the National Association for the Advancement of Colored People (NAACP) or the National Urban League (NUL). Or, some well known personality might be moved to try to come to our children's rescue. That either is likely to occur, however, is doubtful – and certainly we cannot afford just to wait and to hope for either to occur. The combination (inclusively) of tradition, the unique barrier of fictive kinship, and the political correctness of the time almost defy violation.

So, then, the role is likely left to the little known, or to the unknown, which is where the Rempson Foundation enters. As a secondary, and default, goal – contingent on progress made with AMCAP and on resources -- the Foundation would assume the role because if, in particular, the Abandoned among us African Americans are to be uplifted and if, further, we are to solve AMSAC and its inseparable social problems, it is a role that must be filled, but which, otherwise, might well, ad infinitum, go unfilled. Who knows when, or if, someone will come along to fill it.

To address, generally, our need for better leadership, regardless of Movement leadership, resources permitting (perhaps dedicated funding would be sought), the Rempson Foundation would set up a **Booker T. Washington (BTW) Fellows and Leadership Training Program**. The program would draw upon the concepts of both the MacArthur Fellows Program and the Ibrahim Prize for Achievement in African Leadership (see website of each), and would add a training component. The former rewards exceptional talent, the latter exceptional governance. The Foundation would designate a Director to develop and administer the program – which would be based on Washington's leadership attributes -- whose goals would be to train Movement leaders, to reward those providing Washington-like leadership in the Movement, to set up a process and structure to promote cross-fertilization among them, and to enlist them in shared efforts to advance the Movement's agenda. In BTW fashion, stringent standards would be upheld, and, if none were eligible for a reward, none would be given; there would be no ritualized annual or other time-determined granting of rewards.

As the Movement leader, the Rempson Foundation would create the position of **Coordinator for the Child Family Rights Movement**, who, at the same time, would assume overall responsibility for Foundation activities. The African American Male Career Pathway Program (AMCAP)'s Director would serve as one of his two Assistant Coordinators, the other Assistant Coordinator position, to be staffed by an African American female, being created to coordinate African American Parenting Skills Activities. The intent would be to pair an African American male and an African American female, working with the Director of the Foundation's African-American-male-conducted trademark program, AMCAP, in a team effort to reach and work, as appropriate, separately and jointly, with both our African American males and African American females. Depending on resources and needs, other Assistant Directors might be periodically added, such as an Assistant Director for Student AMCAPs.

This structure and staffing reflect the special role envisaged for our African American females. Because it is mainly we black males who are the problem, the proposal is for us to do the heavy lifting, so to speak, in the Movement. But -- the call goes out for our females, since they are the best qualified to do so, to tackle our female-centered problems. That is what Booker T. Washington's wife, Maggie, did for him in her work with black women, and her example is still worthy of emulation.

One other proposed position would be crucial. The rise of the NAACP and BuBois's role in that rise as its Director of Publicity points to the need for publicity as an integral part of leadership. DuBois used the Crisis to put the NAACP on the black map, and it is suggested that, just as we need a substitute for Washington, we also need a substitute for DuBois: a **Director of Publicity and Publications** (to make DuBois's title more encompassing) for the Movement. The intent of the Rempson Foundation, for example, to fund a tentatively entitled book, Black Progress the Booker T. Washington Way (with the Endorsement of Dr. Martin Luther King Jr): Brains, Property, and Character, however contributory, alone is highly unlikely to generate the readership sought. Interest must be generated for the book and other related initiatives. There is, further, a need for someone to oversee its publication and to administer the range of publicity and publication needs of the Foundation. Today there are more means of reaching our people than in DuBois's time and a Director of Publicity and Publications (with the needed staff) should be charged with making effective use of those means, two of which merit special mention: the black church and the internet. With the Southern Christian Leadership Conference (SCLC) of Dr. King providing the lead, our black churches were in the vanguard of the Civil Rights Movement, and they, likewise, can be – and should be -- in the vanguard of a Child Family Rights Movement; and the internet has proven to be an invaluable tool of social action.

It would be easy to see the Movement, if not led by the NAACP or the National Urban League, or by some personality, as in competition with those organizations and with other groups variously working to uplift the race, but such competition is not envisaged. Rather, the goal would be to forge, with all groups and individuals, cooperative and supportive relationships. Both the NAACP and the National Urban League, for example, have the structure and resources to make indispensable contributions to the Movement, and it would be shortsighted not to try to utilize their assistance, whatever the ideological or other differences.

By whomever led, what follows is the remainder of a quasi-master plan for the Movement. No attempt to devise an actual plan has being made, only to convey some of its possible elements. Resources permitting, a number of those elements pertain to what the Foundation would do in its conduct of AMCAP, in the process of which the Movement would be fostered.

Goals

The Movement would: (1) seek to secure for our children their right to grow up in intact homes wherein they are provided a 'hallowed presence" (security and love), and are prepared for school and life; (2) promote a black education agenda, herein termed **Black Advocacy of School Do's and Don'ts**; and (3) advocate a black crime agenda, herein termed **Black Blueprint for Crime Prevention and Punishment**. The Movement would give more common direction and cohesion to a variety of existent and prospective efforts to achieve these goals. The key measure of its success could be its effect on our most devastating problem, our 72 percent out-of-wedlock birthrate, its reduction to under 50 percent being the goal. At present, the national rate is 48 percent.

Message

A movement needs a message -- a statement of what it is trying to do, why, and how. That proposed message appears below.

Method: The Tradition of Choice, with Dr. King-Washington holiday as yardstick and turning point

As indicated, the "how" would be a return to **The Tradition of Choice** whereby self-help would replace civil rights as our zeitgeist, the focus of that self-help centered on the family rights of our children. Several initiatives or activities come to mind which can contribute to that return.

Washington's success was based, not on rhetoric, but, as discussed in Chapter 17, on "results." So must the revitalization of his tradition. It must not rest on a public relations campaign; it can only succeed if it is anchored on demonstrable results. Concrete and substantial progress in the conduct of the herein proposed African American Male Career Pathway Project (AMCAP) can be one such result; so might be the BTW High School, discussed in Chapter 16. Perhaps a BTW Education Consortium can be formed, composed of a number of schools and projects which embody his legacy. The Consortium could model and foster the professional development of its members and engage in dissemination activities.

It is hoped that this book, as well, can contribute to the Movement. But to serve that purpose widely, it may be too comprehensive and too academic. Something is needed which is more targeted and has more general public appeal. Therefore, resources permitting, the Rempson Foundation would fund the research and writing of a book which would embody the Movement's tradition and ideology, perhaps entitled <u>Black Progress the Booker T. Washington Way (with the Endorsement of Dr. Martin Luther King Jr): Brains, Property, and Character</u>. To be published as soon as possible, it might give a brief summary of Washington's life, an overview of Dr. King's support, and, then, in a structured form, such as chapters divided into enumerated sections, use Washington's direct quotes and experiences to convey his teachings. Written for mass consumption, it would help to personify the Movement and provide it a common source of authority and ideology.

As, perhaps, a simultaneous or subsequent project, the Foundation would undertake what Harlan reports Emmett Scott was in the process of negotiating with his publishers a few days before Washington's death: a film version of <u>Up from Slavery</u> (109:435). Scott's idea was to promote a picture of black life to combat the white superiority/black inferiority theme (blacks depicted as beastly) of the film, *The Birth of a Nation*, which, during the time, became wildly popular in the South and remained popular up to the 1950s (109:431-35; 192:413-14). Of course, today, there would be differences: the focus would be on Washington's self-help *and* civil rights legacy, not just on <u>Up from Slavery</u>, and Dr. King's support could be featured. An enormous undertaking, it would require special funding and judicious pursuit. Those factors should not be inhibiting, however; we have a crisis and we must treat it as such.

As a film can help to give life to a renewal of our **Tradition of Choice**, so can a favorite weapon of ours: marches. As we have had, and continue to have, civil rights marches, why not convert them to **Child Family Right Movement marches**. Instead of our usual protest marches, let us engage in internally-directed marches on behalf of our children, an example being provided by the **300 Men March** in Baltimore, Maryland (see below).

As a capstone, a **Second Million Man March** could be staged. Some among us will recall the **Million Man March of 1995**. Organized by Louis Farrakham of the Nation of Islam, and directed by former NAACP Executive Director, Benjamin F. Chavis Jr., the march consisted of black men from across the nation (estimated crowd size of 440,000 to 1.1 million) who gathered in Washington, D.C. "to bring about a spiritual renewal that would instill a sense of personal responsibility in African American men for improving the condition of African Americans" (414a). Like the author, some may recall the excitement and enthusiasm that surrounded the event, from which one got a feeling of renewal, the coming of a new day for us African American men. For many, the author included, it was truly a moment of great pride and awakening. But no significant national follow-up to that historic event has occurred. Insofar as can be ascertained, a lot of words, but minimal deeds, the National Urban League's publication on the plight of the black male years later (2007) being an example of such words (143). Perhaps many individual lives were changed, Oglesby's book being an example. But, as Dr. King emphasized, those changes need to be complemented with collective action.

The idea was a good one, however, and it provides an indication of what might be possible. It shows that we can get African American male participation; the challenge is the substance. That participation has to be translated into concrete follow-up activities and periodic follow-up conferences. If either chooses, that is where the NAACP or the National Urban League can enter. With its headquarters and some 2,000 local units, the NAACP has the needed organizational structure for the task. To a far lesser extent, so does the National Urban League with its over 100 affiliates. Either could designate a **Child Family Rights Movement Coordinator** to lead the way.

Some might consider our second Million Man March to have been the thousands who, in October 2015, gathered at the site of the March to celebrate its 20th anniversary, but that celebration had an expanded composition and focus (446d). Diverse groups, with diverse agendas, were represented. This recommendation is about a continuation of the restricted composition and agenda of the original March.

The accomplishment of the revival of our **Tradition of Choice** would be the establishment of a joint **Dr. King-Washington holiday**, just as we have what some states designate a Washington and Lincoln Day (commonly called Presidents' Day). The pursuit of its establishment would give personification to the movement and its message of renewal and refocus, and, further, could be a contributory, invigorating, and solidifying force. We can think of it as the potential Gettysburg of the Movement, its achievement being a turning point in our cultural war to end our second bondage in much the same way as the real Gettysburg was the turning point in the civil war that brought an end to our first bondage. After a conceivably prolonged struggle, the establishment of a combined holiday would represent, as the real Gettysburg, a tipping point wherein in this instance the Self-Responsibility forces would have gained the upper hand. It would be a return to the emerging dominance of our Self-Responsibility Tradition in a yin-yang relationship with our System-Responsibility Tradition, both working together, "dedicated to the great task remaining before us" (to borrow words from the Gettysburg Address) -- that great task being to end AMSAC and normalize its inseparable social problems, perhaps a two-generation or more outcome. Integral to that outcome would be a gradual ending of our second bondage, Victimology – and, along with it, the ending of the vitiation of our manhood, on which rests the strengthening of the black family and, thereby, the securement of our children's family rights.

While not equivalent to a Dr. King-Washington holiday, the creation of a **Booker T. Washington (BTW) Library and Self-Help Center** -- a la the W. E. B. Du Bois Institute and The King Center -- would be a monumental milestone in the war. In time, it could become the base of the leadership of the Movement.

Joe L. Rempson

Content

Our **72 percent out-of-wedlock birthrate** provides the origin and bedrock of the Movement. Its first step must be the propagation of a community norm which breaks with the traditional silence about our out-of-wedlock births, replaced by the public promotion of wedlock births. That is, the Movement ought to promote what we favor, rather than condemn what we oppose, consistent with the **practice of the art of loving**, assuming a positive tone versus a negative one. Based on his review of the evaluation of Fatherhood-Renewal Programs, United States Department of Health and Human Services Assistant Secretary for Children and Families, Wade F. Horn, provides a lesson in this regard. He notes that few of these programs discuss the topic of marriage. His conclusion:

> By avoiding discussions about the importance of marriage to fatherhood, we may be losing the opportunity both to prevent unwed fathers from fathering additional children out-of-wedlock (and thereby further reducing their ability to fulfill their responsibilities as fathers) and to communicate the ideal of married fatherhood to the next generation of fathers (127a:149).

Eugene Robinson, however, is probably right to suggest that in view of single-parent households becoming a society-wide phenomenon, it is unrealistic to think of marriage as "the cure for Abandoned black America's parlous condition" (227:133). He gets ample support from an impressive article by Natalie Angier in her <u>New York Times</u> article (November 25, 2013), "The Changing American Family" (301a). Drawing upon census data, the research literature, experts in the field, and personal interviews, Angier provides this overview of the change:

> In increasing numbers, blacks marry whites, atheists marry Baptists, men marry men and women women, Democrats marry Republicans and start talk shows. Good friends join forces as part of the 'voluntary kin' movement, sharing medical directives, wills, even adopting one another legally.

Single people live alone and proudly consider themselves families of one -- more generous and civic-minded than so-called 'greedy marrieds.'

While these national changes, indeed, point to the unrealism of banking on marriage as a cure for our "parlous condition," they must not preclude making it the centerpiece of a cure formula. We cannot treat black family life as if it were simply part of a national trend; we are confronted with black family issues which have been the subject of analysis and scholarship since we emerged from slavery and which, along with their fallout, were dramatically documented in 1965 by the Moynihan Report. For us blacks, the family changes reported by Angier merely compound those issues.

Important to observe, Angier emphasizes that the changes she reports notwithstanding, traditional marriage is still the American ideal. And it must be the black ideal as well -- and for more than just idealistic reasons. We ought equally to hold up marriage for its material and health benefits (127a:148-50; 414b). Marriage has documented advantages and we ought to tout those advantages. Many of our males may think that they are better off single, the same being true for some of our females as well, but the research shows that they are wrong -- and we should let them know it.

To those who do not subscribe to the ideal American family model, we must, nevertheless, stress family. Emphasis must be placed on the *need and importance of having a family* and on *family values*, those values that pertain to the *family rights* of our children being foremost. While the form of that family life has changed, the needs for the care, connection, and protection which it provides have not. The imperative must be to place family at the forefront of the black agenda, no one and no form being excluded from its benefits, nor from its responsibilities. Even if one lives by oneself, for example, there is a need for a family -- as it were, a self-constructed family. As Angier's article suggests, such a family can serve the same functions as any other family, and, if that is one's choice, we must respect it and provide education and assistance in making it viable.

Whatever form the family takes, we must not condone out-of-wedlock births; except for those where there has been adequate care arrangements, we must stigmatize them. It is irresponsible of us, in effect, to say that it is OK to bring children into the world and be almost totally unprepared to care for them. To father children here and there (the "rolling stones" among us) with absolutely no intention of helping to take care of them -- to say nothing of the material means or the emotional stability to do so -- is primitive behavior. The new zeitgeist must call for a different attitude. No more do-your-own-thing and the begotten children and the rest of us pay the price. Maladaptive and hedonistic, that lifestyle amounts to moral bankruptcy and degeneration. We black males are not wild animals and, foremost, to yourselves, we must validate our humanity. No mas!

However we can reasonably and effectively do it, we must lay down the hammer. The tone must he helping and supportive, yet insistent and serious. Too much is at stake for all involved for it to be otherwise. Among other things, that seriousness should entail making use of birth control a major, continuous, and intensive campaign with special attention to women on public assistance. Birth control medications, Depo-Provera and Norplant, are available; low-cost long-lasting reversible contraceptive implants are also available. We must have our own black women take the leadership in aggressively promoting their use. Starting early and working closely with the schools, many of which have sex education programs, is a must. At the same time, we must work to provide our children and youth a range of social and recreational activities which will afford them constructive outlets, working with parents to maximize participation. We have a choice: expend our time and resources on such initiatives as these, in which case we would not have, for example, a perceived need for a Black Lives Matter movement -- or -- expend them on all of the problems of delinquency, crime, and anti-social behavior that result from the uncared- for children we too typically get from out-of-wedlock births, which leads us to embark, for example, upon a Black Lives Matter movement as a security blanket to exonerate ourselves from responsibility.

As additions to this bedrock focus, the Movement ought, also, to target **parenting skills** and **neighborhood cleanliness and noise**. The need for a parenting skills focus is intrinsic to our 72 percent out-of-wedlock birthrate problem, and the proposal for a Movement Assistant Coordinator to coordinate African American Parenting Skills Activities is a response to it.

Parenting skills (cognitive outcomes). Research cited shows that poor children are hindered in their development, not by their material disadvantages, but by parent interactions and practices. From their analysis of the research, as already noted, Jencks and Phillips have concluded that "changing the way parents deal with their children *may be the single most important thing we can do* to improve children's cognitive skill" because "the cognitive disparities between black and white preschool children are currently so large that it is hard to imagine how school alone could eliminate them" [emphasis added] (136: 45-46). Ronald Ferguson's previously cited review of the research provides hope on this score. He concludes that the evidence shows that through parent programs for the poor we can change the way they deal with their children, and that the change shows promise of improving the academic performance of their children.

Parenting skills (emotional outcomes). Nor do just the cognitive skills outcomes of these parenting interactions and practices put our children at risk; equally, if not more so, do the character or emotional skills outcomes. Most crucial to stress is the parent-child attachment during the early years wherein the child is provided security and love, or a "hallowed presence." More generally, John Ogbu, for example, has cited several counterproductive outcomes of low-income parenting practices which need to be addressed: dependency, compliance, and manipulation. Previously cited George Taylor has written an entire book to address the deficient coping skills which our males bring to school (255).

School family-life instruction. Good parenting begins with good preparation, and for our students, that preparation needs to begin in high school. Our high school students ought to be *required* to take a family life course which, using an organic and case study approach – versus an academically-structured one -- would address various family and family-related topics, such as choosing a mate, interpersonal skills, conflict resolution, money management, and planning and decision-making. The idea would be to make it as real as possible, centering it around the students' interests, concerns, and experiences, for example, bringing in parents and family care providers as guests. As regards our youth, in particular, we cannot continue to leave familyhood and parenthood to chance.

Bill Cosby and Dr. Poussaint. It could be that aforementioned <u>Come on People</u> by Bill Cosby and Dr. Alvin Poussaint could serve as the centerpiece for popularizing and conducting a parenting skills crusade. It speaks to the training needs of our parents while also addressing related concerns. As Dr. Benjamin Spock's book, <u>Baby and Child Care</u>, has revolutionized parenting generally, perhaps Bill Cosby and Dr. Poussaint's book can do the same for African American parents in our poor neighborhoods -- and beyond.

The second addition, **neighborhood cleanliness and noise**, addresses two of the stark, readily noticeable differences between our poor neighborhoods and better neighborhoods. The streets in our poor neighborhoods are usually filthy and its stores give the same appearance, to say nothing of the noise, both day and night, especially, it seems, at night when an attempt is made to rest. It has been observed that, historically, cleanliness is a measure of a society's or civilization's development, and maybe it is this realization which led Washington to make cleanliness a fetish (415a). Noise control, on the other hand, is not just something desirable, noise, as the work of Cantor in the New York public schools shows (see Chapter 7), retards the learning and emotional health of our children (a major concern for a **Child Family Rights Movement**). Noise also impairs our own health and functioning (471w). To do something about cleanliness, perhaps, among other things, just as we have traffic cops, we should have sanitary cops, and we ought, maybe, give our regular police more responsibility for noise control. Making headway on both factors could pay huge dividends, having a ripple effect on a range of counterproductive behaviors exhibited by the poor. The Movement ought to designate a task force to flush out this focus and come up with a more detailed plan of action.

With our **72 percent out-of-wedlock birthrate**, together with its two appendages, **parenting skills** and **neighborhood cleanliness and noise**, as the bedrock of the Movement, the renewed message conveys the related content to be addressed. It is a matter of concretely flushing out that content. The idea would be to develop something like an initial 5-Year Plan that would include a Million Man March. Based on surveys and other data-gathering means, the Plan could suggest an array of activities which might constitute what can be called a **Child Family Rights Movement Resource Guide** with objectives, general content, and materials. It could give some background, lay out the philosophy, and give general direction. Localities would have a concrete guide and something to plug them into their role in the Movement. Their other central-dependent need could be training and assistance, something that the **Child Family Rights Movement Coordinator** and his staff could provide through the establishment of on-site training and assistance units.

One supportive document envisioned by the Rempson Foundation is a **Practice of the Art of Loving Guide**. Resources permitting, the Foundation will fund the writing, publication, and distribution of a pocket-size guide to provide (perhaps through brief illustrative stories) an understanding of the meaning and application of the **practice of the art of loving**. Intended to be attractive and easily readable, it would be distributed at a minimal cost, if not free, in selected poverty areas and made generally available. The guide would also promote the Child Family Rights Movement.

Some of the other specific activities which the Movement might advocate follows, but first a couple of guidelines.

One such guideline has been followed in the formulation of the herein proposed experimental program, the **African American Male Career Pathway Program (AMCAP)**. In an Op-Ed Contribution in the <u>New York Times</u>, it has been also highlighted by by Ron Haskins, co-director of the Center on Children and Families at the Brookings Institute. Haskins's advocates an *"evidence-based approach" as a prerequisite for any program to get federal dollars"* [emphasis added] (367c). Haskins advocacy derives from his revelation that "... 75 percent of programs or practices that are intended to help people do better at school or at work have little or no effect," which means that millions, even billions or trillions of dollars, have been wasted. President Barak Obams's administration, Haskins points out, has continued what President George Bush's administration began: honoring this guideline by giving primary funding emphasis to programs shown by rigorous research to work. The **Child Family Rights Movement** ought, strongly, to endorse this policy and to apply its principle to the initiatives which it undertakes or support.

The second recommended guideline is somewhat related to the first one. In the fashion of a well-run political campaign, the Movement must be highly organized and have a targeted, sophisticated approach. Specific subsections of our black population, such as the working poor, need to be targeted with tailored messages and methods. Without the tools available to us today, Washington did a masterful job of managing Tuskegee, which made its success possible; with those tools, we shuld be able to rival his success.

Washington, D. C. Department of Health: Home Support Centers prototype. The research evidence tells us the earlier we begin the better. The message and its Movement, then, must give priority to the early years. If we are to turn things around, we must meet the challenge of the absent father and the unready mother. Perhaps the Department of Health in Washington, D.C. provides the germ of a prototype of how it can be met (451b). As reported in the New York Times, the Department has been able to reduce the District's infant mortality rate to a historic low and, at the same, time reduce teenage pregnancy. Its success is attributed to coordinated efforts on part of the Department and community organizations to reach more families in need of parenting help and to provide education and assistance through a city-run home-visit program.

Perhaps these departments can be at the core of Home Support Centers for prenatal care and child medical care up to age 6, each servicing a limited zone in order to personalize its services and create a sense of community. Staffed mainly by trained indigenous lay personnel, male and female, who might receive a stipend, the centers could provide an array of home support services such as day care, home visitors, parent training, shopping and nutrition workshops, counseling, and recreational and educational activities for children. To a considerable extent, this is a matter of surveying and documenting what exists and trying to bring it together on a community-centered basis (which would involve the leadership getting together and working together) so that it services a limited family zone in a way which integrates available and created services *within a given small geographic area* – and promotes their use. Though having a headquarters, the Center would not be in one location. Its various *community* components could function as a single unit, a kind of family social support supermarket. It would be reminiscent of the telephone number 311 concept in New York City, the number serving as the main source of information for government and non-emergency services.

The Commission on Children at Risk provides an appealing way of viewing these centers: as *authoritative communities* -- "groups that live out the types of connectedness that our children increasingly lack" (41). The Commission has in mind institutions which service children and youth, these institutions providing them connections to other people and "deep connections to moral and spiritual meaning." The Home Support Center idea is less encompassing, but embraces the same basic emphases. The **practice of the art of loving** alone, for example, is about connectedness and about moral and spiritual meaning [not religious meaning, but *spiritual* meaning]. And the proposed Center shares the Commission's advocacy of the use, primarily, of lay personnel.

Statewide Family Engagement Centers. As discussed in Chapter 16, since 1994, parent compacts in Title 1 schools have been mandated, and the new law, the Every Students Succeeds Act (ESSA), continues them and further strengthens support of family engagement provisions. We African Americans need to undertake and examination of those provision and determine how we can maximally use them to meet our parenting skills and parental-related needs – a task which might well be led by the Rempson Foundation's proposed Assistant Coordinator for African American Parenting Skills Activities. Like the Department of Health, schools' family engagement programs, supported by the Centers, can provide a means of coordinating and integrating a range of parent-centered activies – both, perhaps, under the umbrella of a Home Support Centers concept.

The brightest and talented. Reference has been made to our supporting school initiatives to identify and educate the brightest and most talented among our African American students rather than crying about their paucity in special programs. If our students do not meet the criteria, they should not be in them, period. At the same time, a program recently learned about is a reminder of what we African Americans need to do broadly to find and support our brightest and talented (as well, incidentally, as the less bright and less talented along with them). The program, El Sistema, is the free music program for the poor which was started in Venezuela in 1975 by economist and musician Jose Antonio Abreu. It has spread to a number of countries, including the United States. Such a program can tap into one of our strengths, and other similar programs can do likewise, such as a program to get more African Americans interested in baseball and tennis, for example. The idea is to do a much better job of positively creating and forging our own identity and of enhancing our character, finding and promoting our brightest and talented being one of the best ways to do it. Our Talented Tenth must step up and, *we ourselves*, in the fashion of El Sistema, must go about mining the diverse racial resources that we have in the person of our children and youth. Must that task be so commonly left to the other race, as in the case of El Sistema, for example?

Disorder. Our out-of-wedlock births demon raises another far less discussed headwind of which it is reflective: **disorder**. In one of his talks to his students, Washington reminds us of the necessity of order in our life. Scott and Stowe quote him as saying to his students: "'In many cases you have come from homes where there was no regular time for getting up in the morning, no regular time for eating your meals, and no regular time for going to bed.'" He then proceeds:

Now the basis of civilization is system, order, regularity. A race or an individual which has no fixed habits, no fixed place to abode, no time for going to bed, for getting up in the morning, for going to work; no arrangement, order, or system in all the ordinary business of life, such a race and such an individual are lacking in self-control, lacking in some of the fundamentals of civilization.... (234:343).

And what applied to Washington's students also applies to many of our students and to many of our people; and for the reason he gave, we must give it top ranking on the Movement's agenda. Our children have a right to an ordered life; it is intrinsic to their sense of being loved and of feeling secure.

Stepping it up by the middle class. As intimated in Chapter 1, quoting Dr. King, our black middle class needs to step it up and undertake an aggressive role in the Movement. The story of **U St. NW** is indicative of a harmful, if understandable, role it has played. Reminiscent of the lads in Paul Willis's study: many have left the the poor by themselves to reproduce themselves. What E. Franklin Frazier said of the black middle class of his day, the 1950s, applies to many in black middle class of our day: no less than those in the white middle class, many seek to escape from the black masses. Why is understandable. We owe ourselves and our family as good a life as possible and that means getting away from that which plagues our poor neighborhoods: the noise, the decrepit houses and filthy streets, the crime, the deficient services, the poor schools, and more. However, it leaves them without the leadership, models, and diversity -- and thus the kind of "**average expectable environments**" which could help improve their life chances. The result is that those left behind have less of an opportunity to acquire the kind of social capital which Glenn Loury cites as so essential, or the kind of connections explained by Nicholas Christakis and James Fowler, and that were possessed by the successful students in Farrell's two studies. Maybe William Julius Wilson best captures what happens.

> The basic thesis is not that ghetto culture went unchecked following the removal of higher-income families in the inner city, but that the removal of these families made it more difficult to sustain the basic institutions in the inner city (including churches, stores, schools, recreational facilities, etc.) in the face of prolonged joblessness. And as the basic institutions declined, the social organization of the inner-city neighborhoods (defined here to include a sense of community, positive neighborhood identification, and explicit norms and sanctions against aberrant behavior) likewise declined (285a:144).

Joe L. Rempson

One sees gentrification changing a black community like Central Harlem in New York City and wonders what might similarly be done as regards other similar black neighborhoods. Could we have a black gentrification movement whereby we get our middle-class blacks to move back to or stay in poor neighborhoods?

In answer to the question, however, recent research indicates that, often, no such effort is necessary because black middle-class families, unlike white and Asian-American middle-class families, tend to live in distinctly lower-income neighborhoods (395d). In what is termed the *neighborhood gap*, "even among white and black families with similar incomes, white families are much more likely to live in good neighborhoods – with high-quality schools, day-care options, parks, playgrounds, and transportation options." And, in one study, it was found that children who grew up in the better neighborhoods "fared much better as adults than otherwise similar children from worse neighborhoods." To state this result in the context of this book, the children fared better as adults who grew up in **"average expectable environments."**

The challenge facing the black middle class, then, is to be assertive in fighting to create or maintain **"average expectable environments"** in lower-income areas where we live, not, in the first place, if avoidable, leaving those areas. Circumstances permitting, let us in the black middle class, aggressively, try to force the poor to meet our standards rather than the poor forcing us to move away from them because of their lower standards. We know that neighborhoods can differ block by block, several houses or blocks contaminating a neighborhood and making it a struggle to establish or maintain standards. But we must motivate and sustain ourselves with the reminder that, often, the poor do great and avoidable harm to themselves, their children, and the rest of us, and that – in reponse -- destiny has bestowed upon some of us a responsibility to do something about it. Ally with the "decent" (to borrow a category from Elijah Anderson's <u>Code of the Street</u>) among them and, together, possibly, we can tip the odds in our favor.

Soul and Body of Proposal

The **practice of the art of loving**, drawn from the previously cited late world famous psychoanalyst Erich Fromm's <u>The Art of Loving</u> is regarded as the soul of what is proposed (98). Fromm says that loving is a skill, and that, as is the case with any skill, with due diligence and the exercise of certain attributes, we can all learn it. He defines love as **care, responsibility, respect,** and **knowledge**. It is considered the soul of the proposed Movement because it can take us off the pathway now traveled by far too many of us: the *pathway of self-sabotage* which is paved with the quicksand of victimhood and its associated anger, aggression, protest, and dependency. It can put us on a *pathway of adaptation*. Paved with the **practice of the art of loving**, that pathway can enhance our values and enrich our human spirit. Enhanced values and an enriched human spirit in turn will likely provide us the drive and energy required to create the **"average expectable environments"** which will nurture in us the development of a positive core identity. From a positive core identity will ensue a healthy personality or character. And from a healthy personality or character, we will be able to make the kind of adaptations on which school and life success depend.

Integral to these accomplishments, potentially, **"average expectable environments"** can do something else: raise our IQ. As discussed, the research suggests that, if we can raise our IQ, we can do it through an enriched environment which includes prenatal and parental care. And that is what the **practice of the art of loving** can enable us to do: enrich our environment. In sum, provide our young with **"average expectable environments,"** and we attack, and, over time, likely conquer our **three major demons**: *IQ lag-- fatherless families--crime.*

Crime

As part of this dynamic whole, no mention has been made of the last of the three: **crime**. Implemented, the belief is that the proposals made would lead to the normalization of our crime problems, including black male fratricide, and thus to crime becoming a matter of customary law enforcement, as is the case when we have **"average expectable environments."** But that is a longer-term solution and we have a present and persistent crime problem. Its effect on our children is devastating and it must be on the Movement's agenda – but in a positive and affirmative context. We can label it: **Black Blueprint for Crime Prevention and Management**. A specially designated Task Force could outline key practices and policies to be advocated, guided by the **practice of the art of loving** and drawing upon enlightened criminal justice practices. Here are a few guiding thoughts.

1. Be specific and emphasize the practical.
2. Make families and neighborhoods more accountable.
3. Replace community-police conflict with community-police cooperation, for example, by stressing the importance of our conduct in police encounters, not just that of the police.
4. Aggressively and strictly address drug sales and use.
5. Give special attention to low-income housing complex crime and disorder.
6. Replace or modify punishment with prevention, management, and rehabilitation
7. Review crime classification and sentencing.
8. Make education and self-discovery experiences a part of prison life.

In the interim, an example of something practical which can be done is provided by the **300 Men March** in Baltimore, Maryland, the site of a recent race riot ignited by the death of a black male (Freddie Gray) from injuries suffered while under police custody (471v). Founded by Munir Bahar, Executive Director of COR Health Institute, a community health organization, it was active during the riot, and, reportedly, (among other things perhaps) regularly marches on Friday evenings to promote personal and community responsibility, and to urge black males to stop killing one another (310d). The March represents black males themselves coming together to tackle our black male crime problem. The group appears to be at the fledgling stage, but nevertheless provides an example of an activity worthy of emulation.

Reward: "The Morning Cometh" / "I Have a Dream"

The African American Career Pathway Program (AMCAP) is designed to help tip the scales in the debate over the African-American Male School Adaptability Crisis (AMSAC) by fostering the kind of cultural adaptation by our black males which can be a watershed in our adaptation journey. That adaptation is unlikely to occur on a massive scale, however, unless it is supported by the black community. To secure its support, as well as to secure a range of complementary objectives, A **Child Family Rights Movement** is proposed. The Movement, of which AMCAP would be part, can help us to fulfill our long-held dream to become unqualified Americans, to see "The End of Blackness," to borrow the title of Debra Dickerson's book -- no hyphenation or other notation, just Americans, like other groups that make up this multiracial/multiethnic society.

This dream is deeply rooted in the African American story. It was articulated by all four of our famous leaders -- Douglass, Washington, DuBois, and Dr. King -- and the two traditions embody it. To solve AMSAC and its inseparable social problems, we are faced with a challenge: continuing the tradition that has run its course -- or -- renewing the one that had hardly begun its course but which has demonstrated such great promise and whose roots remain. At stake is the standing of our race. One choice seals our fate; the other choice puts us in command of it.

Of course, guarantees in life are few, if any. Some of us (and others) feel that the day will *never* come when we are "an example for all the world" or when "this nation will rise up and live out the true meaning of its creed." But such deeply held aspirations may be so ingrained that giving them up is not subject to voluntary action. Perhaps, however, we can put them in a state of suspension and concentrate instead on the soul of our proposed Movement: **practice of the art of loving**.

Practice of the art of loving: soul of proposal. As explained, loving (as Erich Fromm taught) is a skill, nurtured over a lifetime and likely never fully developed, but which enables us to exercise **CARE, RESPONSIBILITY, RESPECT, and KNOWLEDGE** in regard to self, others, and the environment. Sufficiently acquired, we will find that the perceived esteem and equality we seek is within us, rather than in the eyes of others, or in the laws or regulations that we get enacted and, which, though perhaps necessary, are not sufficient. Sufficiently acquired, as the need for external validation is extinguished, the ingrained external search for that esteem and equality will cease. It is perhaps at that attenuated juncture when that which we seek will instead come to us. In the prolonged meantime, we spare ourselves the dis-ease and continual complaining that ensues from trying to engineer something ("artificial forcing," Washington called it, and the "social engineering of attitudes," Lasch-Quinn calls it) that ultimately emanates from the heart. In the words of Debra Dickerson:

Blacks must look inside themselves and decide that they're tired of being the designated losers, tired of coming in last in every race, tired of fratricide, tired of making their peace with criminality and hopelessness, tired of fractured families, tired of watching the newly arrived outdo them, tired of underachievement, tired of soulless consumerism, tired of trying to make others love them, tired of being afraid to try. They must decide that they're ready to love themselves (58:253).

Well put, Ms. Dickerson -- and if a colloquialism is permitted -- you go girl!

- Down with low self-esteem and aggression!
- Down with frustration and anger!
- Down with Victimology -- and Separatism, and Anti-intellectualism!
- Down with self-pity, dependency, and responsibility-resistance!
- Down with our civil-rights fixation!
- Down with being half free!
- Down with our **three major demons**: *fatherless families*, IQ lag, and *crime*!
- Down with making the school a scapegoat!
- Down with stereotype threat!
- Down with arguably putting our greatest black hero in an "accommodation box"!
- Down with a present-fatalistic and past-negative time perspective!
- Down with "think black"! -- that is, with Victimology and the associated fallout: a never subsiding "generational sense of complaint and outrage"
- Down with the vitiation of our manhood!

- Down with feeling equality!
- Down with the **The BTW Meme**!

And

- Up with the Father Rice **Tinkersville School Founding** spirit!
- Up with the **$15 Washington Gold Watch Pawning** spirit!
- Up with the Victor Frankl responsibility-for-finding-meaning spirit!
- Up with the Jerry McGil forgiveness and choosing-life spirit!
- Up with Jimmy Butler's not-wanting-to-be-pitied spirit!
- Up with a future and past-positive time perspective!
- Up with "think white"! -- that is, with adaptation and the associated brains, property, and character message of Booker T. Washington
- Up with careerhood!
- Up with characterhood!
- Up with providing our children a "hallowed presence"!

And, the beat could go on, so to speak, but here is the keynote:

- Up with the **practice of the art of loving!**
- and with the positive core identity and sound character which can ensue from it.

The love of ourselves about which Dickerson writes can be derived through the **practice of the art of loving**. It requires us to exercise **CARE, RESPONSIBILITY, RESPECT, and KNOWLEDGE** equally in the way we treat ourselves, others, and our environment. Not at some juncture in time, but at all times. For Fromm teaches that to cultivate the art of loving, we must practice it at *all* times in *all* that we do. We must stay plugged in! If we do, the drive and energy which we derive from being plugged in will enable us to adapt and to reach our personal and racial potential. As a result, the whole world might not be ours (as the adage goes), but enough of it will be ours so as to bring us a state of bliss that could make the whole world, while not ours, feel as if it were. For in the end, it is how we *feel inside* that will make the difference.

In his book, <u>Super Rich</u>, that is also the message of one of our own, Russell Simmons, hip hop mogul, philanthropist, New Age Guide, and bestselling author. His language and details are different, but the essence of his message is similar. To "be truly happy and realize the full potential of your life," he urges us to "move toward enlightenment." Enlightenment is "A state where you are fully conscious of and connected to the world around you and the God inside you." When that happens, he teaches, "you'll be so attractive to the world that every toy, every material possession, will find its way to you" (236:7). That is what can happen as well with the **practice of the art of loving**. It can move us "toward enlightenment," make us "fully conscious of and connected to the world around us" and to the "God inside" us, however we may define or describe God. At that juncture – whether "every toy…" etc. "will find its way to you" is another question -- but that which is part of our destiny will.

To many of us this may understandably sound like dreaming, a beautiful but unrealistic idea -- something for which one does not have time and which, anyway, does not work in the real world. However, it can and does! Most notably in our history, it worked for Booker T. Washington. More important, perhaps, without our having given it that much thought, at least not from the perspective of a skill, it works for each of us. In numerous ways, each of us practices it. It is a matter, however, of being conscientious about it and taking it to ever increasingly higher levels, as is possible and typically desirable with any skill.

Hill Harper's book (along with the other self-help books cited) provides an excellent example of its practice. Chances are that Harper does not think of himself as **practicing the art of loving**, but his book demonstrates that he is doing exactly that. One infers that he thinks of it, not as a skill, but simply as an act of the heart -- something you do because you have been taught it and have come to believe. For him, that something is serving others. Only serving others is engaging in the **practice of the art of loving**. That Harper applies the practice to himself personally is evident from what he shares about his life, and his mentoring book is an example of his application of its practice to others. We see his practice reflected in his thoughts when his composite Young Brotha asks him, "What are the qualities of a good man?," he answers in part, "A good man is honest, lives his life with integrity, and behaves responsibly." He goes on to add: "A good man is not defined by what he has--be that money, cars, or girls. A good man is ultimately defined by what he does" (113b:8). Wanting to convey the response of others as well, Harper turned to the rapper, Nas, who highlighted knowledge and wisdom, observing that, "A man plays a major role in society and the world." He also turned to the former National Football League star running back, Curtis Martin, who, in part, responded, "Put God first, family second, and yourself third. Respect others, but remain true to yourself" (113b: 9). So Harper, along with a couple of friends to whom he turned, engages in the **practice of the art of loving**. Like Harper and his friends (and we are assuming that at least to some extent they practice what they preach), all of us inevitably engage in the **practice of the art of loving**; daily living requires it. The call here is to elevate that practice into a *conscious, articulated skill* which is daily and constantly practiced in all we do just as we daily practice eating (if we can think of it as a practice – but no doubt you get the idea).

Be assured, then, we are not talking here about becoming reclusive or engaging in some special or esoteric training or endeavor. Rather, we are talking about something that we do already. It is a matter of making that something a conscious, articulated practice -- yes, *a practice, a practice*, not an idea -- part of, not apart from, our routine daily living. Again, practice requires that, day in and day out, in all in that we do, we exercise **CARE, RESPONSIBILITY, RESPECT, and KNOWLEDGE** [each explained in Chapter 12] in the way we treat ourselves, others, and our environment. Although it is something that we already do, it is not easy! In fact, though we do it, and it is doable, it is difficult and challenging, that is, if we are to do it well and constantly, not randomly. **To achieve proficiency, it requires daily, continual, lifelong *practice***. Successful practice, on the other hand, while it requires no special knowledge or training, does require certain character attributes, those traits having been enumerated in our discussion of Washington's possession of them in Chapter 17.

Given those traits, we can well understand why Fromm says that the **practice of the art of loving** is a skill that must be nurtured over a lifetime and is never likely to be fully developed. Nonetheless, with the exercise and cultivation of the stipulated attributes, it can be sufficiently developed to make us *feel* that the whole world is ours -- maybe even feel "super rich," as Russell Simmons terms it.

It is possible to think of the **practice of the art of loving** as the conscientious might think of religion. We know a particular religion's basic teachings and, due to the rewards that these teachings can bring, we try, perhaps increasingly, to live by them, even though we might have come to realize how difficult it is do so. The **practice of the art of loving** is similar. In fact, it may sound something like spiritual science or prosperity gospel, both of which have their place, but the **practice of the art of loving** is neither. ***It is about our attitude and character and about the way we habitually approach life -- <u>all</u> life***. It is not a substitute for that which goes into building a foundation for living, for without such a foundation, not much else falls into place. Rather, it is intended to help enable us to build our foundation. It has a concrete, and yes, material goal. However, it is not limited to the concrete and material -- to foundation-building. It both encompasses and transcends foundation-building, enabling us simultaneously to build a foundation for ourselves and, at the same time, meaningfully connect with all else in a giving, sharing, affirming, energizing relationship.

It must be kept in mind that the concern herein is with the tangible and concrete: AMSAC and its inseparable social problems. We are trying to penetrate all the noise so as to understand better why, especially with respect to our Abandoned one-fourth, we have, so far, made so little headway despite, especially during and since the 1960s and 1970s, the multiplicity of efforts. Having concluded that the reason is that we have not adequately addressed neither the main cause (our character deficits) nor the root cause (our fragile and flawed personal and group core identity), we are proposing a solution. The ***practice*** **of the art of loving** is an integral component of that proposal. It does not embody an escape from reality but a confrontation with it. It is not otherworldly; it is grounded in the here and now. It is about more effectively facing the **three major demons** which confront us in our struggles to consummate our adaptation: *IQ lag-- fatherless families--crime*. Face them and we free ourselves to conquer them.

The **practice of the art of loving** is an indispensably ubiquitous part of a gestalt. We cannot talk, march, wish, or think our way into solving

AMSAC and its inseparable social problems and, thereby, into building a foundation for ourselves -- and our race. That outcome can only ensue from a strengthened black family, which is made possible through the **practice of the art of loving**. The practice is not divorced from the qualities essential for foundation-building, but intrinsic to them. It provides guidance, inspiration, and energy. What we can expect to get when we integrate it into our daily living, and when we see the fruition of that integration, is a driven, energized black personality with a positive core identity, possessed of its own subculture, yet fully adapted to the American way of life and, as a co-product, possessed of an elevated sense of connection to the seen and unseen alike.

Practicality

Our role

It has been said that an idea is only as good as it is practical, and the saying can be applied to the proposed **Child Family Rights Movement** and the self-help thrust which it embodies. As popular as he was, not even Dr. King was able to renew Washington's Self-Responsibility Tradition, and there was the **Moynihan Family Initiative** of 1963, the **Million Man March** of 1995, and **Bill Cosby's Brown Anniversary (Pound Cake) Speech** of 2004 – in essence, all failed attempts to do the same. Given that these attempts involved some powerful and popular personalities, how would a proposal coming from a personality with neither power nor popularity have any chance?

A fair question. The answer is that Booker T. Washington, at first an unknown, tried it and it worked back then and there is no reason to believe that it cannot work now. He had to sell his concept of industrial education to many because, as he says in his classic Up from Slavery, "the chief ambition among a large proportion of them [the students] was to get an education so that they would not have to work any longer with their hands" (271:283). He elsewhere elaborates:

> Quite a number of letters came from parents protesting against their children engaging in labour while they were in school. Other parents came to the school to protest in person. Most of the new students brought a written or a verbal request from their parents

to the effect that they wanted their children taught nothing but books. The more books, the larger they were, and the longer the titles printed upon them, the better pleased the students and their parents seemed to be (271:298).

Nevertheless, Washington proceeded to make labor a successful part of their industrial education. Therefore, students and parents came to accept it, as they and most blacks, seeing their fruits, came also to accept the other ideas in his message. For him, the result was the Age of Booker T. Washington, 1880-1915, and the emergence -- in the previously quoted words of his definitive biographer, Louis R. Harlan – of "the most powerful black American of his time and perhaps of all time," and – through the previously quoted revisionist eyes of recent biographer, Robert J. Norrell, of what must be considered "among the most heroic efforts in American history" [note, not black history but American history]. Or, as historian David H. Jackson Jr. puts it, "the virtual boss of black America."

The point is that Washington succeeded, not because he was some powerful or popular figure, but because his ideas turned out to be powerful, popular – and *productive*! The proposed Movement is about the same ideas. He summed them up in three words -- brains, property, and character -- and the proposed Movement compresses his message into two words: career and character (career operationally encompassing the attributes of brains and property) -- a career to be able to take care of self and family and, inseparably, the character to be able and driven to do so. And as Washington demonstrated their efficacy for his time, it is up to us to demonstrate their efficacy for our time. If we do – and we can if we follow in Washington's footsteps – as he, we can win their acceptance.

If, nevertheless, it all sounds idealistic and impractical, let us remember that it is often only those, such as Washington, who have pursued the seemingly ideal and impractical who, at least over time, have become transformative figures. Some students, parents, and others did not think his ideas were practical, but through determined effort he succeeded in making Tuskegee the preeminent black-founded, black-taught, and black-administered higher education institution in our history. With the same kind of investment, over time (generations), the same can be done through the proposed **Child Family Rights Movement** and its generated school and community cultural offensives.

That is what Washington conducted: school and community offensives. Tuskegee and the other schools he was responsible for starting represent the school component of his offensive. His Southern Educational Tours, 1908-1912, and various community outreach programs (to farmers, teachers, businessmen, ministers, and others) its community component. Not only did his Tuskegee Institute have its own outreach programs (in addition to his own personal outreach), but the 18 to 20 schools established by its graduates and modeled after Tuskegee were expected, though not required, to do likewise (234:426-34). Under the auspices of a Division of Records and Research set up by Washington to keep in touch with and gather information about all its graduates, these schools were periodically observed and a written report on the observation was sent to Washington. One portion of that observation report was as follows:

> 4. Community work.
>   (a) Extension activities carried on by the school,
>   (b) The efficiency of these activities.

In a letter to one of his graduates, this is how he expressed this emphasis:

> 'I trust that wherever you are located you will do all that you can for community uplift. Be active in church and Sunday-school work, help to improve public schools, assist in bettering health conditions, help the people to secure property, to buy homes and improve them. In doing all these things, you will be carrying out the Tuskegee idea' (234:431-32)

Apparently, Washington realized what we must come to realize: that to solve our crisis and its inseparable social problems, we must focus on both school and community. Our <u>African American Male Career Pathway Program (AMCAP) Task Guide</u> gives a detailed understanding of how it can work with our male students, and in addition to the proposals herein, there is no shortage of relevant sources upon which to draw. They include reaching out to the community, as Washington did through his Tuskegee staff, as Bill Cosby and Dr. Alvin Poussaint, for example, have done through their Call-Outs, and as Shawn Dove is doing in his Campaign for Black Male Achievement.

The roots of the proposed Movement were enshrined during the Age of Booker T. Washington from 1880-1915. Although not embraced by our national leaders ("Father, forgive them; for they know not what they do"),[37] those roots are alive and well among the majority of us African Americans. If we make the soul of those roots the **practice of the art of loving**, we can give them new life, the life which they had during the Age of Booker T. Washington because that is what he did; he practiced **the art of loving**.

The role of whites

In describing the public discourse on racial matters, in his award-winning book, The Content of Our Character: A New Vision of Race in America, black Stanford University Hoover Institution Fellow Shelby Steele touches on a crucial aspect of the practicality of the proposed Movement: white support. He offers this assessment of the then state of public discussion in which blacks were expected to exhibit victimization and a sense of entitlement:

> Racism had to be offered as the greatest barrier to black progress, and blacks themselves had still to be seen primarily as racial victims. Whites, on the other hand, had to show both concern and a measure of befuddlement at how other whites could still be racist. There also had to be in whites a clear deference to the greater racial authority of blacks, whose color translated into a certain racial expertise. If there was more than one black, whites usually receded into the role of moderators while the black "experts" argued (247a:ix).

That was in 1990 and, over a generation later, the research herein reveals that nothing has changed. As Lasch-Quinn chronicles, the charade continues. She captures much of that charade in her chapter title, "The New Racial Etiquette: The Ritual of Racial Reprimand" (150a:1). The result, as she asserts, is a focus, not on fundamentals, but on feelings.

---

[37] Luke 23:34.

That must change. Whites may not have as much at stake in our crisis and problems as we do, but most share our concerns and, although *we must be the chief bearers and must provide the leadership*, as DuBois argued, the burden does indeed belong to the entire nation. And it is the entire nation which has always borne it. All of the major thrusts in our upward climb have been supported, or in some cases led, by our fellow white Americans -- from the ending of slavery, to the self-help program of Booker T. Washington, to the founding of the National Association for the Advancement of Colored People (NAACP, to the Civil Rights Movement, to the War on Poverty.

To whites, we then say, the proposed Movement is another thrust in our upward climb and, to facilitate its success, the charade must end. Conscience must not be permitted to fall victim to condescension. It is far past time that many more of you get past any feeling of guilt or fear of repercussions if you support something which puts you in the position of being accused of being insensitive, racist, or supremacists. It is better to be an *equity white liberal* than an *egalitarian white liberal*. It must be remembered that these days, it does not take much to be labeled a racist. A simple word or phrase -- stated, implied, or inferred, it should be added -- can be enough. Lasch-Quinn refers to it as "a world of endless slights" (150a:161-93). So, too often all that tends to get a fair hearing are the same faulty analyses and failed prescriptions. The Arthur Jensens, Patrick Moynihans, Richard Hernsteins, Charles Murrays, Thomas Sowells, and Shelby Steeles among us are demonized, ostracized, and penalized.

Yet, history shows that much of human progress is owed to those who, like them, dare to differ and to devise new thoughtways and new pathways. With this in mind, along with us blacks, many more of you, too, need to man up. Rather than kowtowing to the civil rights establishment and its like-minded, or misreading the meaning of equal humanity, give a fair hearing to themes of the proposed Movement and related cultural offensives, and treat us blacks as you would want your race to be treated under similar circumstances, not as helpless, pitied, and pitiful victims, but as human beings who must bare their own burden and make their own way, recognizing, of course, the need for government and others to play a helping role. But a helping role is not the same as a responsibility role.

Joe L. Rempson

The price, of course, can be great. In "a world of endless slights," the most innocent behavior is often perceived as "racist" and reacted to in such hyperbolic fashion as to seem tantamount to an adjudicated capital offense -- evoking investigations, firings, resignations, boycotts, demonstrations, and so on. If, however, *together*, we blacks and you whites of a like mind stand up and make our voices heard (and there are various ways of doing so), we can reduce that price. Along with those listed by John McWhorter and Dinesh D'Souza, this book is intended to be one of those voices.

Imagine, for example, how different our plight might be if President Lyndon Johnson -- rather than having as his legacy the aforementioned **President Johnson's Validation Omission** -- had transcended therapeutic sensibility, stood up to the civil rights and liberal establishment, and insisted on acting on the Moynihan Report; with whatever effect, he would, at least, have addressed our main internal problem. In contrast, that is what President Bill Clinton did, addressing an aspect of our main problem. After faltering several times, he stood up to the obstructionists and gave us welfare reform through the Personal Responsibility and Work Opportunity Reconciliation Act of 1996 (PRWORA). Even if its success is open to interpretation, at least he sought to address a major internal problem by putting into practice a value too commonly violated among our poor: work over welfare. The focus here, however, is not so much on success or failure, but on whether whites, generally, and those in decision-making positions particularly, are willing to stand up for and support black self-help initiatives at the risk of being accused of racism, or of losing black friendship, or support. Bill Clinton finally was willing, and we can call his willingness the **Bill Clinton Risk** and urge other whites to take it in support of the proposed **Child Family Rights Movement** and related efforts.

Some words to ponder

To help spur both to action, as we near the end, some words are in order from Dr. King, Thomas Rochon, and President Ronald Reagan. In urging Christians to protest the Vietnam War in 1967, Dr. King used the phrase "fierce urgency of now."[38] Since our crisis and problems do not dominate our television and computer screens as did the Vietnam War, for example, we may feel no such "fierce urgency of now" in regard to them. But think, for example, of a couple of our mnemonics – **72** and **young black male fratricide: 13% - 50+% - 85% - 94%** -- and we might at least be led to ponder: Should our current crisis and problems evoke a similar "fierce urgency of now" feeling or, as Eugene Robinson suggests, more of less, have we just abandoned the poor and lost that shared sense of suffering?

Should the latter be the case, we might want to remember the words of Thomas Rochon, cited earlier in the chapter. Those words were that there are times when "… we must change in order to survive," "… when human communities face the need to adapt, and to do so quickly." Do the couple of mnemonics cited remind us that we live in just such times?

As for what we ought to do, as suggested in Chapter 17, some might recall candidate Ronald Reagan's famous line to voters which he used in his attempt to unseat then President, Jimmy Carter, in the 1980 election: "Are you better off than you were four year ago?" In similar fashion, it might be asked: **Are we better off today under our System-Responsibility Tradition than we would have been under our Self-Responsibility Tradition?**. Moreover, since present perspective can be gained by looking at the future, in similar fashion we can ask: **Are we likely to be better off, say, fifty years from now under our System-Responsibility Tradition than we would be under our Self-Responsibility Tradition?**

A Renewed Message and An Adjustable Agenda For Our Time

This final chapter started with a recapitulation and a summary of our mnemonics to remind us of why we undertook this ethnographic-like journey and of some of our major encounters. We near its end with a reminder of what, in continuation, we ought to do. Washington succeeded because he had a message and an agenda suited for his time, the broad outlines of which he laid out in his Atlanta Compromise

---

[38] Source: http://www.npr.org/templates/story/story.php?storyId=122610865 15 January 2010. 8 December 2014.

Address of 1895. On his Southern Educational Tours, he put them in concrete terms. Scott and Stowe tell us that, in his own words, these were his terms:

> 'Make your own little heaven right here and now. Do it by putting business methods into your farming, by growing things in your garden the year round, by building and keeping attractive and comfortable homes for your children so they will stay home and not go to the cities, by keeping your bodies and your surroundings clean, by staying in one place, by getting a good teacher and a good preacher, by building good school and church, by letting your wife be your partner in all you do, by keeping out of debt, by cultivating friendly relations with your neighbors both white and black' (234:209-10).

How different from the victim-laden and race-laden messages of today from so many of our "spotlight" black leaders. This book should serve as a reminder of how much we have regressed. No change and our situation can only worsen, leaving us ever more mired, as Lasch-Quinn puts it, "in a generational sense of complaint and outrage that never seems to subside."

But we black males, along with our black females and our nation, can do something about that. Booker T. Washington taught and preached what it is. It is the embrace of a brains, property, and character message and agenda, different from Washington's only in its particulars. Maintaining its essence and spirit (so vividly captured in the foregoing Washington quote), we merely update the specifics. The focus on self-initiatives to strengthen the black family and community remain unchanged. Here and there on the foregoing pages, what, in addition, that message and agenda ought to be has been variously stated or implied. We now articulate and snapshot both, with the understanding that there are other ways, and perhaps better ways, of expressing them.

The renewed message for our time

Driven by a 72 percent out-of-wedlock birthrate, we African Americans are being devastated by the African American Male School Adaptability Crisis (AMSAC) and its inseparable social problems. To remedy the devastation, we must return to our self-help tradition under which, on our own and under the most adverse conditions, we made such great progress during the Age of Booker T. Washington when we were guided by the gospel of brains, property, and character, a gospel which, today, we can recast as the gospel of career and character, a recasting which requires us to replace our victim mindset, which has vitiated our manhood, with a growth mindset which will enable us to reclaim that manhood, and which - to anchor and energize ourselves – requires us daily to *practice the art of loving* (care, responsibility, respect, and knowledge) so that we can enhance our human spirit and provide the intact homes and "hallowed presence" (security and love) – along with school and life preparation -- to which our children have a right and which is required if they are to forge a positive core identity, develop a sound character, and succeed in the discovery and pursuit of a career pathway.

What we seek

Self-respect and to be, as Washington expressed it, "… an example for all the world in usefulness, law abiding habits and high character"

The adjustable agenda for our time

The common and fixed subject: CHILD FAMILY RIGHTS

The pervasive and situational topics:
- INTACT FAMILY
- CAREER
- CHARACTER
- BLACK ADVOCACY OF SCHOOL DO'S and DON'TS
- BLACK BLUEPRINT FOR CRIME

Joe L. Rempson

PREVENTION AND MANAGEMENT

The pervasive topic: PRACTICE OF THE ART OF LOVING

The nagging question: WHAT AM I DOING FOR MYSELF, AND DO I NEED TO DO MORE; AND WHAT AM I DOING FOR MY CHILD (OR CHILDREN), AND DO I NEED TO DO MORE?
(intended to foster reflection on the message and agenda)

The constant exhortation: As expressed by Dr. King,
"This is the Negro dilemma. He who starts behind in a race must forever remain behind or run faster than the man in front." So, we must run faster!

Condensed

The Movement is about our obligation to secure for our children their family rights to security, love, and life preparation through a return to Washington's Self-Responsibility Tradition whereby – in daily practice of the art of loving (care, responsibility, respect, and knowledge) – we replace our victimhood and system mindset with a growth and manhood mindset and make central in our life an intact family, career, character, black advocacy of school do's and don'ts, and a black blueprint for crime prevention and punishment.

We can think of the ***nagging question*** as the question which the Movement might encourage each of us constantly to ask ourselves. It can be empowering, leading each of us daily to plug into the message and agenda and, thereby, focus our attention and energy. Potentially, it forces at least as much attention to the needs of the child (or children) as to the needs of self, rather than, as too often happens, having the child's (or children's) needs subordinated. Its self-help theme embodies the core of the Movement, and the common use of it could help to forge and foster it.

A Dream Fulfilled

The renewed message and agenda refocus the practicality issue. Here is the conclusion: the proposed **Child Family Rights Movement** can be productive if we blacks follow in the footsteps of Washington and if whites facilitate and support our efforts. That done, in its fulfillment, we can conceive of the dream of which Booker T. Washington and Dr. King spoke as follows: our having, yes, inevitably our own subcultural identity, only a positive one, but also an unqualified American identity which in its manifestations is indeed "an example for all the world" and which would have shown that "this nation will rise up and live out the true meaning of its creed." It could turn out that the proposed Movement, tapping into a black reawakening triggered by a drive for a combined King-Washington holiday, can help us to achieve this lofty goal. But it addresses a need far more immediate and concrete, our family breakdown; yet, in doing so, it speaks to this dream, a dream embedded in the life force of our race. These two leaders memorialized this dream in their famous speeches delivered in memory of the man who symbolizes our emancipation, Abraham Lincoln. African American males have a special place in that dream and a special responsibility to give it life. The proposed **Child Family Rights Movement**, with the **practice of the art of loving** as its soul, can help us to exercise that responsibility.

So let us, *ourselves*, we African American males, with the help of our females and of our nation, confront our **three major demons** -- *IQ lag--fatherless families--crime* -- and **"Take Arms Against [Our] Sea of Troubles."** Those arms consist of the renewal of **The Tradition of Choice** (the Self-Responsibility Tradition of Booker Taliaferro Washington) and the **Child Family Rights Movement**, together with the foundation-building activities undertaken by it. Powerful ammunition can be provided by our black male athletes and entertainers if they support Student AMCAPs and propagate among our African American males the motto of the proposed evidence-based experimental program, AMCAP: **DISCOVER AND PURSUE YOUR CAREER PATHWAY.** Fail to bear these arms, or use our powerful ammunition, and our people are doomed, in perpetuity, to "suffer the slings and arrows of [our] outrageous fortune" and forever to look back without forgiveness to our African American Garden of Eden. May The Force be with us!

Appendix

Appendix

Appendix A

Washington's Compromise Address Of 1895*

Booker T. Washington's "Atlanta Compromise" Speech
18 September 1895

African American Booker T. Washington (1856–1915) increased his fame in 1895 after delivering the following speech commonly referred to as the "Atlanta Compromise." A former slave who was committed to the education of African Americans, Washington worked as a teacher and principal at schools such as the Tuskegee Institute. Believing that Reconstruction failed by offering African Americans too much too soon, he stressed industrial education to his pupils; similarly, he felt that African Americans should become productive citizens and property owners before pursuing careers in politics. Washington expressed these beliefs in the following address he delivered at an exposition held in Atlanta, Georgia, where he was asked to speak by Southern leaders in an attempt to show the North the progress they had made in terms of racial relations. His speech received a positive reaction from the press and primarily white crowd with many African Americans accepting his beliefs as well. Delivered in an era of deep racial prejudice, this speech has been seen as accepting the principle of "separate but equal" that the U.S. Supreme Court would articulate the next year. –Renata Fengler

Bibliography: Samuel R. Spencer, Jr., *Booker T. Washington and the Negro's Place in American Life* (Boston: Little, Brown and Co., 1955), 14, 48–52, 102–105.

Mr. President, Gentlemen of the Board of Directors and Citizens:

[1] One third of the population of the South is of the Negro race. No enterprise seeking the material, civil or moral welfare of this section can disregard this element of our population and reach the highest success. I but convey to you, Mr. President and Directors, the sentiment of the masses of my race, when I say that in no way have the value and [manhood] of the American Negro been more fittingly and generously recognized, than by the managers of this magnificent Exposition at every stage of its progress. It is a recognition which will do more to cement the friendship of the two races than any occurrence since the dawn of our freedom.

[2] Not only this, but the opportunity here afforded will awaken among us a new era of industrial progress. Ignorant and inexperienced, it is not strange that in the first years of our new life we began at the top instead of the bottom, that a seat in Congress or the State Legislature was more sought than real-estate or industrial skill, that the political convention, or stump speaking had more attractions [than] starting a dairy farm or truck garden.

[3] A ship lost at sea for many days suddenly sighted a friendly vessel. From the mast of the unfortunate vessel was seen the signal: "Water, water, we die of thirst." The answer from the friendly vessel at once came back, "Cast down your bucket where you are."… The captain of the distressed vessel, at last heeding the injunction, cast down his bucket and it came up full of fresh, sparkling water from the mouth of the Amazon River. To those of my race who depend on bettering their condition in a foreign land, or who underestimate the importance of cultivating friendly relations with the Southern white man who is their next door neighbor, I would say cast

Joe L. Rempson

down your bucket where you are[;] cast it down in making friends in every manly way of the people of all races by whom we are surrounded.

[4] Cast it down in agriculture, in mechanics, in commerce, in domestic service and in the professions. And in this connection it is well to bear in mind that whatever other sins the South may be called upon to bear, that when it comes to business pure and simple, it is in the South that the Negro is given a man's chance in the commercial world, and in nothing is this Exposition more eloquent than in emphasizing this chance.

[5] Our greatest danger is, that in the great leap from slavery to freedom we may overlook the fact that the masses of us are to live by the productions of our hands, and fail to keep in mind that we shall prosper in proportion as we learn to dignify and glorify common labor and put brains and skill into the common occupations of life... No race can prosper till it learns that there is as much dignity in tilling a field as in writing a poem. It is at the bottom of life we must begin and not the top. Nor should we permit our grievances to overshadow our opportunities.

[6] To those of the white race who look to the incoming of those of foreign birth and strange tongue and habits for the prosperity of the South, were I permitted, I would repeat what I say to my own race. "Cast down your bucket where you are." Cast it down among the 8,000,000 Negroes whose habits you know, whose loyalty and love you have tested in days when to have proved treacherous [meant] the ruin of your firesides.

[7] Cast it down among these people who have without strikes and labor wars tilled your fields, cleared your forests, built your railroads and cities, and brought forth treasures from the bowels of the earth and helped make possible this magnificent representation of the progress of the South. Casting down your bucket [among] my people, helping and encouraging them as you are doing on these grounds, and to [the] education of head, hand, and heart, you will find that they will buy your surplus land, make blossom the waste places in your fields, and run your factories.

[8] While doing this you can be sure in the future, as you have been in the past, that you and your families will be surrounded by the most patient, faithful, law-abiding and unresentful people that the world has seen. As we have proven our loyalty to you in the past, in nursing your children, watching by the sick bed of your mothers and fathers, and often following them with tear dimmed eyes to their graves, so in the future in our humble way, we shall stand by you with a devotion that no foreigner can approach, ready to lay down our lives, if need be, in defense of yours, interlacing our industrial, commercial, civil and religious life with yours in a way that shall make the interests of both races one. In all things that are purely social we can be as separate as the fingers, yet one as the hand in all things essential to mutual progress.

[9] There is no defense or security for any of us except in the highest intelligence and development of all. If anywhere there are efforts tending to curtail the fullest growth of the Negro, let these efforts be turned into stimulating, encouraging and making him the most useful and intelligent citizen. Effort or means so invested will pay a thousand per cent interest. These efforts will be twice blessed—"Blessing him that gives and him that takes."

[10] Nearly sixteen millions of hands will aid you [in] pulling the load upwards, or they will pull against you the load downwards. We shall constitute one third and much more of the ignorance and crime of the South or one third [of] its intelligence and progress, we shall contribute one third to the business and industrial prosperity of the South, or we shall prove a veritable body of death, stagnating, depressing, retarding every effort to advance the body politic.

[11] The wisest among my race understand that the agitation of questions of social equality is the [extremist] folly and that progress in the enjoyment of all the privileges that will come to us, must be the result of severe and [constant] struggle, rather than of artificial forcing… It is important and right that all privileges of the law be ours, but it is vastly more important that we be prepared for the exercise of these privileges. The opportunity to earn a dollar in a factory just now is worth infinitely more than the opportunity to spend a dollar in an opera house.

Discussion Questions:

1. What was Washington urging African Americans to do? What was he urging white Americans to do?

2. What statements in this address made this speech appropriate for a white audience? Explain.

3. What were Washington's long-term goals for African Americans?

SOURCE: B.T. Washington, *Atlanta Exposition Speech* (Sept. 18. 1895). Retrieved January 5, 2006 from the Library of Congress' *African American Odyssey* database on the World Wide Web: <http://memory.loc.gov/ammem/aaohtml/exhibit/aopart6.html#0605>. Paragraph numbers have been added.

[This text was created by Renata Fengler as part of the "Documenting American History" project, supervised by Professor David Voelker at the University of Wisconsin–Green Bay. This project had support from UWGB's Research Council.]

This electronic text is © 2006 David J. Voelker. Permission is granted to reproduce this text freely for educational, non-commercial purposes only. All users must retain this notice and cite http://www.historytools.org.

*Reprinted by email permission from Dr. David Voelker, dated October 18, 2013.

Appendix B

President Barak Obama: Trayvon Martin Case Remarks*

The New York Times

Transcript: Obama Speaks of Verdict Through the Prism of African-American Experience

Following is a transcript of President Obama's remarks on race in America in the White House briefing room. (Transcript courtesy of Federal News Service.)

PRESIDENT OBAMA: Well, I — I wanted to come out here first of all to tell you that Jay is prepared for all your questions and is — is very much looking forward to the session.

Second thing is I want to let you know that over the next couple of weeks there are going to obviously be a whole range of issues — immigration, economics, et cetera — we'll try to arrange a fuller press conference to address your questions.

The reason I actually wanted to come out today is not to take questions, but to speak to an issue that obviously has gotten a lot of attention over the course of the last week, the issue of the Trayvon Martin ruling. I gave an — a preliminary statement right after the ruling on Sunday, but watching the debate over the course of the last week I thought it might be useful for me to expand on my thoughts a little bit.

First of all, you know, I — I want to make sure that, once again, I send my thoughts and prayers, as well as Michelle's, to the family of Trayvon Martin, and to remark on the incredible grace and dignity with which they've dealt with the entire situation. I can only imagine what they're going through, and it's — it's remarkable how they've handled it.

The second thing I want to say is to reiterate what I said on Sunday, which is there are going to be a lot of arguments about the legal — legal issues in the case. I'll let all the legal analysts and talking heads address those issues.

The judge conducted the trial in a professional manner. The prosecution and the defense made their arguments. The juries were properly instructed that in a — in a case such as this, reasonable doubt was relevant, and they rendered a verdict. And once the jury's spoken, that's how our system works.

But I did want to just talk a little bit about context and how people have responded to it and how people are feeling. You know, when Trayvon Martin was first shot, I said that this could have been my son. Another way of saying that is Trayvon Martin could have been me 35 years ago. And when you think about why, in the African-American community at least, there's a lot of pain around what happened here, I think it's important to recognize that the African-American community is looking at this issue through a set of experiences and a history that — that doesn't go away.

There are very few African-American men in this country who haven't had the experience of being followed when they were shopping in a department store. That includes me.

And there are very few African-American men who haven't had the experience of walking across the street and hearing the locks click on the doors of cars. That happens to me, at least before I was a senator. There are very few African-Americans who haven't had the experience of getting on an elevator and a woman clutching her purse nervously and holding her breath until she had a chance to get off. That happens often.

And you know, I don't want to exaggerate this, but those sets of experiences inform how the African-American community interprets what happened one night in Florida. And it's inescapable for people to bring those experiences to bear.

The African-American community is also knowledgeable that there is a history of racial disparities in the application of our criminal laws, everything from the death penalty to enforcement of our drug laws. And that ends up having an impact in terms of how people interpret the case.

Now, this isn't to say that the African-American community is naïve about the fact that African-American young men are disproportionately involved in the criminal justice system, that they are disproportionately both victims and perpetrators of violence. It's not to make excuses for that fact, although black folks do interpret the reasons for that in a historical context.

We understand that some of the violence that takes place in poor black neighborhoods around the country is born out of a very violent past in this country, and that the poverty and dysfunction that we see in those communities can be traced to a very difficult history.

And so the fact that sometimes that's unacknowledged adds to the frustration. And the fact that a lot of African-American boys are painted with a broad brush and the excuse is given, well, there are these statistics out there that show that African-American boys are more violent — using that as an excuse to then see sons treated differently causes pain.

I think the African-American community is also not naïve in understanding that statistically somebody like Trayvon Martin was probably statistically more likely to be shot by a peer than he was by somebody else.

So — so folks understand the challenges that exist for African-American boys, but they get frustrated, I think, if they feel that there's no context for it or — and that context is being denied. And — and that all contributes, I think, to a sense that if a white male teen was involved in the same kind of scenario, that, from top to bottom, both the outcome and the aftermath might have been different.

Now, the question for me at least, and I think, for a lot of folks is, where do we take this? How do we learn some lessons from this and move in a positive direction? You know, I think it's understandable that there have been demonstrations and vigils and protests, and some of that stuff is just going to have to work its way through as long as it remains nonviolent. If I see any violence, then I will remind folks that that dishonors what happened to Trayvon Martin and his family.

But beyond protests or vigils, the question is, are there some concrete things that we might be able to do? I know that Eric Holder is reviewing what happened down there, but I think it's important for people to have some clear expectations here. Traditionally, these are issues of state and local government — the criminal code. And law enforcement has traditionally done it at the state and local levels, not at the federal levels.

That doesn't mean, though, that as a nation, we can't do some things that I think would be productive. So let me just give a couple of specifics that I'm still bouncing around with my staff so we're not rolling out some five-point plan, but some areas where I think all of us could potentially focus.

Number one, precisely because law enforcement is often determined at the state and local level, I think it'd be productive for the Justice Department — governors, mayors to work with law enforcement about training at the state and local levels in order to reduce the kind of mistrust in the system that sometimes currently exists.

You know, when I was in Illinois I passed racial profiling legislation. And it actually did just two simple things. One, it collected data on traffic stops and the race of the person who was stopped. But the other thing was it resourced us training police departments across the state on how to think about potential racial bias and ways to further professionalize what they were doing.

And initially, the police departments across the state were resistant, but actually they came to recognize that if it was done in a fair, straightforward way, that it would allow them to do their jobs better and communities would have more confidence in them and in turn be more helpful in applying the law. And obviously law enforcement's got a very tough job.

So that's one area where I think there are a lot of resources and best practices that could be brought to bear if state and local governments are receptive. And I think a lot of them would be. And — and let's figure out other ways for us to push out that kind of training.

Along the same lines, I think it would be useful for us to examine some state and local laws to see if it — if they are designed in such a way that they may encourage the kinds of altercations and confrontations and tragedies that we saw in the Florida case, rather than defuse potential altercations.

I know that there's been commentary about the fact that the Stand Your Ground laws in Florida were not used as a defense in the case.

On the other hand, if we're sending a message as a society in our communities that someone who is armed potentially has the right to use those firearms even if there's a way for them to exit from a situation, is that really going to be contributing to the kind of peace and security and order that we'd like to see?

And for those who resist that idea that we should think about something like these Stand Your Ground laws, I just ask people to consider if Trayvon Martin was of age and armed, could he have stood his ground on that sidewalk? And do we actually think that he would have been justified in shooting Mr. Zimmerman, who had followed him in a car, because he felt threatened?

And if the answer to that question is at least ambiguous, it seems to me that we might want to examine those kinds of laws.

Number three — and this is a long-term project: We need to spend some time in thinking about how do we bolster and reinforce our African-American boys? And this is something that Michelle and I talk a lot about. There are a lot of kids out there who need help who are getting a lot of negative reinforcement. And is there more that we can do to give them the sense that their country cares about them and values them and is willing to invest in them?

You know, I'm not naïve about the prospects of some brand-new federal program.

I'm not sure that that's what we're talking about here. But I do recognize that as president, I've got some convening power.

And there are a lot of good programs that are being done across the country on this front. And for us to be able to gather together business leaders and local elected officials and clergy and celebrities and athletes and figure out how are we doing a better job helping young African-American men feel that they're a full part of this society and that — and that they've got pathways and avenues to succeed — you know, I think that would be a pretty good outcome from what was obviously a tragic situation. And we're going to spend some time working on that and thinking about that.

And then finally, I think it's going to be important for all of us to do some soul-searching. You know, there have been talk about should we convene a conversation on race. I haven't seen that be particularly productive when politicians try to organize conversations. They end up being stilted and politicized, and folks are locked into the positions they already have.

On the other hand, in families and churches and workplaces, there's a possibility that people are a little bit more honest, and at least you ask yourself your own questions about, am I wringing as much bias out of myself as I can; am I judging people, as much as I can, based on not the color of their skin but the content of their character? That would, I think, be an appropriate exercise in the wake of this tragedy.

And let me just leave you with — with a final thought, that as difficult and challenging as this whole episode has been for a lot of people, I don't want us to lose sight that things are getting better. Each successive generation seems to be making progress in changing attitudes when it comes to race. I doesn't mean that we're in a postracial society. It doesn't mean that racism is eliminated. But you know, when I talk to Malia and Sasha and I listen to their friends and I see them interact, they're better than we are. They're better than we were on these issues. And that's true in every community that I've visited all across the country.

And so, you know, we have to be vigilant and we have to work on these issues, and those of us in authority should be doing everything we can to encourage the better angels of our nature as opposed to using these episodes to heighten divisions. But we should also have confidence that kids these days I think have more sense than we did back then, and certainly more than our parents did or our grandparents did, and that along this long, difficult journey, you know, we're becoming a more perfect union — not a perfect union, but a more perfect union.

All right? Thank you, guys.

Copyright © 2013 by Federal News Service, LLC, 1120 G Street NW, Suite 990, Washington, DC 20005-3801 USA. Federal News Service is a private firm not affiliated with the federal government. No portion of this transcript may be copied, sold or retransmitted without the written authority of Federal News Service, LLC. Copyright is not claimed as to any part of the original work prepared by a United States government officer or employee as a part of that person's official duties. For information on subscribing to the FNS Transcripts Database or any other FNS product, please email info@fednews.com or call 1-202-347-1400.

*Reprinted with permission of FNS, October 11, 2013.

References

(References are alphabetically arranged in each of the two sections (A and B), however, due to continual additions, where necessary, the numbers themselves have been alphabetized to accommodate the additions.)

A. BOOKS and PERIODICALS

1. Ainsworth, James W. and Greg Wiggan. "Reconsidering "Material Conditions": How Neighborhood Context Can Shape Educational Outcomes across Racial Groups." In <u>Beyond Acting White: Reframing the Debate on Black Student Achievement</u>, p. 159-75. Edited by Erin McNamara Horvat and Carla O'Connor. New York: Rowman & Littlefield Publishers, Inc., 2006.

2. Aird, Enola G. "Making the Wounded Whole: Marriage as Civil Right and Civic Responsibility." In <u>Black Fathers in Contemporary American Society: Strengths, Weaknesses, and Strategies for Change</u>, p. 153-64. Edited by Obie Clayton, Ronald B. Mincy, and David Blankenhorn. New York: Russell Sage Foundation, 2003.

3. Akom, A.A. "Reexamining Resistance as Oppositional Behavior: The Nation of Islam and the Creation of a Black Achievement Ideology (The Remix). In <u>Minority Status, Oppositional Culture, & Schooling</u>, p. 190-213. Edited by John U. Ogbu. New York: Routledge, 2008.

4. Amen, Daniel G. <u>Mind Coach: How to Teach Kids and Teenagers to Think Positive and Feel Good</u>. Newport Beach, CA: Mindworks Press, 2002. 39p.

5. Anderson, Elijah. Code of the Street: Decency, Violence, and the Moral Life of the Inner City. New York: W. W. Norton & Company, 1999. 352p.

6. Baker, Ray Stannard. Following the Color Line: An Account of Negro Citizenship in the American Democracy. New York: Doubleday, 1908. Quoted in August Meier, Negro Thought in America, 1889-1915: Racial Ideologies in the Age of Booker T.Washington, p. 179-180. New Introduction. Ann Arbor: The University of Michigan Press, 1963. Also quoted in Norrell, Robert J. Up from History: The Life of Booker T. Washington, p. 381-84. Cambridge: The Belknap Press of Harvard University Press, 2009.

6a. _____. R. S. Baker Notehook. Entries for Feb. 9, 13, 1915. Ray Stannard Baker Papers, Library of Congress. Quoted in Louis R. Harlan, Booker T. Washington: The Wizard of Tuskegee, 1901-1915, p. 367. New York: Oxford University Press, 1983.

6b. Baumeister, Roy F. and John Tierney. Willpower. New York: The Penguin Press, 2011. 291p.

6c. Becker, Ernest. The Denial of Death. New York: Free Press, 1973. Quoted in Philip Zimbardo and John Boyd, The Time Paradox: The New Psychology of Time That Will Change Your Life, p. 21. New York: Free Press, 2008.

7. Bergen, David A. and Helen C. Cooks. "High School Students of Color Talk about Accusations of 'Acting White'." In Minority Status, Oppositional Culture, & Schooling, p. 145-66. Edited by John U. Ogbu. New York: Routledge, 2008.

8. Bernard, Jessie. Marriage and Family Among Negroes. Englewood Cliffs: Prentice-Hall, 1966. 160p.

9. Billingsley, Andrew. Black Families in White America. Englewood Cliffs: Prentice-Hall, Inc., 1968. 218p.

10. Billson, Janet Mancini. Pathways to Manhood: Young Black Males Struggle for Identity, expanded second edition. New Brunswick: Transaction Publishers, 1996. 367p.

11. Blankenhorn, David. Fatherless America: Confronting Our Most Urgent Social Problem. New York: Harper Perennial, 1996. 328p.

12. Bloodworth, Venice. Key to Yourself. Marina del Rey, California: DeVorss & Company, 1952. 141p.

13. Bloom, Benjamin S. Stability and Change in Human Characteristics. New York: Wiley, 1964. Quoted in Barry Silverstein and Ronald Krate, Children of the Dark Ghetto: A Developmental Psychology, p. 230. New York: Praeger Publishers, 1975.

14. Bly, Robert. Iron John: A Book About Men. New York: Addison-Wesley Publishing Company, Inc., 1990. 271p.

15. Boles, Mark A. "Breaking the "Hip Hop" Hold: Looking Beyond the Media Hype." In The State of Black America 2007: Portrait of the Black Male: Portrait of the Black Male, p. 239-41. Edited by Stephanie J. Jones and staff. An Official Publication of the National Urban League. Foreword by Senator Barack Obama. New York: The National Urban League, 2007.

15a. BTW Papers. BTW to George B. Ward., President of Board of Commissioners, City of Birmingham, Alabama, July 13, 1914; Ward to BTW, July 16, 1914 (525). Quoted in Raymond W. Smock, ed., Booker T. Washington in Perspective: Essays of Louis R. Harlan, p. 124-25. Jackson: University Press of Mississippi, 1988.

16. The Booker T. Washington Reader. An African American Heritage Book. Up from Slavery: An Autobiography; My Larger Education; Character Building; The Negro Problem. Radford, VA: Wilder Publications, LLC, 2008. 415p.

17. Borman, Geoffrey D, Samuel C. Stringfield, and Robert E. Slavin. "Preface." In Title I: Compensatory Education at the Crossroads, p. ix-xvi. Edited by Geoffrey D. Samuel, Samuel C. Stringfield,

and Robert E. Slavin. Mahwah, New Jersey: Lawrence Erlbaum Associates, Publishers, 2001.

18. Borman, Geoffrey D., Samuel C. Stringfield, and Robert E. Slavin., eds. Title I: Compensatory Education at the Crossroads. Mahwah, New Jersey: Lawrence Erlbaum Associates, Publishers, 2001. 274p.

19. Bracey, John H. "Frazier's *Black Bourgeoisie*: Talented Tenth or a Parasitic Class?" In E. Franklin Frazier and Black Bourgeoisie, p. 85-101. Edited by James E. Teele. Columbia: University of Missouri Press, 2002.

20. Braddock II, Jomills Henry. "Athletics, Academics, and African American Males." In Educating African American Males: Voices from the Field, p. 255-83. Edited by Olatomkunbo S. Fashola. Thousand Oaks, California: Corwin Press, 2005.

20b. Branch, Taylor. The King Years: Historic Moments in the Civil Rights Movement. New York: Simon and Schuster, 2013. 210p.

20a. Brawley, Benjamin. "The Negro Genius." Southern Workman, XLIV (May, 1915): 305-08. Quoted in August Meier, Negro Thought in America, 1889-1915: Racial Ideologies in the Age of Booker T. Washington, p. 267-68. New Introduction. Ann Arbor: The University of Michigan Press, 1963.

21. Brazziel, William F. "A Letter from the South." Harvard Educational Review, 39 (Spring, 1969): 348-56.

21a. Breger, Louis. From Instinct to Identity: The Development of Personality. With a new Introduction by the author. New Brunswick (U.S.A.): Transaction Publishers, 2009. 371p.

22. Britt, Donna. "Brothercool." In Being a Black Man in America: At the Corner of Progress and Peril, p. 227-37. Edited by Staff of the Washington Post. Introduction by Edward P. Jones. New York: Public Affairs, 2007.

22a. Bronfenbrenner, Urie. "The Psychological Costs of Quality and Equality of Education." Child Development, 38 (1967): 909-25. Quoted in Arthur A. Jensen, How Much Can We Boost IQ and Scholastic Achievement?, Harvard Educational Review, 39 (Winter, 1969): 87.

23. Brooks, David. The Social Animal; The Hidden Sources of Love, Character, and Achievement. New York: Random House, 2011. 424p.

23a. Brown, N. M. "Self Contempt!": A Search for the Identity of Black America. Bloomington, IN: 1st Books Library, 2000 [1998]. 458p.

24. Butterfield, Sherri-Ann P. "To Be Young, Gifted, and Somewhat Foreign: The Role of Ethnicity in Black Student Achievement." In Beyond Acting White: Reframing the Debate on Black Student Achievement, p. 133-55. Edited by Erin McNamara Horvat and Carla O'Connor. New York: Rowman & Littlefield Publishers, Inc., 2006.

25. Canada, Geoffrey. Fist Stick Knife Gun: A Personal History of Violence in America. Boston: Beacon Press, 1995. 179p.

26. _____. Reaching Up for Manhood: Transforming the Lives of Boys in America. Boston: Beacon Press, 1998. 160p.

27. Carnethon, Mercedes R. "Black Male Life Expectancy in the United States: A Multi-level Exploration of Causes." In The State of Black America 2007: Portrait of the Black Male: Portrait of the Black Male, p. 137-50. Edited by Stephanie J. Jones and staff. An Official Publication of the National Urban League. Foreword by Senator Barack Obama. New York: The National Urban League, 2007.

28. Carter, Prudence L. "Intersecting Identities: "Acting White," Gender, and Academic Achievement." In Beyond Acting White: Reframing the Debate on Black Student Achievement, p. 111-32. Edited by Erin McNamara Horvat and Carla O'Connor New York: Rowman & Littlefield Publishers, Inc., 2006.

29. Carter, Samuel Casey. No Excuses: Lessons from 21 High-Performing, High-Poverty Schools. Washington, D.C.: The Heritage Foundation, 214 Massachusetts Ave, NE, 2001. 121p.

30. Castile, George Pierre and Gilbert Kushner, ed. Persistent Peoples: Cultural Enclave in Perspective. Tuscon, Arizona: University of Arizona Press, 1981. 274p.

30a. Cervone, Daniel and Ritu Tripathi. "The Moral Functioning of the Person as a Whole: On Moral Psychology and Personality Science." In Personality, Identity, and Character, p. 30-51. Edited by Darcia Naravaez and Daniel K. Lapsley. New York: Cambridge University Press, 2009.

31. Chapman, Gary. Love as a Way of Life: Seven Keys to Transforming Every Aspect of Your Life. Colorado Springs: WaterBrook Press, 2008. 248p.

32. Chin, Robert and Kenneth D. Benne. "General Strategies for Effecting Changes in Human Systems." In The Planning of Change, 3rd ed., p. 22-45. Edited by Warren G. Bennis, Kenneth D. Benne, Robert Chin, and Kenneth E. Corey. New York: Holt, Rinehart and Winston, 1976.

33. Chopra, Deepak. The Book of Secrets: Unlocking the Hidden Dimensions of Your Life. New York: Harmony Books, 2004. 270p.

34. Christakis, Nicholas A. and James H. Fowler. Connected: The Surprising Power of Our Social Networks and How They Shape Our Lives. New York: Little, Brown and Company, 2009. 338p.

34a. Chua, Amy and Jed Rubenfeld. The Triple Package: How Three Unlikely Traits Explain the Rise and Fall of Cultural Groups in America. New York: The Penguin Press, 2014. 320p.

35. Cibulka, James G. and William Lowe Boyd. "Introduction, Urban Education Reform: Competing Approaches." In The Race Against Time: The Crisis in Urban Schooling, p. vii-xviii. Contemporary Studies in Social and Policy Issues in Education, The David C.

Anchin Center Series. Edited by James G. Cibulka and William Lowe Boyd. IAP LLC, 2003.

36. _____. "Urban Education-Reform Strategies: Comparative analysis and Conclusions." In <u>The Race Against Time: The Crisis in Urban Schooling</u>, p. 205-

24. Contemporary Studies in Social and Policy Issues in Education, The David C. Anchin Center Series. Edited by James G. Cibulka and William Lowe Boyd. IAP LLC, 2003.

37. _____, ed. <u>The Race Against Time: The Crisis in Urban Schooling</u>. Contemporary Studies in Social and Policy Issues in Education, The David C. Anchin Center Series. Edited by James G. Cibulka and William Lowe Boyd. IAP LLC, 2003. 247p.

38. Clayton, Obie, Ronald B. Mincy, and David Blankenhorn, eds. <u>Black Fathers in Contemporary Society: Strengths, Weaknesses, and Strategies for Change</u>. New York: Russell Sage Foundation, 2003. 179p.

39. Clayton, Obie and Joan Moore. "The Effects of Crime and Imprisonment on Family Formation." In <u>Black Fathers in Contemporary Society: Strengths, Weaknesses, and Strategies for Change</u>, p. 84-102. Edited by Obie Clayton, Ronald B. Mincy, and David Blankenhorn. New York: Russell Sage Foundation, 2003.

40. Coleman, James C. and others. <u>Equality of Educational Opportunity</u>. Salem, New Hampshire: Ayer Company, Publishers, Inc., Reprint edition, 1988. 737p.

41. The Commission on Children at Risk. <u>Hardwired to Connect: The New Scientific Case for Authoritative Communities</u>. New York: Institute for American Values, 2003. 82p.

42. Conant, James B. <u>Slums and Suburbs</u>. New York McGraw-Hill Book Company, 1961. 147p.

43. Cook, Philip J. and Jens Ludwig. "The Burden of "Acting White": Do Black Adolescents Disparage Academic Achievement?" In <u>Minority Status, Oppositional Culture, &Schooling</u>, p. 275-97. Edited by John U. Ogbu. New York: Routledge, 2008.

44. Cooper, Robert and Will J. Jordan. "Cultural Issues in Comprehensive School Reform." In <u>Educating African American Males: Voices from the Field</u>, p. 1-18. Edited by Olatomkunbo S. Fashola. Thousand Oaks, California: Corwin Press, 2005.

45. Corbin, Saladin K. and Robert L. Pruitt II. "Who Am I? The Development of the African American Male Identity." In <u>African American Males in School and Society Practices and Policies for Effective Education</u>, p. 68-81. Edited by Vernon C. Polite and James Earl Davis. Introduction by Edmund W. Gordon. New York: Teachers College Press, 1999.

46. Cosby, Bill and Alvin F. Poussaint. <u>Come on People: On the Path from Victims toVictors</u>. Nashville: Thomas Nelson, 2007. 265p.

47. Cose, Ellis. <u>The Rage of the Privileged Class</u>. New York: HarperPerennial, 1993. 192p.

48. _____. <u>The Envy of the World: On Being a Black Man in America</u>. NewYork: Washington Square Press, 2002. 163p.

49. _____. <u>The End of Anger: A New Generation's Take on Race and Rage</u>. NewYork: HarperCollins Publishers, 2011. 320p

50. Cousins, Linwood. "Black Students' Identity and Acting White and Black." In<u>Minority Status, Oppositional Culture, & Schooling</u>, p. 167-89. Edited by John U.Ogbu. New York: Routledge, 2008.

51. Crain, Robert L. and Carol Sachs Weisman. <u>Discrimination, Personality, andAchievement</u>. Quantitative Studies in Social Relations Series. New York:Seminar Press, 1972. 225p.

52. Cremin, Lawrence A. <u>The Transformation of the School: Progressivism in American Education, 1876-1957</u>. New York: Vintage Books, Random House, 1961. 387p.

52a. Cross, William E., Jr. <u>Shades of Black: Diversity in African-American Identity</u>. Philadelphia: Temple University Press, 1991. 272p.

52b. Cruse, Harold. "Behind the Black Power Slogan." In <u>Booker T. Washington and His Critics: Black Leadership in Crisis</u>, 2nd ed., p. 174-83. Reprint from Harold Cruse, <u>Rebellion or Revolution?</u>, p. 198-205, 211, 239, William Morrow & Company, Inc., 1968. Edited by Hugh Hawkins. Lexington, Massachusetts: D.C. Heath and Company, 1974.

53. Curti, Merle <u>The Social Ideas of American Educators</u>. With New Chapter on the Last Twenty-Five Years. Totowa, New Jersey: Littlefield, Adams & Co., 1971. 613p.

54. D'Agostino, Jerome V., Larry V. Hedges, and Geoffrey D. Borman. "Title I Parent-Involvement Programs: Effects on Parenting Practices and Student Achievement." In <u>Title I: Compensatory Education at the Crossroads</u>, p. 117-36. Edited by Geoffrey D. Samuel, Samuel C. Stringfield, and Robert E. Slavin. Mahwah, New Jersey: Lawrence Erlbaum Associates, Publishers, 2001.

55. Davis, James Earl. "Early Schooling and Academic Achievement of African American Males." In <u>Educating African American Males: Voices from the Field</u>, p. 129-50. Edited by Olatomkunbo S. Fashola. Thousand Oaks, California: Corwin Press, 2005.

55a. Davis, Sampson, George Jenkins, and Rameck Hunt. <u>The Bond: Three Young Men Learn to Forgive and Reconnect with Their Fathers</u>. New York: Riverhead Books, 2007.

56. Dentler, Robert A., Bernard Mackler, and Mary Ellen Warshauer, eds. <u>The Urban R's: Race Relations as the Problem in Urban Education</u>. New York: Published for The Center for Urban Education by Frederick A. Praeger, 1967. 304p.

57. Dewey, John. The Child and the Curriculum and The School and Society, with Introduction by Leonard Carmichael. Chicago: The University of Chicago Press, The Child and the Curriculum, 1902; The School and Society, 1900, rev. 1915, by John Dewey 1943; combined reprint, 1956. 159p.

58. Dickerson, Debra J. The End of Blackness: Returning the Souls of Black Folk to Their Rightful Owners. New York: Anchor Books, 2004. 306p.

58a. "Discussion: How Much Can We Boost IQ and Scholastic Achievement?" Harvard Educational Review, 39 (Spring 1969): 273-356.

59. Dobson, James. Bringing Up Boys. Wheaton, Illinois: Tyndale House Publishers, Inc., 1982. 269p.

60. Downey, Douglas B. "A Funny Thing Happened on the Way to Confirming Oppositional Culture Theory." In Minority Status, Oppositional Culture, & Schooling, p. 298-311. Edited by John U. Ogbu. New York: Routledge, 2008.

61. Drake, St. Clair and Horace R. Cayton. Black Metropolis. New York: Harper Torchbook, 1962. Cited in Jessie Bernard, Marriage and Family Among Negroes. Englewood Cliffs: Prentice-Hall, 1966, passim.

62. D'Souza, Dinesh. The End of Racism: Principles for a Multiracial Society. New York: The Free Press, 1995. 724p.

63. DuBois, W. E. B. The Philadelphia Negro. New York: Cosimo Classics, (1899); reprint ed., 2007. 423p.

64. _____. The Souls of Black Folk. New York: Barnes and Noble Classics, (1903); reprint ed., 2003. 212p.

65. _____. "The Conservation of Races" (1897). In The Oxford W.E. B. Du Bois Reader, p. 38-47. Edited by Eric Sundquist. New York: Oxford University Press, 1996.

66. _____. "The Future of the Negro Race in America" (1904). In The Oxford W. E. B. Du Bois Reader, p. 362-73. Edited by Eric Sundquist. New York: Oxford University Press, 1996.

67. _____. Dusk of Dawn [title elsewhere cited as Dusk to Dawn]. New York: Schocken, 1940. Quoted in Robert J. Norrell, Up from History: The Life of Booker T. Washington, p. 425-26. Cambridge: The Belknap Press of Harvard University Press, 2009.

67a. _____. "A Pageant in Seven Decades." An address delivered on his seventieth birthday in 1938. Cited in Basil Mathews, Booker T. Washington: Educator and Interracial Interpreter, p. 293. CreateSpace.com. An Independent Publishing Platform, 2010.

67b. _____. Darkwater. In The Oxford W. E. B. Du Bois Reader, p. 483-623. Edited by Eric Sundquist. New York: Oxford University Press, 1996.

68. Dweck, Carol S. Self-Theories: The Role in Motivation, Personality, and Development. Essays in Social Psychology. New York: Psychology Press, 2000. 195p.

69. _____. Mindset: The New Psychology of Success. New York: Ballantine Books, 2006. 277p.

69a. Dyson, Michael Eric. I May Not Get There with You: The True Martin Luther King, Jr. New York: A Touchstone Book, Published by Simon & Schuster, 2001. 404p.

70. _____. Is Bill Cosby Right? (Or has the Black Middle Class Lost its Mind?). New York: Basic Civitas Books, 2005. 288p.

71. _____. "Sexual Fault Lines: Robbing the Love Between Us." In The State of Black America 2007: Portrait of the Black Male: Portrait of the Black Male, p. 229-37. Edited by Stephanie J. Jones and staff. An Official Publication of the National Urban League. Foreword by Senator Barack Obama. New York: The National Urban League, 2007.

72. _____. April 4, 1968: Martin Luther King Jr.'s Death and How It Changed America. New York: Basic Books, 2008. 290 p.

73. Eagleman, David. Incognito: The Secret Lives of the Brain. New York: Knopf Doubleday, 2011. 304p.

74 Edelman, Marian Wright. "Losing Our Children In America's Cradle to Prison Pipeline." In The State of Black America 2007: Portrait of the Black Male: Portrait of the Black Male, p. 219-27. Edited by Stephanie J. Jones and staff. An Official Publication of the National Urban League. Foreword by Senator Barack Obama. New York: The National Urban League, 2007.

75. Edelman, Peter, Harry J. Holzer, and Paul Offner. Reconnecting Disadvantaged Young Men. Washington, D.C.: The Urban Institute Press, 2006. 156p.

76. Elkins, Stanley M. Slavery: A Problem in American Institutional and Intellectual Life. Introduction by Nathan Glazer. New York: The Universal Library, Grosset & Dunlap, 1959. 248p.

77. Ember, Carol R. and Melvin Ember. Cultural Anthropology, 10th ed. Upper Saddle River, N.J.: Prentice Hall, 2002. 398p.

78. The Encyclopedia of Education, vol. 9, s. v. "Urban Minorities: Education of Immigrants," by Joe L. Rempson.

79. Erikson. Erik H. Identity: Youth and Crisis. New York: W.W. Norton & Co., 1968. 336p.

79a. _____. "The Concept of Identity in Race Relations: Notes and Queries." Daedalus, 95, The Negro American--2 (Winter, 1966): 145-71.

80. Farkas, George. "Quantitative Studies of Oppositional Culture: Arguments and Evidence" In Minority Status, Oppositional Culture, & Schooling, p. 312-47. Edited by John U. Ogbu. New York: Routledge, 2008.

81. Farrell, Edwin. <u>Hanging In and Dropping Out: Voices of At-Risk High School Students</u>. New York: Teachers College Press, 1990. 177p.

82. _____. <u>Self and School Success: Voices and Lore of Inner-City Students</u>. Albany: State University of New York Press, 1994. 173p.

83. Fashola, Olatokunbo. "Developing the Talents of African American Male Students During Nonschool Hours." In <u>Educating African American Males: Voices from the Field</u>, p. 19-49. Edited by Olatomkunbo S. Fashola. Thousand Oaks, California: Corwin Press, 2005.

84. _____, ed. <u>Educating African American Males: Voices from the Field</u>. Thousand Oaks, California: Corwin Press, 2005. 296p.

85. Ferguson, Ronald F. "How Professionals in Community-Based Program Perceive and Respond to the Needs of Black Male Youth." In <u>Nurturing Young Black Males</u>, p. 59-98. Edited by Ronald B. Mincy. Washington, D.C.: The Urban Institute Press, 1994.

85a. _____. "Can Schools Narrow the Black-White Test Score Gap?" In <u>The Black- White Test Score Gap</u>, p. 318-74. Edited by Christopher Jencks and Meredith Phillips. Washington, D.C.: Brookings Institution Press, 1998.

86. _____. "Teachers' Perceptions and Expectations and the Black-White Test Score Gap." In <u>Educating African American Males: Voices from the Field</u>, p. 79- 128. Edited by Olatomkunbo S. Fashola. Thousand Oaks, California: Corwin Press, 2005.

87. _____. <u>Toward Excellence with Equity: An Emerging Vision for Closing the Achievement Gap</u>. Cambridge: Harvard Education Press, 2008. 375p.

88. Fordham, Signithia. "Signithia, You Can Do Better Than That": John Ogbu (and Me) and the Nine Lives People." In <u>Minority</u>

Status, Oppositional Culture, & Schooling, p. 130-42. Edited by John U. Ogbu. New York: Routledge, 2008.

89. Fordham, Signithia and John Ogbu. "Black Students' School Success: Coping with the "Burden of 'Acting White.'" Urban Review, 18 (1986): 176-206.

90. _____. "Black Students' School Success: Coping with the "Burden of 'Acting White.'" In Minority Status, Oppositional Culture, &Schooling, p. 593-627. Edited by John U. Ogbu. New York: Routledge, 2008.

91. Frankl, Victor E. Man's Search for Meaning, revised and updated. New York: Washington Square Press, 1984. 221p.

92. Franklin, John Hope and Alfred A. Moss, Jr. From Slavery to Freedom: A History of African Americans, 8th ed. New York: McGraw Hill, 2000. 712p.

93. Frazier, E. Franklin. The Negro in the United States, rev. ed. New York: The Macmillan Company, 1957. 769p.

94. _____. Black Bourgeoisie: The Rise of a New Middle Class. New York: The Free Press, 1957. 264p.

95. _____. "The Negro Family in America." In The Black Family: Essays and Studies, p. 17-28. Edited by Robert Staples. Belmont: Wadsworth Publishing Co., 1971.

96. _____. "Sex Life of the African and American Negro." In The Black Family: Essays and Studies, p. 109-19. Edited by Robert Staples. Belmont: Wadsworth Publishing Co., 1971.

97. Frey, Daniel R. Miracle or Mirage? Social Science and Educational Reform for African-American Males, Senior thesis, Princeton University, 1992, p. 61. Quoted in Ronnie Hopkins, Educating Black Males:Critical Lessons in Schooling, Community, and Power, p. 15-16. Albany: State University of New York Press, 1997. 145p

98. Fromm, Erich. The Art of Loving. New York: Harper & Row, Publishers, 1956. 118p.

99. Fryer, Roland. "Falling Behind: as Children Move through School, the Black-White Achievement Gap Expands (Research)." Education Next, 22 November 2004.

99b. Garvey, Amy-Jacques. Garvey and Garveyism. United Kingdom: Octagon Books, 1976. Quoted in Harold Cruse, "Behind the Black Power Slogan." In Booker T. Washington and His Critics: Black Leadership in Crisis, 2nd ed., p. 178. Reprint from Harold Cruse, Rebellion or Revolution?, p. 198-205, 211, 239, William Morrow & Company, Inc., 1968. Edited by Hugh Hawkins. Lexington, Massachusetts: D.C. Heath and Company, 1974.

99a. Gates, Henry Louis, Jr. Life Upon These Shores: Looking at African American History, 1513-2008. New York: Alfred A. Knopf, 2011. 487p.

100. Genovese, Eugene D. "Rebelliousness and Docility in the Negro Slave: A Critique of the Elkins Thesis." Reprint from Civil War History, 13-4 (December 1967), p. 293-314. The Bobbs-Merrill Reprint Series in Black Studies. Indianapolis: The Bobbs-Merrill Co. Inc., 1967.

100a. Germany, Kent. "War on Poverty." In Poverty in the United States: An Encyclopedia of History, Politics, and Policy, p. 774-82. Edited by Alice O'Connor and Gwendolyn Mink. Santa Barbara: ABC-Clio, 2004.

101. Gilmore, David D. Manhood in the Making: Cultural Concepts of Masculinity. New Haven: Yale University Press, 1990. 258p.

102. Goleman, Daniel. Emotional Intelligence. New York: Bantam Books, 1995. 352p.

103. _____. Working with Emotional Intelligence. New York: Bantam Books, 1998. 383p.

103a. Gómez, Carlos Andrés. <u>Man Up; Cracking the Code of Manhood</u>. New York: Gotham Books, 2012. 286p.

104. Gopaul-McNicol, Sharon-Ann. <u>Working with West Indian Families</u>. New York: The Guilford Press, 1993. 212p.

104a. Gordon, Edmund W. "Foreword." In Polite, Vernon C. and James Earl Davis, <u>African American Males in School and Society: Practices & Policies for Effective Education</u>, p. ix-xiii. Edited by Vernon C. Polite and James Earl Davis. New York: Teachers College Press, Columbia Univesity, 1999.

105. Gordon, Sol. "Primary Education in Urban Slums." In <u>The Urban R's: Race Relations as the Problem in Urban Education</u>, p. 189-204. Edited by Robert Dentler, Bernard Mackler, and Mary Ellen Warshauer. New York: Published for The Center for Urban Education by Frederick A. Praeger, 1967.

105a. Gutman, Herbert G. <u>The Black Family in Slavery and Freedom 1750-1925</u>. New York: Vintage Books, A Division of Random House, 1976. 664p.

106. Hahn, Andrew B. "Toward a National Youth Development Policy for Young African-American Males: The Choices Policymakers Face." In <u>Nurturing Young Black Males</u>, p. 165-86. Edited by Ronald B. Mincy. Washington, D.C.: The Urban Institute Press, 1994.

107. Hanson, Renee, Mark McArdie, and Valerie Rawlston Wilson. Report from the National Urban League Policy Institute. "Invisible Men: The Urgent Problems of Low-Income African-American Males." In <u>The State of Black America 2007: Portrait of the Black Male: Portrait of the Black Male</u>, p. 209-16. Edited by Stephanie J. Jones and staff. An Official Publication of the National Urban League. Foreword by Senator Barack Obama. New York: The National Urban League, 2007.

108. Harlan, Louis R. Booker T. Washington: The Making of a Black Leader, 1856- 1901. New York: Oxford University Press, 1972. 379p.

109. _____. Booker T. Washington: The Wizard of Tuskegee, 1901-1915. New York: Oxford University Press, 1983. 548p.

110. _____. "Booker T. Washington and the White Man's Burden." In Booker T. Washington in Perspective: Essays of Louis R. Harlan, p. 68-97. Edited by Raymond W. Smock. Jackson: University Press of Mississippi, 1988.

111. _____. "Booker T. Washington and the Politics of Accommodation." In Booker T. Washington in Perspective: Essays of Louis R. Harlan, p. 164-79. Edited by Raymond W. Smock. Jackson: University Press of Mississippi, 1988.

112. _____. "The Secret Life of Booker T. Washington." In Booker T. Washington in Perspective: Essays of Louis R. Harlan, p. 110-132. Edited by Raymond W. Smock. Jackson: University Press of Mississippi, 1988.

113. Harlan, Louis R., ed. The Booker T. Washington Papers, Volume I: The Autobiographical Writings. Chicago: University of Illinois Press, 1972. 469p.

113a. _____. The Booker T. Washington Papers, Volume 2: 1860-1889. Chicago: University of Illinois Press, 1972. Cited in John Hope Franklin and Alfred A. Moss, Jr., From Slavery to Freedom: A History of African Americans, 8th ed., p. 302. New York: McGraw Hill, 2000.

113b. Harper, Hill. Letters to a Young Brother: MANifest Your Destiny. New York: Gotham Books, 2006. 176p.

114. Harrington, Michael. The Other America: Poverty in the United States. Baltimore: Penguin Books, Inc., 1963. 186p.

115. Harris, Judith Rich. <u>The Nurture Assumption: Why Children Turn Out the Way They Do</u>. New York: Free Press, 1998. Cited in Steven Pinker, <u>The Blank Slate: The Modern Denial of Human Nature</u>, p. 381-99. New York: Viking, 2002.

116. Haskins, Ron. "Poor Fathers and Public Policy: What is to Be Done?" In <u>Black Males Left Behind</u>, p. 249-91. Edited by Ronald B. Mincy. Washington, D.C.: The Urban Institute Press, 2006.

117. Havighurst, Robert J. <u>Developmental Tasks and Education</u>, third edition, newly revised. New York: David McKay Company, Inc., 1976. 119p.

118. Hawkins, Joseph A. "An Absence of a Talented Tenth." In <u>African American Males in School and Society: Practices & Policies for Effective Education</u>, p. 108-

121. Edited by Vernon C. Polite and James Earl Davis, with a foreword by Edmund W. Gordon. New York: Teachers College Press, Columbia Univesity,1999.

118a. Heber, R. "Research on Education and Habilitation of the Mentally Retarded." Paper read at Conference on Sociocultural Aspects of Mental Retardation, Peabody College, Nashville, Tenn., June 1968. Cited in Arthur R. Jensen, "How Much Can We Boost IQ and Scholastic Achievement?" <u>Harvard Educational Review</u>, 39 (Winter, 1969): 83.

119. Hemmings, Annette. "Shifting Images of Blackness: Coming of Age as Black Students in Urban and Suburban High Schools." In <u>Beyond Acting White: Reframing the Debate onBlackStudent Achievement</u>, p. 89-90. Edited by Erin McNamara Horvat and Carla O'Connor. New York: Rowman & Littlefield Publishers, Inc., 2006.

120. Henderson, A. T. and N. Berla. <u>A New Generation of Evidence: The Family is Critical to Student Achievement</u>. Washington, D.C.: National Committee for Citizens in Education, 1994. Cited in Glenn Olsen and Mary Lou Fuller, <u>Home- School Relations:</u>

Working Successfully with Parents and Family, 3rd ed. New York: Pearson, 2008, p. 129.

121. Herrnstein, Richard J. and Charles Murray. The Bell Curve: Intelligence and Class Structure in American Life. New York: Simon & Schuster, 1994. 872p.

122. Hirsch, E. D., Jr. Cultural Literacy: What Every American Needs to Know. Updated and Expanded. New York: Vintage Books, 1988. 251p.

122a. Hoffer, Eric. The True Believer: Thought on the Nature of Mass Movements. New York: HarperCollins, 1951. Cited in John McWhorter, Winning the Race: Beyond the Crisis in Black America, p. 165-67. New York: Gotham Books, 2005.

123. Holland, Spencer H. "PROJECT 2000: An Educational Mentoring and Academic Support Model for Inner-City African American Boys." Journal of Negro Education, 65 (3) (1966): 315-321.

124. Holzer, Harry J. "Reconnecting Young Black Men: What Policies Would Help?" In The State of Black America 2007: Portrait of the Black Male: Portrait of the Black Male, p. 75-87. Edited by Stephanie J. Jones and staff. An Official Publication of the National Urban League. Foreword by Senator Barack Obama. New York: The National Urban League, 2007.

125. Holzer, Harry J. and Paul Offner. "Trends in the Employment Outcomes of Young Black Men, 1979-2000." In Black Males Left Behind, p. 11-37. Edited by Ronald B. Mincy. Washington, D.C.: The Urban Institute Press, 2006.

126. Holzer, Harry J., Steven Raphael, and Michael A. Stoll. "How Do Employer Perceptions of Crime and Incarceration Affect the Employment Prospects of Less- Educated Young Black Men?" In Black Males Left Behind, p. 67-85. Edited by Ronald B. Mincy. Washington, D.C.: The Urban Institute Press, 2006.

127. Hopkins, Ronnie. <u>Educating Black Males: Critical Lessons in Schooling, Community, and Power</u>. Albany: State University of New York Press, 1997. 145p.

127a. Horn, Wade F. "Is it Working? Early Evaluations of Fatherhood-Renewal Programs." In <u>Black Fathers in Contemporary Society: Strengths, Weaknesses, and Strategies for Change</u>, p. 138-52. Edited by Obie Clayton, Ronald B. Mincy, and David Blankenhorn. New York: Russell Sage Foundation, 2003.

128. Horvat, Erin McNamara and Carla O'Connor, eds. <u>Beyond Acting White: Reframing the Debate on Black Student Achievement</u>. New York: Rowman & Littlefield Publishers, Inc., 2006. 247 p.

129. Hrabowski III, Freeman A., Kenneth I. Maton, and Geoffrey L. Greif. <u>Beating the Odds: Raising Academically Successful African American Males</u>. New York: Oxford University Press, 1998. 242p.

129a. Hughes, Langston, Milton Meltzer, and C. Eric Lincoln. <u>A Pictorial History of Blackamericans</u>, 5th revised ed. Originally published as <u>A Pictorial History of the Negro in America</u>; 1956, 1963 by Langston Hughes and Milton Meltzer; 1968 by Milton Meltzer and the Estate of Langston Hughes. New York: Crown Publishers, Inc., 1973. 378p.

130. Irving, Miles Anthony and Cynthia Hudley. "Oppositional Identity and Academic Achievement among African American Males." In <u>Minority Status, Oppositional Culture, &Schooling</u>, p. 374-94. Edited by John U. Ogbu. New York: Routledge, 2008.

131. Ivory, Steven. "Universal Fatherhood: Black Men Sharing the Load." In <u>The State of Black America 2007: Portrait of the Black Male: Portrait of the Black Male</u>, p. 243-47. Edited by Stephanie J. Jones and staff. An Official Publication of the National Urban League. Foreword by Senator Barack Obama. New York: The National Urban League, 2007.

132. Jackson, David H., Jr. Booker T. Washington and the Struggle Against White Supremacy: The Southern Educational Tours, 1908-1912. New York: Palgrave Macmillan, 2008. 260p.

133. Jahoda, Marie. "Toward a Social Psychology of Mental Health." Symposium on the Healthy Personality, Supplement II: Problems of Infancy and Childhood, Transactions of Fourth Conference, March, 1950, M.J.E. Benn, ed., New York: Josiah Macy, Jr. Foundation, 1950. Quoted in Erik H. Erikson, Identity: Youth and Crisis, p. 92. New York: W.W. Norton & Co., 1968.

134. James, Muriel and John James. Passion for Life: Psychology and the Human Spirit. New York A Dutton Book, Penguin Books USA Inc., 1991. 303p.

135. Jeff, Morris F.X., Jr. "Afrocentrism and African-American Male Youths." In Nurturing Young Black Males, p. 99-115. Edited by Ronal B. Mincy. Washington, D.C.: The Urban Institute Press, 1994.

136. Jencks, Christopher and Meredith Phillips. "The Black-White Test Score Gap: An Introduction." In The Black-White Test Score Gap, p. 1-51. Edited by Christopher Jencks and Meredith Phillips. Washington, D.C.: Brookings Institution Press, 1998.

137. _____, eds. The Black-White Test Score Gap. Washington, D.C.: Brookings Institution Press, 1998. 523p.

138. Jennings, John F. "Title I: Its Legislative History and Its Promise." In Title I: Compensatory Education at the Crossroads, p. 1-24. Edited by Geoffrey D. Samuel, Samuel C. Stringfield, and Robert E. Slavin. Mahwah, New Jersey: Lawrence Erlbaum Associates, Publishers, 2001.

139. Jensen, Arthur R. "How Much Can We Boost IQ and Scholastic Achievement?" Harvard Educational Review, 39 (Winter, 1969): 1-123.

140. John-Roger and Peter McWilliams. You Can't Afford the Luxury of a Negative Thought: A Book for People with Any Life-Threatening Illness--Including Life. Los Angeles: Prelude Press, 1988. 622p.

141. Johnson, Charles S. "The Social Philosophy of Booker T. Washington." Opportunity: 6 (April 1928): 102-106, 115. Quoted in Robert J. Norrell, Up from History: The Life of Booker T. Washington, p. 424-25, 427. Cambridge: The Belknap Press of Harvard University Press, 2009.

142. Johnson, James W., Booker T. Washington, and William E.B. DuBois. Three Negro Classics: Up from Slavery, The Souls of Black Folk, The Autobiography of an Ex-Colored Man, New York: Avon Books, 1999. Quoted in John Hope Franklin and Alfred A. Moss, Jr., From Slavery to Freedom: A History of African Americans, 8th ed., p. 292-325. New York: McGraw Hill, 2000. 712p. Also quoted in Robert J. Norrell, Up from History: The Life of Booker T. Washington, passim. Cambridge: The Belknap Press of Harvard University Press, 2009.

143. Jones, Stephanie J. and staff, eds. An Official Publication of the National Urban League. Foreword by Senator Barack Obama. The State of Black America 2007: Portrait of the Black Male: Portrait of the Black Male. New York: The National Urban League, 2007. 298p.

144. Kardiner, Abram and Lionel Ovesey. The Mark of Oppression: Explorations in the Personality of the American Negro. New York: The World Publishing Company, 1951. 396p.

144a. Karon, Bertram P. The Negro Personality: A Rigorous Investigation of the Effects of Culture. New York: Springer Publishing Co., Inc., 1958. 184p.

144b. Kennedy, David M. Don't Shoot: One Man, A Street Fellowship, and the End of Violence in Inner-City America. New York: Bloomsbury, 2011. 305p.

145. Kilson, Martin. "E. Franklin Frazier's *Black Bourgeoisie* Reconsidered: Frazier's Analytical Perspective." In E. Franklin Frazier and Black Bourgeoisie, p. 118-36. Edited by James E. Teele. Columbia: University of Missouri Press, 2002.

146. Kimmel, Michael. Manhood in America: A Cultural History. New York: The Free Press, 1997. 544p.

147. King, Martin Luther, Jr. Where Do We Go From Here: Chaos or Community? Boston: Beacon Press, 1968. 223p.

148. Kottak, Conrad Phillip. Cultural Anthropology, 10th ed. New York: McGraw-Hill, 2004. 486p., plus Appendix.

148a. Kunjufu, Jawanza. Reducing the Black Male Dropout Rate. African American Images, 2010. http://AfricanAmericanImages.com. 156p.

149. Lacy, Karyn. Blue-Chip Black: Race, Class, and Status in the New Black Middle Class. Los Angeles: University of California Press, 2007. 281p.

150. Landry, Bart. The New Black Middle Class. Los Angeles: University of California Press, 1987. 250p.

150a. Lasch-Quinn, Elisabeth. Race Experts: How Racial Etiquette, Sensitivity Training, and New Age Therapy Hijacked the Civil Rights Movement. New York: W. W. Norton & Co., 2001. 266p.

150b. Lasch-Quinn, Elisabeth. Race Experts: How Racial Etiquette, SensitivityTraining, and New Age Therapy Hijacked the Civil Rights Movement. New York: W. W. Norton & Co., 2001. Quoted in John McWhorter, Winning the Race: Beyond the Crisis in Black America, p. 168. New York: Gotham Books, 2005.

150c. Leary, Mark R. and June Price Tangney. Handbook of Self and Identity, 2nd ed. New York: The Guilford Press, 2012. 754p.

151. Lee, Carol D. "Foreword." In <u>Beyond Acting White: Reframing the Debate on Black Student Achievement</u>, p. ix-xiii. Edited by Erin McNamara Horvat and Carla O'Connor. New York: Rowman & Littlefield Publishers, Inc., 2006.

152. Lee, Courtland C. "Adolescent Development." In <u>Nurturing Young Black Males</u>, p. 33-44. Edited by Ronald B. Mincy. Washington, D.C.: The Urban Institute Press, 1994.

152a. _____. <u>Saving the Native Son: Empowerment Strategies for Young Males</u>. Greensboro, NC: ERIC Counseling and Student Services Clearinghouse, 1996. 165p.

152b. _____. <u>Empowering Young Black Males--III: A Systematic Modular Training Program for Black Male Children & Adolescents</u>. Greensboro, NC: ERIC Counseling and Student Services Clearinghouse, 2003. 128p.

153. Lewis, Amanda. "Whiteness in School: How Race Shapes Black Students' Opportunities." In <u>Beyond Acting White: Reframing the Debate on Black Student Achievement</u>, p. 176-99. Edited by Erin McNamara Horvat and Carla O'Connor. New York: Rowman & Littlefield Publishers, Inc., 2006.

154. Lewis, Hylan. <u>Blackways of Kent</u>. Chapel Hill, N.C.: University of North Carolina Press, 1955. Quoted in Bernard, Jessie. <u>Marriage and Family Among Negroes</u>, passim. Englewood Cliffs: Prentice-Hall, 1966.

154d. Liebow, Elliot. Foreword by Charles Lemert and Introduction by William Julius Wilson. <u>Tally's Corner: A Study of Negro Street Corner Men</u>, 2nd ed. Boston: Little, Brown and Co., 1967; reprint ed., Lanham, Md: Rowman & Littlefield Publishers, Inc, 2003. 222p.

154a. Locke, Alain, ed. <u>The New Negro</u>. New York: Simon & Schuster, 1925. Cited in August Meier, <u>Negro Thought in America, 1880-1915: Racial Ideologies in the Age of Booker T. Washington</u>, p.

256-57. New Introduction. Ann Arbor: The University of Michigan Press, 1963.

154b. Logan, Rayford W., ed. W.E.B. Du Bois: A :Profile. American Profiles. American Century Series. New York: Hill and Wang, 1971. 324p.

154c. Logan, Rayford W. "Introduction." In Rayford W. Logan, ed. W.E.B. Du Bois: A :Profile, p. vii-xviii. American Profiles. American Century Series. New York: Hill and Wang, 1971.

155. Loury, Glenn C. One by One from the Inside Out: Essays and Reviews on Race and Responsibility in America. New York: The Free Press, 1995. 332p.

156. _____. The Anatomy of Racial Inequality. The W.E.B. Du Bois Lectures. Cambridge, Massachusetts: Harvard University Press, 2002. 226p.

156a. McAdams, Dan P. "The Moral Personality." In Personality, Identity, and Character, p. 11-29. Edited by Darcia Naravaez and Daniel K. Lapsley. New York: Cambridge University Press, 2009.

157. McGill, Jerry. Dear Marcus, Speaking to the Man Who Shot Me. Bloomington, IN: iUniverse, Inc., 2009. 116p.

158. McGovern, Mary Lynne, Astrid Davis, and John U. Ogbu. "The Minority Achievement Committee: Students Leading Students to Greater Success in School." In Minority Status, Oppositional Culture, &Schooling, p. 560-73. Edited by John U. Ogbu. New York: Routledge, 2008.

158a Mackintosh, Barry. Booker T. Washington. Washington, D.C.: Office of Publications, National Park Service, U.S. Department of the Interior, 1972. 78p.

159. Mackler, Bernard. "A Report on the '600' Schools: Dilemmas, Problems, and Solutions." In The Urban R's: Race Relations as the Problem in Urban Education, p. 288-302. Edited by Robert

Dentler, Bernard Mackler, and Mary Ellen Warshauer. New York: Published for The Center for Urban Education by Frederick A. Praeger, 1967.

160. McWhorter, John. <u>Losing the Race: Self-Sabotage in Black America</u>. New York: Perennial, An Imprint of HarperCollins Publishers, 2001. 299p.

161. _____. <u>Winning the Race: Beyond the Crisis in Black America</u>. New York: Gotham Books, 2005. 434p.

162. Marchetti, Domenica. "Bettering the Lives of Black Males: Kellogg Foundation Sponsors a Controversial Plan to Help Men and Boys Reclaim Their Future." The <u>Chronicle of Philanthropy</u>, 30 May 1996, p. 8-11.

163. Markus, Hazel and Paul Nurius. "Possible Selves," <u>American Psychologist</u>, 41 (1986): 954-69. Cited in Edwin Farrell, <u>Self and School Success: Voices and Lore of Inner-City Students</u>, p. 135 Albany: State University of New York Press, 1994.

163a. "Martin Luther King Jr. I Have a Dream." Delivered 28 August 1963 at the Lincoln Memorial, Washington D.C. American Rhetoric. Top 100 Speeches. 1 December 2014. http://www.americanrhetoric.com/speeches/mlkihaveadream.htm

164. Marzano, Robert J. <u>What Works in Schools: Translating Research Into Action</u>. Alexandria, Virginia: Association for Supervision and Curriculum Development, 2003. 219p.

164a. Mathews, Basil. <u>Booker T. Washington: Educator and Interracial Interpreter</u>. CreateSpace.com. An Independent Publishing Platform, 2010. 350p.

165. Matthews, Victoria Earle. <u>Black-Belt Diamonds: Gems from the Speeches, Addresses, and Talks to Students of Booker T. Washington</u>. New York: Fortune and Scott, Publishers, 1898. 115p.

166. Maxwell, John A. Bill Cosby is Right: Silent Genocide. New York: iUniverse, Inc., 2008. 85p.

167. Mehan, Hugh, Lea Hubbard, and Irene Villanueva. "Forming Academic Identities: Accommodation without Assimilation among Involuntary Minorities." In Minority Status, Oppositional Culture, &Schooling, p. 533-59. Edited by John U. Ogbu. New York: Routledge, 2008.

168. Meier, August. Negro Thought in America, 1880-1915: Racial Ideologies in the Age of Booker T. Washington. New Introduction. Ann Arbor: The University of Michigan Press, 1963. 316p.

169. Meier, August and Elliott Rudwick. Black History and the Historical Profession 1915-1980. Urbana: University of Illinois Press, 1986. Quoted in Robert J. Norrell, Up from History: The Life of Booker T. Washington, p. 434. Cambridge: The Belknap Press of Harvard University Press, 2009.

170. Mickelson, Roslyn Arlin. "The Attitude-Achievement Paradox Among Black Adolescents." Sociology of Education, 63 (January 1990): 44-61.

171. _____. "The Structure of Opportunity and Adolescents' Academic Achievement Attitudes and Behaviors." In Minority Status, Oppositional Culture, &Schooling, p. 348-73. Edited by John U. Ogbu. New York: Routledge, 2008.

172. _____. Foreword to Minority Status, Oppositional Culture, & Schooling, p. xv- xxi. Edited by John U. Ogbu. New York: Routledge, 2008.

173. Mickelson, Roslyn and Anne E. Velasco. "Bring It On! Diverse Responses to "Acting White" among Academically Able Black Adolescents." In Beyond Acting White: Reframing the Debate on Black Student Achievement, p. 27-56. Edited by Erin McNamara Horvat and Carla O'Connor. New York: Rowman & Littlefield Publishers, Inc., 2006.

174. Miller, Kelly. The Everlasting Stain. New York: The Associated Publishers, 1968 reprint. Quoted in Robert J. Norrell, Up from History: The Life of Booker T. Washington, p. 424 and passim. Cambridge: The Belknap Press of Harvard University Press, 2009.

175. Mincy, Ronald B. "Conclusions and Implications." In Nurturing Young Black Males, p. 187-203. Edited by Ronald B. Mincy. Washington, D.C.: The Urban Institute Press, 1994.

176. _____. "Introduction." In Nurturing Young Black Males, p. 7-29. Edited by Ronald B. Mincy. Washington, D.C.: The Urban Institute Press, 1994.

177. _____, ed. Nurturing Young Black Males. Washington, D.C.: The Urban Institute Press, 1994. 243p.

178. _____, ed. Black Males Left Behind. Washington, D.C.: The Urban Institute Press, 2006. 326p.

179. Mincy, Ronald B. and Hillard Pouncy. "The Marriage Mystery: Marriage, Assets, and the Expectations of African American Families." In Black Fathers in Contemporary Society: Strengths, Weaknesses, and Strategies for Change, p. 45-70. Edited by Obie Clayton, Ronald B. Mincy, and David Blankenhorn. New York: Russell Sage Foundation, 2003.

180. Mitscherlich, Alexander. Society Without the Father: A Contribution to Social Psychology. Foreword by Robert Bly. New York: HarperPerennial, 1993. 329p.

181. Model, Suzanne. West Indian Immigrants: A Black Success Story? New York: Russell Sage Foundation, 2008. 235p.

181a. Morris, Monique W. Introduction by Khalil Gibran Muhammad. Black Stats: African Americans by the Numbers in the Twenty-First Century. New York: The New Press, 2014. 217p.

182. Moyers, Bill and Robert Bly. "A Gathering of Men." A production of Public Affairs Television, Inc. New York: Public Affairs Television, Inc., l990. 27p.

183. Moynihan, Daniel P. "Daniel P. Moynihan: The Tangle of Pathology." In The Black Family: Essays and Studies, p. 37-58. Edited by Robert Staples. Washington, D. C.: U. S. Government Printing Office, 1965: reprint ed., Belmont: Wadsworth Publishing Co., 1971.

184. _____. "A Family Policy for the Nation." America (September 18): 280-83, 1965. Quoted in Ron Haskins, "Poor Fathers and Public Policy: What is to Be Done?" In Black Males Left Behind, p. 254. Edited by Ronald B. Mincy. Washington, D.C.: The Urban Institute Press, 2006.

184a. Murray, Charles. Losing Ground: American Social Policy, 1950-1980. New York: Basic Books, 1984. 323p.

185. Murray, Charles. Losing Ground: American Social Policy, 1950-1980. New York: Basic Books, 1984. Quoted in Paul Tough, Whatever It Takes: Geoffrey Canada's Quest to Change Harlem and America, p. 28-33 With a New Afterword. New York: Mariner Books, Houghton Mifflin Harcourt, 2008.

186. Myers, David G. Social Psychology, 8th ed. Boston: McGraw Hill, 2005. 663p., plus Appendices.

186a. Naravaez, Darcia and Daniel K. Lapsley. "Introduction." In Personality, Identity, and Character, p. 1-10. Edited by Darcia Naravaez and Daniel K. Lapsley. New York: Cambridge University Press, 2009.

187. National Commission on Excellence in Education. A Nation at Risk: The Imperative for Educational Reform. A Report to the Secretary of Education. Washington, D.C.: U.S. Department of Education, 1983. 115p.

188. Naylor, Larry L. <u>Culture and Change: An Introduction</u>. Westport, Conn.: Bergin & Garvey, 1996. 235p.

188a. Nisbett, Richard E. <u>Intelligence and How to Get It: Why Schools and Cultures Count</u>. New York: W.W. Norton, 2009. 304p.

189. Nock,. Steven L. "Marriage and Fatherhood in the Lives of African American Men." In <u>Black Fathers in Contemporary Society: Strengths, Weaknesses, and Strategies for Change</u>, p. 30-42. Edited by Obie Clayton, Ronald B. Mincy, and David Blankenhorn. New York: Russell Sage Foundation, 2003.

190. Noguera, Pedro A. "The Trouble with Black Boys: The Role and Influence of Environmental and Cultural Factors on the Academic Performance of African American Males." In <u>Educating African American Males: Voices from theField</u>, p. 51-78. Edited by Olatomkunbo S. Fashola. Thousand Oaks, California: Corwin Press, 2005.

191. _____. <u>The Trouble with Black Boys</u>. San Francisco: Jossey-Bass, John Wiley & Sons, Inc., 2008. 324p.

192. Norrell, Robert J. <u>Up from History: The Life of Booker T. Washington</u>. Cambridge: The Belknap Press of Harvard University Press, 2009. 508p.

193. O'Connor, Carla, Erin McNamara Horvat, and Amanda E. Lewis. "Introduction: Framing the Field: Past and Future Research on the Historic Underachievement of Black Students." In <u>Beyond Acting White: Reframing the Debate on Black Student Achievement</u>, p. 1-24. Edited by Erin McNamara Horvat and Carla O'Connor. New York: Rowman & Littlefield Publishers, Inc., 2006.

193a. Oden, Sherri, Lawrence Schweinhart, and David Weikart, with Sue Marcus and YuXie. <u>Into Adulthood: A Study of the Effects of Head Start</u>. Ypsilanti, Michigan: High/Scope Press, 2000. 228p.

194. Ogbu, John U. <u>Minority Education and Caste: The American System in Cross- Cultural Perspective</u>. Carnegie Council on Children Publication. New York: Academic Press, Inc., 1978. 410p.

195. _____. "Minority Coping Responses and School Experience." <u>The Journal of Psychohistory</u>, 18 (Spring, 1991): 433-456.

196. _____. "Collective Identity and the Burden of "Acting White" in Black History, Community, and Education." In <u>Minority Status, Oppositional Culture, & Schooling</u>, p. 29-63. Edited by John U. Ogbu. New York: Routledge, 2008.

197. _____. "The History and Status of a Theoretical Debate." In <u>Minority Status, Oppositional Culture, &Schooling</u>, p. 3-28. Edited by John U. Ogbu. New York: Routledge, 2008.

198. _____. "Ways of Knowing: The Ethnographic Approach to the Study ofCollective Identity and Schooling." In <u>Minority Status, Oppositional Culture, &Schooling</u>, p. 64-88. Edited by John U. Ogbu. New York: Routledge, 2008.

199 _____. "Multiple Sources of Peer Pressures among African American Students." In <u>Minority Status, Oppositional Culture, &Schooling</u>, p. 89-111. Edited by John U. Ogbu. New York: Routledge, 2008.

200. _____. "Language and Collective Identity among Adults and Students in a Black Community." In <u>Minority Status, Oppositional Culture, &Schooling</u>, p. 112-29. Edited by John U. Ogbu. New York: Routledge, 2008.

201. _____, ed. <u>Minority Status, Oppositional Culture, & Schooling</u>. New York: Routledge, 2008. 653p.

201a. Oglesby, K. Thomas. With a Foreword by Tavis Smiley. <u>What Black Men Should Do Now: 100 Simple Truths, Ideas, and Concepts</u>, revised and expanded edition. <u>http://www.kensingtonbooks.dom</u>. Kensington Publishing Corp., 2000, 2002. 205p.

202. Olsen, Glenn and Mary Lou Fuller. Home-School Relations: Working Successfully with Parents and Family, 3rd ed. New York: Pearson, 2008. 394p.

203. Ornish, Dean. With New Foreword. 8 Pathways to Intimacy and Health. New York: HarperCollins, 1998. 298p.

204. Osborne, Jason W. "Race and Academic Disidentification." Journal of Educational Psychology, 89 (1997): 728-35.

205. Page, William H. "Introduction." Up from Slavery. In Up from Slavery: An Autobiography; My Larger Education; Character Building; The Negro Problem, p. 5-9. The Booker T. Washington Reader. An African American Heritage Book. Radford, VA: Wilder Publications, LLC., 2008.

206. Parini, Jay. Promised Land: Thirteen Books that Changed America. New York: Doubleday, 2008. 385p.

207. Passow, A. Harry, ed. Education in Depressed Areas. New York: Teachers College Press, 1963. 359p.

207a. Patterson, James T. Freedom is Not Enough: The Moynihan Report and America's Struggle over Black Family Life from LBJ to Obama. New York: Basic Books, A Member of the Perseus Books Group, 2010. 264p.

208. Patterson, Orlando. Rituals of Blood: Consequences of Slavery in Two American Centuries. Washington, D.C.: Civitas/Counterpoint, 1998. 330p.

208a. Payne, Charles M. So Much Reform, So Little Change: The Persistence of Failure in Urban Schools. Cambridge: Harvard University Press, 2008. 263p.

209. Perry, Steve. Man Up! Nobody is Coming to Save Us. Middletown, CT: A Renegade Book, 2005. 152p.

209a. _____. Push Has Come to Shove: Getting Our Kids the Education They Deserve -- Even if it Means Picking a Fight. New York: Crown Publishing Group, 2011. 272p.

209b. Peterson, Christopher and Martin E. P. Seligman. Character Strengths and Virtues: A Handbook and Classification. New York: Oxford University Press, 2004. 800p.

209c. Peterson, Rev. Jesse Lee, with a foreword by Sean Hannity. Scam: How the Black Leadership Exploits Black America. Nashville: Nelson Current, 2003. 236p.

209d. Pettigrew, Thomas F. A Profile of the American Negro. Princeton: D. Van Nostrand Co., Inc., 1964. 250p.

210. Pinker, Steven. The Blank Slate: The Modern Denial of Human Nature. New York: Viking, 2002. 509p.

211. Platt, Anthony M. "Between Scorn and Longing: Frazier's *Black Bourgeoisie.*" In E. Franklin Frazier and Black Bourgeoisie, p. 71-84. Edited by James E. Teele. Columbia: University of Missouri Press, 2002.

212. Polite, Vernon C. and James Earl Davis, eds., with a foreword by Edmund W. Gordon. African American Males in School and Society: Practices & Policies for Effective Education. New York: Teachers College Press, Columbia Univesity, 1999. 241p.

212a. Poussaint, Alvin F. and Amy Alexander. Lay My Burden Down: Unraveling Suicide and the Mental Health Crisis among African-Americans. Boston: Beacon Press, 2000. 194p.

212b. Powell, Kevin. Keepin' It Real: Post-MTV Reflections on Race, Sex, and Politics. New York: One World, Ballantine Books, 1997. 237p.

212c. _____, ed. Foreword by Hill Harper. The Black Male Handbook: A Blueprint for Life. New York: Atria Books, 2008. 244p.

213. _____. Quoted in Enola G. Aird, "Making the Wounded Whole: Marriage as Civil Right and Civic Responsibility." In <u>Black Fathers in Contemporary Society: Strengths, Weaknesses, and Strategies for Change</u>, p. 156. Edited by Obie Clayton, Ronald B. Mincy, and David Blankenhorn. New York: Russell Sage Foundation, 2003.

214. Quinn, Jane. "Traditional Youth Service Systems and Their Work with Young Black Males." In Ronal B. Mincy, ed., <u>Nurturing Young Black Males</u>, p. 119-49. Washington, D.C.: The Urban Institute Press, 1994.

215. Rainwater, Lee. "Lee Rainwater: Identity Processes in the Family." Printed with permission of <u>Daedalus</u>. From "The Crucible of Identity: The Lower-Class Negro Family," <u>Daedalus</u>: 95 (Winter, 1965): 258-64. In <u>The Black Family: Essays and Studies</u>, p. 257-61. Edited by Robert Staples. Belmont: Wadsworth Publishing Co., 1971.

215a. _____. "The Crucible of Identity: The Lower-Class Negro Family." <u>Daedalus</u>: 95, The Negro American--2 (Winter, 1966): 172-216.

216. Raths, Louis, Hamin Merrill, and Simon Sidney. <u>Values and Teaching</u>. New York: Charles E. Merrill, Columbus, Ohio, 1966. Cited by Sidney B. Simon, Leland W. Howe, and Howard Kirschenbaum in <u>Values Clarification: A Handbook of Practical Strategies for Teachers and Students</u>, p. 19. New York: Hart Publishing Co., Inc., 1972.

217. Ravitch, Diane. <u>The Death and Life of the Great American School System: How Testing and Choice are Undermining Education</u>. New York: Basic Books, 2010. 283p.

218. Reed, Wornie L. "The Middle-Class Black Male." In In <u>E. Franklin Frazier and Black Bourgeoisie</u>, p. 102-17. Edited by James E. Teele. Columbia: University of Missouri Press, 2002.

219. _____ "Fatherlessness in African American Families: Primary, Secondary, and Tertiary Prevention." In <u>Black Fathers in Contemporary Society: Strengths, Weaknesses, and Strategies for Change</u>, p. 125-37. Edited by Obie Clayton, Ronald B. Mincy, and David Blankenhorn. New York: Russell Sage Foundation, 2003.

220. Rempson, Joe L. "For an Elected Local School Board." <u>The Urban Review</u>, 1 (November 1966): 2-15.

221. _____. "Community Control of Local School Boards." <u>Teachers College Record</u>, 68 (April, 1967): 571-18.

222. _____. "School-Parent Programs in Depressed Urban Neighborhoods." In <u>The Urban R's: Race Relations as the Problem in Urban Education</u>, p. 130-57. Edited by Robert Dentler, Bernard Mackler, and Mary Ellen Warshauer. New York: Published for The Center for Urban Education by Frederick A. Praeger, Publishers, 1967.

223. _____. "An Exploratory Study to Help Increase the Number of Parents Who Make In-School Contacts in Low-Income Urban Area Public Elementary Schools." Ed. D. dissertation, Teachers College, Columbia University, 1969. 456p.

223a. _____. "Education of Immigrants." In <u>The Encyclopedia of Education</u>, p. 391-99. Editor-in-chief, Lee C. Deighton. New York: The Macmillan & The Free Press, 1971.

224. _____. "Social Problem: Jung." A Paper Submitted to Dr. Robert Neale as Course Requirement in Theories of Depth Psychology. Union Theological Seminary, New York. November, 1984. 6p. Personal Files of Joe L. Rempson. Bronx, New York.

225. _____ <u>African American Male Career Pathway Program (AMCAP) Task Guide</u>. (The Rempson Foundation: forthcoming)

226. Rempson, Joe L. and Angela Anselmo. "Spirituality: Your Hidden Success Center." In <u>Transitions: The Urban College Student's First</u>

Year Experience, p. 211-30. Edited by Robert C. DeLucia. Needham Heights, MA: Ginn press, 1993.

226a. Robertson, Ian H. The Winner Effect: The Neuroscience of Success and Failure. New York: Thomas Dunne Books, St. Martin's Press, 2012, 305p.

227. Robinson, Eugene. Disintegration: The Splintering of Black America. New York, Doubleday, 2010. 254p.

227a. Robinson, Keith and Angel L. Harris. The Broken Compass: Parental Involvement with Children's Education. Cambridge: Harvard University Press, 2014. 312p.

228. Rochon, Thomas R. Culture Moves: Ideas, Activism, and Changing Values. Princeton: Princeton University Press, 1998. 282p.

229. Roderick, Melissa. "What's Happening to Boys? Early High School Experiences and School Outcomes Among African American Male Adolescents in Chicago." In Educating African American Males: Voices from the Field, p. 151-227. Edited by Olatokunbo S. Fashola. Thousand Oaks, California: Corwin Press, 2005.

229a. Rohrer, John H. and Munro S. Edmonson. The Eighth Generation: Cultures and Personalities of New Orleans Negroes. New York: Harper & Row, 1960. Cited in William E. Cross Jr., Shades of Black: Diversity in African-American Identity, p. 130-32. Philadelphia: Temple University Press, 1991.

229c. Rolfhus, E. I. and P. L. Ackerman. "Assessing Individual Differences in Knowledge: Knowledge, Intelligence, and Related Traits," Journal of Educational Psychology, 91(3): 511-26. Cited in Robert J. Marzano, What Works in Schools: Translating Research Into Action, p. 134. Alexandria, Virginia: Association for Supervision and Curriculum Development, 2003.

229e. Rudwick, Elliott. W.E.B. Du Bois: Voice of the Black Protest Movement. Chicago: University of Illinois Press, 1982. 400p.

229d. Rudwick, Elliott M. "An Accommodationist in Wartime." In Rayford W. Logan, ed., W.E.B. Du Bois: A :Profile, p. 158-82. American Profiles. American Century Series. New York: Hill and Wang, 1971. Reprinted from Elliott M. Rudwick, W.E.B. Du Bois: Progandandist of the Negro Protest, p. 184-207, by permission of Elliott M. Rudwick. Copyright © by Elliott M. Rudwick. Originally published by the University of California Press; reprinted by permission of the Regents of the University of California. Paperback reprint by Atheneum, New York, 1968.

229b. Ryan, William. Blaming the Victim. Revised, updated edition. New York: Vintage Books, a Division of Random House, 1976. 351p.

230. Salomone, Rosemary C. Same, Different, Equal: Rethinking Single-Sex Schooling. New Haven: Yale University Press, 2003. 287p.

231. Samuel, Mark and Sophie Chiche. The Power of Personal Accountability: Achieve What Matters to You. Katonah, NY: Xephor Press, 2004. 133p.

232. Sax, Leonard. Why Gender Matters: What Parents and Teachers Need to Know About the Emerging Science of Sex Differences. New York; Doubleday, 2005. 312p.

233. _____. Boys Adrift. New York: Basic Books, 2007. 273p.

234. Scott, Emmett J. and Lyman Beecher Stowe. Booker T. Washington: Builder of a Civilization. Tutis Digital Publishing Private Limited, 2008 (First published 1916). 496p.

235. Silverstein, Barry and Ronald Krate. Children of the Dark Ghetto: A Developmental Psychology. New York: Praeger Publishers, 1975. 277p.

236. Simmons, Russell with Chris Morrow. Super Rich: A Guide to Having it All. New York: Gotham Books, 2011. 197p.

237. Smiley, Tavis. Introduction. <u>The Covenant. with Black America</u>. Chicago: The Third World Press, 1967. 254p.

238. Smith, Jessie Carney and Carrell Peterson Horton, comp. and eds. <u>Historical Statistics of Black America</u>. 2 vols. New York: Gale Research Inc., 1995.

239. Smock, Raymond W. "Preface." In <u>Booker T. Washington in Perspective: Essays of Louis R. Harlan</u>, p. ix-xi. Edited by Raymond W. Smock. Jackson: University Press of Mississippi, 1988.

240. Solomon, R. Patrick. <u>Black Resistance in High School: Forging a Separatist Culture</u>. Foreword by John U. Ogbu. Albany: State University of New YorkPress, 1992. 159p.

240a. Sowell, Thomas, ed., with assistance of Lynn D. Collins. <u>Essays and Data on American Ethnic Groups</u>. Washington, D.C.: The Urban Institute, 1978. 415p.

241. Sowell, Thomas. "Three Black Histories." In <u>Essays and Data on American Ethnic Groups</u>, p. 7-64. Edited by Thomas Sowell with assistance of Lynn D. Collins. Washington, D.C.: The Urban Institute, 1978.

242. _____. "Race and I.Q. Reconsidered." In <u>Essays and Data on American Ethnic Groups</u>, p. 203-38. Edited by Thomas Sowell with assistance of Lynn D. Collins. Washington, D.C.: The Urban Institute, 1978.

243. Spencer, Margaret Beale and Vinay Harpalani. "What does "Acting White" Actually Mean? Racial Identity, Adolescent Development, and Academic Achievement among African American Youth." In <u>Minority Status, Oppositional Culture, &Schooling</u>, p. 222-39. Edited by John U. Ogbu. New York: Routledge, 2008.

244. Spencer, Samuel R., Jr. <u>Booker T. Washington and the Negro's Place in American Life</u>. The Library of American Biography, edited by Oscar Handlin. Boston: Little, Brown and Company, 1955. 212p.

245. Staff of the Washington Post. <u>Being a Black Man: At the Corner of Progress and</u> <u>Peril</u>. Introduction by Edward P. Jones. New York: Public Affairs, 2007. 355p.

246. Staples, Robert, ed. <u>The Black Family: Essays and Studies</u>. Belmont: Wadsworth Publishing Company, Inc., 1971. 393p.

247. Steele, Claude. <u>Whistling Vivaldi and Other Clues to How Stereotypes Affect Us</u>. New York: W. W. Norton & Company, 2010. 242p.

247a. Steele, Shelby. <u>The Content of Our Character: A New Vision of Race in America</u>. New York: First HarperPerennial edition, 1991; also in hardcover, St. Martin's Press, 1990. 175p.

248. Stein, Sandra J. <u>The Culture of Education Policy</u>. New York: Teachers College Press, 2004. 193p.

249. Steinberg, Laurence. <u>Beyond the Classroom</u>. New York: Touchstone, 1996. Cited by John McWhorter in <u>Losing the Race: Self-Sabotage in Black America</u>, p. 88-89, 114, 130. New York: Perennial, An Imprint of HarperCollins Publishers, 2001.

250. Sundquist, Eric J., ed. <u>The Oxford W. E. B. Du Bois Reader</u>. New York: Oxford University Press, 1996. 680p.

251. Syed, Matthew. <u>Bounce: Mozart, Federer, Picasso, Beckham, and the Science of Success</u>. New York: HarperCollins, 2010. 312p.

252. Taber, Brian J. and Darrell Anthony Luzzo. ACT Research Report Series, 99-3. <u>A Comprehensive Review of Research Evaluating the Effectivenes of DISCOVER in Promoting Career Development</u>. Iowa City: ACT Report Series, 1999. 43p.

253. Taylor, April. "A Quantitative Examination of Oppositional Identity among African American and Latino Middle-School Students." In <u>Minority Status, Oppositional Culture, & Schooling</u>, p. 481-95. Edited by John U. Ogbu. New York: Routledge, 2008.

254. Taylor, Carol. "Frederick Douglass' Views on Education." Term Paper Submitted to Fulfill Course Requirement, December, 18, 1972. Personal Files of Joe L. Rempson, Bronx, New York.

255. Taylor, George R. Practical Application of Social Learning Theories in Educating Young African-American Males. New York: University Press of America, 2003. 208p.

255a. Teague, Bob. The Flip Side of Soul: Letters to My Son. New York: William Morrow and Company, Inc., 1989. 201p.

256. Teele, James E. "Introduction." In E. Franklin Frazier and Black Bourgeoisie, p. 1-13. Edited by James E. Teele. Columbia: University of Missouri Press, 2002.

257. _____, ed. E. Franklin Frazier and Black Bourgeoisie. Columbia: University of Missouri Press, 2002. 170p.

257a. Thurston, Baratunde. How to Be Black. New York: HarperCollins, 2012. 254p.

258. Tough, Paul. Whatever It Takes: Geoffrey Canada's Quest to Change Harlem and America. With a New Afterword. New York: Mariner Books, Houghton Mifflin Harcourt, 2008. 310p.

258a. _____. How Children Succeed: Grit, Curiosity, and the Hidden Power of Character. New York: Houghton Mifflin Harcourt, 2012. 231p.

258b. Toureç. Who's Afraid of Post-Blackness: What It Means to Be Black Now. New York: Free Press, 2011. 251p.

259. Tyre, Peg. The Trouble with Boys. New York: Crown Publishers, 2008. 311p.

260. Tyson, Karolyn. "The Making of a "Burden": Tracing the Development of a "Burden of Acting White" in Schools." In Beyond Acting White: Reframing the Debate on BlackStudent Achievement, p. 57-88. Edited by Erin McNamara Horvat and

Carla O'Connor. New York: Rowman & Littlefield Publishers, Inc., 2006.

261. United States Department of Labor (The Moynihan Report). Office of Policy Planning and Research. The Negro Family: The Case for National Action. Washington, D.C.: U. S. Government Printing Office, March, 1965. 78p.

262. Valett, Robert E. Humanistic Education: Developing the Total Person. Saint Louis: The C. V. Mosby Company, 1977. 232p.

263. Wang, Margaret C., Geneva D. Haertel, and Herbert J. Walberg. "Toward a Knowledge Base for School Learning. Review of Educational Research, 63 (Autumn 1993): 249-94.

263a. Washington, Booker T. The Booker T. Washington Papers. 14 vols. Edited by Louis R. Harlan. New York: University of Illinois Press, 1972-89. Available online. http://www.historycooperative.org/btw/

264. _____. The Story of My Life and Work. In The Booker T. Washington Papers, 15 vols., Vol. 1: The Autobiographical Writings, p. 1-206. Edited by Louis R. Harlan and John W. Blassingame, Assistant Editor. Chicago: University of Illinois Press, reprint ed., 1972; original pub., 1900.

265. _____. Up from Slavery. In The Booker T. Washington Papers, 15 vols. Vol. 1: The Autobiographical Writings, p. 206-385. Edited by Louis R. Harlan and John W. Blassingame, Assistant Editor. Chicago: University of Illinois Press, reprint ed. 1972; original pub., 1901.

265a. _____. Extracts from My Larger Education, 1911. In The Booker T. Washington Papers, 15 vols. Vol. 1: The Autobiographical Writings, p. 418-58. Edited by Louis R. Harlan and John W. Blassingame, Assistant Editor. Chicago: University of Illinois Press, reprint ed. 1972; original pub., 1911.

266. _____. The Case of the Negro. Tuskegee, 1902. Cited in Meier, August Meier, Negro Thought in America, 1889-1915: Racial Ideologies in the Age of Booker T. Washington, p. 105. New Introduction. Ann Arbor: The University of Michigan Press, reprint ed., 1963.

267. _____. Character Building: Being Addresses Delivered on Sunday Evenings to the Students of Tuskegee Institute. Reprints. Bottom of the Hill Publishing: www.BottomofHillPublishing.com, reprint ed., 2010. 148p.

268. Washington, Booker T. Reader. Up from Slavery: An Autobiography; My Larger Education; Character Building; The Negro Problem. Reprints. Radford, VA: Wilder Publications, LLC., 2008. 415p.

269. _____. "Last Words." In Up from Slavery: An Autobiography; My Larger Education; Character Building; The Negro Problem, p. 351-53. The Booker T. Washington Reader. Reprints. An African American Heritage Book. Radford, VA: Wilder Publications, LLC., 2008.

270. _____. "Industrial Education for the Negro." In Up from Slavery: An Autobiography; My Larger Education; Character Building; The Negro Problem, p. 355-60. The Booker T. Washington Reader. Reprints. An African American Heritage Book. Radford, VA: Wilder Publications, LLC., 2008.

271. _____. "Growth." In Up from Slavery: An Autobiography; My Larger Education; Character Building; The Negro Problem, p. 349-50. The Booker T. Washington Reader. Reprints. An African American Heritage Book. Radford, VA: Wilder Publications, LLC., 2008.

272. _____. "Getting Down to Mother Earth." In Up from Slavery: An Autobiography; My Larger Education; Character Building; The Negro Problem, p. 342-44. The Booker T. Washington Reader. Reprints. An African American Heritage Book. Radford, VA: Wilder Publications, LLC., 2008.

273. _____. "What is to be Our Future?" In Up from Slavery: An Autobiography; My Larger Education; Character Building; The Negro Problem, p. 307-09. The Booker T. Washington Reader. Reprints. An African American Heritage Book. Radford, VA: Wilder Publications, LLC., 2008.

274. _____. "Two Sides of Life." In Up from Slavery: An Autobiography; My Larger Education; Character Building; The Negro Problem, p. 249-251. The Booker T. Washington Reader. Reprints. An African American Heritage Book. Radford, VA: Wilder Publications, LLC., 2008.

275. _____. "European Impressions." In Up from Slavery: An Autobiography; My Larger Education; Character Building; The Negro Problem, p. 274-76. The Booker T. Washington Reader. Reprints. An African American Heritage Book. Radford, VA: Wilder Publications, LLC., 2008.

276. _____. "Education that Educates." In Up from Slavery: An Autobiography; My Larger Education; Character Building; The Negro Problem, p. 283-84. The Booker T. Washington Reader. Reprints. An African American Heritage Book. Radford, VA: Wilder Publications, LLC., 2008.

277. _____. "The Gospel of Service." In Up from Slavery: An Autobiography; My Larger Education; Character Building; The Negro Problem, p. 301-03. The Booker T. Washington Reader. Reprints. An African American Heritage Book. Radford, VA: Wilder Publications, LLC., 2008.

278. _____. The Case of the Negro, Tuskegee, 1902. Quoted in August Meier, Negro Thought in America, 1889-1915: Racial Ideologies in the Age of Booker T. Washington, p. 105. New Introduction. Ann Arbor: The University of Michigan Press, 1963.

279. _____. "Is the Negro Having a Fair Chance?" Kessinger Publishing Rare Reprints. No publication data given, but reprint of 1912 article in magazine, Century. Publisher's website: http://www.kessinger.net

279b. _____. "On Getting a Home." In <u>Character Building: Being Addresses Delivered on Sunday Evenings to the Students of Tuskegee Institute</u>, p. 34-36. Reprints. Bottom of the Hill Publishing: <u>www.BottomofHillPublishing.com</u>, reprint ed., 2010.

279d _____. "Calling Things by Their Right Name." In <u>Character Building: Being Addresses Delivered on Sunday Evenings to the Students of Tuskegee Institute</u>, p. 37-40. Reprints. Bottom of the Hill Publishing: <u>www.BottomofHillPublishing.com</u>, reprint ed., 2010.

279c. _____. "The Value of System in Home Life." In <u>Character Building: Being Addresses Delivered on Sunday Evenings to the Students of Tuskegee Institute</u>, p. 45-47. Reprints. Bottom of the Hill Publishing: <u>www.BottomofHillPublishing.com</u>, reprint ed., 2010.

279a. Washington, E. Davidson, ed. <u>Selected Speeches of Booker T. Washington</u>. New York, 1932. Quoted in August Meier, <u>Negro Thought in America, 1889-1915: Racial Ideologies in the Age of Booker T. Washington</u>, p. 107. New Introduction. Ann Arbor: The University of Michigan Press, 1963.

280. Waxman, Hersholt C., Yolanda N. Padron, and Karen M. Arnold. "Effective Instructional Practices for Students at Risk of Academic Failure." In <u>Title I: Compensatory Education at the Crossroads</u>, p. 137-70. Edited by Geoffrey D. Samuel, Samuel C. Stringfield, and Robert E. Slavin. Mahwah, New Jersey: Lawrence Erlbaum Associates, Publishers, 2001.

281. Weis, Lois. "'Excellence' and Student Class, Race, and Gender Cultures." In <u>Minority Status, Oppositional Culture, & Schooling</u>, p. 240-56. Edited by John U. Ogbu. New York: Routledge, 2008.

281a. White, R. K. "Black Boy: A Value Analysis," <u>Journal of Abnormal and Social Psychology</u>, 42 (1947): 440-61. Cited in Thomas F. Pettigrew, <u>A Profile of the American Negro</u>, p. 9. Princeton: D. Van Nostrand Co., Inc., 1964.

282. Willens, Michele. "Breaking a Stereotype, More Men Are Being Hired as Nannies," New York Times, May 13, 1993, p. C-6. Quoted in David Blankenhorn, Fatherless America: Confronting Our Most Urgent Social Problem, p. 198. New York: Harper Perennial, 1996.

283. Williams, Juan. Enough: The Phony Leaders, Dead-End Movements, and Culture of Failure That are Undermining Black America--and What We Can Do About It. New York: Three Rivers Press, 2006. 243p.

283a _____. Muzzled: The Assault on Honest Debate. New York: Crown Publishing Group, 2011. 304p.

283b. Williams, Terri M. Black Pain: It Just Looks Like We're Not Hurting. New York: Scribner, 2008 [paperback edition, 2009]. Cited in Toureȼ, Who's Afraid of Post-Blackness: What It Means to Be Black Now, p. 141-43. New York: Free Press, 2011.

284. Willis, Paul. Learning to Labor: How Working Class Kids Get Working Class Jobs. New York: Columbia University Press, 1977. 226p.

285. Wilson, William Julius. "The Woes of the Inner-City African American Father." In Black Fathers in Contemporary Society: Strengths, Weaknesses, and Strategies for Change, p. 9-29. Edited by Obie Clayton, Ronald B. Mincy, and David Blankenhorn. New York: Russell Sage Foundation, 2003.

285a. _____. The Truly Disadvantaged: The Inner City, the Underclass, and Public Policy. Chicago: University of Chicago Press, 1987. 254p.

286. _____. The Truly Disadvantaged: The Inner City, the Underclass, and Public Policy. Chicago: University of Chicago Press, 1987. Quoted in Tough, Paul, Whatever It Takes: Geoffrey Canada'sQuest to Change Harlem and America, p. 29-33. With a New Afterword. New York: Mariner Books, Houghton Mifflin Harcourt, 2008.

287. _____. <u>More Than Just Race: Being Black and Poor in the Inner City</u>. New York: W. W. Norton & Company, 2009. 190p.

288. Wilson, Valerie Rawlston. "On Equal Ground: Causes and Solutions for lower College Completion Rates Among Black Males." In <u>The State of Black America 2007: Portrait of the Black Male: Portrait of the Black Male</u>, p. 123-35. Edited by Stephanie J. Jones and staff. An Official Publication of the National Urban League. Foreword by Senator Barack Obama. New York: The National Urban League, 2007.

289. Witherspoon, Karen McCurtis, Suzette L. Speight, and Anita Jones Thomas. "Racial Identity Attitudes, School Achievement, and Academic Self-Efficacy among African-American High School Students." In <u>Minority Status, Oppositional Culture, &Schooling</u>, p. 257-71. Edited by John U. Ogbu. New York: Routledge, 2008.

290. Woodson, Carter G. <u>The Negro in Our History (1922)</u>. Washington, D.C.: The Associated Publishers, Inc., 1922. 393p.

291. Woodward, C. Vann. <u>Origins of the New South, 1877-1913</u>. Baton Rouge: Louisiana State University Press, 1951. Quoted in Norrell, Robert J. <u>Up from History: The Life of Booker T. Washington</u>, p. 434-36, 438. Cambridge: The Belknap Press of Harvard University Press, 2009.

292. Wright, Willie J. "The Endangered Black Male Child." <u>Educational Leadership</u>, 49 (April 1992): 14-16.

293. Zimbardo, Philip and Ebbe B. Ebbesen. In Collaboration with Christina Maslach. <u>Influencing Attitudes and Changing Behavior: A Basic Introduction to Relevant Methodology, Theory, and Applications</u>, revised printing. Reading, Massachusetts: Addison-Wesley Publishing Company, 1970. 162p.

294. Zimbardo, Philip and John Boyd. <u>The Time Paradox: The New Psychology of Time That Will Change Your Life</u>. New York: Free Press, 2008. 358p.

B. NEWSPAPER and INTERNET-ACCESSED SOURCES
(Internet-accessed sources are subject to citation changes, so some sources might not be found at the website address shown – or might not even any longer be internet-accessible, an author/subject search being advisable in such instances)

295a. Adams, Portia. "Self-Esteem Research in Black Communities: "On the Whole, I'm Satisfied with Myself." Perspectives. 10 November 2013. Retrieved on 15 November 2013 from http://www.rcgd.isr.umich.edu/prba/perspectives/springsummer2004/adams.pdf

295b. "African American Employment." BlackDemographics.com. 1 May 2015. Retrieved on 4 May 2015 from http://blackdemographics.com/economics/employment/

295c. "African American Income." BlackDemographics.com. 1 May 2015. Retrieved on 4 May 2015 from http://blackdemographics.com/households/african-american-income/

295. Africana: The Encyclopedia of the African and African-American Experience. "Amenia Conference of 1916." Mywire.com. 12 January 2010. Retrieved on 20 January 2010 from http://www.mywire.com/a/Africana/Amenia-Conference-1916/9444688/

296. Afterschool Alliance. Policy and Action Center. "21st Century Community Learning Centers Federal Afterschool Initiative." Afterschoolalliance.org. 13 March 2011. Retrieved on 13 March 2011 from http://www.afterschoolalliance.org/policy21stcclc.cfm

297. Afterschool.gov. "Federal Funding Basics." Afterschool.gov. 13 March 2011. Retrieved on 13 March 2011 from http://www.afterschool.gov/docs/federalFunding.html

298. Ainsworth-Darnell, James W. and Douglas B. Downey. "Assessing the Oppositional Culture Explanation for Racial/Ethnic Differences in School Performance." American Sociological Review, 63 (August, 1998): 536-53. Thestudyofracialism.org. Retrieved on 16 March 2007 from http://thestudyofracialism.org/forum/store/ainsworth01.pdf

298a. AllPsych Online. The Virtual Psychology Classroom. Psychology 101. Chapter 4: Learning Theory and Behavioral Psychology. Section 3: Reinforcement. 29 November 2011. Allpsych.com. Retrieved on 4 July 2012 from http://allpsych.com/psychology

299. Altman, Lawrence K. "U.S. Blacks, if a Nation, Would Rank High on AIDS." The New YorkTimes. 30 July 2008. NYTimes.com. Retrieved on 31 July 2008 from http://www.nytimes.com/2008/07/30/health/research/30aids.html?

299a. American Association of School Superintendents (AASA) [The School Superintendents Association]. "Every Student Succeeds Act: AASA Summary & Overview." Contact information: Noelle Ellerson, Associate Executive Director, Policy and Advocacy, Nellerson@aasa.org. Retrieved on 13 December 2015 from http://www.sammt.org/cms/lib03/MT15000278/Centricity/Domain/223/AASA%20ESSA%20Overview%2011-30-15.pdf

300. American College Testing Program(ACT). "The Path to Career Success: High School Achievement, Certainty of Career Choice, and College Readiness Make a Difference." Act.org. Retrieved on 5 June 2010 from http://www.act.org/research/policymakers/pdf/PathCareerSuccess.pdf

301. Anderson, Michael L. "Multiple Inference and Gender Differences in the Effects of Early Intervention: A Reevaluation of the Abecedarian, Perry Preschool, and Early Training Projects." Berkeley.edu. Retrieved on 8 September 2010 from http://www.are.berkeley.edu/~anderson/pdf/Anderson%20Preschool.pdf

301a. Angier, Natalie. "The Changing American Family." 25 November 2013. NYTimes.com. Retrieved on 26 November 2013 from http://www.nytimes.com/2013/11/26/health/families.html

302. Applebome, Peter. "For Youths, Fear of Crime is Pervasive and Powerful: Worries Force New Behavior, Study Finds." New York Times, 12 January 1996, p. A12.

303. Arenson, Karen W. "Colleges Struggle to Help Black Men Stay Enrolled." The New York Times. 30 December 2003. NYTimes.com. Retrieved on 30 December 2003 from http://www.nytimes.com/2003/12/30/education/30BLAC.html

304. Associated Press. "NY High School Graduation Rates Rise Slowly." New York Post. 11 August 2008. Nypost.com. Received on 22 June 2009 from http://www.nypost.com/seven/08112008/news/regionalnews/ny_high_school_graduation_r…

304d. ABC Staff. "Crying Shame: 10 Black Celebs Expressing Self-Hate." Atlanta Black Star. 9 September 2013. Atlantablackstar.com. Retrieved on 8 November 2013 from http://atlantablackstar.com/2013/09/09/crying-shame-10-black-celebs-expressing-self-hate/#wrap

304c. Baker, Nicholson. "Wrong Answer: The Case Against Algebra II." Harper's Magazine, September 2013, pp. 31-38. Retrieved on 12 October 2013 from http://www.robertferrell.net/wp-content/uploads/2013/08/Nicholson-Baker-Wrong-Answer-Harpers-Sept.-201

304e. Baker, Peter. "Obama Unveils Nonprofit for Young Minorities After Baltimore Unrest." New York Times. 4 May 2015. NYTimes.com. Retrieved on 4 May 2015 from http://www.nytimes.com/2015/05/05/us/politics/obama-my-brothers-keeper-alliance-minorities.html?hp&action=click&pgtype=Homepage&module=first-column-region&region=top-news&WT.nav=top-news&_r=0

304a. Barnett, Steven W., and Jason T. Hustedt. "Head Start's Lasting Benefits." Infants & Young Children, 18 (2005): 16-24. From the National Institute for Early Education Research, Rutgers, the State University of New Jersey, Brunswick. Retrieved on 23 November 2011 from http://depts.washington.edu/isei/iyc/barnett_hustedt18.1.pdf

304b. Baumeister, Roy F. "Chapter 9: Self-Concept, Self-Esteem, and Identity." Numerons.in. Retrieved on 14 January 2012 from http://numerons.files.wordpress.com/2012/04/self-concept-self-esteem-and-identity.pdf

305. Baumeister, Roy F., Jennifer D. Campbell, Joachim I. Krueger, and Kathleen D. Vohs. "Does High Self-Esteem Cause Better Performance, Interpersonal Success, Happiness, or Healthier Lifestyles?" Psychological Science in the Public Interest, 4 (May, 2003). Csom.umn.edu. Retrieved on 5 July 2010 from http://www.csom.umn.edu/Assets/71496.pdf

306. Bausell, R. Barker, William B. Moody, and Richard Crouse. "The Effect of Teaching on Teacher Learning." Journal of Research in Mathematics Education, 6 (March, 1975): 69-76. Jstor.org. Retrieved on 20 March 2010 from http://www.jstor.org/pss/748608

306a. Bennett, John T. "Critical Race Theory: A Cult of Anti-White Resentment." 22 March 2012. Americanthinker.com. Retrieved on 22 November 2013 from http://www.americanthinker.com/printpage/?url=http://www.americanthinker.com/articles/./2012/03/critical_race_theory_a_cult_of_anti-white_resentment.html

306b. Bill Cosby Speech Transcript. "Dr. Bill Cosby Speaks at the 50th Anniversary Commemoration of the Brown vs Topeka Board of Education Supreme Court Decision." Transcript kindly provided by Dr. Bill Cosby's public relations representatives. Eightcitiesmap.com. Retrieved on 23 May 2009 from http://www.eightcitiesmap.com/transcript_bc.htm

307. Blassingame, John W. The Slave Community: Plantation Life in the Antebellum South. New York: Oxford University Press, 1971; rev. ed., 1979. Quoted in Wikipedia contributors. Wikipedia, The Free Encyclopedia. "The Slave Community." Wikipedia.org. Retrieved on 24 October 2009 from http://en.wikipedia.org/wiki/The_Slave_Community

308. Bolton, Jessica Beth. "Examining the Effectiveness of a Social Learning Curriculum for Improving Social Skills and Self-Regulation Behaviors in Middle School Boys with Autism Spectrum Disorder or Social Skills Deficits." 2010. Psychology Dissertations. Paper 14. Digitalcommons.pcom. Retrieved on 12 August 2010 from http://digitalcommons.pcom.edu/psychology_dissertations/14

308a. The Booker T. Washington Society. Society Website. Retrieved on 4 October 2011 from http://btwsociety.org

308b. Boorstein, Michelle. "Pope says children have a right to grow up in a family with a father and a mother." 17 November 2014. Washingtonpost.com. Retrieved on 18 November 2014 from http://www.washingtonpost.com/local/pope-says-children-have-a-right-to-grow-up-in-a-family-with-a-father-and-a-mother/2014/11/17/4edebdc0-6e97-11e4-893f-86bd390a3340_story.html?wpisrc=nl-headlines&wpmm=1

309. Borman, Geoffrey D. and Laura T. Rachuba. "Academic Success Among Poor and Minority Students." Center for Research on the Education of Students Placed At Risk. Report No. 52. February 2001. Csos.jhu.edu. Retrieved on 3 November 2010 from http://www.csos.jhu.edu/crespar/techReports/Report52.pdf

309a. Bornstein, David. "Overcoming Poverty's Damage to Learning." The New York Times. 17 April 2015. NYTimes.com. Retrieved on 17 April 2015 from http://opinionator.blogs.nytimes.com/2015/04/17/overcoming-povertys-damage-to-learning/?_r=0

310. Brainy Quote. "W. E. B. Du Bois Quotes." Brainyquote.com. Retrieved on 2 January 2010 from http://www.brainyquote.com/quotes/authors/w/w_e_b_du_bois.html

310b. Broadwater, Luke. "300 Men March seeks to reclaim neighborhoods, one corner at a time." The Baltimore Sun. 6 May 2015. BaltimoreSun.com. Retrieved on 11 May 2015 from http://www.baltimoresun.com/news/maryland/baltimore-city/bs-md-ci-300-men-20150506-story.html#page=1

310a. Brooks, Arthur A. "A Formula for Happiness." The New York Times. 14 December 2013. NYTimes.com. Retrieved on 15 December 2013 from http://www.nytimes.com/2013/12/15/opinion/sunday/a-formula-for-happiness.html?_r=0

311. Brooks, David. "Mind over Muscle." The New York Times. 16 October 2005. NYTimes.com. Retrieved on 16 October 2005 from

http://www.select.nytimes.com/2005/10/16/opinion/16brooks.html?

312. _____. "The Underlying Tragedy." <u>The New York Times</u>. 15 January 2010. NYTimes.com. Retrieved on 15 January 2010 from http://www.nytimes.com/2010/01/15/opinion/15brooks.html?pagewanted=print

312a. _____. "Stairway to Wisdom." <u>The New York Times</u>. 15 May 2014. NYTimes.com. Retrieved on 16 May 2014 from http://www.nytimes.com/2014/05/16/opinion/brooks-stairway-to-wisdom.html?hp&rref=opinion&_r=0

313. Brown, William O., Steven B. Frates, Ian S. Rudge, and Richard L.Tradewell. "The Costs and Benefits of After School Programs: The Estimated Effects of the *After7 School Education and Safety Program Act of 2002.*" September, 2002. Daremontmakenna.edu. Retrieved on 11 December 2010 from http://www.daremontmakenna.edu/rose/publications/pdf/after_school.pdf

314. Brunner, Borgna. "Timeline of Affirmative Action Milestones." Infoplease.com. Retrieved on 28 May 2009 from. http://www.infoplease.com/spot/affirmativeactiontimeline1.html

314a. Bundy, Trey. "A Place at School Where Students Can Unload Stress and Worry." <u>The New York Times</u>. 3 November 2011. NYTimes.com. Retrieved on 4 November 201 1from http://www.nytimes.com/2011/11/04/us/a-place -at- school -where -students -can-unload-stress...

314c. Burke, Lindsey M. "The Every Student Succeeds Act: More Programs and Federal Intervention in Pre-K and K-12 Education." The Heritage Foundation, <u>Backgrounder</u>. No. 3085. 2 December 2015. Heritage.org. Retrieved on 14 December 2015 from http://www.heritage.org/research/reports/2015/12/the-every-student-succeeds-act-more-programs-and-federal-intervention-in-pre-k-and-k12-education

314b. Caldwell, Leon D., ed. "Academic Success for School-age Black Males." Special issue. Summer 2009. The Journal of Negro Education, 78 (3).

315. Carey, Benedict. "Brain Power: Studying Young Minds, and How to Teach Them." The New York Times. 21 December 2009. NYTimes.com. Retrieved on 21 December 2009 from http://www.nytimes.com/2009/12/21/health/research/21brain.html?_=1&ref=us&pagewa

315d. _____. "Diagnosis: Battered but Vibrant." The New York Times. 7 January 2013. NYTimes.com. Retrieved on 8 January 2013 from http://www.nytimes.com/2013/01/08/science/lessons-in-community-from-chicagos-south-si... 315c. Carlson, Helen B. "Identity and Character Formation." American Journal of Psychiatry, 111 (January 1, 1966): 821-23.

315e. Center for Research on Education Outcomes (CREDO). Stanford University. "National Charter School Study 2013." Retrieved on 13 July 2013 from http://credo.stanford.edu

315a. Cherry, Kendra. "'What is Emotional Intelligence? Definitions, History, and Measures of Emotional Intelligence." Psychology.about.com Guide. Retrieved on 26 December 2011 from http://psychology.about.com/od/personalitydevelopment/a/emotionalintell.htm?p=1

315f. Chavous, Tabbye M., Debra Hilkene Bernat, Karen Schmeelk-Cone, Cleopatra H. Caldwell, Laura Kohn-Wood, and Marc A. Zimmerman. "Racial Identity and Academic Attainment Among African American Adolescents." Child Development, 74(July/August 2003): 1076-90.

315b. Chetty, Raj, John N. Friedman, and Jonah Rockoff. "The Long-Term Impacts of Teachers: Teacher Value-Added and Students' Outcomes in Adulthood." December 2011. Obs.rc.fas.Harvard.eduk. Retrieved on 6 January 2012 from. http://obs.rc.fas.harvard.edu/va_exec_summ.pdf

316. Ciotti, P. "Money and School Performance: Lessons from the Kansas City Desegregation Experiment." <u>Cato Policy Analysis 298</u>. Cato.org. Retrieved on 25 July 2009 from <u>http://www.cato.org/pubs/pas/pa-298.html</u>

316a. Coalition for Evidence-Based Policy. "Complete List of Interventions and Study Reports Reviewed Under the Top Tier Evidence Initiative as of February 2009." February 2009. Retrieved on 22 November 2011 from <u>http://www.evidencebasedpolicy.org/docs/Comprehensive%20List%20of%Early%20Childhood%20Studies20Feb09.pdf</u>

317. Cohen, Patricia. "'Culture of Poverty' Makes a Comeback." <u>The New York Times</u>. 18 October 2010. NYTimes.com. Retrieved on 18 October 2010 from <u>http://www.nytimes.com/2010/10/18/us/18poverty.html?ref=us&pagewanted=print</u>

318. Collins, William J. and Robert A. Margo. "Race and Home Ownership, 1900 to 1990." <u>NBER Working Paper No. 7277</u>. August, 1999. Nber.org. Retrieved on February 2010 from <u>http://www.nber.org/papers/w7277</u>

318b. Commons.wikimedia.org. "File:Booker T. Washington.jpg." 3 June 2014. Commons.wikimedia.org. Retrieved on 1 January 2015 from <u>http://commons.wikimedia.org/wiki/File:Booker T. Washington.jpg</u>

318c. _____. "File: Booker T. Washington c1899 by Strohmeyer & Wyman.png." 3 June 2014. Commons.wikimedia.org. Retrieved on 1 January 2015 from <u>http://commons.wikimedia.org/wiki/File:Booker T Washington c1899 by Strohmeyer %26 Wyman.png</u>

318d. _____. "File:Madison County, Alabama. (African-American) agents and rural nurse with movable school. (The Booker T. Washington... --NARA—512801.tif." 18 December 2014. Commons.wikimedia.org. Retrieved on 1 January 2015 from <u>http://commons.wikimedia.org/wiki/File:Madison County, Alabama. (African-American) agents and rural nurse with</u>

movable school. (The Booker T. Washington... - NARA - 512801.tif#filehistory

318e. _____. "File:Booker Washington and Theodore Roosevelt at Tuskegie [sic] Institute.jpg." 30 May 2012. Commons.wikimedia.org. Retrieved on 1 January 2015 from http://commons.wikimedia.org/wiki/File:Booker_Washington_and_Theodore_Roosevelt_at_Tuskegie_Institute.jpg

318f. _____. "File: Tuskegee Institute – faculty.jpg." 9 December 2012. Commons.wikimedia.org. Retrieved on 2 January 2015 from http://commons.wikimedia.org/wiki/File:Tuskegee_Institute_-_faculty.jpg

318g. _____. "File:Booker T. Washington Lecture, 1906, JPG." 28 November 2014. Commons.wikimedia.org. Retrieved on 2 January 2015 from http://commons.wikimedia.org/wiki/File:Booker_T._Washington_Lecture,_1906.JPG

318h. _____. "File:BookerTWashington1909VAVWtour.jpg." 28 November 2014. Commons.wikimedia.org. Retrieved on 2 January 2014 from http://commons.wikimedia.org/wiki/File:BookerTWashington1909VAVWtour.jpg

318i. _____. "File:Booker T Washington New Orleans 1915.jpg." 14 February 2012. Commons.wikimedia.org. Retrieved on 2 January 2015 from http://commons.wikimedia.org/wiki/File:Booker_T_Washington_New_Orleans_1915.jpg

318j. _____. "File:Booker T Washington burial 3c11868r.jpg." 17 December 2013. Commons.wikimedia.org. Retrieved on 2 January 2015 from http://commons.wikimedia.org/wiki/File:Booker_T_Washington_burial_3c11868r.jpg

318k. _____. "File: Booker T Washington 1940 Issue-10c/jpg." 11 June 2014. Commons.wikimedia.org. Retrieved on 2 January 2015 from http://commons.wikimedia.org/wiki/File:Booker_T_Washington_1940_Issue-10c.jpg

318l. Wikimedia Commons. "File: Frederick Douglass Portrait.jpg." 4 November 2014. Commons.wikimedia.org. Retrieved on 3 January 2015 from http://commons.wikimedia.org/wiki/File:Frederick_Douglass_portrait.jpg

318m. _____. "File: Martin Luther King Jr NYWTS.jpg." 3 March 2014. Commons.wikimedia.org. Retrieved on 3 January 2015 from http://commons.wikimedia.org/wiki/File:Martin_Luther_King_Jr_NYWTS.jpg.

318n. _____. "File:WEB DuBois 1918.jpg." 19 May 2014. Commons.wikimedia.org. Retrieved on 3 January 2015 from http://commons.wikimedia.org/wiki/File:WEB_DuBois_1918.jpg

318o. _____. "File: Booker T Washington retouched flattened-crop.jpg." 28 January 2014. Commons.wikimedia.org. Retrieved on 3 January 2015 from http://commons.wikimedia.org/wiki/File:Booker_T_Washington_retouched_flattened-crop.jpg

318a. Conger, R.D., G.H. Elder, F.O. Loren, K.J. Conger, R.L. Simons, L.B. Whitbeck, S. Huck, and J. Melby. "Linking Economic Hardship to Marital Quality and Instability." Journal of Marriage and the Family, 52 (1990): 643-56.

319. The Conservative Beacon. "Henry Louis Gates Jr.: Race Baiter." 27 July 2009. Theconservativebeacon.net. Retrieved on 20 November 2010 from http://www.theconservativebeacon.net/2009/07/27/henry-louis-gates-jr-race-baiter/

320. Cook, Philip J. and Jens Ludwig. "The Burden of 'Acting White': Do Black Adolescents Disparage Academic Achievement?" In The Black-White Test Score Gap, Ch. 10, p. 375-400. Edited by Christopher Jencks and Meredith Philips. Brookings Institution Press, 1998. Books.google.com. Retrieved on 14 July 2008 from http://books.google.com/books?id=Ywb7r1oOxJYC

320a. Council on Foundations. "Thinking About Becoming a Private Foundation? Let's Run the Numbers." Prepared by the Council on Foundations. March 28, 2003. Retrieved on 7 July 2010 from http://www.twintierscf.org/images/pdfs/LetsRuntheNumbers.pdf

321. Council of the Great City Schools. A Call for Change: The Social and Educational Factors Contributing to the Outcomes of Black Males in Urban Schools. Washington, D.C.: 1301 Pennsylvania Avenue, NW, Suite 702, 120p. Cgcs.org. Retrieved on 8 December 2010 from http://www.cgcs.org/cgcs/Call_For_Change.pdf

321c. The Council of Independent Colleges. "Stipends and Vouchers." Cic.edu. Retrieved on 20 December 2014 from http://www.cic.edu/Programs-and-Services/Programs/Walmart-College-Success/Pages/Stipends-Vouchers.aspx

321a. Cowell, Alan. "Again, No African Leader Wins Annual Good Governance Prize." The New York Times. 14 October 2013. NYTimes.com. Retrieved on 15 October 2013 from http://www.nytimes.com/2013/10/15/world/africa/african-governance-prize-again- withhe…

321b. Craigie, Terry-Ann, Jeanne Brooks-Gunn, and Jane Waldfogel. "Family Structure, Family Stability and Early Child Wellbeing." Center for Research on Child Wellbeing, Princeton University, Princeton NJ 08544. Retrieved on 6 June 2014 from http://crcw.princeton.edu/workingpapers/WP10-14-FF.pdf

322. The Crisis Magazine. "History." Thecrisimagazine.com. Retrieved on 25 April 2010 from http://www.thecrisismagazine.com/TheCrisisHistory2.html

322a. Cruz, Julissa. "Marriage: More than a Century of Change (FP-13-13)." 2013. National Center for Family and Marriage Research. Retrieved on 9 May 2015 from http://ncfmr.bgsu.edu/pdf/family_profiles/file131529.pdf.

323. Dads4kids.com. "Statistics of a Fatherless America." Photius.com. Retrieved on 24 February 2011 from http://www.photius.com/feminocracy/facts_on_fatherless_kids.html

323b. Dee, Thomas and Brian A. Jacob. "Evaluating NCLB." Summer 2010, Vol. 10, No.3. Educationnext.org. Retrieved on 3 May 2014 from http://educationnext.org/evaluating-nclb/

323a. Delgado, Richard and Jean Stefancic. "from Critical Race Theory: An Introduction." 27 November 2006. Nyupress.org. Retrieved on 22 November 2013 from http://www.odec.umd.edu/CD/RACE/CRT.PDF

324. DeParle, Jason. "Project to Rescue Needy Stumbles Against the Persistence of Poverty." <u>New York Times</u>, 15 May 1999, p. A1.

325. Diamond, John B. "Are We Barking Up the Up the Wrong Tree? Rethinking Oppositional Culture Explanations for the Black/White Achievement Gap." Agi.Harvard.edu. Retrieved on 5 September 2009 from www.agi.harvard.edu/events/download.php?id=79.

325b. Dickens, William T. and James R. Flynn. "Black Americans Reduce the Racial IQ Gap: Evidence from Standardized Samples." <u>Psychological Science</u>, 17 (October, 2006): 913-20. Brookings.edu. Retrieved on 20 December 2012 from http://www.brookings.edu/views/papers/dickens/20060619_IQ.pdf

325a. Dickerson, Debra J. "Colorblind: Barack Obama Would Be the Great Black Hope in the Next Presidential Race -- If He Were Actually Black." 22 January 2007. Salon.com. Retrieved on 11 February 2012 from http://www.salon.com/2007/01/22/obama_161/print/

325c. Dienst, Jonathan. "Gunman "Assinates" 2 NYPD Officers in Brooklyn, Kills Self: Officials." 21 December 2014. Nbcnewyork.com. Retrieved on 21 December 2014 from http://www.nbcnewyork.com/news/local/2-Police-Officers-Shot-in-Brooklyn-Myrtle-Avenue-Tompkins-Avenue-286463091.html

326. Dillon, Sam. "Persistent Racial Gap Seen in Students' Test Scores." <u>The New York Times</u>. 28 April 2009. NYTimes.com. Retrieved on 29 April 2009 from http://www.nytimes.com/2009/04/29/education/29scores.html?_r=1&hp=&pagewanted=pr...

327. _____. "Report Questions Duncan's Policy of Closing Failing Schools." The New York Times. 29 October 2009. NYTimes.org. Retrieved on 29 October 2009 from http://www.nytimes.com/2009/10/29/education/29schools.html?ref=education&pagewant...

328. _____. "Method to Grade Teachers Provokes Battles." The New York Times. NYTimes.org. Retrieved on 1 September 2010 from http://www.nytimes.com/2010/09/01/education/01teacher.html?ref=us&src=me&pagewante...

328a. Dodd, Aileen. Georgia Charter Schools Association (GCSA). An Impact Paper. "Single-Gender Education: A Strategy to Help Boys in Urban Charter Schools Achieve." Retrieved on 24 November 2015 from http://www.gacharters.org/wp-content/uploads/SingleGenderEducation_Impact20151.pdf

329. Doolittle, Peter E. and William G. Camp. "Constructivism: The Career and Technical Education Perspective." Journal of Vocational and Technical Education, 16 (Fall 1999): 23-46. Scholar.lib.vt.edu. Retrieved on 15 February 2011 from http://www.scholar.lib.vt.edu/ejournals/JVTE/vl6n1/doolittle.html

329a. Dove, Shawn. "Sponsor's Comment: The Campaign for Black Male Achievement." The Journal of Negro Education, 78 (Summer 2009): 193-94. Academic Success for School-age Black Males [Special issue].

330. Downey, Douglas B. and James W. Ainsworth-Darnell. "The Search for Oppositional Culture among Black Students." American Sociological Review, 67 (February, 2002): 156-64. Jstor.org. Retrieved on 21 March 2008 from http://links.jstor.org/sici?sici=0003-1224%2820020 2%2967%3A1%3C156% 3ATSFOCA%3E2.0.CO%3B2-Y

330a. Dubner, Stephen J. "Toward a Unified Theory of Black America." New York Times Magazine. 20 March 2005. NYTimes.com. Retrieved on 20 March 2005 from http://www.nytimes.com/2005/03/20/magazine/20HARVARD.html?pagewanted=all

331. DuBois, W. E. Burghardt. "The Talented Tenth." September 1903. Retrieved on 11 July 2009 from http://teachingamericanhistory.org/library/document/the-talented-tenth/.

332. _____. "A Litany of Atlanta: Done at Atlanta, in the Day of Death, 1906." In The Book of Negro Poetry. Edited by James Weldon Johnson. New York: Harcourt, Brace and Company, 1922. Bartleby.com. October 2002. Retrieved on 1 November 2010 from http://www. bartleby.com/269/26.html

332a. Duckworth, Angela L. "Grit: Perseverance and Passion for Long-Term Goals." Minnesota Youth Hockey Coaches Association e-Newsletter. Assets.ngin.com. Retrieved on 10 January 2012 from http://assets.ngin.com/attachments/documents/0005/2337/Grit.pdf

332b. Duckworth, Angela L., C. Peterson, M. D. Matthews, and D. R. Kelly. "Grit: Perseverance and Passion for Long-Term Goals." 2007. Sas.upenn.edu. Retrieved on 8 January 2012 from http://www.sas.upenn.edu/~duckwort/images/Grit%20JPSP.pdf

333. Duncan, Greg J., Hans Bos, Lisa A. Gennetian, and Heather Hill. "New Hope: A Thoughtful and Effective Approach to "Make Work Pay."" Northwestern Journal of Law and Social Policy, 4 (Winter, 2009): 101-15. Law.northwestern.edu. Retrieved on 13 April 2010 from http://www.law.northwestern.edu/journals/njlsp/v4/n1/6/6Duncan.pdf

334. Durlak, Joseph A. and Roger P. Weissberg. "The Impact of After-School Programs That Promote Personal and Social Skills." Collaborative for Academic, Social, and Emotional Learning (CASEL), 2007. Casel.org. Retrieved on 16 November 2010 from http;//www.casel.org/downloads/ASP.Full.pdf

334a. Dynarski, Susan. "Urban Charter Schools Often Succeed. Suburban Ones Often Don't." The New York Times. 20 November 2015. NYTimes.com. Retrieved on 22 November 2015 from http://www.nytimes.com/2015/11/22/upshot/a-suburban-urban-divide-in-charter-school-success-rates.html?_r=0

335. Eckholm, Erik. "Plight Deepens for Black Men, Studies Warn." The New York Times. 20 March 2006. NYTimes.com. Retrieved on 20 March 2006 from http://www.nytimes.com/2006/03/20/national/20blackmen.html?

336. _____. "The Smoking Scourge Among Urban Blacks." The New York Times. 20 October 2007. NYTimes.com. Retrieved on 20 October 2007 from http://www.nytimes.com/2007/10/20/health/20tobacco.html?

337. _____. "Murders by Black Teenagers Rise, Bucking a Trend." The New York Times. 29 December 2008. NYTimes.com. Retrieved on 29 December 2008 from http://www.nytimes.com/2008/12/29/us/29homicide.html?

338. Education Week. Research Center "After-School Programs." 10 September 2004. Edweek.org. Retrieved on 19 June 2009 from http://www.edweek.org/re/issues/after-school-programs/?print=1

339. Ehrenhalt, Alan. "Remember when Profanity Meant Something?" [Health societies need a decent supply of verbal taboos, if only as yardsticks by which ordinary people can measure and define themselves.] USA Today, 9 October 1996, p. 13A.

340. Eightcitiesmap.com. "Dr. Bill Cosby Speaks." Bill Cosby Speech Transcript at 50th Anniversary Commemoration of the Brown vs. Topeka Board of Education Supreme Court Decision. Delivered 17 May 2004. Eightcitiesmap.com. Retrieved on 23 May 2010 from http://www.eightcitiesmap.com/transcript_bc.htm

341. Elias, Mary. "Academics Lose Relevance for Black Boys." USA Today, 2 December 1997, p. D1.

341b. Eligon, John. "One Slogan, Many Methods: Black Lives Matter Enters Politics." The New York Times. 18 November 2015. NYTimes.com. Retrieved on 19 November 2015 from http://www.nytimes.com/2015/11/19/us/one-slogan-many-methods-black-lives-matter-enters-politics.html?_r=0

341a. Elliott, Diana B., Kristy Krivickas, Matthew W. Brault, and Rose M. Kreider. United States Census Bureau. "Historical Marriage Trends from 1890-2010: A Focus on Race Differences." 7 May 2015. Retrieved on 7 May 2015 from http://www.census.gov/hhes/socdemo/marriage/data/acs/ElliottetalPAA2012presentation.pdf

342. Engel, Susan. "Teach Your Teachers Well." The New York Times. 2 November 2009. NYTimes.com. Retrieved on 16 November 2009 from http://www.nytimes.com/2009/11/02/opinion/02engel.html?pagewanted=print

343. Farkas, George, Christy Lleras, and Steve Maczuga. "Does Oppositional Culture Exist in Minority and Poverty Peer Groups?" American Sociological Review, 67:148-55. Cited in Karolyn Tyson, William Darity Jr., and Domini R. Castellino, "It's Not 'A Black Thing': Understanding the Burden of Acting White and Other Dilemmas of High Achievement," American Sociological Review, 70 (August, 2005): 582-605. Tc.columbia.edu. Retrieved on 10 April 2009 from http://www.tc.columbia.edu/students/see/events/Darity et al Understanding Burden Acting White.pdf

344. Favro, Tony. "Black American men hardest hit by dysfunctional US inner cities." Excerpted from The New York Times. 20 March 2006. City Mayors Society. Citymayors.com. Retrieved on 2 July 2007 from http://www.citymayors.com/society/us_blackmen.html.

344a. Ferdman, Roberto A. "The remarkable thing that happens to poor kids when you give their parents a little money." The Washington Post. 8 October 2015. Washingtonpost.com. Retrieved on 9 October 2015 from https://www.washingtonpost.com/news/wonk/wp/2015/10/08/the-remarkable-ways-a-little-money-can-change-a-childs-personality-for-life/

345. Ferguson, Ronald F. "A Diagnostic Analysis of Black-White GPA Disparities in Shaker Heights, Ohio." The College Board. In Brookings Papers on Education, 2001, p. 347-414. Edited by Diane Ravitch. Washington, D.C.: Brookings Institute Press, 2001. Collegeboard.com. Retrieved on 19 June 2009 from http://www.

collegeboard.com/about/association/academic/pdf/ronaldferguson.pdf

346. _____. "Addressing Racial Disparities in High-Achieving Suburban Schools." NCREL Policy Issues. A Research-Based Analysis of Education Issues. Issue 13, December 2002. Ncrel.org. Retrieved on 19 June 2009 from http://www.ncrel.org/policy/pubs/pdfs/pivol13.pdf

347. _____. "Toward Skilled Parenting & Transformed Schools Inside a National Movement for *EXCELLENCE WITH EQUITY.*" Wiener Center for Social Policy, John F. Kennedy School of Government, Harvard University. October 21, 2005. Accessednetwork.org. Retrieved on 8 August 2009 from http://www.accessednetwork.org/news/policy/71_Ferguson_paper.ed.pdf

348. _____. "Parenting practices, teenage lifestyles, and academic achievement among African American children." Focus, 25 (Spring-Summer, 2007). Irp.wisc.edu. Retrieved on 12 September 2010 from http://www.irp.wisc.edu/publications/focus/pdfs/foc251c.pdf

349. Fetzer Institute. "Research on Love and Forgiveness." Fetzer.org. Retrieved on 26 June 2010 from http://www.fetzer.org/loveandforgive/about/about-research-on-love-a-forgiveness

349b. Fields, Jason M. and Kristin E. Smith. "Poverty, Family Structure, and Child Well-Being: Indicators From the SIPP." Population Division Working Paper No. 23. U.S. Bureau of Census, Population Division, Washington, D.C. April 1998. Retrieved on 7 June 2014 from http://www.census.gov/population/www/documentation/twps0023/twps0023.html

349a. Fisher, Max. "Why Kenyans Make Such Great Runners: A Story of Genes and Cultures: How an ethnic minority that makes up 0.06% of the world's population came to dominate most of its long-distance races." Theatlantic.com. Retrieved on 28 July 2012 from http://www.theatlantic.com/international/print/2012/why-kenyans-make-such-great-run...

350. Flashman, Jennifer. "Are Black Students Punished for 'Acting White"?: Race, Academic Achievement, and Friendship Choices." California Center for Population Research, University of California-Los Angeles. On-Line Working Paper Series. Last revised: October, 2008. Ccpr.uda.edu. Retrieved on 3 August 2009 from http://papers.ccpr.uda.edu/papers/PWP-CCPR-2008-065/PWP-CCPR-2008-065.pdf

350a. _____. "Academic Achievement and Its Impact on Friend Dynamics." Sociology of Education, 85 (January 2012): 61-80. Originally published online 15 August 2011. Sagepublications.com. Retrieved on 26 June 2012 from http://www.soe.sagepub.com/content/85/1/61

350b. _____. "Different Preferences or Different Opportunities? Explaining Race Differentials in the Academic Achievement of Friends." Social Science Research, 41 (July 2012): 888-903. Elsevier.com. Retrieved on 26 June 2012 from http://dx.doi.org/10.1016/j.ssresearch.2012.03.001

350e. _____. "Friend Effects and Racial Disparities in Academic Achievement." Sociological Science, 1: (July 7, 2014): 260-76. Retrieved on 4 December 2014 from http://www.sociologicalscience.com/articles-vol1-17-260/

350c. Flynt, Cynthia J. "Predicting Academic Achievement from Classroom Behaviors." Dissertation submitted to the Faculty of the Virginia Polytechnic Institute and State University in partial fulfillment of the requirements for the degree of Doctor of Philosophy. August 28, 2008. Retrieved on 20 December 2012 from http://scholar.lib.vat.edu/theses/available/etd-09162008-100711/unrestricted/Dissertation.pdf

350d. Ford, Chad. "Jimmy Butler Finds a New Home, Hope." ESPN.com. 18 June 2011. Retrieved on 25 June 2011 from http://espn.go.com/espn/print?id=6676517&type=Columnist&imagePrint=off

351. Ford, Donna Y. and J. John Harris. "Perceptions and Attitudes of Black Students toward School, Achievement, and Other Educational

Variables." Child Development, 67 (1996): 1`141-52. Cited in Karolyn Tyson, William Darity Jr., and Domini R. Castellino, "It's Not 'A Black Thing': Understanding the Burden of Acting White and Other Dilemmas of High Achievement," American Sociological Review, 70 (August, 2005): 582-605. Tc.columbia.edu. Retrieved on 5 December 2009 from http://www.tc.columbia.edu/students/see/events/Darity et al Understanding Burden Acting White.pdf

352. Ford, Richard Thompson. "Why the Poor Stay Poor." Book Review: More than Just Race: Being Black and Poor in the Inner City, by William Julius Wilson. New York: W. W. Norton & Company, 2009. NYTimes.com. Retrieved on 2 January 2010 from http://www.nytimes.com/2009/03/08/books/review/Ford-t.html?_r=1&pagewanted=print

353. Freedman, Samuel G. "Little-Noticed Crisis at Black Colleges." The New York Times. 3 August 2005. NYTimes.com. Retrieved on 3 August 2005 from http://www.nytimes.com/2005/08/03/education/03education.html?

353a. Fryer, Roland G., Jr. "An Empirical Analysis of 'Acting White.' Harvard University and NBER. Economics. harvard.edu. July 2009. Retrieved on 14 June 2012 from http://www.economics.harvard.edu/faculty/fryer/files/Empirical%2Banalysis%2Bof%2B%2527acting%2Bwhi

353b. _____. "Acting White": The Social Price Paid by the Best and Brightest Minority Students." Education Next, 6 (Winter 2006). Educationnext.org. Retrieved on 4 December 2009 from http://educationnext.org/actingwhite/

354. Fryer, Roland G., Jr. and Paul Torelli. "An Empirical Analysis of 'Acting White.'" NBER Working Paper No. 11334. Agi.Harvard.edu. Retrieved on 1 May 2005 from http://www.agi.harvard.edu/Search/download.php?id=94

355. Gabriel, Trip. "Despite Push, Success at Charter Schools is Mixed." The New York Times. 2 May 2010. NYTimes.com. Retrieved

on 4 May 2010 from http://www.nytimes.com/2010/05/02/education/02charters.html?ref=us&src=me&pagewant ...

356. _____. "Proficiency of Black Students is Found to be Far Lower than Expected." The New York Times. 9 November 2010. NYTimes.com. Retrieved on 9 November 2010 from http://www.nytimes.com/2010/11/09/education/09gap.html?ref=us&src=me&pagewanted

357. Gale Reference Team. "Black males' Rampant Joblessness, high drop-out rate, incarceration dooming black community: study.(NATIONAL REPORT)(Statistical data)." Jet, 26 March 2007. Media-server.amazon.com. Retrieved on 16 July 2007 from http://media-server.amazon.com/exec/drm/amzproxy.cgi/McQOIBHj+oiV8yi/4gcOI8QksC...

358. Gayl, Chrisanne L. "After-School Programs: Expanding Access and Ensuring Equality." Progressive Policy Institute. Policy Report. July, 2004. Ppionline.org. Retrieved on 4 December 2010 from http://www.ppionline.org/documents/afterschool.0704.pdf

358b. Genju, Lynette. "Personal Identity." Bodhi Leaf. Reflections on the Dharma. 12 January 2010. Bodhileaf.wordpress.com. Retrieved on 8 October 2013 from http://bodhileaf.wordpress.com/2010/01/12/personal-identity/

358a. Germany, Kent. "War on Poverty." University of Virginia faculty website. 1960s. Faculty.virginia.edu. Retrieved on 18 September 2012 from http://www.faculty.virginia.edu/sixties/readings/War%20on%20Poverty%20entry%20Poverty%Encyclopedia.pdf

359. Gollan, Jennifer. "Willie Brown Academy, Born in 1992 with High Hopes, Will Close in May, a Failure." The New York Times. 17 April 2011. NYTimes.com. Retrieved on 18 April 2011 from http://www.nytimes.com/2011/04/17/us/17bcshort.html?ref=education&pagewanted=print

360. Goodman, Walter. "TELEVISION REVIEW; Wisdom Won Behind Bars: 'It's Us Who's Killing Us.'" The New

York Times. 4 May 1999. NYTimes.com. Retrieved on 18 April 2011 from http://www.nytimes.com/gst/fullpage.html?res=9901E2D6173CF937A3576COA961F9582...

361. Gootman, Elissa. "Few Minorities Get Best High School Diplomas." The New York Times. 30 November 2005. NYTimes.com Retrieved on 30 November 2005 from http://www.nytimes.com/2005/11/30/education/30graduates.html?

362. _____. "Mixed Results on Paying City Students to Pass Tests." The New York Times. 20 August 2008. NYTimes.com. Retrieved on 20 August 2008 from http://www.nytimes.com/2008/08/20/education/20cash.html?

363. Gould, Emily. "Kanye West to George W. Bush: I'm really, really sorry. Kind of. Really." NYDailyNews.com. Retrieved on 12 November 2010 from http://www.nydailynews.com/fdcp?1295725420468

363a. Greelman, James. New York *World*, September, 1895. Cited in Louis R. Harlan, Booker T. Washington: The Making of a Black Leader, 1856-1901, p. 219-20. New York: Oxford University Press, 1972.

364. Green, Elizabeth. "Roland Fryer Returns, Study: $75M teacher pay initiative did not improve achievement." 7 January 2011. Gothamschoolsorg. Retrieved on 4 April 2011 from http://gothamschools.org/2011/03/07/study -75m - teacher -pay- initiative-did-not-improve-achievement/

365. Greene, Jay P. and Marcus A. Winters. "Leaving Boys Behind: Public High School Graduation Rates." Center for Civic Innovation a the Manhattan Institute. Civic Report No. 48. April 2006. Files.eric.ed.gov. Retrieved on 9 November 2013 from. http://files.eric.ed.gov/fulltext/ED491633.pdf

365a. Guyana.org. "The Following is a Message from Al Sharpton to Herman Cain." Guyana News and Information Discussion Forums. Political Discussions. 11 November 2011. Guyanafriends.

com. Retrieved on 23 November 2011 from http://guyanafriends.com/eve/forums/a/tpc/f/860694972/m/28920119051

365b. Haberman, Clyde. "Back in New York With the Same Passion, but to Less Fire and Smoke." 1 December 2013. NYTimes.com. Retrieved on 2 December 2013 from http://www.nytimes.com/2013/12/02/nyregion/back-in-new-york-with-the-same-passion-but-less-fire-and-smoke.html?_r=0

365c. Hall, Allan. "Now Oprah says sorry: Chat show queen says she regrets ever mentioning the racist handbag incident and insists it got blown up after Swiss sales assistant brands her a liar." 13 August 2013. Dailymail.co.uk. Retrieved on 4 December 2014 from http://www.dailymail.co.uk/news/article-2391313/Oprah-Winfrey-says-regrets-mentioning-handbag-racism-incident-Zurich.html

366. Hall, L. Michael. "Super-Charge Your Ego-Strength." Neurosemantics.com. Retrieved on 19 January 2010 from http://www.neurosemantics.com/ns-model/super-charge-your-ego-strength

366b. Hamdan, Sara. "Children Thrive in Rural Colombia's Flexible Schools." The New YorkTimes. 10 November 2013. NYTimes.com. Retrieved on 10 November 2013 from http://www.nytimes.com/2013/11/11/world/americas/children-thrive-in-rural-colombias-flexible-schools.html?ref=education

366a. Hanushek, Eric A. "How Well Do We Understand Achievement Gaps." Stanford University, NBER, and CESifo. May 2010. Retrieved on 21 November 2011 from http://www.sesp.northwestern.edu/docs/how_well_do_we_understand_achievement_gaps_pdf

367. Harlem Children's Zone (HCZ). "The Harlem Children's Zone Project." Hcz.org. Retrieved on 23 January 2008 from http://www.hcz.org//programs/the-hcz-project

367b. Harper, Brian E. and Bruce W. Tuckman. "Racial Identity Beliefs and Academic Achievement: Does Being Black Hold Students Back?" Social Psychology of Education, 9 (2006): 381-403.

367a. Harris, Angel L. "I (Don't) Hate School: Revisiting Oppositional Culture Theory of Blacks' Resistance to Schooling." Social Forces, 85 (December 2006): 797-833. Project MUSE. Published by The University of North Carolina Press. Princeton.edu. Retrieved on 8 June 2012 from http://www.princeton.edu/~angelh/Website/Studies/Article%203%20(Social%20Forces%20'06).pdf

367d. Harris, Elizabeth A. "Suspension Rules Altered in New York City's Revision of School Discipline Code." The New York Times. 13 February 2015. NYTimes.com. Retrieved on 19 February 2015 from http://www.nytimes.com/2015/02/14/nyregion/suspension-rules-altered-in-new-york-citys-revision-of-school-discipline-code.html

367e. Harris, Gardner. "Obama, Pushing Criminal Justice Reform, Defends 'Black Lives Matter.'" The New York Times. 22 October 2015. NYTimes.com. Retrieved on 23 October 2015 from http://www.nytimes.com/2015/10/23/us/politics/obama-in-call-for-reform-defends-the-black-lives-matter-movement.html

367c. Haskins, Ron. "Social Programs That Work." The New York Times. 31 December 2014. NYTimes.com. Retrieved on 31 December 2014 from. http://www.nytimes.com/2015/01/01/opinion/social-programs-that-work.html

368. Heckman, James J. and Paul A. Fontaine. "The American High School Graduation Rate: Trends and Levels." Institute for the Study of Labor (IZA). Discussion Paper No. 3216. December, 2007. Buildingbrighterfutures.net. Retrieved on 7 November 2009 from http://ftp.iza.org/dp3216.pdf

369. Heckman, James, Seong Hyeok Moon, Rodrigo Pinto, Peter Savelyev, and Adam Yavitz. Centre for Microdata Methods and Practice. "Analyzing Social Experiments as Implemented: Evidence from the HighScope Perry Preschool Program." In Quantitative Economics, 1 (July, 2010): 1-46. Qeconomics.org. Retrieved on 3 December 2010 from http://www.qeconomics.org/supp/8/supplement.pdf

370. Henry, Tamara. "Black Graduates Answer Calling." USA Today, 30 September 1997, p. D1.

371. Herbert, Bob. "Death at an Early Age." New York Times, 2 December 1996, p. A15.

372. _____. "Young, Jobless, Hopeless." New York Times, 6 February 2003, p. A39.

373. _____. "Breakin. g Away." New York Times, 10 July 2003. NYTimes.com. Retrieved on 10 July 2003 from http://www.nytimes.com/2003/07/10/opinion/10HERB.html

374. _____. "Blowing the Whistle on Gangsta Culture." The New York Times. 22 December 2005. NYTimes.com. Retrieved on 22 December 2005 from http://www.select.nytimes.com/2005/12/22/opinion/22herbert.html?

375, _____. "A New Civil Rights Movement." The New York Times. 26 December 2005. NYTimes.com. Retrieved on 26 December 2005 from http://select.nytimes.com/2005/12/26/opinion/26herbert.html?

376. _____. "The Lost Children." The New York Times. 30 January 2006. NYTimes.com. Retrieved on 30 January 2006 from http://select.nytimes.com/2006/01/30/opinion/30herbert.html?

377. _____. "Education, Education, Education." The New York Times. 5 March 2007. NYTimes.com. Retrieved on 5 March 2007 from http://www.nytimes.com/2007/03/05/opinion/05herbert.html?hp=&pagewanted=print.

378. _____. "Tough, Sad and Smart." The New York Times. 16 October 2007. NYTimes.com. Retrieved on 17 October 2007 from http://www.nytimes.com/2007/10/16/opinion/16

379. _____. "In Search of Education Leaders." The New York Times. 5 December 2009. NYTimes.com. Retrieved on 5

December 2009 from http://www.nytimes.com/2009/12/05/opinion/05herbert.htl?_r=1&hp=&pagewanted=print

380. Hernandez, Javier C. "City's Graduation Rates Improve." The New York Times. 22 June 2009. City Room. Blogging from the Five Boroughs. Cityroom.blogs.nytimes.com. Retrieved on 22 June 2009 from http://cityroom.blogs.nytimes.com/2009/06/22/citys-graduation-rates-improve/?pagemode

380a. Hevesi, Dennis. "William Raspberry, Prizewinning Columnist, Dies at 76." The New York Times. 17 July 2012. NYTimes.com. Retrieved on 18 July 2012 from http://www.nytimes.com/2012/07/18/us/william-raspberry-columnist-dies-at-76.html?page...

380b. HighScope Educational Research Foundation. "Long-Term Benefits of Head Start Study Fact Sheet." 2011. Highscope.org. Retrieved on 21 November 2011 from http://www.highscope.org/conent.asp?contentid=260

381. History and Politics Out Loud. "Martin Luther King Jr. "I Have a Dream" speech. 28 August 1963. Hpol.org. Retrieved on 7 June 2009 from http://www.hpol.org/transcript.php?id=72

382. History Tools.org. "Booker T. Washington's 'Atlanta Compromise' Speech, 18 September 1895." Historytools.org. Retrieved on 7 April 2009 from http://www.historytools.org/sources/Washington-Atlanta.pdf

382a. Holder, Eric. "Text of Holder Speech on Trayvon Martin Case." The Wall Street Journal. 16 July 2013. Blogs.wsj.com. Retrieved on 17 July 2013 from http://blogs.wsj.com/washwire/2013/07/16/text-of-holder-speech-on-trayvon-martin-case/t...

383. Holland, Spencer H. "A Radical Approach to Educating Young Black Males." Education Week. 25 March 1987. Edweek.org. Retrieved on 14 June 2009 from http://www.edweek.org/ew/articles/1987/03/25/26holl.h06.html?tkn=QNYFXAe6c30ZW

383b. Hollingsworth, Barbara. "Cost of College Textbooks Is 864 Percent Higher in 2014 Than in 1978." 28 April 2014. Cnsnews.com. Retrieved on 20 December 2014 from http://cnsnews.com/news/article/barbara-hollingsworth/cost-college-textbooks-864-percent-higher-2014-1978

383a. Hopkinson, Natalie. "Why School Choice Fails." The New York Times. 4 December 2011. NYTimes.com. Retrieved on 5 December 2011 from http://www.nytimes.com/2011/12/05/opinion/why-school-choice-fails.html?_r=1&hp=&pa...

384. Horvat, Erin McNamara and Kristine Lewis. "Reassessing the 'Burden of Acting White': The Importance of Peer Groups in Managing Academic Success," Sociology of Education, 76 (2003): 265-80. Cited in Karolyn Tyson, William Darity Jr., and Domini R. Castellino, "It's Not 'A Black Thing': Understanding the Burden of Acting White and Other Dilemmas of High Achievement," American Sociological Review, 70 (August, 2005): 582-605. Tc.columbia.edu. Retrieved on 2 June 2007 from http://www.tc.columbia.edu/students/see/events/Darity_et_al_Understanding_Burden_Acting_White.pdf

385. Hu, Winnie. "To Close Gap, Schools Focus on Black Boys." The New York Times. 9 April 2007. NYTimes.com. Retrieved on 10 April 2007 from http://www.nytimes.com/2007/04/09/nyregion/09school.html?ei=5087%OA&em=&em=&en=Oe...

386. Hudgins, Edward Wren. "Examining the Effectiveness of Affective Education." Psychology in the Schools, 16 (October, 1979): 581-85. Onlinelibrary.wiley.com. Retrieved on 17 August 2010 from http://www.onlinelibrary.wiley.com/doi/10.1002/1520-6807(197910)16:4%3C581::AID-PITS2310160423%3E3.0.CO;2-J/abstract

387. Huggins, Chamicia E. "School Behavioral Programs May Improve Grades." Reuters News Article. 5 December 2005. Reuters.com. Retrieved on 5 December 2005 from http://go.reuters.com/printerFriendlyPopup.jhtml?type=healthNews&storyID=10486828

388. Hughes, Katherine L. and Melinda Mechur Karp. "School-Based Career Development: A Synthesis of the Literature." Institute on Education and the Economy, Teachers College, Columbia University. February, 2004. Columbia.edu. Retrieved on 19 November 2010 from http://www.tc.columbia.edu/centers//iee/PAPERS/Career_Development_2004.pdf

389. Hymowitz, Kay S. "The Black Family: 40 Years of Lies." Summer 2005. City-journal.org. Retrieved on 3 October 2009 from http://www.city-journal.org/printable.php?id=1824

389b. Institute of Education Sciences. National Center for Education Research. U.S. Department of Education. "Efficacy of Schoolwide Programs to Promote Social and Character Development and Reduce Problem Behavior in Elementary School Children." October, 2010. Ies.ed.gov. Retrieved on 20 October 2012 from http://ies.ed.gov/ncer/pubs/20112001/pdf.20112001/.pdf

389a. Jencks, Christopher and Meredith Phillips. "The Black-White Test Score Gap: Why it Persists and What Can Be Done." Spring 1998. Brookings.edu. Retrieved on 24 August 2011 from http://www.brookings.edu/articles/1998/spring_education_jencks.aspx

390. Johnson, Sheldon. "The Burden of Being Black: Exploring the Inequitable Nature of "Acting White'." 17 December 2007. University of Michigan sitemaker. Retrieved on 8 July 2000 from http://www.sitemaker.umich.edu/educationalequity/files/johnsonsk.actingwhitepaper.pdf

390a. Jones, S. R. "A Qualitative Exploration of the Multiple Dimensions of Identity Development in Women College Students," Journal of College Student Development, 38 (1997): 376-86. Cited in Susan R. Jones and Mrylu K. McEwen, "A Conceptual Model of Multiple Dimensions of Identity," Journal of College Student Development, 41 (July/August, 2000): 405-14. Emergent Recovery.com. Retrieved on 15 March 2012 from http://multipleidentitieslgbtq.wiki.westga.edu/file/view/Jones%26McEwen_2000.pdf

390b. Jones, Susan R. and Marylu K. McEwen. "A Conceptual Model of Multiple Dimensions of Identity," Journal of College Student Development, 41 (July/August, 2000): 405-14. Emergent Recovery. com. Retrieved on 15 March 2012 from http://emergentrecovery.com/Uploads/Conceptual_Model_of_Multiple_Dimensions_of-Identity.pdf

390c. Kahn, Jennifer. "Can Emotional Intelligence be Taught?" The New York Times. 9 September 2013. NYTimes.com. Retrieved on 11 September 2013 from http://www.nytimes.com/2013/09/15/magazine/can-emotional-intelligence-be-taught.html?...

391. Kao, Grace, Marta Tienda, and Barbara Schneider. "Racial and Ethnic Variation in Academic Performance," Research in Sociology of Education and Socialization, 11: 263-97. Cited in Karolyn Tyson, William Darity Jr., and Domini R. Castellino, "It's Not 'A Black Thing': Understanding the Burden of Acting White and Other Dilemmas of High Achievement," American Sociological Review, 70 (August, 2005): 582-605. Tc.education.edu. Retrieved on 24 July 2009 from http://www.tc.education.edu/students/see/events/Darity_et_al_Understanding_Burden_Acting_White.pdf

392. Kerckhoff, Alan C. and Richard T. Campbell. "Black-White Differences in the Educational Attainment Process." In Sociology of Education, 30 (January 1977): 15-27. Jstor.org. Retrieved on 17 August 2009 from http://www.jstor.org/stable/2112641

392a. Kidd, Celeste, Holly Palmer, and Richard N. Aslin. "Rational Snacking: Young Children's Decision-Making on the Marshmallow Task is Moderated by Beliefs About Environmental Reliability." In Cognition, 126 (January 2013): 109-14. Retrieved on 12 March 2014 from http://dx.doi.org/10.1016/j.cognition.2012.08.004. http://www.sciencedirect.com/science/article/pii/S0010027712001849

392b. Kim, Meeri. "Mice May Inherit Traumatic Experiences, Study Shows." 7 December 2013. Washingtonpost.com. Retrieved on 8 December 2013 from http://www.washingtonpost.com/national/health-science/

study-finds-that-fear-can-travel-quickly-through-generations-of-mice-dna/2013/12/07/94dc97f2-5e8e-11e3-bc56-c6ca94801fac_story.html

392c. King, Martin Luther Jr. "I Have a Dream" Speech." Ashbrook Center at Ashland University. TeachingAmericanHistory.org. Retrieved on 13 July 2015 from http://teachingamericanhistory.org/library/document/i-have-a-dream-speech/

392d. Klein, Alyson. "ESEA Reauthorization: The Every Student Succeeds Act Explained." Education Week, November 30, 2015. Blogs.edweek.org. Retrieved on 13 December 2015 from http://blogs.edweek.org/edweek/campaign-k-12/2015/11/esea_reauthorization_the_every.html

393. Knight, Fahim A. "W.E.B. Dubois and Booker T. Washington: The Great Debate." Dailygrail.com. Retrieved on 24 October 2009 from http://www.dailygrail.com/node/5764

393c. Kolata, Gina. "Scientific Articles Accepted (Personal Checks, Too)." The New York Times. 7 April 2013. NYTimes.com. Retrieved on 9 April 2013 from http://www.nytimes.com/2013/04/08/health/for-scientists-an-exploding-world-of-pseudo-ac...

393a. La Griffe du Lion [pseud.]. "The Politics of Mental Retardation: A Tail of the Bell Curve." Vol. 2, Number 9, September 2000. Metapedia.org/wiki. Retrieved on 13 March 2015 from http://en.metapedia.org/wiki/La_Griffe_du_Lion

393b. Laitsch, Dan. "Self-Discipline and Student Academic Achievement." Research Brief, vol. 4, no. 6. 26 June 2006. ASCD.org. Retrieved on 7 July 2011 from http://www.ascd.org/publications/researchbrief/y4n06/toc.aspz

394. Lankarani, Nazanin. "Transforming Africa Through Higher Education." The New York Times. 17 January 2011. NYTimes.com. Retrieved on 17 January 2011 from http://www.nytimes.com/2011/01/17/world/africa/17iht-educSide17.html?ref=education&...

395. Lawrence, Jill. "Wanted: Good Citizens, Close Communities." USA Today, 16 December 1996, p. 1A.

395d. Leonhardt, David. "Middle-Class Black Families, in Low-Income Neighborhoods." The New York Times. 24 June 2015. Retrieved on 25 June 2015 from. http://www.nytimes.com/2015/06/25/upshot/middle-class-black-families-in-low-income-neighborhoods.html?_r=0&abt=0002&abg=0

395a. Levin, Henry M. and Heather L. Schwartz. "What is the Cost of a Preschool Program?" National Center for the Study of Privatization in Education, Teachers College, Columbia University. 23 March 2007. Cbcse.org. Retrieved on 22 November 2011 from http://www.cbcse.org/media/download_gallery/Cost%20of%20Preschool.pdf

395c. Lewin, Alisa C. and Sloan Center for Working Families. "The Effect of Economic Stability on Family Stability Among Welfare Recipients." Alfred P. Sloan Center for Working Families at the University of Chicago. June 2005. Also published in Evaluation Review, 29(30): 223-40. alewin@uchicago.edu. Retrieved on 7 June 2014 from http://www.northwestern.edu/rc19/Lewin.pdf

395b. Lewin, Tamar. "Study Assails Merits of Single-Sex Education." The New York Times. 22 September 2011. NYTimes.com. Retrieved on 22 September 2011 from http://www.nytimes.com/2011/09/23/education/23single.html?_r=1&hp=&pagewanted=pr...

396. Lewis, Anthony. "The Noble Experiment." New York Times, 5 January 1998, p.A19.

397. Lewis, Neil A. "For Black Scholars Wedded to Prism of Race, New and Separate Goals." New York Times, 5 May 1997, p. B9.

398. Lewis, Sharon, Candace Simon, Renata Uzzell, Amanda Horwitz, and Michael Casserly. A Call for Change: The Social and Educational Factors Contributing to the Outcomes of Black Males in Urban Schools. Research Conducted by The Council of the Great City Schools. October 2010. 108p. Council of the Great

City Schools. Retrieved on 6 November 2010 from http://www. Call_For_Change_pdf

399. Lewin, Tamar. "Research Finds a High Rate of Expulsion in Preschool." The New York Times. 17 May 2005. NYTimes.com. Retrieved on 17 May 2005 from http://www.nytimes.com/2005/05/17/education/17expel.html?

399a. Library of Congress. Prints & Photographs Online Catalog (PPOC). "Statue of Booker T. Washington 'Lifting the Veil of Ignorance.'" 7 March 2010. Retrieved on 6 December 2011 from http://www.loc.gov/pictures/resource/highsm.05991/

399b. Lickerman, Alex. "Happiness in this World: Personality and Character." 3 April 2011. Psychologytoday.com. Retrieved on 15 October 2012 from http://www.psychologytoday.com/blog/happiness-in-world/201104/personality-vs-charac…

399c. Lindsay, Robert. "Black Females Have Higher IQ's Than Black Males." Beyond Highbrow – Robert Lindsay. 13 August 2014. Robertlindsay.wordpress.com. Retrieved on 13 January 2016 from https://robertlindsay.wordpress.com/2014/08/13/black-females-have-higher-iqs-than-black-males/

400. Liptak, Adam. "1 in 100 U.S. Adults Behind Bars, New Study Says." The New York Times. 28 February 2008. NYTimes.com. Retrieved on 28 February 2008 from http://www.nytimescom/2008/02/28/us/28cnd-prison.htlml?

400a. Lofquist, Daphne, Terry Lugaila, Martin O'Connell, and Sarah Feliz. "Households and Families: 2010, 2010 Census Briefs." U. S. Census Bureau. U. S. Department of Commerce, Economic and Statistics Administration. April 2012. Retrieved on 4 May 2015 from http://www.census.gov/prod/cen2010/briefs/c2010br-14.pdf

400b. Lopez, Mark Hugo and Ana Gonzalez Barrera. "Women's College Enrollment Gains Leave Men Behind." Pew Research Center. 6 March 2014. Pewresearch.org. Retrieved on 14 May

2015 from http://www.pewresearch.org/fact-tank/2014/03/06/womens-college-enrollment-gains-leave-men-behind/

401. Loury, Glenn C. "Free at Last? A Personal Perspective on Race and Identity in America." In <u>Lure and Loathing: Essays on Race, Identity and the Ambivalence of Assimilation</u>, p. 1-12. New York: The Penguin Press, 1993. Quoted in K. Michelle Scott, "A Perennial Mourning: Identity Conflict and the Transgenerational Transmission of Trauma Within the African American Community." Papers. 2 March 2009. Healthsystem.Virginia.edu. Retrieved on 14 June 2008 from http://www.healthsystem.virginia.edu/internet/csmhi/scott.cfm

402. Lovett, Ian. "Teacher's Death Exposes Tensions in L.A. Schools." <u>The New York Times</u>. 9 November 2010. NYTimes.com. Retrieved on 10 November 2010 from http://www.nytimes.com/2010/11/10/education/10teacher.html?_r=1&hp=&pagewanted=p...

402a. Lowrey, Annie. "Big Study Links Good Teachers to Lasting Gains." <u>The New York Times Reprints</u>. 6 January 2012. NYTimes.com. Retrieved on 6 January 2012 from http://www.nytimes.com/2012/01/06/education/big-study-links-good-teachers-to-lasting-gai...

402c. "McCain's Concession Speech." Transcript. <u>The New York Times</u>. 5 November 2008. NYTimes.com. Retrieved on 10 November 2010 from http://www.nytimes.com/2008/11/04/us/politics/04text-mccain.html?pagewanted=all&_r=0

402b. McGee, J. W. Quoted in Indianapolis *Freeman*, July 29, 1899. Cited in Louis R. Harlan, <u>Booker T. Washington: The Making of a Black Leader, 1856-1901</u>, p. 216-17. New York: Oxford University Press, 1972.

403. McKinnon, Jesse. <u>The Black Population in the United States: March 2002</u>. U. S. Census Bureau, Current Population Reports, Series P20-541. Washington, D. C., 2003. Census.gov. Retrieved on 18 August 2009 from http://www.census.gov/prod/2003/pubs/p20-541.pdf

403a. McWhirter, Cameron and Gary Fields. "Communities Struggle to Buck a Grim Cycle of Killing." 18 August 2012. Online.wsj.com. Retrieved on 8 January 2013 from http://online.wsj.com/article/SB10001424052702394830704577496501048197464.html

404. Malone-Colon, Linda and Alex Roberts. "Marriage and the Well-Being of African American Boys." <u>Research Brief No. 2</u>, September 2006. Institute for American Values, Center for Marriage and Family. Americanvalues.org. Retrieved on 7 July 2010 from http://www.americanvalues.org/pdf/researchbrief2.pdf

405. Mapp, Karen L. "Title I and Parent Involvement Lessons from the Past, Recommendations for the Future." Draft. Prepared for conference sponsored by Center for American Progress and the American Enterprise Institute for Public Policy Research. Americanprogress.org. Retrieved on 11 March 2011 from http://www.americanprogress.org/events/2011/03/av/parental_involvement.pdf

405a. Mare, Robert D. "Socioeconomic Change and the Decline of Marriage for Blacks and Whites." Wjh.harvard.edu. Retrieved on 30 September 2012 from http://www.wjh.harvard.edu/soc/faculty/winship/decline_black_marriage.pdf

406. Matus, Ron. "The Invisible Men." <u>St. Petersburg Times Online Tampa Bay</u>, April 17, 2005. Sptimes.com. Retrieved on 2 October 2010 from http://www.sptimes.com/2005/04/17/news_pf/Worldandnation/The_invisible_men.shtml

406a. Mayer, John D. and contributors. "Emotional Intelligence Information: A Site Dedicated to Communicating Scientific Information about Emotional Intelligence, Including Relevant Aspects of Emotions, Cognition, and Personality." unh.edu. Retrieved on 24 December 2011 from http://www.unh.edu/emotional_intelligence/index.html

406a. "The Meaning of Yin-Yang." "Yin and Yang in Medical Theory." From Patricia "Ebrey, <u>Chinese Civilization: A Sourcebook</u>, 2d ed. (New York: Free Press, 1993), p. 77-79. Translated by Mark

Coyle. Fly.cc.fer.hr. Retrieved on 27 July 2011 from http://fly.cc.fer.hr/~shlede/ying/yang.html

407. Medina, Jennifer. "Teacher Training Termed Mediocre." The New York Times. 23 October 2009. NYTimes.com. Retrieved on 1 January 2010 from http://www.nytimes.com/2009/10/23/education/23teachers.html?_r=1&pagewanted=print

408. Mello, Zena R. "Tomorrow's Forecast: Future Orientation As a Protective Factor Among Low-Income African American Adolescents." African American Success Foundation, November 9, 2002. Blacksuccessfoundation.org. Retrieved on 6 March 2011 from http://www.blacksuccessfoundation.org/sci_report-future%20orientation-zena_mello.htm

409. Memphis City Schools. Booker T. Washington: Home of the Warriors. "School Administration." Mcsk12.net. Retrieved on 16 May 2011 from http://www.mcsk12.net/schools/btwashington.hs/site/administration.shtml

410. _____. "School Mission and Vision Statement." Mcsk12.net. Retrieved on 16 May 2011 from http://www.mcsk12.net/schools/btwashington.hs/site/mission.shtml

411. _____. "Courses." Mcsk12.net. Retrieved on 24 May 2011 from http://www.mcsk12.net/schools/btwashington.hs/site/courses.shtml

412. _____. "Recognition Page. Final Video." Mcsk12.net. Retrieved on 24 May 2011 from http://www.mcsk12.net/schools/btwashington.hs/site/recognition.shtml 413. Michigan Department of Education. "What Research Says About Parent Involvement in Children's Education *in Relation to Academic Achievement*" 2001. Michigan.gov. Retrieved on 10 November 2010 from http://www.michigan.gov/documents/Final_Parent_Involvement_Fact_Sheet_14732_7.pdf

414. Mickelson, Roslyn Arlin. "The Attitude-Achievement Paradox among Black Adolescents." Sociology of Education, 63 (January,

1990): 44-61. Jstor.org. Retrieved on 21 August 2008 from http://www.jstor.org/pss/2112896

414b. Miller, Claire Cain. "Study Finds More Reasons to Get and Stay Married." The New York Times. 8 October 2015. NYTimes.com. Retrieved on 8 January 2015 from http://www.nytimes.com/2015/01/08/upshot/study-finds-more-reasons-to-get-and-stay-married.html?_r=0&abt=0002&abg=1

414a. "Million Man March (History)." Encyclopedia Britannica. Encyclopaedia Britannica Online. Encyclopaedia Britannica, Inc., 2011. Retrieved on 13 November 2011 from http://www.britannica.com/EBchecked/topic/382949/Million-Man-March

415. Munro, John. "Black Bourgeoisie at 50: Class, Civil Rights, and the Cold War in Black America." Seven Oaks Magazine, March 1, 2005. Seven Oaks. Sevenoaksmag.com. Retrieved on 5 October 2009 from http://www.sevenoaksmag.com/commentary/53_com1.html

415a. Musofer, Muhammad Ali. "Importance of Cleanliness." Dawn. 15 August 2013. Dawn.com. Retrieved on 14 July 2015 from http://www.dawn.com/news/752560/importance-of-cleanliness

416. Myers, Gloria and A.V. Margavio. "The Black Bourgeoisie and Reference Group Change: A Content Analysis of Ebony." Abstract. In Qualitative Sociology, 6 (Winter, 1983): 291-307. Springerlink.com. Retrieved on 4 March 2007 from http://www.springerlink.com/content/q232445j5303793p/

417. Nagourney, Adam. "Ex-Congressman Tells Blacks Not to be Victims." New York Times, 19 January 1999, p. B3.

418. National Association for Single Sex Public Education (NASSPE). "The Legal Status of Single-Sex Public Education." 11 March 2011. Singlesexschools.org. Retrieved on 11 March 2011 from http://www.singlesexschools.org/legal.html

419. National Center for Education Statistics. U. S. Department of Education "Fast Facts." 5 August 2010. Nces.gov. Retrieved on 5 August 2010 from http://nces.gov/fastfacts/display.asp?id=66

420. _____. U. S. Department of Education. "Participation in Education: Table A-3-3. Percentage distribution of students in private schools, by selected school characteristics and race/ethnicity: School year 2007-08." 6 May 2011. Nces.ed.gov. Retrieved on 6 May 2011 from http://nces.ed.gov/programs/coe/2010/sectioon1/table-pri-3/asp

420a. _____. U. S. Department of Education. 2013 Tables and Figures. "Tabl 219.70. Percentage of high school dropouts among persons 16 through 24 years old (status dropout rate), by sex and race/ethnicity: Selected years, 1960 through 2012." 6 May 2015. Nces.ed.gov. Retrieved on 6 May 2015 from https://nces.ed.gov/programs/digest/d13/tables/dt13_219.70.asp

420b. _____. U. S. Department of Education. Institute of Education Sciences. "Table 326.10. Graduation rates of first-time bachelor's degree-seeking students at 4-year postsecondary institutions, by race/ethnicity, time to completion, sex, and control of institution, 1996 through 20006." Nces.ed.gov. Retrieved on 14 May 2015 from http://nces.ed.gov/programs/digest/d13/tables/dt13_326.10.asp

421. The National Center for Higher Education Management Systems Information Center. "Public School Graduation Rates: For the Year 2006." 17 June 2009. Higheredinfo.org. Retrieved on 17 June 2009 from http://www.higheredinfo.org/dbrowser/indexx.php?measure=23

422. National Institute of Health. "The Power of Love." 26 June 2010. Enotalone.com. Retrieved on 26 June 2010 from http://www.enotalone.com/article/11869.html

422a. National PTA. "National PTA Lauds President Obama's Signing of Landmark Every Student Succeeds Act." 14 December 2015.

Pta.org. Retrieved on 14 December 2015 from http://www.pta.org/newsevents/newsdetail.cfm?ItemNumber=4682

423. Neal-Barnett, Angela. "Being Black: New Thoughts on the Old Phenomenon of Acting White." In Forging Links: African American Children: Clinical Developmental Perspectives, p. 75-87. Edited by A. Neal-Barnett, J.M. Contreras, and K.A. Kerns. Westport, CT: Praeger, 2001. Cited in Karolyn Tyson, William Darity Jr., and Domini R. Castellino, "It's Not 'A Black Thing': Understanding the Burden of Acting White and Other Dilemmas of High Achievement," American Sociological Review, 70 (August, 2005): 582-605. Tc.columbia.edu. Retrieved on 2 April 2009 from http://www.tc.columbia.edu/students/see/events/Darity_et_al_Understanding_Burden_Acting_White.pdf

424. Neill, James. "What is Locus of Control?" December 6, 2006. Wilderdom.com. Retrieved on 5 February 2011 from http://www.wilderdom.com/psychology/loc/LocusOfControlWhatIs.html

424a. Neisser, Ulric and others. Report of a Task Force Established by the American Psychological Association. "Intelligence: Knowns and Unknowns," American Psychologist, 51 (February, 1996):77-101. Gifted.uconn.edu. Retrieved on 1 December 2012 from http://www.gifted.uconn.edu/siegle/research/correlation/intelligence.pdf

424b. Nevitt, Thomas. American Association of Professional Hypnotherapists. "The Victim Mentality." 2011. Aaph.org. Retrieved on 20 December 2013 from http://aaph.org/node/214

425. New Pittsburgh Courier Online. "White House Launches 2011 'Race to the Top Commencement Challenge.'" 25 February 2011. Newpittsburghcourieronline.com. Retrieved on 20 May 2011 from http://www.newpittsburghcourieronline.com/index.php?option=com_content&view=articl...

426. New York City Department of Education. "Parent Coordinators." Schools.nyc.gov. Retrieved on 11 May 2011 from http://www.schools.nyc.gov/Offices/OFEA/SupportforFamilies/ParentCoordinators/default.htm

426b. Obama, Barack. "Transcript: Barack Obama's Speech on Race." The New York Times. 18 March 2008. NYTimes.com. Retrieved on 3 August 2013 from http://www.nytimes.com/2008/03/18/us/politics/18text-obama.html?pagewanted=print

426c. _____. "Transcript: Obama Speaks of Verdict Through the Prism of African-American Experience." The New York Times. 20 July 2013. NYTimes.com. Retrieved on 3 August 2013 from http://www.nytimes.com/2013/07/20/us/politics/transcript-obama-speaks-of-verdict-through

426e. _____. "Transcript: Charleston: Full text of President Obama's eulogy for Clementa Pinckney." The Denver Post. 26 June 2015. Denverpost.com. Retrieved on 26 June 2015 from http://www.denverpost.com/politics/ci_28390441/charleston-full-text-president-obamas-eulogy-clementa-pinckney?source=infinite

426d. O'Loughlin, Michael. "Pope Francis: Kids Must Have Moms and Dads." 11 April 2014. Advocate.com. Retrieved on 1 May 2015 http://www.advocate.com/print/politics/religion/2014/04/11/pope-francis-kids-must-have-moms-and-dads

426a. Open Society Foundations. U. S. Programs. Campaign for Black Male Achievement. "About the Campaign." Soros.org. Retrieved on 20 December 2011 from http://www.soros.org/initiatives/usprograms/focus/cbma/about?skin=printable

427. Otterman, Sharon. "A Quiet End for Boys Choir of Harlem." The New York Times. 22 December 2009. NYTimes.com. Retrieved on 23 December 2009 from http://nytimes.com/2009/12/23/nyregion/23choir.html?_r=1&em=&pagewanted=pr ...

428. _____. "Lauded Harlem Schools Have Their Own Problems." The New York Times. 13 October 2010. NYTimes.com. Retrieved on 13 October 2010 from http://www.nytimes.com/2010/10/13/education/13harlem.html?hp=&pagewanted=print

429. Otterman, Sharon and Robert Gebeloff. "Triumph Fades on Racial Gap in City Schools." The New York Times. 16

August 2010. NYTimes.com. Retrieved on 16 August 2010 from http://www.nytimes.com/2010/08/16/nyregion/16gap.html?ref=nyregion&pagewanted=print

430. Parker-Pope, Tara. "Raising I.Q. in Toddlers with Autism." The New York Times. 22 December 2009. NYTimes.com. Retrieved on 22 December 2009 from http://well.blogs.nytimes.com/2009/12/22/iq-boost-for-toddlers-with-autism/?pagemode=...

431. Patterson, Orlando. "A Poverty of the Mind." March 26, 2006. The New York Times. 26 March 2006. NYTimes.com. Retrieved on 12 February 2010 from http://www.nytimes.com/2006/03/26/opinion/26patterson.html?_r=1&sq=a poverty of the ...

432. Perera, Karl. "Personal Identity." More-Selfesteem.com. September 2007. Retrieved on 12 January 2010 from http://www.more-selfesteem.com/personal_identity_article.htm

432c. Perils, Margaret M. "5 Characteristics of Grit -- How Many Do You Have?" Forbes. Leadership. 29 October 2013. Forbes.com. Retrieved on 18 March 2014 http://www.forbes.com/sites/margaretperlis/2013/10/29/5-characteristics-of-grit-what-it-is-why-you-need-it-and-do-you-have-it/

432a. Pew Research Center. Survey Conducted in Association with National Public Radio. "Blacks See Growing Values Gap Between Poor and Middle Class." A Social & Demographic Trends Report. Retrieved on 13 November 2007 from http://www.pewsocialtrends.org/files/2010/10/Race-2007.pdf

432b. Phillips, Anna M. "Calming Schools by Focusing on Well-Being of Troubled Students." New York Times. 14 November 2011. NYTimes.com. Retrieved on 15 November 2011 from http://www.nytimes.com/2011/11/15/nyregion/calming-schools-through-a-sociological-a...

433. Phillips, Ulrich Bonnell. American Negro Slavery (1918). New York: D. Appleton and Co., 1918; Temecula, CA: Reprint Services, 2008. Quoted in Wikipedia contributors. The Slave Community

[Internet]. Wikipedia, The Free Encyclopedia. Wikipedia.org. Retrieved on 24 October 2009 from http://en.wikipedia.org/wiki/The_Slave_Community

433c. PolitiFact.com. Tampa Bay Times. Truth-O-Meter. "CNN's Don Lemon says more than 72 percent of African-American births are out of wedlock." 29 July 2013. Policifact.com. Retrieved on 19 October 2013 from http://www.politifact.com/truth-o-meter/statements/2013/jul/29/don-lemon/cnns-don-lem...

433e. "Poverty." BlackDemographics.com. Retrieved on 1 May 2015 from http://blackdemographics.com/households/poverty/

433a. Promising Practices Network. "Programs that Work: Child-Parent Centers." September 2008. Promisingpractices.net. Retrieved on 11 May 2011 from http://www.promisingpractices.net/program.asp?programid=98

433d. PR Newswire. "BLACK ENTERPRISE Publishes Rankings of the Nation's Largest Black-Owned Businesses." 19 August 2013. Prnewswire.com. Retrieved on 13 November 2013 from http://www.prnewswire.com/news-releases/black-enterprise-publishes-rankings-of-the-nations-largest-black-owned-businesses-220249331.html#

433b. Psychometric-success.com. "Emotional Intelligence: Can Emotional Intelligence be Developed?" Psychometric-success.com. Retrieved on 26 December 2011 from http://www.psychometric-success.com/emotional-intelligence/developing-emotional-intel...

434. Pungello, E. P., F. A. Campbell, and W. S. Barnett. "Poverty and Early Childhood Intervention." FPG Snapshot: 42 (April, 2007). Fpg.unc.edu. Retrieved on 5 June 2010 from http://www.fpg.unc.edu/~snapshots/snap42.pdf

435. Purnick, Joyce. "Kids Today? Sharpton Grimaces." New York Times, 7 November 2002, p. B18.

436. The Quotations Page. "Carl Sandburg: Quotation #3811." Cole's Quotables. Quotationspage.com. January 2008. Retrieved on 12 March 2010 from http://www.quotationspage.com/quote/3811.html

436a. Ray, Justin. "Obama: "No Black Male My Age" Hasn't Been Mistaken for a Valet." 17 December 2014. Nbcnewyork.com. Retrieved on 21 December 2014 from http://www.nbcnewyork.com/news/national-international/Barack-Obama-Michelle-Obama-People-Race-Prejudice-286092111.html

437. Reisner, Elizabeth R., Richard N. White, Christina A. Russell, and Jennifer Birmingham. Policy Studies Associates, Inc. "Building Quality, Scale, and Effectiveness in After-School Programs." 3 November 2004. Afterschoolresources.org. September 2010. Retrieved on 20 March 2011 from http://www.afterschoolresources.org/kernel/images/psapaper.pdf

437a. Religionfacts.com. "Yin and Yang in Chinese Religion." Source: "yin-yang," Encyclopedia Britannica Premium Service. 18 January 2005. Britannica.com. Retrieved on 28 July 2011 from http://www.britannica.com/eb/article?tocid=9077972 http://www.religionfacts.com/chinese_religion/beliefs/yin_yang.htm

438. Roberts, Sam. "Two-Parent Families Showing Gains." The New York Times. 17 December 2008. NYTimes.com. Retrieved on 24 December 2008 from http://www.nytimes.com/2008/12/17/us/17census.html?

438g. Robinson, Keith and Angel L. Harris. "Parental Involvement is Overrated." The New York Times. 12 April 2014. NYTimes.com. Retrieved on 12 April 2014 from http://opinionator.blogs.nytimes.com/2014/04/12/parental-involvement-is-overrated/?action=click&module=Search&region=searchResults&mabReward=relbias%3Ar&url=http%3A%2F%2Fquery.nytimes.com%2Fsearch%2Fsitesearch%2F%3Faction%3Dclick%26region%3DMasthead%26pgtype%3DHomepage%26module%3DSearchSubmit%26content

Collection%3 DHomepage%26t%3Dqry 453%23%2Fparental+involvement+is+overrated

438f. Romero, Simon. "After Years in Solitary, an Austere Life as Uruguay's President." The New York Times. 4 January 2013. NYTimes.com. Retrieved on 5 January 2013 from http://www.nytimes.com/2013/01/05/world/americas/after-years-in-solitary-an-austere-life-...

438e. Rotherham, Andrew J. "KIPP Schools: A Reform Triumph, or Disappointment? <u>Time</u>. 27 April 2011. Time.com. Retrieved on 8 November 2012 from http://www.time.com/time/printout/0,8816,2067941,00.html

438a. Rushton, J. Philippe. <u>Race, Evolution, and Behavior: A Life History Perspective</u>. 2nd Special Abridged Edition. Charles Darwin Research Institute, Port Huron, Michigan. Charlesdarwinresearch.org. Retrieved on 13 July 2012 from http://psychology.uwo.ca/faculty/rushtonpdfs/Race_Evolution_Behavior.pdf

438b. Rushton, J. Philippe and Arthur R. Jensen. "Thirty Years of Research on Race Differences in Cognitive Ability." Psychology, Public Policy, and Law, 11 (2005): 235-94. Psychology.uwo.ca. Retrieved on 19 August 2011 from http://psychology.uwo.ca/faculty/rushtonpdfs/ppp11.pdf

438c. _____. "Race and IQ: A Theory-Based Review of the Research in Richard Nisbett's <u>Intelligence and How to Get It</u>." <u>The Open Psychology Journal</u>, 3 (2010): 9-35. Charlesdarwinresearch.org. Retrieved on 19 August 2011 from http://www.charlesdarwinresearch.org/2010%20Review%20of%20Nisbett.pdf

438e. Sailer, Steve. "Do Black Women Have Higher IQs than Black Men?" <u>Steve Sailer: iSteve</u>. 7 December 2005. iSteve blog. Retrieved on 13 January 2016 from http://isteve.blogspot.com/2005/12/do-black-women-have-higher-iqs-than.html

438d. Salovey, Peter and John D. Mayer. "Emotional Intelligence." Baywood Publishing Co., Inc., 1990. Retrieved on 31 December

2011 from http://www.unh.edu/emotional_intelligence/EI%20 Assets/Reprints...EI%Proper/EI1990%20Emotional%20 Intelligence.pdf

439. Samad, Anthony Asadullah (The Black Commentator). "The Bruce Gordon Resignation: You Can't Know the NAACP if You've Never Been in the NAACP." 15 March 2007. Hartford Web Publishing, World History Archives. Hartford- hwp.com. Retrieved on 13 October 2009 from http://www.hartford-hwp.com/archives/45a/742.html

439a. School of Arts & Sciences, University of Pennsylvania. "KIPP Character Report Card and Supporting Materials." Sas.upen.edu. Retrieved on 19 January 2012 from http://www.sas.upen.edu/~duckwort/images/KIPP%20NYC%20Character%20 Report%Card%20and%20Supporting%20Materials.pdf

440. Schott Foundation for Public Education. Yes We Can: The Schott 50 State Report on Public Education and Black Males, 2010. Schott Foundation for Public Education. 678 Massachusetts Avenue, Suite 301. Cambridge, MA 02139. Schottfoundation.org. Retrieved on 31 July 2012 from http://www.schottfoundation.org http://www.blackboysreport.org/files/schott_50statesreport-execsummary.pdf

440a. Schwartzman, Paul. "The Reality: Daunting Difficulties for the Children Promised College Scholarships." A three-part series on the fate of 59 fifth-graders who were given an extraordinary gift: the promise of a college education paid for by two wealthy businessmen. The Seat Pleasant 59: The Legacy. 17 December 2011. Washingtonpost.com. Retrieved on 19 December 2011 from http://www.washingtonpost.com/local/for-the-seat-pleasant-59-giddy-promise-is-replaced-by-sobering-reality/2011/12/15/gIQAQ13eyO_story.html?sub=AR

441. Schweinhart, Lawrence J. "How to Take the High/Scope Perry Preschool to Scale." Abstract of presentation at National Invitational Conference of the Early Childhood Research Collaborative. 7-8 December 2007. Earlychildhoodrc.org. Retrieved on 10 February

2010 from http://www.earlychildhoodrc.org/events/presentations/schweinhart.pdf

442. Schweinhart, Lawrence J., H. V. Barnes, and D. P. Weikart. "High/Scope Perry Preschool: Ysilanti, MI." Monographs of the High/Scope Educational Research Foundation. No. Ten, 1993. Aypf.org. Retrieved on 10 February 2010 from http://www.aypf.org/publications/compendium/C2S45.pdf

443. Scott, Imani Michelle (formerly K. Michelle Scott). "A Perennial Mourning: Identity Conflict and the Transgenerational Transmission of Trauma Within the African American Community." University of Virginia Health Systems Paper. 22 September 2002. Healthsystem.virginia. Retrieved on 2 March 2009 from. http://www.healthsystem.virginia.edu/internet/csmhi/scott.cfm

444. Seiler, Casey. "Deal Reached on Mayoral Control of NYC Schools." 24 July 2009. Timesunion.com Capitol Confidential. Blog.times union. com. Retrieved on 27 January 2010 from http://blog.timesunion.com/capitol/archive/17061/deal-reached-o-mayoral-control-of-ny...

444a. Seligman, Daniel. "Black-White IQ Differences." Excerpted from National Review, December 5, 1994, 48-50. Library.flawlesslogic.com. Retrieved on 25 August 2011 from http://library.flawlesslogic.com/iq.htm

444b. Sellers, Robert M., Tabbye M. Chavos, and Deanna Y. Cooke. "Racial Ideology and Racial Centrality as Predictors of African American College Students' Academic Performance." Journal of Black Psychology, 24 (1998): 8-27.

444c. Sellers, Robert M., Mia A. Smith, J. Nicole Shelton, Stephanie A. J. Rowley, and Tabbye M. Chavos. "Multidimensional Model of Racial Identity: A Reconceptualization of African American Racial Identity." Personality and Social Psychology Review, 2 (1998): 18-39.

445. Shatz, Adam. "Glenn Loury's About Face." The New York Times Magazine. 20 January 2002. NYTimes.com. Retrieved

on 7 October 2009 from http://www.nytimes.com/2002/01/20/magazine/20LOURY.htl?pagewanted=all

445a. Shui, Feng. "Meaning of Yin Yang." Absolutely Feng Shui. 2003-2010. Retrieved on 27 July 2011 from http://www.absolutelyfengshui.com/fengshui/feng-shui-yin-yin-yang.php

446. Shyu, Jessica. "Academic Programs Targeting Black Boys Fall Off, But Some Predict a Resurgence." 21 May 2004. Maryland Newsline. Newsline.umd.edu. Retrieved on 7 February 2009 from http://www.newsline.umd.edu/schools/specialreports/brownvs.board/blackboysprograms 051...

446e. Singer, Alan. "Will Every Student Succeed? Not With This New Law." Huff Post: Education, December 13, 2015. Retrieved on 13 December 2015 from http://www.huffingtonpost.com/alan-singer/will-every-student-succee_b_8730956.html

446c. "Small Schools Work in New York." The Editorial Board. The New York Times. 17 October 2014. NYTimes.com. Retrieved on 18 October 2014 from http://nyti.ms/1FeROMO

446d. Smith, Jada F. "Echoing Calls for Justice of Million Man March, but Widening Audience." The New York Times. 10 October 2015. NYTimes.com. Retrieved on 11 October 2015 from http://www.nytimes.com/2015/10/11/us/echoing-calls-of-justice-of-million-man-march-but-widening-audience.html?_r=0

446a. Snyderman, Mark and Stanley Rothman. The IQ Controversy, the Media and Public Policy. New Jersey: Transaction Publishers, 1988. 323 p. Cited in Wikipedia Contributors. "The IQ Controversy, the Media and Public Policy (book)." Wikipedia, The Free Encyclopedia. 3 August 2011. Wikipedia.og. Retrieved on 29 August 2011 from http://en.wikipedia.org/wiki/The_IQ_Controversy,_the_Media_and_Public_Policy_(book)

446b. Sohn, Kitae. "Acting White: A Critical Review." Urban Review, 43 (2011): 217-34. Springerlink.com. Retrieved on 19 June 2012 from http://www.springerlink.com/content/rgn5605r23t2p224/fulltext.pdf

447. Starkey, Brando Simeo and Susan Eaton. "The Fear of "Acting White" and the Achievement Gap: Is There Really a Relationship?" Charles Hamilton Houston Institute for Race & Justice. Harvard Law School. 20 October 2008. Charleshamiltonhouston.org. November 2009. Retrieved on 10 July 2010 from http://www.charleshamiltonhouston.org/wp-content/uploads/2013/11/BRIEF-Acting-White-STARKEY-FINAL.pdf

448. Steele, Claude "Thin Ice: Stereotype Threat and Black College Students." The Atlantic Online. August 1999. Theatlantic.com. Retrieved on 19 March 2009 from http://www.theatlantic.com/doc/print/199908/student-stereotype.

449. Steele, Claude and Joshua Aronson. "Stereotype Threat and the Test Performance of Academically Successful African Americans." In The Black-White Test Score Gap, p. 401-28. Edited by Christopher Jencks and Meredith Phillips. Brookings Institution Press, 1998. Books.google.com. March 2009. Retrieved on 16 April 2010 from http://www.books.google.com/books?isbn=0815746091.

450. Steinberg, Laurence, Sanford Dornbusch, & Bradford Brown. "Ethnic Differences in Adolescent Achievement: An Ecological Perspective." American Psychologist, 47 (June, 1992): 723-29. Des.emory.edu. Retrieved on 23 April 2010 from http://www.des.emory.edu/mfp/302/302EthnicDiff.pdf

450a. Stevenhein.com. Emotional Intelligence. "Critical Reviews of Daniel Goleman: How He misled the public; Notes from his books; Copies of some of his articles; Notes on his background." Retrieved on 24 December 2011 from http://eqi.org/gole.htm#ReviewsofGolemanswriting

451. Strein, William. "Classroom-based Elementary School Affective Education Programs: A Critical Review." Abstract. Retrieved on 14 February 2006 from Onlinelibrary.wiley.com. November 2010. http://www.onlinelibrary.wiley.com/doi/10.1002/1520-6807

(198807)25:3%3C288::AID-PITS2310250310%3E3.0.CO;2-L/abstract

451a. Stys, Yvonne and Shelley L. Brown. "A Review of the Emotional Intelligence Literature and Implications for Corrections." Research Report. Research Branch, Correctional Service of Canada. March 2004. Retrieved on 10 October 2011 from http://www.csc-scc.gc.ca/text/rsrch/reports/r150_e.pdf

451b. Sun, Lena H. "D.C. Infant Mortality Rate at Historic Low." 26 April 2012. NYTimes.com. Retrieved on 27 April 2012 from http://www.washingtonpost.com/national/health-science/dc-infant-mortality-rate-at-histori...

451d. Tavernise, Sabrina. "Project to Improve Intellect of Poor Children Led to Better Health, Too, Research Finds." The New York Times. NYTimes.com. Retrieved on 27 March 2014 from http://nyti.ms/1pdjEEq

451e. _____. "Rise in Suicide by Black Children Surprises Researchers." The New York Times. 18 May 2015. NYTimes.com. Retrieved on 19 May 2015 from http://www.nytimes.com/2015/05/19/health/suicide-rate-for-black-children-surged-in-2-decades-study-says.html?src=me&_r=0

451c. Texas Youth Commission. Prevention Summary. "Significant Benefits: The High/Scope Perry Preschool Study Through Age 27." 19 July 2004. Retrieved on 20 November 2011 from http://www.tykc.state.tx.us/prevention/hiscpope.html

452. Texeira, Erin. "NAACP President Resigns after 19 Months." Associated Press. 4 March 2007. Afgate.com. Retrieved on 13 October 2009 from http://www.sfgate.com/cgi-bin/article.cgi?f=/n/a/2007/03/04/national/a112225S23.DTL&...

453. Tierney, John. "Computing the Cost of 'Acting White.'" The New York Times. 19 November 2005. NYTimes.com. Retrieved on 19 November 2005 from http://www.selectnytimes.com/2005/11/19/opinion/19tierney.html?

454. TimesPeople. Associated Press. "Single-Parent Homes: The Effect on Schooling." 29 June 1988. NYTimes.com. Retrieved on 20 January 2009 from http://query.nytimes.com/gst/fullpage.htl?res=94DE3DA1F93AA15755COA96E94...

454a. Toldson, Ivory A. Breaking Barriers: Plotting the Path to Academic Success for School-age African-American Males. Washington, D.C.: Congressional Black Caucus Foundation, Inc., 2008. 52p. Retrieved on 13 October 2009 from http://cbcfinc.org/newsroom/publications.html

455. Toppo, Greg. "Big-city Schools Struggle with Graduation Rates." USA Today. 20 June 2006. Usatoday.printthis.clickability.com. Retrieved on 22 June 2009 from http://www.usatoday.printthis.clickability.com/pt/cpt?action=cpt&title=USATODAY.com+-+Bi

455a. Tough, Paul. "What if the Secret to Success Is Failure?" The New York Times Magazine Reprints. 14 September 2011. NYTimes.com. Retrieved on 14 December 2011 from http://www.nytimes.com/2011/09/18/magazine/what-if-the-secret-to-success-is-failure.hatml?pagewanted=printg

456. Truth and Reconciliation Commission Website. "Truth and Reconciliation Commission." Justice.gov. Retrieved on 27 May 2011 from http://www.justice.gov.za/trc/

457. Tyson, Karolyn, William Darity Jr., and Domini R. Castellino, "It's Not 'A Black Thing': Understanding the Burden of Acting White and Other Dilemmas of High Achievement," American Sociological Review, 70 (August, 2005): 582-605. Tc.columbia.edu. September 2008. Retrieved on 10 June 2010 from http://www.tc.columbia.edu/students/see/events/Darity_et_al_Understanding_Burden_Acting_White.pdf

458. UNICEF (United Nations Children's Fund). "Children's Rights." Adopted from Teaching About Human Rights, United Nations, 1992, and contributed by UNICEF. Un.org. September 2010. Retrieved on 10 November 2011 from http://www.un.org/cyberschoolbus/briefing/children/children.pdf

459. USA Today "Employer Expectations are Increasing." Supplement. 28 August 1997.

459f. U. S. Census Bureau. Statistical Abstract of the United States: 2012. "Labor Force, Employment, and Earnings." 5 May 2015. Retrieved on 5 May 2015 from http://www.census.gov/compendia/statab/2012/tables/12s0627.pdf

459c. U. S. Constitution Online. "The I Have a Dream Speech." 3 March 2010. Usconstitution.net. Retrieved on 8 May 2014 from http://www.usconstitution.net/dream.html

459d. U. S. Decennial Census (1890-2000); American Community Survey (2010). "Figure 5. Percent Never Married among Those Aged 35 and Older by Sex and Race: 1890 to 2010." Retrieved on 3 May 2015 from http://www.census.gov/hhes/socdemo/marriage/data/acs/ElliottetalPAA2012figs.pdf

459g. U. S. Department of Education. Elementary and Secondary Education. "SEC. 1118. Parental Involvement." Ed.gov. 21 June 2005. Retrieved on 21 June 2015 from http://www2.ed.gov/policy/elsec/leg/esea02/pg2.html#sec1118

459e. U. S. Department of Health and Human Services. "Information on Poverty and Income Statistics Tables." Aspe.hhs.gov. 5 May 2015. Retrieved on 5 May 2015 from http://aspe.hhs.gov/hsp/12/povertyandincomeest/longdesc.shtml

459a. U. S. Department of Health and Human Services, Administration for Children and Families, Office of Planning, Research and Evaluation. "Head Start Research: Head Start Impact Study, Final Report, Executive Summary." Retrieved on January 2010. Retrieved on 20 November 2011 from http://www.acf.hhs.gov/programs/opre/hs/impact_study/reports/impact_study/executive_summary_final.pdf

459b. U. S. Department of Justice, Civil Rights Division and U. S. Department of Education, Office for Civil Rights. "Dear Colleague Letter: Nondiscriminatory Administration of School Discipline."

January 8, 2014. Retrieved on 11 January 2014 from http://www2.ed.gov/about/offices/list/ocr/letters/colleague-201401-title-vi.pdf

460. United States Department of Labor. History. Chapter III: "The Roots of the Problem." In <u>The Negro Family: The Case for National Action</u>. March, 1965. Dol.gov. Retrieved on 24 October 2009 from http://www.dol.gov/oasam/programs/history/moynchapter3.htm

460e. U. S. Senate. "ESSA Final Conference Report.pdf." November 30, 2015. Retrieved on 13 December 2015 from http://www.help.senate.gov/imo/media/doc/ESSA%20FINAL%20Conference%20Report.pdf

460b. Umass Amherst Libraries. Special Collections & University Archives (SCAU). "W. E. B. Du Bois Photographs: 390. Du Bois, W. E. B., ca. 1907." Retrieved on 6 December 2011 from http://www.library.umass.edu

460a. University of Rochester. "The Marshmallow Study Revisited." October 11, 2012. Rochester.edu. Retrieved on 12 March 2014 from http://www.rochester.edu/news/show.php?id=4622

460c. Unterman, Rebecca. "Headed to College: The Effects of New York City's Small High Schools of Choice on Postsecondary Enrollment." MDRC. Building Knowledge to Improve Social Policy. October 2014. Mdrc.org. Retrieved on 18 October 2014 from http://www.mdrc.org/sites/default/files/Headed_to_College_PB.pdf

460d. Valbrun, Marjorie. "Black Males Missing from College Campuses." 14 May 015. Americaswire.org. Maynard Media Center on Structural Inequity. Retrieved on 14 May 2015 from http://americaswire.org/drupal7/?q=content/black-males-missing-college-campuses

461. Vandell, Deborah Lowe, Elizabeth R. Reisner, and Kim M. Pierce. "Outcomes Linked to High-Quality Afterschool Programs: Longitudinal Findings from the Study of Promising Afterschool Programs." Policy Studies Associates, Inc. October 2007. Policystudies.com. December 2010. Retrieved on 10 February 2011

from http://www.policystudies.com/studies/youth/Promising%20Programs%20FINAL.pdf

461b. Villavicencio, Adriana and William H. Marinell. "Inside Success: Strategies of 25 Effective Small High Schools in NYC." The Research Alliance for New York City Schools. July 2014. Media. ranycs.org. Retrieved on 18 October 2014 from http://media.ranycs.org/2014/007

461a. Visher, Mary G., Rajika Bhandari, and Elliott Medrich. "High School Career Exploration Programs: Do They Work?" Phi Delta Kappan, 86 (October, 2004): 135-38.

462. Wade, Nicholas. "Human Culture, an Evolutionary Force." The New York Times. 1 March 2010. NYTimes.com. Retrieved on 2 March 2010 from http://www.nytimes.com/2010/03/02/science/02evo.html?hp=&pagewanted=print

462c. Walker, Lee H. "The Real Importance of Barak Obama's Presidential Run." 6 May 2008. News.heartland.org. Retrieved on 13 January 2015 from http://news.heartland.org/editorial/2008/05/06/real-importance-barack-obamas-presidential-run

462a. Wang, Margaret C, Geneva D. Haertel, and Herbert J. Walberg. "What Helps Students Learn?" Educational Leadership, December 1993/January 1994. Retrieved on 17 December 2012 from http://www.ascd.org/publications/educational-leadership/dec93/vol51/num04/Synthesis-of-Research---What-Helps-Students-Learn%C2%A2.aspx

462d. Washington, Booker T. "A National Negro Business League Address, Wednesday Evening, August 20, 1913." BTW Society. Btwsociety.org. Retrieved on 13 July 2015 from http://btwsociety.org/library/speeches/09.php

462b. Weinger, Mackenzie. "Poll: Blacks Say Whites Have an Edge." 28 August 2013. Politico.com. Print View. Retrieved on 3 December 2013 from http://dyn.politico.com/printstory.cfm?uuid=9A4E7C0B-BEEC-4149-B7FF-F1C06F408683

463. Wells-Wilbon, Rhonda and Spencer Holland. "Social Learning Theory and the Influence of Male Role Models on African American Children in PROJECT 2000." The Qualitative Report, 6 (December, 2001). Nova.edu. Retrieved on 19 January 2009 from http://www.nova.edu/ssss/QR/QR6-4/wellswilbon.html.

463a. Westchester Institute for Human Services Research. The Balanced View: Research-based Information on Timely Topics. "Early Childhood Education, Part 2: Characteristics of Effective Programs." Vol. 1, June 1997. Retrieved on 10 April 2009 from http://www.sharingsuccess.org/code/by/earlychildhood2.pdf

464. The White House. "Commencement Challenge." Whitehouse.gov. Retrieved on 18 May 2011 from http://www.whitehouse.gov/commencement/info

464a. _____. "FACT SHEET: Congress Acts to Fix No Child Left Behind. Retrieved on 13 December 2015 from https://www.whitehouse.gov/the-press-office/2015/12/03/fact-sheet-congress-acts-fix-no-child-left-behind

465. Wikipedia contributors. "Stereotype Threat." Wikipedia, The Free Encyclopedia. 20 Feb 2009. Wikipedia.org. Retrieved on 20 Mar 2009 from http://en.wikipedia.org/w/index.php?title=Stereotype_threat&oldid=272040127.

466. _____. "Self-Help" Wikipedia, The Free Encyclopedia. 28 June 2009. Wikipedia.org. Retrieved on 13 July 2009 from http://en.wikipedia.org/wiki/Self-help

467. _____. "The Slave Community." Wikipedia, The Free Encyclopedia. 5 October 2009. Wikipedia.org. Retrieved on 14 October 2009 from http://en.wikipedia.org/wiki/The_Slave_Community

468. _____. "Samuel Smiles" Wikipedia, The Free Encyclopedia. 21 September 2009. Wikipedia.org Retrieved on 24 October 2009 from http://en.wikipedia.org/wiki/Samuel_Smiles

469. _____. "Theory of Multiple Intelligences." <u>Wikipedia. The Free Encyclopedia</u>. 2009 30 December 2009. Wikipedia.org. Retrieved on 30 December 2009 from : http://en.wikipedia.org/wiki/Theory_of_multiple_intelligences

470. _____. "Booker T. Washington." <u>Wikipedia, The Free Encyclopedia</u>. 10 March 2010. Wikipedia.org. Retrieved on 14 March 2010 from http://en.wikipedia.org/wiki/Booker_T._Washington

471. _____. "Truth and Reconciliation Commission (South Africa). <u>Wikipedia, The Free Encyclopedia</u>. 27 May 2011. Wikipedia.org. Retrieved on 27 May 2011 from http://www.wikipedia.org/wiki/Truth_and_Reconciliation_Commission_(South_Africa)

471a._____. "The Bell Curve." 2 August 2011. <u>Wikipedia, The Free Encyclopedia</u>. 6 August 2011. Wikipedia.org. Retrieved on 6 August 2011 http://en.wikipedia.org/wild/The_Bell_Curve

471b. _____. "Race and Intelligence." <u>Wikipedia, The Free Encyclopedia</u>. 16 August 2011. Wikipedia.org. Retrieved on 16 August 2011 from http://en.wikipedia.org/wiki/Race_and_intelligence

471c. _____. "The IQ Controversy, the Media and Public Policy (book)." <u>Wikipedia, The Free Encyclopedia</u>. 3 August 2011. Wikipedia.og. Retrieved on 29 August 2011 from http://en.wikipedia.org/wiki/The_IQ_Controversy,_the_Media_and_Public_Policy_(book)

471d. _____. "Emotional Intelligence." <u>Wikipedia, The Free Encyclopedia</u>. 30 December 2011. Wikipedia.og. Retrieved on 1 January 2011 from http://en.wikipedia.org/wiki/Emotional_intelligence

471e. _____. "Stanford Marshmallow Experiment." <u>Wikipedia, The Free Encyclopedia</u>. 5 January 2012 Wikipedia.og. Retrieved on 5 January 2012 from http://en.wikipedia.org/Stanford_marshmallow_experiment

471f. _____. "Grit (Personality Trait)." <u>Wikipedia, The Free Encyclopedia</u>. 1 December 2011. Wikipedia.og. Retrieved on 10 January 2012 from <u>http://en.wikipedia.org/wiki/ Grit (personality trait)</u>

471h. _____. "The Shooting of Trayvon Martin." <u>Wikipedia, The Free Encyclopedia</u>. 4 August 2013. Wikipedia.og. Retrieved on 4 August 2013 from <u>http://en.wikipedia.org/wiki/ Grit (personality trait)</u>

471i. _____. "The Flynn Effect." <u>Wikipedia, The Free Encyclopedia</u>. 20 September 2013. Wikipedia.og. Retrieved on 21 September 2013 from <u>http://en.wikipedia.org/wiki/Flynn effect</u>

471j. _____. "List of Largest Companies by Revenue." <u>Wikipedia, The Free Encyclopedia</u>. 13 November 2013. Wikipedia.og. Retrieved on 13 November 2013 from <u>http://en.wikipedia.org/ wiki/List of largest companies by revenue</u>

471k. _____. "Critical Race Theory." <u>Wikipedia, The Free Encyclopedia</u>. 3 September 2013. Wikipedia.org. Retrieved on 21 November 2013 from <u>http://en.wikipedia.org/wiki/ Critical race theory</u>

471l. _____. "Victim Mentality." <u>Wikipedia, The Free Encyclopedia</u>. 12 December 2013. Wikipedia.org. Retrieved on 20 December 2013 from <u>http://en.wikipedia.org/wiki/ Victim mentality</u>

471m. _____. "IQ Classification." <u>Wikipedia, The Free Encyclopedia</u>. 25 February 2014. Wikipedia.org. Retrieved on 8 March 2014 from <u>http://en.wikipedia.org/wiki/IQ classification</u>

471n. _____. "Stanford Marshmallow Experiment." <u>Wikipedia, The Free Encyclopedia</u>. 2 March 2014. Wikipedia.org. Retrieved on 12 March 2014 from <u>http://en.wikipedia.org/wiki/ Stanford marshmallow experimenthttp://en.wikipedia.org/wiki/ Stanford marshmallow experiment</u>

471o. _____. "Victim Mentality." <u>Wikipedia, The Free Encyclopedia</u>. 13 March 2014. Wikipedia.org. Retrieved on 13 March 2014 from http://en.wikipedia.org/wiki/Victim_mentality

471p. _____. "Reality Principle." <u>Wikipedia, The Free Encyclopedia</u>. 29 January 2014. Wikipedia.org. Retrieved on 13 March 2014 from http://en.wikipedia.org/wiki/Reality_principle

471q. _____. "No Child Left Behind." <u>Wikipedia, The Free Encyclopedia</u>. 3 May 2014. Wikipedia.org. Retrieved on 3 May 2014 from http://en.wikipedia.org/wiki/No_Child_Left_Behind_Act

471r. _____. "Gratitude." <u>Wikipedia, The Free Encyclopedia</u>. 30 July 2014. Wikipedia.org. Retrieved on 9 September 2014 from http://en.wikipedia.org/wiki/Gratitude

471s. _____. "W. E. B. Du Bois." <u>Wikipedia, The Free Encyclopedia</u>. 29 December 2014. Wikipedia.org. Retrieved on 31 December 2014 from http://en.wikipedia.org/wiki/_W._E._B._Du_Bois

471t. _____. "Up from Slavery." <u>Wikipedia, The Free Encyclopedia</u>. 26 December 2014. Wikipedia.org. Retrieved on 13 January 2015 from http://en.wikipedia.org/wiki/Up_from_Slavery

471u. _____. "Underclass." <u>Wikipedia, The Free Encyclopedia</u>. 20 November 2014. Wikipedia.org. Retrieved on 15 January 2015 from http://en.wikipedia.org/wiki/Underclass

471v. _____. "2015 Baltimore Protests." <u>Wikipedia, The Free Encyclopedia</u>. 14 May 2015. Wikipedia.org. Retrieved on 14 May 2015 from http://en.wikipedia.org/wiki/2015_Baltimore_protests

471w. _____. "Health Effects of Noise." <u>Wikipedia, The Free Encyclopedia</u>. 14 July 2015. Wikipedia.org. Retrieved on 14 July 2015 from https://en.wikipedia.org/wiki/Health_effects_from_noise

471g. Williams, Walter E. "Should Black People Tolerate This?" 23 May 2012. Townhall.com. Retrieved on 11 January 2013 from http://townhall.com/columnists/walterwilliams/2012/05/23/should_black_people_tolerate...

472. Wilson, Roy. "The Lumbpen-Black-Bourgeoisie Exposed!" 14 November 2007. Amazon.com Customer Review. Amazon.com. Retrieved on 5 October 2009 from http://www.amazon.com/review/R16SJLV73B5TVO

473. Winerip, Michael. "How One Suburb's Black Students Gain." The New York Times. 14 December 2005. NYTimes.com. Retrieved on 14 December 2005 frp, http://www.nytimes.com/2005/12/14/education/14education.html?

474. Wonacott, Michael E. "Myths and Realities: Dropouts and Career and Technical Education." Educational Resources Information Center (ERIC). Clearinghouse on Adult, Career, and Vocational Education. No. 23-2002. Aysps.gsu.edu. January 2011. Retrieved on 5 June 2011 from http://www.aysps.gsu.edu/ghpc/files/Handout_on_Dropouts_and_Career_Education.pdf

474b. Wang, Kun. "Racial Identity of Minority Adolescents: A Review of Empirical Research." Paper based on a program accepted at the 2011 American Counseling Association Conference, New Orleans, LA, March 25, 2011. Retrieved on 17 December 2013 from http://counselingoutfitters.com/vistas/vistas11/Article_73.pdf

474c. Wolfers, Justin, David Leonhardt, and Kevin Ouealy. The Upshot, "1.5 Million Missing Black Men." The New York Times. 20 April 2015. NYTimes.com. Retrieved on 20 April 2015 from http://www.nytimes.com/_interactive/2015/04/20/upshot/missing-_black-men.html?action=click&contentCollection=The%20Upshot&module=MostEmailed&version=_Full&region=Marginalia&src=_me&pgtype_=article&abt=0002&abg=_1

474a. Wood, Robert G. "Marriage rates and Marriageable Men: A Test of the Wilson Hypothesis (includes appendices)." Journal of Human Resources, January 1, 1995. AccessMyLibrary.com. Retrieved on 30 September 2012 from http://www.accessmylibrary.com/article-1G1-16662258/marriage-rates-and-marriageable.html

475. Wright, Willie J. "The Endangered Black Male Child." Association for Supervision and Curriculum Development from Educational Leadership, 49 (December 1991/January 1992): 14-16. Ascd.org. September 2008. Retrieved on 9 February 2009 from http://www.ascd.org/ASCD/pdf/journals/ed_lead/el_199112_wright.pdf

475a. Yan, Holly and Gabriella Schwarz. "GOP Candidates Caught in Slavery Controversy." CNN Political Ticker. 11 July 2011. CNN.com Blogs. Retrieved on 13 July 2011 from http://www.politicalticker.blogs.cnn.com/2011/07/11/gop-candidates-caught-in-slavery-controve…

476. Yates, Scott, Angel Harris, Ricardo Sabates, and Jeremy Staff. "Early Occupational Aspirations and Fractured Transitions: A Study of Entry into 'NEET' Status in the UK." Journal of Social Policy, 40 (October, 2010). Cambridge Journals. Princeton.edu. Retrieved on 25 August 2010 from http://www.princeton.edu/~angelh/Website/Studies/Article%2010%20(Journal%20Social%20Policy%20-%20LSE%20'10).PDF

477. Yost, Phil. "Learning to Teach to Bridge the Achievement Gap." 20 November 2009. NYTimes.com Retrieved on 20 November 2009 from http://www.nytimes.com/2009/11/20/education/20sfschool.html?ref=education&pagewan

478. YouTube. "Martin Luther King III and Bernice King: Speeches at Michael Jackson Memorial." 7 July 2009. YouTube. Retrieved on 8 July 2009 from http://www.youtube.com/watch?v=TQ6_DCeoRLM

479. Zeigler, Jenifer. "War on Poverty Needs New Strategy." Fox News. 1 September 2004. Foxnews.com. Retrieved on 21 February 2010 from http://www.foxnews.com/printer_friendly_story/0,3566,131174,00.html

480. Zezima, Katie. "A Vote to Fire All Teachers at a Failing High School." The New York Times. 23 February 2010. NYTimes.com. Retrieved on 24 February 2010 from http://www.nytimes.com/2010/02/24/education/24teacher.html?em=&pagewanted=print

480a. Zimmer, Amy and Nigel Chiwaya. "Racial Gap Persists as School Test Scores Edge Up." DNAinfo. New York. Harlem Education. 12 August 2015. DNAinfo.com. Retrieved on 7 January 2016 from http://www.dnainfo.com/new-york/20150812/central-harlem/scores-on-state-tests-edge-up-but-racial-gap-persists

About the Author

Retired Dean of Students at Bronx Community College, City University of New York, author has doctorate from Teachers College, Columbia University, and has been a public school teacher, college professor, and special educational programs administrator. Among his other publications: "Spirituality: Your Hidden Success Center" and "Urban Minorities: Education of Immigrants."

Index

$15 Washington Gold Watch Pawning 638, 767
21st Century Community Learning Centers Act (21CCLC) 578
300 Men March 750, 764
10,000-Hour Rule 496

A

Abecedarian Early Childhood Intervention Project 563
abstract beliefs versus concrete beliefs 241
accommodating and subservient versus realistic and savvy 158
acculturated and the externally adapted 270
"acting white" 20-1, 24, 207-9, 211-12, 215-17, 219-22, 224-7, 246-7, 249-64, 267-8, 321, 379, 397-9, 406-8, 456
"acting white" effect 251, 263, 729
activities of the Age of Booker T. Washington 637
Adams, Lewis 99-100
adaptation fathers 98
Adaptation Requirements 27, 31, 335, 338, 484-5, 634, 657, 686, 700
adaptive slave family 277

The adjustable agenda for our time 779
Affirmative Action 8, 294, 440, 459-61, 635, 684, 704, 728
African American Core Identity 371, 421, 622
African American Garden of Eden 8, 27, 30, 34, 65, 94, 96, 98, 109, 149, 164, 175, 177, 181, 725-6
African American Male Career Pathway Program (AMCAP) ix, 2, 35, 66, 94, 465, 512, 523, 525, 527, 531, 552, 571, 583, 616
African American male guides 569, 583-4
African American Male School Adaptability Crisis (AMSAC) 33, 41, 51-3, 65-6, 75-7, 89-91, 233, 553-5, 581-3, 593-5, 689-91, 697-9, 701-3, 735-7, 739-41
African American males as target 525
Afristocracy 72, 171, 286
Afro-American Council 31, 134, 157
Afrocentrism 6, 296, 401, 406, 434, 436, 481, 622, 734
Afterschool Alliance 544-5, 578
The Age of Booker T. Washington 108, 675

Ainsworth-Darnell, James W. 209, 222-3, 225-50, 255, 257, 260, 262, 321, 359, 379
Ainsworth-Darnell and Downey 222-3, 225-50, 255, 257, 260, 262, 321, 359, 379
Ainsworth-Darnell and Downey study 223, 225-6, 230, 242, 248, 255, 321
Akom, A. A. 223
Akom study 223
Alexander, Brian 411
alternative identity 259, 261
AMCAP Code 535, 568-9, 577
AMCAP content: tasks 533
AMCAP cost 544
AMCAP High School Transition Plan 36, 549
AMCAP hypotheses 124
AMCAP K-8 548-9
AMCAP organization 538
AMCAP Success Control Tasks 555, 562
Amen, Daniel 508, 536, 576
Amen Clinic 576
Amenia Conference of 1916 145-6, 165, 727
American Psychological Association 80, 325, 342, 603
Anderson, Elijah 52, 243, 265-7, 297, 398, 598, 669, 737
Anderson, Michael 574
Angier, Natalie 752-3
Anselmo, Angela 19, 25
anti-intellectualism 26, 202, 263, 280, 401, 409, 427, 431, 588, 690, 728, 766
Appiah, Anthony 419, 738
Armstrong, Samuel C. 100

Aronson, Joshua 261, 393, 477
Art of Loving (AOL) schools 40, 42, 599, 613, 628
Asante, Molefi Kete 434
Asian-Americans' IQ 302
associative learning 310, 348, 353-4
Atlanta Compromise Address of 1895 104, 130, 427, 444, 451, 652, 708, 777
Atlanta Riot of 1906 687
An attempt at compromise over combat 164
attributes of a healthy personality 371
authoritative communities 333, 491, 519, 570, 759
authoritative-supportive teaching 617
"average expectable environments" 17-20, 31, 37, 66, 276, 340, 368-9, 416, 731-2, 761-3
AVID, Advancement Via Individual Determination 742

B

BabySteps Project 624
Baden-Powell, R. S. S. 584
Baker, Ray Stannard 116, 179, 643, 683, 687, 700, 708, 731
Baker's visits 675, 687, 689, 731
Baumeister, Roy F. 302, 364-5, 498, 500-1, 564-5
Bernard, Jessie 269, 467, 588
Bill Clinton Risk 725, 732, 776
Bill Cosby Brown Anniversary (Pound Cake) Speech 170
Billson, Janet Mancini 198, 400, 797
Birmingham Letter 129, 131-2, 160, 648-50, 655, 716, 726
"The Birth of a Nation" 749

Black Advocacy of School Do's and Don'ts 40, 748
black attitude-behavior paradox 232
Black Blueprint for Crime Prevention and Punishment 748
Black lives Matter 48, 437-9, 754
black male culture 15, 63
black male-female differences 14, 55
black male fratricide 8, 374, 453, 730, 763, 777
black middle-class flight 625
Black Muslims (Nation of Islam) 434
black personality syndrome 467-8
Black Power 6, 29, 66, 151-2, 296, 373, 377, 388, 390, 401, 434, 436
black student attitude 227
black-white academic achievement gap 24, 89, 603, 613-14
Black-White IQ Differences 311, 315, 317, 321-2, 324, 350
Black-White IQ-Disparity Generalizations 340
black-white IQ gap 21, 312, 318-20, 325-6, 333-4, 342, 346
Blankenhorn, David 588
Blasio, Bill de 461
Blassingame, John 274-5
Bloom, Benjamin 219, 572
Bloomberg, Michael 618
Bly, Robert 584-6, 592-3
Bollettieri, Nick 497
Booker T. Washington (BTW) Fellows and Leadership Training Program 746
Booker T. Washington (BTW) Library and Self-Help Center 35, 751
Booker T. Washington: Builder of a Civilization 650, 700
Booker T. Washington High School 169, 509, 606, 616, 620
Borman, Geoffrey D. 86, 567, 608, 624
Borman, Stringfield, and Slavin 86, 624
Boston Guardian assault 136
"Boston riot" of 1903 137
Boyd, John 124-6, 450, 454, 493, 559-60
Boyd, William L. 86
Bracey, John H. 284, 286, 288, 291-2
brain plasticity 490
Brainology 495, 508
brains, property, and character 28, 31, 33, 98, 128-9, 146-8, 163, 166, 174, 429, 547, 675, 677, 679, 778-9
Branch, Taylor 135, 718
Brazziel, William F. 316-18, 353
bread-and-butter curriculum 40, 615-16, 628
Breger, Louis 369
brightest and talented 759-60
Bronfenbrenner, Eric 56
Brooks, David 39, 65, 123, 341, 411, 414, 490-2, 504, 506, 514, 519-21
Brown, Dorothy 435
Brown, Michael 453-4
Brown, N. M. 385-6, 691
Brown, Tony 738
Brown vs. Board of Education 77, 133, 523, 603, 635
Brownsville decision 139
BTW Education Consortium 749

The BTW Meme   140, 646, 726, 767
BTW Society   37, 168-70, 174,
    551, 731
burden of self-responsibility   449
burden of understanding   448-9
Bush, George W.   87-8, 365-6, 375,
    609, 757
Butler, Jimmy   454, 464-5, 767
Butler, John Sibley   738

C

Caldwell, Bettye   83
Caldwell, Malcolm   386
California Middle School Program
    595, 597
Campaign for Black Male
    Achievement   774
Campbell, Joseph   16
Campbell, Richard T.   234, 236, 238,
    241-4
Canada, Geoffrey   71, 78, 83, 200,
    202-6, 265-7, 496-8, 520, 619
Cantor, Pamela   298-300, 619, 756
Capp, Jefferson   745
career-motivation linkage   556
Carmichael, Stokely   434
Carnegie Hall Agenda   138, 164
Carter, Casey   561, 567, 575
Carter, Stephen   739
Carter study   223
Caruso, David   510-11
Cashin, Sheryll   737
caste system-induced incongruent
    adaptation   214
Cattell, Raymond   22, 331
Center on Children and Families   757
Centrality of Family   4
character development   38, 247, 613
character education   506, 508-11, 732

character education programs   508-9
character or personality trait
    heritability   489
Character Strengths and
    Virtues: A Handbook and
    Classification   489
Characterology   449
charter schools   40, 504, 509, 527,
    600-1, 604-5, 610, 613, 619,
    621, 628
Chatham, on Chicago'   4
Chavis, Benjamin F., Jr.   750
Chavos   407-8
Chavos, Tabbye   407-8
Chicago Child-Parent Centers Program
    548, 572, 608
Chiche, Sophie   444, 462-3, 465-6
Child Family Rights Movement   ix,
    13, 34-5, 37, 39, 41, 66, 343,
    521, 633, 685, 706-9, 743-7,
    756-8, 781
Chopra, Deepak   514
Christakis, Nicholas   556, 583, 761
Chua, Amy   301-2, 432, 500, 561,
    564-5
Chuck D   386
Cibulka and Boyd   86
Civil Rights Act of 1964   78, 460-1,
    635, 658, 740
civil-rights cure-allers   30, 706,
    718, 722
Clark, Kenneth   377, 380
Clark, Mamie   377
Clay, Henry   105, 159
Clayton, Mincy, and
    Blankenhorn   277
cleanliness and noise   754, 756
Clinton, Bill   624, 725, 776
Colbert, Clara Victoria (Vicky) de   618

Coleman, James S. 78
Coleman Report 78-80, 85, 246, 466, 603
collateral support for thesis 412
collective fatherhood 14, 51
collective self-help 287-8, 291
college attendance and graduation 52
colorism 373
Commission on Children at Risk 39, 333-4, 359, 370, 489-91, 493-4, 519, 558, 570, 759
community culture 59, 269
Compromise attempt 138
Conant, James 62-4, 523, 599
Confederate flag 388, 455
Congress of Racial Equality (CORE) 135
Contee, Cheryl 387
The Content of Our Character 385, 477, 774
Cook, Philip J. 223, 225-6, 246-50, 255
Cook and Ludwig study 223, 255
Cook-Ludwig 225-6, 246-50
Cooke, Deanna Y. 407-8
core identity and other identities 376
Core Identity Theory of Disproportionate Maladaptation Among African Americans 33, 416
correlation between IQ scores and school grades 325-6
Cosby, Bill 26, 69-74, 76, 91, 170-1, 178, 268, 286, 423, 457-8, 677, 687, 692, 742-3, 756
Cose, Ellis 19, 51, 60, 172, 286, 288, 292, 386, 393, 397, 405, 469, 601, 621, 684-5
Court, Ronald 168, 174-5, 731

Cousins study 223
Cremin, Lawrence A. 129
Crenshaw, Kimberle 435
Criminal Justice 17, 63, 147, 439, 445, 598, 764
crisis xi, 7, 31-3, 52, 75-7, 85-6, 103, 133, 141, 241, 305-6, 605, 685-6, 733, 747
critical community 736-41, 744
critical race theory (CRT) 434
criticisms of Fordham-Ogbu study 225
Cross Jr., William E. 376-81, 383-6, 389-90, 396-8, 401, 405, 434, 468
Crouch, Stanley 738
Cruse, Harold 152
crystallized intelligence 22, 310, 328, 331-2, 334, 494
cultivation of the most gifted 348
cultural change sought 584
cultural literacy 622-3
Curti, Merle 162, 353, 518

D

D'Agostino, Hedges, and Borman 567, 608
D'Agostino, Jerome 567, 607-8
Darity 223, 264
Darity, William, Jr. 223, 264
Data to judge our two traditions 657
definition of emotional intelligence 488
Delgado, Richard 435
developmental and peer needs 623
developmental tasks 532, 553, 561
Dewey, John 129, 354, 578, 620
Diamond, John 77, 85, 255-6, 341

Dickerson, Debra J.   385-6, 392, 396-9, 405-6, 765-7
disabilities differential   59, 729
disciplinary problem   206
DISCOVER   14, 36, 546, 553, 575, 781
disidentification   206, 267-8, 304, 351, 410, 476-80
disorder   25, 63-4, 290, 299, 389, 394, 466, 477, 760, 764
divergent racial-attribute outcomes of the caste system   214
dominant role of our hidden, inaccessible, inner mind   492
Douglass, Frederick   98, 106, 108, 177, 179, 351, 415, 485, 642, 709, 712, 765
Dove   774
Dove, Shawn   774
Downey, Douglas B.   178, 209, 222-3, 225-50, 255, 257, 260, 262, 321, 359, 379
Dr. King's 5-point program   720-1
Dreamers   55, 244, 413, 725
D'Souza, Dinesh   287, 291, 738, 776
DuBois, W. E. B.   26-32, 94-9, 108-23, 125-8, 132-46, 149-51, 153-62, 164-8, 177-9, 181-3, 424-7, 646-9, 653-6, 686-9, 708-12
 of 1899   709
 post-1903   709, 712
 pre-1903   709
DuBois: two divisive issues   118
DuBois/Washington: time perspective and core identity   123
DuBois's Washington Demonization   29, 154, 183, 646
Duckworth, Angela   24, 38, 358, 498, 501-2, 504, 507-8, 510

Duckworth and Washington   504
Duncan, Arne   605, 608, 610
Duster, Troy   738
Dweck, Carol   493-5, 497-8, 508, 561, 565
Dyson, Michael Eric   69-70, 72-4, 76, 171, 178, 258, 280-1, 286, 384, 386-7, 405-6, 423, 677, 714, 737

E

Eagleman, David   39, 341, 411, 414, 490, 492
Early, Gerald   738
early intervention   85, 553, 571-3, 575, 623-5
Early Training Project   572
Economic Opportunity Act of 1964   658
education and industry   419-20
Effects of Fatherless Homes   592
egalitarian white liberals   706, 735
El Sistema   760
Elementary and Secondary Education Act (ESEA)   86, 523, 578, 608-9, 659
Elkins, Stanley   274-5, 301, 468, 705
Enhanced Cultural-Ecological Framework (CEM)   218-19
Environmental vulnerability of males   591
environmentalists   321, 324
epigenetic principle   363
equity white liberals   706
Erikson, Erik   18-19, 25-6, 92, 276, 362-4, 368-70, 374-6, 381, 390, 396, 399, 401, 417, 555, 557-8
ethnic strengths   349, 353-4
Every Student Succeeds Act (ESSA)   88

extraverted sensation type personality 338, 468-70

F

factors found to account for school achievement 80
"Facts, Figures, and More: Adapted Excerpts" 378, 383
fade-out effect 628
Farah, Martha 83
Farkas, George 223, 225, 229-30, 232, 238-9, 243, 252, 261-2
Farkas study 223
Farrakham, Louis 750
Farrell, Edwin 50, 409, 413, 498-500, 521, 554-7, 566-7, 589, 725, 761
Fashola, Olatokunbo 525, 569
Father Rice 484, 767
fatherless families 6-7, 21, 24, 32, 34-5, 41, 70, 97, 203, 306, 530, 604, 613, 727, 734-5
female-headed families 47, 414, 665-7, 670-1, 673
Ferguson, Ronald 69-70, 76, 78, 85, 89-90, 203, 223, 228-9, 242-3, 245-6, 478-9, 567, 624, 755
Ferguson study 223
fictive kinship 211, 216-20, 222, 260, 263, 398-9, 406, 415, 707, 714, 724, 729, 741, 745
Fitch, Nancy 738
Five Success Character Traits 493, 503, 511
fixed mindset 494
Flashman, Jennifer 223, 232, 248-53, 255, 260-1
Flashman study 223, 250, 252-3, 260-1

fluid intelligence 310, 328, 331-2, 494, 621
For DuBois, being a man 424
forced resignation in 2007 of Bruce Gordon 705
Ford, Harold, Jr. 386, 407
Fordham, Signithia 20, 170, 208-11, 215-22, 224-8, 244, 246, 248-52, 254-5, 258-64, 267, 284, 321, 398-9, 456
Fordham-Ogbu 170, 209-10, 215-20, 222, 224-8, 244, 246, 248-52, 259, 261-4, 267, 284, 321, 398-9, 456
Fordham-Ogbu thesis 215, 222, 224, 226-7, 248-50, 252, 262, 264
Fortune, Timothy Thomas 179
Foster, Wilbur F. 99, 225, 720
Founding Fathers 98-9, 105, 113, 159
Fowler, James 556, 583, 761
Frankl, Victor 462-3, 465, 767
Franklin, John Hope 105, 434, 635, 656
Frazier, E. Franklin x, 6, 11, 105, 258, 263, 267-8, 276-80, 282-7, 289-94, 296, 337-8, 399, 467-8, 635
Freeman, Alan 435
Freud, Sigmund 17, 417, 432, 500
Fromm, Erich 37, 504, 514-15, 519, 763, 765, 767, 769
Fryer, Roland G., Jr. 223
Fryer and Torelli study 223
Fuller, Mary Lou 567, 594

G

Gardner, Howard 352, 486-7
Garner, Eric 438, 453-4
Garrison, William Lloyd 7, 141, 639
Garvey, Marcus 152, 174, 404

Garza, Alicia 437
Gates, Henry Louis, Jr. 105, 122, 294, 386, 419, 635
gender imbalance 57
Germany, Kent 658
Gettysburg Address 29, 104-6, 653, 751
Gettysburg Address of African American History 104
Gilmore, David 15, 588
Gordon, Edmund 53, 458-9, 694
gradualism versus immediacy 157
Gray, Freddie 764
grit 84, 501-2, 504
Gutman, Herbert G. 277

H

Haitian earthquake 64-5, 730
"hallowed presence" 33, 92, 369, 416, 707, 767, 779
Halpern, Diane F. 571
Hamblin, Ken 738
Hamer, Dean 411
Harlan, Louis R. 29, 107, 122, 131-2, 137-43, 148-9, 151-3, 159-61, 177, 182, 510, 646-51, 654-5, 683, 772
Harlem Children's Zone (HCZ) 78
Harpalani, Vinay 258
Harper, Brian E. 9, 407
Harper, Hill 480, 587, 592, 742, 768
Harper-Tuckman study 9, 407
Harrington, Michael 61, 297
Harris, Cheryl I. 435
Harris, Judith Rich 566
Harris, Thomas A. 131, 648-50, 655, 726
Hart, Betty 83
Hartmann, Heinz 26, 368

Haskins, Ron 757
Havighurst 555, 561-2, 736
Havighurst, Robert 555, 736
Hawkins, Joseph 59-60, 271
Haynes, Ulric 288
Head Start 573-4, 659
healthy character 26
Heckman, James 58, 508, 573
Hedges, Larry V. 567, 608
Hendricks, Barkley L. 386
Herbert, Bob 206, 612
hereditarians 321, 324-5, 341
Herrnstein, Richard 21-2, 306, 311, 316-19, 321, 325, 332-6, 339, 345, 347-9, 351, 353, 355, 493-5, 615
Herrnstein-Murray 21, 316-19, 321, 325, 333, 335-6, 339, 347-9, 351, 353, 355, 414, 493-5, 511
Hidden Success Center 512-13, 535, 542-4, 899
high-performing, high-poverty schools 567
high school dropout rate 52, 54, 57-8, 458
high school graduation rate 15, 55, 58, 528
higher education controversy 119
Hirsch, Eric Donald, Jr. 622-3
Hofstadter, Richard 281
Holder, Eric 443, 445
hole in the black American soul 389
Holland, Spencer 571, 590, 595
home-community support 553, 567
Home Support Centers 758-9
Hopkins, Ronnie 200, 590
Hopkinson, Natalie 603
Horowitz, Eugene 377
Horowitz, Ruth 377

Horvat, Erin   220, 223, 246
Horvat and Lewis study   223
how we black males view ourselves   202
Hudley, Cynthia   224
human spirit   19, 25, 37, 476, 486, 503, 511-14, 519, 521, 559, 614, 702, 763, 779
humanistic education   563
Hymowitz, Kay   705
hypothalamic-pituitary-adrenal axis   91-2

I

"I Have a Dream" Speech   108
Ibrahim Prize for Achievement in African Leadership   746
identity and character   26, 33, 361, 416, 613, 633, 735
identity formation   42, 368, 381, 408, 418, 421, 646
identity meanings and related terms   364
identity quandary   272
Incognito: The Secret Lives of the Brain   39, 411, 492
industrial education   18, 32, 98, 101, 112, 119, 121-2, 129-30, 146, 159, 354, 482, 642, 656, 771-2
inimical environment   272
Instruments of self-help   128
Instruments of system-help   132
IQ as cause of black student poor school performance   329
IQ Basics   326
IQ Immutability   333
Irving, Miles Anthony   224
Irving and Hudley study   224

"Is the Negro Having a Fair Chance?"   143-4, 653
Ivory, Steven   14, 50-1

J

Jackson, David, Jr.   102, 148, 158, 648-9
Jackson, Janet   383
Jackson, Jesse   386, 651, 692
Jackson, John   53
James, Muriel and John James   513
Jealous, Benjamin Todd   181
Jencks, Christopher   40, 84, 91, 755
Jenkins, George   17-18, 586-7, 592
Jensen, Arthur R.   21, 56, 219, 306-7, 316, 318-21, 325, 327, 329, 331, 333, 347-8, 353-5, 493-5, 615-16
job ceiling   201, 211, 220, 239
Job Corps   36, 549-50, 659
John Brown's Raid   134
Johnson, Charles S.   158
Johnson, James Weldon   142, 145
Johnson, Lyndon B.   63, 73, 523, 609, 635, 656, 659, 702-5, 732, 776
Jones, Camara Phyllis   435
Jones, Reginald   168
Jones, Susan R.   366, 368
Jung, Carl   468-9

K

Kahn, Jennifer   509-10
Kansas City school system   88
Kardiner-Ovesey   380, 467-9
Kelley, Robin D. G.   738
Kennedy, David M.   17-18, 32, 41, 580, 598, 619, 682, 725
Kennedy, Randall   738

Kerckhoff, Alan 234, 236, 238, 241-4, 412, 414
Kerckhoff-Campbell study 238, 240, 242
Keyes, Alan 738
Kilson, Martin L. 284-6, 291-2
Kimmel, Michael 344
Kiner, Alisha 606
King, Coretta Scott 181, 721
King, Martin Luther, Jr. 30, 51, 97-8, 104, 135, 167-8, 174-5, 284, 377, 652, 699, 712-16, 718-23, 740-1, 747-51
King held Washington in high esteem 715
King-Washington holiday 35, 748, 751, 781
the King Years 25, 133, 135, 718
King's self-help legacy 714, 718, 728
KIPP (Knowledge is Power Program) 346, 504, 619
Klein, Joel I. 93
Krate, Ronald 84, 199-200, 205, 572, 577, 586, 588, 592

L

Lacy, Karyn 285-6, 405
Ladson-Billings, Gloria J. 435
Lareau, Annette 83
Lasch-Quinn, Elisabeth 8, 295, 307, 324, 385-6, 388-9, 391-3, 395-6, 433, 443-4, 446-7, 615-16, 684, 727, 774-5
Lawrence, Charles 435
Legacy Survival 167
legality of single-sex classes and schools 570
Lemon, Don 48
Lewis, Amanda 220, 247

Lewis, Hylan 270
Lewis, Kristine 223
Lewis, Sharon 54, 58, 525, 567
"Lifting the Veil of Ignorance" 196, 419
link between family structure and child poverty 594
Locke, Alain 170
locus of control and self-esteem 526, 553, 563, 571
looking-glass self 363
Loury, Glenn C. 69-70, 76, 78, 85, 89-90, 174, 181, 317-18, 348-9, 398, 405, 511, 703-4, 721, 738
Love defined 514
low-effort syndrome 201, 209, 358, 559, 561
low self-esteem and aggression 466-7, 690, 766
Ludwig, Jens 223, 225-6, 246-50, 255
Luzzo, Darrell Anthony 576

M

MacArthur Fellows Program 501, 746
make-believe world 7, 282-3, 294
male-female divide 57
man of paradoxes 150, 709
Mandela, Nelson 156, 159, 691
Mapp, Karen 607-8
Marable, Manning 738
Margavio, A. V. 286-7
Martin, Granville 109, 134, 136-8, 141, 145, 149-50, 156-7, 165, 222
Martin, Trayvon 8, 399, 436-7, 440-1, 444-5, 447, 451, 453-5, 459, 461, 622, 728, 788
Massey, Douglas 737
Mathews, Basil 451

Mathis, Deborah   738
Matsuda, Mari   435
Mayer, John D.   488
McAdams, Dan P.   364, 366, 368
McEwen, Mrylu K.   366, 368
McGill, Jerry   463, 465, 516
McWhorter, John   ix-x, 7-8, 14, 26, 60, 172-3, 255-7, 280-1, 388-93, 401-3, 405-6, 431-4, 449, 656, 690
"meaning system"   554-5
Measures of Emotional Intelligence   488
meme   12, 140, 257, 388-91, 402, 646, 648, 654, 714-15, 724, 726, 728, 767
Meyers, Michael   739
Mickelson, Roslyn   221, 223-4, 234-8, 240-3, 245-7, 253, 260
Mickelson, Roslyn Arlin   221, 223-5, 234-8, 240-3, 245-7, 253, 260
Mickelson and Velasco study   223-4
Mickelson study   224
middle-class anger   684
middle class culture   278, 291
middle-class exodus   289
Milholland, John   142
Miller, Arthur   363
Miller, Kelly   178
Million Man March   740, 743, 750-1, 757, 771
Mincy, Ronald   287
Mind Coach   508, 536, 553, 576
Minority Student School Achievement Network (MSAN)   60, 245, 257, 729
missing black males   298
Mitscherlich, Alexander   61, 486

mnemonic   32, 48, 57, 59-60, 65, 92, 109, 111, 140, 145, 158, 165, 437, 650, 687-9
mnemonics summary   725
Model, Suzanne   301
Moss, Alfred A., Jr.   99, 105, 434, 635, 656
movements   34, 111, 154, 497, 645, 692, 708, 737, 739-40
Moyers, Bill   584
Moynihan   64, 85, 584, 702-5, 719
Moynihan, Daniel Patrick   63-4, 277, 702-5, 719
Moynihan Family Initiative Obstruction   423
Moynihan Report   5, 78, 532, 702-4, 709, 716, 719, 732, 753, 776
Mozart, Wolfgang   495
Muhammad, Elijah   434
Mujica, José   691
multiple intelligences   352, 476, 486, 511, 513
Murray, Charles   21-2, 71, 73-4, 306, 316-19, 332-6, 339, 347-9, 353-5, 435-6, 493-5, 615, 657-8, 665, 667-74
Murray and Wilson   665
Murray's thesis   93, 667, 670-2, 674
Myers, David   229, 361, 564
Myers, Gloria   286-7
Myers and Margavio study   286-7

N

narrative identity   364
Nation of Islam   224, 434, 750
National Association for the Advancement of Colored People (NAACP)   15, 35, 70, 98, 419,

443, 605, 626, 634, 697, 705, 721, 745
National Center for Higher Education Management Systems Information Center 528
National Negro Committee 142
National Urban Coalition 181, 721
nature versus nurture 333, 492
Neal-Barnett, Angela 223-4, 406
Neal-Barnett study 223
Negro achievements 351
Negro Business League 137, 169, 222, 358, 645, 716, 723
Negro self-hatred 377
new black identity 403
new black teenage culture 256
New Hope Project 592
The New Negro 170, 404
New School 618-19
Niagara Movement 133-4, 138-9, 156, 170, 605
nigrescence fallout 401
Nigrescence versus Americanism 396
Nisbett, Richard 56, 319-21
Njeri, Itabari 739
No Child Left Behind (NCLB) 604
No ignominious ending 147
"the nod" 406, 409
Noguera, Pedro A. 60, 205-6, 243, 265-7, 375-6, 457-9, 567, 694
Norrell, Robert ix-xi, 29, 102, 109-11, 121, 136-44, 146-54, 157-61, 165-6, 174-6, 349, 643-4, 650-1, 689, 715-18

O

Obama, Barak 8, 29, 169-71, 220-1, 385, 399, 405, 430, 441, 459, 604-5, 609-10, 651-2, 703-4, 788
obsessive-compulsive disorder (OCD) 394
O'Connor, Carla 220, 246
O'Connor, Horvat, and Lewis 220
Office for Civil Rights 597
Ogbu, John 20, 201-2, 206-22, 224-8, 230-2, 238-41, 246, 248-55, 258-64, 267-9, 303, 398-400, 408-9, 456-7, 478
Ogbu's earlier thinking 213
Oglesby, K. Thomas 742-3, 750
Olsen, Glenn 567, 594
Olsen and Fuller 567, 594
Operation Ceasefire 580, 619
Oppositional Cultural Framework (OCF) 210
oppositional culture 21, 198, 206, 210, 212, 216-17, 219, 221, 225, 227-9, 249, 252-3, 262-3, 267-8, 425
out-of-wedlock births 8, 278, 337, 373, 416, 453, 468, 485, 552, 661, 667, 671, 679, 707, 754
Overt Market strategy 580

P

Page, Clarence 739
Pan-Africanism 151
Panel of Publications Weigh Current Black Identity 385
parent and community involvement 580
parent participation 612
parenting skills 609, 743, 746, 754-6, 759
Parini, Jay 109-10

Parks, Rosa 156
Passion for Life: Psychology and the Human Spirit 513
Paterson, Basil 601
Patterson, James T. 703
Patterson, Orlando 532, 738
Payne, Charles 88
Payne, Charles M. 88, 90, 524
Payne, Wayne 487
Pearson, Hugh 739
peer pressure 254, 532, 537, 539, 553, 566
peer support 201, 207, 304, 326, 553, 566, 568, 577, 617, 742
Pegler, Westbrook 9
Perry, Steve 41, 76, 78, 178, 627, 692
Perry Preschool Program 546, 548, 563, 572, 620, 628
persistent opposition to family focus 705
personality, identity, and character 362
Perspectives Charter School in Chicago 621
Peterson, Christopher 489-90, 493, 503-4, 508-9
Peterson, Jesse Lee 169, 692, 696
Peterson and Seligman 489-90, 493, 503-4, 508-9
Pettigrew, Thomas 380-2, 409
Phillips, Meredith 40, 84, 91, 755
Phillips, Ulrich 274
physical differences among the races 322
Pinker, Steven 76, 303, 316, 566
Pope Francis 34, 707
popular culture influences 624
positive core identity *see* Scott, Imani Michelle and Erickson, Erik

Poussaint, Alvin 71, 386, 388, 457-8, 742-3, 756, 773
Powell, Colin 738
Powell, Kevin 360, 369, 374, 382, 386, 587, 592-3, 742
practice of the art of loving ix, 36-8, 40, 92, 369, 513-14, 517-20, 558-9, 576, 613-14, 637-9, 757, 763-5, 767-71, 780-1
Pratt, Sharon 386
President Barak Obama's education agenda 604
President Johnson's Validation Omission 704, 732, 776
President Obama 170-1, 399, 445, 451, 459, 461, 609, 622, 651-2, 704, 728
President Obama's Washington Omission in His First Inaugural Address 170, 651, 704
Price, Hugh 739
principals 62, 199-200, 567, 611, 613, 617-18, 626, 629
prisonization 20, 63, 438, 730
problem-solving approach 621, 623
progress-resistant cultural influences 65
PROJECT 2000 571-2, 595-6, 598
protest agenda 132-3, 141, 143, 146, 148, 182, 636, 648, 708
public discourse on racial matters 774
Public Enemy 386
pushout rate 53
Pyke, Karen 435

Q

Quinn, Jane 575

R

r/K Selection theory 322, 337
Race to the Top High School Commencement Challenge 169, 481, 509, 605
Racism as objective correlative and recomposition 394
Racism as security blanket 12
Rainwater, Lee 4-5, 275, 298, 382, 396, 510-11, 602
Raising IQ to Raise Achievement 330
Raspberry, William 596, 624, 696, 739
Raths, Louis 247
Raver, C. Cybele 299
Ravitch, Diane 40, 601, 604-5, 611-12, 628
reaction to the world of make-believe 283
Recapitulation of Book 724
recomposition 9, 394-6, 431, 450, 694
Reed, Ishmael 737
references to Washington in Harlan's Preface 153
Reisner and his colleagues' evaluation 569
rejection of genetic and cultural deficit explanations 218
The renewed message for our time 779
response to nigrescence fallout 405
revisionist nigrescence 376, 385
Rice, Lewis 484
Risley, Todd R. 83
Robinson, Eugene 8, 17, 60-1, 64, 271, 286, 290-1, 294, 297, 384, 392, 395, 397-8, 406, 684-5
Robinson, Jackie 156, 159, 161
Robinson, Keith 84, 568, 608-9
Rochon, Thomas 707, 737, 776-7
Roderick, Melissa 498, 566-7
Rohrer, John H. and Munro S. Edmonson 379-80, 468
Roosevelt, Franklin 2
Roosevelt, Franklin D. 2
Roosevelt, Theodore 139-40, 147, 187, 650-1
Rose, Tricia 738
rote learning 621
Rothman, Stanley 324-5
Rubenfeld, Jed 301-2, 432, 500, 561, 564-5
Rudwick, Elliott 138, 146
Rushton, J. Philippe 319-24, 327, 337
Ryan, William 53, 437, 532, 673, 703

S

Salovey, Peter 488
Salovey and Mayer 488
Sambo personality 273-5, 304-5, 425
Samuel, Mark 444, 462-3, 465-6
Samuel and Chiche 444, 462-3, 465-6
Santigold 386
Sax, Leonard 58, 587, 592
school choice 40, 87, 314
school discipline 8, 440, 459-61, 728
school-parent compact 607
Schwartzman, Paul 55, 244, 413
science of human strengths 489
Scott, Emmett 145, 749
Scott, Imani Michelle (formerly K. Michelle Scott) ix, 25-6, 123, 244, 365-6, 372-6, 378-81, 383-9, 393, 395-6, 400-1, 407-11, 415, 422, 429-31, 466, 468, 693, 720

second birth or soul union 585
Second Million Man March 750
secure versus insecure attachment 369
security blanket 11-12, 297, 395, 706, 728, 754
self-as-my-work 555-7
self-help books 711, 742, 768
Self-Help Center 35, 751
self-help ethos 171, 173, 287
self-help roots laid by Washington 741
Seligman, Martin 38, 489-90, 493, 503-4, 508-9
Sellers 384, 407-8
Sellers, Robert 384, 407-8
Sellers-Chavos-Cooke study 407-8
Separatism 26, 401, 409, 427, 431, 449, 588, 622-3, 690, 696, 728, 766
shackling of Dr. King 30, 42
Shaker Heights study 228, 242
Shatz, Adam 398
Silverstein, Barry 84, 200, 205, 572, 577, 586, 588, 592
Silverstein and Krate 84, 200, 205, 572, 577, 586, 588, 592
Simmons, Russell 768, 770
single-sex education 570-1
Slavin, Robert E. 86, 624
smaller specialized high schools in New York City 618
Smiley, Tavis 178, 221, 690, 738
Snyderman, Mark 324-5
social skills curriculum 742
Sojourner Truth 156
Solomon, R. Patrick 205, 223
Solomon study 205, 223
soul and body of proposal 763

The Souls of Black Folk 31, 94, 98, 109-11, 113-14, 118, 135-6, 159, 168, 227, 280, 399, 426, 726
Southern Christian Leadership Conference (SCLC) 135, 747
Southern Educational Tours 148, 188, 642, 773, 778
Sowell, Thomas 277, 288, 300, 315, 738
specialized high schools in New York City 618
Spencer, Margaret 258
Spencer Jr., Samuel 114, 127, 136, 145, 150, 178, 318, 353, 427-8, 712
Spingarn, Joel 145, 182
Springfield 145
Springfield Race Riot 139
Standout and complementary data:
  Self-Responsibility Tradition 674
  System-Responsibility Tradition 676
Stanford Marshmallow Experiment 500
Steele, Claude 261, 477
Steele, Shelby 9, 330, 376, 385-6, 431, 445, 450, 477, 694, 736, 738, 774
Stefancic, Jean 435
Stein, Gertrude 374
Stein, Sandra 86, 604
Steinberg, Dornbusch, and Brown study 201, 224
stereotype threat 256, 267, 393, 410, 476-9, 766
Stringfield, Samuel C. 86, 624
student behavior 83, 199, 509, 611, 617
Student Nonviolent Coordinating Committee (SNCC) 135

successor to Washington 30, 167
suicide rate among black children 299-300, 730
Sunday Evening Talks 64, 448-9, 507, 510, 708-9
Swain, Carol 738
Syed, Matthew 495-6
symbolism in the passing of our tradition fathers 419

T

Taber, Brian J. 576
Taber and Luzzo 576
Taft, William Howard 139
Talented Tenth 8, 21, 114, 118, 122, 133-4, 163, 263, 268, 348, 356, 440-1, 455-6, 459, 728-9
Tavis Smiley Show 221
Taylor, George 616, 755
teacher accountability 40, 603-5, 610, 628
teacher expectations 256, 410, 478-80
teacher training 20, 122, 523, 610, 618, 623, 644
teaching character 507
Teague 9
Teague, Bob 9
Teele, James 284, 292
therapeutic alienation 166, 181, 257, 296, 403, 452, 627, 656, 724
therapeutic sensibility 15, 444, 468, 615, 776
thingification of the past 358, 392, 415, 429
Thomas, Clarence 738
Thomas A. Harris Rescue 131, 648-50, 655, 726
those who embrace our Self-Responsibility Tradition 738
Those who embrace our System-Responsibility Tradition 737-8
three major demons 6-7, 17, 21, 23-4, 28, 32, 41, 70, 97, 306, 351, 356, 530, 604, 734-5
Three racial flareups 140
three restraints on Dr. King 714
Thurston, Baratunde 386-7, 396, 398, 405-7
Tinkersville School Founding 484-5, 767
Title I parent involvement 605-6
Torelli, Paul 223
total system 611
Tough, Paul ix, 36, 71, 83-5, 89-92, 200, 297-8, 359, 369-70, 413, 502-4, 508-9, 520, 528, 573
Touré 172, 384-9, 392-6, 398-9, 405-7, 410, 685
tradition effect on the four crucial factors: family, manhood, race, and intelligence 421
Tradition of Choice 32, 42, 70, 74, 633, 652, 687, 696, 699, 702, 722, 748, 750-1, 781
Trayvon Martin Case 8, 399, 436-7, 440-1, 444-5, 451, 453-5, 459, 461, 728, 788
The Triple Package 301-2
Trotter, Monroe 109, 134, 136-8, 141, 145, 149-50, 156-7, 165, 222
Tuckman, Bruce W. 9, 407
Tuskegee Army Air Field 645
Tuskegee had an Academic Department 122
Tuskegee Institute 28, 75, 98-9, 102, 109, 128, 185, 195, 422, 506, 617, 620, 625-6, 637, 697
two cultures from slavery 269

two-ness 74, 399-401, 404-5, 415, 420, 426, 429, 622-3, 694
Tyre, Peg 57, 571
Tyson, Karolyn 247, 264
Tyson and Darity study 264
Tyson study 223

U

U. S. Department of Justice 440, 459
U St. NW 290, 688-9, 731, 761
Ulrich, Henry 139-41, 143
unconscious forces 410, 414, 469
Understanding and Solutions 733
Unified Theory of Black America 33, 416
Unity Platform 145-6
universal existence of this male hunger 587
Up from Slavery 3, 28, 102, 109-10, 168, 170, 183, 428, 506, 749, 771
urban school reform 85
use of black male teachers 598
use of females 589
using deeds to judge our Self-Responsibility Tradition 637
using deeds to judge our System-Responsibility Tradition 634
using hard data to judge our two traditions 657
using their doctrines to judge our two traditions 679

V

value-added modeling 600
Veil lifted from DuBois 177
Veil lifted from Washington 175
Velasco, Anne E. 223-4

Verdict on our two traditions 686
victimhood 7-8, 27, 32, 227, 233, 356, 401, 421, 430-1, 440, 449, 457-9, 461-2, 465-6, 695-6
Victimology 6-8, 11, 28, 97, 294-6, 401, 408-9, 429-33, 436-41, 449, 459-62, 690, 693, 705-6, 728
Villard, Oswald Garrison 139-42, 605, 643, 687
Volkan, Varnik Volkan 372-3
Voting Rights Act of 1965 635
vouchers 600

W

Walker, Kara 386
Walker, Lee H. 169, 651
waning of the System-Responsibility Tradition 685
war on poverty 6, 15, 73, 93, 435, 440, 448, 452, 523, 635, 657-60, 667-73, 703, 775
warring was really not over substance 150
Washington, Booker T. 26-9, 64-5, 73-5, 95-6, 98-100, 152-3, 167-70, 173-4, 188-9, 195-7, 481, 606, 643-5, 650-2, 734
Washington, D. C. Department of Health 758
Washington and Moynihan 704
Washington Post survey 171, 202
Washington-Roosevelt dinner 651-2
Washington "set us back" 161
Washington's annual Negro Conferences 642
Washington's Atlanta Compromise as Deed 652

Washington's Black Power credentials 152
Washington's character emphasis 131, 510
Washington's civil rights leadership 649
Washington's practice of the art of loving 518, 639, 721
Wellness Centers in 15 San Francisco high schools 563
West, Cornel 11, 178, 221-2, 738
West, Kanye 375
West African culture 337
What we seek 779
Where Do We Go from Here: Chaos or Community? 699, 715
white support 15, 296, 732, 774
Wiley, George 670
Williams, Armstrong 738
Williams, Juan 386, 692, 739
Williams, Patricia 435
Williams, Serena 495
Williams, Terrie 387, 393, 397
Williams, Venus 495
Williams, Walter E. 373, 738
Willie Brown Academy 88-9, 93
Willis, Paul 204-5, 761
willpower 38, 409, 493, 498-501, 553, 561, 620-1
Wilson, William Julius 71, 174, 290, 413, 456, 459, 469, 533, 625, 657, 694, 737, 761

Winfrey, Oprah 394
Woods, Tiger 495
Woodson, Carter G. 121, 175, 354
Woodson, Robert 738
Woodward, C. Vann 29, 153, 159-60, 428, 646, 648
Work, Monroe 639
world of make-believe 6, 11, 282-5, 291-2, 296, 329, 384
world of make-believe today (the interpretation) 284
Wortham, Anne 738
Wright, Elizabeth 738
Wright, Jeremiah 172, 450
Wright, Richard 381, 409
Wright Black-White Male Teacher Experiment 595-6

Y

yin-yang 696, 700-1, 751
Young, Larry 411
young black male fratricide 8, 374, 453, 730, 777
young black radicals 30, 714, 718, 722, 728

Z

Zimbardo, Philip 123-6, 450, 454, 493, 559-60, 647
Zimmerman, George 440-4, 447-8

Printed in the United States
By Bookmasters